MW00426620

COUNTDOWN TO D-DAY: THE GERMAN PERSPECTIVE

COUNTDOWN TO D-DAY

The German Perspective

PETER MARGARITIS

CASEMATE

Philadelphia & Oxford

Published in the United States of America and Great Britain in 2019 by
CASEMATE PUBLISHERS
1950 Lawrence Road, Havertown, PA 19083, USA
and
The Old Music Hall, 106–108 Cowley Road, Oxford OX4 1JE, UK

Hardback Edition: ISBN 978-1-61200-769-4
Digital Edition: ISBN 978-1-61200-770-0 (ePub)

A CIP record for this book is available from the British Library

Printed and bound in the United States of America

Typeset in India by Versatile PreMedia Services. www.versatilepremedia.com

For a complete list of Casemate titles, please contact:

CASEMATE PUBLISHERS (US)
Telephone (610) 853-9131
Fax (610) 853-9146
Email: casemate@casematepublishers.com
www.casematepublishers.com

CASEMATE PUBLISHERS (UK)
Telephone (01865) 241249
Email: casemate-uk@casematepublishers.co.uk
www.casematepublishers.co.uk

Back cover: Bundesarchiv_Bild_101I-719-0247-17A

Contents

Foreword

Nearly two decades ago, as part of an email discussion group on World War II, I came across a series entitled "We Remember." Overseen by William L. Howard, it chronicled key events that occurred on each particular day in World War II. At the time, I had started developing a book detailing activities of the German High Command on the Western Front in the months leading up to the Normandy invasion.

Wanting to contribute this point of view in the spirit of Howard's work, I began a subseries to the daily log, entitling it *D-Day Countdown: The German Perspective*. It depicted a day-by-day summary of the activities of the German military leaders in Occupied France and in the German Supreme Command as the Allied invasion drew near. My email series addition to the discussion group originally began on December 8, 1999 and ended June 7 the next year.

My daily postings were short and spotty. They were often hastily written in the evening and sketchy on specifics (I was a fulltime technical writer during the day). Thus, they were sometimes not completely accurate. Still, many in the email group found them informative and enlightening.

Strangely, as I wrote them, I found myself slipping into a strongly anecdotal style that increasingly began taking over the details as I delved deeper into the lives of these men. I realized with pleasure that this development made the daily log theme flow much better. And writing the daily particulars in the present tense highlighted the experience even more. As interesting to me were the new individual facts that I discovered from one day to the next as I researched each day to make my postings richer in detail.

The email series was quite a rewarding experience for me, and when it was over, I felt a sense of accomplishment as I went back to my original book, tentatively entitled *Heeresgruppe B*. Unfortunately, an intense technical writing career and American Legion activities over the next decade substantially slowed the development of that work.

It had been styled originally as another history book written in the classic chronological format so prevalent in the thousands of volumes on military history, and so common in the few hundred that had so far been written on the Normandy invasion. Some twelve years later, though, armed with a good deal of additional research (historical and personal information), and using the contributions of many other authors and their fine works, I found myself coming back to the idea of writing, initially as a companion to my main work, a daily log counting down to the invasion as seen from the German side, and focusing as much on the minutiae of the officers' lives as on the military events that they undertook.

As the idea of focusing more on minor personal details again took hold, I began updating, editing, augmenting, and in general revamping the previous material that I had originally submitted in emails, a bit of which by now had made its way to the Internet. Thus, although it follows a conventional chronological layout, this story is somewhat different than the usual yet not ineffectual accounts of the invasion. It is told exclusively from the viewpoint of the Germans, in a similar vein to (and borrowing elements from) Paul Carell's *Invasion! They're Coming! (Sie Kommen!)*. I tried, though, to mold some style along the lines of Cornelius Ryan's great classic, *The Longest Day* (his exhaustive notes for which I was fortunate enough to mine extensively).

I was intrigued by all the missing personal details regarding what the Germans were doing in those critical months when the Allies were finalizing their operational plans. I hope this work fills in many of those gaps. Unfortunately for Rommel, he was asleep at home in Germany when the invasion began. Still, his part in the story is more critical than anyone's, because he was in operational command, and it was his plan that was at stake: would it be followed, or not?

Joseph E. Perisco wrote in the introduction to his excellent book, *Nuremberg—Infamy on Trial*, about the style of his account. I considered this writing style somewhat similar to my own, so it bears repeating:

> My treatment of [this story] is intended for the lay reader and general student of history more than for the academic or legal historian. For that reason, I have chosen a strongly narrative style… The style does not influence the factual foundations of the book… When I have described subjects of the present work as thinking, saying, or doing something, I have drawn from their own writings, letters, oral and written histories, and from other books, archival documents, contemporary press accounts … [and] interviews… The account is narrative supported by historic fact.

Like him, I chose a strong narrative style, although I have kept it strictly within the bounds of historical accuracy. Everything that people in this book do, say and think is based on factual sources. By choosing this style of writing, I hope to present an accurate account, bringing to life characters that, in the last few decades, have become dry figures who lived some seventy years ago during a long-past war. These people, good or bad, right or wrong, were still living human beings with human failings, caught up in a world war that they had helped create through their own shortsightedness and hubris, embroiled in a conflict that now threatened to destroy their country, their families, and ultimately, their own lives.

While this book is, first and foremost, a chronicle of German lives and deeds, I have at times briefly described what the Allies were up to on a particular date.

I believe this is helpful sometimes to add context and to make sense of German responses to Allied operations. Passages set in italics refer to the Allies' movements.

My wife often accuses me of being "wordy" ("I am a tech writer dear," I point out with a smile), and this effort seems to underscore that statement (I am sure my publisher would agree). As further narratives were added to the countdown and my interest in this approach grew, with a substantial part of the added information coming from my original work, *Heeresgruppe B,* the relatively short 180-page countdown grew expansively. I finally realized that my countdown, especially when I added maps and photos, had overtaken the original work and become the final outcome.

I hope though that, in the end, this just makes for better reading. Most of the original information herein is now clearer and much more accurate, and a huge amount of new detail gives the log a much more complete image of the German day-to-day events of the time. I also strove to give the narrative that strong slant towards the personal experiences of those involved, if for no other reason than to make the account more personable and realistic, and not come off as yet another dry history book. After all, the history of the invasion has been recounted time and time again. This account centers exclusively on the day-to-day activities of the German officers as the huge, impending, inevitable enemy invasion loomed ever nearer.

Peter Margaritis, January 30, 2019

Prelude: 1943

Status of the West

By the late fall of 1943, World War II had dragged into its fifth year. Germany, once by far the dominant force in the war, was now struggling hard to defend its Third Reich. Though its forces had once been augmented by Italy and several Eastern European allies, the Reich now stood alone. Its armies, still strong but now beleaguered, braced against many powerful enemies arrayed against them on several fronts.

In the East, the Reich faced a constantly strengthening Soviet Union, a phenomenon that baffled a German High Command that had at once considered the Russians inferior and on the brink of defeat. In collapsed Italy, German divisions defended themselves halfway down the peninsula against a modern American army and a British army, both of which were well supplied by sea and air.

At sea, Germany's dwindling naval assets were bottled up in various harbors, often in the process of repair, owing to either breakdown or enemy attack. The once majestic Italian Navy was now a ghost fleet. In the Atlantic, the U-boats battled feebly against numerically and technologically superior Allied naval task forces. Hunter-killer carrier groups sailed everywhere and rendered every patch of sea dangerous for submarines. In the skies over occupied Europe, the once-powerful Luftwaffe now struggled savagely, desperately, against an Allied bombing campaign that pummeled the Reich's industry by day and by night.

All the while, the German High Command worriedly eyed Western Europe. The buildup of forces in England continued intermittently, but relentlessly, as the Western Allies developed their plans for the long-expected invasion of Europe. This was the major campaign that the Russians grumbled was two years overdue. Still, everyone knew it would inevitably come, and strategists on both sides believed that if successful, it would signal the beginning of the end for the Third Reich.

The German fronts were divided geographically, with titles mostly given from a sense of direction. Each front had an assigned top commander, usually a field marshal. He was responsible for the coordinated operations of all services in that area. Field Marshal Kesselring, for instance, was *Oberbefehlshaber Süd*, the Mediterranean Theater commander. The vast Eastern Front had at any one time at least three front commanders. In Western Europe, the title of *Oberbefehlshaber West* (OB West) gave full command of all German forces there.

Although each commander was directly responsible for his area, his multi-force total command authority was in reality quite limited to in-theater regular, reserve, or training Army units, and very limited operational aspects for units of other services, such as marine battalions, SS units, *Schnelleboote* squadrons, Luftwaffe squadrons, airborne units, police or odd service battalions. Direct aspects of authority over these non-army units were retained by their service commands, including occasional command aspects from special high administrative authorities of that service or political branch. And of course, overall control came from the German High Command and the Führer himself. These muddled lines of authority often resulted in unwieldy, confusing, and ineffective command chains.

The current *Oberbefehlshaber West* was 66-year-old *Generalfeldmarschall* Gerd Von Rundstedt. By the time he had been reappointed OB West in March of 1942, he had become a legend in the Wehrmacht.[1] He had led Germany to victory over Norway and the Low Countries in the spring of 1940, and subsequently in May and June, over longtime rival France. After his wildly successful *blitzkrieg* across that country had forced the stunned, humiliated French to surrender, he had been promoted to field marshal on July 19. He was then immediately tasked with planning *Operation Sealion* (*Seelöwe*), the invasion of Great Britain. However, the Luftwaffe never could gain control of the skies over England, and in mid-September, the Führer reluctantly decided to postpone the invasion. On October 10 though, instead of being able to retire, von Rundstedt was appointed *Oberbefehlshaber West* and given command of the forces in Western Europe. He was tasked with developing a defensive barrier all along the coast. He did very little though to build up defenses in those five and a half months, his excuse being a shortage of materials. Besides, the downfall of England seemed just a matter of time.

At the beginning of April 1941, he had relinquished command of the Western Theater[2] to become, reluctantly, one of the major architects of *Unternehmen (Operation) Barbarossa*. His assigned command became *Heeresgruppe Süd*.[3] This epic invasion of Russia, initially a magnificent success that started in late June, had however stalled by December as a harsh Russian winter set in. The field marshal became embroiled in a dispute with the Führer over whether to withdraw his spent units and regroup. Angry and fed up with this upstart leader, von Rundstedt had angrily demanded, and was granted, permission to be relieved, his excuse being his health. Hitler soon realized, though, that he had been wrong in their quarrel and had lost a valuable leadership asset. So eventually, he forced himself to swallow his pride and persuaded the field marshal to serve yet again the next spring, this time coming back again as the overall commander of the forces on the Western Front.

Now back again as OB West, von Rundstedt made sure that coastal defenses were always a point on his agenda. Still, in the spring of 1943, after a short rest at the Bad Tölz spa, he traveled to the Berghof in Bavaria[4] for a war conference. There he was to confer with the Führer[5] on a number of subjects, mostly the defense of the West, which he had outlined in War Directive No. 40, dated March 23, 1942. It was his major concern, even though he still monitored the situation in the East.

During that April trip to the Berghof, von Rundstedt's operations chief, *Oberst* Bodo Zimmermann,[6] briefed him on what to say there. Zimmermann, a pleasant fellow of medium build and height, with a short, clipped mustache, had been sent to Bad Tölz at the last minute by Günther Blumentritt, the OB West chief of staff, on a special mission. Zimmermann was to convince the old man to use this opportunity to convince the Führer that construction of defenses in the West was lagging, and that they needed help.

At the subsequent meeting with the Führer, von Rundstedt expressed his dissatisfaction with the existing level of defenses. He complained about a lack of materials, and shortages of manpower. Also, units coming to France stayed only long enough to recuperate before they were off to the East.

Hitler's response held a general lack of interest. To him, the West was a backwater theater, and thus a low priority. All of his attention was on the grave, situation in the East. Stalingrad had fallen to the surprisingly ferocious Soviet Army a couple months before, and Hitler, still bristling from the defeat and the surrender of his entire élite Sixth Army, was hell-bent on revenge, impatient for the spring thaws to come. Then the Reich would initiate a mighty, vengeful counteroffensive in what he was sure would end up a decisive victory over those "Russian mongrels." He bragged glowingly about how in a few months, his smashing attack with some two thousand panzers would wipe out over 90 Russian divisions.

Hitler then spoke somewhat cynically about Italy. Things were not good there politically or economically, and getting worse by the day. Mussolini would probably soon be thrown out and the Italians would then turn against the Reich.

"And if that happens," he continued with a frown, "I'll have to disarm the Italian Fourth Army and take over its area with our own troops… Our own troops…" he trailed off. Then there were the units in Greece…

Perhaps sensing at that point that von Rundstedt was getting ready to launch into a speech about his own area, Hitler suddenly ended the discussion by thanking him and wishing him a safe trip back. Thrown off balance, von Rundstedt clumsily thanked him for his time. Hitler then bid him farewell and the field marshal was politely but unceremoniously dismissed to go back to Paris and somehow deal with his problems. He confusedly mumbled his goodbyes and left. The problems in the West would just have to wait.

On the return trip to France, the field marshal bitterly reflected on Hitler's callous dismissal of his problems. An aristocratic Prussian, von Rundstedt had never believed the Führer to be a brilliant strategist, not even way back in 1940. And he hated to be around that Bohemian corporal[7] when his cutthroat, toady, fanatical, uncouth, cacophonous Nazi minions were present. Von Rundstedt had once confided to his chief of staff, Günther Blumentritt, that he wanted no part of the New Order's high command. He just wanted to be head of the Heeres, to be in parades, and to ride his horse around in Potsdam. After all, at 67 years of age, he could easily retire if he wanted to.

So why did he continue to serve?

"The Fatherland is in danger," he had once groused, "and like an old cavalry horse, if I stayed at home, I would feel ashamed." He certainly was not still in uniform for any riches or decorations, or even for rank. He already had plenty of each. "One cannot be higher than a field marshal!" he had once boasted.

Now, unsettled by Hitler's attitude and remembering his own dealings with the Führer in the past, von Rundstedt returned to Paris, convinced that his troubles in the West would rebound on him many times over when the Allies finally invaded. And the invasion could very well come in a few months.

To convince Hitler of the gravity of his situation, the field marshal ordered an extensive survey of the coastal positions all along the English Channel, the Atlantic seaboard, and the Mediterranean. He wanted the study to show how many defensive positions there actually were, their state of completion, a detailed order of battle for all branches of service, and an analysis of the men in his units. The report would be sent to the Führer when it was ready.

Maybe then they would get some cooperation.

---

1   Lit. "War machine." The term was used from 1935 on to describe the combined German Armed Forces and included the Army (Heer), Air Force (Luftwaffe), the Navy (Kriegsmarine), and the Waffen SS, which in wartime was attached to the Army.

2   *Feldmarschall* Erwin von Witzleben took over a month later.

3   Army Group South.

4   The Berghof was a chalet by design, formerly owned by the Wachenfeld family. Hitler purchased it in the mid-1930s and expanded the layout over the years, paid for in part by some of the proceeds from his famous testimonial, *Mein Kampf.* At the onset of the war, he began using it as his mountain getaway and out-of-country residence. As the war continued and Berlin came under attack from bombers, the Berghof became a secondary seat of power as he isolated himself more and more from the Reich. Speer and Bormann oversaw expansion of the complex to include villas for senior party officials and generals, security checkpoints, anti-aircraft positions, quarters for policemen, troops, and auxiliary staff, bunkers for air raid shelters, and the infrastructure to support this massive contingent.

5   Hitler's full title was *Der Führer und Oberste Befehlshaber der Wehrmacht des Grossdeutschen Reichs.*

6   Fifty-six-year-old Bodo Zimmermann was a World War I veteran. In 1920, he started a publishing firm that produced military publications, including training manuals. Re-entering the Army before war broke out, he was appointed to the staff of the First Army and saw service on the Western Front. When von Witzleben in October 1940 took over command in Western Europe of the newly-formed *Heeresgruppe D* (First, Sixth, and Seventh Armies), Zimmermann was appointed to its general staff. After von Rundstedt took command in the spring of 1941 and given the title

of Commander, Western Theater, Zimmermann was promoted to colonel at the beginning of December 1942 and became von Rundstedt's chief of operations.

7   Von Rundstedt himself had often dubbed Hitler "*Dieser böhmische Gefreiter*," having picked the phrase up in the early 1930s from World War I hero Chancellor Paul von Hindenburg. The older field marshal, when first told that Hitler's home town was Braunau, mistook it for another town with that identical name in Bohemia, and not Austria. After their initial meeting (in which each at once took a strong dislike to the other), von Hindenburg would often use the expression "that Austrian corporal," although as time went on, he leaned towards replacing the adjective "Austrian" with the more pejorative adjective "Bohemian." After all, he mused, Bohemians were essentially gypsies, and not as wholesome or refined as the cultured Austrians, much less the highbrow Prussians. To these aristocrats, this nickname was of course viewed as a keen slur. Naturally, von Rundstedt grimly found the insult fitting and adopted it himself.

In an interview between author Cornelius Ryan and Rommel's operations officer, Hans-Georg von Tempelhoff on March 26, 1958, von Tempelhoff was quoted as saying, "You know, it is a very strange thing that I believe it was [*Field Marshal Wilhelm*] Keitel who once said to Hitler, 'Do you realize that Rundstedt called you a Bohemian corporal?' and Hitler said 'Yes, but he's still the best field marshal I have.'"

OB West Summary Report, 1943

The next month (May), OB West began an intensive survey of its Western defenses. The staff conducted a series of queries and analyses that took some time, especially since there was no immediate deadline. The study involved extensive planning, organizing, surveying, investigations, and meetings to draw appropriate conclusions. The detailed findings were finally completed five months later. During that time, von Rundstedt looked over the drafts several times, editing them for content and adding snippets of information or clarity here and there. Knowing his audience, he wanted to get across his own points about the situation on the Western Front and the level of preparedness of the Atlantic Wall in the most effective (and tactfully safest) way.

Finally, towards the end of October, the field marshal was ready to release his official in-depth report. In its opening, the memorandum stated that its purpose was to show how the West's sideline status would radically change in the next year. Von Rundstedt knew that his findings were more negatively realistic than optimistic and would not be favorably received. Still, he felt that they were necessary. His biggest concern was that his conclusions would be glossed over (as his concerns had been that spring at the Berghof), and he wanted to minimize that risk. After all, to the High Command, the fighting in the West, raging in the skies over Europe and in the stormy Atlantic, was still viewed as much less critical than the desperate struggle against Russia. However, von Rundstedt knew that this would change in the months to come when the Allied invasion began.

Because of his concerns, the field marshal, before submitting his findings, first contacted the OKW[1] chief of staff, *Generalfeldmarschall* Wilhelm Keitel. Von Rundstedt told him that he knew that the Führer had a busy daily agenda and at present had his hands full with the situations in the East and in Italy. Nevertheless, the field marshal would consider it a favor it if the Führer at least took the time to read his report.

The situation in the West, he explained to Keitel, was soon going to be serious as well, and von Rundstedt was just doing his job by informing the High Command of this fact. If, down the road, defeat were to come in France, von Rundstedt did not afterward want the Führer to accuse him of not having informed him of the fundamental problems that had been facing them. Of course he did not add that this type of accusation had been leveled against him back in December 1941, when they had faced their first setbacks in the Soviet Union.

His report, dated October 25, 1943, reflected the field marshal's concerns. The Allied landings would certainly come within the next year and start probably in the spring or summer. The obvious location for the main invasion was the Pas-de-Calais because of its short supply line and air routes to England and its relatively direct distance straight into Germany. However, given the enemy's enormous logistical forces, this was by no means the only possibility. There were other potential landing areas in either Normandy or Brittany. He reported that the enemy had him outmanned, both in numbers of divisions and in the quality of their soldiers. And of course, he had to state the obvious nature of the Allied forces' overwhelming air and naval superiority. This gave them not only the capacity to cover and supply any invasion along the coast, but also the flexibility to conduct more than one landing, although one specific area would be the main effort.

Von Rundstedt prided himself among other things on being pragmatic. He knew that, given the dynamics of mobility, he would not be able to fight an active defense behind the Atlantic Wall the same way static defenses had been effectively used in previous wars. The upcoming campaign would incorporate all the advanced concepts of a modern conflict. As such, he contended in the report that strongpoints along a rigid position would not be nearly enough. To defeat the enemy, the Atlantic Wall defenses would have to be considerably more extensive, especially in critical areas. Sufficient reinforcements would have to be readily available, and above all, a powerful mobile reserve would be needed to mount a crushing counterattack.

He then pointed out that he was sadly lacking in all those features, and that he could therefore not at this time defeat any invasion that the enemy might launch. His static fortifications were few and far between, and the coastal defense line lacked any appreciable depth to it. Any reinforcements that he created were usually siphoned off to Italy or the East. And he had no significant reserve.

Various sections in his 30-page report outlined his concerns. Among other things, in support of his static line argument, he detailed the long length of his front and the lack of units at his disposal to man a fixed line, especially compared to World War I.

> A defense in the true sense of the word is not possible on many portions of the front of the Western Command, but only a security, and on the First Army and Nineteenth Army fronts merely a reinforced observation. This fact is a direct result of the general situation. We must make the best of it and try with all means to apply the type of defense that offers us the greatest likelihood of success...
>
> We cannot and may not fall back in the West, because the space separating the Channel from the Western German frontier is too restricted...

He addressed in general the subject of fortresses and fixed defensive strongpoints:

> In spite of all fortifications, a rigid defense of the long stretch of coast is impossible for any considerable length of time.
>
> This fact must be kept in mind...
>
> The defense therefore is based primarily on the general reserves, especially of tanks and motorized units. Without them it is impossible to hold the coasts permanently. But these reserves must not only be available in sufficient number; they must be of such quality that they can attack against the Anglo-Americans, that is, against their materiel, otherwise the counter-attack will not go through...
>
> Fixed fortifications are indispensable and valuable for battle, as well as for propaganda. But it must not be imagined that this wall cannot be overcome when the enemy attacks it with the most powerful weapons of American might from the sea, from the air, and from the

rear. With the available means in men and matériel, and in the time at our disposal, it is out of the question to erect a deep continuous wall of permanent construction.

It is therefore a question of accepting limitations dictated by a proportioned, sober reckoning of time and availability in personnel and materiel...

After detailing supply shortages and the shortcomings of the navy and the air force, von Rundstedt listed the units in his theater and their compositions. Then he discussed equipment, supply problems, and troop morale. He also pointed out the risks of using "liberated" prisoners:[2]

I have accepted the Turk battalions in exchange for German battalions for the East in order to have some men to show on the thin fronts. Everything will depend on their reliability, about which we cannot judge yet today. If they prove unsatisfactory, then they will constitute more of a liability than an asset.

He then contrasted the present situation with that of the year before:

The enemy is in a position to attack from England across the channel at any time...In comparison with 1942, the situation in the West must also be considered much more critical in view of the general situation. In 1944, O.B. West must expect large-scale attacks on his fronts...

After recapping his conclusions, he closed on a positive note for the Führer:

If the day of the large-scale attack arrives, we shall not hesitate to do everything in our power that can be done with the means then available, down to the last man!

(signed) von Rundstedt
Oberbefehlshaber West

***

Near the end of October, a day after the report was sent, 53-year-old *Generaloberst* Alfred Jodl, the balding, square-framed operations chief of staff for OKW, received two personal letters backing up von Rundstedt's concerns.

The first one, initially sent to Jodl's assistant, Walther Warlimont, was from *Fremde Heeres West*[3] commander *Oberstleutnant* Alexis *Freiherr* von Roenne.[4] His letter described a troubling picture of enemy buildup in England. The Allies, Roenne estimated, had some 43 front-line enemy divisions available for a landing—two dozen infantry, a dozen armor, three airborne divisions, and several specialized, independent brigades. Opposing them were only 26 German divisions of any comparable value. A report included in the letter listed several intelligence claims of numerous possible landing sites for an invasion, and recent intelligence reports confirming that Allied landing craft were leaving the Mediterranean, probably headed for England.

The second letter, far more colorful in its language, was from Fifteenth Army commander *Generaloberst* Hans von Salmuth.[5] It came attached to a copy of an original assessment that he had previously sent to OB West in Paris. The accompanying letter was a frank, personal note, addressed to Jodl himself. In it, von Salmuth pulled no punches. He bluntly stated his case, emphasizing points here and there with double and even triple exclamation points. In his judgment, the collection and positioning of both personnel and matériel on the coast at present did not amount to much:

> The forces NOW available are adequate neither in size nor in quality. The draining away process must cease...
>
> ...There must be no "ostrich-like" policy; otherwise there may be a very unpleasant awakening! No enemy invasion will be shattered at the Atlantic Wall!!!

His letter scorned the navy with its "prima donna-like" behavior and farcical chain of command. He also attacked the army's long-standing practice of weakening the West to help the other fronts. His conclusions were forthright and callously direct:

> The Atlantic Wall is no wall!! Rather is it like a thin, in many places fragile, length of cord, which has a few small knots at isolated points, such as Dieppe and Dunkirk...
>
> When I visit the positions, I invariably receive the report: "... workers have been transferred to OT construction work for the Air force—usually, of course, "on the Führer's orders." Hell! Are we soldiers of the Army just dirt?? We are supposed to stand, up to the last man, up to the last cartridge. And we do it. Then they should treat us accordingly!

Von Salmuth also addressed the issue of enacting forced labor laws. After detailing several other important items—again peppered here and there with sarcasm and exclamation points—the Fifteenth Army commander concluded:

> My dear Jodl, this letter has been very frank on all points. It gives neither a pessimistic nor an optimistic viewpoint, but a purely realistic one. I feel myself bound to put things into words as I see them, and to make the requests which I deem necessary. I am aware that you cannot fulfill all my requests; for that the cloth is too thin everywhere. But with good will, much can still be accomplished here which will benefit the situation as a whole.
>
> Heil und Sieg!
>
> Yours,
> (signed) von Salmuth

Von Salmuth's assessment went out to OKW on October 28, and Jodl formally presented both von Rundstedt's study and von Salmuth's addition to the Führer at the daily conference two days later.

Hitler went over von Rundstedt's negative (although quite comprehensive) study in detail for several reasons. First, of course, was the field marshal's request that he do so. Anyway, the crisis on the Eastern Front had temporarily subsided. Winter was setting in, and the Russians had paused to replenish and consolidate their recent gains. They would not begin any major campaigns until the spring thaws next year. The recent three-week Moscow Conference[6] had just concluded, extensively reported by enemy radio broadcasts. The Allies called for unconditional surrender by the Axis, all but convincing Hitler that an invasion in the West was now just a matter of time. Up until that point, he and Jodl had still fervently hoped that they might in one way or another be able to reason with the Western Allies, and despite long odds, manage to agree upon some type of honorable peace accord. Not now, though. The news was quite specific on that.

Thus, faced with an all-or-nothing proposition, Hitler, Jodl, and Field Marshal Keitel now took the time to discuss in detail von Rundstedt's report, along with von Salmuth's communiqué. If all the disturbing facts given were for the most part correct, the Atlantic Wall was not nearly as formidable as they had imagined. If what the old man had written was really true, the inevitable Allied invasion of France, which could come as early as next spring, would have little chance of failing. At that point, the opening of a new front in the West to complement the two in Italy and Russia would forever remove any long-term chance of winning the war. The Reich would be doomed and would not survive.

With hopes of a last chance for peace gone, the thought of a successful invasion of Europe depressed Hitler. Just as Napoleon had assumed he had decisively taken the Prussians out of action in the early phase of the battle of Waterloo, Hitler had essentially assumed after the fall of France in 1940 that he had won the war in the West. He had not really changed his opinion about this, despite the fact that England had managed to survive and then hold its own these last three years, especially with America now in the war. Hitler had long accepted the arrogant mindset that he would not have to worry about a major land campaign on that front. Now, it looked like he might very well lose Western Europe at a time to be chosen by the enemy.

So what then had von Rundstedt been doing for the last two years? Where was that iron barrier that Hitler had wanted finished last May? Hitler only wondered.

---

1   *Oberkommando der Wehrmacht.* The German supreme command for all the armed forces.

2   In September 1943, OKW decided on trading German battalions stationed in France for Öst newly organized battalions in a ratio of two-to-one. During September and October, about forty-five Cossack, Georgian, North Caucasian, Turkoman, Armenian, Volga-Tatar, Azerbaijanian, Volga-Finn, and other miscellaneous Eastern Europe battalions were transferred to the West. By May of 1944, the Seventh Army alone would have nearly two dozen of these battalions, about a sixth of the entire army's rifle battalions.

3   Foreign Armies West, the German Army's Intelligence branch. See Glossary.

4   Forty-three-year-old von Roenne was a decorated wounded hero of World War I. His Foreign Armies West was actually a part of the Army High Command, directly responsible for all the military intelligence in the Western Theater. A devout Catholic who despised the Nazi regime, he would later play a part in the July plot of 1944.

5   Von Salmuth, born in Metz, was a stocky, self-confident leader with a reputation for being outspoken. Like most of his peers, he was a veteran of World War I. Now at 55 years old, he had accumulated plenty of wartime experience. When World War II broke out, he initially served as chief of staff to General von Bock commanding *Heeresgruppe Nord* in the invasion of Poland (*Fall Weiss*—"Case White"), and then later in the Dutch invasion of 1940. In the spring of 1941, on

the Östfront, he took over command of 30th Corps and later served in the opening invasion of Russia and the Sevastopol campaign. The next summer, he was given command of the Second Army, and was part of the drive on Stalingrad, covering the northern flank of von Weich's army group. He later took part in the fierce Russian counterattack in November.

Then, in January of 1943, his command was attacked and encircled by a mighty Russian winter counteroffensive. It found itself on the brink of a smaller Stalingrad. Von Salmuth, a practical fellow (who had learned from von Paulus' fateful decision to hold fast), rejected the Führer's usual "stand-and-hold" order. Instead, in a daring counterattack, he led his men in a hard-fought breakout that rescued his army. Still, he had disobeyed orders, unfortunately in the same month that von Paulus surrendered to the Russians. Hitler had still not learned the harsh lessons of the Sixth Army's fate, so in early February, von Salmuth was cashiered, a humiliating experience that left him bitter and resentful. Eventually, OKW begrudged him the possibility that he had done the right thing and he had after all saved his army. So four months later, he was restored to duty and given command of the Fourth Army on the Russian Front while its commander, Gotthard Heinrici, went on sick leave. His previous defiance to orders though, had earned him the disfavor of the Führer and had made him a number of enemies. So after the failed Kurst offensive in July 1943 and after Heinrici had returned from leave, von Salmuth relinquished his command.

He was eventually reassigned to the West and posted to command the Fifteenth Army on August 1, 1943. His hatred of Hitler and the Nazis though, after being (in his mind) unjustly fired that time in Russia, never left him. Since then, he shared a number of conversations with fellow officers who were a part of the resistance against Hitler.

6   This was a large symposium held by the Allies between October 18 and November 11, 1943. Attending were the senior diplomats, generals, and foreign ministers of the United States, Great Britain, and the Soviet Union. The opening statement called them to "continue hostilities against those Axis powers with which they respectively are at war until such powers have laid down their arms on the basis of unconditional surrender." The outcome included resolutions to eliminate Italian fascism, the restoration of Austrian, Greek, and Yugoslavian independence, recognition of German atrocities and a resolve to see the perpetrators punished, and the creation of a Big Four postwar organization (The United States, Great Britain, the Soviet Union, and the Republic of China).

An In-depth Inspection of the Coast—The Reluctant Messenger

With this new and disconcerting study coming from the West, it seemed that someone from the High Command would have to fly to France and verify von Rundstedt's findings. Alfred Jodl unenthusiastically figured that it would probably end up being him, because this type of task had so many times in the past landed on his shoulders.

Jodl did not want to take the trip for a number of reasons. First of all, he would have to be away from the critical operational aspects of the High Command for about a month. Without him there, and with Keitel in full charge, his absence might prove to be operationally fatal.

Second, winter was coming. Jodl had a nice, convenient, comfortable working environment at the Berghof, and in his quarters, a special villa in the Berghof compound, he had all the comforts of home. He wanted for naught.

In contrast, it would be wet, chilly and blustery walking along that exposed coastline, and there was a great deal of coastline that he would have to cover: realistically, this would not be a short trip. Depending upon how detailed an inspection he made, he could very well be gone for weeks. All that time away from home, and his family; away from High Command operations where he was so badly needed; staying every night in a different set of uncomfortable quarters; walking out in the cold along dreary beaches, and always so near the shores of an active enemy.

Besides, there was a third reason for not wanting to be the one to go, to him a critically important personal one. He was not sure how the Führer would react to the results he knew in his heart he would probably have to convey. The Führer had acquired a bad habit of sometimes picking on the messenger, and Jodl believed that this might be very well be one of those occasions. The Führer had boasted about the Atlantic Wall publically and privately for well over a year; not just in private circles, but officially, through Goebbels' propaganda organization. He would be furious to find out that the bristling steel and concrete defense belt along the coast was just a paper tiger. And if that happened, there was a definite chance that the herald would be targeted along with the message.

It had happened a number of times in the past, as he knew from personal experience. Jodl had made such an inspection trip a year ago, with near-disastrous results to his career and possibly even to his life. The event had certainly changed his once-close relationship with the Führer, as well as with the High Command.

Jodl thought back…

In early September of 1942, at Hitler's insistence, Jodl had flown to southern Russia to scope out the enemy defenses in the area around Tuapse, a strategic port on the Black Sea. OKW was planning a large airborne landing around that area to threaten the Russian rear and to force them back. This operation was designed to motivate *Feldmarschall* Wilhelm List, the general in charge of that front, to make a move and order his alpine units through the steep passes of the Caucasus mountains and onward, downward, towards the Black Sea. From there, bolstered by an airborne landing, they could easily capture the crucial Maikop and Grozny oil fields, thus bringing welcome relief to the Reich's critically short petrol supply. Additionally, they would deprive the Russians of important ports. List was to be given his instructions in no uncertain terms. Hitler did not trust the Heeres chief of staff, 59-year-old Franz Halder, to do his bidding for this task. Besides, the Führer and Jodl had worked well together up until now, and he trusted Jodl's judgment implicitly.

So Jodl had dutifully left the *Werwolf*[1] and flown out to Stalino very early on the Monday morning of September 7 to study the brutal rocky terrain at first hand. An experienced mountain artillery officer from World War I, he had talked at length to List, his headquarters staff, and to General Konrad, commanding the 49 *Gebirgskorps* engaged against the enemy.[2] Jodl had found out that, contrary to what Hitler believed (which was influenced by the fact that Hitler had never really taken a liking to List anyway), the field marshal was indeed doing nearly as well as possible, given the enormity of his task and his limited resources.[3] Jodl concluded that any strategic air landing would fail, especially in the face of strong Soviet forces in the area. And because of the spread-out deployment of List's tired and depleted units, they would never be able to relieve the paratroopers.

Jodl dutifully flew all the way back to the *Werwolf* that same day, and he reported his findings to the Führer late that evening. Hitler though, expecting to hear good news, did not take the report well. He had assumed that Jodl on his behalf would jump down List's back and sternly impose the Führer's will; that the field marshal would do whatever was needed to start making substantial progress in his advance any way that he could. A move forward was critically needed to make sure that the upcoming airborne landing would be successful.

Jodl explained that an airborne landing would be doomed, because List could not at present advance to relieve the paratroopers. Furthermore, there were substantial enemy units in the potential drop zones. In response, Hitler became angry, more than anything because Jodl had taken List's pessimistic position over his own.

As Jodl only later found out, the Führer that day was in no mood for what he now considered insolence. He had over the last couple weeks become even more frustrated with the Russian campaign. The enemy was not only stubbornly holding out but apparently actually getting stronger every week, and Hitler had become increasingly impatient, his moods fouler. Only two weeks ago,[4] Army Chief Franz Halder had reported that Walter Model's Ninth Army near Rzhev[5] was battered and tired, had been heavily assaulted by Soviets and was in a state of near collapse. Halder insisted they be allowed to withdraw to defend a shorter line. Hitler had exploded in a fiery temper.

"You always seem to make the same suggestion—retreat!" he had shouted. "I expect my commanders to be as tough as the fighting troops!"

Halder for once had lost his temper. He had icily retorted that German *Feldgrau* and lieutenants were falling by the thousands just because their commanders were not being allowed to make the only reasonable, possible command decisions.

Hitler, infuriated, had shouted back, "*Generaloberst* Halder, how *dare* you use language like that in front of me! Do you think you can teach *me* what the man at the front is thinking?!? What do *you* know about what goes on at the front?!? Where were *you* in the First World War? You were as chairbound in that one as you are in this one! You don't even have a wound stripe on your uniform! And you try to pretend to me that I don't understand what it's like at the front. I won't stand that! It's outrageous."

He had been referring of course to Halder's lack of combat experience, Halder having served in World War I first as an ordnance officer, then as a staff officer. Hitler had later remarked, "If I listen to General Halder much longer, I'll become a pacifist." And then just a few days previously, the Führer had complained again about Halder, adding, "With Jodl, I know where I stand. He says what he thinks."

Now though, it seemed that his own operations chief was turning on him. And now, as he had several times before with other generals in other critical situations, Hitler turned his wrath on a surprised Jodl. He called him a defeatist and bluntly accused him of having wasted their time. Here, like so many other defeatist generals, Jodl too was now presenting him with another "cannot-be-done" attitude, and unlike the Führer's senior Nazi and SS leaders, was also giving him some Army insolence to go with it—just like Halder had done. Raising his eyes to the ceiling and throwing his arms out dramatically, Hitler declared mordantly, "As soon as one of my senior commanders gets out of my sight, he seems to fall under some sort of alien spell. I can't count on anyone, unless I'm standing right next to him at all times."

In the cold silence following his remark, Hitler paused and then, looking at the map, grumbled that List should never have divided his forces in the first place. In typical *blitzkrieg* doctrine, he should have massed his mobile units at one strategic point and smashed through the Russian lines.

After a short pause, Jodl pointed out that it was the Führer himself who had ordered List to move forward all along a broader front, forcing him in doing so to spread his men out. The implication was that it had been the Führer's own hubris that had convinced him to change their grand strategy to try and take both Stalingrad and the Caucasus at the same time. And that is what had put them where they were now—losing the one and failing to take the other.

Hitler became wide-eyed at this apparent betrayal and had barked "That's a lie!" He growled that he never had given such an order.

Jodl, tired and irritated after his long round trip and this unexpected, unfounded indignation in front of the others (including several subordinates), straightened his wiry frame and again coldly defended his assessments. He insisted that List's performance was as good as could be expected, given the enormity of his task, logistical problems (their supplies had to go over mountain roads by mule), a strong enemy presence, tired resources, and the treacherous mountain terrain he was in.

Hitler snarled back, "I didn't send you Jodl, to hear you report on all the difficulties. You were supposed to represent my view that paratroopers were to be landed in Tuapse. THAT was your job!" His eyes blazing, he added, "Instead of that, you come back here, completely under the influence of the frontline commanders. You're nothing but the megaphone of these gentlemen! I didn't need to send you there for that."

To make matters worse, earlier that day OKW had received a message from that mountain corps that they were starting to withdraw their recon units from the mountain passes. "Apparently," Hitler concluded spitefully, "that is the only success of your flight."

Jodl had a sharp Bavarian temper, and he rarely minced his words. Yet he nearly always had maintained a substantial degree of tact and control in his work, especially to the Führer whom he had until now respected. However, after that last biting remark in this tirade, one aimed directly at him, he tensed up, infuriated at the accusation of being just another Nazi toady.

Throwing caution to the winds, he replied frostily, "If you want to lose your paratroopers, then drop them on Tuapse. And the same thing will happen to the Alpine troops if they have to move over those mountain passes at this time of year." Pausing, he had added stonily, "Apart from that, I wasn't sent down there just to hand over your orders, but to make a study of the situation."

The room had become deathly quiet as he concluded, "If all you want is an orderly, then you don't need me, when you can use any rank-and-file private."[6]

The Führer, already fuming, became livid at this outright insolence in front of the others. He yelled back, "You should have forced them to accept my orders in spite of all their objections, which I so often get. That was your *mission*, General Jodl, and you have failed to carry it out. Thank you. You are *dismissed*."

Glaring, Jodl curtly turned and stormed out of the room, slamming the door behind him.[7] He found out later that Hitler turned to his army adjutant, Rudolf Schmundt, and growled that he would never again eat at the same table with Jodl and Keitel. He then stalked out of the room himself. Several senior officers present quietly shook their heads. It was soon reported that Hitler after the meeting bitterly remarked that not since World War I had an army been so betrayed.

Hitler from then on ruthlessly and coldly excommunicated all of his generals and admirals—officially, emotionally, and of course, socially. The atmosphere at the forest headquarters for the next week or so was icy. Hitler holed himself up in his dark blockhouse and never emerged until late at night, not to be seen, and definitely not to be approached. Conferences were conducted only in his hut, and with only a few individuals.

At these small subsequent staff meetings, Hitler pointedly ignored both Jodl and Keitel, his superior, as if they were not there. He no longer addressed Jodl by name as he had before, and would not shake hands with him, or with any other general for that matter. And he never again took his meals in the headquarters mess hall.

The ever-loyal, acquiescent Keitel, who was totally taken in by the Führer and had catered to his every whim for years,[8] took this rebuke hard. For days on end, he would walk about the headquarters, brooding and sulking.

A short time later, Hitler ordered Martin Bormann (who now arrogantly sat in Jodl's chair at meals) to get a half-dozen or so stenographers to be present at each conference to record the proceedings. That way, the Führer could never again stand accused of saying something not written down, and in turn, those present could be held accountable for everything that they said or were told.[9]

As expected, General List had been sacked soon afterward—two days later, on September 9, getting the dismissal by telephone from Keitel.[10] It was assumed that Jodl would shortly follow suit, although no one had the faintest idea of who they would or even could get to replace him. Jodl had been a critically important, central part of OKW operations since before the war had begun. And yet, to openly defy the Führer like that—no, essential or not, Jodl's days at OKW would soon end.[11]

Jodl himself told his operations deputy chief Walther Warlimont about the incident the next day. After summing up the main points of what had happened, he admitted somewhat ruefully that he had been wrong to react to the Führer as he had. He added in a fairly embarrassed tone, "You should never try to point out to a dictator where he has gone wrong, because this will shake his self-confidence; which is the main pillar upon which his personality and actions are based."

They had then discussed his replacement at length. Jodl had concluded, "I just hope he'll try to find a successor for me among the army generals!" He had paused and then added bitterly, "But he will never again have such staunch National-Socials as me and Scherff."[12]

He and Warlimont continued to discuss the matter for a while, Jodl now regretful over losing his temper the way he had. He finally looked at Warlimont and said, "Keep yourself out of the briefing conferences from now on. It's too depressing having to go through that."

Indeed to Jodl, his days at OKW indeed seemed numbered, like those of General Halder, who had been sacked just a week before. Surprisingly though, Jodl was not dismissed. Hitler, egotistical as he was, had the common sense to realize how indispensable Jodl was to his staff. Naturally though, having exchanged such harsh words with the leader (and especially in the presence of others), Jodl continued to be on his bad side from then on, the common fate of most military commanders who dared question the Führer, much less argue with him. Certainly no Nazi party member or SS leader would ever dream of doing such a thing.

Jodl found out six months later that Keitel had been slated to be dismissed as well, to be replaced by Kesselring. Jodl himself was to have been replaced by General von Paulus as soon as the Sixth Army had taken Stalingrad. Von Paulus though, had of course ultimately surrendered his forces and had shamefully been taken prisoner, so the change never occurred.

Yes, things had indeed been brittle for quite a while. The Führer rarely socialized with his officers after that, and continued dining alone in his private blockhouse, seldom leaving it, except after dark.

***

Now, some 14 months later, the episode was behind them, but for Jodl it had indeed been a close call.[13] It had also permanently corrupted Jodl's relationship with the Führer, who even now never shook hands with him, nor ever addressed him by name. Still, Hitler and Jodl were at least back on speaking terms, although their relationship would probably never be as relaxed and affable as it had been before.[14] No, Jodl definitely did not want to risk such an episode again for this inspection trip. Someone else would have to go instead. Somebody qualified, whose opinion the Führer would respect.

When he had first read von Rundstedt's report, Jodl immediately thought about *Generalfeldmarschall* Erwin Rommel. He was just recently out of a job, because the Führer had relieved him from the Northern Italian Front, and these days, he was sometimes present at OKW. Once considered likely to become *OB Südouest*,[15] he had lost out when the Führer had instead decided to give command of the Italian Front to optimistic *Generalfeldmarschall* Albert Kesselring ("Smiling Albert," they sometimes called him), whose plans to defend Italy were much more proactively aggressive.

Now Rommel's occasional, relatively inactive presence at OKW made for a somewhat awkward situation, especially since the war situation was getting worse. If von Rundstedt's claims about the Atlantic coastline were right, Rommel was certainly available to go there and make a painstaking inspection to confirm them (and of course, possibly take some of the heat for the bad news) or deny them. In any event, he could then stay to revitalize the defensive effort on the coast along with his also-out-of-work army group staff, which the Führer had insisted remain intact for any unexpected contingencies.

It all made good sense. By sending Rommel, Jodl would be killing two birds with one stone, so to speak. At the same time, Jodl could later take some credit for getting an accurate assessment of the coastal defenses and of getting Rommel both gainfully employed once more, and back in the Führer's good graces. Besides, who knew more about fighting the Western Allies (especially the Americans) than Rommel? Well, maybe Kesselring, but he was fully engaged holding them back in Italy.

Jodl quickly had a proposal drafted up at the end of October that called for Rommel and his staff to become the cadre for an inspection group,[16] which might eventually become a new army group. Its purpose would be to counterstrike against the Western Allies, wherever they chose to invade. This new army group staff would, at least for now, answer directly to OKW.

When Jodl first proposed the idea to the Führer, he did not at first enthusiastically endorse it, although he did find it intriguing. He and Jodl discussed the pros and cons of sending Rommel for a couple days before Hitler finally agreed to it. Rommel would be tasked only with inspecting the Atlantic Wall. Possibly, eventually, he might be given area command of its defense, though the Führer insisted that the initial order should only give him power to make "study assignments." The theater commander would of course remain von Rundstedt, because putting the junior field marshal over the old Prussian would not be appropriate. And anyway, Hitler was not quite sure that Rommel had overcome his defeatist depression, his *Afrikanische Krankheit*[17] from North Africa. No, let him just go out there for now and look around. Working together with von Rundstedt, his observations would be helpful.

Consequently, Rommel was to be given the assignment. The Desert Fox would once more be on the move, inspecting and formulating ideas for better defenses against the enemy, only now it would be against the inevitable upcoming invasion in the West. He was to draw up possible plans for a counterattack, based on different scenarios, as well as make suggestions for improving the defenses. He was also to come up with ideas to create additional fighting units out of the reserve or auxiliary units, as well as suggestions for moving troops from quiet areas to those directly threatened. Lastly, he was to provide guidance on the best possible disposition of the panzer forces to allow them the fastest, most powerful reaction to the landing, whenever or wherever it took place.

At the Führer's behest, OKW sent for Rommel to report to the *Wolfsschanze* in East Prussia.[18] In the meantime though, Hitler and Jodl realized that the risk of a weak coastal defensive system in the West had to be addressed on a broad spectrum, and without delay. In the absence of evidence to the contrary, they had to assume for the moment that von Rundstedt's report was accurate. After all, stubborn and rebellious though he might be, the old man usually was usually accurate in his military assessments.

So Hitler directed Jodl to draft a general directive for the Western commanders to follow, stressing the need for preparation to meet the expected invasion. The order, *Führerweisung Nr. 51*,[19] was dated November 3, 1943. It essentially accepted most of the field marshal's conclusions and acknowledged the presence of this new threat from the Western Allies. Unlike the Eastern Front, where any setback could be partially offset by a modest retreat, a breakthrough in the West would have immediate, dire consequences on the direction of the war. Thus, a solid Western shield had to be developed quickly.

The directive went on to list specific instructions to all commands and all the different branches of service (including the Waffen-SS) on steps to take to build the defenses in the West. Details included unit types, movement policies, buildup plans, and general battle strategies to be followed. Also, no unit could be transferred out of Western Europe without Hitler's permission. At the same time, OB West was directed to minimize garrisons in areas of low threat and to improve the counterattack capabilities of his forces (including all the static units) by somehow improving their mobility through internal resources.

The directive cited the strong evidence that the Allies would invade France in the upcoming year, most likely by spring, and that the most likely area was the Pas-de-Calais.

> Should the enemy, by concentrating his armed might, succeed in landing, he must be hit by the full fury of our counterattack. The problem will be, by the rapid concentration of adequate forces and material, as well as intensive training, to form available large units into an offensive reserve of high fighting quality, attacking power and mobility. The counterattack of these units will prevent the enemy from exploiting the landing, and throw him back into the sea.
>
> I can therefore no longer take responsibility for further weakening the West, in favor of other theaters of war. I have therefore decided to reinforce its defenses, particularly those places from which the long-range bombardment of England will begin. For it is here that the enemy must and will attack, and it is here—unless all indications are misleading—that the decisive battle against the landing forces will be fought...
>
> [Therefore] all persons in authority will guard against wasting time and energy in useless quibbling about jurisdictional matters and will direct all efforts toward strengthening our defensive and offensive power.

---

1   Hitler's Werewolf headquarters, located in a dense pinewood area, about 15km northeast of the central Ukrainian town of Vinnitsa, and abut 260km from its capital, Kiev. Started in December 1941, it was finished the next June under a mantle of secrecy. (Rumors had spread that the site was to be a sanatorium for officers.)

2   *General der Gebirgstruppe* Rudolf Konrad, commanding the XLIX Mountain Corps. Konrad was eventually relieved of his command in the late spring of 1944 for losing the Crimea and Sevastopol. He was given a number of lesser commands for the rest of the war, until he was captured in May 1945 and spent two years in prison.

3   Wilhelm List, who had played a major role in both the French campaign of 1940 and the invasion of Greece in 1941, had been recalled to active service as recently as late June to command this front. Hitler split Army Group South into two smaller groups: Army Group A and Army Group B. List was given Army Group A and charged with taking the critical port of Rostov, capturing the oilfields, and then taking Baku. The offensive had started in July, but had bogged down. In late August, List gave a lackluster report to Hitler at his Werewolf headquarters in Vinnitsa, and, while the Führer was pleasant enough to the field marshal, he afterwards complained about he had been duped into appointing this man to the position.

4 Field Marshal Halder and historian John Toland put the date as August 24. Irving put it at September 7.

5 A Russian city on the Volga, about 183 kilometers northwest of Moscow.

6 One source quoted Jodl as saying, "If you had wanted a mere messenger, why hadn't you sent a young lieutenant?"

7 Irving writes that it was Hitler who first "stalked out," but other sources (including Jodl himself) claim otherwise.

8 One time Hitler, consumed by a wild rage, had thrown a file down onto the floor in the presence of Keitel, Jodl, and Warlimont. Keitel, frozen with fear, had just stood there, a look of terror on his face.

9 Nearly a dozen stenographers arrived from the Reichstag 48 hours later. They were at once put in uniform, ordered to take the oath of allegiance to the Führer (given by Hitler personally), and set up in a wooden hut nearby. They were then given a rotation schedule in which two of them would be present to record proceedings at each conference.

10 List spent the remainder of the war at his home near Garmisch-Partenkirchen.

11 Jodl had indeed been slated to be replaced by General von Paulus as soon as the Sixth Army took Stalingrad. Von Paulus of course had never made it out of Stalingrad, and the change had not occurred.

12 General Walter Scherff, the chief OKW historian, appointed by Hitler in 1942 to document the Reich's war history.

13 Warlimont later wrote that both Keitel and Jodl now seemed to be able to find the time to confide in him and to seek his opinions, something they had haughtily never bothered to do before. Keitel had once despondently asked him how he could possibly continue as Wehrmacht Chief of Staff and still keep his self-respect. Warlimont had responded by telling him that only he could answer that.

14 See daily entry for January 30, 1944.

15 The army group in Italy had been designated in 1941 as *Heeresgruppe Süd*. In 1943, it was redesignated *Heeresgruppe Südwest* to avoid confusion with *Heeresgruppe Süd* in Russia.

16 Jodl's initial entry on October 28 for the idea first referred to Rommel's staff as *Eingreifsstab Rommel* (Intervention Staff-Rommel). Its purpose would be twofold: to act as Inspector-General for coastal defenses, and to command defenses in Western Europe if the enemy invaded,

17 "African sickness." It was a term coined by Hitler in reference to Rommel's pronounced change in attitude into a seemingly pessimistic, defeatist mood during his last few months in North Africa.

18 "Wolf's Lair," the Führer's first, advanced strategic headquarters on the Eastern Front, designed so that he could better direct the Eastern Front operations. Surrounded by mines and barbed wire, it was a 1.5 × 2km compound, surrounded by a breezeless, dense pine forest, about 8km east of Rastenburg, East Prussia (now Ketrzyn, Poland). Hot and humid in the summer and cold and damp in the winter, it was isolated from the pulse of the Reich's daily governmental and military functions. Jodl once referred to it as "a mixture of cloister and concentration camp."
Most of his major advance headquarters bore the word "wolf" in their title.

19 War Directive No. 51. The War Directives (*Führerweisungen*) were strategic orders issued by Hitler himself. Covering an assortment of topics, each was written to provide instructions for an upcoming campaign, strategic direction, political policy, or management of occupied territories. A total of 80 were issued. A *Weisung* was not to be confused with a Direct Order (*Führerbefehl*) which was a special instructive edict, more immediate and imperative in nature.

Rommel is Given His Assignment

Generalfeldmarschall Johannes Erwin Eugen Rommel, a week and a half away from his 52nd birthday, reported to the *Wolfsschanze* in Bavaria on November 5, 1943. Together with General Jodl and Field Marshal Keitel, the Führer himself began their proposal by first reviewing the situation in the West. Hitler told Rommel about OB West's troubling summary of October 25, which stated that their celebrated Atlantic Wall was anything but formidable. And Army Intelligence had confirmed that the invasion of Western Europe was only a matter of months away.

The field marshal listened attentively as the Führer went on. Until such time as the new *Wunderwaffe* (miracle weapons)[1] came into full production, the Reich simply had to hold off the Allies. Unfortunately, most of their armies were committed to stemming off those accursed Russians. The few units in Italy were just barely holding their own. If a third front were opened now in the West, it would finish them off. And von Rundstedt's recent assessment indicated that they were wide open out there. Hitler needed a reliable, competent officer to assess the situation locally and come up with a badly needed plan to shore up their defenses if they were to have any hope at all of repulsing the British and the Americans.

So to that effect, the Führer told Rommel in his best encouraging tone that he had an inspiring answer to their dilemma: he wanted his best western commander to go to France and ascertain the situation himself by thoroughly inspecting the Channel coast. He wanted Rommel to verify or disavow von Rundstedt's troubling report, and in any case, provide logical and effective suggestions to improve their defenses. Rommel was to take his now-displaced army group staff and extensively tour the entire western coastline, from Denmark down to the southwestern French seashores, and across to the French Mediterranean coast. The Führer of course put his best spin on the idea and stressed how critical a task this was. The fate of the Reich, he concluded solemnly, depended on what Rommel could do.

At the end of their discussion, the Führer decided to give him some more incentive. He indirectly suggested that perhaps, just perhaps, Rommel himself might be given tactical command of the battle when it began; under the Führer's guidance, of course. He had not entirely accepted Jodl's objections after all.

This series of meetings had a profoundly positive impact on the field marshal, who had by now begun to wonder how badly he had fallen in favor. Now though, he was relieved that he was still critically needed.

The operational orders were drafted and officially issued the next day, November 6. Rommel was appointed *Befehlshaber, Heeresgruppe B.z.b.v.*[2] This army group would be answerable directly to the Führer and receive its instructions through Jodl's Operational Staff at OKW.

Rommel's group was given two directives:

- Study the defense preparedness of the coasts occupied by the Reich and then submit proposals for improvement

- Create options for offensive operations against an enemy landing.

The operational orders called for his first tour to start in Denmark; he should evaluate the defenses there, and submit his findings. Similarly, he was to check out the Artois, the Netherlands, Normandy, the Cotentin peninsula, and then Brittany. All commands in the area were to be instructed to fully cooperate with him.

As Rommel began his planning though, his new enthusiasm seemed to fluctuate. A day or so after the appointment, he attended another conference. He, Jodl, and the Führer further discussed the situation in the West, and how best to defend against the inevitable landing that would come next year. Rommel, considered by most as an expert in techniques for fighting the Western Allies, was convinced that the enemy had to be defeated right on the coast.

The Führer, bolstered by the theories of the General Staff and his experiences in Italy, was not so sure. He questioned putting all their units right up front, where the enemy could easily batter them with their command of the sea and air. Rommel was irritated that the Führer sided on this matter with the General Staff (which in his mind, had been traditionally antagonistic towards him). What had happened to his confidence in Rommel's judgment?

The meeting finally ended, the issue unsettled, and Hitler accompanied him outside the bunker. Rommel heard strains of music coming from one of the nearby quarters. Although he could not hear the needle scratches, it was probably a record: the Führer did not encourage much radio listening, especially from enemy broadcasts. Churchill's speeches in particular rankled him.

They continued talking as they walked, the Führer's overinflated optimism about repelling the invasion clearly evident as he talked. Rommel was still somewhat frustrated over the unresolved general strategy. And some analysis of von Rundstedt's report pointed to the probability that the old Prussian's assessment was accurate, and so this new assignment would be a losing proposition. The Atlantic coast seemed woefully ill-prepared to meet any sort of major landing. He tried gently but firmly to point this out. Then he again tried to win his point on general strategy.

"*Mein Führer*, we must repulse the enemy at his first landing site. Those pillboxes around the ports don't do the trick. Only primitive but effective barriers and obstacles all along the coast can make the landing so difficult that our countermeasures will be effective." The Führer said nothing. Reacting to this, Rommel pushed further. Maybe a low dose of reality here.

"If we don't manage to throw them back at once, the invasion will succeed, in spite of *der Atlantikwall*."

"Perhaps when we mount an effective counterattack—"

Rommel interrupted him. "We won't be able to. Overwhelming enemy airpower will take care of that. I know. I've seen it."

"You know, Rommel, we've seen before that airpower does have its limitations. Even our mighty Luftwaffe was stopped in 1940 by that pitiful RAF."

"Yes, but large numbers make a big difference," replied Rommel patiently, omitting the "*mein Führer*" he so regularly used. He was trying hard to be polite, but his frustration was welling up inside.

"Remember, I've seen first-hand what overwhelming enemy airpower can do to ground units. Towards the end in Tripoli and Tunis, the bombs were dropped in such concentrations that even our best troops were demoralized. And if you cannot halt the bombing, all the other methods to stop them will be ineffective—even the barriers." Perhaps he had gone too far.

The Führer's immediate reaction startled him. Hitler broke out into a big smile and gently grabbed Rommel's sleeve. He said eagerly, "Here is something I wanted to show you today in that connection, Field Marshal."

Hitler guided him over to an open range for his next appointment with the new Armaments Minister, Albert Speer, and his assistant, Karl Saur. A short distance away, there was what appeared to be some sort of experimental heavy-duty truck. It was lightly armored, and mounted in the back was an 88mm Flak-41 gun, nearly identical to the ones Rommel had used so effectively against the British armor in North Africa.

They stood silently and watched as an army officer got in the truck and drove it around the range to demonstrate its mobility. Saur began explaining the unit's features to them. After a few laps, the truck was parked. More soldiers rushed over to it and deployed the flak gun. It was fired several times into the air, as if against enemy aircraft, to show its rapid rate of fire. Stabilizing features that prevented the truck from lurching sideways when the gun was fired were pointed out.

Rommel watched the demonstration patiently, unimpressed. This makeshift weapon was all right, but it did not solve his problems. To counter just the air threat, he would need a thousand or more of those flak vehicles. And it surely would not be the definitive answer to defeat the invasion. No, Rommel needed hundreds of fighters and bombers along the coast, ready in a flash to tear into an invasion fleet and to protect his supply lines from bombing raids.

Unlike Rommel, Hitler was excited by the demonstration. He turned to Saur, and asked, "How many of these can you deliver in the next few months, Herr Saur?"

Saur vowed that they could make three or four hundred. Animated, Hitler turned back to Rommel, searching to see the optimism he was feeling. "You see, *Feldmarschall?*" he had said proudly. "With this armored flak weapon, we can take care of the concentration of bombers over our divisions."

Rommel stared back at the Führer, clearly unconvinced. To him, this flak truck was a totally inadequate remedy. Knowing that the Führer was waiting for a reaction, he finally smiled, but the doubt was plain on his face.

Hitler read his response, and his smile abruptly vanished. Grumbling, "Good day, *Feldmarschall*," he angrily stomped off towards his bunker, Speer and Saur following him as they talked. Rommel silently watched the Führer depart. While he regretted his reaction, he still knew that Hitler clearly was not facing reality. A few flak trucks were not going to do the trick.

Rommel's optimistic mood had been shaken, especially since he became aware of a rumor that the Führer's protégé was never going to get a combat command again. He had lost North Africa, and the Italians did not want him in their theater, because his occasional negative remarks about the incompetence of certain Italian officers had branded him an "Italian hater." No, to some, this was just Hitler's way of putting him in semi-retirement, as had happened to so many other generals before.

Saddened by the rumor, he wrote to his wife Lucie on November 9:

> *I am in a depressed mood. I am not sure whether my new assignment does not mean that I have been shelved. It is being judged that way in some quarters. I refuse to believe it. The Führer gave me an altogether different impression. But so many people are jealous of me. And yet the times are so serious there is really no room for envy and quarrel.*

He left the next day to gather his staff. It took them about a week to wrap things up in Northern Italy and get organized for the move to Western Europe. Finally, on November 21, he was ready to leave the Italian peninsula. He officially turned over his few responsibilities for this area to Albert Kesselring and then made a brief stop in Rome to tell Mussolini *ciao*. At that point he was finished, and departed. He would first go home on leave though, before starting his new task.

He was taken over to the Villafranca airfield, where he boarded his two-engine green and yellow Heinkel 111, designated DH-YA, his pilot Leutnant Hermann Giesen.[3] It took off from a partly cloudy airfield, escorted by two ME-109s, which were needed because of the real danger of being attacked by enemy aircraft. Three years ago of course, they would not have been necessary. But now it was late November 1943. The Allies ruled the skies.

He flew home to rest before starting his task in Western Europe. He and Lucie would celebrate their 27th anniversary on November 27. Maybe the numerical coincidence would be a symbol of good luck for them in the next year. He hoped so. He needed some luck.

In early December, Rommel's inspection tour would begin.

---

1   Hitler was referring to military technological improvements that he felt would turn the tide of war. One was a long-range bomber that could fly across the Atlantic, bomb the US, and come back again. Another was the schnorkel device that allowed a U-boat to remain submerged, and yet still run on its diesel engines. In addition, this category included new German jet aircraft, supertanks and one of superbattleships, glide bombs, a sun gun that could focus intense sunlight on one spot, and of course the Vengeance weapons (V-1 and V-2).

2   *Heeresgruppe B—zur besonderer Verwendung.* "Army Group B—For Special Purposes." See Glossary.

3   Rommel's He-111, classified as a medium-range bomber, had been converted to carry passengers in comfort—in this case, one particular army commander.

PART ONE

Der Atlantikwall

December 1943

Wednesday, December 1

After a restful ten-day leave at his beautiful cottage home in the quaint town of Herrlingen in Baden-Württemberg, *Generalfeldmarschall* Erwin Rommel had traveled for two days by car to Munich the night before to meet his chief of staff and his skeleton army group staff. This morning, he joins them and rides with them to the railroad station, where a special train that has been set aside just for him is waiting. They all board the train with their luggage and boxes of supplies, and are shown their accommodation.

Now in the conference car, Rommel formally meets with his staff, and they all sit down to finalize the schedule that they had laid out the night before. Shortly thereafter, *Heeresgruppe B.z.v.b*'s special train sets off for a 1,100km trip to the coast of Denmark.

Aside from scheduling a number of administrative meetings, they go over more details for their inspection tour at various times that day, As the countryside rolls by, Rommel has occasion to talk to each member of this experienced staff of experts, these trusted officers that he will heavily rely on over the next few months.

His army group chief of staff, fondly called *Der Chef* by the others, is *Generalleutnant* Alfred Gause. He has been with Rommel since North Africa as his chief of staff.[1] He is dependable, intelligent, resourceful, and a decent man. He is a good friend, very familiar with the field marshal's moods and temperament. Rommel in turn trusts him and knows that Gause is completely dedicated to him.

Handsome, debonair, 36-year-old *Oberstleutnant* Hans-Georg von Tempelhoff is their Ia, the chief operations officer.[2] Rommel had first met him back in 1938, when the young man was still a member of the *Hitlerjugend*,[3] although not what could be considered an ardent Nazi. Interestingly, his wife Marianne is English-born, a point that von Tempelhoff is often ribbed about; sometimes though, in a more serious tone. He is a good soldier, having distinguished himself on the Russian front. Joining Rommel in Italy in 1943, he accompanied the field marshal on many inspections, and on a number of occasions they had candidly discussed the progress of the war. Over those months, they had formed a good relationship. Rommel will now count on von Tempelhoff to help him in Western Europe as he did in Italy.

Fifty-four-year-old *Generalleutnant* Ernst Gehrke is their *Höherer Nachrichtenführer.*[4] Gehrke in the early part of 1943 had served under Rommel in North Africa in that same role for the *Panzerarmee Afrika*. Besides commanding and overseeing the staff's signals unit, all theater reconnaissance operations and reports, all communications channels, and radar activities, he will also command the headquarters reconnaissance personnel; that is of course, when he is eventually assigned more men.

Oberst Freyberg is the IIa, their adjutant, in charge of assigning those personnel. *Generalmajor* Dr. Wilhelm Meise will advise Rommel on engineering matters. Even though Meise is a professional engineer, he is constantly amazed at the technical knowledge that Rommel displays about setting up defensive structures.

Oberst Hans Lattman is in charge of the weapons branch and is also Rommel's artillery specialist. Lattman has been a personal friend of the Rommel family for several years, and his admiration for the field marshal is undeniable.

Rounding out the staff is *Oberstleutnant* Wolfgang Queissner, their Luftwaffe operations coordinator, and Rommel's aide, Leutnant Norbert Hammermann, a decorated Eastern Front veteran who was badly wounded in the summer of 1942 and lost one eye.

A further member of the staff who will join them in a day or two is their naval advisor, *Vizeadmiral* Friedrich Ruge. Rommel chose the affable 49-year-old admiral less than a month ago because he has an impressive background.[5] Ruge had organized the naval defensive forces in France, before being transferred to Italy in mid-1943. There he took over command of the scant German naval forces on the Italian peninsula and oversaw their valiant but unsuccessful operations against the enemy invasions. It was during that time that Ruge had met the field marshal. Ruge, also a Swabian, was an uncomplicated man, and so it was no surprise that the two of them had quickly become good friends. And the admiral seemed to be an officer that the field marshal felt he could confide in. So when Gause proposed appointing him their *Obermarineberater*,[6] Rommel did not hesitate to give Ruge the job.

Also soon to join the army group staff on the train will be *Oberst* Anton Staubwasser, their Intelligence Officer (Ic).[7] Recently recruited from the English Section of the *Fremde Heeres West*, he had been a student of Rommel's some thirteen years ago at the Dresden Infantry School. Staubwasser is an easy-going fellow, not a schemer, and considered an authority on the British military. He will be a welcome addition to the staff, although his section only consists right now of a couple interpreters and some clerks. Hopefully, he will be able to get more personnel in a few weeks.

All of Rommel's officers are military men. Although he himself is a loyal member of the National Socialist Party, Rommel (strangely to some) does not want a political officer in his group. This is unusual, because an edict had just come down last week from OKW instructing that a political officer was now required for each command staff. Still, Rommel chooses to ignore the directive to allow his men the flexibility to show initiative, to speak their minds, and to better work together. A sort of harmony has emanated from these men because of their freedom to speak their minds in front of him, and he is not going to change that by including some die-hard Nazi in the team.

Another personal rule of his is that he never has a woman on his staff. The field marshal is always extremely polite to ladies, treats them with great respect, and does not consider himself a chauvinist. However, to him, they have no place in the army, and certainly not in his headquarters staff.

The train travels on all day and stops that night for the men to get out and find quarters in town.

***

British bombers for months have steadily pounded German cities by night. *Reichsmarschall* Hermann Göring grits his teeth at the thought of Germans contemptuously calling him "Meier" behind his back.[8] Today, in a desperate attempt to get his once-vaunted Luftwaffe back in good standing, he will start planning a new blitz against the English cities.

His decision is partly the culmination of a massive enemy campaign that has targeted large German urban centers in the last six months—the devastating raids on Hamburg in July and Schweinfurt in August and October, Wilhelmshaven in early November. More than anything though, this new German counteroffensive is to be in direct retaliation for a series of five recent, devastating RAF raids on Berlin that had started on November 18. Thousands of Germans had been killed. Several historic buildings had been destroyed, including the famous Kaiserhof Hotel. Even the Führer's own Chancellery had sustained a great deal of damage.

Making matters much worse though, had been the snafu that occurred late on November 24.

On that night, nearly 200 German night fighters had been dispatched to intercept the enemy bomber formations headed for the capital. To let them do their job effectively and keep them from being shot at by their own ground units, Göring had ordered the Berlin flak batteries to withhold their fire until the bombers were right over the city. The flak units had reluctantly complied. As it turned out though, the intercepting fighters had arrived too late to effectively interdict against the raiders. Thus, the bombers had come in nearly untouched, even though they had used the same flight path as the night before. When the flak units had finally opened up, it was too little, too late. The resulting damage from the raid had been devastating, and several intensive firestorms had broken out in the city center, slaughtering hundreds.

By the end of November, Hitler had pretty much had enough. He had angrily ordered the Reichsmarshal to violently reply in kind, no matter what air assets would have to be diverted from their other missions.

So today, Göring on his special train *Asia* meets with his two planning officers to exhort them into immediately gathering the forces necessary to strike back at England. Planning the operation with Göring is his *Chef der Luftwaffenführungsstab*,[9] Karl Koller.[10] In charge of the operation will be 29-year-old *Oberst* Dietrich Pelz,[11] the commander of the IX Fliegerkorps and the currently designated *Angriffsführer England*.[12] Göring tells them to gather whatever bombers they can.

Pelz replies, "Anything that can carry bombs is good enough for me."

Their campaign calls for some nine *Kampfgruppen* representing a wide assortment of bomber types to take part in the assault. The first night's raid will consist of three waves of attacks. The first wave of 300 bombers will target industrial complexes and key ports, followed by a second wave of 200 more. A third pre-dawn wave of 150 bombers will hit wherever the first two have missed.

Pelz suggests that ten specially-equipped Heinkel 177s[13] be loaded with a pair of Trialen-filled[14] 2,500kg S-bombs—called "Big Max"—to specifically target Parliament. Göring of course eagerly agrees. "Just imagine the effect," he sniggers, "of twenty Big Maxes thumping down with this super explosive in them!"

* * *

Today, Field Marshal Keitel, chief of staff for *Oberkommando der Wehrmacht*, releases orders to activate a new Army unit, 65th Corps, for a special assignment. Its mission is to "prepare and execute the long-range engagement of England with all such secret weapons as might come into consideration for that purpose."

The new corps will oversee the creation and operation of all of the *Vergeltungswaffen*, from the V-1s to the V-3s, in the new offensive against England.[15] It will be a singular OKW command directly under the authority of OB West. The corps' first commander is to be an older artillery officer, *Generalleutnant* Erich Heinemann. *Oberst* Max Wachtel will command Flak Regiment 155, overseeing production of the V1 flying bombs. Forty-eight-year-old *Generalmajor* Dr. Walter Dornberger, the head of the V-2 rocket project, will devote his efforts to its development. *Generalleutnant* Erich Schneider will concentrate on the V-3 development.

---

1   Gause was wounded in the desert in 1942. He later came back and served Rommel in Italy in the newly formed *Heeresgruppe B* staff.

2   The Ia was the First General Staff Officer (*Generalstabsoffizier*) in a unit headquarters. See Glossary.

3   The "Hitler Youth." A paramilitary youth association created and strictly controlled by the Nazi Party in 1933 to indoctrinate and motivate male teenagers into Nazi culture and ideals and prepare them for military service, especially into the SS (*Schutzstaffel*). Membership was initially suggested,

then increasingly coerced through peer pressure, until it became mandatory in 1939. The 12th SS Panzer Division later took this title, since it was composed mainly of young men from this organization.

4 Chief Signals Advisor, in charge of signal units for signal communications.

5 Ruge, while serving on a destroyer in World War I, had become an expert on mine warfare. Since 1939, he had commanded various minesweeper squadrons along the English Channel.

6 Chief Naval Advisor.

7 The Ic, the Third General Staff Officer (*Generalstabsoffizier*) in a unit headquarters, was the critically important chief Intelligence officer. See Glossary.

8 On August 9, 1939, less than a month before the start of World War II, Göring, now the head of the largest, most modern, most powerful air force in the world, had been talking about potential war with England and France to an audience of Luftwaffe officers. When the subject of possible air raids over Germany had come up, the bombastic Reichsmarshal had haughtily bragged that, "The Ruhr will not be subjected to a single bomb. If an enemy bomber reaches the Ruhr, my name is not Hermann Göring: you can call me Meier!" The name "Meier" (and its variants, e.g., "Meyer") of course was very common, and many considered it Jewish in ethnic origin. Thus, reference to it carried a considerable amount of derision in the Third Reich, and using the phrase, equivalent to the American idiom of "then you can call me a monkey's uncle," was a promissory boast.

Naturally, German cities were bombed (some as early as the fall of 1939), and as the war progressed and urban areas and industries began to get hammered from the air, the quote came back to haunt him. His reputation in the Armed Forces and his standing in the Nazi party (and of course with Hitler) plummeted. People began calling him "Herr Meier" or "Hermann Meier," even hissing it to his face or in catcalls. As a result, he started avoiding being seen in public and shunned public engagements. To further their contempt, the air raid sirens that now went off frequently during the day to warn of American bombers, and again at night to signal incoming British formations, began being bitterly referred to by those seeking shelter below ground as "Meier's trumpets" or "Meier's hunting horns." When Göring complained, Hitler told him that he had brought this scorn on himself, even more so because had also early on in the war made several other such idiotic boasts, including once claiming that if one enemy bomber ever reached the Reich capital, he would "eat a broomstick." Thus, late in the war, he was also referred to sometimes as "Meier the Broom."

9 Air Force operations chief of staff.

10 Forty-five-year-old *Generalmajor* Karl Koller was a highly decorated pilot who had seen action in World War I. He later served as Hugo Sperrles' chief of staff for *Luftflotte 3*, and had been in on the planning for *Unternehmen Seelöwe*. He survived the war and died in his hometown of Glonn on December 22, 1951.

11 Twenty-nine-year-old Dietrich Pelz (also spelled in some sources as Peltz), was the *Angriffsführer England* and commander of IX Fliegerkorps. Although he was promoted from colonel to *Generalmajor* in October 1943, the rank would not take effect until May 1944. He survived the war, eventually achieving the rank of *General der Luftwaffe*. He died in Munich on August 10, 2001.

12 Attack Leader, England. This was a special air combat command ordered by Hitler and created by the Luftwaffe in early March, 1943 (just after a series of devastating RAF bombings on Berlin, Munich, and Stuttgart) to carry out offensive bombing raids against Great Britain. The unit itself was eventually merged into the IX Fliegerkorps some four months later, but Pelz kept the title.

13 The Heinkel 177 was Germany's only successful strategic bomber developed in World War II. With a crew of six, it could carry a 6,000kg bomb load at a speed of 500km/hr, and had a range of 1,500km. The model was fraught with a number of design and mechanical problems in its

development and early deployment, especially with its two engines; so much so, the crews cynical nicknamed it the *Luftwaffefeuerzeug*—The "Air Force lighter."

14 Trialen 105 was a specially developed German explosive, almost twice as powerful as typical British explosives. It consisted of 15% RDX (hexogen cyclonite), 70% TNT, and 15% powdered aluminum to increase the blast effects.

15 Lit. "Vengeance force," a reference to Hitler's innovative, technologically new revenge weapons that were to be launched against the English civilian population in retribution for the Allied bombings of Germany. See Glossary.

Thursday, December 2

Feldmarschall Rommel's special train is en route to Denmark so that he may begin inspection of the Atlantic Wall. The train is not on any time schedule, so it progresses at a leisurely rate.

As they travel northward, the field marshal and his *Heeresgruppe B.z.b.v* command have several sessions during the day to map out their inspection schedule and to discuss what they will be looking for regarding defensive construction.

That evening, the train pulls into the Silkeborg[1] railroad station for the night. There they are joined by their new naval advisor, *Vizeadmiral* Friedrich Ruge. He and *Oberstleutnant* Queissner are the only senior officers in the staff that are not army officers like the others. They will soon pick up the nickname of *Hilsfvölker*—auxiliary tribes.

Rommel and his staff welcome the admiral on board, and that evening, they all enjoy a luxurious dinner. Afterwards, they relax in their conference car for the rest of the evening.

***

Tonight, for the fifth time in a month, Berlin is subject to a British air raid. Over two thousand tons of bombs fall onto the capital. Still, Propaganda Minister Goebbels, overseeing the city's defense, remains upbeat about Germany's plight. Tonight he writes in the weekly magazine *Das Reich*:

> When the skies darken and there is scarcely a gleam of light, then the people's gaze turns unbidden to the Führer. He is the rock in the surging seas of time.

CBS radio host Edward R. Murrow though, who is riding along as an observer in a Lancaster bomber, literally sees the air raid differently. Tomorrow on his show, he will describe it in detail. Near the end of it, he will observe, "Men die in the sky while others are roasted alive in their cellars. Berlin last night wasn't a pretty sight. In about 35 minutes it was hit with about three times the amount of stuff that ever came down on London in a night-long blitz."

---

1   On the Danish mainland, about 240km west-northwest of Copenhagen.

Friday, December 3

Some 460 British bombers again pounded Berlin last night. *Reichsmarschall* "Meier" Göring is once again the source of bitter ridicule. Today though, he is striking back. Today he signs the orders for the new blitz on England. Unfortunately, because of the pressing war effort in the East and in Italy, Pelz and Koller will need time to amass enough night bombers to launch any kind of air offensive. Still, Göring tells them to proceed. Dubbing the plan "*Unternehmen Steinbock*,"[1] he commands that every possible Heinkel, Junkers, and Dornier bomber be scrounged up for the campaign. The Reichsmarshal himself will travel to Paris in a few days to organize the operation himself, and to push his subordinates there to get the required aircraft together.

Of course, while in the French capital, he will spend several days partaking of the city's delights and picking up some rare art treasures. Then it will be back to Carinhall[2] for an elegant Christmas and New Year with his family.

***

Today, *Generalfeldmarschall* Rommel's special train reaches the coast in Denmark. He and his staff leave the train and go to a central conference center. There, the field marshal and his command staff attend a number of informative introductory lectures and planning sessions by area senior commanders. General von Hannecken[3] starts off at 8 a.m. with a welcome and a general lecture on what to expect when the enemy invades. He is followed by a report on the Kriegsmarine by Admiral Wurmbach[4], who lists a small force of a few minesweepers and patrol boats. The Luftwaffe liaison then gives a report on his air order of battle, which includes a complement of a few fighters, some bombers, and a number of training aircraft.

Next, the commanding officer of the army Coastal Artillery Regiment 180[5] gives a report on his battery, and the local director of the OT[6] then gives his report too.

Following a short lunch, the reports continue, starting with *Generalleutnant* Wolff, the Luftwaffe administrative commander for this area, giving a summary of enemy air activity in the area; then a number of reports on ground units. Rommel is told that there are six divisions on the Jutland peninsula. Unfortunately, one is just being organized, three are "grenadier" training divisions, and the one panzer reserve division hardly deserves the title, listing only a few wildly assorted older model tanks. The last ground unit covered is a Luftwaffe field division, currently being trained to move by bicycle.

Overall, the forces in the area are woefully small. Fortunately, there is little likelihood that the enemy will land here, mainly because it is out of the immediate range of their fighters.

The long reports continue on into the evening. They finally finish around 9 p.m., and Rommel's group wearily return to their special train. Over dinner, they plan their route and their routine for the next few days. They outline what they will look for, and what points they will want to analyze.

Rommel of course is given the spacious main bedroom. General Gause and Admiral Ruge are assigned sleeping rooms in a parlor car adorned with a mysterious Cyrillic script, lending credence to the theory that the previous owner was some Balkan ruler. This will have them guessing for days. That and of course, the function of that strange bell in the bathroom that can be rung while on the toilet...

Tomorrow, they will start their inspections.

---

1   "*Operation Capricorn*," so named because the offensive was to begin in January, and because it also happened to be Göring's astrological sign.

2   Carinhall is Göring's expansive hunting estate, located northeast of Berlin in the Schorfheide forest. It was named after his first wife, who was Swedish. Stricken with tuberculosis, Carin died of a heart attack on October 17, 1931.

3   Fifty-four-year-old *General der Infanterie* Hermann von Hannecken, the Wehrmacht Supreme Commander in Denmark.

4   Fifty-two-year-old *Vizeadmiral* Hans-Heinrich Wurmbach, commanding the naval forces in Denmark.

5   The regiment was equipped with three batteries of captured French 105 cm guns. The 1st at Thisted had four, the 2nd at Varde had six, and 3rd at Hjørring had two.

6   *Organization Todt*, a paramilitary government construction force. See Glossary.

Saturday, December 4

Generalfeldmarschall Rommel and his staff are ready to start their inspection of the Atlantic Wall in Denmark. He has begun here mostly because it had been suggested to him; a logical choice, since Denmark is geographically at the top of the Western Theater. It is the furthest point north open to invasion; excluding of course, Norway.

This morning, despite a long day of briefings yesterday, he and his staff are up early, and their first inspection has been scheduled for 8 a.m.[1] While they were sleeping in the night, their special train had moved to their point of departure: Esbjerg. This is Denmark's only significant port on the west coast of the Jutland peninsula. If the Allies do decide to land in Denmark, this will be a likely target.[2]

Rommel comes into the dining car for breakfast. Ruge, his naval advisor, is already seated at the table. The other staff members remain standing until the field marshal has sat down. While they are being waited on, Ruge notices an odd red spot on the field marshal's face. He comments on it and asks the field marshal how he got it.

Rommel smiles. "That spot," he confesses somewhat sheepishly, "always seems to appear after I've used hot water." The staff officers nod in response. Thinking about it, Rommel concludes, "I suppose that now my staff will know whenever I've washed my face." The officers chuckle at this.

Over breakfast, they go over their itinerary for the day. Rommel has given strict instructions that the workers here are to continue on with their tasks. Only the local commanders are to take time to report to him.

They are still in the dining car at 7:55, but just five minutes later, the dining car has been cleared; except for Admiral Ruge who, suddenly realizing he is alone, jumps up and rushes outside, barely getting the last seat in the fairly appreciable auto procession to their first stop.

They travel to Esbjerg to inspect the fortifications around it. Rommel notes with satisfaction a 200mm naval battery in place. They continue on.

That afternoon, the vehicles cross over by ferry to the northern tip of Fanö Island, which faces Esbjerg's harbor. After a nice lunch from a field kitchen, the entourage gets to observe a landing exercise on a wide, open, flat beach. Rommel notes with a frown how a large number of men could under ideal circumstances land in such an area and be able to quickly move inland. Because there is a shortage of weapons here to defend the area, he instructs his staff to take notes on creating wooden obstacles to counter any amphibious and air landings.

Rommel makes some more quick observations of the coastline. They quit work around 4 p.m. and retire to their special train to have dinner, go over their notes, and discuss the day's activity.

1   Times listed in this work are given in German Central Time (GCT), rather than British Double Summer Time (BDST, also sometimes abbreviated to DBST), which most American and British sources use. The idea for establishing British Summer Time (BST) began during World War I, when it was thought that if it was still light outside at 11 p.m., men would continue working, rather than go to the pub.

    German Central Time was also invariably one hour ahead of Greenwich Mean Time (GMT). In comparison, from the summer of 1940 to the summer of 1945, clocks in England were put not just one hour ahead but two hours ahead of GMT for the summer months (Emergency Powers, Defence Summertime Acts SR&O 1040 No. 1883 and SR&O 1944 No. 932). This became known as British Double Summer Time. For the rest of the year and through the winter, Britain remained merely one hour ahead of GMT in what was known as British Summer Time (BST), a practice finally discontinued in 1971.

    Thus, German Central Time (GCT) for this book is one hour behind British Double Summer Time (BDST-1, or DBST-1).

2   The British had done a number of studies of landing here in the late 1890s in case they ever went to war with Germany. Such a landing would a) open a secondary front, b) secure a good seaport, c) allow a raiding party to destroy the Kieler Canal.

Sunday, December 5

Today, Rommel continues his inspection of positions from the port of Esbjerg, Denmark northward along the Jutland peninsula. They pass the Ringkøbing Fjord and continue up the western coast, stopping occasionally to take notes.

They rise, dine in the train, and then depart by auto for the tour. They spend the day inspecting, and finally rejoin their relocated train in the evening.

B-26 bombers of the US 9th Air Force fly the first mission of Operation Crossbow, the Allied air campaign against the German V weapon sites. Targeted are three V-1 launch sites, including those at Ligescourt and St. Josse au Bois.[1] Two hundred bombers have to abort because of bad weather, but 52 make it through to the target.

---

1   Ligescourt is 51km south-southeast of Boulogne; St. Josse au Bois is 47km southeast of that city.

Monday, December 6

Today, the weather is cold and dismal as *Generalfeldmarschall* Rommel and his staff continue their inspection of the Danish portion of the Atlantic Wall.

Rommel makes some quick observations of the coastline. Overall, he is not impressed with the defenses he sees. Today he and his party drive to the Hanstholm battery, covering the southern part of the Skagerrak Strait. The huge 600-man battery consists of four 380mm naval guns, each mounted in a 3,000m² bunker. The site includes its own radar fire control facility and powerhouse.

Impressed, Rommel and his staff continue touring up the Jutland peninsula.

Far over their heads, many formations of US Army Air Corps B-17s, B-24s, and B-26s meet stiff flak and fighter resistance as they cross over the coast headed inland, resuming their daylight bombing raids against the Reich. The Flying Fortresses and Liberators, despite having a considerable escort of P-47s and P-38s, are hit hard, and lose a dozen aircraft. The B-26 Marauders, escorted by RAF fighters, fare better. German targets are hit hard, and it is a sure thing that the Allied bombers will return tomorrow.

Reichsmarschall Hermann Göring is honoring Paris today with his presence. He first meets with his subordinates to plan for *Unternehmen Steinbock*," Germany's retaliatory air blitz against English cities for the recent bombings of Berlin.

Despite delays in trying to get together a formidable air attack force, the Luftwaffe plan is taking shape. Dietrich Pelz, in charge of the offensive, is putting together an air group that already comprises over 400 aircraft, including seven *Gruppen*[1] of Ju-88s (including a few that have been withdrawn from Italy for this operation). Also integrated into the plan are some other odd formations, including nearly three dozen new long-range He-177 bombers.

The strikes will consist of a number of short powerful air raids over major cities like London. Göring's plans called for bomb loads that will be three-quarters composed of incendiary bombs with the last quarter made up of huge blockbusters—sardonically referred to as "English Mixtures."

---

1 A German *Gruppe* consisted of three or four *Staffel* (squadrons) for a total of 30 to 50 aircraft.

Tuesday, December 7

Rommel and his staff continue touring the Danish shore on their initial inspection of the Atlantic Wall. The weather continues cold and with a brisk wind.

Traveling through the coastal area, they pass dozens of small rustic valleys and hollows. Staring from his automobile at these quaint landscapes, the field marshal remarks on how they remind him of his native Swabia.

Today they make it to the tip of the Jutland peninsula, reviewing the positions at Skagen. Then they start down the eastern shores of the peninsula. They reach the town of Frederikshavn where they stop for the evening.

Their routine is becoming simple. In the morning, their train takes them to a start point. From there, they leave at 8 a.m. and travel by auto to inspect the positions. After a short break for lunch, usually delivered by a field kitchen, they continue on until dusk. Then it is back to the train for the night.

Today, Rommel writes to his wife, Lucie:

> *I move about every day, and what I see on my inspections does not satisfy me very much.*

***

This morning, General Dwight D. Eisenhower of the United States Army stands on the tarmac of the Al Aoudina airport in Tunis, watching members of a US presidential delegation, on its way back to the States from the just finished Cairo Conference, deboard their plane. Finally, President Franklin D. Roosevelt himself is hoisted in his wheelchair out of the fuselage and rolled backward down the ramp. Eisenhower and the president shake hands and then get into the rear of the president's limousine, which is actually an upgraded staff car. After a pause, the president, turns to Eisenhower and tells him, "Well Ike, you are going to command Overlord.*"*

It is exactly three years after Pearl Harbor.

The decision to appoint the overall invasion commander had originally been given to the president by the other Allies, because three quarters of the invasion force would be American. Roosevelt has not made his final decision easily. General George C. Marshall, the Chairman of the Joint Chiefs of Staff, wanted the appointment badly. Roosevelt though, has decided not to give it to him for several reasons.

First of all, whoever commanded the invasion would still not be given a chair on the Allied Combined Chiefs of Staff (insisted on by the British), and that would be an insult to Marshall.

Second, Roosevelt felt that he could not spare Marshall from his present duties to direct Overlord, *because he would have to do so overseas and he would probably have to continue in that capacity as theater commander for the rest of the war. He would thus not be in charge of the military in Washington, something that Roosevelt felt the general had done well up until now. Besides, with Marshall in Europe, Eisenhower, his* subordinate, would have to take over as Chairman of the Joint Chiefs in Washington. That would thereby technically make Eisenhower Marshall's superior.

Third, Eisenhower, who currently commanded all the American forces in the Mediterranean, had not hesitated to relieve Patton of his command for slapping a soldier in Sicily. To Roosevelt, this showed that Eisenhower would not hesitate to relieve any subordinate if he felt that it was necessary. That was something that would certainly be needed (especially to preserve Allied détente) as the war progressed.

As much as anything though, both Roosevelt and the British High Command felt that there was a good chance the invasion of Europe might end up a disaster. If that were to happen, the war effort would be much better served if the theater commander was sacrificed and relieved. Roosevelt felt that the country would be much better off if that were Eisenhower instead of Marshall.

So after careful consideration, Roosevelt has reluctantly decided to give the job of supreme commander for the invasion to Eisenhower.[1]

Now Eisenhower stares intently back at his leader and replies, "Mr. President, I realize that such an appointment involved difficult decisions." He pauses and adds, "I hope you will not be disappointed."[2]

---

1   Churchill was surprised when Roosevelt told him on December 5 that he still had not decided between Marshall and Eisenhower. Churchill had until then assumed that Marshall would get the appointment.

2   It would not be until February 12, 1944, that the Allied Combined Chiefs of Staff would issue a directive making his appointment official.

Wednesday, December 8

Feldmarschall Rommel and his staff stay on the move all day as they travel along the Danish seashore, frequently writing observations as they assess what they can see of the coastal positions or areas where they are under construction or lacking.

Finally that evening, their train pulls in for the night at Aalborg, and they set up a makeshift command post. After all, they are at this time strictly a mobile command center and nothing more. They have been told though, that they have been scheduled to get a permanent headquarters location around December 20.

While auxiliaries prepare their meal, they set up their communications and message traffic begins to come in. The senior staff members clean up a bit before sitting down to an excellent dinner. As they eat they discuss the day's activities and summarize their findings. After dinner, they retire to the lounge car and continue their discussions. Rommel gives them pointers for tomorrow, and they offer suggestions on certain points.

That day, Rommel writes his wife:

> *Dearest Lu:*
>
> *We're off again to-day up to the northernmost point. The round trip will be over in a couple of days and then paper work will begin. Hard fighting still in the east and south. I need not tell you with what feelings I look on from a distance.*
>
> *I hear that the call-up is going to be extended to the 14-year-olds. The lads will be sent to labor service or defense according to their size and physique...*

Rommel has good reason to be worried. His own son, Manfred, is fifteen, and now qualifies for conscription into the war.

Thursday, December 9

This morning, Rommel gets a full report from the nearby airbase's Luftwaffe field division commander, followed by that of the local reserve panzer division.[1]

From there, the senior staff members are flown to the Grove airport, and then on to the historic city of Copenhagen. Even after several years of occupation, the Danish capital remains unlike most of the other capitals in Europe, because it is amply stocked and the people well fed. Obviously, the Danes have not suffered nearly as heavily in this war as other Europeans. Most still earn a fair wage, and the country, because of the German affinity to their close racial cousins, has not been forced to pay the Reich any reparations.[2]

Rommel gazes at the people on the streets and in their shops. He senses a spirit of normalcy in their lives. He watches them go about what are probably the same routines they had before the war, ignoring their occupiers for the most part. And why not? The war has had little impact here. Even better is the fact that underlying this sense of normal routine is the fact that Denmark is an unlikely location for an Allied invasion.

Rommel and his staff are amazed at the Danish lifestyles, and stop at a promising, nearby restaurant. They are rewarded by seeing and smelling the culinary delights inside. Delicacies abound, even after four years of occupation. After the tasty meal, the staff members leave the restaurant and spread out, bent on shopping for some personal items. After all, Christmas is close, and the capital seems well-stocked with goods for sale. Rommel takes advantage of this to do some shopping of his own, and this is an excellent opportunity to pick up a nice, unusual present. He chooses a number of scarce, top-quality items, although making the purchases turns out to be somewhat difficult. Being a German, he has a few problems getting the vendors to sell to him, his rank notwithstanding, In the end though, they let him buy, even though he is German.

When they all return from shopping, they are somewhat dismayed to find out that SS intelligence has intercepted a covert plan to attack his train. Some security will have to be provided by the Gestapo, something he is definitely against, but powerless to refuse. Still, Rommel will make sure that their presence is very limited at best once he gets his own headquarters location.

That afternoon, Rommel calls on the local commander, General von Hannecken,[3] and they discuss both the military and the political situation in Denmark over tea. They then talk about defense matters. Later that evening, they feast on a bountiful dinner with the Danish commissioner, 41-year-old SS *Obergruppenführer* Dr. Werner Best.[4]

The doctor's conversation reinforces for them what they have seen all day long: conditions in Denmark are relatively relaxed. Dr. Best tells them that he wants to ensure that Germany maintains good relations with the Danes, in hopes that those in other occupied countries (and the rest of the world) see what life in the Reich can be like. And that includes fair treatment of the Danish Jews. The visitors assure him that he is doing a fine job.

The ironic part is that Best was once a key Gestapo leader who helped developing the RSHA[5] as the executor of the Nazi party's Jewish policy.

---

1 The 233rd Panzer Reserve Division. It would remain in Denmark until the end of the war.

2 Denmark had never actually declared war on Germany, though this was mostly because the swift German advance did not give them time to do so. Germany had little interest in the resources of the country, and from the king down to the citizens, the Danes never offered any resistance to occupation. Because of these factors and that Denmark was considered a 'Germanic cousin', the country was allowed to function as it had. Even after Germany declared martial law for Denmark in the fall of 1943 (because of increased resistance and government resistance), the Danes were for the most part left alone, although a few thousand did die as a result of the occupation.

3 Fifty-four-year-old *General der Infanterie* Hermann von Hannecken, the Wehrmacht Supreme Commander in Denmark.

4 The Reich Commissioner for Denmark, appointed in November 1942. His actual title was that of Plenipotentiary (*Reichsbevollmächtigter*).

5 The *Reichssicherheitshauptamt* (Reich Security Main Office).

Friday, December 10

Generalfeldmarschall Rommel and his staff continue to tour the Danish coast in their special train, which has by now caught up with them. Leaving Copenhagen on the main island of Seeland, they proceed with the next leg of their tour. They drive northward along the eastern shore of the country, dubbed the "Danish Riviera," admiring the lovely harbor views. They travel up to the tip of Seeland, to Helsingør, and briefly stop to gaze across the Strait of Øresund, here only 5km wide, to view the town of Helgeborg in neutral Sweden.

Rommel is discovering that the defense line along the Danish shore up here is woefully inadequate. Fortunately, an enemy invasion of Denmark is very unlikely, especially at this point. Farther from England than Calais, there simply are too few beaches to support a successful amphibious landing. And several key German air bases are far too close. Still, the preparedness of the troops is terrible. To them life seems like one big holiday.

No, he is not satisfied at all. And if this is any indication of what he will find in France...

Saturday, December 11

Today, because of critical developments with *Heeresgruppe Süd* in the Crimea, OKW orders the 60th *Panzergrenadier* Division reforming in Southern France to the Eastern Front. France is going to be shorted another mobile division.

***

After a splendid breakfast, *Generalfeldmarschall* Rommel and his staff conclude their tour of the Danish coast, with their special train ending up back in the Silkeborg railroad station. They have been at it for over a week now, inspecting coastal positions.

The army group staff, based on their discussions with the field marshal and the many notes that they have compiled, begin to draft the official report that Rommel will send to the Führer. The status and placement of the coastal positions have been very unimpressive. If most of the mighty Atlantic Wall is like this, there are serious problems on this front.

First of all, they have found that the control structures here are weak. The chains of command are both disorganized and decentralized. And area defenses have been set up by the local commanders as they see fit, although at least they all get along—for the most part.

If a unit is transferred (usually east), the next one coming to the area has to take over their defensive plan. Usually, this boils down to just a matter of "Hold on for dear life, and pray that the reinforcements come soon."

This is of course, a futile prayer. There is no real mobile reserve in Denmark, and most of the units (as Rommel records) have little transportation and not nearly enough equipment. Many formations are close to capacity in personnel, but the men are usually too green or too old to be very effective. There is a definite lack of combat experience in most of the units there.

Although the vital, strategic major ports each have a well-rounded defense plan, he has found that a good deal of the positions are either incomplete or in some cases, not even started. And viable ports will be critical targets, because the Allies would need at least one as soon as possible, if their landing was to have any hope of success.

That day, Rommel writes to his wife:

> *Dearest Lu:*
>
> *We're now back from the capital. A few days' written work and then the job will continue.*
> *You can still buy everything you want here in Denmark. Of course, the Danes will only sell to their own compatriots. I've bought a few things for Christmas, so far as the money went.*

Even a field marshal who comes from a modest upbringing is not lavished with an extraordinary income.

Sunday, December 12

Generalfeldmarschall Rommel, still in Silkeborg, Denmark, continues his report on his findings along the Danish coast. For a successful defense there, he recommends reorganizing all of the units and reinforcements of men and matériel.

He also adds that they must establish some overall master plan to simultaneously strengthen and yet still effectively defend this so-called Atlantic Wall—either that, or they should just give up France now.

***

Over 1,200 kilometers away to the southwest, the commander-in-chief of all Wehrmacht forces in Western Europe is finishing up a number of administrative details before the holidays.

And today is his birthday. *Generalfeldmarschall* Gerd von Rundstedt, today turning 69 years old, is the oldest man in the Wehrmacht to hold the privileged rank of field marshal—a good reason that he also carries the weighty title of *Oberbefehlshaber West*.

The theater commander is working in his study. He has, along with his country, gone through some stressful times, including being at the center of two world wars. The crusty elderly man is a product of the old-school Prussian corps, with his family going back through Prussian military history for well over 800 years. His war experiences have been paralleled in modern history by only a few. Nearly everyone would concede that he is still a competent theater commander. In his career, despite his aristocratic rigidity in old-style war doctrine, he has adapted to and excelled in conducting mobile, open warfare. This is perhaps one reason he despises espionage and subterfuge of any type. So it is small wonder to those who are close to him that he usually does not seriously take into account information acquired by spies.

A curmudgeon, the strains of his career have left their mark upon his physique. Although he looks grand in his uniform, his frame is frail, and his thin face seems accentuated by the serious expression he nearly always wears. Looking at him, he gives the impression of an old guardsman who had seen too much of war and what it has done to mankind.

Although he now lives in lavish quarters in the Hôtel Georges V just off the Champs-Élysées, he would prefer instead the quiet surroundings of his summer residence in nearby St.-Germain-en-Laye to Paris itself. There he has secured for himself a comfortable villa, uphill from his strategic headquarters, which is a new massive block structure that lies partly underground, dug into the side of a hill.

These days, because of his age, prestige, background, and senior status in the Reich, he is a man used to expensive tastes and fine living. On a personal level, he is a patrician, relishing the finer luxuries in life—an affluent taste no doubt acquired during his earlier, aristocratic life.

Today, even though it is his birthday, *Der Rundstedt* (as Rommel calls him) is in a foul mood. He is upset at Rommel's recent intrusion into his command. "Marshal Laddie," he sarcastically calls him. When the old Prussian had learned that Rommel was coming west to inspect his shorelines, he had grumbled, "Once more, the relative tranquility of the high command in France is being ruined."

He thinks back now to when he had first been appointed OB West, back in early 1941. At that time, he had hoped for a nice, pleasurable tour in France and six months or so of building his Western forces. Hitler of course, had ruined that idea in short order (as he had so many other grand schemes). The Führer had recalled him for the planning and execution of "*Barbarossa*," an invasion of Russia that von Rundstedt had been dead set against from the start. Despite his grumblings though, he had been told to commit his resources to the project, and grudgingly he and *Feldmarschall* von Manstein had developed a brilliant plan.

When the operation had begun, von Rundstedt played a key role in breaking through the enemy lines, commanding Army Group South. Yes, he had commanded admirably well that summer of 1941 against the Russians. However, late fall had found his tired men deep in enemy country, their vehicles worn and neglected, their supply lines overextended and shaky, their enemy recovering and regrouping before them, and suffering surprisingly cold weather. The fortunes of war had started to turn against them.

In late November, after he had taken Rostov in a bitter engagement, the Russians had gathered their remaining forces in the area and had counterattacked with surprising ferocity. His weary First Panzer Army had been forced to retreat and abandon the city. Assessing the strength of the Russian units facing him and the need for his own forces to take time to recover, he had, with *Generalfeldmarschall* von Brauchitsch's agreement, started to fall back behind the Mius River and had insisted on permission to move back further west to regroup.

Unfortunately, a countermanding order came from the Führer, which forbade any such withdrawal. Instead, Hitler had angrily ordered him instead to immediately halt the retreat, to dig in, and to stay where he was, no matter what. The stubborn old Prussian, aware through intelligence reports of the large Russian units starting to mass against him, had concluded that Hitler did not understand the situation at all. So he had refused to obey him. Indeed, it had been quite a communiqué that he had sent:

IT IS MADNESS TO ATTEMPT TO HOLD. IN THE FIRST PLACE THE TROOPS CANNOT DO IT AND IN THE SECOND PLACE IF THEY DO NOT RETREAT THEY WILL BE DESTROYED. I REPEAT THAT THIS ORDER BE RESCINDED OR THAT YOU FIND SOMEONE ELSE TO COMMAND.

Hitler, by now frustrated with the entire campaign, had become furious at this open defiance and outright insubordination. That same night, Hitler sent a message telling him that he was accepting von Rundstedt's resignation.

Von Rundstedt angrily left the Eastern Front on December 1, swearing at the time that he would never forgive the insult and would never return to the Eastern Front.[1] The Führer replaced him with *Generalfeldmarschall* Walther von Reichenau. However, he also almost immediately afterwards flew down to that sector; after seeing the situation, he changed his mind and sanctioned the step-back.

Hitler slowly realized that the old man had had a valid point, and that they were now losing a valuable command asset: von Rundstedt, the hero of the Polish campaign, the master strategist who had defeated the French. So Hitler had recanted and suggested that instead, von Rundstedt go on sick leave. The old man had, after all, actually suffered a minor heart attack earlier that very month.[2]

Four months later, in March of 1942, the old Prussian had been ordered back to France again, to resume his old command title there. And things had been relatively good since then, with France being a sort of rest-and-relaxation back area. It became a good balm for those shattered divisions coming across from the East, badly needing a break and reorganization. But with the Allies now gathering themselves in England, it looked today as though the war would soon be coming back to France. And Rommel's irritating presence was perhaps the most ominous sign of that.

The worst of it was that von Rundstedt was—at least for a few months—stuck with him. And Rommel had recently been openly (although not blatantly) boasting about his close ties with the Führer, even despite his failures in North Africa.

It seems to this old rooster that Marshal Laddie is out to steal his barnyard...

---

1   He never did.
2   In an interview with Basil Liddell Hart after the war, von Rundstedt recalled the story and added, "Significantly, the Mius River line was the only sector of the front that was not taken during the winter of 1941–42."

Monday, December 13

Generalfeldmarschall Rommel, satisfied with his tour and with his initial findings on his inspection of the Danish coast finally complete, submits his report to OKW. In it, he recommends restructuring the units for more efficient operations. Optimistically, he concludes that Denmark can be successfully defended if these restructuring points are done.

***

Generalfeldmarschall von Rundstedt is still mulling over Rommel's assignment to France and its impact upon him. While the crusty Prussian has no personal animosity towards the Swabian, he does have misgivings about how the younger field marshal will handle his critical assignment. And Supreme High Command is considering creating a separate army group command for northern France, and it looks like Rommel might get it. If he does, von Rundstedt will lose a considerable amount of his command power in France, even though Wilhelm Keitel, the OKW chief of staff, came to visit him late last month about this very subject.

Von Rundstedt thinks back to that visit late last November. He did not think Keitel's trip west was for any good reason. And Keitel would never have made the decision to come himself. So this was only a visit of protocol, ordered by the Führer.

At 6'1", solidly built, square-jawed Wilhelm Bodewin Johann Gustav Keitel was the Armed Forces Chief of Staff. He had held that position since 1938. At the end of 1937, Werner von Blomberg, who had commanded the Wehrmacht at the time, suddenly became a target of scandal that centered on his engagement to a young women who Göring and Himmler conveniently found had had a pornographic past. Blomberg was forced to resign in January. When Hitler, out of respect for the man, asked him who he would recommend as his successor, Blomberg suggested that Hitler himself take over the job. Hitler immediately seized on this opportunity to take command of the Armed Forces himself.

But who to get for his chief of staff? He needed someone that would follow orders without hesitation, and allow himself to be controlled. Hitler directed the question to von Blomberg. The old general, depressed over his own dismissal, had again not been able to suggest anyone.

"Well," Hitler had pressed, "who is yours?"

Von Blomberg had looked at him and replied, "Wilhem Keitel."

"Keitel," Hitler had echoed, trying to place the name. "Ah, yes…"

"But," von Blomberg had protested, "he's just the man who runs my office." Keitel was also his son-in-law, but he did not add that.

Hitler had turned to him at that remark, snapped his fingers, and had exclaimed, "That's EXACTLY the man I'm looking for."

So on February 4, Keitel had stepped into the inner circle of power, to the astonishment of the entire General Staff; including Keitel himself. Hitler himself took over as Commander-in-chief of the Armed Forces. The German War Ministry had been replaced by the *Oberkommando der Wehrmacht,* with Keitel its chief of staff, one of the most powerful positions within the Reich.

And yet, it was not for this reason that he was so unpopular with his army peers. Most officers in the General Staff and serving in the field saw him as Hitler's blindingly loyal toady. He was firm in dealing with others only when he was trying to carry out the Führer's wishes. They even had a nickname for him. Behind his back, they dubbed him "*Laikeitel.*"[1] They also sometimes called him "*Nichgeselle,*"[2] which referred to a popular metal toy donkey that always nodded its head up and down from dipping it in a small water container. They even saw personal weakness in his walk, which was a quick but hesitating sort of step.

Keitel, well aware of the opinions held by his peers, often expressed misery in having to do the Führer's bidding. Still, he was after all a Prussian, and orders were orders. Hitler was satisfied with that. In fact, back in early 1938 when he had decided to take over command of the armed forces, he had chosen Keitel to be his chief of staff for that very reason.

The first few years, Hitler had even chided him with teasing remarks like, "You know, von Blomberg would never have let me get away with that." As the war turned against Germany though, Hitler was reported as often lashing out at Keitel, who in turn would merely stand there and take the verbal abuse.[3] Von Rundstedt had heard through the grapevine that one time Keitel's name had come up while Hitler was conversing with some high-ranking officers, and he had characterized him by commenting, "You know, he has the brains of a movie usher."

The general to whom he had been speaking had asked, "So why then, *mein Führer,* did you make him the highest ranking individual in the German army?"

Hitler had turned to the officer with a sly smile, and had replied, "Because the man's as loyal as a dog."

***

In late November of 1943, shortly after Rommel was appointed Inspector-General for the West, Keitel traveled to Paris and arrived at the Hôtel Georges V, a luxurious, historic Parisian establishment that is now a quasi-headquarters and officers' winter quarters for OB West and his staff.[4] Checking in, he had met the Prussian in the grandiose dining room. After an exquisite dinner and a leisurely walk, they had sat down and talked about the soon-to-be arriving new inspector.

Keitel, sporting his monocle and having been pumped up as usual by the Führer, had been true to form. Bombastically, overly optimistic, he claimed that he had come to France for one special purpose: to personally relay Hitler's assurance that no matter what, von Rundstedt would retain the top command post in Western Europe. Rommel was *not* going to relieve him. He was to be strictly subordinate to OB West. Von Rundstedt had nothing to worry about on that account.

Was he lying? Who knew?

As a matter of fact, Keitel had added with a sly smile, von Rundstedt would eventually find Rommel to be a valuable asset for a number of reasons. He was, after all, an excellent tactical commander, and had proven to be a brave leader in combat. And remember, Keitel had reminded him, Rommel had fought well under von Rundstedt once before, referring of course to their 1940 *blitzkrieg* campaign against France.

Lowering his voice as if he were about to divulge some inner confidence, Keitel had tried to spice up his speech with what he hoped would be a little bit of dirt. Hitler, he confided, privately did not consider Rommel to be a great strategist, even though he was indeed a dynamic leader. Von Rundstedt had seen through this con though, and had expressed his concerns, mainly about Rommel gaining influence and power over time.

Von Rundstedt had pointed out that he himself was not in great health. So if he eventually had to go, maybe he might be "coerced" down the road into taking sick leave again, and thus be taken out of command altogether, as he had back in November, 1941 on the Eastern Front.

Keitel was sometimes a bit slow, but he was not stupid. He had picked up von Rundstedt's skepticism, so he had pressed his point home. "Should the time ever come for your replacement because of failing health," he continued, "the Führer wishes you to know that only *Generalfeldmarschall* von Kluge[5] would be in the running to succeed you," which confirmed what von Rundstedt had officially been notified by message a week ago.

Von Rundstedt gritted his teeth upon hearing that. Keitel did not realize that this bit of flattery had only removed what little credibility he might have had up to that point. He did not know that von Rundstedt had his own covert intelligence network—well actually, a refined grapevine. His sources had informed him recently that von Kluge had been wounded last month in Russia, and at this time could not command anything. Keitel was lying, just trying to placate him.[6]

Keitel continued on. "At any rate, Rommel would never replace you," he concluded. Hitler had proclaimed that. Rommel was just not suited for strategic command. He simply was "not supreme commander material." Rather, he was only good for "Seydlitz-type attacks, as at Rossback,"[7] but certainly not competent to command strategic operations. Keitel knew how to spread it when he had to.

Keitel then again had leaned over towards the old man and had stated dryly, "Look, you'll find Rommel a tiresome person because he doesn't like taking orders from anybody. In Africa, of course, he very much ran his own show…" Solemnly, he added, "But the Führer believes that you are the one man to whom even Rommel will show due respect."

Listening to Keitel, von Rundstedt had understood what was going on. This emissary from Berlin was politely inferring that this new rooster, although he would never be Number One in the Western barnyard, was nevertheless here to stay; at least, until the Führer said otherwise.

Von Rundstedt had smiled to Keitel ever-so-politely. He clearly could not believe anything this sycophant had said. He had then cordially excused himself, and retired for the evening to his lavish suite in the hotel. He preferred a good western paperback over listening to this clown. On the way to his room, he had grumbled several unflattering epithets under his breath about Hitler, Rommel, Keitel, and one or two other things while he was at it.

***

Coming back to the present, von Rundstedt worries once more about Rommel's appointment. He still believes this so-called "Desert Fox" will eventually replace him. It has happened too often before.

Secretly, the old man realizes that he does not really know Rommel that well. True, they had occasionally seen each other at Supreme Headquarters in the first year of the war, and the younger man had served under him in that hectic spring of 1940. Even so, the old Prussian had hardly seen him before or during that campaign. Since then, von Rundstedt had followed Rommel's exploits in North Africa, though he has not been too impressed by them. After all, Africa has always been in his opinion just a sideshow to the conflicts in Europe.

And yet, von Rundstedt does grudgingly approve of Rommel as a good German officer and a competent leader in the field. He had become an excellent panzer commander and was a quick learner. But as a Prussian aristocrat, von Rundstedt haughtily looks down on the man's commoner background. He was a Swabian, and spoke in the traditionally thick accent… And he sees Rommel's blatant public style as another failing. Von Rundstedt feels that even a famous German officer should be humble to the public and not seek the limelight, as this man seems to do too often.

Von Rundstedt glowers. Well fine, he grumbles to himself, if Berlin wants to replace him with this young upstart, that is all right with him. If that's the way Hitler wants it, the old man is ready to turn over his headaches to this untrained whippersnapper. Between the worries of coastal defense, playing politics with the occupied French, and having to referee between all of his squabbling German commanders—well, Rommel could have it. Let that foul-mouthed Swabian make some new mistakes. Either way, he is tired of playing Hitler's political games.

Patience has never been his strong suit.

1   The term, a play on Keitel's last name, translates to "lackey."

2   Literally, "nodding donkey."

3   In his defense, Keitel recalled (at the Nuremberg trials) that Hitler "made his accusations, objections and criticisms as a rule at people who were not present. I took the part of the absent person as a matter of principle because he could not defend himself. The result was that the accusations and criticisms were then aimed at me."

4   This was common for the field marshal. He often moved into a Parisian hotel as winter approached. Ostensibly, this was to save on coal and staff operation efficiency. A good part of it though was more than likely for the ambiance and to take advantage of the capital's many pleasurable conveniences.

5   Fifty-one-year-old Günther von Kluge, a World War I artilleryman (he had been at Verdun) had made quite a reputation for himself at the beginning of World War II. Commanding the famed Fourth Army, he had surprisingly distinguished himself in Poland and across France, for which he was promoted to field marshal in the summer of 1940. Despite his old-fashioned approaches to warfare (he was known to be a methodical, cautious commander), he also played a dramatic role in the early stages of Barbarossa. With his army nearly at the gates of Moscow in the summer of 1941, von Kluge, nicknamed *der kluge Hans* ("Clever Hans," an anecdotal reference to a pre-war German horse that supposedly could do arithmetic), had argued with Guderian later that year over some tactical withdrawals that Guderian had ordered. Von Kluge was given command of Army Group Center on December 19, relieving his superior von Bock, who was supposedly ill, but was sacked for failing to take Moscow. Several other generals were fired that day as well, including OKH head *Feldmarschall* von Brauchitsch as head of the OKH, with Hitler himself assuming personal command of the Eastern Front. Guderian was relieved of his command a week later.

6   Von Rundstedt was right. Von Kluge commanded *Heeresgruppe Mitte* (Army Group Center) on the Eastern Front. On October 27, 1943, his staff vehicle skidded on a patch of ice along the road between Minsk and Smolensk. It careened into a ditch and overturned. Von Kluge was mortally injured, and the crash left him an invalid. Replaced by General Ludwig Kübler, he would be out of service for at least seven months.

7   General Friedrich *Freiherr* von Seydlitz—Seydlitz was the lead cavalry commander under Frederick the Great. On November 5, 1757, at the battle of Rossbach, Seydlitz's Prussian cavalry made a surprise charge on the flank of the much larger French–Austrian army. The charge inflicted enormous casualties, and was disastrous for the enemy.

Tuesday, December 14

Generalfeldmarschall Rommel this morning departs the Silkeborg railway station by staff car for a nearby airport. His He-111 will fly him down to his home in Germany for some well-deserved leave. His staff members, still aboard their special train, depart for France, all except his naval advisor. Admiral Ruge is on his way to report to OKM,[1] the Naval High Command headquarters at Eberswalde Germany, some 675km away.

Rommel will enjoy seeing his wife and son. Lucie as always is happy to see him, and young Manfred is more than willing to go on a daily walk with his father.

The family is temporarily staying at the home of a brewer's widow in a small town called Herrlingen, because their new villa is not quite yet ready. Located near Ulm, deep in his native Swabia, Herrlingen is a quiet little town dotted with small, beautiful homes, and surrounded by lovely woods. A gurgling stream wanders through the center of the town.

The family will stay with the widow until the villagers of Herrlingen can get the more suitable quarters ready for their new honored residents. The villa, located at No. 13 Wippengerstrasse, is one of a number of white cottages topped with roofs of red tile. The outside walls of the villa mount sponsons that overflow with varieties of flowers and assorted domestic plants. Once a Jewish rest home,[2] it had been until now vacant, and the city of Ulm was happy to agree to rent it to the field marshal. The landscapers are now working on the lot.

For safety reasons, Rommel had decided that they needed to move back in the fall of 1943. Unfortunately, Lucie has not been happy about leaving their lovely bungalow in Wiener Neustadt, some 61km south of Vienna. She loved their home, and did not want to give it up. Lucie could be resolute in her beliefs and firm in getting her way (although he does not remember her being so when they first married in late 1916). All too often, Rommel, the great panzer hero of North Africa, the legendary Desert Fox, had found himself quietly bowing to her wishes. Well, what was he to do? He loved her.

But by that summer, the lovely area had undergone a radical transformation. The quaint town, once unobtrusive and peaceful, where they could go for a walk, breathe fresh, country air, and get lost in lovely nearby rolling meadows, had unfortunately changed because of the war. Germany's struggle had brought industry into the area, transforming the quiet rural setting into a networked manufacturing center. This included a nearby factory complex to produce their dreaded Messerschmitt fighters.

As the war had progressed and fortune had turned slowly against the Third Reich, more and more targets in Germany had been visited by those ever-growing Allied air formations, dropping their hated destruction upon the land. The proximity of the nearby Messerschmitt factories, the intensifying enemy air raid campaigns, the aerial destruction of Hamburg in late July 1943, the Allied landings in Italy, and then the bombing of Berlin in August had persuaded him to move his family to a more quiet area, no matter how much his wife protested. His mind was made up.

Now as soon as it was finished, they would move in their new home. It would be his last.

---

1   *Oberkommando der Kriegsmarine.* The German Navy's High Command.
2   The structure until 1933 was a boarding school for Jewish children. When the school closed down in 1939, the building was purportedly used by the local Nazi administration for Jewish residents in the area as a Jewish retirement home, until its occupants had "emigrated" (relocated) elsewhere, probably to concentration camps. Confiscated, the home had been converted into a lovely villa, and offered to the Mayor of Ulm to use if ever the city began getting bombed. However, the Nazi party shortly thereafter accused him of deserting his own city, so the mayor was forced to decline the offer. It was then offered as a rental by the city to the field marshal.

Wednesday, December 15

Rommel is enjoying leave at home with his wife and son. They spend a nice day together. Rommel and his son later go on a long walk and discuss a variety of subjects.

During this leave, he and Manfred discuss the boy's draft dilemma. The war has taken its toll on the German male population, and calls for more enlistments keep getting stronger. The latest draft mobilization is digging deep into the younger German male population. Minimum draft age is now the lowest ever, and both father and son know that Manfred will soon either have to enlist or be involuntarily assigned to a military unit.

On one of their talks, Manfred broaches the idea of joining the Waffen-SS. An enlistment drive for this élite arm has started locally, and 15-year-old Manfred, impressionable, feels that its neat, inspiring uniform would look good on him. In the posters going up around the area, the SS men depicted look especially regal, bold, invulnerable. So Manfred suggests to his father that he might join.

The field marshal, caught unaware by the boy's remark, snaps, "Out of the question." Scowling, he quickly adds, "You'll join the same service I did, thirty years ago."

Manfred, noticing the vehemence in his tone, tries to reason with him. After all, his father has usually given him a good deal of latitude in most decisions. Does not the SS get the best of the supplies, he asks.

Rommel, taking a deep breath, admits that this is true. He concludes, "But my decision is final. I will not under any circumstances allow you to serve under a man who I have reason to believe has been carrying out mass killings."

Manfred is silent a few moments as they walk on. He finally asks, "Do you mean Herr Himmler?"

"Yes," Rommel replies. He shakes an index finger. "Under no circumstances are you to say anything about this to anyone, do you understand? You maintain absolute silence about this."

Manfred nods his head. "Look, son," Rommel continues quietly, his voice carrying a strange intensity. "The war, as you know, is not going well for us. I've heard that there are some people like Himmler who are trying to burn the bridges of the German people behind us by committing atrocities like these."

Manfred is surprised at hearing this. Realizing the implications of the statement just made to him—entrusted to him—he vows to keep his dad's revelation a secret. They both agree that another service would do well for Manfred, and the boy promises that he will make a decision soon, before he risked being sacrificed on the Östfront.

Thursday, December 16

Rommel's senior staff members are in Paris, enjoying themselves and preparing their new headquarters at Fontainebleau.

***

Generalfeldmarschall von Rundstedt is preparing for the holidays, staying at the Hôtel Georges V in Paris.[1] He leads a life of leisure, despite his critical position. He often goes out and dines at his favorite restaurant, the Coq Hardi in nearby Bougival.[2] Oh, he is to be sure, still a loyal German officer; but he is also an honorable Prussian; an aristocrat, one of the last of a dying breed. He represents the finest Germany has to offer, and looks down with arrogance upon those uneducated, ill-mannered Nazis. He pities their lack of refinement, especially in their writings and in their artistic expression.

Yes, he knows that his contempt for them is often all too noticeable in his demeanor—especially these last few years, when he has become really cantankerous. Still, despite the fact that Hitler sacked him, von Rundstedt's allegiance (and his ambitions) have always persuaded him to step forward whenever called upon, no matter what he has called the Führer in private. Unfortunately, Hitler, that uncouth World War I corporal, has often kept him from making clear logical military choices. That has infuriated him a number of times.

He remembers once storming into his quarters, fuming in front of his staff. "Without Hitler's consent," he growled to no one in particular, "I can't even move my own sentry from my front door around to the back!"[3]

He is the first to admit that he has been saddled with an impossible task here in France. How can he create a formidable coastal wall of defense with few men, little material, and no commitment from OKW? No matter what, it is a losing proposition.

One the Allies will someday take advantage of.

---

1   Built in 1928 by Joël Hillman, near the Champs-Élysées and close to the Eiffel Tower. Perhaps the finest hotel in France, its cuisine is as good as any in the world, and its wine selection, even during the war, was impressive. This was partly because a number of sections with some of the best vintages were hidden from the Germans by the employees who built brick walls in front of the precious stocks. Over the decades before and then after the war, the hotel had served as a type of "home away from home" for movie stars and other famous personalities. During the liberation of Paris, General Eisenhower himself would use it as a temporary headquarters. Ironically, in 1942, General Hans Speidel (then a colonel), who would in a few months become Rommel's new chief of staff, had often met in this hotel with fellow conspirators to devise a way to overthrow the Nazi regime.

2   The "Dauntless Rooster," a famed inn and restaurant located about 15km west of his hotel, on the Seine River along the Rennequin Sualem Wharf.

3   A comment von Rundstedt would make often, even after the war.

Friday, December 17

Generalfeldmarschall Rommel continues his leave in Herrlingen, Austria. Russian prisoners are digging out a six-meter deep air raid shelter beneath his new villa, and the landscaping around the house is being worked on, even in the cold.

Rommel inspects what has been done on the grounds so far with the man who has been designated his landscaping supervisor—Hermann Aldinger, who is also his private adjutant. While touring the grounds, he runs into the Bürgermeister of Ulm. They chat a while. Then Rommel asks him a strange question. Looking at the mayor, he asks, "Say, are there many Prussians around here?"

The mayor pauses and then answers something like, "Some, I think."

Rommel replies, "Well, don't let so many Prussians come and live here!" A crack no doubt on their aristocratic, superior blue-blood attitudes.

They chat some more, and then Rommel asks him, "What do *you* think of the war?"

The mayor is caught off guard and hesitates. Certainly this is a dangerous question in the Third Reich. One must be careful of the opinions given to others. The mayor cannot think of a safe answer, so he remains silent.

Rommel had put that same question in the fall of 1943 to 52-year-old Oskar Farny,[1] one of his old World War I friends, on his farm in the middle of Bavaria. Rommel had needed someone to keep his papers and special mementos safe. So on August 22 he had persuaded his pilot to fly him up from Italy to Farny's farm in his Storch aircraft to visit his old friend and to ensure his valuables were safely hidden away. They had landed in one of the nearby fields, and Rommel spent a good part of the day visiting with the farmer.

They had talked for a few hours, swapping old stories about their days in the Württemberg mountain battalion, while they dined on a lunch of trout, crab, and afternoon tea.

The conversation had drifted off, and they had sat there in silence for a while. Rommel, deep in thought, had looked at Farny and had impulsively asked him the same question: "Oskar, what do you think about the war?"

Farny, surprised and embarrassed, had also hesitated. Finally, he had looked seriously at Rommel and had said somberly, "If our field marshals start flying out into the country and ask the farmers questions like that, the war isn't going well."

Rommel had nodded in reply, quipping, "No doubt about it."

---

1 Farny was raised in Ravensburg, Württemberg. An infantry lieutenant in World War I, he had met young Erwin Rommel who was in his regiment, and a friendship had begun between them. After the war, he took over his father's acreage and became well known for his cheese and beer products. He modestly became a local conservative political leader in the Reichstag, although he retired from politics and went back to farming when Hitler came into power. Farny had no love for the Nazis, and during the war, he undertook several secret communications with conspirators such as ex-Mayor Karl Goerdeler and Otto Gessler.

Saturday, December 18

Generalfeldmarschall Rommel, his leave now over, journeys by car today to his new headquarters at Fontainebleau, 65km south-southeast of Paris. This is the first time that Rommel has returned to France since mid-February of 1941, when he turned over command of his famed 7th Panzer—the "Ghost" Division—to *General der Panzertruppen* Hans *Freiherr* von Funck.[1]

Ah, the good old days! Barreling through France, overwhelming confused French units. Today though, it is an entirely different story. Great Britain, now joined by the abundantly resourced United States, pounds them continually from the air, with raiding forces sometimes as large as a couple thousand aircraft. The enemy controls the seas, while scores of enemy divisions of all types are drilling right across the Channel, getting ready to assault the Reich's *"Festung Europa."*

It will be up to Rommel to stop them.

In the meantime, he has to get settled in. His lavish, openly decadent quarters, once the bawdy home of the controversial and (in his mind) notorious Madame de Pompadour, are completely beyond what he has expected, despite the stories that he had heard about the palatial settings. Truly, this is a totally different world from that impromptu, fly-infested headquarters tent he had used in the desert some three years before, and he is not thrilled with the idea of his headquarters in the home of such an infamous lady. Well, he does not plan on becoming absorbed in the French good life as his predecessors have done. He is on a mission, and cannot afford to have his head turned by the rich life, his passion for his objectives obscured by the Parisian night lights, or his energy for inspections slowly drained by the theater. He has to stay lean and hard, above the life of luxury.

As he enters the magnificent building in the evening, he is welcomed by his staff. Leading them with a smile is his chief of staff, *Generalleutnant* Alfred Gause; *"Der Chef."* Gause has been at his side since North Africa. The two of them have gone through thick and thin in the desert, and Gause has seen Rommel at his best and at his worst. He has seen him overjoyed and triumphant, and has suffered with him in his heartbreaking defeats.

Rommel's gear is brought to his room, and he immediately calls a meeting with his staff to go over some quick strategies. Tomorrow, he will have to call on his commanding officer—the legendary Gerd von Rundstedt, Commander-in-Chief of the Western Theater. Rommel is not sure how the meeting will go, although he assumes the old man is miffed over his appointment. So Rommel will have to be on his best, most diplomatic behavior. Well, he can do that, so long as the old man accepts his presence and agrees to either cooperate or to stay the hell out of his way...

After a particularly sumptuous dinner and then a social hour, Rommel turns in.

---

1 *General der Panzertruppen* Hans Freiherr von Funck.

Sunday, December 19

Generalfeldmarschall Rommel travels to Paris with some senior staff members to formally call on his new superior, *Generalfeldmarschall* von Rundstedt. He arrives around 11 a.m. at von Rundstedt's winter headquarters, the Hôtel Georges V. The old Prussian greets Rommel formally, somewhat stiffly; each field marshal, of course, is carrying his marshal's baton. Rommel notes that von Rundstedt's staff members are at ease and relaxed. Paris life evidently agrees with them.

After some chitchat,[1] they move to a parlor, while their 1a officers go into conference. Rommel, concerned over the lack of defenses that he has seen so far, is ready to get down to business. He gives his report of the weakly defended Danish coast.

Von Rundstedt counters by giving Rommel a rundown on the military situation. He speaks in short, terse sentences. He explains that they can command at any one time up to fifty divisions in France. Unfortunately, many of them are just here temporarily for rest and refitting before going back to the East. So naturally, for these units, constructing defensive barriers in France is the last thing on their minds. Out of desperation, von Rundstedt had created what were essentially "static" divisions. These were new units made up of inferior, recuperating, and even foreign troops, and lacked any type of mobile transport.

Von Rundstedt explains that the command structure is both an administrative and an operational nightmare. Göring commands the Luftwaffe, so not much help there. He also administratively oversees the Luftwaffe field divisions, and that makes for some logistical red-tape nightmares. The civilian laborers on the coastal defenses are part of Albert Speer's OT. The SS formations, especially the Waffen SS and engineer units, are under *Reichsführer* Heinrich Himmler, who of course, also oversees most of the security forces, including the Gestapo.

Other units, including native country security forces and the local police, are commanded by the military governors, Hermann Hannecken in Denmark, Alexander von Falkenhausen in Belgium, and 57-year-old Carl-Heinrich von Stülpnagel in France. The Kriegsmarine officially controls the naval batteries, marine units, and of course, the fleet units. Dönitz directly controls the U-boats… And there is a total lack of naval craft.

"Technically," von Rundstedt concludes, "I command all the forces in the West; but my deputy is *Feldmarschall* Sperrle, a Luftwaffe commander, and so, all I really control are the army units." He sighs and laments, "How wonderful it would be to control a unified command, like Eisenhower does."

Rommel asks him what he thinks the biggest problem is.

"Well," von Rundstedt replies, "we totally lack any kind of mobile reserve to react to any kind of a landing. And a powerful mobile reserve is the best possible way to defeat the invasion."

They discuss possible strategies. Rommel states that he would like to stop the enemy at the waterline. Von Rundstedt thinks that is impossible, given their resources and the enemy's control of the air and the sea. He would rather counterattack inland, at a point of their own choosing.

"Look," he adds, staring at Rommel, "I understand that we have to make it as hard as possible for the enemy to land; but we simply do not have enough men to protect the entire coast. And the Allies are too powerful in the air and at sea to really prevent an initial landing."

He pauses, then goes on. "But once they regroup and start inland, then we can outflank them with a powerful armored assault that has been organized, say somewhere around Paris. It would smash into their lines and would split the landing in two, driving a wedge of steel that would roll right onto the beachhead itself."

Rommel pauses and then replies, "I don't think that their air force or navy will allow us to maneuver, much less roll down onto their beachhead from any distance. So our entire survival depends on defeating this invasion, and we must do it immediately, before they get a foothold on the continent. And we're going to have to stake everything on a battle that the enemy gets to pick 'where' and 'when'. That means we must be ready everywhere if we're to react decisively without delay."

They pause. "Well, it doesn't make much difference anyway," von Rundstedt concludes glumly. "We have no powerful reserve. Each of the mobile units that refit here in France just recuperates. When they're back up to tolerable strength, they get sent back to the Eastern Front to plug up holes in the lines. So essentially we have no sizable mobile units, especially panzers, that are permanently assigned."

It was true. Just between October of 1942 and October of 1943, some 53 divisions had been ordered to the East, with 12 of them being panzer divisions and another five of them being panzer-grenadier divisions.

"And of course, there's no chance that they can spare any divisions from over there to help us out here in the West." For replacement troops, he often got misfits, walking wounded, and even *Ostruppen*—Russian prisoners of war, each of whom for different reasons was fighting on the side of Germany. Naturally, their motivations were highly suspect, to say the least.

The enemy totally commands the sky and is a common presence above, bombing their forces here and there. Equipment and raw materials are in short supply. And despite all these problems, there seems to be a permanent holiday atmosphere all over the country.

"And, as I have said, I have no panzer reserve," von Rundstedt says softly and sadly. Looking down, he adds, "*Da ist nichts.*"

Rommel gazes at him as he sighs. The old man softly finishes with, "It looks very black to me." Rommel is surprised at this remark, because the Prussian has uttered this last sentence in English.[2]

Rommel tries to reassure him, OKW has not forgotten him, and supplies and men will soon be coming. When the invasion comes, OKW will shift a few infantry units down from Scandinavia, a few from Italy, and some *Jäger* divisions from the Balkans. Plus, a number of panzer units will be put at their disposal.

Rommel says that hopefully he can make a difference and use his influence to make some changes. "In the meantime," he adds, "we can get Goebbels and his men to broadcast my presence here. That ought to stir the other side up some."

Rommel finally changes the subject. He tells von Rundstedt that he is staying at the famous Madame de Pompadour estate at Fontainebleau, but that he would like to move his staff into a headquarters closer to the coast. "That way," he concludes, "I can have easier communications with the units out there."

Von Rundstedt agrees. They chat some more, each trying to get somewhat comfortable speaking to each other. OB West finally invites Rommel to stay for lunch.

They adjourn to the elaborate dining room. Both staffs are somewhat nervous at the luncheon, so if they speak at all, it is in low tones. The field marshals eat in relative silence, broken by the clinking of dinnerware, or an occasional remark, attended by silent waiters. Their senior officers of course follow suit, later they will remember this as one of the strangest lunches of their careers.

The lunch over, they part. Rommel and his staff return to Fontainebleau. Later, Rommel writes to Lucie:

> *Arrived safely yesterday. I've found myself a lovely billet in a chateau which once belonged to Madame de Pompadour. But I won't be here long. I'm already off on a trip tomorrow—as today's news announced. It seems that they can tell the British and Americans soon enough that I'm here.*
>
> *I lunched with R. today. He seems very pleased, and I think it's all going well, but I must first get a picture of the situation and see how things are.*[3]

He does not want her to worry, so he goes back to describing Fontainebleau:

> *The old chateau is a lovely place. The French built very generously and spaciously for their upper classes two centuries ago. We're absolutely provincial in comparison.*

He has deliberately omitted that he was shocked by von Rundstedt's feeling of hopelessness. That isn't going to happen to him. Rommel has resolved that he is going to do his best to negate the lifelessness in OB West by keeping plenty of fire of his own. This he confides to Lucie:

> *I'm going to throw myself into this job with everything I've got, and I'm going to see it turns out a success.*

The letter finished, he then writes out his schedule for the next day. Tomorrow, he and Gause will be back on the road again to the French coast.

1 Irving wrote that the briefing happened after lunch.

2 Making a point in English was evidently a common habit among the German General Staff officers, especially when they wanted to emphasize their statement.

3 Liddell-Hart's *The Rommel Papers* mistakenly dates this letter as December 15.

Monday, December 20

Obergruppenführer und Panzergeneral der Waffen-SS Sepp Dietrich,[1] having put in a good two years on the Eastern Front, arrives in Brussels to set up his headquarters for his returning 1st SS Panzer Corps. As such, he will soon have under his command remnants of the 1st SS Panzer Division, limping back from the East, and the new 12th SS *Hitlerjugend* Panzer Division, currently training in Beverloo, near Antwerp.

***

Generalfeldmarschall Rommel, his mind now made up to totally commit himself to his assignment, today sets off northward with some staff members on a five-day tour of the upper French coast. They are headed for the Somme estuary, and then northeast to the Scheldt.[2]

After a 300km drive, they stop for lunch at Tourcoing, the Fifteenth Army Headquarters, where Rommel calls on its commander, *Generaloberst* Hans von Salmuth. After he leaves, one staff member notes:

> Field Marshal Rommel's view is that our defense forces must be concentrated much closer to the coast. Our reserves are to be brought up forward and thrown into an immediate counterattack. If the British once get a foothold on dry land, they can't be thrown out again.

Rommel has established a set routine for his tours: up at the crack of dawn, gather with his officers for a quick breakfast, and then off with one or more staff members to inspect the coast. Perhaps a few snacks will be taken, although he will seldom eat them. Sometimes he returns that same night and sometimes he stays over somewhere, dining with the commanding officers and visiting with the men of the local unit. Naturally, he sits at the head of the table, and usually Admiral Ruge or Alfred Gause sits on his left.

Rommel makes sure that his dinnertime subjects of conversation vary. Often he tells stories of his exploits, sometimes amusing, sometimes recounting a pivotal point of some campaign, either in this war or the last. Often though, he enjoys reminiscing about North Africa in '41. Rommel will sometimes talk about Tobruk, and his eyes light up as he goes into the fine points of his 1942 offensive against the British. He tries to make sure that there is never any trace of boasting in his stories, and he always strives to tell his accounts objectively and honestly. He prides himself on the fact that he does not hesitate to talk about his mistakes, pointing out to his staff that the main purpose of errors was to set a negative example from which to learn.

Often Gause will take on the roguish job of filling in the details of the general's tales with some humorous, embarrassing, or all-too-human minutiae of the operations. This task, combined with Gause's dry wit, supplies delightful color to the boss's narrative. Add to this the faked anguish—well, maybe not completely—of his staff members who have heard these stories over and over; Rommel's aide Hammermann complained that this was the fifteenth time he had heard Rommel describe how they captured Tobruk.

Wherever he goes, the men flock to him and lay upon him unabashed pride and admiration, bordering upon adoration. He is, after all, there for them. And he is one of their best—He is *der legendare Wüstenfuchs*.

***

At Hitler's noontime war conference, he discusses the subject of the new Me-262 jet with *Reichsmarschall* Göring. He stresses again that he wants this new weapon developed not just as a fighter, but as a fighter-bomber. This is necessary, if they are to turn back the expected enemy invasion in the West.

He repeats this theme to Göring again when they have lunch a couple hours later. Hitler tells him, "Every month that passes makes it more and more probable that we will get at least one squadron of jet aircraft: the most important thing is that they [i.e., the enemy] get some bombs on top of them just as they try to invade. That will force them to take cover. And even if there is only one such aircraft in the air, they will still have to take cover, and in this way they will waste hour after hour!"

He continues. "But after half a day, our reserves will already be on their way. So if we can pin them down on the beaches for just six or eight hours, you can see what that will mean for us."

He continues. "There is no doubt at all that the attack in the West will come in the spring… When they attack, then that attack will decide the war. When that attack is beaten off, the story is over. Then we can take forces away again without delay."

Clearly, he is imagining a terrible fate for the Allies coming ashore.

---

1 Fifty-one-year-old Joseph "Sepp" Dietrich, a World War I artilleryman with limited education, nevertheless became one of the early members of the Nazi Party, joining in 1928. Soon thereafter, he took command of Hitler's special SS bodyguard. Taking on the role of his chauffeur, he went with the leader on many political trips, and as Hitler gained power, Dietrich rose through the SS ranks. When Hitler became chancellor in 1933, Dietrich was given the coveted command of the Führer's SS bodyguard regiment, the *Leibstandarte SS Adolf Hitler* (LSSAH). When the war began, Dietrich's unit began to see military action, and the SS regiment was expanded into a fully functional SS panzer division. In the summer of 1943, the division became the cadre for the 1st SS Panzer Corps, a ruthless, élite unit that would see action in every theater over the course of the war. In 1946, Dietrich was given a life sentence for his connection to the Malmedy Massacre during the Battle of the Bulge, but was released on parole in late October 1955. Shortly after that though, he was again convicted, this time for his involvement in the SA purge during the Night of the Long Knives back in 1934. Released in February 1958 because of health conditions, he still maintained connections with SS veterans until he died of a heart attack on April 21, 1966.

2 The Scheldt River (*Schelde* in Dutch, *Escaut* to the French) flows northeast across western Belgium, past the all-important port of Antwerp, and finally into the North Sea. The Scheldt is also a part of an intricate canal system in that area.

Tuesday, December 21

Rommel continues his tour of the Fifteenth Army positions along the Belgian and northern French coast, von Salmuth accompanying him. He is becoming more and more amazed at his findings. Despite all the Nazi propaganda, there is a decided lack of preparation along the shoreline. There is no overall plan of defense, and no central control. Each of the services is at odds with the others, and cooperation is generally lacking in the face of petty jealousies and varied local resentments. Worse than that, no one really seems to care, other than fervently hoping that the enemy does not decide to land in front of them.

There is only one fully ready panzer division, and its presence in the West is subject to any emergency that might rise in the East. Nearly all the infantry units lack any true kind of transport. Air cover is scant, while enemy air power is growing continually. Fewer than two million mines have been laid on the coast, and many have been down for a couple years now, and are considered unreliable.

The small number of beach obstacles in place are primitive and too few to be really effective. A lot are temporary, and many in or under the water are constantly getting pounded by the waves. Probably only half of them would be effective against armor.

As bad as anything are the *Strandlöwen*[1]—the fortified bunkers with the heavy batteries. Most of the effective ones are along the Pas-de-Calais where the invasion is expected. Because of steel shortages, many are set in stationary concrete bases instead of revolving turrets. So they can only elevate—they cannot traverse, limiting their field of fire.[2] And the guns themselves, the spoils of a defeated Europe, represent nearly thirty different calibers and over forty different makes, with a number of them at odd sizes. Fire control is usually crude, and the gun crews are often older men, averaging in their mid-forties. Others are members of the *Marinehelfer* or *Marinehelferinnen*,[3] many of them are still completing their training via correspondence courses.

At the end of the day, the tired field marshal sighs. Clearly, he has his work cut out for him.

***

Today, a German newspaper, the *Pariser Zeitung*, highlights Rommel's presence in France and, in particular, the new "alliance" between *Generalfeldmarschall* von Rundstedt, the winner of countless campaigns during the war in both the East and the West, and the renowned Desert Fox. The paper reports that this new command "...could attach everlasting glory to their flags in all theaters of war." The old Prussian is portrayed as a, "guarantee for the security of Fortress Europe against all attempts by the Americans and British to infiltrate." Rommel, in turn, is described as the man of action who always commands at the front.

1 "Beach lions."

2 There had been a good deal of construction going on in 1941–43. However, this was primarily limited to the submarine pens at ports like St. Nazaire, and Brest.

3 Naval assistants. See Glossary.

Wednesday, December 22

Generalfeldmarschall Rommel, up early, continues his tour of the northern French Coast, riding in a large 2.3-litre Mercedes 230 Cabriolet. Seeing more coastal positions only drives home the seriousness of the situation. The isolated fortified bunkers with their many different calibers of guns present real supply problems. And the plight of these bunkers typifies the condition of the rest of the coastal defenses.

There are too many different types of weapons, many of them captured. Their ammunition, often no longer manufactured, is hard or impossible to get. Because of this, they cannot be fired in practice.

Transportation is severely lacking, and any transport that units have been able to appropriate is usually a hodgepodge mixture of old civilian and military vehicles. Many unit commanders lack their own personal vehicle to tour their area of responsibility. They must use more simple means of transportation, such as a bicycle or a horse.

Rommel is often stunned by the lack of preparation and decides that he will have to spend the rest of the month in a whirlwind of activity. Then he will have to maintain this high level throughout the rest of the winter.

***

Von Rundstedt has enjoyed a comfortable day at the lavish Hôtel Georges V in Paris. Up at 10 a.m., he has spent the hours leisurely, signing a few reports, and receiving one or two visitors. His own command bunker in the suburb of St.-Germain-en-Laye, to the west, is currently being renovated—not that he cares very much, because he usually stays at his nearby villa, a couple hundred yards away, when the weather is nice, and at his Parisian hotel near the Eiffel Tower in the coldest part of the winter.

He will spend the evening with a nice bottle of some vintage brandy and a Zane Gray western that he started a few days ago. The war to him is far away.

Blumentritt, still in the hotel lounge, is worried about the old man's drinking, which has increased substantially this last year. That in and of itself is not so bad, but the excess alcohol sometimes gives the field marshal a tendency to get a little too frank in any evening conversation with OKW. Some of his staff are worried that some of his more forthright, blunt remarks might get back to the Führer and get him relieved of his command—or even arrested.

Blumentritt finally goes to his room, still worried.

Thursday, December 23

Generalfeldmarschall Rommel is still on his tour of the Fifteenth Army positions on the northern French coast. His staff is hard-pressed to keep up with him, anxious to wrap this inspection trip up. Christmas Eve, after all, is tomorrow.

Oblivious of the holiday, Rommel spends the entire day visiting the area around Montreuil, about 45km south-southeast of Boulogne-sur-Mer. His inspection of the 125th Reserve Division does not impress him. In the evening, he goes back to Montreuil to spend the night.

He does some in-depth analysis that evening. It is obvious that an overall defensive plan against an invasion is needed. To his way of thinking, the most effective thing to do is clearly to just mass everybody—infantry, artillery, staff members, cooks, bottle washers—everybody—into a bristling fortification zone, shielded by mines, obstacles, natural barriers, and anything else that will stop or slow down an advancing enemy. This fortified zone will have to be at least 4.5km wide all along the coastline. The mobile forces that he will somehow have to create and organize will lie in wait just behind them, so that the panzers can charge up to the landing site at a moment's notice and enter the fray.

Since the French road network near the ocean is already well-developed, further construction might allow this short, rapid type of advance to be possible in the short run, even with the enemy control of the air. The critical point, he concludes, is that the panzers must coordinate their fight with the infantry and be right alongside them, and not roaming around the rear lines in massive formations, maneuvering, where air interdiction could pulverize and neutralize the vehicles.

He knows what air power can do to rear areas from personal experience; unfortunately, mostly on the receiving end. He suffered such attacks in North Africa. There had been days when the Afrika Korps was pounded again and again by Allied aircraft. He himself had many times, with bombs falling around him, had to jump into a foxhole or bunker, or leap out of his vehicle into a ditch. How he himself has not been killed or wounded by now is in his mind (as well as in those of his men) nothing short of a miracle. And now the enemy has a much greater number of aircraft to throw against them.

Yes, it would be hell trying to move around behind the lines. And naval gunfire support near the beachhead would triple the problem. No, the best place for his men was to be dug in right there at the very front, mixing it up with the enemy as they struggled to make it ashore and set up their lines.

He and his staff have already begun designing a plan to put this defensive strategy into effect. The problems in getting the massive amount of supplies for this ambitious undertaking will be great.

Of course, it could in the end turn out to be academic. If von Rundstedt cannot be convinced that he is right, his plans might all come to naught. Unless, of course, Rommel can get the Führer to support him…

Friday, December 24

Rommel's inspection party completes its tour of the Fifteenth Army positions. Starting out early in the morning from Montreuil, they begin by inspecting a strong defensive position being constructed by two Waffen SS companies.[1] Then they are off to examine a V-1 launching site carved out of a chalk cliff. Launch ramps would be rolled out to fire the missiles.

Word has leaked out that Rommel is in the area, because a number of drills are being performed as he comes through—exercises that most likely would not have occurred on Christmas Eve if he had not been inspecting. One engineering unit though, unperturbed, has already started celebrating the holidays when he arrives, and the lady auxiliaries there take the opportunity to get the field marshal's autograph.

Around noontime, he attends a conference at the headquarters of the 82nd Corps.[2] Its area of responsibility covers the coastline from the Somme estuary to the Belgian border. He finds the conference enlightening.

At 2 p.m., the inspection group finally heads back to their headquarters, passing through Amiens and at length, Paris. As they drive into to the capital, the weather becomes foggy and they get lost. Tired, Rommel and his staff finally roll into Fontainebleau at 7 p.m.

They have a quick, simple dinner, and then go into a main hall to join in the Christmas celebration initiated by the security force. In addition, all members of staff join in to celebrate Admiral Ruge's birthday, his 50th.

One of the topics discussed during the party is today's news. The Allies have announced that Eisenhower has been promoted to the post of Supreme Commander in Europe. Rommel instructs his staff to update the man's profile immediately.

He then takes time off from the party to call home and wish his family happy holidays. He is especially tender to Manfred, wishing him a heartfelt happy birthday. The boy will tomorrow turn fifteen.

They also discuss his immediate future with the military. Manfred now tells him that he has been assigned to the Luftwaffe as an auxiliary. He reports January 6 to an anti-aircraft battery around Stuttgart. Manfred seems happy about it.

After the phone call, the field marshal spends some more time celebrating with his staff, then retires. He has a busy day lined up for the holiday: Christmas morning with his staff, starting his report, and then going out to spend some time with his troops. After all, he is still Rommel.

---

1   Admiral Ruge in his work (*Rommel in Normandy: Reminiscences*) claims that these were units of the 9th SS Panzer Division *Hohenstaufen*. This is quite possible, even though the division itself was at the time fighting in the East, because some replacement units to the division were at the same time being formed in the West.

2   Fifty-six-year-old *General der Artillerie* Johann Sinnhuber, commanding.

Saturday—Christmas Day

Generalfeldmarschall von Rundstedt enjoys a quiet holiday in his luxurious suite at the Hôtel Georges V. He goes out for a sumptuous dinner at one of his favorite restaurants, and then enjoys the rest of Christmas Day at the hotel.

***

Generalfeldmarschall Rommel, after briefly enjoying a Christmas morning get-together with his army group staff, spends most of his day catching up on the mountain of paperwork on his desk. He also works on his summary report to the Führer on the readiness of what he has seen so far of the Atlantic Wall. He has not been impressed.

He and his staff have settled in to their new quarters. Rommel, Gause, von Tempelhoff, and all their aides are lodging in Madame Pompadour's old château. His naval staff officers are quartered in a nearby boarding house, and the rest of their personnel are in quarters around the estate.

As they do most evenings, Rommel and his staff take their meals in the main dining salon of the Maison Pompadour. The meals are usually simple. This often frustrates their artistic dining officer, who before the war oversaw the exquisite restaurant of an internationally famed hotel. Of course when they have special guests, he is allowed to flex his talents. Still, Rommel seldom has more than one guest visit at a time, and never allows more than two. At such times, the guest usually sits at the table to the field marshal's right (Admiral Ruge dutifully moves down one chair).

The field marshal often relaxes during the evening meal with talk about military subjects and the many different types of people he has met in his life. Still, he does not like to dominate the conversation and often allows staff members to carry on the dialogue. The atmosphere around the table is usually relaxed, and because the field marshal enjoys a good joke (although nothing crude or dirty), the talk is sometimes punctuated with laughter. Rommel allows his staff to smoke, although he does not, and seldom drinks any alcohol.

Tonight after dinner, he takes time out to write to his family. To Lucie he writes:

> It was grand that the telephone call worked so well last night and that I now know that things are all right with you both. The big news was Manfred's call-up on January 6. He is sure to be pleased, but for us, and above all, for you, it's painful to see the youngster leave home, and it will take us a long time to get used to the idea.
>
> I wish you both a happy Christmas. Enjoy the time you still have together... I spent yesterday evening with the officers of my staff and afterwards with the men, though it's difficult to be really cheerful at the moment.

He finishes his letter to her, and then begins one to his son.

Dear Manfred:

In a fortnight, you'll be leaving your parental home to enlist as a Luftwaffe auxiliary. So life begins in earnest for you. I hope you bring us as much joy in uniform as you have up until now.

A new way of life is starting for you. You must learn to obey the orders of your superior quickly and without answering back. Often there'll be orders which you don't like, often you won't understand the point of them. Obey without question. A superior cannot go into a long discussion about his orders with his subordinates. There just isn't time to give reasons for every order...

Now that the instructions are over, he summarizes.

Remember your moral upbringing, and don't fall into bad company. I've talked with you often enough about that. You know the importance I attach particularly to this question of conduct.

He finishes his letter, guilty that the boy has grown so much over the last few years and that he has missed so much of it. Now he is going into the military, and Rommel is missing that, too...

He leaves his office and, to cheer up, he joins his staff for a while, celebrating the holidays. But he is homesick, and is not in much of a mood for festivities. He goes to bed early.

***

Adolf Hitler, Führer of the Third Reich, spends Christmas with most of his senior leaders at his *Wolfsschanze* in East Prussia. He is in a funk of depression. Another Soviet offensive began yesterday, and it looks as though things are going to get really bad in the East.

Clearly, the rest of the war is not going well either. Africa is lost. Italy has surrendered, and Hungary is considering a similar solution. The Wehrmacht has been crippled with nearly two million casualties in just the last year, and given the way the war is going, it looks like there will be at least that many this next year. American bombers pound the Reich's cities by day and British bombers take their turn at night. The struggle in the Atlantic has turned decisively against them, and his surface navy is a ghost of what it once was. On top of everything else, it appears to him that his generals and admirals are doing little to change these fortunes of war.

Dejected, Hitler decides that the holiday will not be celebrated. He has ordered that no Christmas tree be put up, and he does not allow a single candle to be lit. OKW Chief of Staff *Generalfeldmarschall* Keitel makes sure that this policy is followed.

The Führer, his entire command staff, and everyone at the *Wolfsschanze* go through a sad, dismal Christmas Day working as usual.

Sunday, December 26

Generalfeldmarschall Rommel spends the day after Christmas at his palatial head-quarters in Fontainebleau. He goes over the notes and summaries that he and his staff have written up on their last two inspections of the coast. In a few days, he will start writing his report to the High Command. After all, that is really what he is there for. No one as yet has officially told him that he will be taking over the northern area. Right now, he is just an inspector for the Führer.

One disturbing factor out here is the varying sizes of the divisions. So many are either being formed, being refitted, or just struggling to hold onto their own numbers, given the huge drain of manpower on the Eastern and Southern fronts. So the divisions in Western Europe vary greatly in number and types of men, vehicles, and formations.

The panzer divisions were typically created around an initial, small cadre of experienced *Panzermänner*. Initially labeled Reserve Panzer Divisions, they would struggle to acquire resources to grow and then train for combat. After several weeks, they would either reach a reasonable size (at least 12,000 men) and a minimal level of efficiency, or be combined into another larger unit. Sometimes a unit might be able to beg, borrow, or steal enough transport of any kind, including wagons, carts, and bicycles, to be considered "mobile." If they could commandeer enough old or captured tanks to be loosely considered a panzer force, they might suddenly find themselves given an allotment of moderately good tanks (but still no transport). Unfortunately, they are usually then shipped off to the Eastern Front to play in the big leagues.

Some units are already large enough, and just struggle to get into shape to fight. The 156th Reserve Division, as an example, has a nearly full complement of some 14,000 men. And they are usually in good shape too, trained, many with combat experience. But their equipment is pathetic; little motor transport, old decrepit weapons, and a supply setup that is primitive at best.

Then there are the Luftwaffe field divisions.

There are at present several of them stationed in France. The idea for these unique units began in the winter of 1941–42, when the situation on the Eastern Front had first become critical and manpower shortages had begun to have an effect on the Heer. The army was starting to have difficulties getting fresh bodies to fill their divisions. In comparison, Herman Göring's Luftwaffe, shrunken down by heavy combat losses in all theaters, now had spare ground personnel who were, to all intents and purposes, out of a job.

The vain Reichsmarshal, rather than turn these 200,000–250,000 men over to the army, decided to use them to create his own field divisions. And naturally, the Luftwaffe would retain operational control of them.[1] The program to establish these new units had been offered to Hitler as a present on his 53rd birthday in April 1942. Creation of the divisions started in October.

Rommel scowls as he thinks of these divisions. Air force personnel trained as infantry! Two of the divisions are doing a lackluster job in Italy. Those here in France are no better. Some are undersized. The 18th Luftwaffe Field Division for instance, defending the coast northeast of Calais, has fewer than 9,000 men.

Rommel had inspected one of these Luftwaffe field units back in Italy. It was an odd thing to see air force personnel committed in ground combat roles. Their officers were incompetent and inexperienced in land warfare. The senior officers were usually old veterans of World War I. The junior field officers had little training to lead men on ground maneuvers, and the few noncoms lacked any combat experience. The one positive virtue of these divisions though, was that most of the men were healthy and had at least some type of war training, even if it was usually tied to air operations.

Still, Rommel would rather see these inadequate divisions disbanded and their men used to flesh out other, weaker army units. The units would benefit from the fresh influx of good manpower, and the airmen would in turn benefit from the experience of their army cohorts.

But Göring would not hear of such a preposterous idea. Dump his élite Luftwaffe men in with the "cannon fodder?" *Ha! Niemals!*

***

This morning in the freezing North Sea, the German battlecruiser *Scharnhorst*, having put to sea yesterday with five Z-class destroyers in Operation *Östfront*, is having no luck trying to find a couple eastbound convoys northwest of Norway and headed for Russia. The battlegroup, commanded by Konteradmiral Erich Bey, does not know that the convoys are bait sent to lure him out to sea. The Royal Navy, forewarned of *Scharnhorst's* departure by Ultra intercepts from London, has sent a battle force out to catch it. So in the process of looking for and trying to intercept the merchant ships, Bey instead meets at North Cape a British cruiser force.[2] The British cruisers keep the German vessel from engaging a convoy to the north and hold it off until more ships can arrive. The *Scharnhorst*, now alone, having sent its destroyers home to escape in the heavy seas, attempts to return to base southeastward, but is cut off a couple hours later by the battleship *Duke of York* and cruiser *Jamaica*.

In the late afternoon, a three-hour running gun battle ensues. Outnumbered, outgunned, far outclassed technologically by the superior British radar, and crippled by a couple lucky hits early on, *Scharnhorst* is beaten down. Although she is damaged by several torpedoes from British destroyers, she can still make 12 knots. Then the light cruisers *Jamaica* and *Belfast* close in for the kill, and after several more torpedo hits, she goes down by the bow at 7:45 p.m., her props still proudly turning. Out of a crew of nearly two thousand, just 36 crewmen are picked up in the frigid waters. None are officers.

At the *Wolfsschanze*, *Großadmiral* Erich Raeder informs the Führer of the loss later that night.

1   These units initially remained under Luftwaffe control, but not for long. While the Luftwaffe retained administrative control of them, operational control was soon handed over to the Heer. The divisions were able to retain their original numbers and a Luftwaffe designator was attached to them, thus distinguishing them from similarly numbered army units already created. However, they were operationally controlled by Army headquarters.

2   The British had intercepted *Scharnhorst*'s battle orders by wireless before she had sailed, and had just enough time to move in sufficient vessels to trap her.

Monday, December 27

Generalfeldmarschall Rommel goes on the road again. He has a noontime meeting with corps commander *General der Artillerie* Erich Heinemann. The general, at 56 more than three years older than Rommel, had retired from the army back in '37. Recalled to serve again in 1940, he commanded artillery on the Eastern Front for a couple years before he was given command of the new 65th Corps just 26 days ago. He has also, by special order of OKW, been put in charge of the German V-1 program. Rommel discusses with him the locations where the "vengeance weapon" sites will be built.

Later that afternoon, Rommel travels to Paris with Alfred Gause, his chief of staff, and Hans-Georg von Tempelhoff, his Ia. They call on von Rundstedt at his hotel headquarters, and over tea, they go over Rommel's initial findings in respect of the Atlantic Wall.

The enemy has conducted a few landing exercises, and will more than likely do more. Regarding the enemy fleet, intelligence reports that the combat vessels in southern ports are mainly destroyers, escorts, and auxiliary craft. Cruisers and battleships are nested in the central and northern ports, away from German bombers and prying eyes. These ships might unite at any point up there, concealed from the few German recon flights that are completed.

They then discuss possible defensive strategies. The invasion is expected to occur sometime between next spring and fall, when the weather is good. Rommel thinks the invasion will most likely be near Boulogne and the Somme estuary. The Cherbourg and Brittany peninsulas are too remote. In any event, he wants to put all available forces on the coast and build a chain of massive fortifications, interlaced with minefields and obstacles. He wants the panzer divisions brought forward too, with at least one to support each infantry corps.

Von Rundstedt disagrees. There just is too much coastline to cover, and not nearly enough men. Better to let the enemy first land, and then conduct a mobile defense around them.

Still, the old Prussian does not voice too many objections. He partially accepts Rommel's theory of defending the coast despite his own personal views. He is willing to put infantry close to the coastline. And he further agrees that the Somme is a likely target. He does though object to the placement of the panzers. He wants them further inland, where they can be free of naval gunfire and be allowed to maneuver. So he forbids putting them so near the beaches. He states, "for me too there is no doubt whatever that the main invasion will most probably come either side of the Somme." However, if the Allies do land in a different area, then the panzers would not be able to quickly move to get to the landing area.

After Rommel leaves, von Rundstedt repeats his concerns in a reply to an extensive communiqué he has received from von Salmuth. The Fifteenth Army commander's suggestions echo those of Rommel, who toured his area just a few days ago. Von Salmuth, in a detailed report, recommends a) strengthening the coastal defenses, b) expanding the minefields with additional labor and engineer units, and c) concentrating units close to the coast, because the issue would need to be resolved immediately, and reserves would arrive too late. He also adds that the mobile reserves should be formed into large formations and positioned in key "focal points."

Von Rundstedt starts off on a positive note:

> Far be it from me, not to assess the suggestions of responsible commanders-in-chief from a purely technical standpoint, and with a view to the general good. You may therefore rest assured that I welcome every suggestion and every proposal, and that I will have their practicability examined.

And he does agree that time would be of the essence. However, his intentions regarding the positioning of the panzers, as with Rommel, remain the same:

> I have … intentionally avoided placing panzer divisions in particular too far forward, in order still to allow an advance from the rear areas, or a lateral movement without too great a sacrifice.

He adds a note of hope to his report for von Salmuth:

> Circumstances may change, if—as OKW foresees—additional forces, including mechanized formations, are placed at OB. West's disposal within the next few weeks. I will then place large bodies of troops, including mechanized or armored formations at the disposal of Fifteenth Army too as operational reserve divisions, and I shall perhaps also be able to strengthen the forces on the coast.

Still, he has no intention of putting his mobile units up front, where they would be stuck, and where enemy naval and air forces could decimate them. No, the panzers will stay inland, under his command.

This point of contention between the two field marshals will persist until the invasion.

Tuesday, December 28

A meeting in Fontainebleau today is to be attended by the operations officers (Ia) for all the major commands in the West. Attendants include OB West's Bodo Zimmermann, von Tempelhoff, and the operations officers from each of the Seventh, Fifteenth, and First Armies.

Rommel does not stay for the meeting, though. He leaves with his chief of staff and Queissner. They drive to Hugo Sperrle's headquarters at the Palais du Luxembourg in Paris, once the residence of Marie de Medici.[1] Sperrle commands Luftflotte 3, and all other air units in the West. Additionally, he is *Stellvertretender OB West*.[2]

Sperrle, along with Albert Kesselring, had been a key player in the 1940 Battle of Britain. Now, over three years of the easy, Parisian life has left him out of shape, spoiled, relaxed, and generally unconcerned about the war. With his bulky legs propped up on a map on his desk, his monocle in one eye, he tells Rommel that the Luftwaffe will not be much of a factor in the upcoming invasion. As a matter of fact, on the first day, it will not even be around.

Rommel is astounded. Oh, the ground support system for the aircraft is there and will be ready. But the actual air units will not start coming in until a few days after the landing.

Take for instance, the II Fliegerkorps.[3] It had been transferred a couple weeks ago from the Italian front, and was to be the core unit to assault the landing when it came. The headquarters unit had even moved to France. However, the air squadrons were still in Germany, getting refitted and reorganized.

Sperrle tries to interject a positive note. When the invasion takes place, ten *Geschwader*,[4] now in Germany undergoing refitting and a good deal of intensive reorganization (which more than likely that means an influx of new, green kids) would immediately be moved into the area to begin operating against the enemy.[5]

Clearly, Field Marshal Sperrle is planning a long campaign,

Rommel gets the feeling that Sperrle has already decided that they are going to lose the war. Tomorrow, Rommel will call on the Kriegsmarine. Maybe they will be more optimistic.

---

1 Marie de Medici (1575–1642) was a French queen, second wife of King Henry IV and part of the influential House of Medici. When the king was stabbed to death in 1610, she became regent for her son, Louis XIII for seven years, until he came of age.
2 Deputy Commander, Western Theater.
3 2nd Air Corps.
4 An air wing, ranging from 80 to 120 aircraft.
5 By D-Day, the 2nd Air Corps would still be without aircraft; eventually, some five or six wings arrived, piecemeal. They were thrown into the battle that way, and therefore did little to change the situation on the ground.

Wednesday, December 29

The Führer at his Wolf's Lair in East Prussia holds his daily noontime war conference. After the many problems of the Eastern Front are discussed, he turns to the subject of the Western invasion. Three critical issues are discussed:

1. Is all the bombaast being broadcast by the Allies about an invasion this year even to be taken seriously? The many victory speeches that are being made—the speculative articles being written in magazines and newspapers—was this all to be taken for real? Or was it just an elaborate hoax to lure units away from the Eastern Front or prevent Germany from reinforcing that front at the crucial moment of the Soviet winter offensive?
2. Is perhaps the invasion threat to France a hoax to cover another landing to take place somewhere south in the Mediterranean? Perhaps in Crete, Rhodes, the Aegean, or via Turkey, or both? The Turks might have decided to throw their lot in with the Allies and agreed to let them go through her territory. Or maybe the Allies with their huge naval forces are working on a number of landings in any of those areas.
3. Might the invasion be a hoax to cover a possible landing in the north? Maybe Denmark or Norway.

All agree that the danger in the West is just as serious as in the East. While the Russians have a much larger ground force than their Western counterparts, and it is in direct contact with Germany's forces, the Reich can afford to give up large expanses of land if they must to retreat and regroup. As his earlier Directive No. 51 of November 3 states:

> Not so in the West! ... I can therefore no longer tolerate the weakening of the West in favor of other theaters of war.

There are only a few bright points in the conference. One is Turkey's persistent, stubborn refusal to declare war on the Reich. German intelligence confirms the angry protests that have been lodged by the British and Russian governments to the Turkish leaders.

Hitler, thinking again later about the inevitable invasion in the West, exclaims, "If only they would land half a million men and then foul weather and storms cut them off in the rear—then everything would be all right!"

***

Rommel today continues his official report to Hitler about the condition of the Atlantic Wall. Among other things, he requests that he be given the command of the northern units along the coast, so that his recommendations could be carried out faster. This is a polite way of asking to be let back into the fray.

He then writes a quick letter to Lucie, adding:

Yesterday I was in Paris again and had a conference with Field Marshal Sperrle. The prospects here aren't good at all. From all I had heard previously, I expected a lot more from this branch of the services. We'll have to make up for that deficiency in some other way. Today I am going to see the navy.

A couple hours later, accompanied by Admiral Ruge and their adjutants, he drives to Paris to call on Admiral Krancke.[1] As *Befehlshaber* (Commander) *Marinegruppenkommandos West*,[2] he is essentially von Rundstedt's naval counterpart, and as such directly answerable only to Dönitz and OKM. Krancke's headquarters is a nicely furnished building along the Bois de Boulogne.

Rommel's group stays through lunch. The visit goes well enough, although the two naval officers intensely dislike each other. Krancke, a fervent Nazi, cannot see what Ruge is doing attached to an army command, and Ruge, not so ardent politically, resents the undertone that he should be serving at sea or as a flunky on someone's naval staff.

Krancke tells Rommel that there is very little "navy" left in the West. *Bismarck* has been gone for two and a half years now. Her sister, *Tirpitz,* is living on borrowed time, hiding in the Norwegian fjords. The battlecruiser *Scharnhorst* was sunk off North Cape only a few days ago, and her sister ship *Gneisenau* is still under repair, having been badly crippled by British air raids back in April 1942.[3] The few surviving cruisers still commissioned in the Kriegsmarine have been delegated to critical (and safer) jobs in the East.[4] The main force of U-boats is deployed in the Atlantic. What German Navy is left in the West consists of the light cruiser *Emden* in Norway, a couple destroyers, some eight fleet torpedo boats,[5] eight or nine squadrons of E-boats,[6] a number of mine trawlers, and various auxiliaries. There are also some three dozen coastal U-boats, although of course, they are under Dönitz's direct command. Existing minefields can be updated and some new ones laid, but only if the mines are available to do so, and that may not always be the case.

Rommel leaves Paris dejected. He sees that the navy, like the air force, will not be able to do much when the invasion comes. Clearly, the army is on its own.

---

1   Fifty-year-old Admiral Theodor Krancke was a torpedo boat veteran of World War I and as such had participated in the Battle of Jutland. When World War II began, this successful Kriegsmarine officer gave up running the Naval Academy to take part in naval operations. As chief naval advisor to Admiral Raeder, he oversaw planning of the 1940 invasions of Norway and Denmark. Two months later, he was given command of the pocket battleship *Admiral Scheer*. In late October 1940, he began a successful 5½-month North Atlantic raid, capturing three merchant ships and sinking a total of 13 merchant vessels and the auxiliary cruiser HMS *Jervis Bay*. He later served as a naval advisor at OKW before being appointed commander of Naval Forces West on April 20, 1943. Captured by the British in late August 1945, he was released in October 1947. He died on June 18, 1973.

2   Supreme Commander, Naval Forces, Western Theater. See Glossary.

3   *Gneisenau* would never again sail against the enemy. She was eventually towed to Gdynia, Poland at the end of the war and turned into a defensive blockship.

4   Heavy cruisers *Prinz Eugen* and *Admiral Hipper*, the light cruisers *Nürnberg* and *Leipzig*, and the pocket battleship (*Panzerschiffe*) *Admiral Scheer*. One additional vessel, the pocket battleship *Lützow*, was currently being refitted in Germany and would soon join them in the East. The light cruiser *Köln* was decommissioned in the winter of 1943.

5   Equivalent to a US Navy destroyer escort.

6   Mainly a mixture of *R-bootes* of 100–200 tons and smaller *S-bootes*. See Glossary.

Thursday, December 30

Von Rundstedt has recommended to OKW that Rommel's Army Group B headquarters be subordinated to OB West, and that the Seventh and Fifteenth Armies be then put under Rommel's command. Rommel of course wants this too.

Hitler is not crazy about the idea of giving Rommel direct command of Army Group B under von Rundstedt. He and Jodl had discussed the idea in early November and had decided on sending Rommel out just as an inspector. Hitler had then balked at the idea of eventually giving Rommel any actual command. For one thing, he was not sure that Rommel had overcome his defeatist depression from North Africa. No, let him just go out there for now and look around.

On the other hand, if they did relent and let Rommel eventually take charge of the threatened area, Hitler himself could take charge of the battle, since Rommel could remain directly subordinate to OKW, bypassing OB West. Von Rundstedt would be furious, but that would be too bad. Rommel after all was a man of action, and von Rundstedt had been sitting around in Paris too long. Creating competition between the two commanders, one of Hitler's favorite ploys, would inspire them both to greater efforts. He thought that this was a necessary expedient. After all, he had split commands like that before.

Jodl of course, predictably (but respectfully) opposed the idea. For one thing, the theater command OKW would be bypassing was just too important. And von Rundstedt was too senior a general to be subjected to such a ploy. The officers of all the services in the West would be simply furious at this blatant breach of etiquette. Anyway, Rommel's staff was too small to be directly controlled by Supreme Headquarters.

Hitler finally agrees to put Rommel under von Rundstedt. However, he states that he reserves the right to transfer Rommel and his Army Group B headquarters staff to the Russian Front if he ever really needs them there. Von Rundstedt has absolutely no problem with that.

***

Generalfeldmarschall Rommel continues writing his report to Hitler. He has sadly concluded that von Rundstedt had been right in his original assessment. The great Atlantic Wall was indeed a joke, or as he aptly described it, a "figment of Hitler's *Wolkenkuckucksheim*."[1] Its main effect seemed to be propaganda in nature, and to deceive the enemy too if possible. Rommel had smiled when he had heard that the grouchy von Rundstedt had claimed that this charade was "...more for the German people than for the enemy." Pausing, he added dryly, "And the enemy, through his agents, knows more about it than we do."

Now he looks over some of what he has down so far:

The focus of the enemy landing operation will probably be directed against Fifteenth Army's sector (the Pas de Calais), largely because it is from this sector that much of our long-range V1 and V2 attack rockets on England and central London will be launched...

The timing of the enemy attack is uncertain, but he will make every effort to launch the operation before the start of our long-range attack on England. If, due to bad weather or unfavorable sea conditions, he fails in this, he will launch his attack either at the beginning or shortly after the beginning of our long-range campaign...

The landing will probably be preceded by very heavy attacks from the air and be made under cover of a smoke-screen and of intense fire from many warships, with simultaneous heavy-bomber attacks. In addition to the seaborne landing, airborne troops will probably be dropped close behind the coastal defenses in the main attack sectors, to break up the defenses from the rear and create a major bridgehead in the shortest possible time.

On the coast, our defense line, thin as it is at present, will suffer severely from the enemy bombs and artillery, and it seems very doubtful whether, after this battering, it will be capable of beating off the enemy, whose forces will be approaching over a wide front, in hundreds of armored assault craft and landing-craft, and under cover of darkness or fog. But if the landing is not beaten off, our thinly held and shallow front will soon be pierced, and contact will be established with the airborne troops behind.

Rommel, with the exception of pointing out Calais as a likely target, is writing his army group's fate.

***

At the *Wolfsschanze* headquarters in Eastern Prussia, the Führer has a conference with several officials about the deteriorating socio-political situation in Denmark. Those present include the three German leaders for Occupied Denmark: head Gestapo leader *SS Gruppenführer* Günther Pancke, the German plenipotentiary for Denmark Dr. Werner Best, and the Wehrmacht military governor and supreme commander for Denmark, *General der Infanterie* Hermann Hannecken. Also present at the meeting are *SS Reichsführer* Heinrich Himmler, *SS Reichssicherheitshauptamt* leader Ernst Kaltenbrunner, OKW Chief of Staff Keitel and Operations Chief Jodl, von Ribbentrop of the German Foreign Office, and the German Army adjutant, General Rudolf Schmundt.[2]

As the meeting begins, the Führer is in an angry mood. The reports that he has been reading of the Danes paint a dark picture of a traitorous local populace, resentful and rebellious; clearly not the attitude of a people who are supposed to enjoy a close affinity to their German cousins.

The question of sabotage and the recent execution of several Germans by Danish terrorists are brought up. General Pancke and Dr. Best propose they swiftly try the accused in either open or secret courts. Hitler strongly disagrees, stating in a heated tone that there can be absolutely no question of judging saboteurs in a courtroom. He adds that such a policy will only glamorize the defendants and make them heroes. No, there is only one way to deal with this scum: to execute them, preferably right when they commit the act, or just afterward. If not, then kill them when they are arrested.

Keitel speaks up and supportively proposes that the entire country be punished for collaborating with these traitors by lowering their relatively generous food rations to the level of those in Germany. The three Danish leaders, Pancke, Best, and Hannecken, object strenuously, pointing out that this measure would only inflame the people even more. That was certainly something that the Reich did not need at this point in time.

Hitler relents on this line of reasoning, but he is inflexible on the saboteur issue. He personally orders Pancke and Best to undertake a series of "compensatory" murders, targeting suspects and possible accomplices. General Pancke points out that it is not easy and is often risky to shoot people when they are arrested, because one cannot be sure at that point in time if the people arrested are the actual saboteurs.

Hitler snaps back that he does not care. He wants reprisal executions in the ratio of five-to-one. For every German killed, five Danes must die.

The meeting goes on, and General Hannecken reports on the military situation. Hitler tells him that he is no longer to treat the Danes as Reich citizens. Instead, he is to treat them as a sullen, occupied enemy, like the French.

As the discussion ends, Hitler once more reminds the Danish representatives of his reprisal order. They will get the order in writing shortly.

After this meeting, Dr. Best goes off to talk to von Ribbentrop, while SS General Pancke meets privately with his superior, Himmler. The Reichsführer reminds him again of this new order, and that the Führer himself has just instructed him on how Pancke is to act when he returns. His Gestapo is to be harsh and unrelenting toward the Danes. They are to round up suspects and close friends, and destroy their homes. Himmler adds (no doubt, as a veiled show of support) that he personally is confident that he can rely on Pancke to carry out the Führer's order. And it had been the Führer himself who had personally directed him to brief Pancke. Up until now, Himmler points out, he had only been carrying out Himmler's orders. Now it was the Führer himself who was commanding him.

Himmler's instructions are quite clear. Pancke is to now be ruthless to the Danes—or else.

---

1   "Cloud cuckoo-land."

2   Forty-three-year-old *Generalleutnant* Rudolf Schmundt had been a major back in 1938, when he had been called on to personally serve the Führer. His predecessor, *Oberst* Friedrich Hossbach, had held this critical position since August of 1934. Hossbach though, was dismissed in January 1938, after he launched into a heated debate with Hitler over charges of homosexual misconduct against army commander General Werner von Fritsch. Schmundt was a likable fellow, compassionate, competent, and not at all manipulative. However, he also lacked self-assurance and was not the sort to stand up against anyone. He found a hero to look up to in the Führer, and thus was not inclined to stick up for the army ranks in any debate with his superiors or senior officers of other services.

Friday—New Year's Eve

Rommel finishes his report to the Führer on the condition of the Atlantic Wall. He writes:

> We can hardly expect a counterattack by the few reserves we have behind the coast at the moment, with no self-propelled guns and an inadequate quantity of all forms of anti-tank weapons, to succeed in destroying the powerful force which the enemy will land…
>
> With the coastline held as thinly as it is at present, the enemy will probably succeed in creating bridge-heads at several different points and in achieving a major penetration of our coastal defenses. Once this has happened it will only be by the rapid intervention of our operational reserves that he will be thrown back into the sea. This requires that these forces should be held very close behind the coast defenses.
>
> If, on the other hand, our principal reserves have to be brought up from well back inland, the move will not only require a great deal of time—time which the enemy will probably use to reinforce himself at his point of penetration and either organize his forces for defense or press the attack farther inland—but will also be under constant danger from the air. Bearing in mind the numerical and material superiority of the enemy striking forces… victory in a major battle on the continent seems doubtful. [Allied] superiority in the air alone has again and again been so effective that all movement of major formations has been rendered completely impossible… and our own air force has only on very rare occasions been able to make any appearance in support of our operations…

Rommel senses that he is dead on.[1]

He finishes by asking that he be given full command over all ground elements along the coast—including naval and air ground units—and be allowed to incorporate defensive measures that he has in mind. A bit brazen perhaps, but the lack of preparedness that he has seen has disturbed him.

When the report is finished, he joins his staff in celebrating the coming of the New Year with two modest glasses of claret. Then he goes to bed.

---

1   He was.

January 1944

Saturday, January 1

On New Year's Day, *Generalfeldmarschall* Rommel takes a couple of staff members with him and leaves for another inspection tour, this time to the coasts of Belgium and Holland. Up there he will spend the next four days appraising the defenses.

The Wehrmacht units in these two occupied countries, while under the overall control of OB West, still have their own individual commands. Belgium, which will become attached to *Heeresgruppe B* if it is indeed created, is currently under the rule of the military governor there, *General der Infanterie* Alexander von Falkenhausen.[1] Holland has its own separate command, the *Wehrmachtbefehlshaber Niederlande*.[2] Rommel will soon call on its commander, *General der Flieger* "Krischen" Christiansen,[3] at The Hague. Like *Generalfeldmarschall* Kesselring (*OB Süd*), Christiansen is a pilot in charge of ground forces. He has held the post for over four years now. And like Rommel, he won the distinguished Blue Max in World War I.

In Belgium, Rommel once again marvels at the many delicacies that are readily at hand. Food is plentiful here, even in winter. And as in Denmark, the war does not seem to have touched this small country.

He and his staff stay at a nice hotel in Antwerp. Life for now seems good.

***

A message arrives today at OB West from Jodl's staff. Based upon a formal request made by *Generalfeldmarschall* von Rundstedt two days ago, OKW reports that it will integrate Rommel's new army group into von Rundstedt's command. *Heeresgruppe B* will comprise the Netherlands command, von Salmuth's Fifteenth Army, and Dollmann's Seventh Army. Rommel will now no longer report directly to the Führer, but to von Rundstedt.

There are also other instructions from OKW. It was revealed in a conference last week that a buildup of enemy units appeared to be taking place in southern England. It was estimated that the upsurge would be finished by the middle of February. So based on Jodl's recommendations, the Führer decreed on December 27 that starting in January, all available reserves should be moved up to the most likely areas: the entire Fifteenth Army coastline and the right flank of the Seventh Army, including the Cotentin peninsula. To make sure this concentration was not hindered by any attrition to the Eastern Front, the Führer had also decreed in a separate order that it will now be forbidden to withdraw any men or units from either OB West or the Denmark Command without his permission—with a few exceptions, of course, which have been noted in the order.[4]

A nice gesture, but as soon as hell breaks out in Russia again, von Rundstedt is sure that the migration of units to the East will begin once more.

---

1 Sixty-five-year-old *General der Infanterie* Alexander Ernst Alfred Hermann von Falkenhausen, the military governor of Belgium during most World War II, had led a colorful life. Commissioned in 1897, he served during World War I as an attaché to the Turks. He was assigned to the Turkish 2nd Army, and then later as chief of staff to the Turkish 7th Army. He actually fought with that unit against General Allenby in Palestine until the 7th Army was destroyed in the fall of 1918. Von Falkenhausen retired from the German Army at the end of January 1930, and four years later, took on the duties of military advisor to General Chiang Kai-Shek in China. Unfortunately for him, the Nazi regime by then in power decided to politically ally themselves with Japan in 1937, and in the spirit of that friendship alliance, withdrew all political and economic support to China, at war with Japan. Von Falkenhausen was forced to resign his post as military advisor after the Nazis threatened to take action against his family if he did not. Falkenhausen sadly bid his Chinese friends goodbye and promised to do what he could to help their cause, though shortly afterwards he was appointed military attaché in Japan.

Von Falkenhausen was recalled back to active duty in 1938, by now nearly 60. An infantry general now, he was appointed military governor to Belgium in 1940. (Interestingly, he was directly related to Ludwig von Falkenhausen, who had been the German governor-general in Belgium in the last year of World War I.) By now an anti-Hitler conspirator, he would become a close friend of two other conspirators, Carl Friedrich Goerdeler and *Feldmarschall* Erwin von Witzleben.

2 Armed Forces High Command, Netherlands.

3 Sixty-four-year-old Luftwaffe *General der Flieger* Friedrich Christiansen came from a nautical family. A trading vessel captain before the war, he joined the navy in 1913 and trained on torpedo boats, before switching to naval aviation. He became a war ace and was awarded the *Pour le Mérite*—the Blue Max—in 1917 for shooting down 21 enemy aircraft (and helping to sink a submarine in the Thames estuary). He went back to trading vessels after the war before later teaching naval aviation. Under Hitler, Christiansen became the first *Korpsführer* of the NSFK (*Nationalsozialistisches Fliegerkorps*, Germany's pre-Luftwaffe National Socialist Flying Corps). Although not considered a very capable leader, as a close friend of Herman Göring, his rise in the Luftwaffe was assured. After the French campaign in 1940, he was appointed on May 28 as commander of all Wehrmacht forces in the Netherlands. Imprisoned at the end of the war, he was found guilty by a Dutch court three years later of war crimes. He was released early in 1951 because of bad health.

4 In that same order, Hitler stated that besides the major landing in the West, the Allies might also make a secondary landing in Norway because if German resistance collapsed in Western Europe, the British would not want to see the Russians take advantage of that and suddenly appear in Norway to take over there.

Sunday, January 2

With the holidays over now, *Generalfeldmarschall* Rommel continues his inspection tour of the Dutch and Belgian coasts. There is not much fear that the enemy will land up here, because there are too many waterways near the coast. It would be too easy to flood them and impede the enemy's advance.

Word comes down that the Führer has just appointed Rommel to be the Inspector-General in the Western Theater. Although subordinate to von Rundstedt he will report his findings directly to the Führer. His position is now official.

***

Up in the north, it is a trying time in Denmark, despite the ample evidence of plenty of food and sundry supplies. Because the Danish forces had been disarmed last August in the light of mounting terrorist activities, the Reich's "close relatives" in this small country are now responding with an increasing number of small acts of sabotage or defiance. Well, the Danes will soon pay the price for their impudence. They will be subject to harsher policies in answer to this willful disobedience. The Führer has ordered a crackdown by the Gestapo and the SS. Possible terrorist leaders are now being regularly tailed and in some cases, assassinated, although usually discreetly. These new actions drive home the message of the no-nonsense policy that has been initiated.

The German High Command realizes that it will now be forced to defend Denmark's borders more vigorously, from both without and within. The Danish honeymoon is over.

***

At the Wolf's Lair in East Prussia, a final assessment on the loss of the battlecruiser *Scharnhorst* a week ago is completed. Clearly the ship had been outwitted and outmaneuvered because its radar had been quite inferior to the enemy's. Thus while the *Scharnhorst* was mostly in the dark about the whereabouts of the British warships, they had successfully tracked its course and had been able to shadow it until superior forces could arrive to sink it. Clearly, German radar development, currently overseen by the Luftwaffe, needs to be improved.

Pressured by Armaments Minister Albert Speer and *Großadmiral* Dönitz, and with *Reichsmarschall* Göring in disrepute right now, Hitler decides to turn over control of radar development to Speer.

Monday, January 3

Rommel continues inspecting the Dutch and Belgian coasts. He notes that von Rundstedt's policy of defeating the enemy inland has caused the construction of coastal defenses to remain minimal. So Rommel has started planning a complex series of multi-layered defense patterns to compensate for this.

Minefields, consisting of a wide variety of different types of mines, are to be interwoven with variously sized and shaped obstacles, resistance points, barbed wire, artillery positions, natural barriers, and anything else that can be put on the beaches to thwart the enemy. Behind the lines, anti-airborne obstacles will be set.

Current estimates show some 1.7 million mines have been laid. To the astonishment of his staff, Rommel declares that he plans to increase this number at the rate of 2 million mines a month. Phase I of his scheme will eventually require some 20 million mines of all types. Phase II will require double that number. It is a staggering figure.

He plans on having enough panzer divisions deployed near the coast so that, wherever the landing takes place, at least two will be nearby and ready to immediately respond.

Anti-tank weapons will be critical to victory as well. In the absence of panzers at any location, a plethora of small, mobile anti-tank weapons is the next best thing. They do not have the stopping power of a Panther or enjoy its armored protection; but they are easier to hide and better able to be moved around without being spotted by naval support vessels offshore. Always in short supply, they are to be gathered, made, or stolen by the thousands for use against the enemy. But that will not be enough for him. The coastal units will need large numbers of these portable gems if they are going to repulse enemy armored units coming ashore.

His vision though, will be hard to realise. Administrative bottlenecks abound, shortages exist in nearly every category. Outdated defense policies will complicate matters.

On top of that, he is finding out that he is not too popular with some of the unit commanders. They look on him as a newcomer with no real authority, a desert has-been, one who is starting to be a pain in their well-adjusted-to-French-life backsides.

Tuesday, January 4

Adolf Hitler is not thinking much about the West today. Berlin was bombed by the British again last night, although fortunately, not much more damage had been inflicted.

When briefed about progress being made on the new U-boats and jet weapons being designed, Hitler confesses to Albert Speer and to Luftwaffe Air Inspector-General Milch,[1] in charge of aircraft production, that he is heavily relying on their deployment. "If I get the jets in time," he adds, "I can fight off the invasion with them." What he does not realize is that, despite the clear instructions he gave to Göring back on December 20, the Me-262 jet is not being developed as a fighter-bomber as he wants, but instead strictly as a fighter.

His lunch conference mostly centers on the Reich's struggle with the Soviet Union. That afternoon, he gets into a deep argument with *Generalfeldmarschall* von Manstein about the Eastern Front. The angry field marshal insists that his army group in the south be allowed to pull back and regroup. In explaining the situation, he severely criticizes Hitler's recent command decisions, demanding that a military leader be put in overall charge of the entire front.

Hitler glares at him. No one, he retorts, has as much authority over the military as he has. He adds with a growl, "And even I am not obeyed by my field marshals. Do you think they would obey *you* any better?"

No, von Manstein's units must hold out for time; time for the invasion of the West to be defeated; time for the new model U-boats to take over the offensive in the Atlantic; time for relations between Russia and the Western Allies to break down. Where there is a will, he finished, there is a way.

Later that afternoon, he chairs a meeting on the war industry. In the presence of *Generalfeldmarschall* Keitel, Hitler directs Fritz Sauckel[2] to obtain four million new workers from occupied territories for the war industry.

***

Far away in Belgium, *Generalfeldmarschall* Rommel continues his tour of the coast. Today he starts out from Antwerp and inspects the strategically important Walcheren Island at the base of the Scheldt estuary. There, defensive construction has lagged for months, mostly because of concrete shortages. Only about a third of the concrete structures needed have been made operational. He notes the impressive 4-gun 150mm battery near Westkapelle, and observes the defensive positions of part of the Fifteenth Army's reserve and the 19th Luftwaffe Field Division, commanded by *Generalleutnant* Erich Bässler.[3] Rommel makes a point of openly congratulating him on his recent promotion.

He then stops to confer with the island's senior Kriegsmarine officer, the area Sea Defense Commander, *Kapitän-zur-see* Frank Aschmann.[4] Together, they go over the island's inventory of artillery pieces.

To save time, Rommel then travels across the Scheldt in a small patrol boat to Breskens, a pretty seaport that provides the surrounding area with a hearty supply of good fishing. Because of the low tide, the small boat gets stuck on a bar, but the crew, embarrassed in front of their VIP, manages to free the craft and eventually tie up to the dock.

From there, the inspection group goes on to Oostburg and looks over some positions of the 89th Corps.[5] They then call on *Generalmajor* Friedrich-Wilhelm Neumann, commanding the 712 Grenadier Division, and inspect its positions, which extend to the town of Blankenberge along the coast. This includes three huge, imposing railway batteries.

Rommel then goes inland into the Brügge[6] urban complex, where he stops for the night. An inland city founded by the Vikings in the 9th century, Brügge is rich in medieval history. Rommel and his staff marvel at the old architecture in the layout of the city. On a decidedly less artistic and more practical note, they shop for and enjoy the rich abundance of the variety of products in the town's apparently well-stocked marketplaces.

Rommel has noted this economic profusion in a letter written to Lucie the night before:

> *The French, Belgians, have not suffered much from the war... Everywhere the deepest peace. They are well paid, they don't have the crippling taxation that we do, pay no war reparations, and they just can't wait to be liberated from us. Moreover, their towns are beautiful and are spared by the enemy.*
> *It makes you sick, especially when you think how hard our people are having to fight to defend our existence against all comers.*

---

1 Fifty-two-year-old *Generalfeldmarschall* Erhard Milch. An early air veteran of World War I, he commanded an air wing during the invasion of Norway, and was promoted to field marshal after leading *Luftflotte V* in the 1940 invasion of France. He was assigned the title of Air Inspector-General to oversee aircraft production, a job he was barely adequate at, and in which he was to make several critical production planning errors.

2 Forty-nine-year-old Fritz Sauckel was one of the first members of the Nazi party. In 1921, Sauckel was appointed the Gauleiter of Thuringia, and in 1933 when Hitler first rose to power, and later in March of 1942, he took charge of the Reich's manpower procurement program, which included slave labor. Captured in 1945, he was tried at Nuremberg and found guilty of crimes against humanity. He was executed on October 11, 1946.

3 Fifty-three-year-old *Generalleutnant* Erich Baessler took over command of the division on November 12, 1943 and was promoted to *Generalleutnant* on New Year's Day 1944. Later, in December 1944, Baessler was transferred to Norway where he became the *Stadtkommandant* Oslo. He was captured in 1945. He died in May 1957.

4 Aschmann, the senior naval officer on Walcheren, carried the title of Sea Defense Commander for South Holland. Under his command, all naval batteries along the southern Dutch coast were responsible for engaging all enemy sea targets. There was an administrative snag, though. If the targets got close enough to the land that the divisional artillery of General Wilhelm Daser's 165th Reserve Infantry Division could engage them, operational control of the naval batteries would switch to Daser.

5 *General der Infanterie* Baron Werner von und zu Gilsa, commanding.

6 From the Scandinavian word *bryggia*, meaning "harbor."

Wednesday, January 5

Today, Rommel completes his tour of the Dutch and Belgian coastline. Starting out in the morning from his luxurious hotel in picturesque Brügge, he takes a brief detour from his inspection schedule, and for the first time since he began his tour back in December, he takes a couple of hours to do a little bit of sightseeing.

He visits the town's historic cathedral and its city hall. Rommel views with utter fascination the marble Madonna that was sculptured by the famous Michelangelo, and solemnly stares at the sarcophagus of Charles the Bold, before moving on to that of Mary of Burgundy.

He finally gets in his car and leaves Brügge.[1] The inspection party moves southward, down to Tourcoing, where Rommel again calls on *Generaloberst* von Salmuth, commanding the Fifteenth Army. His headquarters complex is located around a picturesque château just outside the town. It is along his sector that Supreme Headquarters believes the enemy invasion is expected to hit.

Rommel, having talked to von Salmuth on the 20th of last month,[2] now reiterates his expectations of these troops. He once again outlines his plans for a fortified network along the coast. The general seems resistant to his ideas. Von Salmuth frankly dislikes this upstart who happens to currently have favor with the Führer.

After meeting with von Salmuth, the inspection group travels on. They stop to have lunch with a group of the *Schlageter* fighter wing, near Lille.[3] The wing is commanded by an animated, expressive veteran pilot, *Oberst* Josef "Pips" Priller. This fighter ace has a remarkable score of 96 aircraft to his credit. The pleasant conversation with this Oak Leaves cluster recipient is animated, and the Desert Fox finds the squadron CO "colorful."[4]

In the afternoon, the entourage has a hectic 110km ride south to Saint-Quentin. Rommel drives his Horch and Admiral Ruge rides next to Leading Seaman Hatzinger in the follow-up Mercury. Always in a hurry, the field marshal today has a lead foot, particularly on the straightaways. Hatzinger just behind him has trouble keeping up, although he manages to close the distance some when they go up a slope. The two vehicles roar on through the rolling hills to Compiègne, and the men finally arrive back at their Fontainebleau headquarters around 8 p.m., exhausted.

This four-day tour has taken Rommel some 480 kilometers.

***

Today, as enemy bombers continue to raid Germany, the OKW Operations staff discuss at length plans for air defenses.

1   Rommel's vehicle of choice was a shiny black Horch 770K Tourenwagen convertible.

2   See entry for December 20, 1943.

3   *Jagdgeschwader* 26. It was named after Albert Leo Schlageter, a veteran of World War I. Arrested for sabotage against the French after they seized the Ruhr Valley in 1923, he was court martialed and shot. The Allies referred to the wing as "The Abbeville Kids," and their aircraft were easily recognizable, because part or all the forward part of their fuselage was usually painted bright yellow.

4   The outspoken Pips Priller and his wingman, Sgt. Heinz Wodarczyk, will be the only two Luftwaffe fighter pilots that manage to strafe the beaches at Normandy on D-Day. This daring exploit will later be dramatized in Daryl F. Zanuck's classic movie, *The Longest Day*, and the aerial scene of that run will contribute to the movie winning two Academy Awards for best cinematography and best special effects.

Thursday, January 6

Generalfeldmarschall von Rundstedt takes advantage of the winter weather to stay indoors at the Hôtel Georges V. Not much to do today, so he relaxes.

***

General der Artillerie Erich Marcks, commander of the 84th Corps in Normandy, writes home to his son. Whereas a few months ago he was relatively sure the invasion, when it came, would strike along the coast to the northeast—perhaps around Boulogne—the general is getting more and more certain the blow will fall in his area.

He has a wicked instinct for knowing these things. It kept him a good staff officer for the invasion of the East, and a great opponent in the *Kriegspiel* that they played in the months before and after the attack. He had realized how risky the campaign against Russia would be, and had been proven right time and time again. Now the alarms were once again going off in the back of his head. More and more it seemed to him that Normandy would be the target... Possibly along the Calvados coast itself,[1] between the Orne and the Vire rivers...

***

Generaloberst Alfred Jodl has arrived on the English Channel coastline and has begun touring the coastal defenses on orders from Hitler himself. The Führer, as Jodl had predicted, had not been at all satisfied with von Rundstedt's October 30 scathing summary regarding the deplorable state of the Atlantic Wall—that had been one of the reasons Rommel had been appointed Inspector-General and sent. However, when Rommel's report of December 31 presented similar distressing results, a real concern had arisen at OKW. Could it be true about the poor status of the Atlantic Wall?

It is a terrible thought to consider. Hitler knows what is riding on the success or failure of the upcoming invasion, and he clearly does not want to believe that his backside shield is in fact a charade. Perhaps Rommel merely wants to be in concurrence with the old Prussian. Or worse, he may still not be cured of his defeatist misgivings—his *Afrikanische Krankheit*.

Still doubting, the Führer finally turned to Jodl. He told him to go out himself to the damned coast and find out once and for all if things were as bad as the two field marshals said. Ironically, Jodl, who had initially thought of sending Rommel to inspect the Atlantic Wall in his stead, has still ended up having to make a trip west. So to back up whatever conclusions he makes, Jodl has decided to take his deputy Walther Warlimont, and Army chief Baron von Buttlar,[2] with him.

For expediency, the three of them have divided the coastal area up into equal sections. Jodl will inspect the Fifteenth Army sector in the northeast. Von Buttlar is assigned the Seventh Army to the southwest, and Warlimont will travel down to the southern coast of France and make his observations of the defenses along there.

The trio had then dutifully made their trip to France and split up. Now they will assess for themselves the state of the Atlantic Wall, and whether the claims of the two field marshals are true or not.

***

Generalfeldmarschall Rommel stays at his headquarters today, going over the results of his recent tour. He has some worry that the Allies might hit up the coast around the Scheldt estuary. Although the geography of that area made it an unlikely target, it would nevertheless yield the rich port of Antwerp, and Rommel knows that the enemy is going to have to capture a port quickly to sustain their massive supply line to the landing area. Besides, landing near the Scheldt would give the enemy close access to the Ruhr Valley.

Still, there are a lot of units up there defending that section of coast, despite the fact that their readiness is incomplete and their planning is half-baked. Even the weakened Luftwaffe would be able to intervene somewhat from nearby air bases set up to defend the German cities from enemy air raids.

There is something else bothering him though, something personal. It is the 6th. Today, Manfred reports to his anti-aircraft battery in Stuttgart. The thought is depressing for Rommel. Not that the boy is going to serve Germany in uniform, but that he has grown so much already. His father has been gone for most of that time, having warred over a good part of Europe and then half of North Africa. He has personally seen hundreds of Germany's finest sons fight and die, far from home, often in blazing heat and under a blistering sun.

Sometimes life isn't fair.

---

1   The popular apple brandy of that name comes from this area.
2   *Generalmajor Freiherr* Horst Trusch von Buttlar-Brandenfels was chief of staff to the Army High Command, OKH (*Oberkommando der Heeres*).

Friday, January 7

Generaloberst Alfred Jodl continues touring the Atlantic coastal defenses on orders from Hitler himself. Today, he writes in his diary about the problems he has observed:

> The best people have been removed. The officers are good and the men are good, but they cannot act. Re-equipment is producing chaos. The (*87th*) Corps has 21 different types of batteries.

***

Rommel is at Fontainebleau again today, dealing with several problems.

His tour of Holland and Belgium has shown him that most of the army coastal batteries lack armor plating. Luckily, most of the naval batteries have some such protection, at least to a certain degree. Armored turrets seem to be the best type of design for survivability. Unfortunately, with metal in great demand, this is out of the question for the army units. Oh, to be sure, camouflage helps some; but armor or some type of protection is a critical component.

He finds that the next best thing to armor is reinforced concrete. Many of the batteries in Denmark had been designed with it, and it does help protect the battery. The drawback is that, to be effective, it must be installed in thick layers, decreasing the traversing angle of the guns—down from 360 degrees to 120, or even 80 degrees, depending on the design. And instead of a moving, narrow gun slit, the firing port must be wide open—exposing the crew to incoming fire.

A second problem is operational control. The naval batteries are run by older members of the Kriegsmarine, and not younger, fresher men. Average age for the gun crews is 40–45, with some gunners over 55 years old. On the other hand, the average American soldier coming ashore will be only about 25 years old. The batteries are told they must destroy all enemy units "at sea." The army batteries are under the command of the Heeres. They are to destroy all enemy units "on land." So where is the transition point? Do naval units disregard landed troops? Must army units withhold fire until the enemy reaches the beaches? Opinions (and policies) varied widely. Cohesion and cooperation are decidedly lacking, not just between services, but often between units in an area. Someone has to take charge, someone who also needs high-powered authority to back them up. And right now, he is just the Inspector-General for the Atlantic Wall.

Then there is the Luftwaffe to consider. Will they provide aerial support when the invasion starts? Again there is the question of coordination. And of course, the air units are not his to command or control.

On top of everything else, he must contend with Jodl's *Wehrmachtführungsstab*,[1] Chief of Staff Keitel, von Rundstedt, and of course, the Führer himself. Day and night they advise, caution, order, warn, and in general interfere with many details, both large and small.

Another problem is smaller but more immediate in nature. He needs to find another location for his headquarters. For one thing, his staff has grown in numbers, and he cannot find quarters in Madame de Pompadour's Fontainebleau palace for all of them. The huge mansion is both beautiful and luxurious. And yet, with all its rooms (which are now mostly for show), it is still too small to billet his entire headquarters garrison. Besides, he feels (true to form) that it is too far from the probable invasion front—wherever that is going to be. He wants to be closer to the coast.

It is a shame, too, because Fontainebleau is a beautiful estate to work in. The ample grounds offer great opportunities for walks in the surrounding woods, complete with small ravines, rocky patches, and fresh springs. An occasional wild boar provides for an infrequent sporting hunt. Still, he is starting to see signs of headquarters opulence, which often leads to relaxed routines and drains one's determination to fight or defend.

He has tentatively picked out a forest camp near Laon, some 130km northeast of Paris. But the location is not closer to the Channel—it is just closer to the Somme River, closer to (although still inland from) its mouth, where he feels the invasion might come. However, it is well away from the "Paris crowd." But today he is informed by Hitler's army adjutant, General Schmundt, that his request to use the forest camp is denied. So the army group staff must now try somewhere else.

He has also become interested in an already-existing headquarters close to Soissons, northeast of Paris. It had been built for Operation *Sealion* back in 1940. But he probably will not get that one either.

As a general area to search, they all decide on looking northwest of Paris, maybe along the path of the Seine River, for a location that would have nearby natural structural cover to protect them from air raids. The caves in the chalk and gypsum cliffs along the Seine offer just such cover.

There is a naval underground torpedo arsenal that Rommel has his eye on.[2] He has inspected it, and he feels it could serve his needs.

He won't get that one either.

---

1   Jodl's OKW operations staff.

2   This might possibly have been the beautiful château that overlooked the Torpedo Arsenal West at Châteaudun, *Kapitän-zur-See* Erich Heymann, commanding. That location though, was much farther inland that Rommel wanted. More likely, he was looking at the underground torpedo arsenal at Houilles, just northwest of Paris, and some 65km from La Roche Guyon.

Saturday, January 8

Today, Rommel remains at his Fontainebleau headquarters. As the appointed Inspector-General for Northern Europe, his advice is being sought by several units on a number of defensive ideas. The teletypes have been clattering, and the number of incoming communiqués is increasing. He and his staff are busy evaluating and answering them.

He has been formalizing his status reports from his last tour. One big concern is that there are a number of problems with the batteries in Holland and Belgium.

In the Brügge-Blankenbourg sector, for instance, there are three railroad batteries. Two batteries consist of 170mm guns, with a range of 13km to 26.5km. The third is a huge 203mm gun with a range of over 36 kilometers—not enough to reach England, but enough to cover most of the Channel there. The guns look imposing, and to the observing eye, quite awesome in their power and construction. But their fire control system is a jury-rigged setup, quite liable to break down under the intensive stress of combat. The sights are old-fashioned and crude. Because of this, the guns can only fire at a moving target if it keeps the same course and speed. Not likely for any naval target.

At Walcheren Island, strategically located at the entrance to the Scheldt estuary, the largest caliber battery is a 12-gun 150mm naval unit. Heavier guns are not available at this time; just a mixed lot of smaller caliber pieces.

General der Infanterie von Gilsa's 89th Corps further down the coast is better off. They have three naval batteries, five army coastal batteries, and six divisional artillery batteries—a total of some 55 guns.

Again, Rommel has been finding out (to his immense satisfaction) that the naval units had insisted on being located right on the coast, because their primary mission was to engage enemy vessels. Rommel knows though, that there is also a drawback. They are too exposed. Experience has taught him that positioning guns not on the shoreline, but behind the coast and well concealed, gives them a much better chance of surviving the initial bombardment. The navy though, would have none of that. Rommel had noted as far back as December 5:

> Antipathy against the artillery's indirect firing methods seems to be universal in the navy.

It is still true a month later. On the other hand, the naval units have much better sighting equipment (and experience) than their army counterparts.[1]

Today, he is visited for the first time by *General der Panzertruppen Freiherr* Leo Geyr von Schweppenburg. At 57, "Geyr," as he is called, is yet another fine product of the German General Staff and has been with the army for almost forty years. A Prussian military aristocrat and excellent horseman, he is intelligent, educated, well read, and sophisticated. He has served as a military attaché to London, Brussels, and The Hague. A close friend of *Generaloberst* Heinz Guderian, the pioneer of the *blitzkrieg*, he transferred to the Panzer Corps in 1937, and commanded the 3rd Panzer Division and subsequently several panzer corps in the East.

In June 1943, he had been transferred to OB West. His duties had initially been limited to supervising training of panzer units in the West and to act as personal advisor to von Rundstedt on all matters pertaining to panzer warfare. Then in the fall, von Rundstedt decided on creating a new command. Designated Panzergruppe West, it was to become a command staff to lead a mighty armored strike force that would undertake a counterattack against the invasion, whenever it came, smashing into any Allied columns from inland. Ostensibly, it would also be in charge of training, supply, and disposition for all the reserve panzer divisions in the West. More importantly, though, it had a voice in determining their positioning. Geyr had been the perfect choice to lead the new command, so in November 1943, he had thus been appointed to this new post.

Rommel talks to Geyr, and tells him in detail of his plans to meet the enemy on the beach. Geyr, no doubt unimpressed by Rommel's reputation, his lack of General Staff training, and absence of any combat experience on the Eastern Front, reacts skeptically. He instead suggests that the panzers be placed inland, away from direct enemy naval gunfire, so that they can move freely and maneuver against the enemy when the landing comes. Panzer units lacking backup transportation could protect the capital from a massive airborne invasion. Rommel disagrees, and they part on that note.

But their disagreement is far from over. In fact, it is just beginning.

---

1   Rommel would find out later that the navy's theory was the best. Inland batteries would prove to be effective only against infantry that had just hit the beach.

Sunday, January 9

Rommel continues summarizing his assessment of the Dutch and Belgian coastline. At noontime, he and his staff receive today's first official visitor: *Oberst* Kurt Hesse, an old friend from the Potsdam Academy.[1] A respected author of a number of military writings, he is now the field commander at St.-Germain. They talk about several books on World War I including Hesse's popular *Feldherr Psychologos* (*Military Psychology*), and the influences on the German youth of today. Rommel's own book, *Infanterie grieft an* (*Infantry Attacks*) is brought up.[2]

The conversation switches to sculptors, and art collections at the Louvre. Some pieces are missing—special presents for the Reichsmarshall, no doubt.

But they talk about command problems, too. The men present are all friends and trust each other, so the conversation is forthright and open. Rommel in a serious tone tells his friend that he plans on asking to make a number of officer changes in some of the lower commands that he has inspected. Shaking his head, he complains somewhat bitterly that in all the time they have been here so far, their units have done almost nothing for their defenses. And the first couple days would be crucial.

He pauses and stares at Hesse. "If we don't succeed in pushing the enemy back into the sea by the fourth day at the latest, then their invasion will have succeeded."

***

Elsewhere at Rommel's headquarters, *Generalmajor* Meise, his chief engineer, writes a report regarding the mine situation. Rommel has learned from experience that a key factor in a successful defense line is the mine. Placed properly, a minefield can considerably bog down even the most determined enemy offensive. He had successfully done this against Montgomery at Alamein. Now Rommel has boldly conceived of an Atlantic Wall carpeted with 50–100 million mines; a formidable undertaking, to say the least. Unfortunately though, his bold design is a far cry from the harsh reality he has to face. Only 1.7 million have been laid so far, and only 40,000 are coming in every month. Requisitions for higher amounts take months to process, and demands on other fronts make them even more difficult to get. And to make matters worse, most of them have a finite time period in which they will work effectively. No, somehow, the minefields have to be augmented, either by other means, or by other sources.

One possible answer is the idea of adapting old enemy munitions into mine-type devices. Stockpiles of captured and obsolete artillery shells, upon initial inquiry, had been reported to have been either destroyed or scrapped. But further investigation outside normal, official channels had yielded some success. A number of caches had been located. Now they must be put to good use.

So today, Meise happily writes that thousands of enemy artillery shells have indeed been found. Some were old French naval shells, stockpiled in ports along the Atlantic and Mediterranean; Russian, Czech, French, British, Belgian, and even Polish design. Others are varieties of old French and German artillery shells sitting in neglect along the old Maginot Line. Burying these shells with attached jury-rig detonators around key defensive points would help considerably.

Additionally, some eleven million enemy mines seized in 1940 have been located. They only need cases and fuses, and simple substitute fuses could be produced without too much effort.

The report gives Rommel a renewed sense of determination.

***

Generalfeldmarschall von Rundstedt enjoys a pleasant leisurely day at his Paris hotel. Perhaps he will take a nice walk in the afternoon, before a fine evening meal.

***

Generaloberst Heinz Guderian, the main architect of the German panzer forces, is today with Hitler at the snowed-in Berghof in Bavaria.[3] Sacked in December of 1941 for his failure to advance far enough in front of Moscow, Guderian had been reprieved and appointed *Generalinspektur der Panzertruppen*.[4] Now, alarmed at the unorganized fashion in which the Army High Command has been dealing with the setbacks on the Eastern Front, he is ready to propose to the Führer a reorganization of the Supreme High Command. He waits for the right time when they are alone (and the Führer is in a good mood) to broach the subject. He will use the command situation in the West to support his idea.

At mid-morning, the Führer, finally up and dressed, invites him to breakfast. "Somebody's sent me a teal,"[5] he says. "You know I'm a vegetarian.[6] Would you like to have breakfast with me and eat the teal?"

Guderian readily agrees, and they sit down together at a table in a somewhat darkened room, the morning daylight shining in from only one window. They are alone, except for the Führer's German shepherd, Blondi. The table has already been prepared for them by Linge,[7] who now wordlessly serves them the food and then quickly, discreetly leaves.

Despite his basic diet, one of Hitler's few joys these days is the cuisine at the Berghof. His cook, 25-year-old Marlene von Exner, is a celebrated Viennese dietitian. She had been bragged about to Hitler by Romania's Marshal Antonescu back in mid-1943, at a time when the Führer's heart condition had been diagnosed as not improving. Hitler had turned to his own doctor, Theodor Morrell, and had instructed him to find an expert dietitian. Morell had gone straight to Fraulein von Exner herself and had coerced her into giving up her practice in Vienna and working exclusively for the Führer.

This talented lady had not only turned out to be a whiz in the kitchen, but also good company, with her sunny, upbeat disposition. Because she too was from Austria, she often shared conversations with the Führer about their native country. She told him stories about her youth, growing up with several brothers and sisters. She occasionally conversed with him about improving the Viennese culture.

On the whole, she is not too happy about his limited diet—vegetarian soup, carrots, potatoes, and on occasion, a couple soft-boiled eggs. Still, she accepts it good-naturedly and has managed to work her menus around this handicap. Her soups and stews are always rich, flavorful, and hearty, enhanced by secret ingredients (one special one, she confided to a close friend, is a bit of bone marrow). At any rate, because of her warm demeanor, she is always a bright spot in the Führer's day, although, unknown to him, she secretly pines for one of the SS adjutants on the mountain.[8]

Alone now at the small table, Hitler and Guderian begin breakfast. Hitler occasionally tears off a small chunk of freshly baked bread and feeds it to the German shepherd, who dutifully eats it out of his hand. Blondi is a vegetarian, too.

The conversation at first is light. But Guderian is resolved to make a point and soon gets to it. He broaches the subject of the upcoming Allied invasion in the West. Guderian and OKW expect it to come in the spring. At present, the reserves there are totally inadequate to meet the threat. A firmer defense in the East is needed, he concludes, so that they can safely release units for the West. He goes on about the problems in Russia, citing a lack of defensive fortifications, but is finally cut off by an angry Hitler.

"Believe me, general," he snarls, "I am the greatest builder of fortifications of all time. I built the West Wall. I built the Atlantic Wall. I have used nineteen million tons of concrete. I know what the building of fortifications involves." He goes on with his harangue about what he feels are the problems in the East, and concludes by telling Guderian that you can only successfully wage a war on two fronts if you can temporarily keep one of them inactive while you stabilize the other.

Guderian suggests that since he has done so well building defenses in the West that he should be able to do so in the East as well.

Hitler responds by lamenting one of his popular themes. His generals on the Eastern Front would simply love to retreat to a series of fortifications in their rear if they were to be constructed. The lack of such a defensive line forces them to stay on the offensive. He is resolute on that point.

The conversation then changes to the High Command. Guderian tells him how incompetent it is and suggests that maybe he can turn over supreme control to a general to clear up chains of command. And his senior staff should be replaced by generals he can trust and who will work efficiently, not constantly bicker between themselves. And he should "get rid of the obscure confusion of command functions that now reign among the Wehrmacht Command Staff, the OKH, the Luftwaffe, the Kriegsmarine, and the Waffen SS..."

Again Hitler cuts him off, bluntly refusing. He will not get rid of Keitel as his chief of staff. He glares at Guderian suspiciously, and asks if Guderian is trying to limit his powers. Guderian of course denies it, but Hitler does not seem to believe him. "Besides," he grumbles, "is there any general that I can really trust?"

Guderian, clearly on the losing side of this conversation, admits that there probably is not. Hitler finally concludes their conversation with a frequent remark of his: "I can't understand why everything has gone wrong for the past two years."

Guderian's answer, unwavering, is the same one he has given before. "Change your methods," he replies curtly.

---

1   *Oberst* Kurt Hesse was a friend of Rommel's, having taught at the Potsdam Academy with him in the 1930s. The exact date of this visit is unknown; the phrase "early in January 1944" was given. [*Auth.*]

2   Rommel's book, published in 1937, was well received, and is today considered a classic of German military literature. It deals with military tactics and is based on his experiences in World War I. After it was published, Rommel told Hesse, "It's astounding, the money there is to be made from such books. I just don't know what to do with all the cash that's flooding in. I can't possibly use it all, I'm happy enough with what I've got already. And I don't like the idea of making money out of writing up how other good men lost their lives."

3   The date for this conversation is not exact, and as Guderian's biographer Kenneth Macksey writes, we only have Guderian's account of this story.

4   Inspector-General of the Armored Forces.

5   A teal is a small, brightly-colored, freshwater duck with a short neck.

6   Hitler firmly believed that consuming meat made him sweat excessively, a trait he did not desire, especially when in public and giving speeches.

7   Thirty-year-old Hauptsturmführer Heinz Linge, the Führer's close personal valet. Personally chosen from Hitler's LSSAH in 1935, he was a dedicated, intelligent but simple-minded orderly who as the *Chef der persönlichen Diensts Beim Führer* (Chief of the Führer's Personal Service), oversaw all aspects of Hitler's daily life. Linge would stay with the Führer until the very end and help burn Hitler's corpse outside the bunker after his suicide.

8   Fraulein Helene Marie "Marlene" Exner would not be at the Berghof very long. Martin Bormann had flirted with her a few times, and she had committed the cardinal sin of spurning him. Soon, revenge in his heart, he decided to get rid of her. All he had to do was find some Jewish blood in her background. He eventually did (using the SD, the security branch of the SS), finding a trace in her great-grandmother, as it turns out.

The story then gets interesting. Traudl Junge, one of Hitler's personal secretaries, later recalled that she became horrified when the news of her friend Marlene's leaving over this "genetic flaw" was broken to her; "not so much because she might lose her job with Hitler," she wrote, "as because now she couldn't possibly become the wife of an SS man." In this case, he was a young Prussian officer named Fritz Darges (who was also admired by Eva Braun's sister, Gretl). As expected, the Führer did fire Marlene over her tinge of Jewish ancestry, although he did so quite reluctantly. He sadly explained, "I cannot make one rule for myself and another for the rest." Still, because of her sweet character and his fondness for her, he ordered Bormann to "Aryanize" her entire family. Bormann, resentful and upset, put this task off indefinitely, hoping the Führer might forget about it.

However, a few weeks later, Fraulein Junge received a letter from the now-departed Marlene, stating that she and her sister had had to abandon their studies in Vienna, and that the careers of her brothers had been sabotaged in some way. Traudl recorded: "I was so angry and indignant that I sat down at the typewriter with the outsize characters [*large font characters, used for speeches—Auth*], typed the letter out on it word for word, and took it to the Führer. He went red in the face with fury and called for Bormann at once. The *Reichsleiter* was red-faced too when he came out of Hitler's room, and he gave me a furious glance. All the same, in March, I received the cheering news that everything was all right again, the whole Exner family was extremely grateful to me, and their 'Aryanization' had finally gone through."

Monday, January 10

Alfred Jodl, *Chef der Generalstab, Wehrmachtführungsstab,* OKW,[1] is touring positions in the Scheldt coastal area. His deputy Operations chief of staff, Warlimont, is currently in southern France, inspecting the defenses down there.

***

In the evening around 6 p.m., a phone conversation occurs between *Heeresgruppe B* and OB West headquarters. At Fontainebleau, Hans-Georg von Tempelhoff, Rommel's operations officer, talks to his counterpart in Paris, *Generalleutnant* Bodo Zimmermann.[2]

Tempelhoff tells Zimmermann that the army group needs some sort of "combat direction" from von Rundstedt. Zimmermann replies by explaining that the standing orders on what the chain of command should be during a battle have been given to the field units time and time again. He points out that these orders are clear, have been gone over many times, and are to remain in effect just as they are. No other views are possible.

Tempelhoff elucidates by pointing out that the directives need clarification for the lower units. Zimmermann replies, "It's all in the standing orders—check the standing orders."

Tempelhoff hangs up, frustrated.

In the meantime, a message comes in to Fontainebleau from Paris. *Generalfeldmarschall* von Rundstedt has turned down a request by Meise, Rommel's chief engineer, that a wide set of coastal areas either be flooded now or be prepared for flooding in the event of a local amphibious landing. OB West has decided that such measures can only be allowed on a severely restricted level, and only so long as communication lines (wires, cables, telephone lines) are not in any way affected.

At 9:45 p.m., General Gause gets on the phone with Walther Warlimont in southern France. Gause asks him whether or not the Führer has read Rommel's report of December 31, and whether or not he agrees in principle with both Rommel's assessment of the situation and the importance of defending the beaches.

Warlimont's reply is tactful. He reminds Gause that Rommel is subordinate to von Rundstedt, and so it might be inappropriate for OKW to give him direction outside of the chain of command.

Warlimont continues. He states that Hitler believes without a doubt that an invasion must be thwarted on the beaches. The High Command, Warlimont adds, has never stated otherwise.

Gause asks about the idea of coastal flooding.

Warlimont replies that, in principle, areas that can be flooded to deny maneuvering space to the enemy should be. If some populaces have to be evacuated because of it, well that's too bad.

Warlimont concludes the conversation by trying to cover himself. He reminds Gause that General Jodl is currently touring positions out there too. He suggests that, if anyone on Rommel's staff needs clarification about this issue of "combat direction," and they can't get it from OB West, that they get it from Jodl himself when he winds up his tour out there.

Gause thanks him. After the phone conversation he talks to Rommel and updates him. The upshot of his phone call: Talk to Jodl.

---

1   Chief of staff, operations office, Armed Forces High Command.

2   At 56, Zimmermann, a veteran of World War I, had in the 1930s purchased and built up a popular military publication, *Offene Worte* (*Frank Words*). Recalled to active duty when the war broke out, he was appointed operations officer to von Witzleben's First Army in the Saarbrucken area. He was later transferred along with Witzleben when the latter became OB West. When von Rundstedt took over in 1942, Zimmermann stayed on.

Tuesday, January 11

Jodl is continuing his inspection of the Atlantic Wall on orders from Hitler himself. During his travels along the Fifteenth Army sector, he has taken the opportunity to talk to a number of the area commanders. Many of them, re-echoing a main grievance of their Army commander General von Salmuth, complain that their men are so busy building defensive fortifications that they have little time or are too tired to undertake critical, required training.

He continues to make notes again in his diary on what he finds. On the 9th, he noted that the once powerful 319th Division (the "Canada" Division) on the Channel Islands now has only about 30 percent of its original strength.

Still concerned, today he writes:

> Transfer of officers to the East must cease. The regimental commanders are new and so are several battalion commanders.
>
> 711 Division has only six battalions, including one Caucasian. It has no modern anti-tank equipment.

General von Buttlar is touring another sector on the coast, and also has talked to a number of unit commanders. One has made a solid impression on him. This is *General der Artillerie* Erich Marcks, commanding the 84th Corps. He bluntly states that he has only two and a half divisions to cover hundreds of kilometers of coast, and that he would not be able to put up even a decent delaying action against an enemy landing, much less an adequate defense. Even if his strength were doubled, his forces would still only be a slim defensive crust that could be cracked open anywhere.

Von Buttlar wryly notes Marcks' comments and moves on. As the Heeres chief of staff, he is along on the inspection strictly as an advisor to OKW, which has operational control of this area, even though most of the units being inspected are army.[1]

It is an affront that the army generals will never forgive.

---

1 Originally, all military operations had been overseen by OKW, but all army operations were conducted under them by OKH. In December of 1941, Hitler, frustrated by not having knocked Russia out of the war, was fuming over what he thought was a lack of motivation for victory on the part of his army generals. So, in a flash of what he considered brilliant expediency, he decided to split responsibilities for the two commands. Hereafter, the Supreme Command itself—OKW— would oversee all operations on the Western Front and Southern Fronts. The OKH, now directed personally by Hitler, would limit its operational command to the Eastern Front, while still being administratively subordinate to OKW.

Wednesday, January 12

Generaloberst Jodl's inspection of the Atlantic Wall is winding down. Today he tours the units of the 10th SS Panzer Division *Frundsberg*, newly arrived from the East. Their first request is to be exempted from construction of defenses along the coast, so that the division can refit. It has taken quite a mauling on the Eastern Front, and has lost much of its equipment. Jodl notes that it is only "semi-mobile."

His deputy, Walther Warlimont, has concluded his part of the tour and is already back in Paris. Army Chief of Staff von Buttlar has joined up with Jodl for the last phase of his tour.

***

Today, Rommel and his staff travel to Paris and meet with von Rundstedt and his staff. They are there to reach some sort of agreement on this matter of "combat direction."

Word has it that Rommel's Army Group B is to take over command of the Seventh and Fifteenth Armies in the north. If true, the timing would be good. Von Rundstedt was supposed to go on leave next month, and Rommel would thus be acting OB West. So it is critical that he knows what strategy von Rundstedt wants to implement. More importantly, Rommel needs to find out whether his strategy plans are "orders" or just "instructions." (Actually, Rommel really wants to see if he can maybe push some of his own theories forth in the old man's absence).

This distinction is important. Tradition in the German Army since World War I held that an "order" was to be carried out without question. An "instruction" though, was not. Rather, it was a guideline issued by the superior officer or parent command. Thus, if von Rundstedt's strategy plan is actually an instruction, Rommel could technically ignore it, and not be accountable. Of course, in the Reich today, if he did make such a decision, he had better be right. Any mistake could result in dismissal—or death. So Rommel has to find out von Rundstedt's commitment to his defense policies and how much leeway he himself would have.

At any rate, tomorrow General Jodl will end his tour and join him, and they will all have a conference.

Thursday, January 13

This morning, *Generalfeldmarschall* Rommel posts a letter to his wife that he wrote the night before about a gift he is getting: a dog. He has written:

> *Just think of it, I am expecting to get a wire-hair Dachshund puppy. It'll be given to me by the OT... They will buy it for me. I should like to housebreak it here.*

***

At the Berghof, Hitler, short of his operations staff, is hampered in dealing with a new Soviet offensive that has begun today across the Vistula River. Problems in the West are not being considered.

***

A large conference is held at the Hôtel Georges V in Paris. In attendance are the senior staff members from Jodl's OKW operations office, from OB West, and from the Inspector-General army group headquarters *Heeresgruppe B.z.b.v.*

Rommel, for the most part, has not had a good relationship with the OKW operations officers. The dislike is mutual. When Rommel was given command of a panzer division back in mid-February 1940, less than three months before they would attack France, Jodl had been shocked and indignant at the appointment of this junior officer. Rommel was not a member of the General Staff, had little training with panzer units, and had spent the entire Polish campaign doing nothing, standing next to the Führer at their headquarters, watching units move eastward on a map.

Rommel does not like Jodl, either. He considers him a cold, professional staff officer. And he always seems to have a pinched look on his face, like he has something sour in his mouth.

Rommel knows that his resentment is returned, and so he will have to be careful in dealing with Jodl. After all, he is the linchpin in OKW, and easily the most powerful man in the Wehrmacht. An excellent clerk, he shrewdly knows when to keep his place and how to stay out of harm's way by keeping his mouth shut and listening. A collected and levelheaded man, a member of the General Staff, he could easily become a powerful enemy.

The other prominent figure in OKW is *General der Artillerie* Walther Warlimont, Jodl's deputy and first assistant. In his late forties, Warlimont is quite handsome, and cuts a dashing figure. Calm and easygoing, he is socially active and highly popular with women. Well educated, clever and and remarkably versatile, he ably takes over for Jodl whenever the latter is ill or on vacation. His intellect includes an in-depth knowledge of wartime economies and basic strategies, both learned as a seasoned member of the *Generalstab*.

Rommel considers Warlimont an ambitious fop and an unethical, glorified opportunistic clerk whose military capabilities are negligible.

Jodl and Warlimont together could present a formidable front against him with the Führer. But Rommel still has some credibility left. Hitler had expressed every confidence in him, and had once even given him a copy of *Mein Kampf.* Rommel remembered the inscription inside: "To General Rommel with pleasant memories."

So today Rommel is on his best behavior as he converses with these two visitors from OKW and their senior officers.

With Rommel going first, each field marshal gives his opinions of how the West should be defended. Rommel argues that they must stop the enemy right on the beaches, and outlines his plan to fortify the coast, including laying some two million mines a month. He also states that the panzers must be placed in strategically vital positions close to the coasts, so that they can move swiftly against the invasion whenever it comes

Von Rundstedt on the other hand, argues that stopping a landing is impossible, and therefore insists on keeping a powerful mobile strategic reserve inland to strike after the enemy had landed. Rommel's view, he argues, is tactical; his on the other hand, is strategic. Rommel's concern for the Channel and his desire to put all available forces there is understandable. But von Rundstedt's concern is bigger and covers all of Western Europe. He must take into account the enemy's strategic reserves and their ability to strike in another area of Europe.

He also goes on to make a number of frank remarks about the command structure in France. In fact, he goes on to berate the entire armed forces command structure as well, and the way they are running things. He is, Warlimont later notes, in rare form.

The air situation is covered as well. Jodl will later note in his diary:

> How on earth is the air war against the invasion going to be conducted? Major action against the enemy air forces is not possible. Fighters can carry out minor attacks against shipping and targets at sea. We must not accept battle with the enemy air force.

The OKW entourage in turn makes a number of valid points. General von Buttlar has observed on his part of the tour that there were large gaps between the resistance nests strung out along the shore. On the Calvados coast, he noted that they were some 1,300 meters apart, and less than 15 percent of them were bombproof. He concludes that if the enemy overran any one of them, they would be able to move inland fairly swiftly through a three- or four-kilometer gap.

Rommel comes away from the conference and notes:

> Met General Jodl, who shares my views of the coastal defense for the most part.

Friday, January 14

Jodl is on his way back to the *Wolfsschanze* to report to Hitler on his findings. Essentially, Rommel and von Rundstedt are right about one thing. The Atlantic Wall is too weak. And with the Russians attacking on the other side, the Führer will not be thrilled to hear this. Once again, Jodl is bringing him bad news. Well, at least this time, Warlimont and von Buttlar can back up his findings.

***

Rommel stays at home and evaluates the conference with Jodl and von Rundstedt. He notes general support for his ideas from the former, but sees implacable resistance from the latter.

***

Von Rundstedt is essentially doing the same as Rommel. He likes the younger field marshal's zest, his energy, his resolve, and his dedication. But he considers him an amateur at strategy.

And why not? Rommel was never a member of the *Generalstab*, and has risen through the ranks mainly as one of Hitler's many "stars," like that SS trash. When it comes to general strategic warfare, Rommel is a slouch. He proved that in North Africa, outstripping his supplies and biting off more than he could chew. And now this kid—*Marshall Bubi,* as von Rundstedt likes to call him—may get half of the Prussian's command.

It is not fair, and it is downright foolish to split the command like that.

Saturday, January 15

General Jodl apprehensively reports to Hitler at the Wolf's Lair on his trip to the Western defenses. Rommel, he states, is correct in his assessments. Jodl tells him that he was not "impressed" by the defensive positions that he inspected. Everyone in France and the Lowlands is too lax. Von Rundstedt has done little to bolster the coastal defenses. The West is inadequately prepared to meet a major enemy landing. To make matters worse, OB West and his staff live in luxury in a swank Parisian hotel, mesmerized by Paris life.[1] Soldiers go out to enjoy themselves along the city streets, often carrying briefcases, parcels, or umbrellas instead of rifles.

The units in the field have picked up this slack behavior as well. Combat battalions transferred from the Östfront are required to do little except to rest and refit. Fraternization with the local populace is commonplace (especially with French women), and despite the Reich's presence, there is little air of military authority in the occupied capital (except of course, at Gestapo headquarters). It is certainly a different world than the frenetic, desperate, savage operational life in Russia. In the meantime, large areas of the defensive positions along the coast are incomplete. And the Luftwaffe has not planned ahead at all.

The Führer is understandably upset at the report (though, thankfully, not at Jodl).

Jodl goes on to support Rommel's efforts, and his concepts of hitting the enemy right on the beaches, The strategy seems sound, although there is good merit in having a panzer reserve as well. But to base their entire strategy on a mobile, inland defense, he concludes, seems foolhardy.

The Führer agrees with him and adds, "The main thing, is that the moment the invasion begins, the enemy must be smothered in bombs. That'll force them to take cover, and even if there's only one jet airborne, they'll still be forced to take cover, and this will delay them hour upon hour. But, in half a day, our reserves will be well on their way!"

He asks Jodl if the once-defeatist Desert Fox would now be able to handle the defense of the West, and Jodl replies that he can. Rommel these days is a flurry of activity, personally overseeing, detailing, and inspecting the massive construction plans to upgrade—no, to build up—the Atlantic Wall. It seems as though they have found their man.

Hitler orders Jodl to write exactly what he has found out in no uncertain terms and to make sure his reports get circulated to the Western commands. He also instructs Jodl to issue the order: Rommel is to officially be put in command of the northern French coast. He is to be given the Fifteenth and the Seventh Armies. Army Group B is to become an operational reality again in the West.

The official word goes out immediately.

***

In the late afternoon at Fontainebleau, word comes down from the High Command that Rommel has officially been appointed commander of *Heeresgruppe B*. Rommel greets the news of his appointment with deep satisfaction. He is back in the saddle again, as the American cowboys say. And with Warlimont's confirmation of OKW's blessings on flooding the coastal plains, damming rivers, knocking down houses in his fields of fire, and generally uprooting the whole countryside as he sees fit, Rommel is now filled with even more resolve. He and his *Atlantikwall des Stahls*[2] will defeat the Allies.

His first order that evening is to increase the number of offshore obstacles, a proposal several subordinates are strongly against. He tells them, "We'll have all sorts of obstacles to stop their landing craft, and at various points. I expect that the enemy will land at high tide. Less open area to charge across, and easier to get across the low-tide obstacles. So we'll start construction at the high water mark, and work our way seawards…" He notes in his diary:

> *I have instructed that the troops ram stakes into the beaches as a barrier against landing craft.*

Yes, Rommel is back in his element.

***

Von Rundstedt, on the other hand, greets the news of Rommel's selection sourly. Well, it was going to happen anyway. No doubt, Rommel will soon get back in the spotlight. The disgusted old Prussian acknowledges the appointment by deciding to go on leave immediately. Let "Marshal Laddie" run the show.

In the meantime, von Rundstedt's chief, Günther Blumentritt, is asked by Speer's deputy to come up with a million Frenchmen to go to work in Germany. That would seriously impair any attempt to strengthen the Atlantic Wall.

Blumentritt promises to give the request every consideration.

Just after midnight, while a disgruntled von Rundstedt is sleeping, set to go on leave in the morning, his counterpart, 54-year-old four-star General Dwight D. Eisenhower, arrives in Scotland from the United States to assume the command of all Allied forces in the European Theater of Operations (ETOUSA). He immediately begins preparations for the Allied invasion of Europe. His new command staff has been waiting for someone to take charge for over nine months now. Eisenhower is of course not to blame. He had been informed of his appointment by the president only five and a half weeks ago.

Sir Bernard Law Montgomery, who is designated at this time to command the assault troops for the landing, has already been in England for 13 days.

---

1   Except in winter, the field marshal lived in St.-Germain-en-Laye (see December 12 entry).
2   "Atlantic Wall of Steel."

Sunday, January 16

Generalfeldmarschall Rommel hits the road again, invigorated by his new appointment—*Befehlshaber, Heeresgruppe B.*

He had already surveyed the Fifteenth Army's section of the coastline in late December when he was still the Führer's inspector, and had laid out specific orders and plans for improving the beach defenses, emphasizing that time was critical. Now he is coming back to check on their progress.

His inspection group drives northwest down the Seine to the coast, and they begin with General Reichert's[1] 711th Division, east of the Orne River. Rommel steps confidently into the division's headquarters, resolved to make sure every unit commander from regimental level up is completely clear on his strategy and intentions. His plans for interconnected, in-depth defensive fortifications to be constructed, and all his anti-invasion measures, will be put into full effect.

Basically, the idyllic French vacation is over. The Allies are coming. It is time to get to work.

The simple lunch that they are served is crowned with an exquisite dessert of apple soufflé. Then he is off again up the coast, into the mist. Cabourg, Deauville, Trouville-sur-Mer; the villages fly by as he stops, observes, and gives out instructions. The inspection group is generally satisfied with the defensive positions that they see, but the weak concentration of minefields is glaring.

By dark, they have worked their way back up the Seine River to Rouen, where Rommel calls on the 81st Corps headquarters just west of the town. Stocky, self-confident *Generaloberst* Hans von Salmuth is present. General Gümbel, filling in for absent corps commander General Kuntzen, tells them that they already have some 253,000 mines down. Most of them have been laid on both sides of Cayeux-sur-Mer,[2] and their minelaying is averaging some 15 kilometers of coastline a day, with some ten mines being laid per sapper.

Having already determined from what he has seen up here that von Salmuth has been slacking off in his defense efforts, Rommel, now displaying attitude to go with his new appointment, curtly orders: "Make that twenty."

And that is it. Once Rommel has made a decision, he expects it to be carried out immediately. Still, later on in the briefing, he orders that the hours these men spend on laying mines are to be increased, even if it means sacrificing time for training.

Von Salmuth looks at him pointedly as he hears this remark, and when a break in the briefing comes shortly thereafter, he tonelessly asks to speak to Rommel privately. The two of them go into an empty room and close the door.

Alone with the field marshal, van Salmuth complains about the amount of work the men are doing. As it is now, he explains in a somewhat imposing tone, they have no time for military training, including the use of weapons and tactics. "When the battle begins," he concludes defiantly, "I want fresh, well-trained soldiers—not physical wrecks."

Rommel is quickly getting mad. Even though his appointment is only a day old, the time has come to establish his authority with his generals. He looks pointedly at von Salmuth and says in a menacing low tone, "Evidently, you don't intend to carry out my orders."

Von Salmuth snorts in derision. "Stick around a bit," he replies patronizingly to this newcomer, "and you'll soon see that you can't do everything at once." He pauses briefly and adds, "Your program is going to take at least a year to complete. If anybody tells you any different, then he's either just trying to flatter you, or he's a *Schweinidiot.*"

Rommel stays tightlipped and follows him out as they return to the briefing. Von Salmuth knows that the field marshal is upset, but he is content that he has made his point. After all, he has had years of experience on the Army General Staff, and more wartime experience than Rommel. And besides, he commands the massive Fifteenth Army—Rommel's largest and most important unit. His opinion should weigh a good deal with the field marshal, who is still a newcomer to the area and somewhat of an outsider.[3]

The briefing continues, although now there is a decided tension in the air. The conference finally ends, and all the staff members file outside, Rommel's own officers heading towards their cars. Rommel tells von Salmuth to stay behind.

When everyone else has cleared out and the door is shut, Rommel turns on the general and launches into a tirade. He lets loose with a vociferous tongue-lashing that can be heard throughout the building. A startled von Salmuth turns red from embarrassed resentment. Angrily, he tries to defend himself. He shouts back that the intensity of Rommel's program is driving the area commanders crazy.

"*I don't care!*" the field marshal roars back. He then continues with his diatribe, cursing at the army commander and dressing him down in several imaginative ways. Von Salmuth suffers through a five-minute verbal onslaught. Finally, red-faced and rasping out of breath, Rommel ends his castigation and once more tells von Salmuth that he will obey his orders.

After an embarrassing silence, a chastened von Salmuth opens the door. The glowering field marshal stomps out wordlessly towards his car, a humiliated von Salmuth walking just behind him. Rommel turns, glances at von Salmuth, and impassively tells him goodbye. He then strides over to his black car and climbs into the front.[4] Admiral Ruge is already in the back. Their driver Daniel[5] then takes off in a trail of dust. The admiral of course stays silent.

After they leave the area and are heading towards Fontainebleau for the night, Rommel, picking up on the awkward silence, drops his glare and turns around to smirk at Admiral Ruge. He hitches his thumb back towards the dwindling building, winks, and chortles, "He's quite a roughneck, that one. That's the only language he understands."

A shocked Ruge can only stare back at him.[6]

1 Fifty-two-year-old *Generalleutnant* Josef Reichert. A colonel when the war broke out, Reichert rose through the command structure. He commanded the 177th and the 714th Infantry Divisions, before taking command of the 711th on March 15, 1943, relieving *Generalleutnant* Friedrich-Wilhelm Deutsch.

2 On the English Channel, about 31km northwest of Abbeville, and some 83km northwest of Amiens.

3 Von Salmuth, with so much wartime experience, no doubt considered himself an expert on warfare. And he had a reputation for being outspoken and directly presenting his views when he thought the need arose. His letter to Jodl back in December 1943 complaining about the Atlantic Wall (see Preface) was ample proof of that.

4 Rommel nearly always sat in the front—riding "shotgun."

5 *Oberfeldwebel* Karl Daniel, a Luftwaffe sergeant who was Rommel's personal driver in Europe.

6 Rommel had once confided to his orderly, Hermann Aldinger, with a slight grin, "It's good to have once been a sergeant and to still remember how to talk like one." It was experience that he sometimes put to good use.

Monday, January 17

Rommel is back on the road again. Reassured by Jodl's apparent support of his theories, he leaves the 81st headquarters and travels northwest to Bolbec, about 30km east-northeast of Le Havre, where he attends a conference at the headquarters of the 17th Luftwaffe Field Division. He notes a large percentage of NCOs in the enlisted ranks, typical of the air force. Once again, he outlines his strategy to the commanders.

Then it is off to the port of Le Havre. He has meetings with the *Hafenkapitän*[1] and the naval coordinator for the area at their headquarters. Again he points out the inferior emplacement design of the army batteries compared to their naval counterparts.

It is then northeast up the coast to Fécamp, to see the massive number of positions being built there. Rommel nods approval. The local area commander is furious at his naval counterpart there, a mild, easy-going fellow. The army officer complains that the navy is a bunch of no-good bureaucrats. Rommel turns on the charm and has the commanders laughing and making up in no time.

After a short lunch in the enlisted mess, he travels up the coast to St.-Valery-en-Caux and his mind takes a trip down memory lane. For it was there in 1940 that his famed 7th Panzer "ghosts"[2] had pushed an entire British division back to the English Channel and forced them to surrender.

Climbing a few hills to reach a Luftwaffe radar station, Rommel finds out that the station had failed to report an air raid to the local army base commander. He reprimands the lieutenant in charge there, only to find out that the man had just returned from leave and had not been present. Still, the point has been made, and the field marshal leaves it at that.

Next, they are off to the port of Dieppe. There, during the long, inevitable conference, held in the officers' mess, everyone is given a hot cup of coffee. Rommel, typically occupied by the talk, forgets to drink his. Chief engineer Meise, sitting beside him, finishes his and starts looking at Rommel's slowly cooling mug with longing.

Admiral Ruge sees Meise eyeing Rommel's coffee cup. Finally taking pity upon the engineer, Ruge casually walks over to where the field marshal is sitting and calmly picks up both Meise's cup and Rommel's cup. The field marshal, engrossed in the briefing, does not notice.

Ruge walks behind one of the large situation maps and pours over half of Rommel's coffee into Meise's empty mug. He then walks back to the table and puts the cups back where they were. Rommel is still oblivious to the incident, but a grateful Meise savors the warm drink.

A few minutes later, the field marshal, perhaps subconsciously triggered by Meise's sipping, reaches for his own cup. As he listens to the briefing before him, he raises the mug to his lips. Glancing down, he is surprised to see it nearly empty. He looks up at the briefing officer, back down at his cup, then around the room for a telltale guilty face. Temporarily distracted, he forces himself to return his attention to the meeting.

After the conference is over, they stay for dinner. They finally tell Rommel what happened to his coffee, and he shares a good laugh with them. After eating, he regales them with stories about his mad dash across France in 1940. He recalls how his panzers assaulted the Maginot Line on a moonless night with his memorable order: "Broadside right, broadside left; just like in the navy."

They spend the night in local French quarters, and some of the staff have trouble getting into bed. It seems that the blankets in typical French style are firmly tucked under the mattresses, and the officers find that to get in, they have to slide in from the top. A French sleeping bag on a frame, one officer grumbles.

---

1   Port commander *Vizeadmiral* Rieve.

2   In the 1940 *blitzkrieg* across France, Rommel commanded the 7th Panzer Division. It was nicknamed *Le Division Fantôme* (the "Ghost Division") by the French because it moved so fast and they never knew where it would turn up, or from what point it would attack. It also amazed them that Rommel was always in front, his command vehicle being a speciallyequipped *PzKw III*. Sometimes, he would even take off in a light Storch observation plane and study the battlefield from above, before landing near his lead tanks.

His amazing movement through enemy lines stunned the French, and sometimes his crazy advance would startle them so much that they would hesitate to shoot at his lead formation. Instead they would just stand back to either side of his column and stare wide-eyed, trying to figure out what the hell was happening. One day, a French officer that Rommel's men had captured asked Rommel the identification of his unit. When Rommel told him, the man smacked his forehead and exclaimed, "*Sacre bleu! Le Division Fantôme encore!* First in Belgium, then at Arras, and on the Somme, and now here, again and again our paths have crossed."

The men of the 7th Panzer were of course thrilled with the compliment, and the nickname Ghost Division (*Gespensterdivision*) stuck. Rommel himself was amusingly referred to as one of the four horsemen of the Apocalypse. The division pushed on through France, hell-bent for the coast and the devil take those in the rear. They averaged a staggering 60 to 80 kilometers a day, and eventually, the 7th Panzer would bag nearly 100,000 enemy prisoners for a loss of only 42 tanks. Rommel later in his letters home to Lucie referred to his smashing operation across the countryside as "a lightning tour of France."

As a result of his success, his name was included in nearly every German paper in print, and his unit truly had earned its nickname. The 7th Panzer's moniker was considered well-deserved even by the German High Command, because Rommel's panzers moved so fast and so unexpectedly that often, like the French, neither OKH nor OKW had any idea where he was. Even the Führer himself later commented that Rommel had cost him a "sleepless night," and after the campaign, greeted (and embarrassed) him with mock distress, bemoaning, "Rommel! We were all very worried for your safety!"

Tuesday, January 18

Rommel continues his tour up the northeast French coast. Starting at Le Tréport,[1] he instructs the uninformed local division commander[2] on how to thwart a landing, and points out serious communication problems for the army batteries there. He notes that an invasion here is unlikely, because of the narrow stony beaches and high cliffs. But a raid is quite possible.

Touring south of the Somme estuary nesr Cayeux-sur-Mer, they stumble across an excellent battery site, complete with fortified bunkers and defensive strongpoints. The only problem is that the bunkers have been partially destroyed, and the area has been abandoned, even though the unused position is still viable. Rommel, enraged, demands that this be rectified immediately.

That afternoon he again meets with a now-chastened General von Salmuth at Montreuil-sur-Mer.[3] They talk a while, and then Rommel moves on to inspect some minefields sown by SS engineers at Hardelot-Plage.

He retires for the evening at an old soldier's home in Le Touquet-Paris-Plage.[4] He discovers that someone has thoughtfully has left a nice variety of good English books in the reading room.

---

1   About 32km northeast up the coast from Dieppe.
2   Probably *Generalmajor* Paul Seyffardt, commanding the 348th Infantry Division.
3   About 40km south of Boulogne-sur-Mer.
4   Just south of Boulogne-sur-Mer.

Wednesday, January 19

At 8 a.m., Rommel's entourage is off again. Leaving Le Touquet-Paris-Plage, they turn southward and drive to nearby Breck-sur-Mer, to inspect some more defensive positions and a few minefields.

The inspection concluded, the entourage speeds for home and arrive back at headquarters early that afternoon.

That evening, Rommel writes to his wife about various subjects:

> Dearest Lu:
>
> Returned today from my long trip. I saw a lot and was very satisfied with the progress that has been made.
> I think for certain that we'll win the defensive battle in the West, provided only that a little more time remains for preparation.
> ... Situation in the East: apparently stabilized.
> ... Situation in the South: severe fighting and more heavy attacks to be met.
> ... In the West: I believe we'll be able to beat off the assault.
> Günther's[1] going off tomorrow with a suitcase and will help you with the move. In 10–12 days, he will return here. He has taken everything along that we—more accurately Hammermann—have been able to get here. When he returns, he should bring back my brown civilian suit and lightweight overcoat with hat, etc. I want to be able to go out sometime without a marshal's baton for once...
> Günther wants two days of leave for his wedding. Give him 300 marks...

***

After a study conducted by OKW, Adolf Hitler today reclassifies a number of areas along the Atlantic Wall categorized as defensive areas (*Verteidigungsberich*) as fortresses (*Festungen*). They include Ijmuiden and the Hoek van Holland in the Netherlands; and in France, Dunkirk, Boulogne, Le Havre, Cherbourg, St. Malo, Brest, Lorient, St. Nazaire, and the Gironde estuary.

---

1   *Obergefreiter* Herbert Günther was Rommel's orderly. He had served under the field marshal since North Africa. In comparison to *Leutnant* Hammermann, Rommel's aide, Guenther performed minor daily functions for the field marshal, such as preparing his uniform, unpacking his suitcase, etc. Hammermann, an officer, acted as his personal assistant in military events, carried his papers, etc.

Thursday, January 20

In the very early morning hours, Berlin is hit hard by the RAF. They dump some 2,400 tons of explosives onto the city, devastating whole sections. Clearly, the enemy can now amass huge bomber armadas to tear into Germany's cities.

In pathetic comparison, it was all the Luftwaffe could do a year ago to transport a hundred tons a day just 330km to Stalingrad.

***

Today, Rommel stays at Fontainebleau and has a number of meetings with his staff. They establish three points:

First, Rommel wants to pursue the concept of "coastal zones of combat." In each zone, the overall commander there will have unlimited authority. This will cut down tremendously on red tape and bureaucratic policies that would slow down construction of defenses, to say nothing of jeopardizing the responsibility of command in the event of an invasion.

About a dozen major port areas are classified as "fortresses." While most are already significantly fortified and defended against the sea, few are capable of withstanding an assault from the land side. Creating the official term now of "fortress commander" bestows upon the man unlimited authority, and gives him a staggering amount of power to conduct his business. On the other hand, it also imposes upon him a terrific responsibility. Loss of his fortress area would now probably mean dismissal, perhaps even arrest and a firing squad.

Second, Rommel tells them to transfer unit command on each side of the Somme estuary to the 67th Corps,[1] and thus not split authority across the river mouth.

Third, the staff must give serious attention to the formation, reorganization, and training of both new and existing panzer divisions.

Rommel gets on the phone and calls Jodl at the Führer's headquarters in Rastenburg. They discuss coastal defenses, and specifically positioning the reorganizing 21st Panzer Division. Rommel wants the 21st employed in the coastal defense immediately. As part of his strategy, he asks that all divisions on the coast be able to initiate counterattacks immediately against a possible landing.

As he did after his inspection of the West, Jodl tentatively agrees with him in principle. However, Rommel does not know that, right after he hangs up with him, Jodl considers the matter and discusses it with Warlimont, his deputy.

Despite Rommel's sound logic, von Rundstedt's belief that the coast is way too long to adequately defend every kilometer has merit. The enemy could in theory concentrate on whatever area he wished and would be able to penetrate at any point, no matter what type of defenses they put up: a sort of amphibious *blitzkrieg*.

The answer, then, might be along von Rundstedt's way of thinking: to put out a few coastal divisions to slow the enemy up, and then hit them with a powerful, mobile, strategic reserve force when they began to advance. And if that does not work, they will just have to defeat them in the French interior itself.

So Jodl calls von Rundstedt's headquarters and speaks to his operations officer. To placate them, he claims that his understanding of this "immediately counterattack" concept only pertains to the infantry—not to the panzer units.

Von Rundstedt's operations officer, Bodo Zimmermann, later calls his counterpart at Army Group B, *Oberstleutnant* von Tempelhoff, and tells him about Jodl's call.

Von Tempelhoff counters that Rommel wants the panzers moved close to the coast immediately to be able to react at once to any invasion. Zimmermann replies that von Rundstedt will never go for that. The reserve panzers must be inland and free to maneuver, since the enemy will no doubt have a number of surprise moves for them; surprises that the panzers will have to meet quickly.

Finally, a small concession is made. The 9th SS, 10th SS, and 21st Panzer will be allowed to move a bit closer to the coast, but not much. And they will have to be ready to move out at a moment's notice to maneuver inland.

---

1   Fifty-four-year-old *General der Infanterie* Walther Fischer von Weikersthal, commanding. A World War I veteran, he served as Dollmann's chief of staff during the French campaign of 1940, later commanding the 35th Infantry Division in Russia. He was considered a ruthless leader who served on the Eastern Front until late January 1942. Then, commanding LIII Infantry Corps, he went against express orders to "hold until the last possible moment" and directed some of his hard-pressed units to retreat. Relieved of his command and placed into the Führerreserve, he was given command of the 67th Infantry Corps in September, 1942 but then relieved of command of July 25, 1944. Captured in early May 1945, he was charged with committing war crimes in Russia. He was finally released from American custody two years later, and died on February 11, 1953.

Friday, January 21

Today, the weather is mild. Rommel's senior officers meet with other staff members and, together with the visiting General Wagner,[1] they critique a recent resupply exercise that had been organized by OB West. It is well noted that a vital means of keeping the front supplied will be the railroads. After the meeting, Ruge leaves to meet with *Vizeadmiral* Schirlitz, the naval commander for Western France.

The field marshal meanwhile is dedicating himself to defeating the upcoming invasion. He is preparing himself for that task by getting himself in shape, both physically and mentally.

The focal point of his physical training becomes small "hunting" walks around Fontainebleau. Once lean and healthy in the desert, his tour in Italy (where he also suffered a bout of appendicitis) has softened him. And Jodl's comments about the rich, easy Parisian life have made him aware of the holiday attitude of the men in France. Now getting out into the cold French woods around his headquarters will harden his body again.

He takes a shotgun along, although his walks are mainly for the exercise. He pushes himself mercilessly, and often comes back to his car out of breath and aching. His routine often exhausts him, but gritting his teeth, he vows to stay on track with his training program. The only things that curtail his sprees are being on an inspection tour or an occasional attack of his lumbago; and of course, the incessant paperwork.

He is also reorienting himself mentally. He simply has to stop the invasion and be victorious. And this will not be a halfway measure. He will either totally win or totally lose. This is Germany's last chance. They are counting on him. His peers, especially those critical snobs of the *Generalstab*, will be watching him—waiting for him to fail or to get discouraged. Well, that is not going to happen. He will show them that he is no defeatist. The stakes here are too important, the odds are against him, and there will be no second place.

His staff members have picked up his frenetic pace and struggle to keep up. *Der Wüstenfuchs* is back on form again. And now he has some company. He glances at them sleeping under his desk: two lovely young dachshunds.

They had been given to him by the Todt Organization on the 20th. Rommel had instantly taken a liking to them. Ajax, the older one, is less energetic than the younger one, Elbo. They have been following him everywhere. Last night, they both slept in his room, Elbo's spot behind the luggage stand, and Ajax's on the carpet close to the door. He writes his wife:

Dearest Lu:

I've been a dog owner since yesterday, when the OT presented me with not one but two dachshunds. One of them (a male) is a year old, longhaired with a proper mustache. The other is only three months. The younger one was very affectionate immediately, but the older one is not so forthcoming.

> *The two of them are now lying beneath my writing desk. The older one barks whenever anyone comes. They both howl occasionally at night. Probably they're homesick for their previous owner. The older dachshund would be just right as watch dog for our house. He reports well. The younger one I would like to keep here.*

He thinks about their move to the new home in Herrlingen and adds:

> *I am anxious to hear from you about the move and how it went. I hope everything goes without a hitch.*

***

The Luftwaffe this evening begins *Unternehmen Steinbock*,"[2] the bombing counteroffensive against England that was conceived in response to the Allies' recent massive air campaign targeting cities and air production centers. It will consist of a series of air raids: a sort of "baby blitz" as the English will soon refer to it. The campaign has been delayed about a month because of bad weather and the time it has taken to gather a sizeable force. Tonight though, it begins. In the first attack, *Unternehmen Mars*, nearly 450 bombers—the largest force assembled to strike England since 1940—and two *Jagdgruppe* fly across the English Channel to try to strike terror into major cities with incendiaries and blockbusters. Unfortunately, even though the pathfinders drop enough flares to identify London from the air, the inexperienced aircrews have trouble finding their targets, so only about 30 tons of the total 270 tons of bombs dropped actually fall over London.

The Führer, as expected, will be furious when he hears this news, especially considering that Allied bombers range nearly a thousand kilometers into Germany and hit their targets accurately. In contrast, London is only 200 kilometers away from the coast.

Today, Eisenhower formally meets for the first time with his SHAEF[3] senior staff officers in London at what will be their new headquarters, the historic Norfolk House.[4] They begin formal preparations for the invasion. Field Marshal Montgomery, the first speaker, somewhat monopolizes the meeting with his broad plan for a landing on the beaches of Normandy.

The American First Army, he states, will land on the right flank, mostly so that they can receive supplies directly from the United States, as well as from England. They are to drive inland, sweep around westward, and capture the port of Cherbourg. The British Second Army, he states, will land on the left flank, immediately seize Caen, and take on the German forces counterattacking from the east and southeast. The two Allied forces will unite somewhere around the town of Bayeux. Montgomery will command both armies, to be identified as the 21st Army Group.

Montgomery then adds, "In the initial stages, we should concentrate on gaining control quickly of the main centers of road communications. We should then push our armored formations between and beyond these centers and deploy them on suitable ground. In this way, it would be difficult for the enemy to bring up his reserves and get them past these armored formations."

Eisenhower will consider the plan.

---

1   Fifty-four-year-old *General der Artillerie* Eduard Wagner, the *Generalquartiermeister der Heeres* (chief quartermaster of the German Army).

2   "Operation *Capricorn*." See entries for December 3 and 6, 1943.

3   Supreme Headquarters, Allied Expeditionary Force.

4   Located at 31 St. James's Square, it was built in 1722 for the Duke of Norfolk. It had for centuries been owned by royalty (King George II was born there). In 1938, the house was demolished and an office building put in its place. It later became the headquarters for SHAEF.

Saturday, January 22

The weather is dreary today. Rommel and several staff officers travel to Le Mans, headquarters of the Seventh Army, commanded by General Dollmann. It is Rommel's first trip to the western sector.[1]

Rommel's naval advisor *Vizeadmiral* Ruge arrives early, and meets with Dollmann and his brilliant career chief of staff, Max Pemsel.[2] He is immediately besieged by both about the lack of naval artillery in this sector of France. Ruge responds by defending the navy. He argues that the responsibility of coastal defense is the army's, and that several naval batteries have already been donated to that task. Besides, the Kriegsmarine had already supplied an abundance of batteries to defend major ports.

Then Rommel arrives, and the conference begins. Pemsel gives a status report and a briefing on unit deployment. Static divisions have been formed out of necessity. Each typically consists of two infantry regiments, made up of second-rate, or "non-line" troops. They are supported by two field batteries, each with a dozen or so older guns, and a third battery of horse-drawn, medium guns. Divisional transport is just a couple dozen trucks and some horses and carts.

Pemsel goes over every possible landing area and gives a shrewd evaluation of each. Brittany is an unlikely area, unless undertaken with a concurrent landing in southern France to cut off the Loire area.

He covers the Calvados coast in detail. It seems logical that the coastal stretch from the Orne River west, around the Cherbourg peninsula to St. Malo, offers the best locations for an enemy landing. He points out that while the Normandy beaches are more rocky and treacherous than those near Calais, many small coves and beach areas on the eastern shoreline are relatively sheltered from heavy winds and high seas, and offer excellent landing areas.

As for possible airborne landing sectors, there are three. Two are in the Calvados area: around the city of Caen, and around Carentan, on the Vire River.[3] The third is in Brittany, around Montagne d'Arée, especially to the west.

Pemsel summarizes by stating that he is convinced the invasion will occur in their sector.

Rommel states that he thinks the best place to invade is further up the coast, closer to the Ruhr Valley. Dollmann counters that the good beaches and inland hedgerow fields in his sector invite an enemy landing. Cherbourg would be a substantial prize, and the area is weakly defended. And in Brittany, two divisions cover a 515km front.

Next they discuss weapon stocks and calibers of shells available.

That afternoon, in a pouring rain, Rommel heads west to Rennes, and then continues on another 135km to call on *General der Infanterie* Erich Straube,[4] commanding the 74th Corps at Guingamp. Several conferences with him and his chief of staff, *Oberst* Ludwig Zoellner, go on into the evening. Once again,

Rommel outlines his general plans for constructing defensive barriers and his basic hold-at-the-waterline strategy.

They stay there for the night, and rest in civilian quarters.

***

Startling reports begin to come in at the Berghof today that the Allies have landed at Nettuno[5] and are pushing inland. Göring's *Unternehmen Steinbock* against London will have to continue minus three *Kampfgruppen*, which are to be returned to Italy immediately.

---

1   *Generalleutnant* Friedrich Dollmann at 62 is a large and physically impressive officer who has shown great political adaptability throughout his career. A World War I veteran, he had served as an aerial observer and artillery battalion commander, and after the war, became a former artillery inspector. A Bavarian Catholic, he had nevertheless been one of the first officers to jump on the Nazi bandwagon. He had even gone as far as to dress down his Catholic chaplains back in 1937 for not having a sufficiently positive attitude toward National Socialism. Given command of the Seventh Army in 1939, the only action he has seen has been at the tail end of the French campaign in 1940. By 1944, he has turned against the Nazi regime, and believes it will be the downfall of Germany.

2   *Generalmajor* Max-Josef Pemsel, having just turned 47 on January 15, is also a veteran of the Great War. When World War II broke out, Pemsel was chief of staff for the 1st Mountain Division, and later for General Beyer's XVIII Mountain Corps. He took over the chief of staff duties for the Seventh Army in January of 1943.

3   These two areas are roughly where the US 82nd and 101st Airborne Divisions would land on the western flank, and the British 6th Airborne Division would land on the right flank.

4   Fifty-six-year-old *General der Infanterie* Erich Straube. For Barbarossa, he commanded the 268th Infantry Division in the Fourth Army. Straube took command of the LXXIV Corps on August 1, 1943.

5   Some battles in World War II are referred to differently by the opposing sides. The Allies referred to this invasion as "Anzio"; the Germans, "Nettuno." Both were towns right at the landing site.

Sunday, January 23

Generalfeldmarschall von Rundstedt is on leave at the spa in Bad Tölz.[1]

***

Generalfeldmarschall Rommel continues his inspection tour of northwest France. Today, he begins a round trip covering the northern coast of Brittany. Traveling westward to the coast at Sibiril, he turns eastward to the ancient town of Paimpol.[2] There are no major ports in this 500km of shoreline, known as the *Cote d'Armor*, and there are fewer roads than in coastal areas.

They discuss mines, and at one spot, when Rommel points out an area that would be ideal for minefields, one staff officer quips, "Yes, this is a great place for 80,000 mines!" Rommel's officers laugh. Then they explain to the other officers accompanying them that this was a standing joke at *Heeresgruppe B*. Two years ago on a beautiful day in North Africa, Rommel and his staff had been standing at the edge of a picturesque desert scene. Gazing at a beautiful wadi, one of the officers had shaken his head in admiration and remarked, "Isn't that a wonderful sight?" Rommel had growled in response, "*Ja*, it will take 80,000 mines."

The 74th Corps located there has put down over 100,000 mines and cannot lay any more; they have run out. Rommel authorizes them another 20,000 to get them going again. The mines will come from army group supplies.

The group inspects many of the resistance points spread out along the shore. About three quarters of the 200-odd batteries are not yet in permanent casements, and this concerns him too.

Traveling south away from the sea some 35km, they return to spend the evening in Guingamp at the 74th's headquarters. They dine that evening with the corps' General Straube and *Oberst* Zoellner.

That evening, the radio reports that in the East, the Russians continue to push west. What little chance OB West had of getting additional units is gone. In fact, they will be lucky to keep the mobile divisions that they have. Then they hear the bad news of the large enemy landings at Anzio in northwest Italy. The German line is now outflanked, and a disaster could result. Despite the usual bombastic, confident tones of the announcer, Rommel is disturbed to find out that the Allies are nevertheless establishing a beachhead, and though they have been ashore now over 24 hours, no German panzer counterattack has as yet hit them.

A critical mistake Rommel definitely does not want to repeat when the enemy invades against him.

***

Today, the Führer has a visit at the Wolf's Lair from Japanese Ambassador Baron Hiroshi Ōshima,[3] and among other things, they discuss matters in the West. By now, news is out that Dwight D. Eisenhower has been appointed the supreme Allied commander in the West. Hitler asks the Japanese attaché, "Doesn't it look like the appointment of Eisenhower, etc., and all this boastful propaganda is a kind of camouflage?"

He pauses and adds, "Still, in view of their relationship with Russia, England and America can't get away without doing anything at all. Even though it might not be a large invasion, I think that they will have to carry out one that they may call in their propaganda a "second front.""

Later in a private meeting, they discuss the invasion again. Hitler begins by saying, "Now, as for the question of the second front, no matter when it comes, or at what point, I have made adequate preparations to meet it. In Finland, we have seven divisions; in Norway, twelve; in Denmark, six; in France and the Low Countries, 62."

He thinks for a moment and continues: "Well, all of those divisions are not, I must admit, of the finest caliber; but I have emphasized that there must be complete mobility. I have gotten together as many armored divisions as possible, including four SS divisions, and the Herman Göring Division."

He begins pacing. "Besides, don't forget our coming retaliation against England. We are going to do it principally with rocket guns. Everything is now ready… and practice shows that they are extremely effective."

Hitler confides that the most effective area for the enemy to land is the Straits of Dover area, but that such a landing would be very difficult, and the Allies are surely not strong enough to undertake such an operation. After a moment he adds thoughtfully, "On the other hand, along the Bordeaux coast and in Portugal, the defenses are relatively weak. So this zone might be a possibility…"

The Führer pauses again, and then continues. "But how vast is that seacoast! It'd be impossible for me to prevent some other sort of landing somewhere or other. I couldn't even stop this recent landing behind our lines in Italy.[4] And they came ashore with little resistance. So another landing in the West is likely."

The Führer pauses and makes a fist as his eyes glint fiercely. "But all the enemy can possibly do is establish a bridgehead. I will stop, absolutely, any real second front."

After some discussion, Hitler walks over to a map of England, where a line has been drawn across the lower part of the country. "Now take this line running to the Birmingham area. That is a good place to start. I cannot tell you when we will begin, but we are really going to do something to the British Isles! And we also have ready two thousand *schnell* bombers, and last night we carried out our first real bombing of London. With all these various factors in play, I believe we can gradually regain the initiative and, seizing our opportunities, turn once again against Russia…"

Eisenhower and his staff have analyzed Montgomery's invasion plan for two days. Pressured to give maximum latitude to maximize a spirit of détente with the British, he has decided to formally authorize the plan. At 11 p.m., through his chief of staff, Bedell Smith, he sends a detailed message to the US Joint Chiefs of Staff for their approval.
Operation Overlord *is born.*

---

1   Bad Tölz is a spa located in the foothills of the Bavarian Alps on the Isar River, about 50km south of Munich. Once a medieval trading center for lumber and salt, it became famous as a pleasure resort when natural springs were discovered in the mid-19th century. The spa district, located on the left bank (the town itself is on the right), includes these natural springs, high in iodine content, with supposedly natural healing and curing properties. The town's claim to fame was enhanced in 1937 with the opening there of an extensive SS *Junkerschule*, complete with a nice sports stadium, indoor sports halls, a heated swimming pool, and a sauna. Labor for the school and some government offices was later provided by a local branch facility of the Dachau concentration camp.

2   On the northern coast of Brittany, about midway between St. Malo and Brest.

3   Fifty-eight-year-old Baron Hiroshi Ōshima had been the Japanese military attaché and ambassador to Germany for some ten years. A staunch supporter of the Third Reich and a personal friend of Foreign Minister Joachim von Ribbentrop, he had quickly became a favorite of Hitler, and as such, he was privy to many strategic meetings and conversations with the Führer and the German High Command. Because the United States had in 1940 cracked the Japanese diplomatic Purple Code that Ōshima used to encrypt his detailed dispatches to Japan (a code the Germans warned him on several occasions was unreliable), the Allies were privy to most of the messages the ambassador radioed to Japan, and by extension, often to many of the German High Command plans and their positions on military situations.

Between 1941 and 1945, nearly all of Ōshima's dispatches—almost 1,500—were intercepted, and most were decoded. Taken into custody by the Americans in 1945, he was later found guilty of war crimes, but was paroled in 1955. He died in 1975, never knowing the extent of intelligence assistance that he had given the Allies during the war. For further reading on this extraordinary individual, refer to Bruce Lee's *Marching Orders: The Untold Story of World War II*.

4   Referring to the Anzio landing of January 22.

Monday, January 24

Rommel and his entourage continue their inspection of Brittany on a stormy day. They start out in Guingamp and travel in a cold, drenching rain some 125km, along the *Cote d'Armor*, eastward to St. Brieuc, and then on to the port of St. Malo. There, one division defends a staggering 250 kilometers of coast.[1]

Included in the division's order of battle are a few Östen battalions, made up of Russian POWs. Rommel is somewhat taken aback to hear their commanding officers make their status reports in crisp Russian. The fighting quality of the troops in these battalions can easily be seen. The men are rough-looking, and only the temperament of their commanding officers keeps them in line. Their quality as reliable, cohesive fighting units though is questionable, and Rommel is under no illusions about what these Russians will do if something goes wrong in their sector.

At St. Lunaire, west of Dinard, an argument breaks out between the local area army and naval commanders about the location of a Russian 122mm battery. It is the now-familiar story about where to put the coastal batteries: along the shoreline as the navy insists, or somewhat inland, as the army wants.

At St. Malo, they inspect the well-constructed fortress of La Cité in a driving rain. They note its intricate tunnel network, with horizontal tunnels to connect the positions and vertical shafts to store extra ammunition and supplies. Despite the fortress' fine design, there are only a few 75mm guns there, along with some automatic weapons. And on the island of Cézembre, just outside the port entrance, the naval battery of four 190mm guns is exposed to the elements—and of course, any naval fire.

The tour continues on to an army battery near the small coastal fishing village of Cancale. The rain does not let up.

That evening, they rest and warm up. Admiral Ruge gets to talk to a few fellow naval officers who have run naval convoys up to and down from the Channel Islands. Naturally, the officers take the opportunity to complain about the lack of support from the Kriegsmarine, and especially the Luftwaffe.

---

1 Admiral Ruge wrote erroneously that they inspected positions of the "71st Corps." He must have meant Straube's 74th Corps. He also mentioned deployment of the 721st Division under *Generalmajor Freiherr* Christoph Stolberg-Stolberg. The author could find no record of this unit.

Tuesday, January 25

Generalfeldmarschall Rommel continues his tour of the coast in Brittany. Admiral Ruge shows up a quarter hour early for the conference at Dol-de-Bretagne[1] so that he can first visit with the commander of the five-month-old 179th Reserve Panzer Division,[2] *Generalleutnant* von Boltenstern.[3]

Ruge chats about manipulating Rommel into visiting charming Mont-St.-Michel after the day's inspections, and showing him the unique historical aspects of the preserved monastery. Boltenstern agrees, and adds to the inspection itinerary a small five-man guard outpost there.

Unfortunately for them, when Rommel arrives, he does not fall for the trick. He listens to the list of stops, and when Boltenstern reads off Mont-St.-Michel, Rommel glances at Ruge with a hint of a smile and tells the division commander to scratch that one off the list. Ruge frowns amusingly in disappointment.

They leave to inspect the still-developing 179th. Originally formed in late 1939, it was classified in January 1940 as the 179th Replacement Division. A year later, it was reclassified as a motorized infantry division, and in April 1943, upgraded to replacement panzer division. Three months later, it transferred from Germany to France. Ever since then, it has struggled to maintain its very existence. Habitually drawn from to flesh out other motorized units, it has never really gained stature. Even now it is but a shadow of the size a true panzer division should be, even by 1944 standards.

In one set of fields, the entourage inspects a makeshift panzer company, an infantry battalion devoid of transport, and a coastal defense battalion, a truly unique formation to be included in a panzer division. Another two regiments of men are training without equipment or transport.

They watch the division's recon unit[4] demonstrate its readiness near the town of Tinteniac. The men carry French rifles, but otherwise lack equipment, and even a change of clothes, which in rainy Brittany is a sad state of affairs.

At noontime, the inspection party dines in Rennes at the 179th's staff quarters. Then it is back to Le Mans, where they go over the results of the tour with Seventh Army Chief of Staff Max Pemsel. To the complaint of lacking supplies, Rommel promises to increase shipments to them and guarantees delivery of some 400,000 mines by the end of the next month.

Rommel then returns to Fontainebleau and finds out from von Tempelhoff that OKW has turned down their request to move the reserve panzer divisions to the coast. Rommel is disappointed, but is determined not to give up.

They need those tanks near the beaches.

---

1   About 28km southeast of St. Malo.
2   In the spring, this unit would combine with the 16th *Panzergrenadier* Division to form the 116th Panzer Division.

3 Fifty-four-year-old *Generalleutnant* Walter Boltenstern. A World War I veteran, he commanded the 71st Motorized Infantry Regiment in the early part of the war, and then served with distinction on the Eastern Front, commanding the 29th Motorized Division. Relieved for health reasons, he later took over the 179th.

4 1. Reserve Panzer Aufklärungs-Abteilung.

Wednesday, January 26

Fontainebleau is visited by one of Gause's old commanding officers, 61-year-old *General der Infanterie* Hermann Geyer.[1] Rommel had been delighted to invite the man, a fellow Swabian, over for dinner. The general had been Gause's superior, in charge of the Fifth Military District before the war.[2] Geyer had been a highly regarded strategist on the *OHL*[3] during World War I and was considered extremely intelligent. Even legendary General Ludendorff had once said so.

Geyer had served in the Reichswehr in the 1930s. In the spring of 1939 he left active duty, upset over the fact that he faced retirement just when his country was about to go to war. But he was reactivated just after the Polish campaign to take over promoted General Dollmann's 9th Infantry Corps. Commanding them, Geyer participated in the 1940 campaign in France, earning him the Knight's Cross.

The next year, in the opening months of the Soviet invasion, Geyer had fought well on the Eastern Front. His 9th Infantry Corps in General Hoth's Fourth Army had advanced through western Russia alongside General Guderian's panzers. Geyer had pushed his men eastward past Borodino, the sight of Napoleon's victory back in 1812, and it was Geyer's infantry that had stood before the gates of Moscow at the end of November. By the time that freezing Russian winter began, they had taken severe casualties during their determined advance.

Geyer had still been in the process of moving his tired forces up alongside Guderian's units for an assault on the capital when the enemy units opposing him had launched a furious counterattack in early December. Assessing the situation—the freezing temperatures, the formidable Russian forces probing before him, his depleted units, the extended, slim, overburdened supply lines, threatened with being cut off—Geyer, like several other conscientious commanders, had reluctantly but prudently ordered his exhausted and depleted corps to fall back out of their threatened pocket before they could be surrounded, to dig in for the cold months, and regroup.

In doing so, he no doubt saved the lives of several thousand men. Politically though, it was the wrong decision to make, and he certainly was not congratulated. Hitler, furious with Geyer about his withdrawal, relieved him of his command on December 31 (along with several dozen other commanding officers, including von Rundstedt), less than a week after Guderian himself had been sacked. He had been unceremoniously fired, curtly told that he was too old to continue leading in the field. To make matters worse, word went around the High Command about how Geyer had criticized the Nazi Party before the war. Since then, Geyer had tried several times to get another command, but had remained inactive. By the time of his visit to Fontainebleau he is effectively in retirement.

After dinner, Rommel and his staff sit and chat with him. Geyer now does little to show his contempt for the Party.[4] He wants to know from them why the senior generals still put up with Hitler and his "type of leadership." Well, someone counters, most of them listen to him because they do not have as much combat experience. Guderian had suggested in December 1941 that experienced front-line generals trade places with the inexperienced ones in OKW and OKH. Hitler had refused to even think about it.

Geyer does not like their answer, and the debate goes on. Rommel is somewhat bored, and his mind seems to wander. Maybe he is wondering about where he can get more mines.

The discussion turns to defending against the invasion. A few people mention having thought about the recent landing at Anzio four days ago, and how the Allies have still not made a follow-up attack from the beachhead. Geyer feels that their reserves near the landing area should be all moved forward, since there are few consolidated enemy positions as yet. He had done something similar in Russia in late 1941. Rommel is only half-listening…

Geyer continues talking about reserves. If you considered their deployment mathematically, he explains, you would discover that there's a direct function of time and space variables. The formulas could get fairly complicated. He states, "The fact that one square kilometer contains one million square meters does not occur to most people."

A million square meters to a kilometer… Rommel raises his head and turns to his chief engineer, Wilhelm Meise.

"Meise," he asks, "how many mines do you think that'd take?"

Meise looks at him, surprised. He hesitates. Rommel does some quick calculations in his head and comes up with roughly one mine per 15 square meters. He concludes, "I figure about 65,000."

Meise nods and notes the figure. The conversation goes on to other subjects, like ammunition safety and better cooperation between the Luftwaffe and the panzer units. Rommel seems preoccupied again, probably drifting back to those 65,000 mines.

The group finally breaks up and General Geyer accepts Rommel's gracious invitation to stay the night at the château.[5]

Later, the field marshal gets to talk to Lucie by phone. Afterward, he writes to her:

I just spoke to you on the telephone. Now the move seems to be pretty much over, and you are in the new home, which I hope is in every way satisfactory.

The job's being very frustrating. Time and again one comes up against bureaucratic and petrified individuals who resist everything new and progressive. But we'll manage it all the same.

My two hounds had to be separated, after the older Ajax had well nigh killed the younger with affection. Ajax, the older one, is now with me, the other one with Böttcher.[6] Ajax is turning into a lovable pain.

1   *General der Infanterie* Hermann *Freiherr* von Geyer. Some sources confuse him with Freiherr Geyr von Schweppenberg, Commander, Panzergruppe West, who happened to visit Rommel the next day.

2   Ruge erroneously reported him as commanding the V Corps.

3   *Oberste Heeresleitung.* The German General Staff and later Supreme Army Command. See Glossary.

4   Geyer was certainly no favorite of Adolf Hitler. He was one of a few scores of generals blacklisted in back in October 1938 as being unreliable, a member of a sweeping list that had included Generals Ludwig Beck and Gerd von Rundstedt.

5   On April 10, 1946, less than a year after the war ended, General Geyer, despondent over the fate of Germany in the war, and guilt-ridden that he had not done enough to resist Hitler, committed suicide by drowning in Wildsee Lake near his home.

6   *Feldwebel* Albert Böttcher, Rommel's longtime secretary. This must have been just a temporaray arrangement, because Rommel will later refer to his "two dogs" again.

Thursday, January 27

Generalfeldmarschall von Rundstedt continues his leave at the spa in Bad Tölz.

***

Rommel remains at Fontainebleau today. His lumbago is giving him problems again, and anyway, he wants to catch up on some paperwork. This includes documenting the latest finds from his inspection in Northwest France.

Besides, he has another problem today. None other than Baron Geyr von Schweppenburg will be coming to visit today. The baron commands Panzergruppe West.

Geyr and von Rundstedt share a number of similarities—background, training, tastes, and most importantly, their theories on the role of armor during an invasion. This partly explains why the old man selected Geyr for his command position. Despite the fact that OB West thinks him a capable leader, the feeling is not mutual. Geyr feels that von Rundstedt has not kept up with the latest developments in modern, mobile warfare, and that despite his critical role in the early *blitzkrieg* theories, he knows less about panzer tactics than most of the younger generals. Geyr considers him an armchair strategist, the last of a dying breed; an infantry dinosaur in a modern, *blitzkrieg* world. The old man, in his opinion, belongs at home.

Nor does Geyr have any respect for Blumentritt, his chief of staff. The man in his view does not have the qualifications or demeanor for his post.

And Rommel? To Geyr, he is an upstart; a johnny-come-lately who, while admittedly having learned the fundamentals of tactical mobility, nevertheless has had no real training in strategic warfare. He had been far luckier than he should have been in North Africa. And Geyr considers him socially just a commoner: Rommel's father had, after all, only been a schoolteacher.[1]

Geyr of course is a strong panzer warfare advocate and colleague of *Generaloberst* Guderian's, having joined the panzer forces in 1937. Having commanded a number of panzer units in France and Russia, he holds the Knight's Cross. He thinks he knew it all, and is prepared to advocate his principles.

He and Rommel have already met once, a brief meeting on January 8. Now, having talked to Jodl at OKW a week ago, Geyr is ready to restate and insist upon his theories.

Geyr enters Rommel's study, and after pleasantries, they get serious. As expected, he and Rommel disagree over the positioning of the panzer divisions. Rommel is already tired of playing this game, having gone a few rounds with von Rundstedt and OKW. The baron, reinforced in his view by OKW, von Rundstedt, and Guderian, insists that the panzers be kept inland, strategically located, ready to strike en masse. Rommel agrees that they should be ready to hit hard and fast, but should be near the coast where they can engage without delay.

Geyr disagrees, pointing out his experience. Rommel counters that he has some too. And yet, experience means little in the face of the technologically advanced Western Allies, with their command of the Channel, their massive air fleets and their modern equipment.

Geyr accuses him of reducing the role of the panzers to semi-mobile artillery. Rommel replies that the danger will not come from swift-moving armor but from masses of infantry moving right off the beaches. He adds that once the enemy gets firmly ashore, there will be no getting rid of them. He cites Salerno and Anzio.

After the meeting, Rommel is perturbed by the encounter. So he drives up to Paris and goes to OB West's staff quarters (von Rundstedt is still on leave). There he talks with von Rundstedt's staff members about the panzer problem. They agree with Rommel that the tanks must hit fast, but support Geyr's general position. Rommel leaves, somewhat frustrated. He is running up against too many brick walls.

---

1   Later, when Rommel got another chief of staff (Hans Speidel), Geyr would dislike him too, claiming that the man has never "commanded anything larger than an infantry company."

Friday, January 28

General Jodl at OKW in the Wolf's Lair is busy worrying about a massive Soviet pincer attack on the Eighth Army at Cherkassy. But his report on his inspection of the West earlier this month has just gone out. On the whole, it supports von Rundstedt's theories but is not flattering to the old man himself, currently on leave at Bad Tölz.

The basis of the report is the level of unpreparedness along the coast, followed up by the premise that there are two strategies on how to deal with the invasion. He covers Rommel's hold-them-at-the-beaches position, and outlines Rommel's experiences with the Afrika Korps and Italy. Rommel's line is, "Don't let them get ashore." Von Rundstedt's on the other hand is, "Hey, let them come."

Jodl then states von Rundstedt's position: that the coast is too long to adequately defend every mile—which is plainly obvious—and that the enemy, with their formidable command of the air and the sea, can concentrate wherever they want and penetrate at any point, no matter what type of defenses are up. The answer then, in the old Prussian's opinion, is to put out along the coast a few dozen static divisions to slow the enemy up, and then hit them with a powerful, mobile, strategic reserve force when they began to advance inland. If that does not work, they will just have to defeat the enemy units in the French interior itself.

Jodl writes that, based upon what he has seen, von Rundstedt is right in one respect: the coast cannot at present be held. However, Jodl also writes that he somewhat agrees with Rommel's theory of hitting the enemy on the beaches (especially since the Führer still favors this strategy). On the other hand, Jodl also states that von Rundstedt's concept of a strategic reserve, centered somewhere around Paris, is a sound one. He adds that OKW is not going to sanction the placement of reserves on the coast because of the "general situation."

On matters of preparation though, the report digs hard at OB West. The rich, soft Parisian lifestyle, Jodl feels, has decayed their fighting ability. He writes in his report with chilly distaste:

> The C-in-C West would do well to exchange his Hotel Georges V for a command post where he can see the blue sky—where the sun shines, and which smells fresher.

And he does not stop there in his derision.

> Lower headquarters and officers' accommodations are a danger not only to security but also to inner attitudes and alertness. The bloom of war is completely missing. Deep armchairs and carpet lead to royal household allures.
>
> As of March 1, all staffs are to move into their command posts. Unfortunately, these too have largely been built next door to fine châteaux.

Jodl has certainly not pulled any punches. And he is not making his point out of envy. No, the officers here are not thinking like warriors—rather, like relaxed gentlemen who are getting ready to go out on the town.

Hitler believes in Rommel's hit-them-at-the-beaches strategy, but is sufficiently persuaded by Jodl's report to let Panzergruppe West continue to exist.

***

Tonight, after a few weeks of reorganizing and replenishment, some 26 aircraft undertake another *Steinbock* air raid against England. Results are paltry. Clearly, the offensive is not having any measurable effect against the enemy. Wisely, General Pelz, commanding the IX Air Corps, suspends the raids again for a few days to regroup.

After over nearly three and a half years of war with England, the Germans have still not learned the lessons of the Battle of Britain.

Saturday, January 29

Despite another bout of lumbago, Rommel rides out to inspect the 84th Corps sector, including the coastline from the Seine Bay west to the Channel Islands, formerly owned by the British. He especially wants to check out that one section of beach west of the Orne River that Pemsel briefed him on a week ago.[1]

The corps is commanded by cantankerous *General der Artillerie* Erich Marcks. Rommel finds the 52-year-old fellow to be a tough but straight bird with a solid army background, and a highly competent strategist.[2] A sharp tactician, he is a product of the old, pre-Nazi officer cadre. Despite his competence in the *Generalstab* though, the Nazis have never really favored him, mainly because of something in his political past.[3]

Marcks is optimistic about being able to turn back the enemy, even though he is responsible for a large area of the coastline. His confidence is surprising to the inspecting group. Rommel though, has a decidedly different feeling about the defenses here, and chides Marcks for his sanguinity. If the invasion comes here, he will find his defenses woefully inadequate.

Marcks points out that he must cover the Seine Bay from the Orne River westward, along the eastern shore of the Cotentin peninsula, through the strategic port of Cherbourg, down the western coast of the peninsula, and lastly, the Channel Islands. This amounts to some 400km of coast, and to cover this long stretch, Marcks has only five divisions.

One of these is the 319th Infantry Division.[4] Though it has been weakened as a fighting unit by experienced men being transferred out into combat divisions, especially those at or bound for the fighting fronts, it is still a capable unit. However, because of its location, it might just as well be stricken from the list of available units in the West. OKW has placed the entire division offshore, way out on the Channel Islands of Guernsey and Jersey, dozens of kilometers west of the Cherbourg peninsula. Although these islands are of little military value outside of protecting coastal traffic around Brittany, their occupation nevertheless carries a significant psychological weight for Hitler, since they are basically the only portions of original British territory that the Reich still controls.

The 319th Infantry is jokingly referred to by the *Feldgrau* on the mainland as the "*die Kanadadivision.*" This is partly because it was felt by most that as soon as the invasion began, the unit would be isolated. It would only be a matter of time before they all became POWs, which were known to get shipped off to Canada. Anyway, it was joked, it might just as well be over there, for all the good that it would do against the enemy landing.[5]

Covering some 90km of coast from the Orne River to the Vire is the second-rate 716th Infantry Division.[6] Commonly classified as a *bodenständig*[7] division, it lacks any type of transport and is made up of second- or third-rate troops. Looking over the maps, Rommel expresses concern that the 716th lacks so much transport and equipment, and yet is stretched across a really vital sector. This beach area obviously must be strengthened.

All around the top of the Cotentin peninsula and situated westward down the coast is the 709th Infantry Division.[8] Including the critically important port of Cherbourg, it presently defends an incredible total of 220km of front line, about thirty times the normal frontage for a division.[9] Rommel tells Marcks that the Allies have plenty of small vessels for supplies. "They won't need to depend upon seizing any large ports immediately."

Sitting in reserve is the 243rd Infantry Division.[10] The static 243rd's regiments only have two battalions, with very limited transport. One regiment uses horses to move its supplies, and another has to rely on bicycles.

The recently created 352nd is actually a composite of other units, survivors of the Eastern Front.[11] Marcks points out the liability of the very limited transport for both divisions, although the 352nd is much better equipped. Unfortunately, the 352nd is slated to relocate to the Eastern Front as soon as it becomes combat ready. The 352nd's sister division, the 353rd, is stationed in Brittany.

Marcks and the field marshal continue a satisfying discussion. Rommel explains his defense plans for this area and Marcks, staggered by the size of the undertaking, still agrees to somehow get it done.

They finally part. Rommel continues with his inspection, and Marcks goes back to his headquarters at St. Lô to prepare their quarters for the evening. His emotions about Rommel are mixed.

The rest of the day is filled with brief stops and quick reports. Some vessels spotted near the Gironde River turn out to be a bunch of fishing boats.

That evening, Rommel returns to St. Lô as planned and dines with Marcks. His chief of staff, *Oberstleutnant* Rudolf von Oppen, a middle-aged Austrian, gives them a number of interesting facts about military and naval history.

Later, Rommel retires to write to Lucie and update her on the war:

> *The situation in the East is still very tense and serious, although we are shooting up masses of enemy tanks; 860 in the last three days, which they'll have a job to replace.*
>
> *The situation in Italy has developed as I always feared it would. The open, unprotected flanks were a great danger. However, I feel certain that we'll manage to restore the situation.*
>
> *I'm having a new coat made in Paris. My old one is too tight and too thin...*

---

1 This is the first time the field marshal would visit the future invasion site.

2 *General der Artillerie* Erich Marcks had taken an active part in the invasion of France of 1940, and his swift capture of the Seine River bridges on June 13th had prevented them (and subsequently parts of Paris) from having to be shelled. In late 1940, Marcks came up with the original master plan for invading Russia. He had later helped spearhead the Russian invasion on June 22, 1941, only to be severely wounded just four days later. He lost his right leg and suffered some head injuries, especially to his eyes. After he recovered and was fitted with a prosthesis, he was reassigned

to command the 337th Infantry Division in France. He was appointed commander of the 84th Infantry Corps in August of 1943.

3   Marcks had made the political mistake of being Press Officer to General Kurt von Schleicher, elected Chancellor of Germany in 1932. Unfortunately, von Schleicher's radical views on sweeping social reform had quickly become unpopular with everyone. He was especially hated by the National Socialist Party, which he repeatedly attacked politically. When his reforms irrevocably lost the backing that they desperately needed to pass, he became a political outcast. With no chance of getting any cooperation from any other government members, von Schleicher was forced to resign. As fate would have it, in the next election, Hitler was appointed to succeed him, and being one to carry a grudge, he never forgot his political enemy and by association, his underlings.

Eventually, von Schleicher was murdered by Hitler's SS henchmen during the Blood Purge of June 20, 1934. Because of Marcks' association with von Schleicher, he was thereafter looked upon by the Nazi party with suspicion. Although no one could doubt Marcks' capabilities as a unit commander, his past had kept him from getting an army command, something that Marcks never forgave.

4   Fifty-three-year-old *Generalleutnant* Rudolf Graf von Schmettow, commanding. Recently promoted that month, he had been appointed Military Governor of the Channel Islands back in September of 1940. In June of 1941, Erich Muller replaced him, and von Schmettow took over command of the 319th.

5   Von Rundstedt, hard-pressed to find more men for his units, suggested to the Kriegsmarine on March 14, 1943, that army personnel manning the batteries on the Channel Islands be replaced with naval personnel. This would free up several hundred men for units in Normandy and Brittany. Naturally, the navy did not relish the idea. Sending sailors so far off the coast, isolated, under army command, was against their instincts. Besides, those men freed up would probably be factored into the slow drain of army personnel to the Eastern Front. So the navy rejected the idea three days later, their excuse being that the navy did not have the men available for such a task.

6   Generalmajor Richter, commanding.

7   "Static" or "defensive" division. See Glossary.

8   *Generalmajor* Karl-Wilhelm von Schlieben, commanding.

9   A good rule of thumb by 1943 was that a front of ten to eleven kilometers was about as much as a normal infantry division could handle. (In comparison, the average frontage for a German corps on the Eastern Front was about 52.3km, about 17.2km per division). The average front coastal divisions in the Fifteenth Army were about 80km. For the Seventh Army, it was an implausible 193km. General Schlieben's 709th Division alone was covering some 65km of coastline. And then there was the entire Atlantic coast to worry about—some 350km for each division.

10 Commanded by 54-year-old *Generalleutnant* Heinz Hellmich. He commanded the 23rd Infantry Division in Poland at the outbreak of the war, which in 1941 became a part of *Barbarossa's* Army Group Center. He was reassigned at the beginning of 1942 when the division was converted into the 26th Panzer Division. Hellmich was given the 243rd at the end of 1944.

11 The 352nd was formed in late 1943 from the cadres of three other units: the 268th Infantry Division, which had fought hard in the East at Cholm and Demyansk; the 321st Infantry Division, which had been ravaged and decimated at Kursk that summer; and the 546th Grenadier Regiment (of the 389th Infantry Division), a rare partial survivor of Stalingrad. The 546th would be the cadre for the 1st and 2nd battalions of the 352nd's 916th Grenadier Regiment. The surviving units were redesignated the 352nd Infantry Division on November 5, 1943.

Sunday, January 30

Generalfeldmarschall Rommel, having spent the night in St. Lô, is up early. He bids goodbye to General Marcks at 8 a.m. and departs to continue his inspection. Today it will be the Cotentin peninsula. He starts at the wide mouth of the Vire River, intending to go up the coast.

The entourage meets the commanding officer of the 709th Division,[1] *Generalmajor* Karl von Schlieben, who was given the division last month.[2] Von Schlieben reports on his division's positions, and Rommel outlines his plans to create an intricate maze of barriers.

The inspection group continues up the coast, running into heavy patches of fog here and there. The ride is bumpy since the roads in this area are bad. They reach Quineville just after low tide. Rommel, gazing out over the wet beaches, spots just offshore a small group of obstacles off in the distance and asks about them. A lieutenant tells him that the obstacles had been out there for a while now, part of a defensive barrier experiment started some two and a half years ago. Rommel immediately marches out to examine them.

Slogging into the low waves, he spies four stakes set in concrete. Three are still effective. Rommel smiles and shows them to his approaching staff. Clearly, offshore obstacles planted even last year would still be effective when the invasion comes.

On the other hand, not too much work has been done in this area, except for some limited flooding. There are not many defensive points in the area, other than a 155mm army battery at Morsalines. The massive naval battery at St. Marcouf is still unfinished.[3]

The inspection party is joined by Admiral Hennecke, who had been detained by the fog,[4] and they continue on, eventually getting to the critical port of Cherbourg, where they have a late lunch at the soldiers' mess hall. They listen to the report of the fortress commandant and inspect the port in the haze, noting several problems. Then they continue westward along the top of the Cotentin peninsula and then down the western coast.

Late in the day, they finally turn around and head back to St. Lô to again quarter for the night with Marcks' staff. Admiral Ruge leaves them to have dinner with Admiral Hennecke in his quarters at Tourlaville, southeast of Cherbourg, and to confer with him on harbor defenses.

Because Rommel has cancelled tomorrow's planned inspection of Mont-St.-Michel, Admiral Ruge separates from the entourage and drives to Admiral Hennecke's headquarters at Tourlaville, the eastern suburb of Cherbourg. There they confer about naval matters including mines and how to make large ports unserviceable if they are about to fall into enemy hands.

Rommel's own entourage though is somewhat upset over tomorrow's schedule. The field marshal has once again crossed the famed Mont-St.-Michel off their itinerary. Shaking their heads, they grumble about how it is so typical of him to pass up famous tourist points in his inspection trips. Months ago, they had done the same thing in Pisa, Italy. They had driven straight through without stopping to admire the world-famous leaning tower.

"How long has the tower been leaning already?" Rommel had asked gruffly. Someone had answered, "Over 150 years."

"Then drive on," he had growled. "It'll still be leaning when the war is over."

***

In a small ceremony at the *Wolfsschanze,* Alfred Jodl is promoted from *General der Artillerie* to *Generaloberst.* Later that evening, Hitler in his quarters sends for him. Standing, Hitler tells him with a smile that he forgives him for his insolence back on September 7, 1942 over List and the Caucasus.[5] The Führer tells him that although he still believes Jodl was wrong on his assessment of the proposed airborne landing, he considers Jodl a competent man and he has come to appreciate his excellent qualities as an officer.

Then in a sort of reconciliation, Hitler presents Jodl with a golden Nazi party badge of honor. Jodl eventually leaves the quarters grateful but wary, his faith in the Führer's sense of justice still low.

He will later decide that his principles cannot be compromised, and that he will still speak out whenever the Führer wrongs any senior officer.[6]

---

1   The 18th Panzer Division, devastated at Kursk, was deactivated in early September, and its components were sent to Lithuania. There they were eventually reorganized into the 18th Artillery Division.

2   Like nearly all German generals, 49-year-old *Generalmajor* Karl-Wilhelm von Schlieben entered the army at the outbreak of the World War I and served with distinction. When World War II began, he was an adjutant in the XIII Military District. During the early part of the war, he commanded the 108th Rifle Regiment and then the 4th Rifle Brigade. Then in mid-May 1943, he was given command of the 18th Panzer Division for the battle of Kursk. In September, he was relieved of his command and placed in the Führer Reserve.

    Samuel Mitcham in his book *The Desert Fox in Normandy* concludes that von Schlieben must have been wounded, since the period of his absence (September 7 to sometime in December) was too long for any leave. It is possible though, that he was also relieved for other reasons, because the 18th Panzer Division, having suffered heavily in the battle, was disbanded at the end of that September, and its units were used to create the 18th Artillery Regiment and the 504th Panzer Battalion.

3   The St. Marcouf battery consisted of four 210mm Skoda K52 Czech guns. These pieces would have a range of some 33km and a field of fire of 120 degrees. For air protection, a battery of six French 75mm anti-aircraft guns and some 20mm anti-aircraft guns would be added. A dozen machine-gun nests would cover them from any airborne assault.

4   Konteradmiral Walther Hennecke, the naval commandant for the peninsula.

5   See Prelude.

6   According to a handwritten document written by Jodl, Office of US Chief of Counsel for the Prosecution of Nazi Criminality, Interrogation Division.

Monday, January 31

In Normandy, there is another morning fog, particularly dense in some areas. At the 84th Corps headquarters in St. Lô, *Generalfeldmarschall* Rommel takes his leave of General Marcks and begins his trip back to his own headquarters at Fontainebleau. Admiral Ruge, separated from the entourage, continues on with his own inspection, starting around the mouth of the Vire River. The weather soon clears, and a hint of spring seems to be in the air.

That evening in Fontainebleau, during a pleasant dinner, Rommel once again states his objections to the idea of knocking down important bunkers just to clear fields of fire. From there, the dinner party goes on to talk of naval traditions in general.

After the meal, they discuss the subject of flares and tracer ammunition before they head off to the designated cinema room, where that night's movie is to be shown.

Checking his mail, Rommel is happy to find correspondence from his 15-year-old son. Manfred, now in the Luftwaffe auxiliary forces, has written the field marshal a letter. Tonight Rommel replies:

> Dear Manfred:
>
> I was particularly pleased with your first letter as Luftwaffe auxiliary, because you have settled in so well to your new conditions. It is not easy for an "only child" to leave home. Perhaps you'll be getting a few days' leave in February, and then you must give us a full report.
>
> There's still an endless amount of work here before I'll be able to say that we're properly prepared for battle. People get lazy and self-satisfied when things are quiet. But the contrast between quiet times and battle will be tough and I feel it essential to prepare for hard times here.
>
> I'm out on the move a lot and raising plenty of dust wherever I go.
>
> All the best to you and warmest greetings,
>
> Your Father

February 1944

Tuesday, February 1

Generalfeldmarschall von Rundstedt is still on leave at the spa in Bad Tölz. While he is away, his villa and command bunker complex are undergoing changes.

Normally, von Rundstedt only stays at the Hôtel Georges V in Paris in the winter, since it offers maximum comfort in the freezing months for his staff at a low cost. Personally though, von Rundstedt has often found living in the crowded Parisian capital to be distasteful. Once he had grumbled that Paris was, "a dirty hole," and that it was, "atrocious, especially during the holidays." So when he was first appointed OB West in the spring of 1941 he had moved his headquarters from Paris to the Pavillon Henri IV in the suburb of St.-Germain-en-Laye.[1] He loves this picturesque western Parisian suburb, where his father had once taken temporary residence back in 1870.

Back in the spring of 1942, a few stray bombs from an RAF air raid had landed aoround his quarters in St.-Germain. When Hitler was told of the air raid, to protect his field marshal, he had ordered a bunker complex to be built for his strategic headquarters command. So von Rundstedt and his staff had chosen a beautiful, discreet, secluded location nearby. The picturesque area included a rolling hill, a nice terrace, a breathtaking little forest, a nearby castle, and several large villas, all which could be requisitioned if necessary for the headquarters staff.[2]

On an old limestone quarry below a hillcrest, at 20–24 Boulevard Victor Hugo, OT laborers divided into three 400-man teams had started working in shifts around the clock for seven months to build a three-floor concrete command bunker. The solid, thick concrete structure was finished in late 1943.[3]

The bunker normally holds over a hundred people, although it can accommodate up to three times that number. Staff members include various administrative and communications personnel, including a number of *Kriegshelferinnen*.[4] All in all, it is an excellent and safe location for the strategic staff charged with overseeing the defense of Western Europe.

Near the bunker has been built a communications center. For air protection, the surrounding area includes a number of anti-aircraft positions, as well as several fire stations. The nearby girls' school had to be partially requisitioned by headquarters for additional personnel to work in the command blockhouse down the hill. Half of the school is now a garrison for German troops, and the mixing of German uniforms and girls in pink overalls around the buildings evokes concern from the locals. Other staff members have quarters in homes on the Rue Thiers and the Rue de Lorraine.

Von Rundstedt's personal quarters are in the Villa David, located behind the girls' école at No. 28 Rue Alexandre Dumas: a petite three-storey, twelve-room villa on a well-landscaped half-acre lot. It sits atop the gentle hill in which the block headquarters building, some 300 yards away, is partially buried. Blumentritt lives with him in the villa.

The field marshal usually works at the villa. He avoids going down to the blockhouse unless there is a pressing situation, conference, or whenever he has to use the communications complex to make a long-distance phone call.

Whenever he does go to the command bunker, he leaves his villa through the back door. He walks across the roomy courtyard, heading for the gate in the railed fence. Next to that back gate is his modest rose garden, tended for him by his gardener, M. Ernest Gavoury.[5] The old servant faithfully tends to all flowers there, and von Rundstedt, who loves gardening, spends many hours of his spare time talking to the old Frenchman and fussing with his roses.

With the field marshal now on leave, the complex is getting expanded, with several more rooms and offices being added to the basement of the command bunker, expanding it to 40 rooms. At the same time, the nearby communications network is being improved. About a dozen 5cm-thick, heavily insulated copper telephone cables now connect the headquarters with Berlin and the Berghof. There are also several other communication cables for teletype and other landline communication links. These lines will eventually connect directly to other commands in Europe, including those of the Luftwaffe and the Kriegsmarine.

Rooms in his nearby villa are also being improved upon or added to in the field marshal's absence. Some of them he will enjoy; some of them he will not.

Take the bomb shelters, for instance.

There had been no protective cellar for him in case of an air raid. Blumentritt, living with him in the villa, was understandably concerned. He had pointed out to the field marshal more than once that a single bomb could take out their entire house. There was little anti-aircraft defense in St.-Germain—a couple of light batteries, manned by the headquarters security unit.

The field marshal though, had totally dismissed the idea of a bomb shelter. He did not want any ugly concrete structure in his backyard, his villa, his garden, or anywhere else nearby. It would just ruin his view. Whenever anybody ventured a comment that he needed SOME sort of air protection, he would growl back, "One can be killed just as comfortably in bed as in the cellar." Besides, bombing the surrounding residential area would be tantamount to bombing Paris itself, which he believed would not go over well with the French, either in occupied Europe or exiled in England.

Surprisingly, the people around town had supported his presence in the area, and he had quite relished that. And because of him, they did not fear air raids. "Our best anti-aircraft protection is Field Marshal von Rundstedt," was a popular phrase of the local folks.

Once as he was walking in the alley behind the park, the air raid sirens had begun. He of course had no interest in going to a shelter but was surprised to see an older housewife out on the street as well. As she calmly walked past him, a shopping basket on her arm, he asked her, "*Mais Madame, vous n'avez pas peur des bombes?*"

She looked at him calmly and replied, "*Pourquoi aurais-je peur, mon maréchal? Ils ne bombarderont pas St.-Germain. Il n'y a aucun objectif militaire ici, et rien ne se passe jamais.*"[6]

Eventually though, the problem of his lack of protection had also come to the attention of the Führer. In response, he had ordered Blumentritt (through Jodl) to see to it that a bomb shelter was built immediately. The chief of staff knew the old man would strongly oppose the idea, and he could be quite cantankerous and obstinate at times. He would most strenuously object, no matter how high the orders originated. And he would raise all kinds of hell when construction began. So, to carry out the Führer's orders and yet not incur the field marshal's renowned wrath, Blumentritt concluded that subterfuge was necessary. He had therefore conspired with the *Organization Todt* to design and then execute the entire project in secret.

The plans were covertly finished in mid-1943, just before von Rundstedt had gone on leave. When he departed for his favorite spa at Bad Tölz, the project had immediately started, and the air raid shelter had been completed in the villa's basement in his absence.

Upon his return, the irate field marshal had reluctantly accepted this *fait accompli*, although he swore that he would never go into the *verdammte* thing. Unfortunately, construction of this sheltered basement had not been enough to satisfy Hitler. He ordered that another, larger, more fortified shelter be built, with specific instructions that this one be outdoors, located, of all places, next to von Rundstedt's beautiful garden. No one could object to the Führer, so reluctantly, the same planning technique had been implemented. Now that the field marshal has again gone on leave, the second shelter is being built.

***

Rommel spends his early morning going over paperwork and has a couple meetings to analyze the observations of his last inspection tour.

In the meantime, his army group staff finishes a directive on how to sabotage the ports and make them unusable by the Allies. Another directive is written on how to defend St. Malo Bay. The two documents instruct the Kriegsmarine to use what few patrol boats they have left to cover critical areas between radar sites. A letter is drafted for Rommel to sign, thanking Admiral Wurmbach[7] for immediately undertaking Rommel's recommendations.[8]

That morning, the field marshal goes to Paris to the Hôtel Georges V and has another talk with Günther Blumentritt in von Rundstedt's absence. Afterward, he has a little free time, so he stops off to buy himself a sharp new black leather topcoat and a brown woolen one. Then he returns to Fontainebleau. When he arrives there, he is annoyed to find out that the already-scheduled meeting on implementing minefields had been delayed until his return.

Later that afternoon, Rommel meets with *Oberst* Höffner of the Army's *Generalstab* and a civilian representative of the French railroad. They discuss problems of transporting supplies.

---

1   About 17km northwest of the capital.

2   Eventually, some 500 homes in St.-Germain were used by the Germans.

3   For more detail on the headquarters complex, see Appendix B, page 598.

4   German female army volunteers. The French nicknamed them *souris grises* ("grey mice").

5   Gavoury, then 59 years old, had been the gardener for the villa's owner, M. Randon. When the Germans requisitioned the residence in 1942, von Rundstedt allowed Gavoury to stay on to tend the garden.

6   "Why would I be afraid, Field Marshal? They won't bomb St.-Germain. There's no military target here, and nothing ever happens here."

7   Fifty-two-year-old *Vizeadmiral* Hans-Heinrich Wurmbach, commanding the naval forces in Denmark.

8   Admiral Ruge also records that on this day, a package of maps was delivered from the 191st Infantry Division. The 191st was part of the 33 Infantry Corps, stationed in occupied Norway.

Wednesday, February 2

The weather at Fontainebleau is nice today. Rommel spends most of the day tackling paperwork, making phone calls, and undertaking a number of meetings to set policy.

No expense is to be spared to get the Atlantic Wall strengthened. Although Rommel does not think highly of them, he has started to actively enlist the aid of the French, Belgian, and Dutch peasants. They in turn seem to be cooperative in helping his men construct the coastal defenses.

He makes sure that his staff and senior unit commanders understand that all civilian assistance is strictly voluntary. He realizes that those working for them are probably not collaborators. He is not deluded on that point. He knows the feelings of the general population regarding the occupation of France. No, they assist him for three reasons.

First, no matter what the civilians personally think about their work, he pays them very good wages and provides their meals while on the job. Second, he insists and ensures that they are treated fairly and honestly. He never lets them get harshly punished or inconvenienced. Third and most importantly, he finds it easy to convince them that the stronger the defenses are in their area, the more likely the Allied invasion will come somewhere else and not ruin their own land. It will be a matter of letting some other Frenchman suffer. "Let the invasion come, but not in my backyard," becomes a common expression.

So the men help with the beach obstacles, while the women fashion rush matting for sand traps, or help put up wooden stakes to snag gliders in the fields just behind the beaches. It is rough labor, especially constructing the obstacles out in the surf, with the wintery waves of seawater often crashing down upon the workers. At times their work is frustrated by the weather, either slowing down their progress, or even worse, undoing some of what they have constructed. More work is created if a two-day storm overturns several obstacles. Often a number of stakes get pulled up by the swells, dragged to shore by the crashing breakers, and rolled up onto the cold beaches.

Now that he has the authority, Rommel orders all the dikes in Holland opened. This floods thousands of acres of farmland with the cold, salty waters of the Atlantic. These surges cause considerable damage to arable lands, destruction that will take several years to undo.

Despite this draconian measure, he is pleasantly surprised to find that the local Dutch folk remain remarkably calm. They discover, just as their counterparts in France have done, that these actions make the invasion much less likely to occur in their area. So they have a better chance of preserving their homes and towns from the ravages of war,[1] while not actually thwarting the Allied war effort. And besides, it would be useless—no, dangerous—for them to resist his edicts.

That afternoon, just for relaxation, Rommel and a couple of his officers go out on an "armed promenade"—a combination of a walk in the woods and a leisure hunt. There are a number of rabbits and small wild boar in the area, and they would make for a nice meal.

During this time, they casually talk over some current items. The conversation is the only fruitful result of the hunt.

***

Today, Seventh Army commander Friedrich Dollmann and his staff celebrate his 62nd birthday.

It will be his last.

---

1   Only too true. By the end of the battle for Normandy, both Caen and St. Lô would be almost totally shattered.

Thursday, February 3

The weather at Fontainebleau is lovely. *Generalfeldmarschall* Rommel, along with his chief engineer and naval advisor, is off again to inspect the Fifteenth Army. Reaching the Channel, they drive northeastward, up towards the Pas-de-Calais. Along the coast, some 8km south of Boulogne, they stop to examine some experimental obstacles put in at the water's edge.

Rommel is pleased to find that the innovative troops there have found a way to make their work much easier. They are efficiently installing the stakes of offshore obstacles at low tide with high-water pressure using fire engine hoses, instead of with a clumsy pile-driver. This, he is told, knocks installation time from 45 minutes down to three or four. The officer in charge complains though, that that the hoses are "ancient," and the high pressure causes them to frequently burst. Rommel promises to see what he can do.

They continue north, and are joined by the commander of 82nd Corps, General Sinnhuber.[1] They survey a number of sites between Boulogne, Calais, and Wissant. They inspect some flat areas where flooding has just been started, to see the effects. Rommel is told that the corps can produce some 300–400 mines a day. The SS units in the area are helping to lay the minefields.

As sunset draws near, Rommel takes over the officers' mess hall in Calais. There he has a talk with the local senior officers and his own group about the day's results and what he expects.

That evening, he invites *Konteradmiral* Frisius, the local naval commander, and newly appointed 47th Infantry Division commander *Generalleutnant* Otto Elfelt to dinner. Rommel likes the two, and the dinner generally is satisfactory.

There is, though, one sore spot to the evening. The new appointee—perhaps in tribute to the field marshal, who is renowned for his makeshift command changes in the field—later remarks that he has no stomach for paperwork, and that it is in his mind a waste of time. Among other things, he will not want to take the time to send *Heeresgruppe B* maps and plans for the installation of his defensive measures in the area.

Rommel glares at him, and in an abrupt tone, sets the man straight right away. As a soldier, he does not cherish paperwork either, but he is not going to be kept in the dark on what his units are doing. Elfelt, chastened, agrees to comply.

Later that night, the field marshal writes to Lucie about his new coat:

> *I bought myself a leather overcoat and a woolen one. Please be so kind and send a check for 350.50 marks to the Verkaufsabteilung der Luftwaffe.[2] Berlin Postal Check account No. 169187, and 157.85 marks to the Heereskleiderkasse.[3] account No. 3522. Both coats are very nice, and I hope I won't get any more Hexenschuss.[4]*

***

Tonight, 280 aircraft fly another *Steinbock* air raid. Bombs are dropped all over the English countryside. Seventeen aircraft are lost, mostly over the Channel. Göring in response orders the raids hereafter to be conducted on moonlit nights, so that aircrews can better navigate. Pelz objects, pointing out that the bombers would be easier to spot and be shot down.

---

1 Fifty-seven-year-old *General der Artillerie* Johann Sinnhuber, who took command of the corps on July 10, 1943. He survived the war and died on October 23, 1974.
2 A type of commissary where Luftwaffe officers could purchase clothing articles.
3 The army commissary.
4 Lit. "witch's shot." A colorful term for neuralgic pains in the back and the shoulders (his lumbago).

Friday, February 4

At 8 a.m., Rommel has finished breakfast and is ready to start the day. The Calais port commander gives him a briefing on the port's defenses. Then Rommel and his entourage, complete with photographers and reporters, leave to inspect them.

They come across one company working on defenses at an unused airfield some 5km from the coast. To him, that is too far from the beaches, and he orders them to work on positions along the shoreline.

The inspection party then drops in on newly appointed General Elfelt's 47th Infantry Division, and finds out that the new CO is out meeting the troops. The good news is that the unit is heavily involved in mine installation. The bad news is that they have not as yet received any orders or instructions on creating offshore obstacles. Rommel corrects this at once, issuing orders right there.

He then immediately leaves and goes east-southeast to Tourcoing, the Fifteenth Army headquarters. There he confers with von Salmuth, no doubt partly about how orders to construct offshore obstacles have not as yet reached some units. They talk privately again, but this time, no one hears any yelling coming from behind the closed door.

On the way back to his headquarters, Rommel (in front next to Daniel, the driver), Meise, and Ruge discuss the problems they have seen with constructing the obstacles and the minelaying. They go on to talk about other things, and Rommel relates to the others a story that took place in the late 1930s. Just an *Oberstleutnant* at that time, he had arranged a meeting between the Minister of Education and the leader of the Hitler Youth. He had wanted to make sure that the schools did not become a battleground between the teachers and the youth leaders. His efforts on this occasion, he recalled, had failed.[1]

***

Today, General Erich Marcks in Normandy writes home to his wife. In the letter, the corps commander tells her about the impression the new army group commander has made upon him:

> *Rommel is the same age as me but looks older, perhaps because Africa and its many trials have left their mark on him. He told me a lot about Africa and Italy. My impression is that although he's very blunt and earnest, he's not just a flash in the pan, but a real general. It's a good thing that A H [Adolf Hitler] holds him in high esteem despite all his outspokenness, and gives him these important jobs.*

---

1   In February of 1937, Rommel was appointed the War Ministry's special liaison officer to Baldur von Schirach, the leader of the Hitler Youth. Rommel's job was to introduce some military training to the boys. The son of a schoolteacher, he perhaps took his job a bit too seriously, and Schirach, 11 years younger and more Westernized, developed a dislike of him. A year or so later, Rommel was transferred to commanding the officer candidate school in Wiener Neustadt, Austria.

Saturday, February 5

Generalfeldmarschall Rommel spends the first part of his day catching up on paperwork. Good news from Supreme Headquarters: he has been granted permission to keep the newly formed 352nd Infantry Division in France, instead of letting it get carted off to Russia. Rommel will assign it to Marcks' sector. In addition, he will petition OKW to let him move the division directly to the coastline, and not sit inland as a reserve unit.

Good news indeed, but there are so many other problems. The current lack of mines to lay weighs heavily on his mind. So he takes some time to travel upriver to Paris and call on General Blumentritt, von Rundstedt's chief of staff. Rommel talks to him about the mine shortage. The OB West chief promises to bring the subject up to his superior when he returns from leave.

Rommel returns to his headquarters and begins another report. He writes that the work along the beaches has progressed and the coast is beginning to take on the semblance of a defensive line.

Obstacles of many different shapes and sizes are beginning to go up everywhere along the waterline. They are of course, positioned to snag landing craft at various stages between high tide and half tide, although his scheme will eventually cover low-tide landings as well.

His master defense plan details a series of four underwater obstacle belts. The first set will be optimally effective in two meters of water during high tide. On the other hand, it will also be the most exposed at low tide. The second obstacle belt will work best in four meters of water and around half tide. The other two belts will work optimally in a low-tide period—one in four meters of water, and the other one in two.

Rommel has ordered his units to complete the high-tide and half-tide belts before proceeding to the low-tide belts. This reasoning, to him, is sound. The invasion will probably come before they are finished with the four belts, most likely in the spring. If it does, and the enemy lands at high tide as he figures they will, he is covered. If they land at half tide, that belt will be effective.

If for some crazy reason the Allies decide to land at low tide before those two belts can be finished, the lack of effective underwater obstacles will be balanced by the prospect of the enemy coming ashore being exposed to defensive fire for longer. They will have to charge over a much greater distance of beach, in the open, and quite vulnerable.

This longer time will give his men on the bluffs a far better opportunity to chew up the incoming assault wave. And there will be other advantages for him if they land at low tide. Both his high-tide and his half-tide belts will still present obstacles that the enemy will have to move around under fire, especially for vehicles and tanks. Another plus for him is the fact that any landing craft that stay too long and leave at half tide will still be exposed to his half-tide and high-tide belts.

And if the enemy gives him enough time to finish the two low-tide belts, his Atlantic Wall will indeed be a very tough nut to crack.

Sunday, February 6

OKW, currently located at the Wolf's Lair in Eastern Prussia, is giving little thought to the problems in the West. The renewed Soviet offensive has their attention. Kanev, Niktopol, and Cherkassy are the names on their agendas, instead of Calais, Brittany, and Normandy.

***

Rommel spends the day at his luxurious Fontainebleau headquarters. At breakfast, his mind as ever on his coastal defenses, he takes time out to make another phone call about the status of his minelaying efforts, particularly in the areas most likely to be hit. He then goes on another one of his casual armed walks in the woods to relax.

Upon his return, he sits down with an important guest: Walther Warlimont, OKW deputy operations chief. Although Rommel is not too fond of the man and considers him an ambitious, self-centered, inexperienced staff officer, he will nevertheless rub elbows with anyone if it can get him more replacements and supplies.

The two sit down in the late morning and discuss coastal defenses. They go over the chain of command problem again, and Warlimont assures Rommel that he will have the command control that he needs when the time comes.

They are then joined by *Vizeadmiral* Ruge and by *Leutnant* Reischauer from Naval Group Headquarters. Once again, they talk about the problems of shortages of mines. Then comes another meeting with Rommel's Luftwaffe advisor, *Oberstleutnant* Wolfgang Queissner,[1] who tells them how weak the Luftwaffe is, and about the depleted air units that now occupy France.

Rommel and his staff then treat their guests to a modest but satisfactory lunch, with Warlimont sitting in Ruge's normal place next to the field marshal. They all talk of their experiences in Italy the year before. Warlimont recalls his couple visits there.

That afternoon, Warlimont and Reischauer depart for Paris with Ruge, who will meet there an OKW naval deputy flying in from southern France.[2] On the way, they discuss Rommel's plans and problems.

Rommel, concerned about his family's move into their new home in Herrlingen, that evening writes to his wife:

> Günther[3] has arrived safely here with everything. Thank you for your letter of 4 February. Now I know that the move went pretty well in general. Even if one does not see the sense of getting newly established in our grave times, one should still be grateful and happy that one has found such a beautiful new home. I will be so happy if I can spend a few days of leave in February with you...
>
> My dachshund [Ajax] is getting to be more and more affectionate. When I take him to the woods, he is crazy with joy. He diverts me from the grave worries that are with me day and night...

***

General Marcks, commanding the 84th Infantry Corps, also writes home, to his son:

> R. [Rommel] has driven us hard to work fast. He is already so experienced here that he unites our warm confidence in him. Nevertheless, his decisions are final, which is something we've needed to poke us along.

---

1 Queissner was a decorated bomber commanding officer.
2 At least one source indicates that Warlimont accompanied Ruge to Paris, where he and the naval deputy parted from Ruge and returned to OKW together.
3 Günther, Rommel's orderly, had been sent to Rommel's home in mid-January to get some civilian clothes for him.

Monday, February 7

Since Rommel is still technically the Inspector-General for the defenses in all of France, he decides to take a tour of southern France. First the Nineteenth Army positions in the southeast. Then they will swing west to the Bay of Biscay and cover the First Army positions there. This tour will also confuse Western Intelligence, and might persuade them that this is his area of command as well.

So at 6 a.m., he leaves with Staubwasser and Queisner in his Horch. They travel southeast, with Rommel himself at the wheel. General Meise and Admiral Ruge, chauffeured by *Matrosenoberstabsgefreiter* (Leading Seaman) Hatzinger, follow him in a Mercury. Behind them are two open cars full of escorting soldiers.

As usual, Rommel is in a hurry, and Hatzinger has a hard time trying to keep up with him. Rommel's car surges ahead on the straightaways, and the trailing Mercury can only barely catch up on the hills. The last two escorting cars behind struggle even more, and they slowly drift back. Finally, the rearmost car gets lost.

Rommel stops (briefly) in the city of Dijon, on the Burgundy canal. From there, they travel south to Chalon-sur-Saône, the wine center Beaujolais, and then on to the lovely city of Lyon, where they stop for lunch along the right bank of the Rhône River. Under a light cool wind, they take shelter behind some advertising signs. They munch on some sandwiches, drink tea, and sip some wine before continuing southward.

They sail past several towns—Tournus, Valence, and Montelimar, the town that created the nougat. Naturally, Rommel does not stop, to the chagrin of his staff.

Onward to Orange, and finally they hit Avignon at half past four in the afternoon. Way above the town west of the Rhône is located the headquarters of *General der Infanterie* Georg von Sodenstern, commanding the Nineteenth Army.[1]

The general briefs Rommel on his construction progress, and the field marshal is satisfied with the work done so far. In turn, Rommel outlines his plans for new defensive measures. Then they leave and tour the French towns at a dizzying tempo, including Marseilles. Members of staff feverishly take notes every time they leave their cars, and often continue writing after they are back on the road again.

That night, after the lost car of escorts has caught up with them, they travel to the exquisite Hôtel d'Europe[2] in the center of Avignon. They will stay there for the night. After checking in, they dine with von Sodenstern in the hotel's fine restaurant. Afterwards, most of the weary travelers turn in.

---

1 This unit used to be *Armee* Felber, named after its commander, *General der Infanterie* Hans-Gustav Felber. After Italy's collapse in August of 1943, Felber was relieved by General Sodenstern, and it was renamed the Nineteenth Army.

2 A lavish four-star hotel on the Place Crillon. Built in 1580 for the Marquis de Graveson and once owned by a female friend of Napoleon, it is laden with rare antiques and stunning rooms.

Tuesday, February 8

Today, after a nice breakfast at the Hôtel d'Europe, *Generalfeldmarschall* Rommel and his entourage start out again at 8 a.m. for the Mediterranean coast. Driving through the Alpilles hills, they reach the coast just south of Fos-sur-Mer. They turn southeast and travel to Port-de Bouc,[1] go west across the mouth of the Rhône River, and finally reach Port St.-Louis-du-Rhône.

The flatland area around the Rhône estuary is rich with large stones and small boulders. Rommel notices that many of these have been gathered and piled into stone mounds called "cairns," to thwart any paratroop attacks there.

In Port St.-Louis, they watch an impressive demonstration of flamethrowers used against a couple old landing craft. The boats go up nicely in billowing columns of smoke as the flames lick at their hulls and interiors.

Then the entourage is off again, continuing west. They stop for lunch around midday. They dine in Montpellier at the headquarters of the IV Luftwaffe Field Corps. The commanding officer, General Petersen,[2] is pleased to play host to the field marshal.

Rommel is shown that the laying of barriers in this area must be different than along the English Channel. The tides down here are very shallow, and as a result the width of the land exposed at low tide is very small. Water pressure hoses down here cannot be used to put in the stakes of the obstacles; it must be done from rafts. On the other hand, the belts themselves can be much narrower and more concentrated.

In every sense, defensive measures here are quite inadequate, and not much is being constructed, except at ports, towns close to the coast, and at chosen resistance points, way too far from each other.

Sodenstern has reported that he has a long 500km stretch of coast to defend with a mere six divisions. The 277th Infantry alone, near the Spanish border, must cover a staggering 200km of coastline. The weather is usually nice, with an occasional chilling "Mistral" wind blowing down from the north.

They travel on southeast to the well-defended port of Sète, then on to Agde, where they make a cursory inspection. As twilight nears, they reach the city of Narbonne near the coast. There they stop for the night.[3]

A nice dinner is followed by summaries of the day's findings, and then off to bed for the tired inspection party.

Rommel makes sure the reporters get several good photos of him.

---

1 About 20km east of Marseilles.
2 Fifty-five-year-old *General der Flieger* Erich Petersen, a decorated veteran of the trenches of World War I. The IV Luftwaffe Field Corps consisted of General Schack's 272nd Infantry Division, Praun's 277th Infantry Division, and Danhauser's 271st Infantry Division.
3 Desmond Young states they stopped in Perpignan.

Wednesday, February 9

After a very early breakfast of tea, jam, and bread in Narbonne, *Generalfeldmarschall* Rommel's inspection of southern France continues. Departing at 6 a.m., his party swiftly rolls southward around the coast under overcast, rainy skies to Perpignan. There they turn westward and travel inland, along the edge of the Pyrenees. Between the bad weather and the trees and brush along the route, the view of the mountains is all but invisible. The chilly rain slows down their pace, although Rommel makes sure they stay at a good clip. More towns: Foix, Tarbes, and Pau. Following the twisting roads, the vehicles often churn down muddy gullies, gorges, and deep ravines. The road begins to lead upward, and it starts to snow as the clouds seem to come down to greet them.

They stop for a makeshift lunch. Standing along the side of the road, eating sandwiches in the cold, they observe the gray skies around them. A check of their fuel tanks shows that there is only enough petrol for two cars to finish the trip. The reserves are split up between Rommel's Horch and Ruge's Mercury, and these two vehicles continue on, leaving the other cars behind.

The two cars reach the outskirts of Bayonne, near the coast, at 2 p.m. There they are briefed by the commander of the 86th Corps.[1] Then Rommel gets up and outlines his program of defensive construction. Immediately afterwards, the group leaves for the Spanish border, the weather hardly letting up for them. Rolling southwest down the coast, they inspect a number of positions en route, including the railway battery at St.-Jean-de-Luz.

The motorcade reaches the border near the harbor town of Hendaye, next to the coast and just a kilometer away from the Spanish border. Actually driving up to the border, they take a cursory look at neutral Spain, each of them silent in his own thoughts. Then they turn around and return up the coast on a fairly good road through flat, swampy forests, some 220km towards First Army headquarters in the lovely provincial city of Bordeaux.

The sky has turned dark, and it is close to 7 p.m. as the two vehicles reach the outskirts of the city, Rommel's Horch naturally in front. The city guide scheduled to meet them and escort them into town is not at the appointed rendezvous point, so the two cars enter the city unescorted. Suddenly, Ruge sees an unmarked car pass his. Accelerating in front of the Mercury, it starts moving up suspiciously towards Rommel's car. The unknown vehicle has no license plate and maneuvers strangely, as though the driver either wants to pass the Horch or force it off the road. Resistance fighters maybe?

Ruge tells his driver that the vehicle is acting suspiciously and, not wanting to take any chances, orders him to cut it off. Acting instinctively, the seaman accelerates and runs the suspect vehicle off the road. They continue on.

The two cars find the First Army headquarters, located at the Palais de la Bourse along the Garronne River. The army commander's quarters are in Hôtel Ballande, across from the mayor's office, inland 0.9km away on Bordeaux's main square, the Place Pey-Berland. Blaskowitz had picked this hotel because of its key location, its beautiful, white, aristocratic layout, and most importantly, because it had been the quarters of his French predecessor.

Rommel's inspection party will be quartered nearby at the Hôtel Splendide.[2]

The inspection party dumps their suitcases in their rooms and immediately goes back to the First Army headquarters for briefings with the army commander, *Generaloberst* Johannes Blaskowitz.[3] Rommel and his staff are treated to some hot chocolate, and Blaskowitz wastes no time getting started. Later on, they find out that the mysterious car was only the city guide, just trying to get ahead of the field marshal to guide him. The poor fellow had been waiting for them at the wrong rendezvous point. Still, Ruge had reacted correctly. Rommel's safety always came first.

Rommel learns that only in a few experimental areas are defensive barriers actually being built, despite his detailed instructions given out when he was just the Inspector-General. The field marshal is not happy. This clearly underscores the fact that his "proposals and suggestions" were taken as that, and not regarded as orders.

At 9 p.m., the group casually breaks for a small snack. Then the army's supply officer gives his report, followed by the signal communications officer, and then the Bordeaux fortress's chief engineer. Then Meise begins, giving instructions on what defensive measures are expected. As the reports drone on, Rommel's staff, steadily winding down since their arrival, grows weary, and several officers slowly fall asleep at the briefing table, including General Meise whose head sinks down quietly onto the tabletop.

The briefing finally ends, and Rommel's staff retires for the night. Rommel sits down with Blaskowitz, and they have a nice, personal chat. Blaskowitz tells him a couple stories, including the main reasons he is still a *Generaloberst*.[4]

Blaskowitz is an even-tempered, happily married, religious man. From his stint as head of the Führer's security back in 1939,[5] Rommel knows that Blaskowitz commanded the Eighth Army in the invasion of Poland, and it was his army that had captured Warsaw late in September.

On October 5, 1939, they had both been a part of the victory celebration in Warsaw, commemorating their quick victory over Poland. Hitler had flown in from Berlin, in his personal Condor. He was met at the airport by Generals Walther von Brauchitsch, Erhard Milch, and Walter von Reichenau.[6] Rommel had gone ahead of him a day or two before, to organize his escort. Also with them had been the three senior army officers who had actually captured the capital. They were 10th Infantry Division commander *Generalleutnant* Conrad von Cochenhausen, his superior, Eighth Army commander Blaskowitz, and his superior officer, army group commander von Rundstedt.

The celebration had been organized as a show of triumph for both the victors and the vanquished. An elaborate victory march and salute to the Führer had been reluctantly prepared by Blaskowitz and an uncooperative von Rundstedt, who found the whole matter disgusting, once referring to it as playing *"Affentheater."*[7]

Blaskowitz recalls, "Personally, I thought it was too early for him to see the city, since it was still in shambles, and I had not had the chance to completely secure it."

There also had been reports that the Polish Resistance had found out that Hitler had been recently touring the battlefields, and was planning an assassination. In any event, Warsaw still had a "pall of death" hanging over it, and the stench of rotting flesh was present here and there. The Führer, however, had remained unmoved by these concerns, and at one point had prophetically remarked to foreign journalists near him, "Take a good look around Warsaw. That is how I can deal with any European city."

The review stand had been set up across from the Belgian embassy (the Belgian flag above still had holes in it from the fighting).[8] Finally, Hitler's entourage had pulled up, the Führer himself in his gray Mercedes, accompanied by Rommel's heavily armed SS guards. General von Reichenau had greeted the German leader stiffly and had said simply, "Führer, I give you Warsaw."

The parade, complete with an elaborate band, had lasted nearly three hours, and included a review of components from each of the six divisions that been involved in taking the city. As the Führer had saluted the lead of each passing division, the steel-helmeted division commanding officers, each in succession, had dismounted his horse, left the parade, and had joined him up on the review stand. Thus as the seemingly endless columns of gray-uniformed troops had marched by, his generals had joined him one by one, and in the end, they had all stood next to him, at attention, an exalted and majestic group.

"Remember the dinner fiasco?" Blaskowitz asks.

Rommel does. Blaskowitz is referring to the banquet given after the ceremonies. Hitler had ordered that the field kitchens back at the Warsaw airfield feed the men who had marched in the parade. Hitler would join them in an open-air lunch.

As commander of the occupying army, Blaskowitz had been in charge of setting this up. Knowing that the Führer himself would visit them, and in what Blaskowitz thought was in line with the spirit of the elaborate fanfare of the parade, he had decided that a more festive occasion was warranted. So taking some initiative, he had told his people beforehand to make considerable efforts to spice up the "atmosphere" in the hangars with some bright tablecloths, flowers, decorations, banners, and extra benches.

While the parade had been going on, Hitler's pilot, *Generalleutnant* Hans Baur, had seen the fancy layout and had warned the major in charge of the hangar that the Führer might not be too thrilled with the arrangement. After all, he was at heart a simple, unpretentious man and preferred simple meals. The major, following Blaskowitz's lead, had replied that it was simply unthinkable to let the Führer eat off an uncovered table.

Sadly for Blaskowitz, his strategy had backfired. Hitler, arriving around 4 p.m., had taken in the elaborate fanfare, including the pretty tablecloths, the bowls of fresh flowers, the large banners, and other garnishes. He had immediately asked in an irritated tone on whose authority all of the decorations had been made. Hitler had grumbled in a sarcastic voice, "Isn't there a *war* going on here, or did someone schedule a state dinner?!?"

The culprit was of course the unsuspecting Blaskowitz. Hitler was already irritated with him because of an inadvertent slur he had made earlier that day regarding the élite SS unit in his command.[9] General von Brauchitsch, panicking, had tried to get Hitler to sit down and dine in the hangar, but to no avail. The Führer had instead decided to walk over to the actual field kitchens outside. Sitting down among them, he had shared a little soup with the men out there, laughing with them and swapping stories. Many felt that this had mostly been done for show. Still, the Führer did as a rule prefer unpretentious meals. Others later theorized that the culmination of seeing recent city images of destruction, in contrast to the pristine, celebratory theme of the hangar (and of course, the impression this would have on both the national foreign journalists, and thus the rest of the world), brought on this remonstrative display. In any event, the snub to the planning staff had been real, especially when the Führer had then immediately departed for Berlin. Blaskowitz had again taken the blame.

In the months afterward, as the Eastern Theater commander, Blaskowitz had witnessed firsthand the atrocities that were soon being committed *en masse* in Poland. These often unspeakable policies carried out by the SS and the Gestapo had simply horrified him. His repeated complaints, first through the chain of command and then eventually around it, had finally stirred up a hornet's nest. He had caught the attention of the senior Army command, senior Nazi party leaders, the international press, Western leaders, and even the Swiss Red Cross.

Blaskowitz concludes that he, naturally, had incurred the wrath of the SS and eventually of Hitler himself, who had never really taken a liking to him anyway. Relieved of his post and exiled to the German Western Frontier, Blaskowitz had sat back and as a bystander, watched the entire Western Campaign of 1940. Even von Rundstedt's steady support and influence had only managed to land him a backwater army command, where he had wasted the rest of the war watching global events unfold.

"And it has continued," Blaskowitz adds. "Last July was my 60th birthday, and my 40th year in the army. As you know, most senior officers get a write-up and their photograph in the papers. And of course, a special letter and gift from the Führer. I got nothing. *Nothing.*"

Rommel sympathizes with his host.

***

Today, Adolf Hitler has a long talk with Heinrich Himmler about Admiral Canaris' counterintelligence group, the Abwehr. He is irritated over the fact that this intelligence service had failed to warn them about recent Allied landings in the Mediterranean, especially Salerno and the latest one, Anzio. Kesselring had reported that he did come across a few indications of an upcoming landing around the middle of last month (a week before the Anzio landing), but Canaris had concluded that these signs were wrong. And now in the last few days, a critical Abwehr agent and his wife in Istanbul have disappeared, presumably going over to the enemy. This has essentially shut down most counterintelligence sources in Turkey.

Hitler, disgusted at this clear lack of support, now tells Himmler that he is fed up with Canaris and that he thinks the man should be dismissed. They need a viable, effective counterintelligence bureau if they are to have any hope of finding out about the upcoming invasion in the West.

Himmler tells him that he will look further into the matter and get back to him in a day or two. He leaves, satisfied that Canaris' days are numbered.

---

1   Fifty-seven-year-old *General der Infanterie* Hans von Obstfelder.

2   Now Le Boutique Hôtel, Bordeaux.

3   General Blaskowitz until now had an interesting wartime career. Leading the Eighth Army during the invasion of Poland, it had been his units that had marched on and occupied Warsaw. Afterwards, when von Rundstedt had turned the appointment down, Blaskowitz had been appointed *Befehlshaber, Oberost* (Commander-in-Chief, Eastern Theater). Eventually transferred to the West, he sat out most of the war commanding the First Army.

4   Blaskowitz was the only general left in the German army who carried that rank at the beginning of the war and who had not been appointed a field marshal.

5   *Generalmajor* Rommel at the time commanded the *Frontgruppe der Führerhauptquartier Truppen*. The unit later evolved into the *Führer Begleit Battaillion*.

6   Walther von Brauchitsch was head of OKH, *Generaloberst* Erhard Milch had commanded the Luftwaffe units in the invasion, and *Generalleutnant* Walther von Reichenau commanded the Tenth Army, which had assisted in the capture of the city.

7   Charades.

8   Peter Hoffmann claims it was the Dutch embassy.

9   In the capture of Warsaw, Blaskowitz had commanded the better part of Hitler's personal SS unit, the motorized regiment *SS Liebstandarte Adolf Hitler*. During the day's victory procession, when the SS unit had marched past the grandstand, Hitler had with a smile asked Blaskowitz how his namesake unit had performed in combat. Blaskowitz was like von Rundstedt, a Prussian aristocrat, never one to flatter or brownnose. So he had replied perhaps a bit tactlessly that, "It was an average unit, still inexperienced, with no unusual qualifications." Hitler's smile had immediately gone away, having of course taken the remark personally. *Reichsführer* Himmler and the unit commander Sepp Dietrich became infuriated upon hearing about the remark.

Thursday, February 10

Rommel has breakfast with General Blaskowitz, and they discuss more of the general's past dealings with the Führer.

After finishing breakfast and some more talk, Rommel finally leaves the general and continues with his trek through Southern France, now heading towards the Atlantic. Leaving Bordeaux at 8 a.m., the two cars, rejoined now with the other cars that had been short on fuel, drive on to the Gironde estuary. There they inspect a number of defensive positions along the Atlantic, including an unusual unit consisting of "free" troops from India. The field marshal examines the fortress position south of the river mouth, where they are joined by the naval commander for the Gascogne area, *Konteradmiral* Michahelles.[1] The southern fort is well equipped with a few good-sized batteries.

At the port of Le Verdon on the southern tip of the Gironde, they stop and have lunch at a field kitchen. Then they traverse the river mouth to get to Royan on the northern bank. The crossing takes an hour, and the westerly wind, combined with some heavy swells, makes a few of the landlubbers in the inspection party somewhat seasick.

As they travel along the northern side of the river, the inspection party, now joined by *Kapitän* Lautenschlager,[2] finds that the strongpoints there are over 3½km apart, manned by Russian contingents—Cossacks, to be exact.

The inspection group winds up somewhere near La Rochelle for the night.

***

Today, at von Rundstedt's winter quarters in the Hôtel Georges V off the Champs-Élysées, the field marshal's staff holds a small soiree for the OB West chief of staff, who is celebrating his 52nd birthday. The officers all enjoy the short party. Then several junior officers leave to continue their festivities in the Parisian nightlife. Blumentritt himself goes up to his room and retires for the night.

---

1 Forty-five-year-old *Konteradmiral* Hans Michahelles, appointed the *Seekommandant* (Commandant of Sea Fortifications) for the Gascogne area in late August.

2 *Kapitän* R. Lautenschlager, the commander of the 4th Security Division.

Friday, February 11

As usual, Rommel is up early. After a simple breakfast of tea, bread and jam, he and his entourage depart and begin looking over the defensive positions around La Rochelle, one of the principal U-boat bases on the Atlantic. Considerable work has been done in the port area, and Rommel is satisfied to see the progress that has been made so far.

The Mediterranean tour pretty much over at this point, Rommel's inspection party departs for home. First though, a long drive northward to Le Mans, headquarters of the Seventh Army. They are expected there for a conference with the commanding officer, General Dollmann. Soon after they arrive, Admiral Ruge leaves them to call on the *FdU West* at Lorient, *Kapitän* Rösing.[1] They are to discuss the role the submarines should play when the invasion begins. With the enemy's advanced techology in anti-submarine warfare, and their control of the seas, only those boats that have snorkels are expected to have a chance of surviving.

Rommel stays long enough to have his conference with Dollmann and is happy to learn that construction of obstacles and minefields along Seventh Army's sector is now in full swing.

The field marshal leaves and finally arrives back at his headquarters in Fontainebleau early in the evening. He is tired from the trip, understandably, since he has traveled over 2,200 kilometers in less than a week.

Inevitably, a lot of paperwork has piled up in his absence. Though night has fallen and he is fatigued, he nevertheless begins tackling the piles. He takes time out though, to call General Jodl at OKW and report to him the findings of his tour.

He tells Jodl that the coastal areas in his opinion are too thinly defended. He recommends that more units be brought up from the inland areas northwest to the Bay of Biscay for the First Army and southward to the Mediterranean shore for the Nineteenth.

He complains that before von Rundstedt had gone on leave, the old man had ordered that an artillery division be created out of existing coastal batteries. Rommel tells Jodl that he objects to this, since it makes no sense. The units would not be able to act as a cohesive unit, and more importantly, they had no transport to move them, either as a unit or individually. They would thus not be able to travel a long distance to the invasion area, and even if they could, they would be cumbersome on the road and vulnerable to attacks by partisans or by air. Better to put them in strategic locations in suspected landing areas.

He segues into complaining once again about their nebulous chain of command. With von Rundstedt on leave, Rommel is effectively in charge of the defense of France. Technically though, the job is being held by the deputy OB West, Luftwaffe General Hugo Sperrle. And administratively, each branch of service controls its own units. So with orders, directives, and policies coming from Rommel, Sperrle,

Blumentritt (OB West chief of staff), Himmler to the SS units, Krancke to the naval shore commands, and Geyr von Schweppenberg to the panzer units, a good deal of confusion is being created.

Jodl replies by telling him that he will bring this command issue to the attention of the Führer.

Rommel then gives Jodl some good news. He informs him that their supply of mines is now better, and they are now being laid down more quickly in a greatly expanded program. Lastly, he gives Jodl a thorough report on his travel arrangements for the upcoming visit to the Führer's headquarters in March.

***

At the Supreme Headquarters, currently located at the *Wolfsschanze* in East Prussia, Hitler has a late-morning talk with Hermann Fegelein, *Reichsführer* Himmler's liaison to the Führer. Several days ago, Foreign Minister von Ribbentrop[2] had complained to the Führer that acts of sabotage by the Abwehr on British ships moored in Spanish ports were endangering their relations with neutral Spain. In response, on February 8th, Hitler had ordered that all such destructive acts, well-meaning or not, were to be stopped immediately. Now today, in incoming messages, he learns that a massive explosion has occurred on a British ship docked in Cartagena, Spain. The vessel was reportedly carrying nothing but oranges.

The Führer is enraged, especially when he learns from the reports that the sabotage was most likely carried out by Abwehr agents, in either direct defiance or ignorance of the new order. The Führer and Fegelein discuss this and other recent intelligence failures of Canaris' organization. Fegelein points out in contrast that it was improved SS covert assets that had originally found out the secret place where Mussolini had been whisked off to by the Italian traitors after they had arrested him in late July 1943. And it was the SS who had subsequently sent in a strike team and freed him in late September.

Taking advantage of Hitler's anger, Fegelein suggests that he might want to turn over the entire incompetent Abwehr organization to the SS. Hitler thinks about it, looks at him, and nods. He sends for Himmler and they talk.

Himmler has long considered the intelligence section of the Heeres to be in direct competition with his own SS/Gestapo network, and while he does not consider Canaris a political enemy (like von Ribbentrop), his concerns about the admiral's loyalties have deepened considerably with each military setback.[3] At the beginning of last month, the Reichsführer had pressed Hitler to consolidate all of the intelligence units into one organization. This would make them more efficient, and rectify the problems in the Abwehr. The Reichsführer would run the organization, of course.

Admiral Canaris in turn had protested, claiming that his recent intelligence failures had been a result of mistakes, superseding, or gross meddling by either the SS or von Ribbentrop's foreign ministry. Himmler's evidence of course shows this is not true, and his information, faked or not, is considerable. Unlike the devoted SS, the loyalties of key Abwehr members are questionable. Dr. Hans von Dohnanyi for instance, the resourceful young lawyer in charge of its special projects, had been arrested last April for treason. Another Abwehr traitor, Hans Oster, had been suspended from military duty and placed under house arrest. To make matters worse, several of Canaris' key leaders had disgustedly left the Abwehr to serve, of all places, on the Russian front.

There were operational letdowns as well. There was the Army's failure to find out beforehand about the landings at Salerno. On the contrary, they had quite recently reassured Kesselring that he could only lightly defend the Italian coast around Nettuno. The Abwehr had totally failed to detect the massive enemy landings on January 22, and the three Allied divisions that came ashore were met by only two German battalions. (When the Führer had asked Kesselring why he had been caught unawares, the field marshal had made dammed sure the blame went to Canaris.)

To make matters even worse for Canaris, less than two weeks ago, Argentina had suddenly broken off formal relations with Germany. Not only had the Abwehr agents there not seen this move coming, but, unknown to them, their secret network had been accidentally discovered by the Argentine government, and this had brought on the official break. Several of their agents, spies, and contacts had been subsequently arrested, their spy ring broken.[4] The Führer had been livid at this sudden, critical setback.

Perhaps though, the final nail in the admiral's coffin came when several recent reports from their ambassador to Spain arrived.[5] The man indicated that the Abwehr organization there was so worthless, top-heavy, generally lazy, and obnoxiously arrogant that the Spanish were now leaning towards joining the Allies. Canaris, he added, is to blame for this, adding that the admiral, far from being the Reich's main influence in keeping the Spanish neutral (as the Führer had thought), was actually hinting to Franco that Germany was losing the war and that he might want to think about saving himself and Spain from the calamity that would probably follow. Spain, heretofore leaning to the side of Germany, had suddenly issued a statement of strict neutrality eight days ago on February 3. A coincidence?

Now Himmler's seemingly reluctant disclosure of Admiral Canaris's fiascos confirms the Führer's suspicions. Already having had a recent confrontation with Canaris,[6] Hitler is now disgusted with him, and decides to sack the man. The Abwehr, he instructs, is essentially to be dissolved. Himmler will take over all counterintelligence activities, and is granted permission to take over the Abwehr and create a new combined intelligence service out of it and its SS counterpart, the *Geheimdienst*.

The Führer will sign the order as soon as a plan for assimilation can be worked out. Himmler is pleased.[7] The plan for merging the two agencies will actually be carried out as an assimilation.

Canaris, who has already been under suspicion of treason by the SS for months, is now clearly a marked man.

1   *Führer der Unterseeboote,* Western Theater (Senior U-boat Officer, Western Theater), 48-year-old Hans-Rudolf Rösing. A Knight's Cross recipient for his exploits commanding U-48, Rösing was finally posted back to Lorient where he became *FdU West.* His "command" consisted of several flotillas out of the major ports in the Atlantic. For a number of reasons, Rösing was disliked or even hated by the U-boat skippers. Historians have often wondered why this position even existed, except perhaps in a strictly advisory or administrative role. All decisions regarding operational orders, tactics, and deployment were issued by Dönitz's staff.

2   He had long been a stiff adversary of Canaris over intelligence operations in North and South America.

3   Some historians speculate that Himmler despised Canaris but did not want to move against him because he feared that undisclosed damning information on him, Heydrich, or the SS might suddenly come to light. One had to be very careful about who one wanted to move against in the Third Reich—even the Reichsführer.

4   American and British intelligence had uncovered the Abwehr's network of spies in and around Buenos Aires. Although Argentina had up until then been an ardent supporter of Germany, the pressure and hostility of the Western Allies—especially the United States—was by now considerable. It included a near-blockade of the country, a number of diplomatic warnings, and public criticism of their government that all but declared it as fascist. The undertone of threats from the Allies (who to the Argentines seemed to be winning the war anyway) was now too great for President Ramírez to ignore. Argentina, Germany's last bastion of alliance on either American continent, was forced to sever relations with the Reich.

   It is interesting to note that Argentina's military leaders reacted strongly to the break in relations. Sympathetic to the Reich, despising the current administration and now worried about German retaliation up to and including a possible declaration of war, they secretly formed a military junta and overthrew the government a month later. Prominent in the military circle was one Colonel Juan Perón, who at the time was the Labor Relations Minister, and whose wife Eva would years later become an Argentine legend.

5   Sixty-year-old Hans-Heinrich Dieckhoff, brother-in-law to Foreign Minister von Ribbentrop. He had been appointed Germany's ambassador to the United States until mid-November 1938 when, in bitter protest over Germany's *Kristallnacht,* the US recalled its ambassador to Germany. Dieckhoff was recalled in response. He was appointed Ambassador to Spain in May 1943.

6   In a previous incident (confirmed, although the date is not definite; but it occurred a couple weeks before February 11), Canaris and Himmler had gone to brief Hitler on the situation in the East. Brandishing several reports in his hand, Canaris had painted a gloomy picture of the situation and on their future prospects there. Hitler, who had slowly been getting angered at his bad news, curt manner, and obvious negativity, had suddenly lurched forward, knocking over a table between them, and had viciously grabbed the admiral by the lapels and yanked them forward. "Are you telling me that I am going to lose the war?!?" he had bellowed.

   A no-doubt startled Canaris had replied, "*Mein Führer,* I have said nothing about the war. I have tried to explain the military situation on the Russian front." His reports, he added, were coming from their own agents in Russia. "Are your Russian agents as trustworthy as the *Veermehrens?*" Hitler had shouted. He was referring to a married German Abwehr couple who had been effective in Turkey until, worried by suspicious Gestapo probings, they had defected to the British (supposedly with important secret Abwehr code books) just a few days before. Canaris was gruffly told to leave his reports and depart.

7   The order was signed a week later on February 18.

Saturday, February 12

This morning, Rommel is back at his headquarters in Fontainebleau. Up since dawn, he is sitting in his study with the backlog of reports, messages, and forms needing his attention. Still tired from having motorcaded all over southern France in the last five days, he is thankful that he is not going anywhere today. On this last long trip, wherever he went, he heard myriad reports, chaired many briefings, made speeches and pep talks, drafted recommendations, and took notes on all the units and positions that he visited. This particular tour though, had been undertaken as much as anything for the benefit of the enemy. He wants again to create for them the illusion that he is everywhere, reorganizing the entire defensive effort in France. That should give Montgomery something to think about.

One point that Rommel finds fascinating is that because of his position and reputation, he never seems to lack for visitors, whether he is on the road or at his headquarters. These callers of course usually interfere with his work, which irritates him at times. And a lot of his meetings with them are just politics. Of course, he can be quite diplomatic and play the model host. Still, he does have many other pressing things to do.

Thinking about it, he shakes his head. As much an annoyance as anything are those who just want to take his picture: the other edge of the celebrity sword again. Some photographers want to go everywhere with him, pestering him for a pose, and habitually getting in the way. Many others though meet him along the way, usually admiring junior officers, administrators, or just unit officers wanting a photo memento. Although they are bothersome, he almost always welcomes them. He patiently allows them to take his picture at various locations along his tour, because he knows that the photos increase the morale of his own men and at the same time, worry his enemies (on both sides of the Channel). And, yes, truth be known, he does like the publicity.[1]

"Do what you like with me," he once told photographers eagerly brandishing their cameras, "if it results in even a one-week postponement of the enemy's invasion." He had made sure that most of the photos taken on this last trip showed him in the new leather overcoat that he had just bought in Paris on February 1. You never knew. Maybe Lucie would get to see him wearing it on the cover of some magazine and smile.

He focuses on the present. He has an important visitor scheduled today. Rommel is not usually nervous about guests, but today's caller is none other than the Panzer Inspector-General himself, *Generaloberst* Heinz Guderian, known to his men as "Heinz the Meteor," or "*Schnelle* Heinz."

The 55-year-old general, Prussian by birth, has become by this time a legend in his own right, regarded by many in Germany and indeed the world as the father of modern armored warfare. Guderian, having already met with von Rundstedt and

Geyr von Schweppenberg, is coming to Fontainebleau to discuss the disposition of the panzer units in France. This meeting is critical for both Guderian and Rommel.

The field marshal knows that he is about to engage in another battle of theories, this time with a contemporary. And Guderian is most enthusiastic about his own views on panzer warfare, as proven by his pre-war bestseller, *Achtung, Panzer!* His theories have been proven successfully time and again in Poland, France, and Russia. And Guderian, considered by many the leading expert on the *blitzkrieg*, is today, as always, going to push his suggestions to the utmost.

Rommel and Guderian are alike in several ways. They are both commoners by ancestry, lacking any aristocratic background. Both are extremely popular and well respected with the populace and with the general ranks, and both are leery of General Staff officers. They are both ferocious leaders in battle, and both usually lead at the front. After all, their two panzer units had raced each other almost side by side in their wild dash across France in 1940.

While Guderian and Rommel are long acquaintances and respect each other, they are not close. Rommel has been told that Guderian does not care for Rommel's flair for being in the limelight.[2] Nevertheless, he, like Rommel, has during the war often been an object of attention of the propagandists. Their common bond is their mastery of the *blitzkrieg*, and the adept way that each has used it in the field has earned the other's professional respect.

They are meeting again today, and unfortunately this time, their experiences of defending a coast will put them on opposite sides of the fence. Rommel is concerned about how adamant Guderian will be. The Russian Front veteran is usually brutally frank, sometimes even with the Führer, and he has been known to get insultingly critical with someone opposed to his point of view. He has another nickname too—"*Brausewetter.*"[3] He has earned that one by giving several rather forward opinions to the Führer.

Well, Rommel can be irascible too, and he really has no desire to argue philosophies. However, he has to make this brilliant *Panzermann* see the strategic picture his way, because Guderian's opinion goes far with the High Command. Rommel knows that his theories are right, and to plan otherwise is courting the final disaster for the Reich.

A knock at Rommel's door startles him out of his reverie. His personal aide Hammermann announces that General Guderian has arrived. Rommel thanks him, adding that he will be right out. He stands up, straightens his uniform, and walks out of the study and down the hallway. He catches sight of Guderian in the main foyer, resplendent in his uniform. They exchange warm greetings as a staff member takes Guderian's coat and hat.

Guderian seems to have aged considerably. The stress of the Russian campaign has clearly taken its toll, evidenced by his heart condition contracted last winter. However, he is still immaculately dressed, and despite looking tired from his recent tours, his eyes continue to flash. And he certainly has kept his wits about him.

They chat easily, making small talk as Rommel escorts him back to his study. They sit down and immediately get down to business. Rommel quickly realizes that his concerns are for nothing. The meeting between the two goes well.

Rommel is pleasantly surprised to find that the Inspector-General agrees with him in principle that committing the panzers in the first few hours of an invasion is critical. He also agrees that intensive mining will also be needed to turn back a landing. Rommel feels the tension within him ease up, and the conversation becomes relaxed and warm. Rommel will later write in his notes:

Guderian agrees with me on the mining and the forward deployment of the panzer reserves.

After some discussion, they arise and go into the dining hall for lunch. Guderian turns out on this occasion to be an excellent luncheon guest. Maybe he is putting on a little bit of a show, but he is still as entertaining as he is charming.

Admiral Ruge brings up the subject of Guderian's latest publication, *Die Tigerfibel*.[4] The general happily discusses his work, and the conversation goes on to a number of lively topics.

Rommel sits back and listens. He is thankful that they are not alienating the Inspector-General. He could be a powerful enemy. Ah, politics. Tomorrow, more of the same. Rommel will have to go to von Rundstedt's headquarters to discuss unit readiness. Well, the day after, he will relax with his staff. They are planning to have a birthday party for Gause. Rommel will naturally give a big speech. He looks forward to that. Later, he will have to find time to write to Lucie and tell her about the work he is doing, and of course today's visitor.

He comes out of his reverie and chides himself for daydreaming and not listening to what his guest is saying. It is a bad habit of his. His attention to a conversation sometimes wanders, especially if it rambles and seems to have no purpose.

He mentally comes back to the table. Guderian goes on about his book.

---

1   Once a very junior officer had addressed the field marshal, asking whether such widespread publicity was wise in "autocratic Germany." Rommel had thanked the officer for the comment, but supposedly for a time after that, there was a substantial decline in his publicity efforts.
2   Early in the war, Guderian had found out that a journalist was doing research for a biography about him, and he had written his wife to warn her not to disclose personal information. "I would not under any circumstances like becoming involved with propaganda, à la Rommel." Guderian once described Rommel as "an open, upright man and a brave soldier...[who] possessed energy and subtlety of appreciation; he had great understanding of men and, in fact, thoroughly deserved the reputation that he had won for himself." Rommel in turn also thought highly of the other man, respecting General Guderian's accomplishments in Russia the last three years.
3   "Hothead."
4   "*The Tiger Primer*." This was a simple, comic-book-styled basic operation and maintenance guide (Publication D656/27) on the complex German Tiger tank (*PzKw VI-a*). Released in August of 1943, it was fully illustrated with simple drawings (including a few risqué images personifying

the tank as a woman named "Elvira"). The text was written in an often humorous or light-hearted fashion, which the tankmen found entertaining, and certainly easier to follow than a mundane, complex instruction manual. It was the first set of German service regulations that was done partly in humorous rhyme. Although Guderian did not actually write the manual (its author was Leutnant Josef von Glatter-Goetz) or illustrate it (two enlisted men provided the diagrams), he authorized, organized, approved, and distributed it. The booklet was soon followed by its Panther (*PzKw V*) counterpart, the *Pantherfibel*. Both became collector's items after the war.

Sunday, February 13

One issue remains pre-eminent all over northern France. The many acres of mine-fields, offshore obstacles, battery positions, resistance nests, clear fields of fire, inland anti-airborne measures, and other countless defensive programs that Rommel has ordered are starting to consume a staggering amount of materials, time, equipment, fuel, and sweat. The soldiers stationed along the coastline, in their continuing struggle to make time for construction of Rommel's barriers, are finding little time for unit combat training. As expected, unit commanders are starting to complain that their men, many of them green, inexperienced, or very young, are simply not getting enough time in on combat maneuvers. Without proper training, they argue, the enemy will slaughter them when they land. And by the way, munitions are short, limiting in scope and effectiveness those training exercises that do occur.

Rommel also has to address several other problems arising out of Seventh Army Headquarters in Le Mans. They have reported that they are pretty much out of wood for the offshore obstacle posts. And the local woodcutters are out of the area, working in the Vosges forests near Belgium.

Then there is the offshore minelaying. There are several main areas just off the western coasts of Brittany that the Seventh Army would like mined. The difficulty is that there is a lot of heavy surf there, making the laying of mines near shore difficult.

Yet another problem concerns the issued anti-landing combat orders for what little naval force exists in the area. The Seventh Army now wants to know what the hell are they supposed to do with them. The Kriegsmarine only takes orders from Dönitz.

Similar problems are coming in from von Salmuth at Fifteenth Army Headquarters in Tourcoing.

To address these issues, Rommel leaves Fontainebleau today and travels northwest up to Paris, to the OB West headquarters hotel. Even though von Rundstedt is still on leave, Rommel discusses with the staff there several compromises that he hopes will keep everyone happy, from the unit commanders on up.

That night, Rommel finds time to send Lucie a photo of his dog:

> *Here is a photograph of "Ajax." Perhaps I'll bring him along and leave him with you.*

***

Tonight, 230 aircraft fly yet another *Steinbock* air raid. Bombs are dropped all over the English countryside. Only a dozen or so actually find and bomb London. Many more bombs fall on English fields. In exchange, ten bombers are lost, mostly over the Channel.

Monday, February 14

Despite the exhausting trip that he has recently completed, *Generalfeldmarschall* Rommel hits the road again for another tour. This time he travels north to check out components of the slowly forming 9th SS Panzer Division *"Hohenstaufen."*[1] He then inspects the Somme area just west of Dieppe. Afterwards, there is a quick tour of the 271st Infantry positions. The 9th SS and the 271st are both to be relocated to the Nineteenth Army area.

He returns to Fontainebleau for a quick hunt and then partakes in a celebration. This evening, his staff is throwing a birthday party for Chief of Staff Gause. While the field marshal rarely attends festivities, he is going to take time out for this occasion. Gause, turning 48, has been with him since the Afrika Korps.

As the dinner begins, Rommel stands up and gives a touching speech on behalf of the guest of honor. His feelings for the man are strong. They have shared so much since North Africa, and Gause is a trusted friend. But there is more to it; Rommel also feels sorry for the man and a little guilty because of his current situation.

Gause has just returned from leave in Germany. His wife, going home on August 23, had found their house a smoldering ruin, bombed to ashes during the first heavy raids on Berlin that last August. The next day, she had called Gause and told him, and he had immediately traveled home to witness the damage himself. Lucie Rommel, sympathetic to his plight, had invited Gause's wife to temporary quarters at the new Rommel residence in Herrlingen, and the chief of staff had been heartily invited to stay there as well during his leave.

Gause, understandably morose over the total loss of his home, had been grateful to accept the offer. Flying to Germany on leave, he had stayed at the field marshal's new home. During his stay, he had engaged in a number of political discussions with Lucie. The mayor of Stuttgart, Dr. Karl Strölin, and his wife had visited during this time, and the chief of staff had been afforded the chance to sit down with the mayor and discuss the war. Despite the hospitality of the Rommel family, Gause had been upset and ill during his leave, partly from the stress of his job, partly from his wife's pessimism, and partly because of the war. However, most of his gloominess stemmed from the loss of his beautiful home and his possessions, including all of his money, which had been destroyed along with the bombed bank it had been sitting in.

Most importantly though, during this stay, Gause had made a critical political error, one which eventually might be the deciding factor in him losing his job.[2]

One early February morning during his stay at Rommel's new home, *Hauptmann* Aldinger, Rommel's private home adjutant, had arrived at the villa later than usual. Aldinger was another long-time friend of the field marshal, their acquaintance going back to World War I. He had also served in Rommel's 7th Panzer Division in 1940, and later had been Rommel's devoted aide in North Africa, where he had earned his present rank of captain. By 1944, as a reservist in his early forties, he had been granted indefinite leave to act as the field marshal's *Ordonnanzoffizer*, a position that was part aide, part private secretary, and part personal assistant. This assignment suited him immensely, because it kept him out of the war and yet allowed him to take care of the field marshal's home.

Ever since the Rommel family had been invited by the village of Herrlingen to rent this frame villa back in December,[3] Aldinger had been there to supervise repairs, direct the landscaping, and in general act on the family's behalf to renovate the lovely little country home. He had also closely assisted Lucie in running the house, doing countless errands for her, and had just been there for her daily on behalf of the field marshal—which of course, even further endeared the aide to her.

Now in early February, despite the weather, his duties had taken him back to the garden again, where he was quite in his element, personally getting the ground around the house ready for spring (not surprising, since as a civilian he had been a landscape architect).

Gause was up quite early that critical morning and noticed that Aldinger had not yet arrived to start the day's work. When the aide came in some time later, Gause happened to catch him preparing to start in on the garden. Gause stopped him and proceeded to chastise him somewhat harshly for being late.

Unfortunately, Lucie overheard the rebuke and immediately took issue with Gause, fiercely defending an embarrassed Aldinger.

Lucie had come away from the incident with a permanent dislike of Gause. Coupled with his bad health, his negativity, and his depression about the war and the loss of his home and possessions, the man was really starting to irritate her.

To make matters worse, Frau Gause had not fared much better with her. Gause's wife was not an easy woman to be around, and recently she had a number of times gotten on Lucie's nerves. Perhaps she had whined too much about losing her home. Maybe she too was overly pessimistic about the war. And anyway, having guests on an extended stay was a pain for any hostess, especially when that home was in the middle of refurbishment.

As the days went on, Lucie had become more and more unsettled with the two of them. She was certainly glad to see the chief of staff go back to France, and told her husband that she definitely did not want Gause or his wife back.

The field marshal does respect his wife's opinion, despite realizing that sometimes he gives in too easily to her requests. It will not take Lucie long to convince her husband that they need to get away from the Gause family, both socially and militarily.

The chief of staff will eventually have to go.

---

1   Named after Frederick Barbarossa von Hohenstaufen, a great 12th-century German hero, part of a noble German dynasty in Swabia that had been the source of a number of German kings. Its creation was as one of two new Waffen-SS divisions, agreed to in theory on New Year's Eve 1942 by Hitler. The sister division is the 10th SS *Frundsburg*, named after the famous 16th-century

German mercenary Georg von Frundsburg. The two units were initially designated *panzergrenadier* divisions and began forming in January 1943 in Berlin. On February 8, several cadre elements were assembled at a *Truppenubungsplatz* (training area) in Mailly-le-Camp (east of Paris, between Châlons-sur-Marne and Troyes). Shortly thereafter, two units from the LSSAH Replacement Battalion in Berlin arrived and SS Brigadefuhrer Wilhelm ("Willi") Bittrich took command of the 9th SS. Throughout the rest of the year the 9th SS and 10th SS continued forming, and in late October, they were designed panzer divisions, if in name only. By early February of 1944, the 9th SS consisted of the 9th SS Panzer Regiment, the 19th and 20th SS *panzergrenadier* regiments, the 9th SS Panzer Artillery Regiment, and ten specialty battalions.

2   One could also argue the change would ultimately cost Rommel his own life eight months later.

3   See entry for December 14, 1943.

Tuesday, February 15

Generalfeldmarschall von Rundstedt is still on leave at the spas in Bad Tölz.

***

Rommel leaves sprawling Fontainebleau again for an inspection of northern France near Dieppe. He visits several positions and receives a report from General Feuchtinger, commanding the reborn 21st Panzer Division. This unit is a sort of phoenix, rising up from the ashes of an earlier bird—one that Rommel had known well. The original 21st Panzer had been one of his key units in the Afrika Korps, but it had mostly been lost in Tunisia. Now it is having problems getting tanks.

Nearly all of the latest-model new units coming off the assembly line are either going to the mayhem on the Eastern Front, or are being sent south to Italy to thwart the Americans and the British. The 21st simply has to make do with whatever they can for now. In addition to 54 German tanks of various models, they have at least 28 captured French Somua tanks (without radios), some three dozen Hotchkiss armored assault units, and some Russian 122mm artillery pieces: hardly the normal allocation for a front-line panzer division.

And the division commander is an unusual breed as well.

Generalmajor Edgar Feuchtinger, a stout 37-year-old career officer, is a Nazi favorite. An early party supporter, he was a key organizer in the yearly Nuremberg Rallies of the 1930s. His military experience has unfortunately only featured the command of a horse-drawn artillery regiment in the East. But his political connections have remained strong, and so his chance to command has now come. What he does with it will remain to be seen.

Still, Feuchtinger is off to a good start. He is working hard to get this unit up to snuff. Having taken what had initially been a light infantry division with no mechanization, he has by hook-or-crook found, appropriated or stolen enough tanks and other odd armored vehicles for the unit to be reclassified as a panzer division, though only in the barest sense of the term. Organized practically from scratch, the unit has had to be completely refitted. Many vehicles are captured enemy equipment, and many of the transports used are commandeered taxicabs, but at least they are mobile. Feuchtinger has been able to get his hands on some German models as well, but these are mostly a couple dozen old *PzKw IIs* and *PzKw IIIs* and 30-odd *PzKw IV Ausf. B* or *C* tanks, with their short, 75mm guns.[1]

The *PzKw IV Ausf. B*, or *Ausf. C* models were the newest models the 21st Panzer was able to get. Unfortunately, at this stage of the war, they were considered to be relatively obsolete. The muzzle velocity of their short, 75mm KwK L/24 guns was only 385 mps, about half that of an *Ausf. G*. The *Ausf. B* weighed only 20 tons, four tons less than the *Ausf. G*. And not only did it lack firepower, but its protection was inferior. Its maximum armor was only 30mm, less than half the 81mm on an American Sherman, and it carried no side skirts. The optics were obsolete, visibility from inside was not that good, and the tracks were a bit narrower than those on a Sherman.

Production of tanks was at a crisis at this point in the war, so the *Ausf. G* and *Ausf. H* models were hard to get. Even more unfortunate was the fact that by now, even the *Ausf. G* and *Ausf. H* models were outdated in comparison to the larger Soviet and American models. However, German technology was not lacking, and the older *PzKw IVs* were being replaced by the *PzKw VIa*, nicknamed the "Tiger," and more slowly by the new renowned *PzKw V Ausf. D*, nicknamed the "Panther."[2]

Rommel tells Feuchtinger that the 21st Panzer getting Tigers and Panthers is of course, out of the question at this time. He then leaves and takes time out to visit the town of Auberville, some 28km northeast of Le Havre. While he is there, he checks out the old quarters that he occupied way back in 1940, during his mad dash across France. Ah, so long ago…

On the way back, he stops at a luxurious château along a loop in the Seine River. It has been chosen as his new headquarters.

He and his men (usually Meise or Gehrcke[3]) have over the past weeks been looking northwest of Paris along the Seine River for a location with caves in the chalk and gypsum cliffs—a type of position that would be naturally protected from air attacks. After permission to use the naval underground torpedo arsenal had been denied by the Kriegsmarine, they had continued looking.

This location that they have found seems to suit his needs. Although somewhat pretentious, it is ideally located. About 64km northwest of Paris, it is roughly halfway between the capital (where the major strategic headquarters are located) and Rouen, and just 165km from Le Havre on the coast. The château is situated in the small town of La Roche-Guyon. It is a splendid villa, although the thought of using the place leaves Rommel indifferent. He does not much care about picking comfortable quarters, and his schedules reflect this. For him, just about any building will do, as long as it is closer to the coast. Having a headquarters farther away from where the fighting will be is totally unsuitable for him.

The large estate has been the home of the Duc du Rochefoucald since the 17th century. The present duke is 60-year-old Jean de La Rochefoucauld. The château is located above the sloping northern bank of the Seine at a large U-shaped river bend. Behind it is a steep chalk cliff in which a few connecting tunnels to the château have been dug. High above and just behind the château is a round, half-ruined Norman tower that dates back to the 11th century.

Next to the château and to its left is the small village of La Roche-Guyon, with about 540 inhabitants. The senior staff will stay at the château. The rest of his men, at least 80, will be quartered in the town.

The complex was administratively taken over on March 17, 1943 by the German forces, who installed a flak battery on the hill above the château.[4] Just down the main street[5] is the town's Kommandant's office. Near the town center is the 15th-century church of St. Samson, on the Rue des Frères Rousse.[6]

Because the bridge next to the château was destroyed in June 1940, anyone wishing to cross the Seine has to take the local ferry.[7] There are also road bridges at the nearby towns of Mantes and Vernon. All in all, the château's location is off the main routes, but within easy access of them, and most of all, it is close to the coast.

It appears that the château will suffice for them. Built somewhere around the 15th century, it is elegant and spacious, although because of its age and solid construction, utilities are somewhat challenging. And considering that an entire army group headquarters will be working there, quarters will be a problem. Obviously, many will have to stay in the town. Some room has been made by digging tunnels adjoining the mansion. Also, there are numerous cellars that they could use in addition to the tunnels. Still, there is much work to be done. Engineers will dig out more tunnels in the cliffs, for such things as extra offices, storage, a makeshift movie theater, and of course, safe air raid shelters.

Yes, all in all, it will do nicely. Rommel returns to Fontainebleau, satisfied.

---

1   *PzKw* stands for *PanzerKampfwagen*, the German military term for tank. Equivalent to the American term "Mark," it was used to denote the tank's model number. Thus the Allies' term "German Mark IV" was based upon the German designator, *PanzerKampfwagen IV* (*PzKw IV*). This model with all its variations was the most-produced German tank of the war. An improved version of the older *PzKw III*, it had in turn undergone during the course of the war a number of different modifications, or *Ausführung*. The earlier versions sported a short, low-velocity 75mm main gun that could not compete with later Allied tanks. *PzKw IV* production lines eventually began turning out the *PzKw IV Ausf. G* or *H*, what the Allies called a "Mark IV Special." At 24 tons, each sported a heavier, 75mm KwK 40 gun (the KwK 40 L/43 gun for the *Ausf. G,* and the improved KwK 40 L/48 for the *Ausf. H*), which could penetrate 84mm of armor at 1,100 meters. Its own armor protection included thicker armor on the front and sides. Some units carried side skirts to absorb the blow from hollow-charge projectiles fired at its sides, but many such skirts were torn off when passing hedges and trees.

2   The Panther is acknowledged by most military experts as the finest-designed tank of the war.

3   *Generalmajor* Gehrcke, Rommel's newly arrived communications officer. He later became Rommel's reconnaissance expert as well.

4   Until then, the villagers were largely left alone by the occupiers, except for occasional work drafts. To avoid them, able workers would often hide in their *boves* (caves dug in the chalk cliff) to escape being deported for work gangs. These few would later leave their hiding places when it was safe, with chalk residue covering them, arising from the caves "white, like endives" (testimony of villager Paulette Lamiral).

5   Address No. 6 on what is now the Rue Paul Dauvergne.

6   "Street of the Red Brothers."

7   See Appendix A, page 595.

Wednesday, February 16

Rommel spends the better part of the day on the phone. The 9th SS Panzer Division is getting ready to reposition itself south, inland, behind the Nineteenth Army while the 271st Infantry Division in contrast is to be repositioned closer to the beaches.

Rommel assesses his work so far. Hundreds of obstacles are popping up all over the coastline, as his men work feverishly to construct his idea of a defensive line. Rommel's toys are many, and quite deadly.

To create havoc with landing craft coming in at high tide, ramming cones with mines attached and steel saws are to be positioned offshore. Scores of thousands of steel girders are to be dumped onto the coastline, fastened in a variety of shapes.

One of these is the *Tschechenigel*,[1] an idea borrowed from old Czechoslovakian defenses. Consisting of angle or rail beams, often old Czech stock, each unit consists of three or four two-meter beams laid out at right angles to each other, connected and reinforced in the center by welds or fasteners. At high water, they rip the bottom out of any landing craft approaching overhead. Another similar contraption that Rommel is borrowing from his enemies is the "Belgian door": large iron gates that are fastened down in the surf, also designed to foul incoming craft. A similar device to this is the "*Rollbock*."[2]

Tetrahedrons are being constructed with a similar purpose, as are other anti-tank obstacles. Simple stakes seem inadequate to stop landing craft, so *Tellermines*[3] are to be attached to their tops and sides to give the Allied boats a nasty surprise.

Everywhere of course, between the miles of interlaced barbed wire and the rolls of concertina, are areas that will be strewn with thousands of land mines. What kind of mine is set down each time depends upon three factors: location, purpose, and availability. Since Rommel wants more than he can get, he arranges for certain types to start being made in France. Against tanks and vehicles in open areas are laid the classic *Tellermines*, as well as wooden mines (the "*Holzmine 42*"), which are much harder to detect by enemy engineers. For advancing troops, especially along trails and paths, the S-mine[4] is to be used, as well as a wooden model called the "*Schumine 42*."

Wherever Rommel travels, he shows his men how to make homemade defensive devices. Here and there, he finds out about captured caches of medium- to large-caliber shells, most of which are now orphan, since the guns that they had been designed for are now either destroyed or in Allied hands. There has to be a way to use them.

So he has created one.

His design is beautifully basic, and he nicknames it *die Nussknackermine*—"the nutcracker mine." In a workshop, a surplus obsolete shell (such as an old French caliber) is carefully set into a small concrete block and covered with a two-piece lid that has a hole in the center. A pivotable heavy wooden or metal stake is affixed with one end around or next to the tip of the shell, and the other end going up through the hole in the housing. The assembly is then planted into the sand at low tide, casing end first, with the stake sticking up.

The theory is simple. When a boat or vessel runs into the stake, it acts like a lever and rams down onto the shell's fuse, exploding it beneath or beside the vessel. In a similar fashion, the engineers design a mechanism for mortar shells that can also be used with contact detonators. These devices will start being laid next month.

This is another place where that fire-hose technique he was shown back on February 3 comes in handy. To expedite installation of his "nutcrackers," instead of pile-driving the stakes into the seabed, water jets are used.

Rommel's engineers and technicians are finding out that he is full of many other such ideas, devices, and fixtures, all designed to slow down or stop the enemy's landing. He toys with the idea of hiding kerosene tanks along some of the exits leading from key beach areas. One easy strike will engulf an approaching column in flames. He orders searchlights to be positioned in strategic, high positions on certain bluffs. They will not only blind and confuse a landing enemy, but help defenders locate incoming targets at night.

Inland from the beaches, he orders certain open fields, pastures, and clearings to be covered by 3–4m stakes and pylons driven into the ground at 30m spacings. These artificial thickets that he first mentioned to Meise as they flew in his Heinkel back in December will prevent glider landings. New artillery shells will eventually be attached to many, if they ever come.[5]

He will later be amused to learn that these inland obstacles have been jokingly dubbed by the men as "*Rommelspargel*"—"Rommel's asparagus."

He constantly exhorts everyone under him to push themselves to the limit. He has no qualms about ruthlessly driving them, working them to a frazzle, and he does not hesitate to chew someone out over any problem. He tirelessly points out open areas, improper troop positions and equipment, or weak or non-existent camouflage schemes for minefields. There is no such thing as too much or too good camouflage for a minefield or block, he tells them. On his tours, he makes sure that he does not limit his inspections to just fixed bunkers and defensive positions. He visits mobile units as well, reinforcing to them his theme of having to strike back quickly.

He arrives, he inspects, he gives out orders, and then he is gone in a cloud of dust. He never takes time out for evening social events such as a concert or play because his schedule is always full. His sleeping periods are short, and his breakneck pace gives his staff fits. He had though, become accustomed to that in the desert, so it did not bother him much now. He never starts his day any later than 8 a.m. Sometimes, he rises before dawn and gathers up a couple escorts for a tour; his aide Hammermann, sometimes Meise, von Tempelhoff, or Ruge. He eats a hurried breakfast and then hits the road, often between 5 and 6 a.m., riding down country roads at high speeds to see some different installation. He seldom takes much food along (another habit picked up in the desert), although he does try to drink two quarts of seltzer water a day. He makes a hurried inspection, his staff members scribble down some notes, and then they leave in a flurry.

And the routine will continue.

---

1 "Czech hedgehog."

2 Named after roll support, which is a piece of railway equipment used to move rail components.

3 The term comes from the appearance of the mine itself. Around 30cm in diameter and 7–10cm in height, with a charge of some 5kg., they resembled large dinner plates—"*teller*," in German.

4 Known by the G.I.s as "Bouncing Betties" because when triggered, the mines popped up about a meter in the air before exploding their deadly steel balls.

5 They never did.

Thursday, February 17

Generalfeldmarschall von Rundstedt is still on leave at the spas in Bad Tölz.

***

Generalfeldmarschall Rommel and *Generaloberst* Heinz Guderian are in Paris for a scheduled wargame—a *Kriegspiel*. Naturally, it centers around a theoretical invasion of the Continent. The command staffs will go through various scenarios and analyze the ability of the German forces to swiftly react to and defeat the enemy attempts, and to test their alarm setup.

The entire exercise is being held at *PanzerGruppe West* in Paris, sponsored by *General der Panzertruppen* Baron Geyr von Schweppenberg. Although von Rundstedt is still on leave, he is represented at the wargame by his staff. Also attending are Rommel's two army commanders, Dollmann and von Salmuth, as well as all of their corps commanders and various senior staff members.

The *Kriegspiel* goes off rather well in Geyr's opinion. Many considerations were factored in, including political and economic factors. Enemy elements included their operational traits or habits, possible points of contention between them, and pre-invasion operations.

Rommel though, is disturbed by what he sees. For one thing, he believes that the invasion target areas picked are unlikely to actually be selected by the enemy. And the set rules of the exercise did not allow nearly enough for the influence and power of the (in his opinion) overwhelming Allied air forces. Granted, no one present that day denies their superiority over the Luftwaffe. Still, the rules forbade the enemy *Jabos*[1] to wreak much damage on the advancing German panzer units, which is something that would very likely occur each day all over the front.

This last point really sticks with him. He painfully remembers countless times that he himself had been forced to hit the ground at El Alamein to dodge strafing runs by enemy tactical aircraft as they pounded the dust around him; seeing men sometimes standing or lying right next to him get hit or killed by bullets or bomb fragments. And now, with Allied aircraft predicted in much greater numbers, it will be far worse. Whole columns will become paralyzed as the enemy slams them from above.

Unfortunately, few in the exercise seem to understand the power of the enemy air forces, despite his efforts to explain to them the gravity and implications of this overlooked critical factor. And unfortunately, the widely varying opinions presented during the discussions by the navy, the air force, and the army do not help.

In the simulation, Geyr as expected held back the panzer reserves inland for several days after the landing, and then picked a killing ground of his own choosing. He then aligned his formations, attacked the enemy line, and annihilated them. Take that ploy, Rommel thinks to himself, and you can kiss Germany's chances goodbye. The enemy *Jabos* will tear you to pieces. He tones down his response though. Fortunately, other generals had shared Rommel's objections.

General Marcks, commanding the 84th Corps in the Normandy area, is one. Marcks had been designated the "enemy" commander in the exercise since he was experienced in such wargames. When his turn to speak comes, he stands with a determined look on his face, and awkwardly stumps over to the huge map that is before them. Using his cane, he whacks the section of the mapboard at the Seine Bay. Normandy, he declares firmly, is where the invasion will probably come. Despite a few frowns and head-shakes, he goes on. From Normandy, he concludes, the Allies can pivot around Caen, a small key industrial town just west of and a couple kilometers inland from the Orne estuary. There will probably be a second landing in Brittany. If that happens, the enemy's objective naturally has to be the huge port of Cherbourg. Capture of this strategic port alone will provide supplies for some three or four armies—more than enough to sustain and break out from a sizeable bridgehead.

Rommel firmly replies that the naval experts have concluded Normandy will not be the target. There are simply too many underwater reefs in the seaward approaches.

Marcks answers that this might be the case on the Cotentin peninsula, but not along the Calvados coast. Rommel scowls, irritated to be corrected. Dollmann tells Marcks that there are some reefs along the Calvados coast too, not to mention a few towering bluffs manned by batteries. Marcks sits down, a stony look on his face.

One point that does come up at today's meetings is Rommel's recent inspection trip to southern France. They discuss at length the lack of preparation along the southern coasts. Coupled to this, they reflect on the enemy's amphibious capabilities in the Mediterranean (evidenced by the landings at Sicily, Salerno, and just last month, Anzio). They analyze possible landing sites.

An important administrative point is announced to all the Western senior commanders. The upcoming conference with the Führer, scheduled to occur in one week at the Wolf's Lair, has been put off for a few weeks until the Führer moves back to the Berghof from East Prussia.

***

Today, the Kriegsmarine releases a half-dozen batteries of 88mm and 150mm naval guns for use on the coast.

It is, in the Army's opinion, not nearly enough.

---

1   Short for *Jagdbomber*, the German term for a tactical fighter-bomber.

Friday, February 18

Generalfeldmarschall von Rundstedt is going to be returning to Paris in a few days. When he does, Rommel will take ten well-deserved days off himself.

***

After a quick breakfast, Rommel is on the road again at 7 a.m., this time to the western coast of Brittany. OKW has indicated that the Führer has become concerned over reports from *Fremde Heeres West* of enemy units concentrating in southwestern England. The invasion might be launched against Brittany and the port of Brest.

Besides Meise and *Vizeadmiral* Ruge, accompanying him on this trip will be von Rundstedt's chief of staff, General Blumentritt. So the entourage drives first southeast along the Seine to the Hôtel Georges V in Paris to pick him up. Then they leave the city, heading west towards the Atlantic coast.

After driving some 450km to the base of the large Brittany peninsula, they begin their inspections at the major U-boat base of St.-Nazaire. By now, the city and port have been all but destroyed by the Allied bombings over the last three years. Buildings are in ruins, businesses have been closed down, churches gutted, and the residential areas have been devastated. But the submarine base, though seriously damaged, is still functional, despite the fact that the U-boat pens provide barely adequate protection from enemy raids. And the small security force located at the base is still quite active.

The inevitable conference begins. First comes a report by General Fahrmbacker,[1] commanding the unit assigned to this section, the XXV Infantry Corps. His southernmost division, the 275th, shows the worst status. It consists of little more than a headquarters, a regimental staff, a unit of artillery, and a couple battalions of old geezers. Rommel orders another regimental staff and another battalion from the 343rd to supplement the division, as well as two remaining battalions from the now-departed 243rd Infantry.

The officers discuss the area units covering all three critical seaports in this area—St.-Nazaire, Lorient, and Brest. Each of the three major ports, despite their strong defensive posture against any seaward attack, only has one actual battalion of regular infantry to guard them from the landward side. So the inspection group goes over all the units for each port—auxiliary troops, dock force, security, balloon crews, smoke-laying units, miscellaneous workers, and the artillery batteries. For each of the three ports, this includes one medium and two heavy army batteries, a couple naval batteries, and five or six naval anti-aircraft batteries. The ground order of battle also, unfortunately to some, includes a couple contingents of those crazy Russians.

After the conference, Rommel's group drives northwest up the coast to inspect a few positions. They travel along the underside of the Brittany peninsula, and about

135km up, they reach the summer port of Quiberon for the night. The town, about 65km southeast of Lorient, is at the end of a smaller peninsula that juts out into the ocean, providing a beautiful view of the sea.

Their quarters, located at the extreme end of this narrow strip of land, are at the site of a famous naval battle. There, in November of 1759, an English fleet of some two dozen vessels under the famed Admiral Hawke had chased a similar-sized unit of French ships through a fierce storm and had defeated them in a decisive battle that had ended at sunset.

***

Today at Fontainebleau, Alfred Gause talks by phone to OKW deputy operations chief Walther Warlimont. He fails once more to persuade him to see Rommel's position on the usage of the panzer divisions close to the coast. Finally Warlimont tells him, "OKW does *not* want them moved from their present areas."

***

General Guderian travels to an area between Nancy and Luneville to attend a training exercise conducted by the newly created *Panzer Lehr* division;[2] Fritz Bayerlein, the good-natured, feisty, stocky commanding officer, oversees the exercise.[3] He took command of this powerful panzer division on January 10, but his senior officers think that they are ready. They have only received copies of Guderian's *Die Tigerfibel*[4] at 11:30 p.m. the night before. Having intensely pored over it, they then practiced a good part of the night. So they hope today goes well.

After a couple basic demonstrations, Guderian divides the men up into three groups to test them individually: first the panzer commanders, then the tank gunners, and lastly, the non-commissioned officers. The test results are mixed, some of them doing well, some failing. Guderian then gives them all a class on gunnery before he leaves, letting them breathe easy once again. Tomorrow, they will have to practice what they have learned in the cold.

***

Tonight, another *Steinbock* air raid: 175 aircraft fly into England, and this time, London is hit hard. It is one of the most damaging raids to the capital in nearly three years. Only nine bombers are lost.

---

1   Fifty-five-year-old *General der Artillerie* Wilhelm Fahrmbacker.
2   "Tank training" Division. See Glossary.
3   Forty-five-year-old *Generalleutnant* Fritz Hermann Bayerlein had been a private in World War I, rising to the rank of *feldwebel* before the war's end. He received a commission in the 21st Cavalry

Regiment in 1922. At the start of World War II, he was General Guderian's Ia during their headlong advances through Poland, France, and then on towards Moscow in 1941. That September, he had been transferred to Rommel's newly named *PanzerGruppe Afrika* in North Africa, where he quickly distinguished himself as chief of staff of the Afrika Korps component. Rommel took to him at once, and the two got along well. On June 1, 1942, Gause was wounded in an artillery barrage. Rommel assigned *Oberst* Bayerlein to be temporary chief of staff of the *PanzerGruppe*, until Gause recuperated. When Gause returned to duty on June 23, Bayerlein returned to his position of chief of staff of the Afrika Korps. However, a month later, he had to again temporarily replace Gause, who had suffered a concussion from a nearby shell burst. On August 31, Afrika Korps commander General Nehring was wounded in an air raid, so Bayerlein temporarily took over as its commander and did so again in November. Bayerlein later took Gause's place again for the *PanzerGruppe*, and eventually *Armeegruppe Afrika*. He did a good job with Rommel until his tearful departure on March 7, 1943. Two days later, Rommel left Africa to fly to the Führer's Rastenburg headquarters to plead for assistance. He did not get it, and was ordered not to return to Africa. Bayerlein would later see him there a number of times over the summer.

4   Guderian's *The Tiger Primer*. See footnote for February 12.

Saturday, February 19

Generalfeldmarschall von Rundstedt is still on leave at the spas in Bad Tölz. In St-Germain-en-Laye, expansion of his headquarters and villa is finishing up. This includes the air raid shelter being built next to his prized garden. Blumentritt expects to see a firestorm erupt over it when von Rundstedt returns.

***

After breakfast, *Generalfeldmarschall* Rommel begins his day with a conference in the enlisted mess hall in the small port of Quiberon. He and his staff go over their inspection points taken at St.-Nazaire and write down their recommendations. Also discussed are possible tactics that can be used against an enemy landing force launched against such a port. Bogus navigational aids are suggested, as are periodic sessions of making smoke.

They talk about tactics and devices that they might incorporate, first as the enemy nears their landing area, and second, as they actually begin landing their troops. Of course, that is assuming one knows when and where the enemy is coming.

The conference moves on to the concept of using extra U-boat crews, dock helpers, and other base personnel against such a landing force. The last topic covered is about how to render such a port useless to enemy shipping if it looks like being captured.

Then the inspection party is off. They first go to a couple bases south of the U-boat port of Lorient before heading up to the famous base itself. Lorient, as expected, has a strong defensive line, surrounded by fortifications and strengthened by a number of batteries. The port has been busy making hedgehogs and other offshore obstacles, and Rommel is satisfied with the progress made.

The motorcade finally leaves the main port area and heads out to Douarnenez Bay. The group notes only a few obstacles up here, and the wide, sandy beaches are defended by only a few companies of Russians. They travel on towards Brest, and the shoreline scenery is beautiful. They stop to inspect a battery in Camaret near the outskirts of the large port, and then move on towards the third U-boat base. They stop for the evening at a soldiers' home in Morgat, on the Crozon peninsula. A few conferences, dinner, some after-dinner talk, and then they retire to bed.

***

Today *Generaloberst* Guderian attends the second day of a training exercise being conducted by Bayerlein's newly created *Panzer Lehr* division in an area between Nancy and Luneville. The men drill with their armored vehicles outside in the icy snow, and General Guderian a few times gets distressed over their results. At one point, he growls at them, "This is the *worst* nonsense I have seen in my entire military career!"

Dissatisfied, he finally leaves the unit. Chastened, they (as one officer later puts it) "console themselves with a first-class dinner."

Sunday, February 20

Although it is the Sabbath, Rommel still has a good deal of work to do. So before dawn he is up, fed, and out the door of the soldiers' home where he stayed overnight. Despite the wet haze and steady rain, his group reaches the key port of Brest early and begins. They find that the seaward approaches to the base are strong, and those facing inland, though fewer, are also well-built.

It looks as though it will rain steadily throughout the day as the group moves on to the northwest tip of Brittany, taking notes as they go: This area is unsatisfactory for a major landing; defenses in that sector seem good. They travel eastward to the well-defended Goolven Bay,[1] and then onward.

Rommel is amused to see that despite the bad weather, the Bretons are out today *en masse*. Dressed in their Sunday outfits and carrying their umbrellas, they casually stroll up and down town streets. The men typically wear broad-brimmed black hats, and the ladies show off various types of white head covers, displaying distinct designs that vary in style from one locale to the next.

Usually the civilians recognize him—it is hard not to, riding in his beautiful dark shiny Horch, a field marshal flag in front, his entourage in their cars behind him. Typically, people first slow down and stare at him as his car drives up. Then they whisper, often wide-eyed, as he emerges in his elegant black leather topcoat, his marshal's baton in hand. It takes only a few moments for them to realize who he is, and you sometimes hear in a low voice *"C'est Rommel!"*

Noontime. They travel inland to the Monts d'Arrée hills, some three dozen kilometers east-northeast of Brest. There they inspect the still-forming 353rd Infantry Division,[2] normally commanded by *Generalmajor* Mahlmann.[3] In his absence, the executive officer and the divisional staff make their report. They detail how, in the event of an invasion, their initial objectives would be to secure the small road networks into their area. Rommel comments that he is not quite sure what the enemy would be doing in this area, far from the main roads.

The weather has not let up much, and so they all sit inside a chilly tent to have dinner. Someone comments dryly that their stew is not much warmer than the tent, and Rommel, usually either affable or gently reproachful to members of his staff when they make such remarks, is strangely quiet and even distant. Even Blumentritt notices the difference in his demeanor.

Later on, someone in their group, talking to a divisional staff member who has been with the core elements that had made up the 353rd for years, discovers the probable reason for the field marshal's icy demeanor. Years before, Mahlmann as a colonel had written a scathing review of the field marshal's book, *Infanterie grief an.*[4]

Rommel has a memory like an elephant.

On the drive home, they stop in Rennes, then head towards in Le Mans to see General Dollmann. They are delayed though, because Rommel's Horch sputters and stalls several times. Corporal Daniel determines that the petrol in the tank is contaminated or low grade. They eventually arrive at Seventh Army headquarters, Rommel discusses his findings with Dollmann and his senior officers. Dollmann, as it turns out, heartily agrees with Rommel's suggestions. The meeting goes well.

The inspection group finally leaves the headquarters. Tired from the long trip and dreary weather, and eager to return home, they walk towards the awaiting vehicles. Naturally, they will have to drop General Blumentritt off in Paris on the way back. Rommel though is himself in no hurry and wants to relax and enjoy the return trip. So he nonchalantly tells the rest of his entourage to directly return to Fontainebleau ahead of him, and asks Blumentritt to ride with him. The two of them pile into Rommel's Horch, which now carries high-grade petrol, and begin a nice leisurely trip home, the field marshal as usual sitting up front.

On the way back, they have a long, interesting talk. Rommel is happy to have an avid listener, and the OB West chief of staff is in turn fascinated with Rommel's schemes for beefing up the coast, especially the highly technical engineering tasks. Rommel, flattered by the interest, admits that engineering had been his favorite subject at the War Academy.

Their subjects vary, and inevitably, Rommel ends up regaling him with some recollections of North Africa. He tells Blumentritt that, as close as they came to the Suez Canal, they finally lost their campaign because their supply lines became just too long, and with Malta still in enemy hands, their stocks could not keep up.

His supplies, he explains, were adequate at first, "but just barely. The problem was that as we pushed the British back to the Egyptian border, their supply points on the Suez Canal became much closer. In the meantime, our lines following the communications lines became so long that keeping up was just impossible. And our losses kept mounting."

"Especially panzers," Blumentritt replies.

"Precisely. It got to where I only had about 80 *Jägers* that were operational. We had very few panzers left. Fuel was desperately low, and ammo was so low that some of the units could only fire a few rounds in a defensive withdrawal."

"Our supplies were being destroyed at sea by the RAF and the British fleet, since we had lost air and sea control. You wouldn't believe how many of our ships were sunk trying to get through to us—ships carrying munitions and fuel…"

"And replacements? What did the High Command do about that?"

"What could they do?" Rommel replies. "I had told the Führer about these problems a number of times earlier in the year, but what supply forces we had were inadequate, and additional air units were committed in Russia. Those that we had were being whittled down by the enemy. Those that made it through could no longer land close to us, because we had advanced into Egypt."

"You had advanced that far?"

"Yes," Rommel replies, his eyes blazing. "There we were one day on the heels of the British, while everyone was cheering us on. The next, we were fighting them off, just trying to survive, screaming for supplies while everyone in Berlin kept dumbly rooting us on."

Of course, not being able to freely command your own troops did not help either. Jodl had frequently put in his few pfennigs' worth of advice. And the command organization had been so screwed up, that just about anybody at Supreme Headquarters had a say in what he did.

"Kesselring gave us directives," he said, ticking off the factors on one of his gloved hand, "because he was Commander-in-Chief, Italy. Göring could dictate commands to us too—at least, when he wasn't drugged out. Mussolini sometimes wanted to butt in, that incompetent clod—even his worthless *Commando Supremo* in Rome wanted to give us orders from time to time!"

Rommel looks back at Blumentritt and asks, "How on earth was I supposed to lead my troops into battle, when so many commanders and authorities could intervene?" They did it frequently too, and often at the most unexpected times. "You know, Blumentritt, it's a wonder we were effective at all."

They both agree that the present command structure in France is not much different. Right now, with von Rundstedt on leave, *Feldmarschall* Sperrle is the ranking authority, and OB West is at his disposal. How strange; a Luftwaffe general in charge of the ground forces! Just like Kesselring in Italy… Of course, Sperrle would have little control of the Navy or the SS, and was subject to operational directives from the Führer or OKW, administrative issues of OKH, guidance from Göring, and so on.

Rommel changes the subject and goes back to North Africa. He recalls his ordeal at El Alamein that crucial early November of 1942. He had decided to take matters in hand. "I flew up to see the Führer," he recalls, "and to tell him in person what was what."

He recalls that day when he had flown from North Africa to make a personal appeal on behalf of his army to be able to fall back. He tells Blumentritt how Keitel and Jodl had met him at the airport, and how coldly they had treated him on the trip back to Supreme Headquarters. He politely glosses over his stormy meeting with the Führer, tactfully stating instead that they had discussed the military situation. He makes sure to criticize the OKW staff though.

However, he then recounts how Hitler had berated him, and had later come out and apologized for his anger. When he and Hitler had at last sat down to tea, the Führer had sympathized with his situation.

Rommel notes with contempt that the OKW staff had then changed their attitudes as well, from hostility to cordiality, abruptly changing their moods like chameleons to their surroundings.

"*Sie sind Arschküsse*," he finishes. "They're ass-kissers."

After telling the story, Rommel pauses and then declares, "Well, that's in the past. Now I have new problems to face." They discuss in detail the problems they have identified. Rommel goes over his pet theory of hitting the enemy at the waterline.

Blumentritt feels his loyalty to his own commanding officer and honorably defends von Rundstedt's position of waiting and striking the enemy is further inland.

"*Generalfeldmarschall* von Rundstedt also assumes that the Allies will employ heavy air power when the invasion comes," he says. "And like you sir, he feels that they will use some sort of saturation bombing of the landing area. That's another reason that he wants to keep the panzers inland. Because, even if we did have a sufficient number of panzers right there among the coastal fortifications, he feels that the concentrated fire from the intense air bombing patterns and from their heavy ships offshore would hem in the panzers and prevent them from being able to maneuver. And if the panzers can't maneuver..."

"*Leichtes Ziel,*" Rommel finishes. Sitting ducks; classic *blitzkrieg* theory.

Blumentritt mentions Italy. He notes that there were several instances where the panzers were put into the line and converted, so to speak, into static pillboxes. Ordered not to maneuver, they were picked off one by one. Just like the French tanks had been back in 1940.

Rommel counters that at Salerno there were also some fortifications along the shore, and with them, they had almost thrown the enemy back into the sea. All they had needed were a few more units—and time.

Blumentritt points out that von Rundstedt still feels that the panzers would be safer inland, and still be able to react to an invasion.

"Yes, well, he wasn't in North Africa like I was," Rommel says grimly. "While I was there, I learned the RAF's *modus operandi*. No doubt they will employ it when they invade. And when they do, our panzers, no matter where they are, will not be able to move by day or by night without incurring attacks by air."

"The only problem,," Blumentritt says, "is that if we put our panzers all near the coast, we will have to correctly guess where the enemy is going to land. If we don't, almost all of them will be in the wrong place, and many hundreds of kilometers away from where the fighting is. And they will then have even more of a difficult time moving to the landing area."

He continues, "That's why *Feldmarschall* von Rundstedt wants a large panzer reserve, so that they can cover a larger area of coast without exposing themselves to the enemy air and sea power."

Rommel looks at his companion and says, "Well, if I do live through this, I'd like to sit around my house for a few years and start a few fruit and vegetable gardens."

Blumentritt nods with a smile. "Von Rundstedt loves gardens, too. He goes berserk if he sees one that has not been tended to."

Rommel smiles. "Wouldn't that be great? You know, grow tomatoes the size of soccer balls!"

"And carrots the size of cannon!" They both laugh heartily.

They go on talking happily about gardens. Rommel tells about his new garden at Herrlingen and about his plans to expand the garden areas.

After a moment of silence, Rommel sighs wistfully. "Well, I just hope that the Allies give me enough time to build up. Up to, oh, the end of May." He stares off into the moving countryside, gazing out into the late afternoon overcast haze, listening to the rain on the car's roof. "Then they can come," he says.

The time goes by, and they suddenly realize that they are in the outskirts of Paris, late in the evening. Rommel drops Blumentritt off at the Hôtel Georges V in Paris, where von Rundstedt is expected to return tomorrow. He then proceeds through the French capital and on down to his headquarters at Fontainebleau.

After he arrives, he has a quick meeting with Gause. His chief of staff has been in contact with Warlimont at OKW, pressing him on the question of who is to command the mobile units, and where they are to be positioned. Warlimont on the 18th had told him that "OKW does not desire their movement from the present areas." A couple days later, Warlimont has responded to the question, and in official language, given OKW's position. Basically, it states that while Rommel should have more say in commanding the panzers, most areas of disagreement should be ironed out between Gause and Blumentritt themselves. Warlimont has done a nice job of keeping OKW on the fence, and Rommel is back to square one on this issue. Great.

Sighing, he drafts a personal letter to his subordinate commands: Seventh Army, Fifteenth Army, and the Netherlands Command. He congratulates them on their efforts so far, and exhorts them to continue as much as possible, using every resource they can—he greatly emphasizes that point—to lay whole fields of mines and set mass numbers of offshore obstacles.

He wants them to be ready.

***

Tonight, in response to the RAF air raid over Leipzig, another *Steinbock* air raid is launched with 165 aircraft. Navigational difficulties limit the damage done over England, and another nine bombers are lost.

---

1   On the upper coast of the Brittany peninsula, about 38km northeast of Brest.

2   The 353rd included small units from the 137th, 328th, 371st, 306th, and 389th Divisions, all of which had been decimated in Russia and withdrawn to reform. The 353rd would eventually include over 1,700 Russian (Öst) troops.

3   Fifty-one-year-old *Generalmajor* Paul Mahlmann, who assumed command November 20, 1943 at the division's inception. An infantry officer in World War I, he rose through the ranks in the postwar years, later taking an active part in the campaigns in France and in Russia.

4   *Infantry Attacks*. Published in 1937 as a military textbook that reflected Rommel's experiences in World War I, it received wide acclaim and has since become a classic primer on military tactics.

Monday, February 21

Generalfeldmarschall von Rundstedt finally returns to his command at the Hôtel Georges V in Paris after his four-week holiday.[1] His headquarters naturally welcomes him back. He eventually retires to his hotel room and sits down with his chief of staff, who proceeds to update him on what's been happening in his absence. The highlight of Blumentritt's briefing is telling him all about his latest tour with Rommel.

***

Rommel meanwhile is back at Fontainebleau, fresh from a long night's rest.

This morning, he and his staff go over their plans for further tours along the coast. The commander-in-chief of the Netherlands forces, Luftwaffe *General der Flieger* Friedrich Christiansen, is informed through his own chief of staff, *Generalleutnant* Heinz Helmuth von Wühlisch, that he can expect the field marshal sometime early in the next month, and that he will be inspecting the progress that has been made so far on the offshore obstacle construction.

Von Wühlisch replies in casual tones that the inspection is really not necessary at this time. The installation of their obstacles is still "in the experimental stage." He adds that the main thing they have found so far was that only stake-type obstacles are suitable for the water.

Rommel is upset at hearing this. Two months nearly wasted on inactivity! To make matters worse, his headquarters finds out today that the order Christiansen was told to give on making ports unserviceable in the event of imminent capture has not yet been issued.

It is true that the Netherlands command is not technically a part of *Heeresgruppe B*. Now evidently, it seems that they do not want to adopt Rommel's spirit of determination either. Frustrated, he grudgingly tells his staff to change his itinerary and to postpone the Netherlands tour until later in the month. In the meantime, he says sternly, he wants *Vizeadmiral* Ruge to make his own tour up there later this week and to emphasize to them in strong terms that Rommel's directives are to be carried out completely and immediately.

On top of all his command frustrations, Rommel is having some personal trouble. The older of his two dachshunds, Ajax, is becoming a real problem. He terrorizes the younger Elbo incessantly. Ajax also has a decided dislike of sabers and for some reason, staff cars, barking loudly whenever he is around either.

He does enjoy shoes though, and has developed an embarrassing habit of chewing on the footgear of whoever happens to be around the field marshal. The dog prefers in particular the shiny leather boots of officers, including visitors.

One of his favorite marks has become Rommel's hapless chief of staff, and it has become clear that Ajax over time has started to wear on the man's nerves. Almost regularly now when Gause is in Rommel's presence, his boots fall prey to the mutt's friendly assault, although the dog will take to task any other human target of opportunity as well. So if someone else walks into the field marshal's study (and Gause is not around), Ajax immediately shifts his attention to their shoes.

Today is no different. When Rommel begins discussing business with a visiting officer in his study, Ajax, lying on the floor under a sofa, quietly eyes the man's boots. The animal's excitement increases, and slowly its willpower drains away.

Rommel spots Ajax going into a crouch, getting ready to move in on his target. Fuming, the field marshal stands up and walks around his desk. Before the dachshund can make its move, Rommel roughly grabs it by its head and tail, drags it over to the doorway, opens the door, and throws the dog bodily out. As he does so, he turns to the visiting officer and grumbles, "*This* is the only one who won't obey my orders."

It has clearly not been a good day.

---

1   See footnote for December 22.

Tuesday, February 22

Von Rundstedt, just returned from a relaxing stay at the spas in Bad Tölz, spends his first day back catching up on paperwork at the Hôtel Georges V in Paris. That evening, he decides to go out for dinner. He usually dines in elegance, sometimes just enjoying the finer dishes of his hotel, and sometimes going out to a fancy restaurant. His favorite place to go to though, is the renowned Maxim's restaurant on the Champs-Elysées.[1] He has become friends with the winemaker there, Henri, who serves him an excellent St. Emilion bordeaux. Most of his officers though, prefer a Pommard '39,[2] which always puzzles him.

"I cannot understand," he sometimes comments wonderingly. "Why do they drink Pommard after a meal, instead of brandy with their coffee?"

To him, it is a matter of strange taste.

***

It is now Rommel's turn to take time off. He departs Fontainebleau for ten days' leave and is driven to the airport. He climbs into his own specially outfitted twin-engine green and yellow Heinkel 111 and, along with its two ME-109 escorts, they take off. Rommel watches the sun through the window, shimmering beautifully over the plane's wings as they fly above the clouds. The converted bomber makes its way southeast, towards Ulm. He normally would travel to Germany by car, since wartime gas rationing is critical at this time, and the enemy controls the skies. The Führer has instructed officers for safety reasons to not fly unless it is an emergency. But high rank does allow some privileges, and right now he wants to get home as quickly as he can to spend some time at his new home in Herrlingen. His recent, charged efforts of the last few weeks have both physically and emotionally drained him.

On this trip, Rommel has finally decided to take Ajax home with him. Now a terror at headquarters, barking noisily at strangers, he will make a good house-dog. Besides, the younger brown-and-black Elbo, as he will later explain to Lucie, is "really too funny, but not yet quite house-trained." Anyway, he knows that she will love Ajax. He will make a good companion.

The plane lands and a waiting car takes him to his new home. When the field marshal walks in with frisky little Ajax, Lucy greets him, and they exchange warm greetings. He then turns to embrace his tall, gangly son Manfred, standing awkwardly near the door, wearing horn-rimmed glasses, a flustered smile on the lad's face. Rommel shakes his head wonderingly as he beams at Manfred. He is constantly being amazed by his growing son. His adjutant Aldinger is there too, smiling, humbly quiet, giving the family its greeting space as he unobtrusively begins unloading the field marshal's luggage.

Inside, Rommel finds the *Oberbürgermeister* of Stuttgart, 54-year-old Dr. Karl Strölin, and an assistant. Rommel suppresses a groan. Not only will he have to entertain, but he will have to talk politics as well. Lucie goes through the formality of properly introducing them, although Strölin is certainly not a stranger to them. The Rommels had met him when they first moved to Herrlingen, and the mayor has visited the house several times since then. Anyway, Strölin had briefly served in Rommel's unit in World War I. Lucie is enthusiastic in her introduction. The field marshal though, is worn out from the job and the trip, and right now he just wants to relax. He is not up to company.

The two men exchange greetings. The mayor, to explain his presence, says that he had come out to visit Lucie earlier in the day to give her a painting, and when she had mentioned to him that her husband was coming home that afternoon, he had begged her to let him stay, so that he might talk to the field marshal on a matter of great importance.

As they go into the living room, Lucie points out the new painting with pride. Rommel does not realize how much Strölin has been courting Lucie's goodwill for a special cause, lavishing her with several visits and special gifts or favors.

Rommel does not care much for the mayor, although he carries no animosity towards him either. What bothers him is the way the man has indirectly wheedled his way into the field marshal's life. Early in the month, when Gause had requested to go on leave and Lucie, ever polite and considerate, had welcomed him to Herrlingen just as she earlier had his wife, Strölin had come over and had talked to Gause and Lucie at length about political changes that were needed. Gause, in bad health, depressed about the war, dejected about losing his home and savings, and feeling helpless about the political situation in his country, was a good listener, openly agreeing with the problems that the mayor either stated or alluded to.

Lucie had been a harder subject for the mayor to win over. She had listened to him during his visits with a degree of skepticism, and he had been careful not to get too radical in his complaints against the government. He had instead wooed her with lavish gifts, including often sending bouquets of flowers to their home. Occasionally, Strölin sent her tickets to the theater, and he made sure that she had an official car available at any time. If she ever chanced to go into Stuttgart for any reason, she was given free boarding whenever she wished at one of the city's most lavish hotels. And of course, now there was that painting, a large representation of Rommel in uniform.

Lucie and Aldinger leave to get refreshments as Rommel, the mayor, and Manfred sit down in the parlor. They begin with some idle chitchat. How Manfred is growing so tall, as the lad sits there smiling. Strölin tells how Stuttgart had been bombed the night before by the RAF.[3] Rommel studies the mayor intently as they talk. He notes that he is chain-smoking and seems somewhat nervous, although he is trying to hide it well behind a smiling countenance and genial behavior.

After a few minutes, the mayor senses that Rommel is fatigued. So he wastes no further time and begins by saying that he has also come out to talk to the field marshal on a matter of great importance. He pulls some documents out of his briefcase and gazing at his audience—Lucie, Manfred, Aldinger, and the expectant field marshal—he begins to speak.

Strölin, once an avid Nazi, is now an anti-government conspirator. As such, he starts off by first condemning the National Socialist regime, calling it a brutal, criminal, runaway abuse of power. It is destroying their country, and will lead them all down the path to total destruction, unless someone like the field marshal himself takes the bull by the horns. Looking directly at Rommel, he solemnly declares, "We need you, *Herr Feldmarschall*, to save the Reich."

Everyone in the room is dead silent as Strölin continues. Hitler's government has to go, he says bluntly. Its illegal and immoral activities are too much for the world to have to take.

And there is more. He speaks to them of horrible crimes being committed against Jews on a scale so large that even he has trouble believing it. To support his claim, he selects a few more documents for Rommel to examine. One of them is a memo to the Ministry of the Interior that shows a number of activities offensive in humanitarian terms. As he passes to Rommel some documents to prove his point, he talks about grisly atrocities against the peoples of the East: massacres, brutality, torture, and outright systematic extermination. Something has to be done, the mayor said grimly.

Strölin goes on, outlining the plans of a small group that he represents. He tells Rommel that a number of senior army officers on the Eastern Front are considering arresting Hitler and forcing him to announce his abdication on the radio.[4] Along with a few other officers, they have met covertly for about a few years now, trying unsuccessfully to overthrow the existing government.[5] Since an inevitable coup d'état would probably trigger civil unrest and political chaos, someone solid would have to take over leadership immediately, someone everybody respected and would readily accept.

He points to Rommel sitting in his chair and tells him that as a war hero well respected by the enemy, he is that man. The facts are obvious. Rommel, the mayor boasts, is their greatest and most popular general, and he is more respected abroad than any other. His loyalty to Germany as well as to the Wehrmacht is beyond question. His good favor with the Allies is a rare and critically important necessity, if the Reich is to have any hope of negotiating a survivable peace. Just as importantly, he is a member in good standing of the Nazi party. Thus many die-hard Nazis would also be willing to accept him. Basically, he is the best choice—indeed, the only choice—for this pivotal job. Strölin tells him, "You are the only one who can prevent civil war in Germany. You must lend your name to the movement." The mayor spends a couple more minutes trying to convince him.

Getting to the end of his speech, he states that the Nazis in power have to be overthrown if Germany is to survive as a country. For this to happen, Hitler has to be killed. "If Hitler does not die," he concludes, "then we are all lost!"

At the mention of assassinating the Führer, Rommel's one-time mentor, the field marshal stiffens. He has found the mayor's remarks up until now distressing enough, but now they have taken quite a dangerous turn. Besides, as far as Rommel is concerned, assassination is totally out of the question. Making things worse is Manfred's presence. It will do no good for his son to hear such things, much less accidentally repeat them to the wrong people. And what type of message does it give him to hear his father considering the idea of killing the leader of the Reich? A man his father, a national hero, has supported for years? No, the mayor has gone too far.

Rommel rises in a dignified fashion and says sternly, "Herr Strölin, I would be grateful if you would refrain from speaking such opinions in the presence of my young son!"

Strölin pauses. Looking around the room, he sees indignation, resentment, and shock on the faces of his audience. He senses that he has perhaps gone too far and begins to put his papers away.

They finally talk a bit more, though there is now a decided chill in the room. Rommel promises to at least think about what the mayor has said, if for no other reason than to get him to leave. Strölin asks Rommel whether or not he will come to Germany's aid if his country needs him.

"Yes," Rommel admits, "I believe it is my duty to come to the rescue of Germany."

"Well sir, your country is in trouble."

"Herr Strölin, I do not need *you* to tell me that," Rommel grumbles.

Embarrassed, Strölin apologizes for intruding on Rommel's homecoming, and beats a hasty withdrawal to his car.[6]

The troubled family soon has dinner with the issue clearly unresolved, Manfred silent on the matter. Later, Rommel discusses it with Lucie. What the mayor said did make some sense, but how on earth could a field marshal turn against the leader of Germany? And not assassination! Out of the question! Pure treason! Such things were far beneath the dignity of a German officer.

Lucie points out the obvious fact that removing the Führer is also a very dangerous undertaking. And besides, she adds, it had been Hitler who had first made him famous. He had put him in charge of his own personal bodyguard. And despite Rommel's lack of experience in armored warfare, he had given him command of a panzer division in 1940 and put him on the leading edge of their early victories in France and North Africa.

The couple finally goes to bed, deep in thought over the idea.

***

Again responding to Allied raids over Germany, a series of *Steinbock* air raids is initiated. It will continue sporadically for three weeks. Although damage to English cities is significant, the offensive is clearly not yielding the results that Göring had hoped for. And the Führer is not impressed.

More occasional raids will continue through May.

---

1 Von Rundstedt invited Rommel a few times to dine with him there, but Rommel turned him down each time.

2 A premier burgundy.

3 About 542 bombers hit the city, although not much serious damage occurred.

4 According to Strölin, Rommel actually agreed in principle with this idea.

5 The group had been dubbed by the Gestapo the *"Schwartz Kapelle"*—the "Black Band," or 'Black Orchestra.' In 1942-43, there had been a "Red Orchestra" (*Rote Kapelle*), so dubbed by the Gestapo's intelligence. This had been a communist-aligned covert intelligence network formed after the German invaded Russia. Its prime mission was not necessarily the removal of the Nazi regime, but rather to secure victory for the Soviet Union over Germany. The name originated in the Spring of 1943. Gestapo investigations, headed by Dr. Manfred Roeder, had centered on certain members of the Abwehr, and a surprise inspection of now-Major Hans Dohnanyi's office yielded incriminating evidence of a plot to overthrow the government. The subsequent inquest by Roeder's section was dubbed by him the "Black Band Investigation," fashioned no doubt after the "Red Band" ring he had helped to break the year before.

6 Although David Irving wrote that Strölin soon left, Samuel Mitcham, based on the material in the book *Rommel* by Richard D. Law and Craig W. H. Luther, indicated Strölin did not leave immediately, and that the discussions lasted over five hours. This seems unlikely since the field marshal had just arrived home and was tired from his trip. Still, it is possible that the mayor stayed for dinner and the dialogue continued on and off well into the evening. Neither Brown (*Bodyguard of Lies*) nor Fraser in his biography indicate how long the mayor stayed, although the latter refers to the meeting as a conversation, and not a long discussion.

Wednesday, February 23

Generalfeldmarschall von Rundstedt, just returned from leave, spends his second day back catching up on paperwork at his winter quarters in the Hôtel Georges V. Of course, it takes more time to catch up when one takes breaks for sumptuous meals and relaxing conversations in the parlor…

***

Generalfeldmarschall Rommel is at his new home in Herrlingen on a ten-day furlough. With him is his fifteen-year-old son, Manfred, who has recently been inducted into the Luftwaffe auxiliary. Today, the two spend time together, and Rommel gets an opportunity to really study the boy. These days, he is often amazed by his teenage son, and every time he sees him, it seems like the boy has grown a little taller and has learned something new. Sometimes, Manfred makes some remark that surprises his father with his complexity and maturity. Yes, Manfred is indeed growing up. As if to confirm this, the field marshal observes that the boy is having some acne problems.

Rommel gently chuckles. No doubt, girls will be next.

***

Vizeadmiral Friedrich Ruge leaves Fontainebleau today for his own tour of the coast of northern Europe. He travels northwest along the Seine, his destination Le Havre. There he calls on the fortress naval commander, Admiral von Tresckow. Afterward, Ruge takes time for a pleasant visit with a former assistant of his, *Korvettenkapitän der Reserve* Kloess, once Ruge's flag lieutenant. Kloess now oversees the Le Havre shipyards.

On his return trip, Ruge follows the Seine eastward to Rouen to see the port captain there and assess the port's defensive stature. Finally, he formally calls on the *Kanalküste* naval commander, *Vizeadmiral* Friedrich Rieve, at his headquarters in the town. Ruge discusses with the admiral and his staff Rommel's expectations for naval defenses and strategy.

***

Adolf Hitler, the subject of Mayor Strölin's plea to Rommel the night before, today leaves his *Wolfsschanze* headquarters in Eastern Prussia to attend an "Old Guard" conference in Munich. From there, he will go to his mountain villa, the Berghof, for a few months. He has a number of reasons for going there. For one thing, the air raid shelters at the Wolf's Lair are inadequate, and if the Allies ever decided to try to kill him by air attack, he would be vulnerable. Leaving will allow its air raid defenses and shelters to be heavily reinforced by the OT without bothering him or his staff.

Another reason for the move is that at the Berghof, he will be closer to the Italian front. He recently said somewhat amusingly, "We have built headquarters in just about every other corner of the Reich, but never dreamed that we would one day need one near Italy!" And anyway, with the hard toll of the war upon him, Hitler feels he deserves a break. Where better to relax than his mountain retreat?

So this morning he has boarded his special train, and now he is on his way, first going by way of Munich. There he will lead the Nazi party in its annual Party Foundation Ceremony. Göring will follow him to the Berghof in about a month.

As the Führer's special, heavily armored train travels southward in secret, the shades are down and the blinds are closed, blocking nearly all of the sunlit view. This is in accordance with his strict orders, because the sunlight hurts his eyes. For a few weeks now, his right eye has been giving him trouble. Vision on that side is sometimes painful and difficult, and the medication that Dr. Morell gives him does not help much. However, his staff secretly knows that his headaches are only part of the reason for the drawn shades. He simply refuses to get himself upset by gazing upon any damage sustained by the many enemy bombing raids. He will not give the enemy that satisfaction.

The trip is uneventful, and his train arrives in Munich that afternoon. He and his entourage attend the rally, and after nightfall, as they all travel the 150km southeast through Bavaria, they are unaware of enemy bomber activity above them in the night sky, as several hundred aircraft fly over the area.[1]

They arrive at the Berghof at 10:15 p.m., tired. Still, the Führer insists on a late conference, which he schedules for 11:30 p.m. It is delayed though, because *Reichsleiter* Martin Bormann and his brother Albert coerce him into first touring the new air raid tunnels built below ground in the last couple months. Finally the Führer returns to the Berghof's main hallway, tersely smiling as he talks to Bormann. The conference begins at 11:45 p.m., and ends a half-hour later.

***

In St. Lô, General Erich Marcks, commanding the 84th Corps, sits in his office, gazing down at his map of Normandy, grumbling about the Supreme Command. The fools! He is probably going to be the corps commander that will be hit by the Allied invasion, and no one above him in the command structure seems to be taking him seriously.

He had tried to tell *Generalfeldmarschall* Rommel his concerns at their regional conference on the 17th, but the field marshal had repeated what the Kriegsmarine had told him—that the invasion would most likely not hit the Calvados coastline because there were just too many underwater reefs along the Normandy shores. Marcks though, feels that this is wrong. If the field marshal really studied the Seine Bay area, he would agree that the reefs there would not pose a significant problem to landing craft. Still, Rommel remains convinced that the invasion will most likely occur somewhere up the coast around the Somme estuary, or as the High Command foolishly believes, farther up along the narrowest Channel gap at Calais.

Marcks however, feels otherwise. The heavily defended Straits of Dover are where OKW expects the enemy, so most likely they will not land there. The Allies are not stupid. And the Somme estuary does not have enough beach area to allow the enemy to land in force and rapidly exploit a quick, mobile strike inland.

Angrily returning from that conference on the 17th, Marcks had scheduled a war game to test his theory. Really, it amounted to little more than a map game, played along with supporting messages between him and his staff. Marcks, taking the part of the Allies, had simulated a landing along the Calvados coast between the Orne and the Vire Rivers.[2] In the war game, he was able with relative ease to push out on his right flank and capture not just Cherbourg and the Cotentin peninsula, but all of Brittany as well.

He had sent the report of the game's results to both Army Group Headquarters and to von Rundstedt's OB West. As yet, they have not replied, so they must not consider his conclusions important.

Marcks grits his teeth and looks back at the map. He is very probably going to catch hell from the enemy, and no one east of Caen seems to care much.

Stupid morons…

---

1   Eighty American B-24s were coming back from hitting the ball-bearing factories in Steyr, Austria, a little over 100km east-northeast of the Berghof. The Luftwaffe, having lost several aircraft intercepting the bombers, persists, and the Americans would lose another 17 aircraft on the way back over the Alps. Also, around this time, some six hundred British bombers were attacking the armament industries in Schweinfurt, northwest of the train's route.

2   Exactly where the Allies were to land on June 6.

Thursday, February 24

Adolf Hitler, after his trip to Munich, has returned to the Berghof on the Obersalzberg mountain. His military entourage, which includes the core members of OKW, has followed him, setting up their field headquarters in the Berchtesgaden train station.

***

Generalfeldmarschall Rommel continues enjoying a 10-day tour of leave at his home in Herrlingen.

***

Vizeadmiral Friedrich Ruge on Rommel's behalf is touring up the northern French coast. Today, Ruge and his aide are in Boulogne-sur-Mer on the coast. There he watches a test run made on an underwater barrier of stakes. A 120-ton British landing craft is run up onto the obstacle. Unfortunately, the tide at that time is too high, and the stakes just scrape the boat's bottom as it sails over the tips.

Ruge is then off for Utrecht in Holland to see *Vizeadmiral* Kleikamp,[1] the commander of all naval forces in Belgium and the Netherlands. Not knowing that the naval headquarters is at the town entrance, Ruge wastes time finding it. He asks a sailor walking down the street with his newlywed wife, but the man is just a visitor. Two Dutchmen plead ignorance as well. When a town citizen also says he does not know where to find the headquarters, Ruge's suspicions are aroused.

Finally he gets hold of a city map and finds that the headquarters is right nearby.

***

Generalfeldmarschall von Rundstedt spends his third day back catching up on paperwork at the Hôtel Georges V. By now, he has developed a general daily schedule. He gets his morning report privately from his chief of staff after breakfast around 10 a.m. Barring any visitors (which he avoids), his next update comes after lunch at 1 p.m., unless he is detained at a nearby restaurant. His third update comes around 4 p.m., followed by tea, and the last around 7:30 that evening. Naturally, any critical issues that come up will be reported at once.

Interestingly, he spends almost as much time studying reports and maps of the Eastern Front as he does the Western Front. Having led the invasion there in 1941, he now keeps up on the military situation, particularly with Army Group South, his old command. He has been studying the recent near-disaster at Cherkassy and the collapse of the Korsun pocket. Estimates are that one out of three German soldiers in the Eighth Army have been killed or captured. Because he has been keeping up to date on how critical the situation in the East is, he is usually agreeable to donating units from his command, even volunteering them from time to time.

Generalfeldmarschall Gerd von Rundstedt; Commander-in-Chief, Western Theater. (German Historical Museum)

Generalfeldmarschall Erwin Rommel; Commander, Army Group B. (German Historical Museum)

Generalleutnant Günther Blumentritt; Chief of Staff, Western Theater. (National Archives)

Generalleutnant Alfred Gause; Chief of Staff, Army Group B. (German Historical Museum)

Generaloberst Friedrich Dollmann; Commander, Seventh Army. (German Historical Museum)

Generaloberst Hans von Salmuth; Commander, Fifteenth Army. (German Historical Museum)

Vizeadmiral Friedrich Ruge; Chief Naval Advisor, Army Group B. (German Naval Museum)

Admiral Theodor Krancke; Commander-in-Chief, Naval Forces, Western Theater. (Bundesarchiv 146-1977-028-03)

Generaloberst Alfred Jodl; Chief of Staff, Operations Office, OKW. (Bundesarchiv 146-1971-033-01)

Generalleutnant Walter Warlimont: Deputy Operations Chief of Staff, OKW. Taken in 1939. (Bundesarchiv 146-1987-104-27)

General der Panzertruppen Freiherr Leo Geyr von Schweppenburg; Panzer Group West. (National Archives)

General der Artillerie Erich Marcks; Commander, 84th Corps. (German Historical Museum)

A small view of the massive French château at Fontainebleu, Rommel's first headquarters. (Wikipedia)

La Roche-Guyon on the Seine River. Rommel's second headquarters, beginning on March 9, 1944. (Musée del'Armée, Paris.)

The Berghof—Hitler's mountain retreat on the Obersalzberg. (David Duggleby/BNPS)

Alfred Jodl, Hitler, and Wilhelm Keitel analyze a map at the Berghof.

Field Marshal von Rundstedt at the Hôtel Georges V in Paris, winter 1944. (*After the Battle,* Vol. 141, Bundesarchiv 717/2/45)

Field Marshal Rommel inspecting Denmark, December, 1943. Admiral Ruge is next to him. (Bundesarchiv_Bild_101I-263-1595-30)

Rommel inspecting the 105mm battery at Saltzwedel near Ostend, December 21, 1943. (Bundesarchiv 1011-295-1596-12)

Conference in Paris, January 13, 1944: Rommel, von Rundstedt Gause, and Zimmermann. (Bundesarchiv 1011-718-0149-12A)

Von Rundstedt and Rommel discuss strategy at 81st Corps headquarters, March 30, 1944. (Bundesarchiv 1011-298-1763-09)

The Rommel family in Herrlingen: Manfred, Lucie, and Erwin. (World War II Foundation)

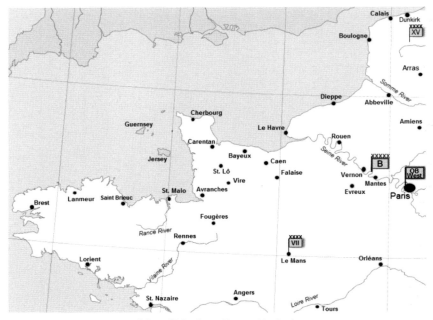

Map of Northern France (Author)

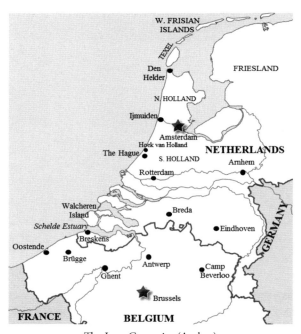

The Low Countries (Author)

Today though, most of his attention is on the West. What are the Allies up to? Information from Naval Group West is scant. There are only a few small vessels to carry out intelligence operations, and the enemy's security forces are far too strong. Daytime air reconnaissance is almost impossible, and the few nightly aircraft that get over the Channel and back find out little. England remains a blank picture, and von Rundstedt these days is usually in the dark when it comes to enemy intentions.

Well, not quite. Some reports from a few remaining scattered, unreliable agents get through from time to time. Isolated observations that usually do not mean much, except the presence of sizeable military forces. He does know that there are two army groups at present in England, one commanded by the American general, Eisenhower, and the other by Rommel's old nemesis, Montgomery.

OB West is certain that there are large numbers of divisions across the Channel, either ready for combat or training vigorously.[2] More are coming from the Mediterranean. From time to time, word of a landing exercise will leak through, or occasionally a convoy is spotted just south of England. Through neutral diplomatic channels, it might be learned that certain British or American senior officers are on leave.

At any rate, none of it means much. And it is just as well. The old Prussian has no spy network of his own, and would not want one anyway; spywork is, in his opinion, skullduggery. He does not believe in subterfuge and undercover work. It is undignified for a soldier, much less a German officer, and almost always unreliable. The distasteful people who do such things are, in his mind, of low moral fiber.

Still, today he has received an espionage report originating from a contact in Spain warning of possible Allied actions against that country. He discusses this with Blumentritt, and they dismiss the report as a feint. Von Rundstedt has seen a number of reports before that indicated the Allies were preparing to go into Spain or Portugal. Each one had in the end turned out to be just a ruse.

Personally, the field marshal does not think such a landing will occur. He has a healthy respect for the Spanish army. He knows that they would defend themselves vigorously against any aggressor. Even if the Allies did get a toehold in Spain or somehow persuaded Franco to ally with them (unlikely) and grant access, where would they go from there? The poor Spanish road complex and rail networks would not help them establish much of a base. And the Pyrenees would be a tremendous obstacle to cross into southern France.

His generals near the border have had several talks with their Spanish counterparts. While the Spaniards would indeed resist a German thrust against them, they do not relish siding with the Allies either. No, Spain will stay neutral. He has told his staff that more than once. "The Allies are not so stupid as to violate Spanish neutrality," he once said, "and the Spaniards themselves would not allow such a thing to happen. Moreover, a layman can see that it is no easy matter to jump from there over the Pyrenees, the Garonne and the Loire. This could be purchased more cheaply on the Channel, with a secure base in England and a short distance to the Ruhr."

Fortunately, the Führer shares his opinion, and has ordered that no action is to be taken that might offend the Spanish. In the meantime though, von Rundstedt orders contingency plans for the occupation of Spain to be updated.

Just in case…

---

1   *Vizeadmiral* Gustav Kleikamp, who took command of naval forces in Belgium and the Netherlands on April 3, 1943. A veteran of World War I, he served in a number of distinctive roles in World War II. He had commanded the obsolete dreadnaught battleship *Schleswig-Holstein* during the invasion of Norway in 1940, and later served as a transport force commander for the never-executed Operation *Sealion*.

    Most interestingly though, Kleikamp had taken a big part in forcing future SS terror leader Reinhard Heydrich out of the German Navy. Heydrich, a naval officer at the time, had become quite the womanizer. In late 1930, he undertook an illicit love affair with the daughter of an important shipyard director and friend of the navy's commander-in-chief, Grand Admiral Erich Raeder. The girl spent several intimate nights with Heydrich and came to believe that he would marry her, especially after she discovered that she was pregnant. When he informed her (callously, by sending her a copy of the engagement announcement) that he had instead become engaged to another woman, one Lina von Osten, she brokenheartedly confessed her affair to her father, who in turn angrily lodged a formal complaint with Admiral Raeder.

    In April 1931, a Court of Honor was convened on the matter. The panel included then Kapitänleutnant Kleikamp and 31-year-old Karl-Jesko von Puttkamer (who would become Hitler's naval advisor in 1935 and remain so until the end of the war). The proceedings found that although Heydrich was technically exonerated, he had acted improperly as a naval officer. A defiant Heydrich bluntly refused to give up his engagement with Miss von Osten to marry this girl, and his cavalier attitude during the proceedings certainly did not help his case. The matter was finally referred back again to Admiral Raeder, who finally forced Heydrich to resign his naval commission for "conduct unbecoming of an officer and a gentleman." With Heydrich's naval career abruptly over and his pension lost, and encouraged by his avid Nazi fiancée, he joined the National Socialist party and vigorously, ruthlessly, turned his attention to its new SS security organization, the *Sicherheitsdienst* (SD). It was a move that would lead him to one of the most infamous roles in the 20th century. He did marry Lina von Osten in December 1931 (after the war, she eventually remarried in 1965, and finally died in 1985). Later, rumors of this infamous scandal included a theory that Heydrich had earlier joined the SS and was actually spying on the Navy for them at the time. Another rumor was that Heydrich was forced to resign from the Navy over homosexual charges. This of course was never proven. Heydrich was assassinated on May 27, 1942 on a Czech country road by partisans. Severely wounded, he died a few days later. A reprisal fell on the small mining village of Lidice, where supposedly a few inhabitants had aided the assassins. On June 10, all 172 males were rounded up and shot, all the women and children sent to a concentration camp, and the village was burned to the ground.

2   Because of successful Allied deceptions, German intelligence grossly overestimated the Allied strength in England. They estimated that the Western Allies had some 80 different-sized divisions and nearly two dozen small brigades across the Channel. Realistically, the Allies only had some two dozen American divisions, a dozen British divisions, three Canadian divisions, and over a dozen brigades. To add to this, senior German army officials at OKH began in 1944 to "pad" enemy estimates to seep some realistic sense into the Führer. It was this image of some five dozen divisions left biding their time in England after the invasion began that would later scare Hitler and OKW into releasing the Fifteenth Army to fight in Normandy.

Friday, February 25

Vizeadmiral Ruge, on Rommel's behalf, is touring up the Northern European coast. Today, the admiral is on the North Holland peninsula, and has a conference at the naval base in Den Helder with Kapitän Stophasius in his headquarters.[1] They talk about mines, and how to effectively sabotage harbors to prevent the enemy from using them.

Then the two of them cross the dike across the Zuider Zee and drive off through Groningen and Nieune-Schas to the town of Leer in Germany.

At sunset, Ruge makes it to Sengwarden.[2] There he calls on Admiral Förste at the *Marineoberkommando Nordsee* (headquarters of the Northern Sea Command).[3] Förste has just come back from leave in Hamburg. Ruge lays out for his staff plans and sketches of Rommel's proposed barriers. He discovers that none of these plans have reached here through official channels. Gritting his teeth, Ruge goes over them with the naval officers, until there is no doubt in anyone's mind what Rommel expects of the navy.

On the other hand, Förste tells Ruge that he has no real authority up here. Förste merely carries out the will of OKW and is under their direct command.

Ruge's tour is not going well.

***

Generalfeldmarschall von Rundstedt has successfully (at least, in his mind) employed a deception for the last three or four months now. Through OB West, false and misleading deployment information has intentionally been leaked to various diplomatic circles in Paris. The "slipped" information has been designed to indicate that large, well-equipped mobile units are being moved to the south of France to discourage an Allied landing down there. Substantial pains have been taken to convince both German and French civilian personnel that the move is underway.

Rundstedt had started this rumor on one of his visits to Germany. Officers coming back from leave in the Reich had been instructed to return with new rumors. Exercise grounds and new quarters have been requested and scoped out in the south, and commands down there have been instructed to stand by to create new units.

Unfortunately, the field marshal knows that the ruse is about up. He senses that, although the Allies might have initially believed this ploy, they are no longer falling for it.

On a more grisly note, in response to the escalated acts of sabotage in the interior of France, he today issues a harsh order regarding the search and capture of Resistance fighters and details for reprisals; he calls the fighters "terrorists." In the order, he writes that if in the course of the pursuit innocent civilians are killed, it will be a "deplorable" condition. The fault though, he adds, will be that of the terrorists.

It is an order that will come back to haunt him after the war.

1   *Kapitän* Stophasius was the North Holland Naval Commander. Den Helder is located at the tip of the North Holland peninsula, about 100km north of Amsterdam.

2   About 8km north of Wilhelmshaven.

3   Fifty-two-year-old Admiral Erich Förste, who headed the Northern Sea Command. A U-boat veteran of World War I, he served aboard various commands between wars, including torpedo boats and the cruisers *Königsberg* and *Karlsruhe*. At the start of World War II, Förste was in command of the battlecruiser *Gneisenau*, which turned out to be his last sea command before he went through a number of desk assignments. He took over the Northern Sea Command at the beginning of March, 1943 and would finally relinquish the command for captivity some two months after the end of the war.

Saturday, February 26

Vizeadmiral Ruge, continuing his tour up the northern European coast, today has a conference with the Deputy Naval Commander, North Sea[1] and his chief of staff[2] at their headquarters in Buxtehude.[3] Ruge is impressed by the large personnel department, complete with "friendly girls" who do not hesitate to give him the Nazi salute.

The talk is about alert levels, and which naval personnel would report for duty with each. The OKW setup as it now stands dictates that most of the men would first mobilize at specific bases in Germany before reporting to their units in Western Europe. Ruge decides to slant his suggestions by recommending that naval personnel transfer inland to man administrative positions, so that their army counterparts can be freed to man the coast.

***

Generalfeldmarschall von Rundstedt today reads a few summaries of the Allied bombings of the French transport infrastructure. These first two months of 1944, the enemy has been targeting a larger area of the French railroads than before. So far, they have taken out some 200 locomotives. Of course, the Resistance has done far worse, having put out of action some 500 locomotives in the same period. The field marshal knows that in the next few months, the situation will just get worse, and with little airpower of his own, there is not much that he can do to stop the bombing trend. Since his divisions already have little motor transport of their own, their dependency upon the railroads for their supplies is even more important, thus compounding the problem.

The French rail system has suffered greatly in the last decade. Even before the war, it struggled because of an economic crisis and a number of scandals. The effective *blitzkrieg* campaign of 1940 had severely crippled it, and the Germans have been picking at its dwindling resources ever since. Overall, the Reich has removed some 4,000 locomotives from France, including many larger engines. In addition, over one third of the rolling stock has been moved to other areas, and over 20 percent of the French rail personnel have been reassigned to "more important duties," including OT activities, factories, and a few to military units.

Small wonder that the French rail system suffers acutely everywhere. Not only must it deal with this shrinkage, but it has now been given the hopelessly huge task of supplying the occupying forces under a strange German–French management setup that is incompetent at best.

To partially offset these problems, von Rundstedt had ordered a very precise, tightly adhered-to priority system be set up for the railroads in early January. The new system is now fully functional. Time will reveal its effectiveness, but it had better work—because if it does not, his men will be unable to get the supplies that they will need to subsist, let alone fight the enemy.

---

1   Fifty-one-year-old *Konteradmiral* Siegfried Engel. He also carries the title of *Admiral der Nordsee*, which oversees Schiffsstamm, *Marinelehr* (naval training), and *Marineersatz* (naval replacement) units. Engel would be taken captive by the British in 1945.

2   *Kapitän zur See* Maximilian Glaser.

3   About 20km west-southwest of Hamburg, and 160km east of Förste's main North Sea headquarters at Sengwarden.

Sunday, February 27

Generalfeldmarschall Rommel is in the middle of a ten-day leave at home. He and his wife privately discuss at length the recent behavior of his chief of staff, who had recently stayed with them.[1] Lucie tells him that Gause had been totally out of line, admonishing Aldinger for being late. Rommel agrees, although he is not too sure what all the fuss is about. Plus (she points out), Gause is so negative about everything. Granted, he lost his house and his savings back on August 23, but he is so down about it. And about the war, his health…

Rommel points out that he was wounded a few times in North Africa, and she nods her head. Still, he does carry on about it.

Lucie then starts in about Gause's wife. She tells him that the woman's stay has about driven her crazy. His wife is also quite negative about the war and life, and Lucie does not like how she has a couple times spoken out indirectly against the Führer. Again, Rommel is at a loss and just listens to his wife's complaints.

Perhaps, he reasons, she is on the right track. Maybe things will be better if Gause goes to another command. Lucie is firmly of this mind and tells him so. Well, it might be time anyway. Rommel will have to think about that.

***

Today, *Vizeadmiral* Ruge is touring the Heligoland Bight. He will stay with the coastal commander there and plans on writing a report about the defenses in that area.

***

It is evening. The Führer is at the Berghof, having returned on the 23rd. Today he has been studying the Russian northern offensive. Rorkhov was taken yesterday. Army Group Center's situation is rapidly deteriorating. Something will have to be done soon. And he will need even more units to brace for the upcoming Russian spring offensive.

As a direct corollary of this, he has all but decided that his ally Hungary must be occupied.

The decision has been a long time in coming. He had courted Hungary in the late 1930s and promised restoration of a good part of its kingdom, lost at the end of World War I. The Hungarian government had been caught in a dilemma. Fearful of a treacherous backstabbing by a Balkan neighbor and intimidated by this new, powerful Germany, they had been coerced into supporting the Axis and had allowed German troops to cross through their territory to set up for the invasion of Poland. As a reward, Hungary had received slices of the southern and eastern portions of Czechoslovakia in 1938 and 1939.

Over the next few years, Hungary had followed Germany like a scared young adolescent too afraid of the bully to tell him no. The Hungarians have been fearful of being overrun by those powerful panzer formations and terror-stricken at the thought of occupation by the fearful SS. Worse, Germany could conspire with Hungary's adversaries, those accursed Romanians to the east, to carve up her territory. So reluctantly, Hungary has been forced to participate in the invasions of Yugoslavia and Russia.

Admiral Horthy, the country's prince-regent,[2] (who Hitler is sure privately dislikes the Nazis), has at times tried to minimize his country's military effort. Hitler had first expressed his outrage at this "lack of enthusiasm" with Horthy in his field headquarters in September, 1941. Horthy had replied that Hungary was saving the bulk of her strength for the upcoming struggle in the Balkans.

As 1942 came in, Hungary, afraid now not only of German retribution but of savage Russian retaliation, still kept its commitment to sending supplies and men to the Eastern Front; but as the months went by and the fortunes of war turned against the Reich, Hungary had begun to try and ease out of its pact with the devil; slowly at first, of course.

In April 1943, Hitler had a meeting with Horthy at his Klessheim Castle in Bavaria.[3] There he indignantly showed Horthy proof, provided by Hitler's foreign minister, von Ribbentrop, that Hungary was secretly conferring with the Allies. Hungary's prime minister, Miklos Kallay, was secretly negotiating with Great Britain to turn Hungary against the Reich and open up the Balkans to the Allies. Hitler demanded that Kallay be dismissed and arrested, and Horthy staunchly defended him.

In September, when Italy had collapsed, Hitler and OKW concluded that the Balkans could very well be the Allies' next target, and resolved that this area would have to be held. With Hungary's wavering attitude in mind, Hitler ordered Jodl's staff to make contingency plans to occupy Hungary or Romania. The operations would be codenamed *Margarethe I* and *Margarethe II* respectively, although Romanian occupation would probably not be necessary. Romania's leader Ion Antonescu had sworn eternal loyalty to the Reich. Horthy though, was another story.

Still, both countries according to German intelligence reports were secretly negotiating with the Allies for a major amphibious landing in their area. The British and Americans would get a friendly reception from the inhabitants, and the liberated countries would in turn be spared the terrors of subjugation and eventual occupation by a vengeful Soviet Union.

An update from Goebbels in November had revealed a worsening situation. Hungary was now all but openly pro-Allied. German agents sent there to stir up pro-German sentiment were being stymied by Hungarian officials, and some were being openly removed from the country.

What directly affected the war effort though was that Hungary was now desperately trying to keep her army intact—no doubt, to turn it against the Germans and assist an Allied liberation, if and when it came. At a time when every available soldier was needed, the Hungarians were trying to withdraw their men from the fighting in the East. Their army chief of staff, Colonel-General Szombathelyi, had begged the Führer in January (which infuriated him) to allow two Hungarian corps to withdraw from the front and return to their country, where they were desperately needed. Admiral Horthy had followed up in a letter dated February 12, demanding the return of nine Hungarian divisions.

Today's morning conference has outlined the need for more units in the East, and how withdrawing Hungarian troops might mean the difference between survival and defeat. And in another meeting later in the day in the castle, Antonescu told him that Romania would not take part in any defense or even occupation of Hungary—unless of course, the Reich returned territories that were ceded to Hungary in 1940. Hitler obviously does not want to do that.

Resolved now on what he has to do, he orders that the planning of *Margarethe I* be finalized. Jodl's office has determined that they will need a total of about a dozen divisions. It had initially been planned that most of the occupying force would be composed of Serb, Croatian, and Romanian (whom the Hungarians hated) troops, centered around one seasoned German division. However, Hitler needs to preserve Hungarian stability, and the presence of thousands of Serbs and Romanians in Hungary would wreak havoc among the population and very likely collapse the Hungarian economy. His meeting with Antonescu has made it clear that this will have to be a German operation, so only German units will be used. Unfortunately, the units that had been pigeonholed for that possibility have long been swept up into the desperate fighting on the Eastern Front.

No matter. Many of the units will just have to come from the peaceful Western Front. After all, the Allied invasion is not scheduled for at least two months. These selected units will just have to do double duty and shuffle between two fronts. Smaller units can be taken from the currently stable Anzio line.

The main assault elements will be composed of one corps headquarters, a number of regular mobile infantry assault units, several police and security components, several assault gun battalions, and Bayerlein's new *Panzer Lehr* division. Since all of the available German mobile units are coming from the West, they will immediately have to be ordered to prepare to move east. *Panzer Lehr* and the mobile infantry units will be followed up with the rest of the Western panzer units, including as part of the reserve, the 21st Panzer Division, currently rebuilding in France. The West will have to be temporarily stripped of its panzers.

The orders go out the next day.

---

1 See entry for February 14.
2 A regent (from the Latin *regens*, "one who reigns") is a formal term for a temporary appointed leader of a country. This usually occurs in a monarchy when the king or queen cannot accept the throne due to injury, serious illness, or being underage. During this period (called a *regency*), the

regent has the full authority to act as the country's head of state, including appointing his or her own cabinet and generals. When the royal heir is competent enough to assume the throne, or if the royal line has died out and a new line is appointed, the regent then is obligated to step down, usually peaceably, although sometimes other darker means are used.

3   Klessheim Castle on the western outskirts of Salzburg is a huge estate, greatly enlarged from a small villa by the famous architect Fischer of Erlach in the early 18th century for Archbishop Johann Thun. It had once belonged to Archduke Ludwig Victor, the younger brother of the late assassinated Emperor, and after *Anschluss* (Germany's annexation of Austria) in March 1938, Hitler had its splendor restored and a permanent detachment of guards assigned there, so that he could use it as a reception palace to receive (and no doubt impress) special guests of the Reich. The expansive rectangular castle consists of three floors, and is approached through a magnificent, well-landscaped courtyard. The outside covered entrance is attained by two enormous, winding, stone staircases that lead to an extravagant foyer on the main floor. Several lavish rooms on the upper floor were used for sleeping quarters.

Monday, February 28

Generalfeldmarschall Rommel is enjoying a 10-day tour of leave at his home in Herrlingen. Still, he has taken time to fly to Brussels to visit the military governor of Northern France and Belgium, *Reichskommissar* Alexander von Faulkenhausen.[1] The military governor finds Rommel energetic and optimistic on the war. He will write after the war, "Our views on the political and military situation could not have been more divergent."

***

Vizeadmiral Ruge, on Rommel's behalf, is inspecting the defenses around the Helgoland Bight. He is staying with the coastal commander there and is working on a report about the defenses in that area.

***

Generalfeldmarschall von Rundstedt has a new, serious problem. OKW is evidently going to take all of his panzers. Hitler has turned his fury upon Hungary and had decided that it must be occupied. And a good part of the troops for this operation will be coming from the West.

To start, one corps headquarters and a number of regular mobile units will be detached from their infantry divisions. And his new *Panzer Lehr* division is to prepare to move east to be ready for the coup immediately. The West is to be temporarily stripped of its panzers.

With Rommel's reinforcement of the Atlantic Wall only a quarter finished, France will, for a month or so, be wide open for an invasion.

---

1   *Reichskommissar* von Faulkenhausen was a silent member of the plot against Hitler.

Tuesday, February 29

Today, leap day, *Vizeadmiral* Ruge is finishing his inspection of Holland's defenses. He is staying with the coastal commander and has finished a report about the defenses and the alert units in that area. He sends the report by teletype to OKM with his recommendations on how to better organize the defenses in the area.

***

At Fontainebleau, in Rommel's absence, his staff is busy carrying out the duties of overseeing the revitalization of the Atlantic Wall. Alfred Gause has made a number of trips to the coast, carrying out his own inspections, making notes for Rommel to review upon his return. On one trip, he stops at the château of La Roche-Guyon and sees how the work is going on the new headquarters. The castle is now a bustle of activity. There are sentry boxes at each of the two gates to the castle, and several others around the perimeter. Above them on the chalky cliffs can be seen machine-gun positions.

Gause continues on up to the coast, to inspect various units there.

In the meantime, the army group staff fields various problems. A message comes from the commander of the 67th Corps, General von Weikersthal.[1] Located around the Somme estuary, he complains that he is having problems with the navy about how they should direct the defense of the coast there. They would like either Rommel or Admiral Ruge to come out there and straighten out the matter.

***

Several conferences have been held by local commands on how to best react to the projected Allied invasion. One such conference is held by the Luftwaffe. *Oberst* Dietrich Pelz's IX Air Corps, made up of a number of bomber squadrons, will be undertaking the *Steinbock* operation against England. In his blitz counteroffensive, he has wisely ignored Göring's orders to bomb on moonlit nights, especially since British nightfighter technology and activity has increased substantially. Naturally, with substantial enemy fighter forces, advanced radar, and strong anti-aircraft batteries, any daylight raids would be decimated. He has sent in an official report, indicating that his forces should continue to only be committed to night battle.

He estimates that if his squadrons begin daylight raids, they will get ripped apart in just two days.

---

1   See entry for January 20.

March 1944

Wednesday, March 1

It is a time for headquarters renovations and changes, from the top command on down.

The Führer's Eastern Front headquarters, the Wolf's Lair in East Prussia, is undergoing a series of building projects. As part of a major expansion program, new buildings are being constructed for the staff. The surrounding area is also getting improved protection with stronger security and more anti-aircraft positions. Hitler's own personal quarters are being refurbished as well, which is why he is presently at the Berghof.

The Berghof complex itself is being actively improved as well, although on a less obtrusive scale, to minimize impact to the surrounding scenery. Under the watchful eyes of Party Secretary Martin Bormann, many of the barracks are getting enlarged, and new operational facilities are being put in. Residential structures are being built or renovated for high-level officials, and several more anti-aircraft defensive measures are being created. Additional underground quarters are being dug out, and several additional security checkpoints are getting set up. The area is a flurry of construction activity, and the once-serene, secluded slope is being turned into a beehive, fortress complex.

In St.-Germain-en-Laye, expansion projects on von Rundstedt's headquarters complex and his nearby villa are finishing up.

In northern France, while Rommel is on leave at home in Herrlingen, his own new quarters at La Roche-Guyon are being prepared for him. All in all, the château is a great choice for his new army group headquarters with a great location. The one drawback is that the bridge that had once stood next to the château had never been rebuilt after its demolition, and so access across the river will have to be out of one's way, upstream across the Mantes bridge, downstream over the Vernon bridge, or across the river by ferry.[1]

Engineers are digging additional tunnel space out of the chalk cliffs adjoining the château and chiseling out sections of the chalky interiors for new rooms. Additional basement areas are being added to those existing ones that are being improved. Pits for anti-aircraft positions are being dug out of the surrounding area, security checkpoints are being constructed at key traffic points, and barriers are being put up along critical sections.

Rommel's headquarters has also just undergone two personnel changes, one of which will affect Rommel's life considerably in the next six months. General Diem has joined the staff as special deputy for supply services and engineers. He has known the field marshal for many years, and had even once been his superior officer.

More importantly though, *Hauptmann* Hellmuth Lang has taken over as Rommel's new aide, replacing Major Hammermann.[2] Rommel had told General Schmundt, Hitler's army adjutant, that had he wanted the replacement to be at least a major in rank. Lang, although a captain, is nevertheless an outstanding panzer officer. He is highly decorated, including the Panzer Combat Badge, the Iron Cross First Class, and just recently, the Knight's Cross for serving with distinction in Russia. Moreover, like Rommel, Lang is a native of the of Württemberg province and speaks Swabian.

An affable fellow, Lang quickly meshes in with the staff, and seems destined to become a close acquaintance and confidant to the field marshal.

Rommel's naval advisor spends part of today at Camp Beverloo in Belgium. Ruge calls on the commanding officer of a naval regiment training there,[3] and finds out that his orders in case of an invasion are contrary to what Rommel wants. So the two of them discuss alert status levels and coordinated defensive efforts in case of an invasion.

***

Today one of General Dollmann's units tests another 120-ton captured British landing craft over a pattern of wooden stakes and a couple Czech hedgehogs. Quite a number are either broken off or just pushed away before the boat is stopped. Seventh Army Headquarters in its report recommends that mines be placed at the end of the stakes. Army Group B will concur.

---

1   For more information on Rommel's headquarters, see Appendix A, page 595.
2   Sources are quite sketchy on why Hammermann was replaced, but they suggest that he had some type of serious falling-out with the field marshal. Hammermann returned to combat, and a month before the end of the war, he was killed around Friesenhagen.
3   This was also the training area for the 12th SS Panzer Division, *Hitlerjugend*, under the command of *Generalleutnant* Fritz Witt. It is possible that Ruge stopped in to see Witt as well, though association between the Kriegsmarine and the SS was not that common.

Thursday, March 2

Generalfeldmarschall Rommel is currently on furlough, enjoying a rest in his renovated house in Herrlingen, a small town just west of Ulm.

***

His naval advisor is still on an inspection tour for the field marshal, traveling today in Belgium. In Brussels, *Vizeadmiral* Ruge has a meeting with an officer on the staff of the military governor of Belgium, General Alexander von Falkenhausen. Driving at night in the capital has become quite a hassle for many, since no street lights are available and one has to drive with severely dimmed headlights. Ruge discusses with the officer possible ways to change the street signs so that they can be seen more easily at night while driving.[1]

Later that afternoon, he returns to Fontainebleau, and discovers that he has an energetic new assistant, one *Kapitän* Peters. He has worked with Ruge before when he was the Cuxhaven Sea Commandant, and Ruge knows that he is an expert on coastal defensive positions. After a couple brief meetings with him, Ruge concludes that they will probably get along just fine.

***

Today, OB West and *Marinegruppenkommandos West* conduct a number of practice alerts. Afterward, they have several meetings to evaluate the alert levels and what the naval units are to do during each. Von Rundstedt's group wants to turn them into riflemen immediately and send them to the invaded area. Krancke's command objects, declaring that each naval component must carry out its assigned special task first (sabotage port facilities, communications, special seagoing operations, etc.) before being committed to land combat.

The navy also insists that some ratings, like for instance submariners awaiting a new U-boat, should remain at their normal duties, nearby landings notwithstanding. OB West here is tactfully reminded that the Kriegsmarine's primary purpose in the war is still to wage unrestricted undersea warfare against the enemy. The navy insists that this guideline be expanded to include naval training personnel (particularly the Second, Third, and Sixth Naval Training Regiments—a couple thousand men at most), some special small tactical units, port authorities, communications personnel, school instructors, and of course, minesweeper crewmen who escort the U-boats out to sea and keep the lanes cleared of enemy mines.

The navy here is defending a position that had been put out in a recent OKM directive. It had angered the army. It stated that these "special forces" were not to be a part of any alert unit, and could only be used in a local defense—and then only if the nearby garrison was directly threatened by a closing enemy force, and the "proper" naval authority agreed. Clearly, the navy was trying to keep some shore units from getting swallowed up in a desperate army *Materialschlacht*[2] to defend the coastline. More importantly though, the navy is worrying that their men will get called to arms too soon, or torn from their duties to perform some menial, local tasks.

Von Rundstedt's assertion is just as critical, though. His staff had countered with their own directive that stated:

> In case of threatening danger, even the last armed man will have to be used for the tasks which Western Command considers necessary. Western Command cannot supply replacements for missing naval forces.

So faced with these opposite positions, Ruge, back at army group headquarters, begins drafting a compromise for both sides. He suggests that during any alert, these "special" naval personnel be available for "security" operations for any fortress or critical strategic target if their unit is located within 100 kilometers of the target's garrison. He sends it off to Krancke's headquarters and copies OKM and a disgruntled OB West.

The sailors have never been so wanted.

---

1   At least one source claims (without stating much foundation) that this was a personal trip, and that a discussion of possible options to change the current government were discussed. If this is true, perhaps Ruge might have met the field marshal there.

Controversial military authority David Irving in his biography *Trail of the Fox* wrote that Rommel also traveled during this leave time to Brussels, and also called on General von Falkenhausen. Irving (perhaps with a slight slant) wrote, "When he met General Alexander von Falkenhausen, the aristocratic military governor of Belgium, in Brussels a few days later, he infuriated that elderly gentleman, an anti-Nazi, with his cheery confidence that he was going to inflict a big defeat on the enemy when they hit the beaches. Besides, field marshals whose whole military reputation is staked on forthcoming victory are unlikely to lend their names to a coup d'état." Could this be the meeting that Ruge referenced in his *Reminiscences?* See footnote for March 23.

2   Lit. "material slaughter." A war of attrition, where large forces of fresh men and material come in on each side and leave the battlefield either dead or wounded on the other; an analogy, no doubt, to the meat-grinder-like butchery of the battles in the trenches during World War I.

Friday, March 3

His leave over, *Generalfeldmarschall* Rommel leaves Herrlingen early for his return to France. Accompanied by his chief engineer, Meise, and his Ia operations officer von Tempelhoff (who has traveled from his home in Munich to meet them in Herrlingen), he drives to the Wurttemberg airport and they take off in Rommel's converted He-111. The aircraft arrives over Paris in the afternoon, flying into a snowstorm.

As the plane touches down, the passengers are harshly jolted when one of the aircraft's tires suddenly suffers a blowout. The startled officers hold their breaths and brace themselves for a ghastly crash as the bomber starts bumping along the runway, lurching to the side, rubber screeching. But the field marshal's luck once again holds as the momentarily surprised pilot manages to keep the plane from crashing and brings the Heinkel to a safe stop. Fortunately as it turns out, the aircraft has not suffered any serious damage, and the passengers, shaken up by the experience, hastily gather their gear and exit the plane.

Rommel is no doubt thinking that, between the Allied fighters, bad weather, and now flat tires—enough of this endangering-your-life-in-the-air crap. Next time, he will go home by car.

They ride off to Fontainebleau in heavy snow.

***

Today, *Generalfeldmarschall* von Rundstedt is again mad, his anger rising from once again being insulted. He is the third generation in a family that has served the Fatherland for nearly sixty years, and yet his solid Prussian loyalty is being questioned. Army adjutant Rudolf Schmundt wants him to sign an oath of allegiance to the Führer.

Schmundt's actions are a culmination of developments that all stem from the fall of Stalingrad over a year ago. When von Paulus' Sixth Army surrendered on February 2, 1943, among the prisoners taken by the Russians were nearly two dozen German generals, including corps commander General Seydlitz-Kurzbach, captured on January 30.[1] Pressured by the Russians and no doubt upset by Hitler's seemingly cold abandonment of their army, he and several other captured generals and colonels decided to cooperate with the enemy and participated in an anti-Nazi propaganda undertaking.

Starting in the summer of 1943, they began to write a number of letters to senior German army generals serving on the Eastern Front, exhorting their compatriots to stop making this terrible war upon the Soviet Union, renounce the Nazi government, and join the "National Committee to Free Germany" movement (*Nationalkomitee Freies Deutschland*) that they were helping to create out of Moscow. Seydlitz-Kurzbach actually spoke of creating a German force of POWs to help liberate Nazi Germany.

When Hitler was later informed that Field Marshal von Paulus himself had joined this "League of German Officers," he was enraged.[2]

Naturally, the generals in the Reich receiving these letters first considered them to be a hoax, or at least that the officers writing them were being forced to do so. But soon, most senior officers became convinced that Seydlitz's campaign was genuine. And it was confirmed that Seydlitz's signature was authentic.

Recently, his group had broadcast their message a number of times to German units trapped in the Cherkassy pocket along the Dnieper River. Before the units' breakout in mid-February, several league officers had tried to coerce the 54,000 embattled troops into surrendering. Some of these traitors to Germany had actually disguised themselves and infiltrated their lines, committing acts of sabotage and delivering notes to corps commanders about giving up.

Hitler, for years paranoid about the loyalty of the senior German military strata, became quite upset over the whole thing. The demons in his head active, he began to wonder if he could trust *any* member of the Heeres officer corps.[3] To allay his fears, Schmundt has finally decided to take action (based on recommendations from Goebbels). In early February, he drew up a written oath of allegiance to the Führer, and promised to get the signatures of the seven most critical army field marshals on it.

So, flying in to Paris today, Schmundt has gone directly to the Hôtel Georges V in the heavy blizzard and has presented von Rundstedt with the purpose of his visit and the letter. After some grumbling and a number of choice resentful comments, von Rundstedt signs the document.

Knowing that his welcome has worn out, Schmundt quickly takes his leave and heads down to Fontainebleau for Rommel's signature. General Gause, who happens to be in Paris talking to OB West staff members about matters of unit deployment and transportation, meets Schmundt and tells him that Rommel has been on leave for the last ten days, but is due back to his headquarters. So he takes Schmundt back with him southeastward through the snowy streets of Paris to Fontainebleau, 80km away.

Rommel has not yet shown up when they arrive, but arrives shortly thereafter in the late afternoon. He stomps the snow from his boots as he steps through the main entrance where Schmundt awaits him. He welcomes Schmundt to his headquarters, and the two of them go into Rommel's study to talk.

The army adjutant tonight wisely avoids mentioning the issue of the oath signature. That evening, they enjoy a happy, sumptuous dinner. At one point, Rommel pushes the conversation a bit when he remarks that "certain people" were once again making problems. His staff hope fervently that he is not talking about the high command in Schmundt's presence.

Later, Rommel calls home to let Lucie know that he made it safely. He asks her how Ajax is doing. He has left the dog in Herrlingen with her to keep her company, and so that she might perhaps better train him. Ajax had shown a wild streak in him, which at times drove the field marshal crazy. This last time that he had been on leave, he had decided to do some skiing, and thought to take Ajax with him. That had turned out to be a mistake. Each time the Rommel had started down the slopes, the dog had taken off after him, barking and going for his skis. He finally had to tie Ajax up, after which the dog would bark, struggle, and then howl as Rommel went down the slope.

Lucie though, tells him his training of the dog is starting to pay off, because Ajax for the most part is minding her. He tells her about the plane's flat tire, and she admonishes him to be more careful.

Before turning in, he writes to his son:

> *I was delighted to see your attitude to duty and everything else in life. Keep it up and do the name of Rommel proud...*
>
> *Only the man who has learned to obey—even against his better instincts and convictions—will make a capable officer, and learn how to master the supreme art of leading other men.*

Things have gone well today. Now, if only the Allies would cooperate...

---

1 Fifty-five-year-old *General der Artillerie* Walther von Seydlitz-Kurzbach, a World War I veteran, had served since 1939 on both fronts. He commanded the 12th Infantry Division in the 1940 French campaign. Taking part in the initial invasion of Russia in 1941, still commanding the 12th, he was awarded the Knight's Cross the next spring when he broke his division out of the Russian Demyansk pocket. Promoted, he eventually took command of Sixth Army's 51st Corps.

   At Stalingrad, arguing unsuccessfully for weeks that the trapped Germans should either try to break out or surrender, he was finally relieved of his command on January 25. Disgusted, he and several other officers deserted over to the enemy lines and were subsequently captured a few days later, less than a week before the Sixth Army itself surrendered.

2 His breach of faith was later scorned by the Germans, the affair being tantamount to their version of America's Robert E. Lee, descendant of Richard Henry Lee (who first proposed and then later signed the Declaration of Independence), seceding with the South against the Union.

3 This was a repeat flare-up of a tirade that came back on January 31, when first Hitler found out that von Paulus was in the process of surrendering the entire Sixth Army. In a desperate attempt to get the general to hold out, Hitler had the day before promoted him to the rank of field marshal, in hopes that since no field marshal in German modern history had ever surrendered, von Paulus would not be the first. But the ploy had not worked and, furious over the subsequent surrender, Hitler had von Paulus sentenced to death in abstentia and bitterly swore that he would never promote another general to the rank of field marshal, because none of his generals could be trusted. Of course, he later changed his mind, and before the end of the war, he promoted two more Army generals to the rank: Walter Model (March 1, 1944) and Ferdinand Schörner (April 5, 1945). In addition, he appointed two Luftwaffe generals to the rank: Wolfram Freiherr von Richthofen (February 16, 1943), and just before Hitler committed suicide, Robert Ritter von Greim (April 25, 1945).

Saturday, March 4

At the Berghof, planning continues for *Unternehmen Margarethe I*—the German occupation of Hungary. Though expected for some time now, it is now a sure thing that, because the occupational forces will have to be mobile units, a large part of them will have to come from the West (though some units will also be drawn from the Italian Front). Slated to be transferred over are the newly formed *Panzer Lehr* division and a number of mobile units from several infantry divisions. Hitler confers with Jodl and Keitel on the details.

Later on, at the daily war conference, in response to reports of Allied preparations for the invasion in the West, Hitler repeats that he has a hunch that the main enemy thrust will be Normandy and Brittany, mostly because they are good areas to establish a beachhead.[1] Jodl makes note of this in his diary:

> *The Führer does not believe the Allies will make cross-Channel attacks at many points. For this their forces are not large enough. As particularly threatened he names Normandy and Brittany, both suitable for establishing bridgeheads. Garrisons of important strongpoints are to be strengthened.*

A message to that effect goes out to OB West and *Heeresgruppe B* later that afternoon.

Though no one dares tell him, the Führer appears exhausted, no doubt from worrying about the East and Italy, as well as the normal matters of state. Deep lines are etching into his forehead, and he is having eye problems, induced he has been told, by stress. His doctor tells him to rest more. Would that he could…

***

Generalfeldmarschall von Rundstedt enjoys a nice weekend in his hotel suite, even though it is in downtown Paris. He knows that most German officers would give plenty to have their duty station in the French capital. But not him. He cannot wait for spring to come, so that he can move back to the outer suburb of St.-Germain-en-Laye. He is not captivated by the Parisian charm, especially during the holidays.

Today, after taking care of business—a cursory look at the latest status reports—he sends a nice "care package" home to his wife, Bila.[2] He then sits down to read a good book.

***

It is a lovely day in central France, and spring is in the air. Just after breakfast, visiting General Rudolf Schmundt confers privately with *Generalfeldmarschall* Rommel in his study.

The straightforward adjutant and Rommel had been friends for years, even more so since the early days of North Africa.[3] The only threat to their relationship had come near the end of the Polish campaign in 1939. Schmundt had become upset with Rommel (actually, it was more like jealousy) because it seemed to Schmundt that Hitler was becoming closer to this new general than he was his own army adjutant. Indeed, several at Supreme Headquarters had felt that way. But that had been straightened out once Rommel had been assigned a combat command in France, and they had stayed good friends ever since.[4]

The years have made their mark upon Schmundt's appearance. Lines of age and stress are clear on his face. The affable, big-eared adjutant had once considered his job the supreme point in his life. Now though, with the war failing, and having slowly realized that his idol had feet of lead, he has suffered more and more bouts of depression. Rumor has it that his binges with alcohol have increased significantly.

Schmundt now explains to Rommel the real purpose of his visit—the Seydlitz affair.

"The Führer is furious at the treachery of certain generals who have been captured by the enemy, or deserted to them, at Stalingrad," Schmundt says. He details the traitorous letters Seydlitz had sent to the many senior army generals. He reveals, "Since the battle of Cherkassy, we now have proof that Seydlitz's signature on them is authentic."

Rommel comments that the Führer must be upset over this.

Schmundt stresses, "What matters now is for the Führer to be sure he can trust his field marshals—to know you all stand loyally behind him." Here he produces the oath of loyalty document, a joint statement from the field marshals disavowing any connection with these turncoats, and swearing undying fidelity to the Führer. Would the field marshal be so good as to sign the document?

Scowling, the field marshal reads it and then pens his signature with a flourish, just below von Rundstedt's fancy scrawl.

Schmundt soon leaves—to get similar signatures from army field marshals Model, von Kleist, Busch, Weichs, and von Manstein.[5]

Unsettled over the letter thing, Rommel and a few staff members go hunting for wild boar that afternoon, using two French sympathizers and their hunting dogs to flush their game for them. They scare up a couple of animals, but the boars manage to get past a few "somewhat inferior" hunters of their party.

That evening, at the invitation of Naval Group West, Rommel and Ruge attend a special dinner soirée at Krancke's lavish quarters in Evry.[6] Also attending is Krancke's superior, none other than *Großadmiral* Karl Dönitz, now Commander-in-Chief of the Kriegsmarine. Surrounded by a host of naval officers, he and Rommel feel each other out over an excellent dinner, and the two leaders afterwards have a stimulating conversation about the general defensive strategies for the coast.

---

1   The "hunch" was partially based upon the information microfilmed by a spy in Ankara, Turkey, code name "Cicero." Hitler though, had at first been skeptical of the information, growling, "Why on earth did the British find it necessary to tell their ambassador in Turkey that?!?"

2 He usually referred to his wife by her middle name, and not her first name—Luise.

3 Back on February 12, 1941, Schmundt, initially (but temporarily) attached to Rommel's staff, had accompanied him on his first flight down to North Africa, when Rommel had assumed command of the newly arriving German contingent there. Their friendship deepened appreciably in the next few weeks.

4 Schmundt had gone on to become Hitler's chief of army personnel and a loyal follower, as well as being his military adjutant.

5 The often-cantankerous von Manstein was the last to sign what he called this "rather curious document." In fact, he was so upset with Hitler at that time over the failed Russian campaign, that he actually considered not endorsing this ludicrous oath of allegiance. In the end, the only reason he actually did sign it was because his name was the last on the list, and he would have looked like a fool if he had refused. But he did tell Schmundt that, all the same, he thought the document was not needed, certainly not from the point of view of the professional German officer. Weichs later wrote in his own diary, "Such a reaffirmation of our oath of allegiance seems unmilitary to me. An officer's loyalty ought to be taken for granted."

6 Evry is located roughly between Paris and Fontainebleau to the southeast. While Krancke and his staff stayed at Evry, they worked during the day in their Paris building on the Bois de Boulogne.

Sunday, March 5

At the Berghof, an enthusiastic Air Inspector-General Milch and Armaments Director Saur report on production of new weapon technology. Their estimates are openly optimistic, despite the pounding German cities have recently been taking by British bombers at night and American bombers during the day. The Führer gives them permission to give fighter production top priority. He further instructs them to make sure that two new underground aircraft assembly factories nearing completion have enough space to include all the facilities needed to completely construct the aircraft underground. To support this, he orders over five dozen miners recently working on his new underground bunkers at the Berghof to be turned over to Saur. Then he orders the hapless armaments director to come up with at least ten thousand more. Germany's war industry, he declares, will be relocated entirely underground, so that enemy bombers will not affect production.

Milch reports to him that of course, V-1 production is already being conducted underground. In an excited tone, he also suggests that they unleash the first wave against England on the Führer's birthday, April 20. Then follow in the next ten days with 1,500 more, and then all the rest that are assembled by the end of the next month. Hitler agrees.

After the meeting, Milch breaks the news to his staff. With a big smile, he chimes, "It will be the most evil torture you can imagine. Just picture for yourselves a large high-explosive bomb falling on London every half-hour, and nobody knowing where the next one will fall! Twenty days of that will have them all folding at the knees!"

***

At his headquarters, *Generalfeldmarschall* Rommel chairs a conference on defensive measures for the Netherlands. Attending from that area are *Generalleutnant* von Wühlisch and *Vizeadmiral* Kleikamp.[1] They go over Rommel's plans, the little progress made so far, and problems faced on a number of subjects. They include units deployed, possible reserves, obstacle construction, areas flooded and possible additions, and of course, the minefields. Rommel's staff by now are thorough, and every point is covered in detail.

After the conference, they have a nice lunch with the field marshal as ever being the gracious host. Although he is charming to his guests, Rommel is still vexed over the lack of development so far in their area. He notes this later in his report.

Rommel then gets together with Gause, and they discuss Gause's phone conversation the day before with Warlimont at Berchtesgaden. The subject again had been the displacement of the reserve panzers. Warlimont had once again defended von Rundstedt's theories about inland deployment, and that the units had to be trained by the organization designed for that purpose—Panzer Group West.

Rommel sees that he somehow has to get through to these idiots that, once the Allies are ashore, they will stay there, and no *Panzergruppe* will be able to budge them—not in the face of overwhelming aerial superiority and massive naval gunfire support.

Owing to the continuing disagreement over this issue, Warlimont had suggested that the two commands meet and thrash it out between themselves. Rommel comments on the futility of that idea. The old Prussian has already made up his mind, and Rommel will not be able to budge him.

A couple positive things, Gause points out. First, Warlimont promised to send him a copy of the letter he sent to Blumentritt, outlining OKW's reasons for siding with OB West. Second, he agreed to pass on Rommel's request that he be allowed to see the Führer on his progress so far. It is a fair request, both in light of the situation, and because of the fact that, as a field marshal, he has the right to ask for a personal audience at any time. True, von Rundstedt will see it for what it is—an end around his immediate superior—but at this point, their choices are limited. Rommel knows he is right, but he does not want history to bear that out at their expense.

To take his mind off this panzer thing, Rommel and a few of his senior officers go out with guns that afternoon,[2] somewhere near Melun. This is more than just an "armed promenade" for him now. Frustrated, he wants to shoot something.

They employ a couple of French farmers and their dogs as game drivers. Rommel of course brings his Elbo. It is a warm afternoon, so they leave their topcoats in the vehicles and start off. The hunters line up and slowly move through the brush. The dogs eventually sniff out a couple wild boars and chase the animals towards the advancing hunters. Three times the boars get close, but each time they somehow escape between a few of the amateurs in the line before any of them can raise their shotguns and shoot.

Tired, sweaty, dirty, and scratched in a few places from thorns that have pierced their trousers, but still determined to shoot something, the men doggedly continue on with the hunt. Eventually, struggling through yet another dense thicket, several of the hunters come out in a grassy meadow. There, off in the distance, they spot a stately 12-point buck.

The sight of this magnificent animal takes their breath away. How arrogantly it struts in their presence! Silently, General Meise takes aim, and Admiral Ruge cocks his own automatic rifle. But at the last moment, the field marshal waves at them to lower their weapons. Perplexed, they just stare at him. He grabs his Wehrmacht hunting license, waves it at them, and then points to it. He is trying to let them know that the animal is out of season. The hunting season for stag had ended back at the beginning of February.

Uncertain what to do, they stand in place, weighing in their consciences the implications of what he has imparted to them against the idea of bagging such a prize. Finally, he calls out to them:. "It's the closed season," he says.

They stare at him. "The season's closed," Rommel repeats louder, his voice now startling the deer. It bounds away. Ruefully, the rest of them watch the beautiful animal disappear into the forest. The field marshal's sense of fair play has cost them several delicious roasts.

Sometimes working for the old man was a real pain.

---

1 Fifty-one-year-old *Generalleutnant* Heinz-Hellmuth von Wühlisch was chief of staff to General Christiansen, the Luftwaffe general commanding the combined German forces in the Netherlands. Forty-eight-year-old *Vizeadmiral* Gustav Kleikamp commanded all naval forces in the Netherlands (see note for February 24).

2 Admiral Ruge wrote that this hunt took place a day earlier, on the 4th.

Monday, March 6

It is early morning, and Rommel is back on the road again. This time he is off on another four-day tour to the west, his destinations the coasts of Normandy and Brittany. With him are his chief of staff, his chief engineer, and of course, Ruge, his naval advisor. Interestingly, the areas slated for his inspection this time are not his choice.

Last Saturday, they received a wire from OKW detailing the Führer's hunch about Normandy and Brittany at the day's war conference. The message had come over the communications teleprinter:

> THE FÜHRER... CONSIDERS NORMANDY AND BRITTANY TO BE PARTICULARLY THREATENED BY INVASION, BECAUSE THEY ARE VERY SUITABLE FOR THE CREATION OF BEACHHEADS.

Rommel was to inspect and re-evaluate these areas at once—thoroughly. What more can he do than he is not already doing? It is bad enough that Berlin is not cooperating with him about furnishing troops and supplies. Now with this message, they are critiquing him as well. Still, a prod from the Führer... Shaking his head, the field marshal phones General Marcks, commanding the 84th Corps along the Calvados coast and partially up the Cotentin peninsula. The corps commander was told he was going to join him on this trip.

After a breakfast of omelets, whipped cream, and fresh coffee, the entourage leaves at 8 a.m. Traveling northwest along the right bank of the Seine, the motorcade crosses over the Mantes bridge and then continues downriver to the coast. There they start inspecting units of *Generalmajor* Reichert's 711th Grenadier Division.[1] Holding the extreme left flank of von Salmuth's Fifteenth Army, the 711th defends the shore between the mouth of the Seine and the Orne River—some two dozen kilometers of coastline.[2] Rommel is told that a little over four kilometers of this sector is already strewn with effective minefields—about six thousand mines for every kilometer of shoreline.

Again, Rommel finds here a coastal unit that has taken the liberty of doing some "independent testing." A 300-ton vessel was steered into an obstacle test area to see how effective the underwater obstacles were. The vessel had pushed through, either bending, breaking, or plowing under the wooden stakes. No one had expected much more, since the vessel was relatively large and the stakes did not have any mines attached to their tops. In a similar test though, using a lighter, 10-ton vessel, the boat ended up stranded on the obstacles.

Rommel calls a halt to all these tests. He declares the last one is good enough. Actually, he wants the men to quit wasting time and get back to installing more obstacles. Besides, to make the stakes really effective, they need mines attached to them. The trouble is, the only effective ones that are available for this task are land mines, and though they are supposed to be waterproof, no one knows if they will be able to survive the constant exposure to water and the incessant pounding of the offshore waves.

Moving west, the inspection party crosses the Orne River and goes into Seventh Army's sector. They travel into the 716th Division's area, which holds the extreme right flank of Marcks' 84th Corps, and meet its commander, *Generalmajor* Richter.[3] They note that only some of the coastal artillery positions have been completed so far, and observe how the holes for the obstacle stakes are being installed efficiently with water jets. In some areas though, where the bottom is densely packed, good old-fashioned pile driving is necessary.

Marcks takes the opportunity to again point out to Rommel that the 716th has some twenty kilometers of shoreline to cover—far too much, especially if this happens to be where the enemy decides to land and concentrate their forces. Richter tells Rommel how he has brought this problem up before. Clearly, another unit is needed to help defend this part of the coast.

The inspection party finally quits around 6 p.m. They travel back eastward to the 716th's divisional headquarters in Caen. There they have a conference and discuss today's observations. They talk about mine shortages and whether or not land mines will remain functional if exposed to water for long periods. Rommel discusses with Marcks and Richter the long sector that the 716th must cover.

Rommel decides that more men are needed, so he gives his staff specific instructions. The experienced 352nd Infantry Division, presently located inland around St. Lô, is to move north to the coast and take up the left half portion of this stretch of beach between the Orne and Vire Rivers. Deployment will start with the repositioning of the division's artillery regiment, the 352nd. The move is scheduled to begin some ten days hence.

The order will turn out to be one of the most important that he will give in this last year of his life.

After the meeting, the officers sit down to dinner at the town's officers' quarters. Unfortunately, Rommel's evening is spoiled afterward by another report of still another offshore "obstacle test." He is told of the test that General Dollman's men had run a week before, thrusting a captured 120-ton British landing craft onto some offshore wooden stakes. The craft had smashed through the stakes with relative ease, pulverising their tops.[4] More wasted time and resources. Rommel reacts angrily to the report. Retiring early, he stomps off to his quarters in a nearby hotel.

The two resolute guards outside his door make absolutely sure that the fuming field marshal is not disturbed.

***

Today, for the first time, Berlin is bombed in broad daylight. Some 750 American bombers take part in the raid, scoring hits on strategic targets. Later that night, as part of the initial support phase for the invasion, RAF bomber command sends 261 Halifaxes and six Mosquitoes to bomb the railyards at Trappes, some 33km west-southwest of downtown Paris. Later RAF recon photos will confirm some 190 hits directly on the tracks, as well as massive damage to rolling stock, engines, sheds, electric lines, and footbridges.

---

1   The title of "Grenadier" was seldom used and often given to these static or *bodenständig* divisions as a matter of prestige. This term was to partially conceal the fact that they were reorganized with less than would be given the standard infantry division. A grenadier division was as a rule comprised of six infantry battalions instead of the normal nine (two per regiment, instead of three), with the addition of a "*füsilier*" battalion to replace the recon unit. The basic rifle companies were smaller, and the division listed only three battalions of artillery instead of four. However, Marcks beefed up those along the Seine Bay with several coastal artillery batteries. The 711th's three regiments (the 731st, 744th, and 763rd) included a couple Russian battalions from the Caucasus.

2   Presumably Marcks, coming east from St. Lô, joined him here.

3   Fifty-two-year-old *Generalmajor* Friedrich-Wilhelm Richter.

4   See entry at the end of March 1.

Tuesday, March 7

Generalfeldmarschall Rommel is on tour again, this time along the Calvados coast with General Meise and Admiral Ruge. This is the second day of his inspection, ordered by the Führer to re-evaluate the Normandy coastal defenses. After breakfasting in the Caen hotel, he and his entourage are off at 7:30 a.m. They first travel northeast to Ouistreham, then onward to the Orne River estuary. General Marcks is once again with them, along with Generals Richter and von Schlieben.[1]

They travel westward from one shore position to another, inspecting the beach obstacles that are going up: wooden stakes, Belgian gates, Czech hedgehogs, tetra-hedrons—the group takes it all in. Construction along this area is lagging, mainly owing to lack of materials. They observe that a couple of areas have been flooded.

Overall, the work appears satisfactory, although Rommel sees a number of areas for improvement. For one thing, along the sandy area just west of the Orne's mouth, there is nothing put down as yet. The unit responsible for this point is currently working with another unit. Rommel curtly orders each battalion to start improvements on its own sector. And those minefields are to be made much wider than the present 1,000 meters. If they run out of mines, they can fill in the back sections with dummy mines. Marcks listens to him and takes notes. When Rommel asks him if he will see that these details get done soon, Marcks assures him that they will do their best.

They move on. He constantly makes observations and his group takes notes on his comments about the different positions. At Quineville, they see an extensive belt of *rollerbocks* positioned to thwart any movement off the beach. The belt, the group is told, is about 5km long. Rommel tells Marcks to pass along his congratulations to the men.

The inspection party moves up the Cotentin peninsula. Here the construction is lighter. Rommel wants a number of improvements made there.

Soon it is time for lunch. They dine at a soldiers' mess hall just outside the main port of Cherbourg. From there, it is off to the west side of the peninsula, southward to Carteret, about halfway down.[2] Rommel is concerned about all the possible open landing areas he sees. And this side of the peninsula is not too heavily defended. True, a landing here would be open to the weather elements coming off the ocean from the west, including a gusty storm. And this area is further from England, which would make air support harder. But a small support landing here coordinated with a large one on the eastern side was entirely possible. Rommel barks some orders. Pencils scribble as more notes are taken.

Rommel continues his inspection. Most of the units he finds inland he orders moved to the coast. He notes several areas needing obstacles; others that are suitable for mines. Small units are to create *Widerstandsnesten*[3] that overlook the various coves and inlets. His officers write down seemingly endless observations.

They continue southward and inland to the old Norman town of Coutances. It is here that Marcks' area of responsibility ends. He bids them farewell and leaves them as they press on into the area defended by General Erich Straube's 74th Corps.[4] They continue on southward: Granville, around the tip of Mont-St.-Michel Bay, past the mouths of the Sienne, See, and Selune rivers.

The cars have to detour at one point, because the coastal road has been mined. Rommel approves of this measure, although locals have complained. They bypass the road and travel westward until they can get back on the main highway, now somewhat inland.

Passing south of the port of St. Malo, they cross the Rance River into Dinan. Turning north, they travel along the river and, long after sunset, they pull into the town of Dinard, just on the western side of the Rance's mouth, opposite St. Malo. The tired group arrives at General Straube's elaborate headquarters at Villa Mond, a stunning château once owned by a British politician.[5]

They check into their quarters, and a short time later, the staff are shown a display of a special, priceless dinnerware collection. They marvel at the exhibit of exquisite china, superb crystal, and fashionable sterling silver set in beautiful showcases. The collection features a special section of famous Sèvres china, vases, and special pottery.[6] The hosts are only too happy to give tours of the priceless items along the hallways, and Gause is only too happy to assist with the tour, hoping to entertain the field marshal with the displays to take his mind off work. He shows the group a number of exquisite examples, verbally admiring each one. Carefully picking up a priceless vase, he holds it out for Rommel to see.

The field marshal, tired from the trip, has graciously suffered through the displays, polite but noticeably lacking in enthusiasm—until looking at the vase, a sudden thought strikes him.

"Porcelain!" he exclaims in wonder. "Meise, why don't we use china for our landmine casings?" After all, porcelain is non-metallic, so it would not be picked up by mine detectors. And being waterproof, the mine should hold up to being moderately handled.

His staff, absorbed by the artistry of the exhibitions, are surprised at his remark. They move on, and Gause resumes his descriptions. Rommel though, is still pondering his idea. After Gause mentions some of the newer products the company is now making, Rommel snickers, turns to Ruge and Meise and comments with a grin, "Maybe they could manufacture mines for us."

Gause, startled at this blasphemy of art, manages to continue, his comments more to himself now. The field marshal is a hopeless case. His staff officers shake their heads and smile as they all walk on.

Rommel finally goes to bed at 10 p.m., while his staff stay up for a few drinks around the fireplace.

***

That evening, General Marcks starts a letter home to his wife and vents his frustration over Rommel's roughshod methods:

> *These visits are very strenuous, because Rommel is a fanatic and it's impossible to do too much on the schemes he's thought up, like the gigantic minefields.*

---

1   Fifty-year-old *Generalmajor* Karl-Wilhelm von Schlieben commanded the 709th Grenadier Division.

2   The town merged with Barneville-sur-Mer in 1964, and is now referred to as Barneville-Carteret.

3   Strong, often isolated self-contained resistance points surrounded by minefields and usually manned by a platoon or company.

4   Admiral Ruge in his biography mistakenly refers to this as the 71st Corps.

5   Owned by British politician, economist, and financier Alfred Moritz Mond (1868–1930) before he converted to Zionism.

6   In 1738, a group of porcelain makers established in a villa near Paris a large porcelain manufactory (the old English term for a factory or plant). King Louis XV developed a keen interest in their lavish products, and so he moved the whole operation to much larger facilities in the Paris suburb of Sèvres—which conveniently happened to be near the residence of Madame de Pompadour (his rumored mistress) and the king's own palace at Versailles. The Sèvres porcelain in subsequent decades became known as the French porcelain of royalty, and then of Napoleon's imperial court. The manufactory went through a series of financial ups and downs throughout French history. Today, the historical building is run by the French Ministry of Culture, and its 18th- and 19th-century products have become priceless collectibles.

Wednesday, March 8

Generalfeldmarschall Rommel is on his third day touring western France, today in the Brittany area. This latest inspection, ordered by the Führer, at least has come at a fortunate time. While he is covering the coastline, his new headquarters back at La Roche-Guyon, downstream from Paris, is being set up for him. Hopefully, he will be able to move right in when he finishes this trip. Those of his staff not with him are already moving their gear over from Fontainebleau.

The inspection group enjoys a robust, early-morning breakfast at General Straube's 74th Corps headquarters, a historic villa in Dinard. They are off by 7:30 a.m. and travel west to Saint-Brieuc, then onward to meet at Belle-Ile-en-Terre with General Sprang,[1] commanding officer of the 266th Infantry Division.[2] The unit dispositions are gone over, and yet again Rommel emphasizes the importance of components being as close to the beach as possible.

They move on. Along the coast northwest of Saint-Brieuc, he meets a unit commander who dares make a complaint. His unit, he argues, is too small to stop any coordinated invasion. He simply cannot defend his long section of shoreline with the few men that he has. Rommel, irritated already at the lack of progress made in this area, chews the officer out. He tells him that he is missing the whole point of their strategy. They must do what they can against whatever is thrown against them. That's all that matters. Naturally, his unit would not be able to stop a major operation. The main enemy effort would probably be against the eastern shore. But against a minor probe (more likely in this region) such as a small diversionary landing or commando raid, his unit would be quite adequate. They must be ready for *anything*, he drills them. And when it comes, they will have to be furious tigers and throw the enemy back into the sea.

The chastened officer replies that he now understands—whether he actually does or not.

More obstacles are inspected and progress is noted near Lannilis. Flat land mines for this sector are in short supply, but on the other hand, the areas around the critical port of Brest are starting to bristle with obstacles of every shape and size. Ruge notes that open areas look "like porcupines." Rommel is satisfied. The group moves on.

More inspections, more wading out from the beach. In some areas, the heavier obstacles, like the Belgian gates, have sunk down into the wet sandy bottom. Rommel bluntly tells the local commander to "fix this."

After sloshing through the surf for a half-hour or so, they walk back to their cars and drive to the rear areas to view some minefields. Rommel criticizes the configurations of a number of them. The patterns laid out are too regular, and in some areas, the mines have been too closely laid. A good barrage would be able to take out whole sections of them. He orders this corrected.

The group turns around and heads back east. Lunch today is brief but stylish, at a lovely villa turned soldiers' mess hall in Pléneuf-Val-Andre, which features picturesque views of the cliffs there.[3] Then it is off again, back to Dinard. There a ferry takes them across the river mouth to the major port of St. Malo. More inspections, more recommendations, more orders. Next comes a short 15km trip eastward across the Alet peninsula, and a breathtaking view of the Bay of Mont St. Michel from the town of Cancale on the northeast tip of the peninsula. At one point, the party stumbles across two SS "geological" companies. The field marshal recommends that the local unit commander use them to help construct their beach obstacles.

They reverse their course and return to St. Malo, crossing back over to stay for the evening again at Straube's villa headquarters in Dinard. There they dine with Oberst Aulock,[4] the St. Malo commandant, an amusing fellow who never seems to mince his words.

***

Back at St. Lô, General Marcks, having just yesterday experienced the Rommel "*Wirbelwind*"[5] again, now writes home to his son:

> R. [Rommel] has a great amount of energy, and is truly fanatic on some things. He was content with us, and told me to pass along his satisfaction to the corps. And said he'd rather be happy after a victory than before one. Still, he makes the men happy saying things like that...

***

Today, Adolf Hitler issues Führer Order No. 11, entitled *Commandants of Fortified Areas and Battle Commandants*. It details the duties and responsibilities of the area commandant, of fortified areas and fortresses, as well as specifying that every fortress is expected to hold out to the last man.

Having long since broken the Japanese Ultra code, the Allies intercept and decrypt another situation report sent by the Japanese military attaché to Germany, currently in France. The message turns out to be critically important. It asserts that, up until December of 1943, the German strategy against the invasion had been to conduct several full-scale counterattacks against the invaders after they have landed. The report then states:

> However, as a result of studying the problem, and because of recommendations which have been made by Marshal Rommel, the Germans have now decided that the coastal lines must be held at all costs and that the enemy must not be permitted to set foot on the continent...
>
> The changes in defense plans are the result of the German experience in Sicily, Salerno, and Nettuno. In Rommel's opinion, it was bad strategy to allow the enemy to land because (1) After the British and American forces had obtained a bridgehead, the Germans did not quickly move into action against them, and (2) With superiority in the air, the enemy makes it

a rule to pound the rear of the defending forces, and that makes impossible a defense in which small units hold the front lines and a large reserve in the rear is used for counterattacks...[6]

The Allies are thankful for the information, and wonder who the military attaché's incredible source for this information is. They will find out only three days later, when another report from him is intercepted. His source again has spoken quite openly about their defensive strategy. The attaché in turn dutifully reports that:

The essence of the German plan of defense for Holland, Belgium, and France can be summed up in these words—Hold on to the beaches. The strategy now is to destroy the enemy landing forces before they ever reach the beaches, or if they do manage to land, to destroy them in areas as close to the coast as possible.

This time, the report does state the information source. It is none other than von Rundstedt's chief of staff, Günther Blumentritt.

---

1   *Generalleutnant* Karl Sprang, who took over command of the 266th on June 1, 1943.
2   The 266th Grenadier (*bodenständig*) Division was officially created in mid-May 1943 at the troop training grounds in Stuttgart. Like many of the static divisions by this time, the 266th had shed its third regiment to help create a mobile infantry unit.
3   On the northern Brittany coastline, about 47km west of St. Malo.
4   *Oberst* Andreas von Aulock. After the Allied breakout from Normandy in early August, he put up a staunch defense of the port area, forcing the Americans to literally blast him out. He declared at that time to the town leaders that, "I was placed in command of this fortress—I did not request it. I will execute the orders I have received and, doing my duty as a soldier, I will fight to the last stone. I will defend St. Malo to the last man even if the last man has to be myself." Horrified, the town leaders requested that he instead declare the port an open city. A relatively fair man, he reluctantly relayed their request to OKW, relayed through OB West. Hitler of course turned it down, declaring that in war there was no such thing as an open city. Aulock in response vowed to fight to the last man. He nearly did. Starting out with some 12,000 defenders, he would finally, arrogantly surrender with fewer than 500 men on August 17.
5   "Whirlwind."
6   Based on intercept SRS 1234, March 8, 1944.

Thursday, March 9

Generalfeldmarschall Rommel begins the final day of his latest tour in northwest France. Starting out early in Festung St. Malo, his inspection party travels east, inland, bypassing Cancale and moving southeast to get to Fougères.[1] There they will inspect the 155th Reserve Panzer Division.[2] Today though, Rommel decides to change the itinerary. By now, his staff have all but given up trying to get him to visit the historic monastery at Mont-St.-Michel. Now as they travel east, having inspected several positions so far, they once again get close to this tourist area. Rommel suddenly announces with a smile, "Today, we'll visit Mont-St-Michel."

His surprised staff are immediately pleased. They turn off towards the famous abbey and travel up the narrow spit of land to the medieval seminary out on the bay. They eagerly get out of their vehicles and begin taking a full tour of the grounds. They marvel at this finely designed abbey of solid granite, and they take in the breathtaking views of the bay. They listen to the history of this Christian "Mecca," and are shown the different rooms and levels within the solid stone structure.

Like his officers, Rommel enjoys the sightseeing. At the end of the tour, he thanks the monks for showing them the sights. Turning to leave, he looks over at his staff, thumps the solid doorway with his boot, and with the hint of a smile, remarks, "Good bunker."

They leave the historic attraction around 10:30 a.m. and move on. The field marshal is unusually hungry because he has not eaten a good breakfast. Anyway, this is the last day of the tour for him. Moving into his new headquarters probably has a lot to do with his easy-going manner. So with this half-holiday, half-hooky sort of attitude, they stop at a locally famous restaurant, Le Poulard. There he and his staff gorge themselves on the specialty of the house—exquisite home-made crêpes. Fascinated, they watch these delicacies get cooked in a long-handled pan over the open wooden fireplace.

As expected, the servings taste wonderful. The innkeeper delights in their satisfaction, although she still has no idea who this important German officer with such an impressive entourage is. She of course realizes he is a bigwig—the general's uniform and his company are obvious. But who he is, she cannot guess. Not knowing him continues to perplex her, which of course, delights him. Still, she does not openly come out and ask who he is; that of course would be rude (and possibly dangerous). So she says very little about it as they sit.

They eat their fill, lean back relaxed and casually converse for a while. Finally, just before noon, they get ready to leave. Rommel smiles, feeling sorry for the old woman. She is now openly frustrated because he has obviously enjoyed the meal, yet she does not know who he is. Relenting, he finally allows the guards to tell her the identity of the high-ranking general who has so recently stuffed himself on her cooking. Her eyes light up like silver dollars when she is told. *"Mon Dieu!"* she yelps in amazement, slowly sinking down into a chair. *"Rommel."*

He grins and motions Daniel that it is time to go.

They arrive at the Fougères castle a few minutes after noontime. The efforts of the 155th Reserve Panzer are coming along, and there are several *PzKw IIIs* and *PzKw IVs* already in its ranks. The commanding officer complains that he is losing his trained men to other units.

On to Le Mans. Rommel tells General Dollmann that his men are doing all right, but that they must continue erecting defenses in all areas, not just the most likely.

They discuss the upcoming move of the 352nd Infantry to the Calvados coast. Rommel suggests only moving up half the division, and leaving the other half inland. While this is going back on his original idea, he hopes that this placates OKW somewhat by leaving some units protected inland. They discuss how this leaves the western sector of the Cotentin peninsula weakly manned, and how they will compensate for this with heavy minefields and obstacles.

Dollmann tells him they only have some 100,000 mines laid, with nearly twice that number on order. They discuss the placement of units, and trying to combat the OT's plan to remove French workers from the coastal defenses and ship them to factories in Germany. Rommel expresses concern that the Seventh Amy is moving slower on carrying out his defensive orders than its counterpart, the Fifteenth Army. They are some six weeks behind in their constructions.

The inspection group finally leaves and drives off to their new home. The motorcade arrives at La Roche-Guyon around 7 p.m. The huge château looks positively beautiful to them as they approach it in the twilight.

The current duke, having no animosity towards the Germans taking over his home,[3] will be permitted to stay, along with his wife and daughter. They will be allowed quarters on the second floor.

The mansion is perfect for Rommel, and is large enough that it can house his immediate staff. The rest of his men will of course have to find quarters in the village. Over the centuries, a number of tunnels and small rooms had been constructed into the chalk cliffs. Rommel's own army engineers, assisted by some Polish POWs, have now enlarged them.

Yes, it will be quite adequate for his needs. He writes to Lucie that night:

> *Tomorrow Gause will fly to the wedding[4] and should bring you this letter. I still happily remember those nice days of my leave with you two and I want to thank you for them.*
>
> *In the meantime I have scheduled numerous days here and we will be looking forward to upcoming events. For the time of the wedding, I gave Gause permission to use the two cars. Aldinger will then take the camouflage-colored one and put the black one in the new garage.*
>
> *How is our Manfred? I hope his stiff neck is alright again. We are now in new quarters. It is very cold, but hopefully spring will come soon to France. A good post is always worth a bit.*
>
> *That's all for today. Have Gause bring some long underwear pants back for me. Aside from that, there is nothing else I need.*

1   About 80km southeast of St. Malo and 50km northeast of Rennes.
2   Originally organized as the 155th Panzer Division, it was redesignated in August of 1943 as the 155th Reserve Panzer Division. The division would disband at the end of April, and its units would become part of the 9th Panzer Division.
3   The Germans had seized the castle a year ago in mid-March, and had installed an anti-aircraft position at the top of the castle.
4   Rommel's niece was getting married.

Friday, March 10

At the Berghof, OKW continues planning for *Margarethe I*, the occupation of Hungary.[1] Two days ago, Hitler had targeted the 19th as the invasion date, and tomorrow, the orders will officially go out. Now, *Panzer Lehr* begins its journey eastward out of France.

In the meantime, OKW is up to its eyeballs in Eastern Front problems. The latest Soviet offensive is just a week old, but battered German lines are staggering in retreat. Many panzer units have been decimated, and the élite 1st SS Panzer Division, nearly surrounded in Galicia, is starting to look like a large regiment. More units have to be brought east to bolster the front. The 161st Division, which had taken part in the Battle of Kursk last year, has been ordered out of Denmark to move back east. It will have to be replaced with some reserve unit.[2]

***

The *Heeresgruppe B* staff spend the day acquainting themselves with their new headquarters.[3] Several auxiliaries are busy in the tunnels, preparing new spaces for additional staff members that will soon join them.

Rommel, having taken an immediate liking to the place because of its aristocratic taste, its old historic flavor, and its charming, out-of-the-way locale, is relaxing today. The rustic quarters have lavish rooms that were once occupied by Princess Zénaïde.[4] They are not overly spacious or luxurious and are comfortable and well furnished. The solid walls are a few meters thick and stay cool, even in the summer. Now in the late winter though, the building is downright cold. Many rooms have not been heated in years, so getting them warm is a slow process, especially when the staff discover how archaic the room fireplaces are. Luckily, wood is plentiful.

Rommel and his senior staff of course get to stay at the château. Junior staff officers and senior enlisted men will stay in a large adjacent building, which is also where the naval advisory staff will work. The remainder of the headquarters personnel will have to find quarters in town.

This morning, Rommel checks the latest message traffic. Dollmann at Seventh Army headquarters in Le Mans was bombed the night before, though the bombers had targeted the railyards. Then he meets with a couple of high-ranking engineering officers in his study.[5] Later in the afternoon, he will see the Luftwaffe field commanding officer for Belgium and Northern France, General Wimmer.[6] Then there are no more meetings, because he will spend the next two days touring up the coast.

The field marshal wastes no time settling in. Even Elbo quickly gets used to the new quarters, allowed to stay in the study in the daytime, though not (to his chagrin) ever allowed in the dining room.

1   A second such plan, *Margarethe II*, called for the occupation of Romania if the government there ever decided to either surrender to or side with the Soviet Union. Despite the fact that Romania indeed surrendered in August 1944, the operation was never undertaken.

2   *Generalmajor* Paul Drechmann's 161st would later be destroyed as a fighting unit in Romania during the Russian August offensive of 1944.

3   See Appendix A, page 595.

4   Zénaïde Julie Bonaparte, the elder daughter of Joseph Bonaparte, who was in turn the elder brother of Napoleon.

5   One of them is *General der Pioniere* Alfred Jakob, chief engineer and fortifications officer for OKH.

6   *Luftwaffe General der Flieger* Wilhelm Wimmer. He oversaw the Luftwaffe field command for Belgium and the Netherlands (*Befehlshaber Luftgau-Kommando Belgien-Nordfrankreich*). In 1942, he helped create a Dutch air unit from the *Nationalsozialisches Kraftfahrkorps* (NSKK) named the *NSKK Gruppe Luftwaffe*. Not to be confused with Undersecretary Friedrich Wimmer (see entry for March 23).

Saturday, March 11

Having enjoyed the different flavor of his new quarters at La Roche-Guyon, *Generalfeldmarschall* Rommel is off on another tour. He takes with him his Ic, *Oberstleutnant* Staubwasser. This will be a two-day trip up the northern coast of France.

As he is leaving, Rommel reconsiders a small problem. His headquarters is on the northern bank of the Seine. Half of his inspections will take him across the river. On top of that, the main garage for his Horch is located on the left bank. The problem is that the splendid bridge here—le pont de La Roche-Guyon—had been destroyed a few years before. Something to think about.

In the meantime, he travels north to the Somme estuary. On the other (northeast) bank, he and Staubwasser inspect Schwalbe's[1] 344th Infantry Division. It is well positioned on the coast, with the reserve regiment not too far inland.

Rommel finds out that an order from Fifteenth Army headquarters has suspended the installation of obstacles. In a stern tone he tells the men to disregard the order and to start putting them in again. They have done quite well on the high-tide barriers. Rommel now wants them to start on the low-tide barriers without delay.

The 344th's neighbor, the 49th Infantry,[2] has also progressed in its defenses quite well. Rommel is satisfied overall with the work that has been done. He can only hope that high-level red tape does not further sabotage his plans.

***

Today at the Berghof, the formal orders for *Margarethe I* go out. The German commanders are instructed to go into Hungary with as little disturbance as possible to occupy the key Hungarian civic and military focal points. On the other hand, if the people show active resistance to them, they are to be disarmed—by force, as needed. Any commanders and political leaders opposing the takeover are to be rounded up and summarily shot.

---

1 Fifty-two-year-old *Generalleutnant* Eugen-Felix Schwalbe (German for "swallow"), who took command September 27, 1942.
2 Fifty-four-year-old *Generalleutnant* Sigfrid Macholtz, commanding.

Sunday, March 12

The village of La Roche-Guyon is alive with gossip over the recent *en masse* arrivals of the German army group headquarters personnel. With quarters at the historic château quite limited, junior staff members cannot stay there[1] and must be housed in the village. The entire area is rapidly turning into an armed camp. Fences are being constructed, guard posts are popping up, and soon no one will be able to enter or leave the town without special papers. Rommel insists that all proper courtesies be extended to the villagers who must quarter members of his staff, and that none of them are to be thrown out of their homes.

Meanwhile, the headquarters potentate, *Generalfeldmarschall* Rommel, is off on the second day of a tour inspecting the northern coast of France. This morning, he begins with the fortress of Boulogne. Its contingent of almost 5,000 defenders includes about two dozen mortar units, over forty anti-tank guns, nearly fifty artillery pieces, and almost three dozen anti-aircraft guns to defend the strategic base. In addition, General Macholtz's[2] 49th Infantry Division, positioned just inland, provides the men in the port with added security. Rommel approves of the defensive barriers the division has created so far and gives Macholtz the go-ahead for more improvements. Rommel feels good about this section of the Atlantic Wall. Here he feels, is one point where he can stop the enemy in the water.

Traveling upward to the neighboring 47th Infantry Division at Calais though, he sees a different picture. He notes that less than a quarter of the coastline here has been worked on. On the other hand, a good part of the shore is rough cliffs, unsuitable for landings. He inspects the local units, their five dozen field pieces, and the reserve division positioned behind them, the 349th Infantry. The 47th's plan is to finish the rest of their coastline defenses here in 90 days. Rommel gives them instructions on how to expedite their construction efforts.

The field marshal then watches yet another demonstration; another landing craft crashing upon offshore obstacles. As predicted, the local naval authorities point out the ineffectiveness of the stakes, adding that even a mine on one or two of them would not do much damage to those well-constructed Allied craft. Rommel disagrees, and argues that even partial damage inflicted during combat would have a decided effect upon the condition and morale of the men inside. And everything would count at the moment of landing.

He attends another conference at the officers' quarters back in Boulogne, and then it is off to look at *Generalleutnant* Viktor von Drabich-Waechter's 326th Infantry Division.[3] The field marshal notes the condition of the three *Festung grenadier* regiments and the pathetically small anti-tank battalion. He finishes inspecting their defenses, content with the work they have done so far.

He returns to La Roche-Guyon and finds that he has to deal with a few Seventh Army concerns regarding that move of the 352nd Infantry northward to the Calvados coast. Some minor issues are resolved, and the division is finally given permission to move northward to secure the left flank of the 716th along the shore.

The addition of the 352nd will be a big improvement to the defenses in this area, but considering the work that has been done in the Calais and Somme sectors, this area of shoreline, the Calvados coast, is clearly still weakly defended. Worse than that, there are no divisions deployed immediately behind and in direct support of the frontline divisions. A landing here, without the nearby active support of a few panzer divisions, would in all probability succeed.

***

General Erich Marcks writes another letter to his wife. He tells her about the reinforcements that have been shipped in to man his positions. As soon as they arrive, he jokes, "I unpack them straightaway from their boxes and set them up."

He tells her how he is pleased that they can still produce such a high caliber of soldier after five years of being at war. He adds that he is optimistic about the future, and only develops a degree of "animus" whenever his birthday comes up—June 6.

---

1 There will eventually be about 80 junior staff members attached to the headquarters.
2 Fifty-four-year-old *Generalleutnant* Sigfrid Macholtz.
3 Fifty-four-year-old *Generalleutnant* Viktor von Drabich-Waechter, who took over on June 1, 1943. He would die in combat on August 2, 1944 during the Allied Operation *Bluecoat*.

Monday, March 13

It is a lovely spring day on the Seine. This morning, Rommel has a phone conference with General von Stülpnagel[1] on the disposition of his forces. In the afternoon, he goes on another one of his "armed promenades," this time on the grounds around his new headquarters. He and a couple of his officers trek up to and then around the old Norman tower above the château. On this lovely crisp day, they take in the beautiful countryside as they wander from the meadows into the surrounding woods.

Unfortunately, the only harvest from their hunt is a bunch of wild primroses.

The owner of the elegant but drafty, chilly château below them, the Duc du Rochfoucauld, for better or worse is getting used to his new tenants. The duke, a rather thin fellow, about 65 years old, is getting acquainted with Rommel and the two men are developing a mutual liking.

The duke's wife is a small woman, by descent a Danish princess. She speaks fluent German, and often socialized with high-placed Germans before the war. Their daughter Charlotte, a young woman of nearly 21, is quickly becoming a favorite of the staff members. Together with his wife, daughter, and sons, the duke begins getting used to the hustle and bustle of busy office sounds on the floor below them. Somehow, for them, life goes on.

That evening, Rommel writes to Lucie to tell her about his chief of staff's return from his trip to Germany:

> *Gause brought everything—also the baton—I will need it soon for an official report. Our new quarters are cold, but soon it will be spring.*

***

Today at the Berghof, during the daily war conference, the subject of defense tactics in the West is discussed. Chairing the conference as he always does, Hitler states that thought should be given to the idea of a second line of infantry divisions as a part of, but just behind, the main line. They would be out of range of enemy naval units and better able to move to trouble spots, even if in a strictly limited sense. Only mobile formations would be held as operational reserves. Exceptions were the areas east of Brest and south of Cherbourg, where there was great danger of landings from the air.

Jodl responds by stating the dangers of cramming so many forces into one big line. Field fortifications, he points out, might be obliterated by bombardment.

Hitler replies though, that his idea could be the best way to conduct an aggressive defense. Perhaps Rommel, he concludes, is right, and that the invasion must be defeated right on the beaches, because once the enemy establishes a firm beachhead, it would be too late to throw them back into the sea.

Rommel at this time seems to have the solid support of the Führer.

***

General Marcks at St. Lô writes another letter home, this time to his son. He describes his recent bout of flu a couple weeks ago.

He goes on to state that he is baffled as to why the army commanders around him cannot understand the gravity of what must be done. Especially because Hitler time and time again has hammered into them how critical it is that no foot of soil be given up to the enemy. He writes about the enemy's impressive air superiority, and that he only hopes that they are lucky enough to beat back the enemy.

---

1   Fifty-eight-year-old *General der Infanterie* Karl-Heinrich von Stülpnagel, *Militärbefehlshaber Frankreich.*

Tuesday, March 14

Rommel is on the road again early, with *Oberfeldwebel* Daniel driving, the field marshal riding in his customary position of "shotgun," and his chief engineer, Wilhelm Meise, in the back. As usual, *Vizeadmiral* Ruge is in the second car. Next to him is a new staff member, Major "Teddy" Behr.[1] The new man, assigned to the headquarters staff on February 15 and having come from the Eastern Front, has saddened them all with the discouraging news from the front.

Their first stop is the 81st Corps headquarters in Canteleu, near Rouen. Rommel's group is greeted by the corps commander, General Kuntzen.[2] After hearing a detailed briefing on their progress, Rommel begins his comments. The divisions are still too spread out, he tells their staff. They must defend the coastline in unison, but each division must operate like its own fortress. All units must fight within their division's tight perimeter, with no expectations of any immediate help or relief. Artillery support will have to be available to everyone, and local movement and maneuvering must be possible for all units. That way, Rommel comments dryly, if the High Command wants to relocate the corps' reserve units in the rear areas to the east into Russia, no one will mind. Of course he muses, if trends continue, they will not have to worry about reserve units being relocated to the East. There just will not be any.

Rommel's inspection party moves on. The 245th Infantry,[3] then the 17th Luftwaffe Field Division,[4] east of Le Havre, are on today's agenda. Rommel notes the steep cliffs and rocky shores, mostly unsuitable for landings. On the other hand, you do not underestimate your enemy. The few beaches, narrow as they are, might still be used for diversionary raids. The cliffs would provide some shelter from the winds, and the tides are negligible.

The field marshal reacts with a slew of instructions. Ravines are to be blocked off. Chunks of cliffs must be blasted into the sea. And mines, mines, mines...

The inspection group travels from one unit to the next, guided successively by the various unit commanders. Their guides though, get the motorcade lost several times, and Rommel gets more and more irritated, growling at their ineptitude. These officers don't even know their own sectors!

The vehicles eventually reach the port towns of Yport and Etretat. Satisfactory defenses... His staff officers make notes to that effect.

Onward they go, working their way roundabout towards the port of Le Havre. They observe one concrete foundation being finished for a large gun, part of a huge 380mm naval battery.[5]

They enter Le Havre and inspect the docks. Port preparations are noted as significant and effective.

Despite the irritations of the day, Rommel is cordial that evening at dinner with the local commanders.[6] He actually becomes jovial for a change as he carries on with various recollections of World War I. He tells them about his first experience with the Kriegsmarine in 1919, just after the war had ended. At the time, he was a company commander, stationed in Friedrichshaven, Germany.

That year, he recalls, a unit of sailors was transferred from Stuttgart to his area. These fellow Swabians had been redeployed because they were unruly and had simply been too much trouble in Stuttgart. Somehow, Rommel got stuck with them. There were no orders given on what to do with them—just keep them in line, he was gruffly told. And they were a rowdy bunch indeed, partly because they were not seasoned salts. Most of them had never even been to sea. He saw right off that they clearly had little respect for authority. When Rommel presented himself to them, sure enough, they were not impressed. And the coveted Blue Max that he had so bravely won meant nothing to them. They rudely referred to it as his *"Blechle."*[7]

Mentally rolling up his sleeves, he tackled the task of winning over these hooligans head-on. Rommel tells his listeners that it had not been easy, and he recounts a number of setbacks. Eventually though, using every element of leadership that he could devise (including some occasional rough abuse), he slowly brought about a metamorphosis. This raucous bunch was transformed into a firm, deadly unit, one that later fought magnificently against Communist components in the Ruhr area.

A few years later, many of these seamen, having transferred together as a small group into the police force, had called upon him, trying to get him to become a cop as well. Not that they had any sense of justice—they just wanted to serve under him again.

Sailors…

***

General Gause today visits Seventh Army headquarters in Le Mans. From there, he phones General Christiansen's headquarters in The Hague.[8] He tells them to supply his staff with updated, detailed strategic and operational maps of the Netherlands by the first of May.

---

1   Twenty-six-year-old Major Winrich Behr. One of Rommel's younger staff officers, Behr had served with Rommel in France in 1940, and then under him in North Africa. In mid-May 1941, he won the Knight's Cross commanding a recon company that had the distinction of being the first German unit to destroy an enemy vehicle (an armored car) in North Africa. Later on in the war, he served in Russia, including on von Paulus' intelligence staff at Stalingrad, briefly acting as special courier between OKW and von Paulus. Traveling back and forth as a go-between, the young officer on the one hand pleaded the general's case to the Führer, and on the other reaffirmed to von Paulus the Führer's orders to stand fast and not retreat. After the fall of Stalingrad, Behr served on the command staff of the 79th Infantry Division before being promoted in January 1944 and assigned to Rommel's staff in mid-February. Behr would stay with the army group command after D-Day, and in September become adjutant to *Feldmarschall* Model during the Allies' Operation *Market*

Garden and the battle for Arnhem. After the war, he would become a military historian. He died April 25, 2011 at the age of 93.

2   Ffity-four-year-old *General der Panzertruppen* Adolf Friedrich Kuntzen. His distinguished career included fighting in Poland, France, and later in Russia.

3   Fifty-two-year-old *Generalleutnant* Erwin Sander, commanding.

4   Forty-nine-year-old *Generalleutnant* Hans Kurt Höcker, commanding.

5   The site was bombed and severely damaged a few days later. As a result, it would not be operational by early June. The Allies were once again lucky, because with its range and caliber, this battery could have wrought havoc with the British soldiers landing at Sword Beach.

6   Fifty-three-year-old *Generalmajor* Walther Leutze, who was in the process of handing over command of the Le Havre fortress to 50-year-old *Generalmajor* Hans Sauerbrey, and Admiral von Tresckow, in charge of the naval squadrons there.

7   A cheap piece of metal found in toy sheriff badges, and the analogy that infers.

8   *Wehrmachtbefehlshaber Niederlande.*

Wednesday, March 15

This morning in Le Havre, Rommel as usual has an early breakfast. He is irritated about some undefended tall bluffs to the east that he had observed yesterday, and the table talk for the morning is about possible enemy landings around these cliffs. Airborne operations and cliff climbing are discussed.

Starting out in a light fog, they arrive in Bolbec and drive to the "nicely situated" headquarters of *Generalmajor* Diestel's[1] 346th Infantry Division, positioned in reserve behind the 17th Luftwaffe Field Division, which they visited the day before. Diestel reports on his division's readiness. Rommel expresses his concern. This unit, like so many on the coast, seems to lack his sense of urgency, often working as though they have all the time in the world. Oh, they realize how important the preparations are, and the field marshal's orders will be carried out to the letter! However, they are awaiting some components, or must delay until some directive gets modified, or have to figure out an easier way to do something else.

Rommel then inspects the 346th's three regiments. Only one has true mobile transport. The others rely on an accumulation of old French vehicles, horse-driven wagons, and hundreds of bicycles. And a few small units have the unpleasant task of having to walk everywhere.

The division does not have a clear set of directives, so Rommel takes over, firing off a volley of instructions. During his visit, he comes across a rear fortified position under construction. He is told that this is a fallback position and is not going to be manned until the battalion is forced to retreat. Rommel tells them to put in a small contingent to man it at all times. The battalion officers just look at him blankly, because this goes against his all-available-troops-on-the-coast doctrine. He patiently explains that an enemy airborne unit could be dropped nearby and seize the position to hold it themselves.

He critiques other divisional positions. Even though the 346th is a backup division, its units are still deployed too far from the coast. He wants them to move closer, and to better cover the steep ravines next to the shoreline. He marks off a number of cliff areas as examples of where to blast some earthslides. But, *Herr Feldmarschall*, would not steep slopes to the ravines better impede any advance made by the enemy troops coming ashore from the landing craft to move inland? Not that much, he elucidates. The sharp drops would impede your line of fire, and better protect the enemy from your counterfire.

He does finds one battery ready at a moment's notice to repel an airborne landing, But one, he points out, is not enough. They all must be able to react instantly to a sudden paratrooper assault. Although they dislike the idea, the men near the coast are to move out of the warm, comfortable local villages and into the fields. Towns make too easy a target for the enemy. His own staff make a few notes, in contrast with the divisional staff officers who are scribbling hurriedly as he lays out instructions.

Suddenly he is gone, and the divisional staff officers breathe a sigh of relief. So much more to do now.

His next victim is Menny's 84th Infantry.[2] The division is still forming, so only a few units are ready to fight. Their boot supply has improved, and the men tell him that the food is good, although a bit insufficient for the younger soldiers and the seasoned *Ostkämpfer*.[3]

Not to worry, though. Menny is one of Rommel's disciples from North Africa. The two of them recall their days at Tobruk. Rommel notes with satisfaction that the experience Menny gained back then is now being reflected in the degree of training of his men. Even though they lack equipment, weapons, and most of them ammunition, they are a well-disciplined, capable unit. One battalion demonstrates for the visitors a charging assault, complete with a number of explosives and grenade salvos. Rommel nods in approval. He praises the group and expresses his undying confidence in them.

By 2 p.m., the motorcade is back at La Roche-Guyon. Gause has been on the phone for most of the morning. He is working out the administrative details between OB West and Marcks' 84th Corps on the redeployment of the 352nd Infantry to the Calvados beaches. In addition, he has been talking to Himmler's SS headquarters, wanting to get permission to redeploy that SS geographical engineer battalion Rommel came across near Cancale back on the 8th, to work in the Mont-St.-Michel area on defenses. The SS agrees, as long as their men can work together and the unit is not split up.

Dealing with the SS is sometimes a tricky business.

More phone calls about new obstacles for the beaches and anti-aircraft protection for the railroad yards. The recent enemy raids seem to be taking a much heavier toll than usual upon the French railway system. And without the railroads, supplies cannot move.

***

During today's pre-noon conference at the Berghof, little attention is given to the West. The focus rather is an update on the planning for *Margarethe I*. Hitler, Keitel, and von Ribbentrop decide that they want Hungary's top military leaders under their roof when the operation takes place—just in case. If the Hungarians decide to resist occupation, at least their top generals will be absent. So today, Admiral Horthy is sent a telegram. In it the Führer carefully expresses his regrets for not being able to attend his holiday.[4] In a counterproposal, he invites the prince-regent to come to Salzburg in three days to confer with him. The Führer wants to discuss certain military matters that the prince-regent had addressed in a February 12 letter.

Hitler hopes that this will get not only Horthy to come, but his top military commanders as well. In any case, Horthy hopefully has no idea that Hitler intends to hold him a virtual hostage while *Margarethe I* begins.

***

The prince-regent of Hungary is disappointed that the Führer did not come to his country to celebrate the anniversary of their revolution. Still, Hitler had been considerate enough to send written regrets, his excuse being that he was needed to oversee pressing war matters. To make up for this, he has invited Horthy to Austria in a few days and to be a guest at Klessheim Castle on the outskirts of Salzburg.[5] The Führer wants to review the war situation with him, to discuss some political concerns that they share, and to settle the issue of Hungarian troops returning to their country for security matters, something Horthy and his staff have been pushing for months.

Horthy though, hesitates to accept the invitation. With the war turning sour and Hungary's deteriorating relations with the Reich, Hitler's true reason for Horthy coming to him—on his ground, so to speak—is probably not good.

Horthy consults with his cabinet on whether he should agree to take the trip. The prime minister (secretly negotiating with the Allies) and his minister of war recommend that he decline. However, his chief of staff and foreign minister disagree. The latter points out that Hitler had just recently received the presidents of Slovakia and Romania.[6] To turn down his invitation (especially since relations with the temperamental Hitler were at present quite cool), would surely invite a swift negative reaction on Germany's part. And anyway, resistance at this point would probably just be futile.

Horthy reluctantly decides to go, if for no other reason than to try to persuade the German leader to let his Hungarian units return from the front. At home they can recover, rest up, and prepare to defend against any breakthrough on the Eastern Front, which could at any time come rolling across the steppes towards their country. He could also in a conciliatory gesture tell Hitler that Hungary has some 100,000 Jewish laborers ready to integrate into the German industrial war machine.

Horthy tells his staff of his decision, and they begin to make preparations for the trip.

---

1 Fifty-one-year-old *Generalmajor* Erich Diestel.
2 Fifty-year-old *Generalleutnant* Erwin Menny, commanding.
3 Lit. "Eastern Combatants." Those veterans who had served on the Eastern Front.
4 March 15 is one of Hungary's most important holidays. The date commemorates the start of the country's uprising in 1848 against the Austrian Habsburg Empire and some 200 years of occupation. The nearly-spontaneous protests that began on this day led to a revolutionary war. Interestingly, although the Hungarians usually celebrate this struggle yearly, the Austrian royalty (with the help of Russia) ultimately prevailed, and the revolution finally failed in August of 1849. Though Hitler was by birth Austrian, he could hardly claim his birthright as an excuse to not attend the holiday celebrations, particularly since he so strongly considered himself German.
5 It is less than an hour's drive from the Berghof.
6 Josef Tiso and Ion Antonescu.

Thursday, March 16

It is a busy time at La Roche-Guyon. Details of the departure of *Panzer Lehr* for an upcoming operation in Eastern Europe are still wrapping up. Chief of Staff Gause is on the phone again, this time with Army Supply. There is a large stock of antipersonnel mines in Germany that are available for the West. The only problem is that they do not have fuses. Gause has to find them—somewhere. In the meantime, he gets authorization to ship the rest of those allotted to France using the *Blitzpfeil* priority.[1]

In the meantime, Rommel has other problems. He has traveled to Paris to sit in on a noontime conference with the commander of *PanzerGruppe West*. On the issue of where to place the panzers, they both seek a meeting of minds—so long as the other meets it on his terms.

While Rommel is occupied with von Schweppenburg, Ruge is a few blocks away with his own problems. He is attending an hour-and-a-half consultation with *Vizeadmiral* Krancke at Naval Group West.

The talk is not going well at all. Rommel's staff want to have a say on the production and distribution of naval mines—in this case, the new deadly *KMA*.[2] They have some ideas on increasing production, and Ruge wants them laid off certain coastal areas around northern France. Krancke flatly refuses, wanting to retain all control over their production and distribution.

Underlying the mine argument though is a rift between the two admirals. Ruge sees Krancke as a pompous mini-dictator, wanting to be lord and master over all naval matters, no matter what their application or his experience on the subject. Krancke had been OKW's chief planner in the 1940 *Weserübung*[3] and still carries considerable influence there. He already runs all naval operations in the area with what meager naval forces he has (except, of course, U-boat operations, which are directly run from OKM in Berlin). Krancke wants to control Ruge's activities too, and Ruge has angrily vowed that he will never get to do that, even though in this case, Ruge is outgunned.

Krancke on the other hand sees what he is doing as his critical duty, his massive responsibility. And anyway, he cannot understand what on earth a senior naval officer is doing in an army group headquarters. And if Ruge is going to work in France, then surely his chain of command should still go through normal naval channels.[4]

Now the two of them are arguing. Krancke is admonishing Ruge because some time back, one of Ruge's assistants had overstepped his authority by giving orders to the *Kanalküste* commander, *Vizeadmiral* Rieve, on how to position light naval batteries. Never mind that the assistant was now gone, replaced by an experienced (and no doubt, more reticent) coastal artillery officer, and that Ruge had later straightened the matter out with Admiral Rieve himself. Krancke is bringing the matter up yet again, no doubt to press home the point that Ruge does not know what he is doing and is out of control, ignoring protocol and command chains. Ruge, his feathers ruffled, argues back. When it comes to coastal defense requirements that *he alone* might deem necessary, he can go straight to Dönitz himself and bypass everyone in the naval chain of command.

As Krancke glares, Ruge concedes that he will be informed of everything that Ruge discusses with Berlin. Krancke is not satisfied, and Ruge is forced to be more conciliatory.

The two part on hostile terms. Furious at his treatment, Ruge goes to the senior officers' quarters of nearby *Sicherung West*[5] and has lunch with some old colleagues to help assuage his anger.

***

The snow still lies heavy on the Obersalzberg. Hitler is having a quiet evening in his Berghof. Propaganda Minister Goebbels is staying with him. They are relaxing, enjoying color home movies that Eva Braun had taken of them back in 1939, and then later in 1942. Hitler has evidently aged badly since then. There is much less spring in his step, and he stoops more while he stands or walks.

The movies over, the two discuss a number of subjects. At one point, Hitler brings up the invasion in the West. He shakes his head tiredly and tells Goebbels that he hopes it comes soon, so that he can just get it over with.

---

1   "Lightning Arrow." It was the highest priority available at the time, a status usually reserved for besieged areas in Italy or Russia. A lightning arrow symbol was used for such a priority shipment.
2   *Küstenminen A* (Coastal Mine, Model A). This was a mine of a simple design, used in various shallow areas such as off Dieppe and south of the Gironde River.
3   "Weser Exercise." The invasion of Norway in early April 1940. The codename was of course a red herring, inferring a harmless practice assault on the Weser River in Germany.
4   This is a classic example of administrative command problems that have haunted the different services of many countries for hundreds of years.
5   Naval Security Command, Western Theater. Created in late October 1940, it was charged with controlling naval coastal security operations for Belgium and France. This entailed command of some small coastal minesweepers and patrol craft.

Friday, March 17

Generalfeldmarschall von Rundstedt prepares for a trip to Berchtesgaden. All the senior commanders in Europe have been ordered there for another large, formal conference with the "Bohemian corporal." Von Rundstedt is determined to make sure that the question of command between Rommel and him, which has been stewing for some time, will now get settled once and for all. That prima donna Rommel has been going around imprudently ordering everything, lock stock and barrel, to move to the coastline. Units there are bound to be defeated when the invasion comes. Well, both field marshals will have a private audience with the Führer, and now they will see just what is what. Either von Rundstedt is in charge or he is not...

Hitler has sent their two staffs a special train to travel in. How kind. Still, providing the train is only the appropriate thing to do; after all, proprieties have to be observed. And truthfully, Hitler always had done special favors like this for the old Prussian because of his rank, his experience, and his past glories early in the war. Besides, Hitler has banned his field marshals from flying. It is no longer safe, what with the enemy now so strong in the air (although the Führer still will never admit that the Allies have achieved air superiority).

Thus, the special train. Von Rundstedt plans to board today or early tomorrow morning.

Once again, the public will get to see him. Surprisingly, although he was the key military leader in their 1940 defeat, he is generally popular with the occupied Parisians, though he does not admit it to anyone.

Once, in the spring of 1942, when he was on leave yet again at his favorite spa in Bad Tölz, Hitler, who had been staying as usual at his Berghof a couple hundred kilometers away, had invited him to take a short trip down for lunch and had provided a special car for him. When von Rundstedt walked out of his villa, he saw a beautiful black limo parked at the curb. It had been waiting for him for several minutes. In doing so, it had drawn the attention of several people passing by. The field marshal, dressed as always in his mufti[1] and accompanied by his wife Bila, walked over to the waiting car. As he did, a throng of smiling civilians gathered near them, of course respectfully keeping their distance. As he poised to get into the vehicle, his wife, surprised at seeing this gathering, paused, turned back to him in wonder, and said with a big smile, "Oh, look how much the people want to see you!"

He hesitated, and turned around to briefly glance at the folks standing around them. He frowned and growled, "Oh, they don't want anything from me—they're just waiting for the bus!"

With that he brusquely entered the car. But he did know better.

***

Generalfeldmarschall Rommel also spends a good part of today preparing for the Führer's upcoming conference at the Berghof. All of the senior commanders will be there, and this is one more chance to (hopefully in private) lay before his mentor the absolute necessity of moving the panzers close to the coast and putting them under the direct command of his army group headquarters. That is the only chance they have of defeating the invasion, and giving those fighting in the East a break.

Before he leaves, he sends another letter off to Lucie, telling her:

> *Here in the West we have every confidence that we can make it—but the East must hold out too.*

Meeting Rommel in the château's main entryway late that afternoon are his Ia von Tempelhoff and his new aide *Hauptmann* Lang, both of whom will be accompanying him on the trip. Their final preparations complete, they walk out to the waiting vehicles, their staff as usual turning out to see them off. Rommel bids them goodbye and the three of them get in the Horch. Daniel drives them off.

They get into Paris that evening and after dinner, they drive to the train station and prepare to board the special train. The cars are decorated in lavish fashion, and the staff find the accommodation quite plush.

Just like von Rundstedt, Rommel spends the night on the train, parked in the Paris railway station. They are scheduled to leave very early the next morning and travel with the other top Western commanders to Salzburg, not far from the Führer's villa. While traveling across Europe, Rommel will not idly watch the countryside go by. He is going to do his homework thoroughly. When his time comes to speak at the conference, he will be quite ready to convincingly lay out his case.

***

This afternoon, after the daily war conference at the Berghof, Hitler gets together with von Ribbentrop, Keitel, Jodl, and Himmler, to plan for the war symposium coming up in two days. Before they get to that though, they discuss the upcoming Hungarian operation, and how Hitler will deal with Admiral Horthy. He tells the others that he will break the news of the occupation to him at some time in the morning. He is going to take a stern attitude with the prince-regent and tell him in no uncertain terms that Hungary, having become reticent about the war and having undertaken secret dealings with the enemy, is skirting with disaster.

Hitler tells these four senior officials that he will carefully observe how Horthy reacts. Around 12:30 p.m., they will break for lunch. At that point, based on Horthy's response to the announcement and his attitude until then, Hitler will determine whether or not the operation will go on as scheduled. Jodl later writes in his diary:

> *If Horthy permits the invasion and there is no resistance then we defer decision on disarming and demobilizing them.*

Hitler tells his generals that they must try hard to find out how Horthy really feels about the news, because he is a slippery fellow. To ensure they get all the prince-regent's reactions and true thoughts—again as a precaution—the Germans make sure that the main rooms that the Hungarian delegation will be given at Klessheim Castle (where the conference is to take place) are all bugged with microphones. The private conversations of the Hungarians will be monitored in the castle's main control room and recorded on circular drums. Clearly, despite their desires, the Germans very much expect the meeting to be explosive.

With the unsettling details mapped out, they go on to discuss the military aspects of the occupation. Hopefully, the Hungarians will not know what has hit them until it is too late.

They eventually get to the relatively unimportant details of the upcoming conference with the Western commanders.

---

1   A military expression originating in the 19th-century colonial British Middle East, referring to any civilian attire worn by a man who normally wore or was entitled to wear a military uniform. It often alluded to soldiers on leave who no doubt enjoyed being able to relax in informal (and sometimes outlandish) attire and forget the stresses of war. Equivalent to the American "civvies."

Saturday, March 18

It is 3 a.m. in the Balkans. German forces, many just arrived from France, wait patiently, just over the Hungarian borders, getting final deployment briefings for Operation *Margarethe I*. A big part in the operation will be the *Panzer Lehr* division and several mobile assault units from the West. A number of SS security and police units will be involved as well—all poised to strike when they are given the word.

***

Predawn in Paris. The entire Wehrmacht senior command for Western Europe is aboard a specially outfitted train in the Parisian railway station, about to leave for a grand conference with the Führer. Most of the generals expect that strategic defense policies will be finalized and set in stone.

The train pulls out of the station in the dark and slowly begins to head southeast across France. It is bound for the far-off city of Salzburg in Austria, and from there it will travel southward down a rail spur to the town of Berchtesgaden in lower Bavaria. The passengers will be given special rooms for the night in the local hotels. Tomorrow, they will travel by car up the Obersalzberg mountain to the Führer's retreat—the Berghof. There they will attend this obviously elaborate conference that has been planned for the Western Theater commanders.

During the day's train ride, Rommel goes over his notes several times and confers with von Tempelhoff on several key points. He wants to be sure that he makes the best impression upon the Führer and that his argument is the most persuasive. No doubt, von Rundstedt will present his inland-defense case with great aplomb and sophisticated authority. Still, there is a good chance the old man will not sway the Führer much. Hitler, with his commoner background, has like Rommel always had a natural resentment of the aristocratic Prussian *Generalstab* caste. Anyway, the Führer for once is thinking the same way Rommel is thinking (or vice-versa)—stop them in their tracks. Rommel certainly hopes so…

***

In the meantime, a different drama is going on at their destination.

The leader of the Third Reich is on his way off the Obersalzberg, headed down the muddy trail toward the Berchtesgaden railway station. He wants to be sure to be that he is there on time to meet Admiral Horthy's train when it pulls in to the station.

Now that Hitler's elaborate plans for this have been set in motion, he has been nervous about this meeting all morning. He has no idea how Horthy will react to the news that his country is about to be occupied. How furious will he be, and more importantly, how will the Hungarians respond?

Hitler has time to think again about this going down the mountain. Sitting in the front passenger seat of his special Mercedes convertible, he impulsively opens the glove compartment in front of him and removes the revolver in there. His mind lost in thought, he examines it, checking to see that it is loaded. He puts the gun down in his lap for a while, before finally deciding to return it to the glove compartment.

Trying to play out today's possibilities, he turns around to Dr. von Sonnleithner[1] and asks him, "Will the admiral have eaten?"

The liaison nods affirmatively. Hitler in response nods his own head.

Soon thereafter, 75-year-old Admiral Miklós Horthy, having started out for Bavaria with his staff by rail the day before, stares at the looming Berchtesgaden railway station as his train slowly pulls in. He sees just inside the station the figures of the Führer, Foreign Minister von Ribbentrop, Wilhelm Keitel, and several other senior German officers and officials. Hitler seems much older than he did on their last visit, as he stands, staring at the train. The cost of waging war on the world, no doubt.

Hopefully, they will resolve the issue about returning some Hungarian divisions from the Eastern Front to recuperate and to defend against any sudden Russian thrust against Hungary. Horthy though, is unsettled over any other purpose this meeting may have and wonders if he should take along his personal small-caliber pistol, just in case. He probably would be able to get away with carrying it. He knows that as a head of state, he will not be searched by the German guards. Twice he hesitatingly picks the loaded weapon up and puts it in his pocket, and twice he takes it out again and puts it back in his suitcase.

Horthy slowly gets off the train. His host walks out of the station to meet him and gives him a lukewarm reception. The two of them climb into Hitler's Mercedes and they roar off towards Klessheim Castle in Salzburg.

Not much is said on the 30-kilometer ride. Horthy asks Hitler if he wants his accompanying Hungarian senior staff members to attend their meeting. Hitler shakes his head and stonily replies no. Clearly, he is not in a good mood. Horthy senses that Hitler is upset with him too.

They arrive at Klessheim and enter the resplendent castle. Horthy precedes Hitler into the Führer's study, followed by Schmidt, the Führer's personal interpreter. Since no interpreter is needed for them to talk, Horthy asks if he needs to be there. Hitler nods at the interpreter, who leaves them alone in the study.

Though Hitler is clearly upset, he hesitates to begin. He starts off grumbling about Italy's betrayal and the difficult situation that has put Germany in. And, he adds in a determined tone, since according to his sources, Hungary also seems to be planning on going over to the enemy, he feels that he must take certain precautionary actions to avoid getting caught the same way again.

He continues. Even in the best of times, Hungary had always been a reluctant partner. Now that the situation is worse militarily, according to reports by the SS, it seems like the Hungarian government wants to ease their way out of the Axis alliance by making contacts with the British.

The admiral, now upset himself, hotly denies any such thing. He replies, "Without my consent, there can never be the change of sides that you have described. Should events force my hand one day so that, to safeguard our very existence, I have to ask the enemy for an armistice, I can assure you that I shall openly and honestly inform the German government of such negotiations beforehand. We would, in any case, never be the first to take up arms against our German comrades."

Hitler calls him a liar, and repeats that he thinks otherwise, and that is why he has to take precautionary measures to protect Germany.

Horthy replies stiffly, "I do not know what you mean. If by that phrase you mean military measures, or in other words the occupation of an independent and sovereign state which has made many sacrifices on Germany's behalf, that would be an unspeakable crime. I can only warn you against the execution of so ill-advised a step, which would cause unparalleled hatred for your regime to flare up."

Hitler replies that he must do what he must do. He declares that in 24 hours, a dozen German divisions will march into Hungary to occupy the country until a better-suited government is set up—one approved of by the Führer himself. Horthy's initial shock quickly turns into anger. He gruffly replies that he would not stand for any such thing. Hitler over the next few minutes bluntly tries to convince him that he has no choice. Horthy threatens to resign, and they argue some more. Hitler finally threatens to take over all of Hungary's economy for his own war effort.

Horthy has heard enough. He barks, "If everything has been decided upon already, there is no point in prolonging this discussion. I am leaving." He turns and storms out of the study. Hitler is still angry but also surprised and flustered at this unexpected act of defiance. He follows the prince-regent out the door.[2]

With Hitler telling him that this is not a wise move, the Hungarian leader nevertheless marches upstairs to the room allocated to him and sends for his staff. He tells them what has happened and informs them that they are leaving immediately and departing as soon as they return to the Berchtesgaden station. Horthy is angry, but mostly worried about what is transpiring. He does not know if the occupying forces have already crossed his border.

Von Ribbentrop, thinking fast, stages a fake air raid, even ordering a smoke screen to simulate a real air attack. With the sirens going off, he apologetically tells Horthy that, for his own safety, he must wait until the air raid is over. The prince-regent, disgusted, reluctantly agrees. Soothingly, von Ribbentrop hands Horthy a note. Hitler has invited him to stay and dine with him, to further discuss the matter that afternoon. With leaving at the moment out of the question, he again consents.

Soon afterward, everyone sits subdued at the well-laid table. Hardly anyone speaks, and if they do so, it is in a very low voice. As the Führer picks unenthusiastically at his vegetarian plate, those around wonder what he is thinking.

After lunch, Hitler sadly tells one of Horthy's aides that he truly regrets the actions he has had to take. He even makes a show of calling for Chief of Staff Keitel and asks him if the occupation order can somehow be called off. Keitel of course plays his part and replies that it cannot. The troops are already on the march.

Hitler and the prince-regent soon have another meeting. Horthy tells him that based on the current situation, he must resign. Hitler surprisingly becomes distressed. Is it an act? Horthy cannot tell. The Führer begins to plead with him. He tells Horthy that he has always loved his country. "And I would not dream of interfering with Hungary's sovereignty."

Hitler pauses again and continues. His military actions, he says apologetically, are only being undertaken to safeguard Hungary and its future. "I give you my word that the German troops shall be withdrawn as soon as a new Hungarian government that has my confidence has been formed."

Horthy replies stiffly that he will have to reserve judgment on that point.

Changing tack, Hitler becomes acrimonious. If Horthy resigns, he states coldly, he will install in his place a radical right-wing puppet government. The veiled threat to the personal safety of Horthy and his staff is implied. And if anyone tries to organize any resistance to the new government, Germany will enlist the aid of Hungary's hated neighbors to subdue them—those damned Romanians and the Slovaks.

On that note, the meeting ends and the prince-regent returns again to his own quarters. Now that the air raids are over, the all clear has sounded, their departure can be made. They might as well stay for dinner though, because their special train (they are told) will now not be ready for them before 8 p.m.

Sometime later, after Horthy has had a chance to cool down and is preparing to leave, von Ribbentrop goes to him. He tells Horthy that he has had a chance to reason with the Führer. If the prince-regent cooperates with the takeover and remains in office, the government changeover will go smoothly. German troops will stay in the country only until a suitable government is installed. The occupational force will then leave—assuming that there is no unrest. Or violence.

Horthy sees that this is probably the best deal he is going to be able to get, and consents. A short time later, von Ribbentrop returns with a draft of the public announcement that he will put out covering the Admiral's visit. He says that the Führer, in a show of solidarity, "wants you to sign this draft communiqué, stating that the decision to occupy Hungary is being made by mutual consent."

Horthy again gets angry at this coercion. He barks, "You might as well have added that I begged Hitler to have Hungary occupied by Slovak and Romanian troops, which is another one of the threats he made!"

The German foreign minister is moderately distressed at Horthy's reaction. Clearly, the deal he is trying to barter for the Führer is not going well. He replies, "Your Majesty, in life, minor untruths are often necessary."

Disgusted, Horthy looks over the communiqué again. Despite the mutual consent phrase, the text is diplomatically worded, of course to lessen the impact of the impending occupation. Still, Horthy insists that the mutual consent part be removed. Ribbentrop, realizing that this is an ultimatum, reluctantly agrees to strike the words.

Horthy, resigned to Hungary's fate, cables his cabinet and instructs them to allow German troops in. In return, Hitler in turn agrees to order his troops not to occupy Budapest—except of course, for a special "honor guard," to protect the prince-regent.

The Hungarians are finally given clearance to depart, and Hitler politely accompanies the coldly silent prince-regent back to the railway station. The special train departs the station at 8 p.m. Horthy does not know it, but his return trip will be delayed for hours, first at Salzburg, and then at Linz. The Germans will still be able to snatch him, in case his cabinet refuses to obey his orders and resists.

The drama over, Hitler returns to the Berghof now to receive his generals.

***

Vizeadmiral Ruge takes advantage of Rommel's absence to visit several naval installations. Starting off at 6 a.m. with *Kapitän* Peters, they leave La Roche-Guyon in the thick, gloomy fog of the morning. With Hatzinger having to sometimes stick his head out his window to see where they are going, they make their way some 340km southwest to the naval engineering school in Angers. There they talk to the commander about various types of mines and mine detectors.

From there, they head south across the Loire River at Le Pont-de-Cé and travel a few kilometers to the town of Murs Erigné, where they call on the naval commander for Western France, *Vizeadmiral* Schirlitz,[3] and his staff. They sit down for nearly an hour and a half and discuss various schemes to thwart the enemy. They talk about ways to destroy port facilities, mining techniques, concrete gun emplacements, and other issues. Ruge stresses to them once again Rommel's main objectives of holding the enemy on the beaches and keeping them from getting a foothold ashore.

That afternoon, they go west to Nantes, and then to St.-Nazaire. They eventually find and call on the fortress commander, *Konteradmiral* Mirow,[4] in his quarters by the shore and have another conference with him about the same issues.

---

1   Thirty-nine-year-old Dr. Edler Franz von Sonnleithner, von Ribbentrop's adjutant in OKW. He was captured at the end of the war and interned for two years. He died April 18, 1981.

2   It is an entertaining notion to speculate just how Horthy might have reacted differently if he had picked up the pistol back on the train and carried it into the study. Of course, any attempt on the Führer's life would have meant his immediate certain death. Still, how history would have been altered if he had.

3   *Vizeadmiral* Ernst Schirlitz; *Kommandierender Admiral, Atlantik Küste.* Later in August he was also designated *Festungkommandant, La Rochelle* until its surrender, May 9, 1945.

4   Forty-nine-year-old *Konteradmiral* Hans Mirow, who took command February 4, 1944.

Sunday, March 19

At midnight, Operation *Margarethe I* begins. At least half the units entering Hungary are from the West, including several mobile assault units, mobile infantry units, and Bayerlein's new division, *Panzer Lehr*. The Hungarian leader, Admiral Miklós Horthy, is still en route to his capital in the early morning hours, delayed by Nazi intrigue. The German columns have of course long preceded him.

By the time he arrives back in Budapest the next morning, his fears are confirmed. He is informed that the German occupying forces have been on the move since midnight. And he finds out later that day that he has been lied to by von Ribbentrop—one of those "minor untruths" often necessary. The offending phrase "mutual consent" has been left in the official German press announcement.

***

The senior generals of the Western Theater are in Berchtesgaden today for their grand military symposium with the Führer. Having stayed the night in luxurious hotels, they spend the morning sightseeing, relaxing, and souvenir shopping.

Early in the afternoon, the guests begin arriving at Hitler's mountain villa. Rommel is driven by limousine from his hotel through the outskirts of Berchtesgaden, and from there up a steep mountain road that unfortunately has a number of potholes. The expanded country manor is situated atop a 1,950-meter mountain, called Obersalzberg, which overlooks and partially rings in the town far below. After some more sharp bends, the car finally reaches the courtyard in front of the Berghof entrance around 2 p.m.

As he gets out of the limo, Rommel takes in the scenery down the mountainside and around the compound. The Führer's villa is shrouded by large sections of camouflage netting, laid down to throw off the aim of any enemy bombers. There are also several smoke generators around, ready to create a thick smoke screen to cover the area during an air raid. And of course, there are several anti-aircraft positions and security guard posts. The place has certainly expanded since he last saw it. Rommel nods in approval.

There have been a number of upgrades to the villa over the years. Some had been done by the Führer himself, often using instruments and tools that he had borrowed from Albert Speer. It is now a beautifully simple, three-storey block building with white walls. The lower floor has been lengthened to form an L-shape, and the roof includes some ornate eaves overhanging the building. The shutters to the petite windows are painted with wide, diagonal stripes.

Standing at the main door of the villa is the Führer himself, personally receiving the guests as they approach. He looks tired, a bit more stooped over than before.

There are countless greetings and introductions, and the rest of the afternoon is wasted as the high-ranking generals and admirals continue to arrive. Most of the socializing is done in the expansive great salon, Hitler's greatest pride. It is a roomy, 18-meter-long lounging area, complete with a thick red carpet and a generous, red marbled fireplace. At one end is a large globe of the world, around which several individuals stand.

Best of all, the huge salon boasts an immense picture window. It can be lowered electrically, but this is done only on fair days. Unfortunately, years ago, Hitler inadvertently had his auto garage built just below. Thus, whenever the window is lowered, the smell of acrid exhaust and petrol fumes wafts up into the great room.

The panorama though, is spectacular. Down the mountain is Berchtesgaden, its population expanded by the Führer's entourage and visitors. The city of Salzburg can be seen in off the distance, including the large railway station.

There is also a magnificent view of the Untersberg mountain, where the legendary Emperor Charlemagne has slept for a thousand years, accompanied by some 5,000 of his best men. Supposedly, this ghostly army waits to emerge from the mountain and save Germany at a critical time, restoring her worldly power. The Führer at times has pointed the peak out, adding with pride, "It's no accident that I have my residence opposite it."

In front of the viewing window is a large, circular, glass-topped dining table. Around it is a beautiful Gobelin tapestry that shows a hunting scene, probably French in origin. Rommel knows from experience that the Führer has his late-morning brunch at this table, surrounded by his regulars, and his guests.

The afternoon stretches on. Some of the conversation is inevitably about the new construction projects around the Berghof. Bormann is clearly overdoing it, in some opinions ruining the landscape. The mountainside has become a huge complex of buildings as countless additional workers, assistants, and supply trucks come into and out of the area. Substantial additional anti-aircraft protection and security have been added to the complex. More chambers have been tunneled in the mountain to make room for aides, security, and the many visitors that come up to see the Führer. Nearby, special quarters have been built for Bormann and Göring. Armaments Minister Albert Speer resides in another smaller villa, away from the main compound.[1] Yes, this is now truly the government's home away from home.

All of the major western commanders are now present. Rommel of course has traveled east with his superior, *"Der Rundstedt"* as Rommel sometimes calls him, now standing out in his gray uniform and polished black boots, his field marshal's baton in hand. Admiral Krancke is in his dark naval uniform. There is overweight Luftwaffe *Feldmarschall* Hugo Sperrle. Pompous Geyr von Schweppenburg is present and of course, Rommel's own army commanders, Dollmann and von Salmuth. The senior officers of the OKW are there too, including Keitel, Jodl, and Warlimont.

Several times during the socializing period, Rommel gets to study the Führer. He entertains his guests, walking about in a conspicuously simple military uniform, beaming, listening, commenting occasionally. Seeing him close, those who know him well can tell the difference that the last few years have made. The stress of a world war seems to have aged him tremendously. His skin is pale, and his frame seems fragile. He is graying, and there are new lines in his tired face. But his cool, blue-gray eyes still have their fire, despite the red rings surrounding them.

He seems to favor his left arm, and a shrewd, discreet observer might occasionally see it tremble slightly, although of course, it is impolite—even perilous—to openly stare. Rumor has it that his personal physician has him on a number of questionable drugs. Of course, no one else really knows what Morrell gives him, but the Führer has on several occasions been given an injection for this or for that. Many feel that Morrell seems a little too generous with his needles. Someone had once contemptuously referred to him as the "Reich Injection Master." All those strange shots—Rommel only wonders.

Now the Führer is politely laughing at someone's amusing story. Being around him frequently for the last five years, Rommel has learned that he almost never tells anecdotes; not that he is humorless—not at all. It is just that he often does not follow complicated jokes and misses a punch line. So he usually leaves humor to others around him, and just smiles politely through the story, even if he does not understand the gag. On the other hand, a practical joke or good slapstick at the misfortune of another can make him laugh to tears. And while he refrains from telling jokes, ridicule is certainly something he frequently indulges or participates in.

Always near him hovers short, dark Bormann, ready to update him, comment on someone, or ask his approval for some detail. A shrewd manipulator, he is suspicious and distrustful of anyone who might be getting close to the Führer. Bormann had even eyed Rommel himself a number of times last summer, when the field marshal had been attached to the supreme headquarters staff after the fall of Tunisia.

That though, was not surprising. Bormann at times behaved like a thug, and because of his character traits, Bormann is not popular with other members of the Führer's inner circle. Speer privately has referred to him as, "The man with the hedge clippers," because Bormann always seems to ensure that no one ever rises above a certain level in popularity.

Finally, late in the afternoon, the program officially begins. It opens with a small ceremony. All the officers gather with Hitler in the great salon, along with the staff of OKW. There is the Führer's yes-man, Keitel—*Der Chef*. Beside him stands hawk-nosed Alfred Jodl, alert and unsmiling. Next to them stands the dashing, young, ambitious Walther Warlimont, smiling, looking confident.

The field marshals form a line and stand at attention, and the room goes quiet as von Rundstedt takes the floor. Clearing his throat, the old Prussian begins reading an oath of loyalty to the Führer. Rommel recognizes it as the one Schmundt had brought for him to sign a few weeks ago over the Seydlitz affair.[2]

The voice of the old Prussian wavers only slightly as he eloquently reads the flowery pledge in the presence of an attentive audience. The Führer listens impassively, his hands folded in front of him.

The field marshal finishes and ceremoniously hands the oath document, signed by all of the army field marshals, over to the Führer, who accepts it graciously. There follows long, tumultuous applause, and then a few words of thanks from him.

There are a number of toasts after that, and the official portion of the day thus ends.

The entire group, now joined by some women and the civil leaders, are slowly guided into the main dining room. There they are treated to a spectacular, lavish dinner, guests of *Reichsführer* Himmler and the SS. One can only imagine the thoughts and misgivings that go through the minds of the army generals about this SS leader as they sit through the meal. Still, the entertainment is quite elegant.

After the dinner, everyone socializes for a bit. Von Rundstedt makes an early evening of it, and Rommel is not far behind him. He and von Tempelhoff put on their coats to leave for the trip down the mountain again, and back to their hotel rooms for the night.

Rommel turns to the operations officer and mutters, "Nice, but a waste of time."

---

1   The Bechstein House.

2   Because of his activities against the Nazi regime while in captivity in Russia, von Seydlitz-Kurzbach understandably became hated by most of his fellow generals (including many who were actually imprisoned with him). Even after the war, most of them considered him a traitor, despite the terrible Nazi deeds that soon came to light. It was certainly no surprise to anyone that Hitler gave him a death sentence in absentia. Still, von Seydlitz was considered by many others to not be a traitor.

Towards the end of the war, he showed no love for the Soviet Union and refused to be a part of their establishing a communist structure whenever the Soviets occupied Germany; he was appalled over the idea of East Prussia being ceded to the Soviet Union. Anyway, the July 1944 assassination attempt convinced the Russians that they did not need his services. So they imprisoned him and eventually sentenced him to death as well. His sentence though was later modified to life in prison, and in October 1955, he was returned to West Germany. Nine months later, his death sentence was reversed. Ultimately, his actions and the German response to them brought on severe sessions of depression, and he died in April 28, 1976, Bremen, a sad and in his mind, misunderstood 88-year-old man.

Monday, March 20

It is the second day of the military conference for the Western Command. After a leisurely early morning of coffee and pastries, more sightseeing, shopping, and general idleness, the senior commanders are driven back up the Obersalzberg to the Berghof.

There is an elaborate late-morning brunch in the great salon, as is the Führer's custom. Then everyone is packed into limousines that set off down the slope for Klessheim Castle just outside Salzburg, some half-dozen kilometers away. It is here that the actual war conference will take place.

While it is not far, the snow and the wet road conditions (especially down the slope) cause the trip to last nearly an hour. Hitler finally arrives around 3 p.m., the snow swirling around him as he gets out of his limo and walks up the elaborate steps.

Standing up before the assembly sitting on wooden chairs before him in the castle's huge hall, Hitler begins an oration that goes on for nearly an hour. In a clear voice, he talks about the future of the Reich. Initially his tone is upbeat, designed to give his generals and admirals renewed hope. Fighter production is up, and he boasts of the progress that has been made in the production of the new jets under Albert Speer's direction. The almost-ready revenge V-rockets will soon wreak havoc upon London. The newer model U-boats currently being built will be able to stay underwater almost indefinitely. These silent killers, he states confidently, will soon reclaim the seas. The new panzers rolling off assembly lines—the panthers, the tigers, and all their *Jagd-* variations—will smash the Allies' attacks.

Then changing subjects, he cautions them to beware of enemy airborne strikes behind their lines. On this note, he brings up the upcoming enemy invasion of Europe. Rommel and von Rundstedt are especially attentive here.

To the surprise of many, the Führer states that he believes the invasion will fall upon the Normandy and Brittany peninsulas, and not at Calais.

"Obviously, an Anglo-American invasion in the West is going to come," he declares in a clear voice. "Just how and where nobody knows, and it isn't possible to speculate."

He stares at them all. "You can't take shipping concentrations at their face value for some kind of clue that their choice has fallen on any particular sector of our long Western Front, from Norway down to the Bay of Biscay... Such concentrations can always be moved or transferred at any time, under cover of bad visibility, and they will obviously be used to dupe us."

He looks dramatically at his audience and declares, "The most suitable landing areas, and hence those that are in most danger, are the two west-coast peninsulas of Cherbourg and Brest. They offer very tempting possibilities for the creation of bridgeheads, which could thereafter be systematically enlarged by the massive use of air power."

He pauses for effect before continuing. "The enemy's entire invasion operation must not, under any circumstances, be allowed to survive longer than hours, or at most, days; that's taking Dieppe as a direct example." Exactly, thinks Rommel. The Führer has just stated the very axiom that he himself has been preaching to his men again and again.

Hitler scans his officers. A defeat in the West, he states, would throw the enemy back many months and discourage them, "Once defeated, the enemy will never again try to invade." An ambitious and seemingly dubious statement to say the least, given the present stage of the war, and many generals no doubt disagree.

"Quite apart from their heavy losses, they would need months to organize a fresh attempt. And an invasion failure would also deliver a crushing blow to British and American morale," Hitler declares. "For one thing, it would prevent Roosevelt from being reelected in America... With any luck, he'd finish up in jail somewhere!"

The audience laughs.

"For another, war weariness would grip Britain even faster, and Churchill, already a sick old man with his influence waning, won't be able to carry through a new invasion operation."

He continues. "We can match the enemy's opposing strength of about 50 to 60 divisions in the shortest period of time. So smashing the enemy's landing attempt will mean not only a decisive final decision on the Western Front, but will also by itself be decisive, not just to end the war, but for the history of warfare itself!"

The audience breaks out into applause.

"The forty-five divisions that we now hold in Europe... are badly needed on the Eastern Front, and as soon as we have forced the decision in the West, we shall have to transfer them there immediately to reverse the situation."

The Führer seems calm and, alert. Now *this* is the Führer that had inspired them in earlier years. Moreover, his argument sounds logical. If they defeat the invasion, that will release 30 divisions to join in the struggle on the Eastern Front. An influx of some thirty fresh divisions, including two panzer corps, in at one or two strategic points, could very well turn the tide in the East.

He goes on. "So the whole outcome of the war depends on every man fighting in the West, and that means the fate of the Reich as well! Each officer and man must therefore be made to feel that everything depends on his individual effort."

His speech has ended, and as the generals applaud, several sets of eyes glance over at Rommel. He will no doubt be commanding the repulsing forces. So it will ultimately be up to him to secure victory. Again massive applause thunders through the hall. Von Rundstedt claps lightly, politely, stone-faced and sullen. That is all right. Rommel resolves that he will not let the Reich down. Like in North Africa, he will once again pull a rabbit out of his hat. He will defeat the invasion, so that they can push the Russians back and hold them off indefinitely. Peace will be inevitable.

A smaller conference then begins, with each of the generals allowed to give their views. When it is Rommel's turn, he is ready. His theme is that the invasion should be immediately crushed on the beaches. The Führer responds by praising him, partly for all the work that he had done so far, and partly because of the confidence that Rommel is exuding. Obviously, he is over his "African sickness." Besides, Rommel is echoing what Hitler has advocated for a while now, as far back as his Directive No. 40 of March 1942. In it, he had said that the objective of the defense was, "the collapse of the enemy attack before, if possible, but at the latest upon the actual landing." His Directive No. 51 of November 1943 merely echoed this theme in a more pressing way. Unfortunately, neither directive had addressed the problem of who would direct the battle on site. Now it seemed obvious who that would be.

Throughout most of the conference, lackluster von Rundstedt is laid-back, kept in the background, sulking all the more as the briefings progress. This is his command that they are talking about, and clearly, his opinion does not seem that important to Hitler. Rommel on the other hand, sensing that things are going his way, uses the spotlight to press his advantage. He requests that Hitler turn over to him command of the reserve panzers. Von Rundstedt seethes at this.

Attention then turns to the south of France. Because of the prodigious work that Rommel has done on the Atlantic Wall thus far, Hitler in the middle of the briefing asks him to help out with the First and Nineteenth Armies down there. The field marshal is to inspect their defenses too, along the Bay of Biscay and the Mediterranean respectively.

At this point, von Rundstedt explodes. He has been a minor participant in the conference until now. Addressing the Führer directly, he barks that it is pointless for him to remain in France as OB West, when Rommel's authority is constantly and infuriatingly being extended.

After the meeting, tea is served. Hitler decides to meet with his two field marshals. Angry, von Rundstedt makes a point of not attending. Hitler sends his stenographer out to fetch the crusty old Prussian anyway.

A short time later, respectfully summoned, von Rundstedt arrives at the door to the conference room and goes in brooding for his private chat. He fiercely emerges in just five minutes, stomping away with a grimace on his face. Grabbing his coat angrily, he starts down the castle stairs, heading back to the special train that will take him back to France. "What's the point?" he says to no one as he stalks out. "The Führer wouldn't let me open my mouth... So I walked out on him."

Rommel, amazed at the old man's actions, then gets his private audience. Because of his upbeat vigor and his recent activities, he gets better treatment, and his meeting lasts a half-hour.[1] Going out on a limb, he brazenly tells Hitler and Jodl that he's sure that he will turn back the invasion. He points out that by the end of April, the entire coastline will be intertwined with enough mines and obstacles to cause heavy losses to any force attempting to land. He concludes that, "In my view, the enemy's not going to succeed in setting foot on dry ground in these sectors."

He continues. He tactfully suggests that, for the best chances of defeating the invasion swiftly and to maximize coordination, all three branches of service in his area should be put under one unified command—preferably his.

He pauses, then goes on. Since the Führer has requested him to inspect the coastal positions of the First and Nineteenth Armies in southern France, Rommel now suggests that he could do this much more effectively if he were to be given a larger measure of control (but not total) over the First and Nineteenth Armies in the south. Hitler sympathetically tells him that he understands, that his request sounds logical, and he might grant it in principle. He also promises to seriously consider the issue of command unification.

Not giving up, Rommel then renews his request to get command of the reserve panzers. If he can just manage to get their control and station them where they would do the most good (which in his mind, is near the coast), his chances for success will increase dramatically.

Rommel seems to score on this point, because Hitler apparently sees the reason in what he is saying. He tells Rommel that his request sounds logical and promises to seriously consider it. Rommel finally departs, believing that Hitler will accede to his request.

---

1   Dr. Theo Morell, the Führer's private physician, was standing next to Rommel's operations officer at the door to the closed conference room. At the end of the meeting, he nudged von Tempelhoff and with a slight grin, commented dryly, "Congratulations. Evidently you're Ia to the new *Oberbefehlshaber West*. Rundstedt lasted only five minutes, and your boss managed thirty." Of course, Morell's prediction was wrong. Von Rundstedt kept his position.

Tuesday, March 21

Vizeadmiral Ruge is, on Rommel's behalf, finishing a three-day tour of the Brittany area, checking out naval ordnance centers and other naval facilities.

***

The conference at the Berghof ended, the major Western commanders return to France by special train. Rommel feels satisfied with the meeting on the whole. However, his positive feelings are peppered by some misgivings, some of them based upon the Führer's past record on fulfilling promises. Rommel has noted in his daily report:

> Satisfied with result. The Führer has completely accepted the commander's [Rommel's] opinion regarding the defense of the coast and agreed to a change in the command organization.

He believes this. After he had left the conference with von Tempelhoff, he had even exclaimed that the Führer had agreed with every one of his points. A half-hour later though, after some inner analysis, he had remarked thoughtfully, "What has he *really* given me?"

He is still wondering about that.

Generalfeldmarschall von Rundstedt understandably still feels slighted by the Führer's behavior at the conference. As a result, he and Rommel speak to each other as little as possible on the return trip. On the other hand, army commanders Dollmann and von Salmuth, having heard from the Führer himself how they must stop the enemy at the water's edge, have renewed their determination in carrying out Rommel's defensive instructions.

The special train arrives back in Paris in the late afternoon. Rommel immediately returns by car to his château and unpacks. Before catching up on his paperwork though, he starts going over the notes he and von Tempelhoff have made at the conference.

In the meantime, his headquarters staff have not been idle. Chief of Staff Gause has been on the phone several times with OKW. The main subject was armor, of course. There are only four panzer divisions left in France,[1] and only two can be considered even somewhat combat-worthy: the 9th SS and the 10th SS, both down south. The still-forming 12th SS *Hitlerjugend* is not yet ready for combat, and the 21st Panzer, still fitting itself, lacks a good deal of its armor as well as most of its transport. Basic training on tank warfare is in full swing. Clearly, the division still needs time to develop. Even so, it had nearly followed *Panzer Lehr* to Hungary, assigned to the operation's strategic reserve. Several of the 21st's components, such as they were, had already entrained and were ready to move east when the order to stand down had come from the top. Operation *Margarethe I* had been completely successful—the 21st Panzer would not be needed.

---

1 Not of course, including scattered reserve panzer battalions in various stages of organization.

Wednesday, March 22

Rommel spends the whole day at his headquarters, further going over conference notes. In addition, a couple of other details need his attention. Fortresses along the coast, for one thing. Again, it is a matter of command control. To a large extent, OKW directives and special orders dictate that each fortress area is to be its own entity, complete in its responsibility, and broad in its control of defense. On the other hand, what about the individual units within the fortification zone? While they may belong operationally to the fortress command, and are subject to reorganization for its benefit, are they not in many ways still connected to parent units (often nearby) and administratively to other organizations on the outside?

Rommel decides that they are. Army and naval ground units within a fortress are to keep their own unit and service identities, and not be reorganized into "fortress units" for the area.

In addition, he wants the fortress commands to undertake the same anti-airborne measures that the other coastal units are pursuing. Up until now, undertaking this measure has been a problem in fortified zones, what with the shortages of material and the priorities of port operations and constructing the beach barriers. Still, work is moving along on airborne barriers, and this problem once again has to be addressed. He calls for implementation of the usual obstacle ensnarements in clear fields, including stakes, barbed wire, and mines, mines, mines…

Late in the morning, a directive comes down from OB West. Offshore obstacle construction is to utilize as much as possible all available geologists in Western France, naturally applying, of course, tact and diplomacy to coordinate this with the Navy.

***

Generalfeldmarschall von Rundstedt is mostly pleased with the relocation of his quarters, and it partially dispels his foul mood from that distasteful conference in Austria. In his absence, his staff have moved his things out of the Hôtel Georges V in downtown Paris and into his main residence, the villa on the Rue Alexandre Dumas in St.-Germain-en-Laye.

He approves most of the changes that have been made, except of course, the air raid shelter in his backyard. The conspiring staff who had overseen the installation had hoped that, like before, the addition would have a minimal impact on his mood. Unfortunately though, they are not as lucky this time. The workers had taken great pains to not damage, ruin, or remove any of his garden or landscape in the area. He would have thrown a fit if they did. They had though made one mistake. A privet hedge[1] had been mauled during construction. As he is being shown the new shelter, he notices the assaulted shrub immediately. True to form, he grouses about it. He will thereafter take pains to point out the poor hedge's damage to his staff every time he passes by.

He goes back to doing most of his work in the villa, spending more time there than at his headquarters; a sort of semi-retirement. He performs most of his daily activities on the first floor, where his bedroom, his study, and the dining room are located. His own room has a view of the girls' school next door. For efficiency, his adjutant and chief of staff both have quarters with him.

As the weather warms up, he will start to spend part of his time outside. The villa is surrounded by a beautiful lawn (woe betide the man who unknowingly steps on it!). There are some pretty hedges, lovely poplars, chestnuts, and beech trees. Lots of room for his dachshund, Flori. And of course, he has designated the area that soon will become his pride and joy—his half-acre garden, which he and the resident gardener, M. Ernest Gavoury, will tend to almost religiously.

Down the hill slope from his villa and mostly underground is his bunker headquarters, built into the hillside. He still only walks down there for official activities and to make long-distance phone calls.

Well, at any rate, he is back now in the villa, and he can really relax. He is glad to be out of Paris. He did not like living in the French capital. Too much hustle and bustle; too many people, dirty streets, occasional offensive odors. And besides, the social nightlife is far beyond his desires. No, he had preferred St.-Germain for years. Only the cold and the severe shortage of coal for heat had driven him to the Parisian hotels for the winter. Now though, he is happily back in his little suburb.

It is getting on to lunchtime. Perhaps he might go for a brisk walk. He considers wandering over to the Pavillon Henri IV at the edge of those beautiful woods to have a few brandies. As always, he takes in his pocket several bars of chocolate for any children he might encounter.

---

1 A hedge-type shrub identified by small, dark-green leaves.

Thursday, March 23

Rommel is on the road again by 6:30 a.m., with a part of his staff. Coming along are engineer Meise, *Oberst* Lattmann, von Tempelhoff, and Ruge, his naval advisor and good friend. They are leaving on a five-day tour up the northern European coast.

They make good time and hit Brussels by noon. Rommel first calls on the district military commander there, *General der Infanterie* Alexander von Falkenhausen. The man is getting on in age, and the style in which he lives underlies the responsibility that he carries. And why not? After all, von Falkenhausen had already been appointed a second lieutenant when Rommel was only six years old. As a young officer, von Falkenhausen had served as a military advisor to, of all people, the Chinese, and it had only been the war that had forced him to come out of retirement. He had been appointed the military governor of Northern France and Belgium back in the spring of 1940, and had been there ever since.

They all dine together, and over a sumptuous lunch, discuss a number of subjects, including some politics. Von Falkenhausen at one point mentions the obvious negative consequence of gaining power, and paraphrases Confucius: "Power corrupts, and total power corrupts totally."

That afternoon after lunch, von Falkenhausen and Rommel adjourn to secluded quarters to have a "private discussion." Most staff members surmise that it is about the war, and that the two are merely airing their frustrations and opinions in seclusion, where they can speak freely. Some think that they are actually exploring possible actions that can be taken.[1] It is of course hard to do that with staff members around, even loyal ones; and though there are no SS or Gestapo members in the area, it would still only take one slip to get into trouble.[2]

After the private talk, Rommel and his staff bid farewell and leave again, off to the headquarters of General Reinhard's LXXXVIII Corps.[3] There he meets with Reinhard, Admiral Förste, and Admiral Kleikamp, commander of the naval forces in the region.

Reinhard briefs them on the construction progress in the area. As part of the effort to maximize the difficulty of attacking specific fortress and fortification defenses, large areas of flat terrain—over a quarter of a million acres—are undergoing flooding. As is to be expected, with spring here, the nearby inhabitants and the local civilian authorities, who had initially been remarkably relaxed over the loss of the farmland and pasture, have realized how much the loss of this land will mean to them this year, and are now irate.

Rommel patiently explains to them all that the protesters will just have to make do with the lands they have. "All interests, economic and otherwise," he declares, "will have to be subordinated to the military requirements, because improving the readiness of the defenses will protect the Netherlands from destruction and any enemy threat." And so he orders Reinhard to continue with the flooding, insisting that he wants it completed by the end of April. After that, good weather will set in. The risk of invasion will increase significantly.

On the rest of their work, Rommel expresses dissatisfaction. The total number of offshore obstacles completed is not high enough. And the fortresses must better prepare surrounding flat areas against possible paratroop landings.

Admiral Kleikamp tries to argue that the area is already well protected by the extensive checkerboard pattern of naval batteries.

Rommel replies that the batteries are still too far inland, irritated by their complacent lack of insight, he energetically restates his well-worn theories about a fortified zone on the coast, no further inland than eight kilometers; about the batteries and reserves also being on the front line. Let the naval training units protect the rear areas.

Reinhard's chief of staff mentions a few areas that already have significant defenses. But when he mentions effective strengths for reserve units, Rommel criticizes the numbers. One corps has a complement of 39,000 men, but is being listed as having an effective strength of only 20,000 because so many are recruits. Rommel rebuffs this practice. Recruits, he claims, can in only a matter of days be shown how to use weapons effectively and defend a position.

Reinhard's staff protests, arguing that recruits should remain in reserve units in the rear until they can be sufficiently trained to be combat efficient. Rommel tells them they are wrong. Even the reserves should be on the front line for maximum initial resistance to the landing.

After the reports and some more discussion (Rommel of course, squelches the protests), the entourage leaves. They travel to see Christiansen in the Netherlands. A large dinner is served, and besides the army group inspection party, Christiansen's guests include Admiral Kleikamp, Admiral Förste, and undersecretary Wimmer. Interesting conversations about the war drift over the evening dinner table.

Rommel and his staff do not stay long after the meal is over. There is too much work to do.[4]

***

OB West today gets an intelligence estimate from OKW that the invasion might be put off. Recent reports received by *Fremde Heeres West* suggest that the Allies might postpone the landing. FHW has dismissed them, concluding that they are delusive, designed to throw the Germans off. But OKW is not so sure, leaning perhaps too heavily on wishful thinking. At any rate, it is more persuasive evidence to transfer badly needed units to the East.

***

At OKW, that subject brings more bad news. The problems in the East are getting worse. The Russian spring offensive has torn significant gaps in three army groups. General Hube's élite but emaciated First Panzer Army is once again in trouble. Fighting in the Carpathian Mountains, they have been assaulted by strong Soviet units.

The front commander, *Feldmarschall* von Manstein, had also attended the Führer's conference back on the 19th and taken part in the oath of allegiance ceremony. However, though the conference was mostly about the West, von Manstein at that time had briefed Hitler on the severity of their problems in the East, and the field marshal had not pulled any punches. The Soviet army, he had pointed out, was advancing all along the Bug River, and if he was going to have any hope of stopping them, he had to pull back and regroup his forces. He had then asked to withdraw them back to the Dniester River and to reinforce the First Panzer and Eighth Army. Hitler, irritated at this distraction from the main purpose of the conference—the West—had not allowed any general withdrawals, and had told von Manstein that reinforcements were not available.

Now though, just four days later, the situation has become critical, and both the First Panzer Army and the Eighth Army could very well be surrounded and neutralized unless help comes. Hitler has already dispatched no fewer than six of the army's newly created infantry divisions to the southern portion of the Eastern Front, but that clearly will not be enough. To extricate Hube's army, they will need sizeable power. All the mobile formations in the East and the South are committed. As with the Hungarian occupation, the relief will again just have to come from the West. Several mobile units in France are put on a list for reassignment to the East. The orders will go out as soon as possible.

As if the military situation is not enough to fret over, Hitler is given another bit of news that sends him into a fury. He is told that the Russians have tried several German officers for crimes against the Soviet Union and, having found them guilty, have executed them.

Yelling over this outrage, he decides to return the favor to the enemy. Only he decides to target the American air crewmen that are devastating his country. He declares that, "British and American war criminals must also be condemned to death and their confessions must also be publicized after their execution." He orders that Allied airmen accused of machine-gunning civilians are to be put on trial.

Jodl suggests that since the enemy routinely executes German agents, they should do the same with the five hundred British and American agents and saboteurs who have been captured in the Hungarian operation.

Hitler agrees, adding that he had read that some of these enemy gangsters had carried out particularly dirty assignments to assassinate Germans, or to spread highly contagious germs to start epidemics.

1 This could be the meeting that David Irving referenced in *Trail of the Fox* (see footnote for March 2). Admiral Ruge remarked of the meeting, "As I found out much later, it was the first time they made contact in order to find ways to end the war and to change political conditions in Germany."

2 Rommel early on refused to have an SS officer or representative anywhere on his staff. This was mainly so that he could be relaxed around his men, although he also never cared much for the flair and aplomb of the SS. Interestingly enough, he also banned the Nazi salute in his headquarters and around the local populace. Once the year before, when Rommel had been speaking rather freely to his own staff, he had noticed that one of the aides was writing down what he had said. "My God, man!" he had shouted at the fellow with a laugh. "Are you trying to get me *hanged*?!?"

3 Forty-six-year-old *General der Infanterie* Hans Wolfgang Reinhard. After serving on the Russian front, he took command of the corps on July 1, 1942. Admiral Ruge in his *Reminiscences* mistakenly refers to him as "Major General Reinhardt, commanding 89th Corps."

4 Undersecretary Dr. Friedrich Wimmer was the *Reichskommisar* (Reich Commissioner General) for Internal Affairs from July 1940 to the end of the war. As such, he participated in the regular weekly official conferences of the Reich Commissioner, along with the general commissioners and the general secretaries. Wimmer was also general commissioner for internal administration and justice in the Netherlands.

Friday, March 24

Von Rundstedt's headquarters is notified in the early morning hours (Rommel, in Brussels, will get the word later) that the 349th Infantry Division is to move east immediately.[1] Along with it are to go the assault gun battalions from three infantry divisions—the 326th, the 346th, the 348th—as well as the one from the 19th Luftwaffe Field Division.

Those small reinforcements though, will not be enough. Panzers are needed. The 1st SS Panzer Corps and most other main panzer units are already in the East, and *Panzer Lehr* is tied up in Hungary. The remaining panzer units in the West are still organizing or training.

Except, that is, for General Hausser's[2] 2nd SS Panzer Corps[3] in southern France...

***

Rommel and his staff are again up early. After breakfast, they head out at 7 a.m. for the strategic naval base at Den Helder near the tip of the North Holland peninsula. Rommel as usual rides in front and Meise sits in the back. In the second vehicle, Ruge rides along with Admiral Förste, the North Sea Naval Commandant. During the ride, they discuss naval defenses in the area.

The group inspects several recently flooded areas, and Rommel notes that this has substantially improved the defensive position there. They get out of their vehicles and walk along some sand dunes to inspect the offshore barriers, Rommel often impatiently stomping ahead of the others.

They stop briefly for a quick lunch at a soldiers' home at Bergen-op-Zee. The staff there is made up mostly of *Kriegshelferinnen*.

In the afternoon, they inspect more coastal positions, galumphing along the sand dunes. Rommel is disturbed that a couple fortresses occupy larger areas than necessary, so he lays out what he feels should be the maximum perimeters for each. Noting that several senior officers live in lavish quarters in the area, he growls that he expects all the division officers to live within their assigned fortress, including the commanding officer.

The day passes slowly as they walk for a while, drive some, and then walk some more. Finally in the late afternoon, they finish and return to their local quarters in Amsterdam. They pass several beautiful, colorful fields blooming with crocuses. Rommel of course hardly notices them, his mind on the problems of defending the fortresses up here.

That evening, it is another dinner with General Christiansen, and again, undersecretary Wimmer attends. The discussion afterwards includes the layout of the areas around the fortresses. Having thought some about it, Rommel has now realized that excessive flooding and minefields, having prevented the local farmers from using the land to grow more crops, will exacerbate local food shortages. So he decides to restrict flooding and mining to a one-kilometer strip around each fortress. The outer three- to seven-kilometer area around it can now be used for agriculture, provided the ground is also staked with obstacles—*Rommelspargel.*

On the other hand, if more land becomes available for farming, fewer people will be available to work on the coastal defenses. So as a concession, Wimmer agrees to discontinue removing workers from the local areas to be hauled off to one of Saukel's slave labor sites in Germany.

In addition, Christiansen adds that for Rommel's worker requests, he will take the initiative to bypass Saukel's labor organization altogether, a tedious and often unrewarding procedure, and openly procure workers himself for the coastal defenses. He is confident that many locals will take up a job offer because, despite the fact that they are helping their occupiers, it is widely known that civilians fortunate enough to work directly for the Wehrmacht—at least in Holland—are paid good wages and enjoy relatively good food. In comparison, those labouring for the OT work long hard hours, are paid low wages, and often experience uncomfortable or harsh working environments. Worse than that though, is the fact that Dutch workers in the OT are often suddenly and without warning transferred to German factories, where many perish from harsh conditions, disease, or air raids. Alternatively, they are simply never heard of again.

Rommel reminds Christensen that Saukel will not be happy with this new arrangement and will likely protest. Christensen replies that he will tell the labor leader that at the present time, getting workers for the Atlantic Wall is a higher priority than for munitions production.

***

In the continuing "mini blitz" against England, the Luftwaffe sends 90 medium bombers to London. Minor damage is done to the capital, and several aircraft are lost.

The force pales in comparison to the 811 British bombers that hit Berlin. They unload some 2,500 tons of bombs and incendiaries that create several huge fires. The Germans in the capital cringe under the onslaught.

---

1   The 349th would end up being all but destroyed in a desperate attempt to stop Russian attacks. Survivors would later be sent back to France to recuperate and become the cadre for the 349th Volksgrenadier Division.

2   Sixty-three-year-old SS Obergruppenführer und *General der Waffen-SS* Paul "Papa" Hausser. A Prussian who had served in World War I, Hauser joined the SS in 1934, and participated in the invasion of Poland, the Low Countries, and then France. He took part in the invasion of Russia, where he lost an eye in 1943. He later took part in the battle of Kursk, and afterwards was given command of the newly-formed 2nd SS Panzer Corps, Consisting of the newly formed 9th SS Panzer Division (*Hohenstaufen*) and 10th SS Panzer Division (*Frundsburg*).

3   Consisting of the newly formed 9th SS Panzer Division (*Hohenstaufen*) and 10th SS Panzer Division (*Frundsburg*).

Saturday, March 25

At the Führer's late-morning conference, it is clear that on the Russian Front, the situation is now nearly out of hand. The last supply line to Hube's First Panzer Army on the Dniester River has been severed. They are now trapped and in danger of being destroyed. A relief force is obviously needed, but not one division can be spared from the rest of the Eastern Front. *Feldmarschall* von Manstein attends Hitler's noon conference, and they have a heated discussion. The field marshal thinks the army should immediately attempt a breakout, and Hitler argues that they should stay where they are until they are rescued. Just like they did at Stalingrad, von Manstein points out bitterly.

After having argued for some time and received at least one threat from von Manstein that he will resign his commission, the Führer grudgingly makes two critical concessions. First, the "stand-and-fight" order is rescinded for General Hube. He has permission to try and break out on the west side of the pocket. Second, von Manstein is assured that a relief force from Western Europe will soon be on its way to the East. General Hausser's 2nd SS Panzer Corps, still deployed around Alençon, France,[1] will immediately entrain to go to Hube's rescue. Rommel and von Rundstedt will be informed today. Jodl so notes it in his diary.

Unfortunately, when this corps moves out for Serbia, the only panzer divisions available to fight off any enemy invasion will be the 12th SS Panzer and the 21st Panzer. Making matters worse, both units are still in the process of formation and training, and neither division has anywhere near the tanks needed for combat. Part of the 21st Panzer's force includes a bunch of captured light French Somua tanks; no radios in them, by the way. Well, maybe they can salvage the chassis and mount a German gun on each. In the meantime, the new but outdated *PzKw IVs* are very slow in coming.

***

As usual, Rommel starts out early, continuing his tour of the Netherlands and Belgium. Heading southward down the North Holland peninsula, he inspects the *Schnelleboote* bunkers and then the massive naval batteries at Ijmuiden. Here, inter-service cooperation seems to be working.

Onward, driving southward to Wassenaar, he sees more evidence of effective flooding. New obstacles and minefields. More briefings with fortress commanders. More units "discovered" to be deployed too far inland (to him, they are hiding). Move them forward, Rommel orders.

They take time out for lunch, then continue on. But not before Rommel finds out about certain reserve units in training that have not been listed on the unit rosters. Deliberately withheld, he concludes. As this morning, he again orders them immediately transferred up to the fortified, front areas.

The inspection group continues down to the fortress of Scheveningen. The commander briefs them on their construction activities, impressing the field marshal with an accurate, visually elaborate sandbox model. The commanding officer of the *Kriegsmarine 1. Sicherungs-Division*[2] goes over their deployment. The inspection group had observed a good deal of flooding and a number of offshore obstacles, and the briefing now elaborates on them. Rommel expresses his satisfaction at the work that has been done.

Contingency plans are made for the SS panzer[3] and naval units training up here. In the event of a nearby invasion, they are to move inland immediately and reorganize to meet an attack.

That evening, the inspection party drives some 30km to the city of Rotterdam and stays at the Park Hotel.[4] After checking in, the field marshal joins his group in a crowded coffeehouse for a late cup of coffee. They all sit, relax, and study the traffic of pedestrians, bicycles, motorbikes, and autos bustling through the downtown area. All around them is a flurry of activity. The economy in this historic city is obviously thriving.

They then go to the naval officers' mess for dinner. There, they are joined by General Wahle[5] and the Rotterdam port commander, a talkative, boisterous sort of fellow. He recalls for them his many exploits as a World War I submarine skipper and later on as head of Paraguay's navy. Amusingly, the officer with him, representing the local naval headquarters, says hardly a thing through dinner.

***

This evening, Rommel's chief of staff talks to the aide-de-camp of Jodl's OKW Operations staff. Gause explains to him that, while von Schweppenburg's *PanzerGruppe West* is directly subordinate to OB West, the Führer's latest decision—that being, of course, his tacit agreement at the March 20 conference to turn over command of the reserve panzers to Rommel—must take precedence.

***

Today Eisenhower, talking to his staff about possible air strategies, decides to concentrate on Western Europe's transportation network instead of going for fuel production and delivery. He hopes with this plan, which includes hitting all the major river bridges and nearly 80 major railway centers, to isolate the invasion area and to retard enemy support arriving there. Forcing the Germans to funnel their reinforcements and supplies through fewer transportation lines will also better expose them to air attacks and slow down industrial activity.[6]

Some air force generals protest his decision. Utilizing heavy bombers, especially the British night air wings, against bridges and other smaller targets will require more

262 • COUNTDOWN TO D-DAY

262 • COUNTDOWN TO D-DAY

262 • COUNTDOWN TO D-DAY

training. Also, use of these assets against transportation targets in Western Europe will weaken the Allied effort in the air campaign over the Reich. German fuel supplies are desperately short. Their petroleum production and supply infrastructure, especially for synthetic fuels, is complicated, vulnerable, and hard to replace. Diverting heavy bomber units from hitting them does not seem wise to some senior air officers. Perhaps the transportation plan could be undertaken by just medium and tactical bombers? Besides, they argue, German reinforcements moving in on the first few days after the landing would most likely be traveling on roads, so hitting bridges and rail lines would not accomplish much at the onset.

Eisenhower though, remains adamant. European transportation lines and networks will be given top priority, along with German air bases near the coast. After more protests, he allows some refinery targets to be included as well.

---

1   Located about halfway between Rennes and Paris.

2   1st Naval Security Division. Some Belgian and French coastal sectors were assigned a security division that was responsible for protecting the naval bases in its sector, requisitioning boats, forming new and maintaining existing flotillas, and carrying out missions assigned to it such as assigning coastal convoy protection and mine-laying, dragging accesses to ports, anti-submarine missions, and barge traffic. They usually consisted of two regiments or several battalions.

3   Sepp Dietrich's 1st SS Panzer Corps, which at the moment, consisted only of the 12th SS Panzer Division (*Hitlerjugend*).

4   The Bilderberg Parkhotel on Westersingel Avenue, constructed in 1922.

5   *Generalmajor* Carl Wahle, the commanding officer of the 719th Infantry Division.

6   In just the first 10 days of March, the Germans had lost some 50 locomotives by air attack. Significantly, another 79 were destroyed by the Resistance.

Sunday, March 26

It is early morning at the Obersalzberg. OKW is completely focused on critical problems, few of which have anything to do with the West. On the Eastern Front, the Russian spring offensive is continuing in full force, and Hube's First Panzer Army—the remnants of over twenty divisions, eight of which are panzer[1]—is trapped in a pocket near Skala-Podolskaya, west of the Bug River. Hausser's 2nd SS Panzer Corps has already started to entrain in southern France, getting ready to go east and relieve them. Their official orders go out today.

In Italy, a full-scale British and American assault on Monte Cassino has just failed, but the cost of victory for the Germans in terms of supplies used and casualties taken has been extensive. And while the Anzio beachhead is stable for now, no one can say whether or not a renewed assault will stretch or break the German cordon around the landing area.

Now, on top of the issues revolving around conducting the war on three and a half fronts (the "half front," the West, is relatively idle), OKW is confronted with a new problem. Word has come in of a massive breakout that occurred over the weekend from a British prisoner-of-war camp. Over 70 British *Gefangene* have escaped from their compound in Sagan, Poland,[2] and are now fleeing all over Central Europe. At the Berghof, Himmler informs Hitler of the escape.

An irate Führer orders a special early-morning conference with Himmler, Göring, and Keitel. Unlike the normal daily military conferences though, this is a small private meeting. Stenographers are not even allowed in, and so no minutes are taken.

Hitler in an angry tone informs Göring and Keitel of the prisoner breakout. Himmler, immediately trying to cover himself, blames Keitel. Göring jumps on the bandwagon, and Keitel, flushed now with anger at being openly ganged upon with these accusations, loudly defends himself. The three argue over the blame for a minute while their stewing leader only half-listens to them.

Himmler estimates that the recapture will take something like 70,000 policemen for each escaped prisoner, and one hell of a long time to round all these POWs up again. More discussion follows. Keitel finally looks at Göring and states that, since the prisoners had been guarded by Luftwaffe personnel, the blame for the escape is in the end his alone. Furthermore, Keitel adds haughtily, he will not listen to any more groundless accusations against him, especially in the Führer's presence.

Hitler interrupts, telling them to stop bickering. He looks at all three of them and snaps, "They are all to be shot when they're recaptured."

There is a stony silence following this announcement. Göring is aware that the blame for the breakout is mainly his. But the prisoners are fellow airmen, and he is clearly uncomfortable with the idea. He tries as tactfully as possible to object; not that the concept of shooting prisoners bothers him in principle. After all, it was Göring himself who had initially created the Gestapo back in the 1930s. No, he reasons, political considerations have to be taken into account. As the Führer glares at him, he continues. You see, he explains, if all the prisoners are shot, the official excuse that they were killed on recapture will look transparent and blatantly cruel. No one in the world will believe that the shootings were anything other than cold-blooded, calculated murder. That, he concludes, would have a terrible effect on world opinion, especially among the neutrals. And who knows what reprisals the Allies might then take upon their own captured men? Any rerpisals against German prisoners would strike a heavy blow to morale at home.

The Führer pauses a moment as this sinks in. He reluctantly sees the reasoning. "In that case," he decides, "more than half of them are to be shot." He tells them that all of these prisoners that are recaptured are to be turned over to the Gestapo. He turns to the Reichsführer and says sternly, "Himmler, you are not to let the escaped airmen out of your control!"

Göring comprehends that this is the best deal he is going to get, and along with the other two, accepts this pronouncement. After the meeting, Keitel and Himmler get together to iron out the details. Later, Keitel finds his army staff officer in charge of prisoners of war, *Generalmajor* Hans von Graevenitz. Keitel informs him that over half of the prisoners recaptured are to be shot.[3]

Von Graevenitz is clearly upset with this decision. Stunned, he replies, "We cannot just shoot these officers."

Keitel, angry over the entire incident and his part in it, yells back, "The time has come for an example to be made, or we will not be able to cope with these escapes!" He pauses and adds, "This ought to be such a shock that prisoners won't escape any more. Every prisoner must be told about it, understand? Every prisoner."

Von Graevenitz is told that the Himmler's SS will carry out the executions. He just has to coordinate the roundup with them and be sure that the word gets out to the POW camps.[4]

***

Today, Rommel continues his tour of the Netherlands. Starting at 7 a.m., he leaves the Park Hotel in Rotterdam and travels westward to the coast to visit Hoek van Holland.[5] There he hears the reports of the *Festungkommandant* and the port commander. Again, a lack of supplies has suspended their minelaying program. Still, the effort so far has been good, with some 140,000 mines laid over or around some eight layers of barriers. Considering that the tides here are shallow, this is a formidable feat.

To compensate for the shortage of mines, the local unit has undertaken a program of deception. Certain areas where minefields have been planned are already posted with warning signs. To lend credence to the ruse, a few rumors have been spread about a number of accidents that have occurred in these fields while laying down mines. Rommel smiles and gives his approval.

They leave the *Festungkommandant's* headquarters and make a number of further inspections along the coast; the fortified peninsula at De Beer; across the river to Voorne and the nearby flooded areas; across the Moordijk and Willemstad bridges to Breda, General Wahle's 719th Infantry Division headquarters. Rommel commends Wahle for all their efforts.

One final briefing with his group, Wahle, 88th Corps Commander General Reinhardt, and Admiral Kleikamp, the naval commandant for the Netherlands. The field marshal again stresses the need to move units inland closer to the coast. Again Kleikamp tells him that even in the event of a landing, the Kriegsmarine High Command will still refuse to dispatch naval training units to any combat areas—as if they will be able to continue training with full-scale combat going on nearby.

The meeting finally concludes, and the inspection party returns to the Park Hotel, which by now has been totally emptied of guests to accommodate Rommel's inspection party, something Rommel had not at all intended. Because of these evictions, word has leaked out of his presence, and upon their return, they find a good-sized crowd of onlookers waiting to see him. As soon as the officers get out of their vehicles, a pair of fulltime armed guards is assigned to each one of them, opening their rooms for them, and accompanying them everywhere.

Rommel sighs. That's the price of popularity in a war. But it does not bother him too much.

---

1 This included the 1st SS Panzer Division, *Leibstandarte Adolf Hitler.*
2 About 170km southeast of Berlin.
3 Keitel later testified at Nuremberg that he had tried to keep the report of the escape from Hitler to keep him from "reacting vengefully," but Himmler had already told him. He also claimed that it was he who convinced him not to have all the recaptured prisoners shot.
4 Of the 76 prisoners who escaped, only three ever made it to freedom. The rest were recaptured, and 50 of them were eventually coldly executed in small groups. The breakout later became the basis for Paul Brickhill's famous book, *The Great Escape*, which in turn was made in 1963 into the blockbuster United Artists movie.
5 "The Hook of Holland." Officially designated a fortress, it boasted a concentration of anti-aircraft weapons, used to regularly fire at the Allied bombers coming and going across the Channel on bombing raids inland.

Monday, March 27

OKW today again has little time to address issues in the West, being still heavily involved with the crisis on the Eastern Front. *Feldmarschall* von Kleist, following in von Manstein's footsteps, goes to the Berghof and begs Hitler to let him withdraw his own *Heeresgruppe A* away from the massive Russian attacks. Today, Hitler decides to hell with them. He replaces both generals.

Later that morning, the Operations deputy chief of staff, Warlimont, gets yet another call from the *Heeresgruppe B* chief of staff. Gause starts by reminding Warlimont that he had talked to his aide-de-camp two days ago about the panzer issue. Gause then plays his ace. He reminds Warlimont that the Führer had promised both Rommel and Gause personally at the Berghof a week ago that he would give the field marshal control of the panzers, instead of leaving them under strategic control of *PanzerGruppe West* in Paris. Gause adds tactfully that OKW has to get off its administrative butt and make the decision official.

Warlimont manages to stall him again. He replies that "the OKW is determined to regulate command relations in accord with the Führer's decision." However, OKW has not yet received a copy from OB West of the actual orders putting *PanzerGruppe West* under his direct authority. They were prepared to wait until such time as they received these orders by courier before making any changes to them.

Warlimont is obviously buying time. The Führer seems to be vacillating on his decision—helped, no doubt, by the minions around him, and clouded by more pressing problems in the East and in Italy.

***

Rommel and his staff, having spent the night in their specially set-aside hotel in Amsterdam, start off early again.

First, a trip to the headquarters of the 88th Corps.[1] There they hear the report of the local corps commander, *General der Infanterie* Hans Reinhard. His big problem is that Amsterdam is a major strategic port. Although it is occupied by over a hundred units, most of them are small, and altogether only about 13,000 men are committed to its defense. And the outer defenses, where much of the ammo and food supplies are stored, can only be guarded by a few security units. So the port's defensive perimeter will just have to be tightened.

Reinhard has flooded some of the city suburbs in the northwest, and this had helped; but a better defensive plan is needed. And for safety reasons, the minefields preventing access to the critical mouth of the Scheldt River are almost all dummies.

The conference goes on, and a mix-up in the schedule is discovered. The 165th Infantry Division is scheduled for inspection, but the 48th is inspected instead.[2]

And on the way to the 48th, Rommel makes an unscheduled stop to inspect the totally unprepared units of the 712th Infantry.

Caught unawares, they suffer a number of inspection "hits." Rommel examines a beach that he had looked over back in January, and finds only a slim line of Belgian gates installed. In harsh language, Rommel orders the commander to have thousands of wooden stakes installed immediately, with mines attached to the tops. The hapless commander tells him that there is not enough wood around to do the job, and Rommel roars in anger. He wants no excuses. Just results. The commander finally backs off. Fortunately, the entourage's army photographer has the good sense to not photograph Rommel chewing the local commander out.

They travel down the coast through Belgium. Things look better at the 48th Division, and Rommel's mood improves. They finally dine at the soldiers' mess in Adinkerque,[3] and Rommel loosens up. He invites the local naval commander, *Konteradmiral* Frisius,[4] to join the inspection party.

They continue southwest down the coast to Calais. They find the work in progress there adequate. This is logical, since it is here that the High Command believes the invasion will come.

At one stop, the members of the group get out of their cars to have a particular defensive position shown to them. Suddenly, out of the blue a motorcycle with a sidecar approaches them, barreling down the road hell for leather.

As it speeds towards them, the group sees that the motorcyclist is a young army soldier. Riding in the sidecar is a beautiful young local woman. The enlisted man, drawing near, spots the entourage of senior officers stopped alongside the road and slows down.

Although several officers smile, a number of them grimace at the sight of this open fraternization. Taking it all in and thinking fast, the corporal brings the motorbike to a gravel-rattling halt. He and the girl dismount, and he hands control of the bike over to her.

Turning around, he hesitates, then gives Rommel a crisp, boot-camp salute and barks, "*Herr Generalfeldmarschall! Gefreiter* Schmidt and the regiment's laundress on their way to work!"

Aware of the slack-jawed, astonished looks around him, Rommel fights back a chuckle, and with a twinkle in his eyes, he solemnly returns the salute. The corporal gives him a big, adulatory grin, and with that, he and the girl jump back on the motorcycle. They take off in a flurry of small pebbles before anyone else can recover and reply—or ask embarrassing questions.

Shaking their heads (some of them still smiling), the group continues the inspection. They go on to Abbeville, then back to the beaches at the town of Ault to call on another unsuspecting unit, the 348th.[5] They inspect more open dunes. More notes and more terse instructions. Then it is back to La Roche-Guyon.

That night, Rommel writes to Lucie:

Back for two days in my quarters. Lovely spring weather. My little dog is really coming along. He now reports when someone comes. The little fellow is so cute. I must often laugh over him. Much work and trouble! Everything just doesn't work out the way one thinks and then one must face the issue, and that means burning up extra energy...

Rommel has little idea of how both the job and the dog are going to vex him in the next couple of weeks.

As he writes though, some frustration comes out:

Things just aren't going as I would like, and this means I've got to use my elbows, which really takes it out of me.

---

1 Admiral Ruge, in his notes, mistakenly refers to this as the 89th Corps.

2 Daser's 165th Infantry had been slated for the inspection, but when the message went out, as part of the coding, only the sum of the division's digits was broadcast. Since the sums of digits for the 48th and for the 165th are identical (12), the mistake was understandable.

3 In Belgium, along the coastal road, about 3km from the French border.

4 Forty-nine-year-old Frederick Frisius. *Kommandant* of the naval fortifications at the Pas-de-Calais. Six months later, he would lead the 226th Infantry Division in defending *Festung Dunkerque* successfully until the end of the war (he was promoted to *Vizeadmiral* for doing so).

5 The 348th Infantry Division, *Generalleutnant* Paul Seyffardt, commanding. Part of the 67th Corps.

Tuesday, March 28

It is another busy day at La Roche-Guyon. Rommel's chief of staff tries unsuccessfully to reach Warlimont at OKW for another follow-up to their conversations yesterday and back on the 25th. Gause is determined to get OKW's acknowledgement of the Führer's promise to give the field marshal control of the panzers. Rommel tells Gause to press the issue and try again.

Unfortunately, Warlimont is still unavailable. It seems he is avoiding Gause.

***

Actually, Warlimont had discussed the issue with Jodl a few times yesterday. Today they discuss the matter again. Jodl flatly does not want to turn the panzers over to Rommel, trusting seasoned von Rundstedt's judgment instead. Obviously, they have to get Hitler to change his mind.

Warlimont does not know how to take his Operations chief. Professionally, they have worked with each other since 1939. For five years they had seen the Reich go to war, triumphing over Poland, Scandinavia, Europe, and the Balkans, only to watch it slowly stop and retreat, bleeding over North Africa, Italy, and the vast plains of Russia. And with the Americans in the war, things are much worse.

On a personal level, the two men do not get along that well. Warlimont does not care too much for his boss. For one thing, Jodl definitely tries to cover his butt, and he does it well, too. So he sometimes has a hard time making a decision, often postponing one until the solution becomes painfully obvious. His chances of being right increase the longer he hesitates to make a pronouncement, and therefore he does not look bad in the Führer's eyes.

Warlimont does not like that Jodl tries to model his OKW Operations staff after Hitler's own personal staff. He has tried to surround himself with subordinates who generally agree with him and are not supposed to have thoughts different than his own. They exist merely to carry out the orders that are given. While this is most efficient, it clouds good judgment. Unfortunately, since Warlimont is somewhat self-willed, occasional friction arises between them.

There had been one such conflict recently. A few months ago, Warlimont had received a coded warning from an industrialist relative of his who happened to be close to *Reichsmarschall* Göring. The warning was that the Reichsmarshal had been overheard claiming that he had been informed of some disturbing news about both Warlimont and *Feldmarschall* von Manstein. Supposedly, the two of them were leading secret lives as members of some Catholic freemason society. According to the claim, their covert organization was trying to undermine the Nazi party.

Warlimont had of course found this charge preposterous. Hell, von Manstein was not even Catholic. Still, *der Dicke* ("Fatso") must have put some credence in the information, because Warlimont found that the big man had begun to avoid him. When Warlimont one day greeted him with a warm "Good morning, *Reichsmarschall*," Göring just ignored him.

Warlimont had worried about this for a few days, and finally decided to tell Jodl about it. That was a mistake. Warlimont went to his superior's office and related the entire story. The operations chief listened in stony silence. Warlimont finished by asking Jodl to personally straighten things out on his behalf.

Instead of agreeing to do that though, Jodl, who possibly had also heard the rumor, unexpectedly replied in a frosty tone, "Well, if it's true, your place is in a concentration camp, not in the Führer's headquarters."

Warlimont was caught off guard, because he had expected a sympathetic ear and support, not this accusatory, curt tone. He looked his superior in the eyes and asked him point blank if he believed the rumor.

True to form and pressured to commit himself, Jodl hesitated. He finally answered, "Well... I am not saying that I believe it. I am only saying that if it *is* true, I think that you belong in a concentration camp."

Warlimont was disgusted with this reply and abruptly stood up. Turning to leave, he curtly remarked, "That was hardly the answer that I expected from someone that I had worked for so long with."

Jodl, seeing his open anger, relented somewhat. "Look," he began, apparently trying now to mollify. "Maybe you'd better talk about it to Bodenschatz."[1]

Opening the door, Warlimont briefly glanced back and replied coldly, "Fine. I will." He then strode out, closing the door none too gently behind him.

Bodenschatz had been more sympathetic than Jodl, and the Luftwaffe liaison officer had started to try to clear up the misunderstanding with Göring. Still, Warlimont had remained angry over the entire affair, mostly because of Jodl's reaction. Still flushed with anger, Warlimont had gone to their superior, *Feldmarschall* Keitel, and requested that he be transferred from OKW immediately. Keitel politely but firmly denied the request. Times were rough, he explained. Quoting the Führer, he stated that staff officers like Warlimont were desperately needed if OKW was to be able to efficiently continue conducting the war.

While the explanation was actually a compliment, Warlimont had not been satisfied. Still, he had resigned himself to the fact that that was the best answer he was going to get. So he had thanked the field marshal and had departed.

Since then, Warlimont has kept his distance from Jodl and watched his own backside. Now, knowing how Jodl feels about the panzers in Europe, he is not going to push Gause's argument.

---

1   Fifty-three-year-old *General der Flieger* Karl-Heinrich Bodenschatz. He was Göring's liaison officer with the Führer.

Wednesday, March 29

It is another day of reports, phone calls, and administrative duties at La Roche-Guyon. One concern of Rommel's is over recent reports that he has been receiving about Allied air raids on the French railway system. The attacks have stepped up noticeably in the last three months, and March so far has turned out to be far worse than the previous two. Rommel sees a coordinated air effort going on here to stymie the German supply system to the outlying units.

A prelude to the invasion? Maybe.

Today, he receives a special visitor. It is 61-year-old General Herman Geyer again, who has recently retired from active service.[1] He is on his way back to Germany, and has stopped off to bid farewell.[2]

Rommel invites him to stay for lunch, and afterwards, they go on to discuss a number of things: territorial claims of the Soviet Union, especially towards Turkey and Iran; the Italian fleet, and its general failure as a fighting force; the merits of certain strategic bases in the Mediterranean; the old Zeebrügge raid of April 1918; the question of the best coastal defense strategy, which the army and the navy kept bandying about with each other. They talk about Admiral Gladisch,[3] and later, Geyer tells Rommel some interesting stories about a recent festival in Ulm that he attended.

The conversation turns to the defense of the coast, and Rommel is pleased to learn that Geyer feels as he does—destroy the enemy at the water's edge.

Geyer finally departs, and later that afternoon, some more officers arrive for meetings. The adjutant to the commander of the 10th Minesweeper Flotilla arrives to see Ruge and his assistant Peters about training and weapons supplies. Meanwhile, Rommel meets with some senior engineering officers and they talk about special assignments and better support. Rommel stresses the need to increase their effort on the defensive efforts going on in their respective areas.

It has been a busy day.

***

This evening, after having dined with his son Hans Gerd, von Rundstedt hears air raid sirens go off. A short time later, Zimmermann[4] reports that enemy aircraft have been spotted dropping flares over St.-Germain. Obviously, their bombers are approaching. He asks the field marshal to go down into his new air raid shelter. Although he has vowed to never go down into that *verfluchtes Kaff* next to his garden, his son, after a good deal of cajoling, persuades his father to go; for the safety of both of them. Grumbling, the old man heads down to the shelter.

The subsequent air raid never hits St.-Germain. Zimmermann gets on the telephone. With several calls to field, he stays on it for some time and totally forgets about the field marshal. About an hour later, just as he gets off the phone, it rings again. Answering it, he hears von Rundstedt's voice. The field marshal (surprisingly) politely asks him, "Zimmermann, can I please come out now?"

---

1   See entry for Wednesday, January 26.
2   Geyer survived the war, but committed suicide in April 1946.
3   Sixty-two-year-old Walter Gladisch, a World War I veteran, commanded the *Kriegsmarine* from October 1, 1931 to September 30, 1933. Retired by the time World War II began, he served as a Reich Commissioner until he was permanently retired in June 1943. He died in March 1954.
4   Fifty-seven-year-old *Oberst* Bodo Zimmermann, the OB West Ia (Operations Officer).

Thursday, March 30

Today at the Berghof, another ceremony is held and promotions awarded. General Ferdinand Schörner is promoted to *Generaloberst*[1] and General Walther Model is promoted to *Generalfeldmarschall.* The Führer personally presents him with his baton.

In August, Model will be transferred to the Western Front and take over not only Rommel's job, but von Rundstedt's as well.

***

Today, *Generalfeldmarschall* Rommel rides with Gause on a northwest tour to the Seine Bay to inspect the new barriers going up along the shoreline there. During the trip, Rommel takes up the delicate matter of discussing a replacement for his chief of staff. Rommel had decided, urged by Lucie, to replace him back in mid-March. He had written to her on the 17th:

> *Let's draw a line underneath it all... I am going to. Perhaps G. will find another post. Of course, it's a tough decision for me to have to change my chief at a time like this.*

He had meant what he had written. However, he was unsure of making the decision to relieve Gause, because in many respects, he was indeed reluctant to let Gause go. On the record of course, Rommel would only have the highest praise for the man.

He had then sent word by letter to Hitler's army adjutant, General Schmundt, that he needed a new chief of staff. He wanted someone who had extensive experience in mobile warfare and had spent time in the *Generalstab*. Rommel recommended that Gause be given command of a panzer division.

In response to his request, OKW had given Rommel a shortlist of two general officers. Rommel had picked Hans Speidel immediately, mostly because he was a fellow Swabian. But Rommel also knew him. They had served in the Argonne Forest in 1915, and after the war, Rommel had run across him serving in the 13th Württemberg Regiment. Now Speidel has been ordered to Berchtesgaden to be briefed about his new post.

Rommel and Gause are alone now,[2] traveling in Rommel's Horch. Perhaps the field marshal gives him the need-to-move-on speech. A sensitive and usually not tactless leader, Rommel probably does not tell his trusted chief of staff about Lucie's recent disenchantment with him, nor about his "nerve-wracking" wife. Maybe, Rommel tells him, it is time for Gause to rearrange his life, considering that his home had been bombed out last year, leaving him nothing. Maybe it is time for Gause to further his career, to move up to a more important posting, perhaps somewhere in von Rundstedt's command, where he can be Rommel's confidant. When the invasion comes, Gause will probably get his own panzer division to command.

Gause is of course upset about the move. He has been with the field marshal since their initial North African operations in the summer of 1941. Perhaps he feels abandoned when he hears about the replacement, but he tries to be stoic about it, if not for himself, then to make it easier on the field marshal.

They begin inspecting the defenses of Reichert's 711th Grenadier Division,[3] holding the left flank of von Salmuth's Fifteenth Army. Again, Rommel finds that a number of his instructions have not filtered down to this divisional headquarters. A good deal of the construction that Rommel anticipated seeing has not yet begun.

Next they view a few positions of Richter's 716th Division along the Normandy coastline. After the inspections are over, Rommel travels to Caen where he is met by 84th Corps commander Erich Marcks, General Kraiss, commanding the 352nd Infantry[4] (now moved up to the Calvados coastline alongside the 716th), and General Reichert. A number of moves are discussed. The 709th and the 716th Grenadier are now fully committed to defending the Seine Bay, as is the 352nd Infantry (which means it is no longer considered in reserve). General Hellmich's 243rd has been moved northward, and the newly arrived 3rd Parachute Division under General Meindl[5] has been put into Brittany, somewhat east of the critical port of Brest.

Rommel then leaves the coast and travels eastward to Rouen to attend a large conference at the headquarters of Kuntzen's 81st Corps (of which the 711th is a part). At 7 p.m., *Generalfeldmarschall* von Rundstedt, in a rare trip to the coast, joins up with Rommel at Kuntzen's headquarters. Together with Gause, Kuntzen, and the Fifteenth Army's chief of staff,[6] they discuss the new deployments. Rommel, his inspection of the 711th Division fresh in his mind, mentions again how some of his orders are not filtering down to the divisional level, and von Rundstedt calmly promises to look into it.

Something else, though, is bothering the old Prussian. He is upset because, of the four remaining special railway engineer battalions attached to OB West, he must now give one up to Kesselring in Italy. Losing units to the Eastern Front is one thing—but for Italy, that is another thing entirely. And with the Allies stepping up their raids on the French railroads, this reassignment does not sit well with him. It is bad enough that the Allies are crippling his railway supply system, without OKW helping them out.

Rommel sympathizes and offers some suggestions on improving the rail network. That night Rommel writes another letter to his wife:

> How are we doing with our taxes? I guess we will have to pay taxes for Ajax too. How is the mutt doing? The little one[7] is too cute for words and I believe he will be a good hunting dog. He is not yet quite housetrained. But I can't spend very much time with him...
>
> Now March is nearing its end without the Anglo-Americans having started their attack. I believe they have lost confidence in their cause.

1 Fifty-one-year-old *General der Gebirgstruppe* Ferdinand Schörner, commanding *Heeresgruppe A* on the Southern Front in Russia.

2 Except, of course, for Rommel's driver, Korporal Daniel.

3 See footnote for March 6.

4 The 352nd's sister division, the 353rd, was stationed in Brittany. The Germans had four rating levels for their infantry divisions: Level I (full attack capability), Level II (limited attack capability), Level III (full defense), or Level IV (limited defense). The veteran 352nd carried a Level I rating, but was not considered a top-notch division. The *bodenständig* divisions were all Level III or IV.

5 *General der Fallschirmtruppen* Eugen Mendl.

6 *Generalleutnant* Rudolf Hofmann.

7 His dog Elbo.

Friday, March 31

General Dr. Hans Speidel leaves his position as Chief of Staff, Eighth Army on the Eastern Front and travels southwest by train across the muddy Russian steppes. He is headed for Berchtesgaden, where he is to be decorated for recently helping to save the Eighth Army as its chief of staff. He is also going to be briefed on his new position in the West—*Chef der Generalstab, Heeresgruppe B.*

***

General der Flieger Kurt Student, commander of the vaunted airborne arm of the Luftwaffe, has set up his new headquarters at the Parachute High Command in Nancy. His orders are to create additional airborne units in France, even though he must still administer those currently in Russia and Italy.

***

Today on *Heldengedenktag,*[1] some good news comes to the Berghof. Last night, a large RAF night bombing raid against the party's famous rally city of Nuremburg was met with fierce resistance. Although the night air had been cold, visibility was excellent as the enemy bombers had approached the city. Using a new radar and following the bomber condensation trails in the night sky, German nightfighters closed with the enemy *Terrorflieger* formations and ripped into them. Of some seven hundred enemy bombers, about a hundred were brought down. The Führer is pleased.

General Erhard Milch, in charge of aircraft production, calls this the turning point in the air war over Germany, just like September 1940 had been for the enemy in the Battle of Britain. Milch confidently adds that as England had survived past that critical point, Germany would survive past this one.

***

This morning, Rommel gets on the phone with Jodl about the reserve panzers. He tells him that they need to be under the unified command of one Western commander; namely, him.

Jodl replies that he has not yet received the confirmation from von Rundstedt and when he does, the order will go to the Führer for confirmation.

Rommel points out that he had talked to von Rundstedt the day before at a conference with the 81st Corps officers at Caen. Von Rundstedt, he tells Jodl, saw the logic of having the tanks under one commander. Of course, the old Prussian still assumes that this should be von Schweppenburg, who technically takes orders from him. Rommel does not point this out.

Jodl again reassures Rommel, and says that the Führer will look into this matter this afternoon. Rommel thanks him, and asks him to notify him when the Führer finally does give his permission. He then hangs up, muttering under his breath.

Later, OB West calls. *Heeresgruppe B* is ordered to transfer the still-forming 12th SS Panzer Division to the boundary between the Seventh and Fifteenth Armies. They are also instructed to create a new unit from the 155th and 179th Reserve Panzer Divisions. After this new unit moves to its training area, the 21st Panzer is to be moved to their old area.

Rommel asks about the status of the 2nd SS Panzer Corps, getting ready to head east. He is told that two nights before, part of it had been caught by British bombers just east of Paris in its assembly area at the Vaires railroad yard and pummeled.

Rommel asks for details. Blumentritt replies that the 10th SS had been caught out in the open. What made things worse was that a nearby train of sea mines was also hit, and the mines were touched off in a chain reaction of explosions that tore into the panzer troops. Estimated casualties were over a thousand.

Rommel thanks him and hangs up.

At about 10:30 a.m., a special guest arrives at La Roche-Guyon: Admiral Krancke, *Marinegruppenkommandos West*. He and Admiral Ruge, now backed by Rommel, have a morning conference regarding the mine situation off France. Rommel wants some new fields laid in the Seine Bay.

Krancke explains that there are several priorities in other areas that must come first. American supplies arriving in a steady stream of Allied convoys to Northern Russia are taking a heavy toll on German land forces there. Krancke's top priority right now is to work with Dönitz's crippled U-boat arm to somehow stem the flow of merchant ships going up there. Minefields off France will have to wait.

Rommel counters by telling him that the Allies have not mined the bay for quite some time. They are sweeping the Straits of Dover, but not near where they have recently laid down three new fields. Rommel thinks this is significant.

Rommel mentions the Bay of the Seine. What about new minefields there? Krancke replies that they cannot do much right now. Because of heavy enemy air activity, and the fact that they are short of mines, he has had to cancel the program of replacing the 1943 fields in the middle of the Channel. He feels that those laid in deep water will be no good by the middle of June.

Rommel persists. What about Normandy? They turn to a map of the Calvados coast. Krancke points out that the coastline here is really too rocky for a successful invasion, and so it does not need to be mined. Rommel is skeptical.

Krancke tells him he will take his suggestions under advisement. They then talk about another ongoing issue, the alert status conditions for the coastal naval batteries. Rommel states that he wants naval units in training to be moved closer to the coastline. Krancke says that is not practical.

The meeting ends on that sour note. Although Krancke stays for lunch, the atmosphere in the dining room is somewhat tense. The admiral's antagonistic attitude towards Ruge continues, and Rommel is again caught between defending his naval advisor while trying to smooth over Krancke to get some cooperation from the man without asserting his rank.

That afternoon, after Krancke leaves, Rommel, Gause, and von Tempelhoff discuss a number of details with Günther Blumentritt. Rommel would like more rear areas to be secured against paratroop landings, especially the deployment areas of the panzers. He feels that the critical port of Antwerp should be more fortified, based upon his latest observations there.

He also tells Blumentritt that the Nineteenth Army units in southern France must be better organized, and of course, he adds that he wants more mines. He then requests intelligence updates from OB West, and wants to get some artillery for the 3rd Parachute Division. They were supposed to get a couple batteries of 88mm flak guns, but Sperrle at Third Air Fleet had turned them down.

He goes on with his requests. Too many obstacles have been placed around the airfields. This is a waste. He wants some of them removed and installed on his beaches. And while he is at it, he mentions some Luftwaffe combat engineer battalions that he wants to use.

Still, he adds more. He wants permission to have the Dives River dammed to flood some outlying key areas. More importantly, he also wants to relocate the 12th SS Panzer (forming in Belgium), and the 21st Panzer (forming near St. Lô), both to be repositioned closer to the coast. After all, they are now the only panzer formations in France. If the Allies were to invade now…

Rommel has some questions regarding Directive No. 40. He is looking to extend his command influence, and to clear up hazy areas regarding policy.

At the end of the meeting, Rommel and Gause both congratulate Blumentritt on his promotion to *General der Infanterie*. The promotion officially goes into effect tomorrow, April 1. They have a small toast in celebration, and finally Blumentritt returns to his headquarters with his hands full.

That evening, Rommel writes home again to Lucie:

Dearest Lu:

No news of importance. Stalin seems to have made all manner of demands to his Allies, such as supplying him with a fleet of strength equivalent to the former Italian Mediterranean Fleet…

It would be fine if it were true. I saw plenty to cheer me here yesterday. Although we've still a lot of weaknesses, we're looking forward full of confidence to what's coming…

---

1 Lit. "Memory of Heroes Day." Originally observed as *Volkstrauertag* ("The People's Mourning Day"), the name was changed by the new Nazi party at the end of February 1934. Essentially equivalent to the US Memorial Day, it too was originally started as a national holiday to commemorate those servicemen who died fighting for their country in World War I. The Nazis though changed the focus of the memorialization to German heroes, rather than all slain servicemen. After the war, the event reverted to its original name.

PART TWO

Les Sanglots Longs

Spring

By the beginning of April, *Generalfeldmarschall* Erwin Rommel was firmly in control of *Heeresgruppe B*. He had shown OKW that he was no commander to sit idly by and run his units from a desk. He had been a whirlwind of activity, touring up and down the coast, inspecting divisions, taking notes, giving orders. Despite several stalls and some grudging resentment from some senior officers, his efforts were starting to pay off. The Atlantic Wall was quickly turning into a stalwart defensive barrier. All along the coastline, as unit commanders tried desperately to carry out his extensive plans, hundreds of thousands of men prepared formidable defenses. Some though, were not convinced that the reception planned for the landings would make all that much of a difference.

Rommel of course knew differently. "The war will be won or lost on the beaches," he had once told his new aide, *Hauptmann* Lang, on a chilly day, as they overlooked a deserted beach in their greatcoats. "We'll have only one chance to stop the enemy, and that's while he's in the water… struggling to get ashore."

By now he had developed a rigorous routine. Coastal inspections and meetings with subordinate officers were exhaustive. He traveled regularly, and often the ritual of getting in and out of the Horch, not to mention tramping around various sites, sometimes for hours, played hell with his lumbago. Still, he dealt with the discomfort stoically and kept up his active, hectic schedule. He had to. It was the only way that he could even hope to have his men ready.

As usual, his staff found it hard to keep up with him, especially when he traveled. Most of them usually stayed at headquarters to tackle administrative details, and to coordinate the efforts of the units with each other and with higher commands. That was not to say though, that he always inspected the positions with a small entourage. On the contrary, he was often accompanied by many officers, including of course, the commanders of the positions that he was inspecting. In addition, he was often followed by reporters and photographers representing newspapers and magazines published throughout the Reich. So some of his stops turned out to be borderline newsreel sideshows for Goebbels' propaganda machine. Still, he did not mind the theatrics. He had come to realize the value of publicity to both the home front and to the men in uniform. The articles inspired confidence in his men and the country, while at the same time it worried the enemy's intelligence organizations.

He felt, almost guiltily, that he had to travel nearly every day. Contrary to the encouraging updates that he conveyed to the Führer, there were just too many reasons to be dissatisfied with the work that was going on along the coast, and his eyes, even though mismatched in vision,[1] were sharp enough to pick out problem areas at construction sites in a way that seemed uncanny to his subordinates.

Many problem areas were obvious. The emplacement of the big coastal guns by *Organization Todt* was proceeding far too slowly. Concrete shortage was the biggest reason. Then there were the foreigners that had been pressed into forced labor to help build the positions. They were not very enthusiastic about their work. Some were local one-time soldiers or sailors, now civilians working for the Reich. The projects to build large fortifications to help defeat the Allies did not thrill them at all, although they were in no position to argue about it. So they usually worked as slowly and leisurely as they dared, and their workmanship was often not up to par.

Constructing defense points in the Seventh Army sector was going slower than in the Fifteenth Army sector, where the invasion was expected to come. By April, only 31 of the planned defensive strongpoints there were finished. Marcks' men were doing their best, but it was not enough. And it was way too slow for Rommel.

Perhaps what bothered him most though was that privately, even he had serious doubts about whether they could stop the Allies from coming ashore. If they failed, the war would be lost for sure. He had known (as many generals did) for months that they could not now win the war outright. At most, they could force a peace.

He knew that deep down, the Führer realized this as well. Rommel had seen a glimpse of this one day back in the late spring of 1943. At Hitler's chalet in Bavaria, Rommel had been studying the overall strategic situation with Hitler. They were relatively alone, and Rommel once again became depressed over what he was seeing on the maps and the reports they were getting daily. The staggering losses on the Eastern Front; the wholesale surrenders at Stalingrad and Tunis; the Allies poised to invade Italy or Greece. Enemy bomber formations now flew regularly over the Reich, growing stronger every day, dealing out death and destruction both day and night. Germany had dramatically lost the Battle of the Atlantic with the introduction of sophisticated enemy electronics and escort carrier groups.

Rommel sadly shook his head, and they talked quite a while about what seemed to him to be a losing situation. Rommel went over the impressive material strengths of the British and the Americans. Hitler listened to him quietly, looking down continuously at the floor, asking an occasional question.

They moved on to the general situation of the war. The Führer was clearly worried; the updates on all theaters were discouraging. Rommel wanted to make a good point, and this seemed the right time to do just that. There was just such a combination of rationality, calm, and depression in the Führer that maybe, just maybe, Rommel's point might hit home.

He entered into it carefully. His tone was quiet, almost wondering as he ticked off the details of their situation. He stated that they were now at war with England, all of North America, and the entire British Commonwealth, which included Australia, India, New Zealand, and massive Canada. Over half of Africa was against them, and of course, there was that behemoth to the east, the Soviet Union. There were even a couple countries in South America fighting them. Their Japanese allies were losing islands in the Pacific as the Americans gained the initiative. The Italian economy was in chaos, and Germany itself was experiencing shortages and losing hundreds of men a day.

Rommel repeated what Admiral Dönitz had recently told him. They were losing some thirty U-boats a month in the North Atlantic as tonnage sunk decreased dramatically. With American escort carrier groups ranging across the Atlantic, their radar-equipped aircraft could now attack submarines anywhere and at any time.

Probably more disturbing than anything else was the fact that the Allies, despite all of the severe military setbacks that they had suffered, still seemed to have a great deal of material strength left to keep them going. Most of it was coming from Canada and the untouched manufacturing might of the United States; but even battered Russia was continuing to produce material and conscript men in substantial quantities. Of course, their own efforts to full mobilization in 1943 would now increase their production of war supplies.

"But then," he added, "can we keep pace with the whole world?" How long would they be able to sustain their high-energy output? A recent fiery British night air raid over Germany was just a taste of what was to come. With Allied air strength increasing, their production centers would soon be under heavier bombing attacks.

The Führer, wearing his tan, undecorated uniform blouse, still sadly looked down at the floor, leaning against a map table. Suddenly, he glanced up, the stress of the last three years all over his face. He then spoke slowly, sullenly, "I know that there is very little chance now of winning the war."

Rommel was amazed and yet heartened to hear Hitler admit this. Perhaps he was not out of touch with reality after all.

"Unfortunately," the Führer then added, "those in the West would never agree to make peace with me—certainly not the ones who are at present at the helm… And those that would negotiate with me have no power."

Glancing over at Rommel, his voice strengthened and his eyes hardened as he continued. "I never wanted a war with the West," he said defiantly, "But they did. Well, now the West will have its war, and they shall have it to the end!"

Rommel did not reply.

Then a couple months later, the Führer's frustration, his contempt for their failure to win, and this growing determination never to sue for peace had come out on an even more alarming occasion, one that had made Rommel start to wonder if psychologically the Führer was becoming ill from the stress of the war.

In July, with the battle of Kursk raging, Hitler and a couple senior officers had been assessing the overall strategic picture in Russia. They had been evaluating their chances of a final victory in the East, one that would win them the war. On this particular occasion, he once again took up a favorite theme—the ultimate effort. He said that he was convinced Germany could still win the war. He believed this would happen naturally, if only the Germans would rise and be the great warriors that he knew they were, to make the same supreme effort that he himself, their leader, was making every day.

Energized by his own words, his piercing eyes blazed as he looked at Rommel. He stated that Germany had up until now been putting forth only a half-hearted effort. They had to strive harder as a people to overcome their enemies.

Sensing something within him, the Führer suddenly become defiantly bitter. "Well, if the German people are incapable of winning the war," he said vehemently, "then they can *rot*."[2]

Rommel was stunned to hear him say that.

"In any case,' he added, "the best of them are already dead. If I'm to be beaten, then I will fight for every single house. Absolutely nothing will be left standing."

He looked directly at Rommel and read the surprise in his face. "A great people," he explained, "must die heroically." He evidently believed this to be a known truth and the result was inevitable. He added, "It's a historic necessity, you know."

No one had replied, and Rommel had naturally been troubled by this speech. He had later mentioned the conversation to his son, who had also found it hard to believe the Führer's words. Rommel had looked directly at Manfred and had added, "You know, sometimes you feel that he's no longer quite normal."[3]

---

1   Rommel was near-sighted in one eye and somewhat far-sighted in the other. In cadet school in Danzig, he sometimes used a monocle with the one (also, it was a fashion often sported by the Prussian military aristocracy). Of course, whenever he came across a senior officer, he would snatch it away and hide it, so as not to look foolish. As a field marshal, he rarely wore glasses in public, in case he was photographed or filmed.

2   This was not the first time Hitler had made such comments. On November 2, 1941, Quartermaster General Wagner had occasion to report to him that the Wehrmacht had come to "the end of our human and material forces." Both Hitler and Jodl had then realized that the war could probably not be won. Later that night, miserable and moody, Hitler remarked to a visitor, "If the German people are no longer so strong and ready for sacrifice that they will stake their own blood on their existence, they deserve to pass away and be annihilated by another, stronger power." Later he added callously, "If that is the case, I would not shed a tear for the German people."

3   Charles Marshall confirms this quote, adding that Rommel then said, "Eighty million Germans should not have to die for this man's demonical hate." Since the first sentence was repeated a number of times by Lucie and Manfred later, it's probable that this additional comment was spoken sometime during the last few months of his life, when his revulsion for the Führer had heightened considerably.

April 1944

Saturday, April 1

Generalmajor Doctor Hans Speidel arrives at the Berghof for duty. After reporting in, he is taken under the wing of *Generaloberst* Jodl. They begin by talking about the West. Since Speidel has spent some of his past career in France, including a stint early in the war with the military governor, Jodl asks him about that and Speidel recalls his experiences.

To his surprise, this briefing is then followed by a small ceremony. Speidel is to get a medal in recognition of his heroic actions as chief of staff for the Eighth Army during their recent breakout from Cherkassy. He had played a critical part in helping them make a successful retreat, thereby saving the army from being surrounded and annihilated by the Russians. He is promoted to the rank of *Generalleutnant*. Adolf Hitler personally awards him the Knight's Cross of the Iron Cross.[1]

Then he is told officially that he has been appointed chief of staff to *Heeresgruppe B* in France.

Speidel inquires about his new role. He politely asks the Führer what instructions or directive he is to transmit to *Generalfeldmarschall* Rommel, especially regarding military strategy.

"Directive?" repeats the Führer. He pauses and then replies, "Any kind of directive would be superfluous."

Jodl elaborates. OB West and *Heeresgruppe B* already have rigid instructions. The coastline is to be fiercely defended. No retreat will be made, and no free space for "mobile maneuvering" is to be allowed. Wherever the enemy lands, he is to be defeated at the water's edge and driven back. The mistakes of Salerno and Anzio are not going to be repeated.

Those are two critical landings that OKW has come to realize were strategically mishandled. Both times they had allowed the enemy time to get ashore and to build up a defensive bridgehead. And both times, the enemy had been in the end able to hold on to the landing area, taking full advantage of their superior airpower and naval gunfire. Reserve panzers had been too scattered and too far away to intervene effectively in time, and enemy strafing raids had hit their columns hard on the way to the beaches. Well, this time is going to be different. This time, the enemy is going to be stopped in his tracks.

The lack of panzer support in the West is briefly mentioned. The Führer promises though, that when the invasion comes, Rommel will have eight to ten full-strength panzer divisions stationed near Paris under the unified command of *PanzerGruppe West*, but completely at the field marshal's disposal.

Right after the ceremony, Speidel is ushered into a private room to confer with Jodl and Warlimont. Speidel is to report to his new command immediately.

That evening, Speidel returns to his hotel room, his mind a whirl of information and ideas.

***

Today, Rommel is in Paris inspecting a concrete plant at an engineering depot. Fascinated, he watches reinforced concrete and revolving gun turrets made of cement under construction. He is told at one point that the turret he is looking at has been tested and could take a 150mm shell. He enjoys the tour and expresses regret that he did not know about these earlier. Unfortunately, production of the turret foundations is slow; again, due to concrete shortages.

He returns to La Roche-Guyon, and that afternoon, he and some of his senior staff go off for one of their "armed promenades." Traipsing through the woods does not go well on his lumbago, but he keeps up. They scare up a few rabbits, but nothing more.

Outgoing Chief of Staff Alfred Gause is busy on the telephone a good part of the day, trying to drum up some transport for the static divisions. This is an especially hard task. Nearly all the military vehicles are east, either in Hungary, Italy, or in the Soviet Union. He could procure a few dozen bicycles and some horses, although not the men to tend them…

That evening, Admiral Ruge leaves the army group headquarters for two weeks' leave. He is going to the minesweepers' recreation home in the Taunus Hills of Germany. His assistant, *Kapitän* Peters, will take over his duties in his absence.

***

Today, OB West Chief of Staff Günther Blumentritt is officially promoted to *General der Infanterie*. Von Rundstedt's staff holds a small ceremony on his behalf.

---

1   Ironically, a little over five months later, Hitler would have Speidel arrested for treason.

Sunday, April 2

Generalleutnant Hans Speidel continues another day of briefing at the Führer's chalet. After the daily noon conference, *Generaloberst* Jodl meets with him, and they go over further details regarding Speidel's new assignment as Rommel's chief of staff. Along with some new details, Jodl reiterates what Speidel has been told the day before—that the defense of the coast is to be rigid. Again, Speidel asks if there is anything specific to pass on.

Jodl calmly replies, "There's no need. If there is any sort of a local landing, just drive the enemy into the sea. It's that simple."

The new chief of staff is told once more that when the invasion occurs, some ten panzer divisions will be "brought up in time" to help deal with the landing. In addition, a revolutionary new class of U-boats will be sent into the English Channel to viciously deal with the enemy fleet. Lastly, he is briefed on several new types of special "reprisal" weapons that are being readied to exact a savage toll on the English population.

Jodl also goes over the current political situation in the West. Talking about the ground order of battle, Jodl asks him if, in his opinion, the Western Allies will ever invade.

After taking a few seconds to think about the question (and how it was put), Speidel carefully answers yes. Jodl responds with more assurances. He boasts confidently that whenever the invasion comes, the Luftwaffe will have a thousand fighters put at their disposal. This includes several squadrons of the new jet fighters to deal with the Allied bombers.

And what about Rommel himself? On a personal level, Jodl takes Speidel aside and asks him—begs him, in fact—to try to bolster the field marshal's morale. He needs to be cheered up, if for no other reason than for the sake of the Reich.

"Do what you can to cure him of his bouts of pessimism,[1] *ja?* He has suffered from them ever since Africa." The appointee agrees to do so. How he is to cheer up the field marshal is left entirely up to him.

Jodl of course does not know that Speidel is indirectly in on the plot to overthrow the Führer. Since he wants Rommel to join their cause, cheering him up about the war would be the last thing he would want to do.

***

Generalmajor Feuchtinger's 21st Panzer Division continues having problems outfitting its units. Over half of the allotment of panzers have indeed arrived. Some are the more modern 75mm *PzKw IVs,* although most of these are the older *Ausf. C* or *D* models, with their shorter 75mm KwK 37 gun.[2] Unfortunately, many of the panzers are also old *PzKw IIs* and *PzKw IIIs,* and many are old French Somua medium tanks that had been captured back in 1940. The division also lacks anti-tank units; it has perhaps a few older assault guns, like the *StG III Auf. A.*[3] Also, transport for the *panzergrenadier* units remains a serious problem.

The division still has those French Somua light tanks, quite outdated. What could be done with them? Or those old French Hotchkiss and Lorraine armored vehicles?

It is regarding these captured French units that the division's assault gun battalion has come up with a genius—Alfred Becker.[4] A reservist, the man is a resourceful engineer. His family is wealthy, owning the Alfred Becker Werke factory in Krefeld, Germany, near Düsseldorf. Starting in 1943, using some of the firm's own resources, Alfred set up a branch *Baukommando*[5] near Paris to work on these old French armored units.

Using tracked chassis that he had found at the Hotchkiss factory in Paris, they began converting some into assault guns by mounting heavy guns. They also experimented by adding guns to some Lorraine 37L prime movers and other odd tracked vehicles. Several will be outfitted to carry 75mm PaK40 anti-tank guns and function as makeshift tank destroyers. Other units are being equipped with less armor and mounting 105mm leFH16 guns and 150mm s. FH13 howitzers, to function as self-propelled artillery. For protection, they affix to the sides some jury-rigged armor. Overall, Becker has something like 90 frames to convert, so his work is cut out for him.

For some units, the top portion of the armor structure is being built by Alkett, and the anti-tank gun assembly built by Reinmetall in Düsseldorf. All of the components are being put together by Becker's detachment in Paris and shipped out to the field—mostly to his division, the 21st Panzer.

Becker plans soon to add rocket launchers to the remaining old vehicles to create a fleet of oddly shaped but deadly self-propelled weapons. His branch location is now referred to as *Sonderkommando* Becker (Special HQ Becker).

Other unit commanders in the division are struggling to get transport as well. Old buses, trucks, cars—whatever can propel itself down the road is "appropriated," under the watchful eyes of the divisional commander, *Generalmajor* Edgar Feuchtinger.[6]

***

Today, *Generalfeldmarschall* Rommel stays in his headquarters and catches up on paperwork.

---

1   Rommel's *Afrikanische Krankheit* ("African sickness")—the chronic, pessimistic mood that enveloped him late in 1942 after his defeat at El Alamein.

2   The 75mm KwK (*Kampfwagenkanone*) 37 gun was indeed deadly against infantry, vehicles, and light tanks. However, because of its short barrel and low muzzle velocity, it was not as potent a weapon to use against the enemy's newer heavy tanks.

The 24-ton *PzKw IV Ausf. G* or *H* (referred to by the Allies as a "Mk. IV Special") sported a heavier, longer-barreled 75mm KwK 40 gun. Its shell, about twice as long as the KwK 37's, had a greater velocity (792mps) and could penetrate 84mm of armor at 1,100 meters. The *Ausf. H's* own armor protection included 80mm frontal, and 30mm side. Some units carried side skirts to absorb the blow from hollow-charge projectiles fired at its sides, but many such skirts were torn off by the hedges and trees. Only in mid-May would the division start getting *PzKw IV Ausf. H* models—five tons heavier with thicker armor, mounting the longer, higher-velocity 75 mm Kw.K. 40 L/48 barrel—outdated models, but more than a match for a US Sherman.

3 The *Sturmgeschütz III Ausf. A* (Sd. KDZ.142) was a four-man, 20-ton, self-propelled assault gun created early in the war to support ground troops. Built on a *PzKw III Ausf. F* chassis, it mounted a 75mm Sk 40 L/43 gun in a fixed casemate, and thus could only shoot forward. (The 360-degree traversing capability of a turret was sacrificed for additional armor, protection, and simplicity in manufacture.) Because of their versatility, over time these units became anti-tank units, often replacing actual tanks in depleted panzer units.

4 *Major* Alfred Becker commanded *Panzerjäger Abteilung 200*, attached to Feuchtinger's *21. Panzer Division*. Becker, first and foremost an engineer, had served in World War I and had by this time amassed a number of distinctions fighting for the Third Reich as well.

5 Becker's "Construction Command" in Paris was (in cooperation with Alkett in Berlin) an ad hoc branch of the main plant, in Krefeld.

6 Feuchtinger, a favored member of the Nazi party, had been the key organizer of the military portion of the *Reichsparteitage*, the massive annual Nuremberg rally that had been held before the war had begun. The Nazi party had in turn reciprocated by giving him a high officer's rank within the Wehrmacht.

Monday, April 3

Generalleutnant Alfred Gause today chairs a conference at La Roche-Guyon. The main subject is the placement of artillery batteries. Recent inspection results show that areas near the Scheldt and Somme river estuaries are still not strong enough. More batteries are needed.

Reports and summaries of the Allied landing at Nettuno are discussed. The engaging German divisions there had minimal artillery support. The panzer forces, located too far inland, had initially taken precious time to gather themselves for a major counterattack. In almost every instance, the preparation and subsequent assault had been crippled or severely slowed down by Allied airpower.

Another point is reviewed. Studies find that the Allied infantry on those beaches did not attack or even advance when there was "reasonably heavy artillery fire." This revelation is to be driven home to each of Rommel's division commanders. Regrettably, though, the figures for their divisional artillery are not impressive. Even at the Pas-de-Calais, the most heavily fortified area on the Channel, artillery dispositions average at best one battery for every thousand meters. It is true that the presence of several railroad and naval batteries has made a big difference. Still, they do no good to the outlying areas. More batteries are needed, especially in the Somme estuary.

***

Rommel is on tour again. Today he is at Tréport, near Dieppe, accompanied by the 67th Corps commander, General von Weikersthal.[1] He inspects the positions of *Generalmajor* Paul Seyffardt's 348th Infantry Division.[2] Although the unit have made good progress in their barrier construction, they are still working on obstacles too far from the shoreline. Nevertheless, Rommel thanks them for their effort.

He finds considerable results at his next set of stops, the positions of *Generalleutnant* Schwalbe's 344th Infantry Division. He is satisfied with the work progress at the 344th and notes in his daily report:

> It is amazing what has been done here, thanks to the initiative of the commander.

***

President Roosevelt rejects a modification to the unconditional surrender policy demanded of the Axis. The revision, submitted by the Joint Chiefs of Staff, defines and elucidates certain minimal prerequisites to an alternate surrender that might be considered, one much more favorable for the German generals to accept. Details such as steps towards demilitarization, removing all Nazis from political positions, religious freedom, and arrests of potential war criminals are laid out. Acceptance of Allied authority and the relocation or return of various ethnic or political sects that have been persecuted or forced into labor are spelled out in detail.

Roosevelt has his reasons for rejecting the proposal. He is mindful of how their enemy has taken a path of aggression twice now in this century and many times before. He no doubt reflects upon the many millions who have died because of this war. He remarks that it will take some two generations to change the war-like attitudes of the German people.

He therefore decides against the option. "No," he growls, "I'm not willing at this time to say that we do not intend to destroy the German nation."

Eisenhower and the Joint Chiefs, mindful of a number of indirect contacts their people have made with the anti-Hitler conspirators, understand the importance of key generals like von Rundstedt and General von Falkenhausen in Belgium to the Allied plans. Both men reportedly want to rid their country of the Nazi party, and their assistance would dramatically shorten the war if they could be coerced into working with the West. Besides, privately, Eisenhower is unsure that the upcoming invasion will even succeed. So he would just as soon prefer that over the next year the Germans simply open the Western Front up to them.

---

1 See footnote for January 20.
2 Admiral Ruge in his account mistakenly refers to this unit as the 384th Infantry, transposing the 8 and the 4.

Tuesday, April 4

Rommel continues his tour of the northern French coast. He begins by inspecting the rest of the 344th Infantry Division. He then visits positions held by the 82nd Corps,[1] inspecting their artillery batteries. On his previous tour, he had noted three dozen guns in position, although many of the casements had not been finished. Today, he is pleased to find out that more are done, and that another dozen are being put in.[2]

Rommel tries to increase battery versatility. He would like those guns that are on wheels or some sort of mobile platform to be somehow able to easily traverse, so that they can be fired at positions threatening the flanks. For those without wheels, he asks about using those revolving concrete turrets that he saw being made at the concrete factory near Paris the other day—sort of like a *Panzerstellung*[3] for artillery.

That evening, Rommel returns to his headquarters on the Seine. In the updates he receives, he is pleasantly surprised to find out two things. First, OKW has officially notified them that Hans Speidel, Rommel's first choice to replace Alfred Gause, has been approved and will report to *Heeresgruppe B* on April 15. Second, he discovers in his mail that he has received a check for royalties from his pre-war bestseller, *Infanterie greift an.*

That night he writes Lucie about replacing Gause:

> G. [Gause] will be replaced by Generalleutnant Dr. Speidel about the middle of the month. His brother was once with me in the machinegun company...
> P.S. Mittler & Son4 has sent a check for 3,575 marks to my account at Wiener Neustadt.

---

1   *General der Artillerie* Johann Sinnhuber, commanding.
2   There would be a total of 52 guns by the end of the month.
3   Lit. "Armored emplacement or position." This was a small fixed defensive position that consisted of a tank turret affixed to the ground in a small fortified position (as opposed to a *Schadpanzer*, in which the entire tank was permanently mounted into the ground). Low to the ground and armored, these positions were often difficult to destroy, and made deadly defense points to take, especially by armor.

    The boxed fortification below the turret was typically made of steel and/or concrete, and was entered from the side or the rear. The turret itself typically consisted of a tank gun, sometimes with a machine gun mounted next to it. The turret was bolted, riveted, or welded to a thick metal plate, which had wheels or bearings below and was manually rotated. The Germans used whatever turrets they could find. Country of manufacture was not important, so long as the gun had shells to fire. Typically along the Atlantic Wall, turrets of captured French Renault 35s were used, although as the war progressed, turrets of other knocked-out tanks were mounted as well, including even some German ones.
4   The publishing house handling his book *Infanterie Grief an.*

Wednesday, April 5

Generalfeldmarschall Rommel goes on another inspection tour. Today, just south of Boulogne, he visits the 49th Infantry Division,[1] starting with the headquarters at Montreuil-sur-Mer. For once, the teacher's itinerary is outdone by the student's. He finds their plans for laying minefields are somewhat too—well, ambitious. Bemused by their enthusiasm, he tones down their plans a bit, both in field density and in size. Besides, mines are becoming short in supply. He gives them a scaled-down plan to use. He reduces the size of their too-large defensive zones and narrows the strip of coast to be defended. He orders those outlying units in the rear areas to move much closer to the shoreline—including the divisional headquarters, 14km from the coast.

No doubt, the divisional commander quietly sighs to himself as he replies with the dutiful, "*Jawohl, Herr Feldmarschall.*"

Rommel continues his inspection. A number of positions have been well constructed. Grateful to the men, he resorts to handing out rewards—something he did occasionally a couple of months ago. He has again secured for himself a supply of musical instruments—some harmonicas and concertinas.[2]

He hands out a number of them, and then moves on.

***

Today, General Marcks writes home to his son some cynical comments about Rommel:

> *Rommel is cantankerous and frequently blows his top—he scares the daylights out of his commanders. The first one that reports to him each morning gets eaten for breakfast; the next ones after that get off lighter.*

***

A disquieting teletype from Admiral Krancke at *Marinegruppenkommandos West* comes in to *Heeresgruppe B* today. It reports intensive naval activity by enemy light vessels in English Channel areas west and northwest of the closest point to England, between Boulogne, Cap Gris Nez, and Calais. Krancke concludes that these are concentrated minesweeping operations, probably the initial steps of an amphibious landing in the narrows of the Channel. This of course, is supporting evidence for that theory, long supported by OKW and at times, the Führer, about the invasion coming at the Pas-de-Calais. Krancke writes that the enemy vessels could not be engaged by coastal batteries because the radar interference was too strong. As an excuse, he adds that sometimes this happens to the Luftwaffe's radar as well.

1   *Generalmajor* Siegfried Macholz, commanding.

2   A concertina is a small, hexagonal, free-reed, bellows-driven musical instrument, sometimes referred to jokingly as a "squeezebox." The bellows are worked by pushing the ends in and pulling out with your arms, while the musical tones are played by pushing buttons on each side, as opposed to the customary side keyboard for a regular larger accordion. The German style differs from its English counterpart in that when a button is pressed, one note is played when the bellows are pushed, and a different tone when they are pulled out. The field marshal sometimes handed these small instruments out as gifts to the men when they had done a particularly good job. Usually none of the men knew how to play the charming things, but the instruments were popular (especially with the naval units), and the men always appreciated the gifts, especially when they were personally handed out by Rommel.

Thursday, April 6

The late-morning daily military conference at the Berghof has ended. Adolf Hitler is in the main salon, talking to Jodl and Warlimont. By now, despite the fact that the Russians surged into Romania four days ago, it is evident that their massive spring offensive is slowing down. The upcoming spring thaws and resulting seas of mud are grinding the enemy formations to a halt. So today, the Führer's attention turns to the West.

He has just read a number of intelligence reports. A couple indicate the detection of troop movements into southeast England. Increased radio traffic has been picked up out of that area, close to the Straits of Dover and von Salmuth's Fifteenth Army. There are other reports of public buildings southeast of London being requisitioned or appropriated. The Führer, so often suspicious of anything, has studied these messages and now comments that he smells a rat. Jodl replies that he isn't so sure.

Hitler turns to him. "The whole way that the British are serving all this up to us—it just looks phony," he says. "This latest news about the restrictions they're ordering, their security clamp down, and so on. Now you don't normally go in for all of that if you're really up to something..."

The Führer gazes off into the distance, almost oblivious to the two officers standing next to him, then suddenly looks back at Jodl. "I cannot help but feel that the whole show the British are putting on looks suspiciously like a charade to me."

They discuss this matter further. A while later, Hitler is shown another report. As he reads it, he grunts with a slight smile on his face. He hands the message to Jodl, who in turn reads it silently, those around him watching his face for a reaction. Jodl wordlessly passes the paper on to Warlimont. The message reports more troop movements in England, mainly headed towards the southeastern area. Hitler addresses them again.

"Another message about troops moving towards the Pas-de-Calais, *ja?*" He looks at them penetratingly. "Now," he continues, "what I ask myself is this: Why make such a song and dance about it? We wouldn't, I guarantee you!" He stops for a moment, lost in thought, and absent-mindedly adjusts his glasses. He slowly walks over to the map depicting Western Europe, then continues.

"And they don't need to either, do they?" he comments. "They could perfectly well marshal their forces over here," he says, pointing to southeast England, "then load them on board and ship them over to here," moving his finger dramatically down to the stretch of coast along Normandy. "We've no real way of finding out what they're really up to over there."

His staff officers agree with that. Reconnaissance photos have been scant, and those that have come in often lack detail, often because the pilot was in too much of a hurry, weather was bad, or altitude was too high. Too often the pilot, whether inexperienced, gun-shy or overcome by wanting to get his images back safely, settles for any old shot, considers himself lucky, and bolts for home. With Allied airpower being what it is, no one can really blame him. Especially since the Luftwaffe has suffered staggering losses in the first three months of the year, losing over 5,500 aircraft, along with many experienced pilots and their invaluable experience. Competent flyers are becoming a rare breed.

"No," Hitler concludes, "I can't help feeling the whole thing will turn out to be a shameless charade." A few minutes later, Hitler looks up and declares," I'm in favor of pushing all our forces into here," once again pointing to the Normandy area.

Jodl gives Warlimont a significant look. Normandy? Is this possibly where the landing will take place?

***

Rommel spends this day at his headquarters, catching up on paperwork and making the usual administrative phone calls. Today, he meets with the Nineteenth Army's chief of staff[1] and chief engineer. They discuss problems with unit placement along the coast, mine shortages, and the return of the battered 2nd SS Panzer Division from Russia to Southern France.

That night, he writes Lucie:

> *Here, the tension is growing from day to day. It will probably be only weeks that separate us from the decisive events...*
>
> *My little dachshund has grown a lot and is coming along nicely. He accompanies me—when I'm at my quarters—on my walks...*

He also finds time to write to his son Manfred, repeating some of what he wrote to his wife:

> *In a few weeks—the favorable weather for landing and air operations starts in May—we will be facing the decisive battle. We are moderately armed and are going into the battle with confidence. It will be tough, but we'll manage...*
>
> *My second dachshund that is only half a year old is coming along nicely and accompanies me occasionally on my hunting walks...*

***

Generalfeldmarschall von Rundstedt's attention is diverted to the Atlantic defenses by a report from the First Army commander, General Blaskowitz. He writes that his area is:

> "[an] absolute point of weakness in the defense of the occupied French land, and it will not change."

Blaskowitz is quick to point out that the Allies will discover this weakness, writing:

> This will not remain a secret to the Anglo-American leadership and investigation. It is probably already known to them.

The field marshal shares Blaskowitz's concern. Granted, the chances of the main invasion coming to his area are small. On the other hand, his four divisions[2] have to cover some 860 kilometers—far too thin a spread to make any kind of effective defense.

First Army needs more units, and thus, more men. He had better complain to Keitel at OKW again, though it will probably do him little good...

---

1 *Generalmajor* Walter Botsch.
2 The 158th Reserve Infantry Division, the 708th [*bodenständige*] Infantry, the 159th Reserve Infantry, and the 276th Infantry.

Friday, April 7

Rommel travels in his Horch north-northwest today, again to the Dieppe area, with Daniel driving, and Rommel as usual sitting up front beside him. They arrive at the headquarters of the 245th Infantry Division,[1] which is a backup to *Generalmajor* Seyffardt's 348th Division and *Generalleutnant* Menny's 84th Division along the coast. After the customary briefing, he moves to the coast and inspects a number of positions. Some work has indeed been done, but he does not see much of a concerted effort being made. Part of the problem though, lies in the fact that some projects must be delayed until additional batteries arrive, and getting artillery from the OT these days is difficult.

Rommel is courteous enough to thank the men for their work so far and moves on northeastward 240km to Tourcoing, *Generaloberst* von Salmuth's headquarters. There the field marshal chairs a Fifteenth Army conference. It is announced that a "specialist" group has been attached to the army to help them come up with innovative ideas to use natural and artificial camouflage over the positions. The group includes representatives from the natural sciences and a few special engineering experts in panzer and artillery defense.

The army is also getting an additional two construction battalions to assist in constructing defensive positions. Rommel pushes the officers to get their men to put more time in on the shoreline defenses. Von Salmuth's men are already averaging three or four days a week on these infernal barriers, but he has learned that Rommel is the boss. Whatever he says, goes.

Test reports regarding the shelling of minefields are discussed. It has been determined that mines laid within a 20-meter radius of a shell exploding in shallow water are subject to going off themselves. Appropriate corrective action is to be taken.

Rommel heads back to his headquarters late that afternoon.

---

1 *Generalmajor* Erwin Sander, commanding.

Saturday, April 8

Fortresses.

Again, the subject plagues *Generalfeldmarschall* von Rundstedt's mind and fouls his mood. This damned problem has been a thorn in his side for months now. He personally thinks these monstrosities are archaic and not worth the effort to build and maintain, especially with limited resources.

Hitler of course feels differently. He wants the entire coast stiffly defended, utilizing a series of citadels to be established and strengthened. And while he is not particularly fond of prepared fortifications in the field, he is an avid disciple of steel and concrete bunkers in principle, and thus simply enamored of the concept of the impenetrable fortress. To him, they imply resolute bastions that can be relied upon to hold indefinitely against any determined enemy.

Von Rundstedt does not agree at all, but unfortunately, OKW does (naturally). So the directives have gone out. Because of these, von Rundstedt must cover selected portions of the coast that are either immediately threatened or considered by him to be likely targets for a landing.

One such area is obviously the Straits of Dover. Closest to England and a straight shot into the industrial Ruhr Valley, it naturally invites some type of enemy landing, even if diversionary. Besides, that is the area where the new V-1 and V-2 rocket sites are being located. Surely the enemy through their photographic reconnaissance would know about them by now.

The estuaries of the Seine and Somme Rivers—these too are likely targets. Also considered vital are the many large French ports being used by the Kriegsmarine for their soon-to-be-revitalized U-boat campaign: Bordeaux, Lorient, St. Nazaire, La Rochelle, and Brest, all in the Seventh Army Sector. These main harbors have also been designated by the Führer to be "fortresses" and now have to be reinforced as such. Also in Seventh Army sector are Cherbourg and St. Malo.

In the Netherlands sector are Ijmuiden and the Hook of Holland. In the Fifteenth Army sector, there are the vital ports of Dunkirk, Boulogne, and Le Havre. And of course, the politically critical but militarily useless Channel Islands.

Hitler over time has re-emphasized the importance of strengthening all these ports. He has started to refer to them with pride as his powerful fortresses within his grand *Festung Europa*. Clearly, the man is infatuated with the term. And even *"Marschall Bubi"* has picked up the tune. Army Group B has added Vlissingen, Ostende, and Calais to the list.

Well, the hell with them all. He has already argued a number of times with OKW against expanding them. In his opinion, fortresses are just a waste of time and limited resources. Have those idiots already forgotten how they outflanked and neutralized the Maginot Line in May of 1940? Have they forgotten that those monstrous, intricate French bunker positions ended up being little use to the enemy? Or what

Frederick the Great (whom his ancestors had served valiantly) once said: "He who defends everything defends nothing." Well, this is a classic case.

But this is different, they counter. These would be along the coast, against an amphibious landing. A fortress would stop the enemy from establishing a nearby beachhead.

Sure it would, he thinks sourly. A halfway-intelligent enemy would just land a bit down the coast from one (or drop an airborne detachment behind the lines), cut the fortress off, and either take it from the landward side, or besiege it until it surrendered. His staff have a standing joke about these land elephants. If a commander wants to improve the defense of a particular position, all he has to do is designate it a "fortress." The sad part is that this is to a certain extent true. Redefining a port as a fortress means that it will now automatically have extra supplies and reinforcements allocated to its garrison, resources that could go to better fortify retaliating units.

According to OKW, each fortress is to have garrisoned within its walls one to two infantry divisions. *Ha! Reine Wahnsinn!* ("Pure madness!") He will be lucky to find two or three coastal battalions to defend each one. Unfortunately, as far as OKW is concerned, the shortage of troops does not affect the responsibilities of the garrison commanders. Each has been personally appointed by the Führer. As a fortress commandant, each had to sign a sworn affidavit stating that he would hold his fortress to the last man, no matter what orders he received from a higher command, or how woefully inadequate his defense force might be. The penalty for disobeying was of course, implied in the very nature of the affidavit.

To make matters worse, each commandant quickly found out that controlling his own fortress units was difficult. His authority over his charged area was somewhat limited, since the navy, air force, and of course, the SS also had some control over their units under him, even if their power was only administrative. Thus, if a matter of discipline arose with one of these units, the respective service higher authority had to be coerced into taking action. Naturally, if an enemy force engaged the garrison, the commandant had the authority to assume all facets of command for every unit within his garrison. Of course by then, it would be too late to do anything more than just try to hang on and hope for a rescue.

Over the last four months, OB West has tried to strengthen the fortresses with additional detachments. Dubbed "alarm units" (*Alarmeinheiten*), they were supposed to assist in training and augment a fortress's defense during an invasion. In reality, they were little more than inexperienced dock workers, poorly armed but in uniform.

Any way you looked at it, a fortress commandant was in a tricky position.

Von Rundstedt is at least thankful about one thing. Despite all their differences in defensive theories, Rommel firmly agrees with him that the independent fortress concept is a bad idea. They both believe that each fortress should remain under the command of the local division rather than become autonomous organizations. Militarily this is common sense, but naturally, the Führer will not relent. He wants his fortresses independent and directly under OKW control. Another chain-of-command problem that must be worked out. Another example of Hitler diluting, dividing, and confusing the authority chain below him.

Amateurs…

Sunday, April 9

Generaloberst Alfred Jodl reports to the Führer about concrete shortages for defensive works on the Atlantic Wall. When Hitler grouses that OKW should have apportioned enough allotments in the first place, Jodl points out (is his tone perhaps a bit smug?) that it was the Führer himself who had picked the target figure of 1.3 million cubic meters of concrete last year. Since the war conferences were by then being meticulously recorded by stenographers (Jodl reflects on their wild run-in back in September of 1942),[1] the number picked is of course available for review. Fuming, Hitler tells him to appropriate special measures to get more concrete.

Jodl makes a note to inform *Heeresgruppe B.*

***

Although it is Easter, today is a busy day at La Roche-Guyon. An early communiqué comes in from OKW concerning Holland. OKW has given them permission to move any mobile formations in that area (including the still still-forming 12th SS *Hitlerjugend*) forward. Local SS detachments are not to be worried about because, should any landing occur nearby, they will automatically move against the enemy. Permission to use the Hermann Göring Panzer Regiment, currently reorganizing in Tuscany but slated to move to France, will of course, have to come from the Reichsmarshal himself.

Günther Blumentritt shows up for a noontime conference. The topic for discussion is the rapid deployment of the mobile units—again, the panzer reserve issue. Where to put both the 12th SS and the 2nd Panzer, which has been recently refitted?[2]

In the afternoon, General Baron Geyr von Schweppenburg arrives to talk to Rommel.[3] Actually, with few panzers left in France, he finds himself with hardly any large units to train for inland maneuvers. But about strategy—the question of placing panzer units close to the sea—well, Rommel would just have to see the light.

Unfortunately for the baron, he has picked the wrong day to try to change the field marshal's mind. Rommel is not in a good mood. And since Rommel's senior staff members have seen a confrontation coming for a while now, harsh words are likely.

Both men have impressive backgrounds, their war deeds impressive. Rommel though is a field marshal; von Schweppenburg is a *General der Panzertruppen*. Still, Geyr is a prime example of the Western Theater Command. Perhaps his aristocratic Brandenburg demeanor and General Staff training lead him to feel that he has an edge over this common Swabian who had been somewhat lucky in remote, primitive North Africa against limited Allied forces. Or perhaps it is his experiences on the Eastern Front, something the so-called "Desert Fox" lacks entirely. Geyr also considers his experience under von Rundstedt (a close friend), and his present command role, qualifications to be able to freely exchange theories with the field marshal. In any case, Geyr could be in for a small shock.

Rommel has long known the score regarding Allied naval and air capabilities in paralyzing armored movement, and has experienced too many air raids himself, often in an open, uncomfortably prone position. So he is in no mood to listen to this upstart.[4] Although aware of the many panzer divisions lost against Russia, he is also tired of hearing from these Eastern Front veterans about the great capabilities of powerful mobile reserves. These fellows do not know what they are up against. Effective air power will knock the stuffing out of their columns long before they reach their targets. He knows. He has lived through it, with men sometimes getting hit right next to him.

Gause ushers Geyr into Rommel's office. The baron wastes no time and begins stating his case on why the panzers have to be moved inland and grouped for maneuvers.

Rommel, ready for the worst, listens to the general begin his arguments, but he does not pay attention for long. Geyr only gets to expound his generally accepted theories for a few minutes, mentioning what experiences have taught panzer commanders in Russia, when the field marshal loses his temper.

"Listen," he snarls in a frustrated tone, interrupting the baron in mid-sentence. "I am an experienced tank commander too. You and I do not see eye to eye on anything. I *refuse* to work with you anymore."

After a moment of silence, he snaps, "I propose to draw the appropriate conclusions." Had he been able to, Rommel would have fired him then and there.

Cut short by the field marshal, Geyr, obviously dismissed, is speechless with rage. Gathering what little ego he has left, he salutes the field marshal sharply, does an about face and marches out of the room. On the way out he repeats in his mind that he will never let himself be insulted like that by Rommel again. And he will never again speak to the field marshal, unless he absolutely has to.

Rommel's summary in the war diary of the incident is a dry and laconic remark:

> Strong difference of opinion, with no positive result.

That night, Rommel has dismissed the incident and his mood has improved. He writes:

> An endless amount of work must be done around here in order that we are 100 percent ready when the battle starts. Many weak points will have to be strengthened by then.
> Yesterday I was boar hunting. We shot four sows and one fox. The former will improve our rations.

Today General Marcks, commanding the 84th Corps in Normandy, writes to his mother, telling her that he is well and hopes she is too. He sends her a small photo of himself posing with Rommel. The field marshal is not smiling, and Marcks explains to her:

> As you can see in the small picture, Rommel does not usually look friendly. He is usually very serious, and if someone displeases him, he becomes quite coarse in his rude, pigheaded Swabian way.

1 See Prelude.

2 According to Nafziger's detailed volume on German panzer formations, the 2nd Panzer was taken out of combat in the middle of January 1944, refitted (including conversion of one panzer battalion to Panther Mark Vs), and made operational again by the end of February.

3 Irving wrote that this meeting took place on March 29. Ruge also thoroughly documented Rommel's itinerary for March 29 in his book, and Geyr von Schweppenburg does not appear anywhere in it. There are though, confirmed accounts of a visit by General Hermann Geyer, who had stopped by to say goodbye to Rommel. Irving probably got the names (and thus the dates) mixed up, which is understandable. Admiral Ruge wrote that although Rommel and von Schweppenburg indeed had two such conferences; one around March 16 and the other on April 9; he suggests that this particular conference took place on April 9. This is reinforced by the fact that the two had only just briefly met each other in March.

4 Geyr had only just turned 48, and although he had experience on the General Staff, his combat command had never been higher than a panzer corps—the 24th, the 20th, and finally the 58th—all on the Eastern Front.

Monday April 10

Rommel and Gause leave to meet with von Rundstedt and Blumentritt at their bunker headquarters in St.-Germain-en-Laye. They start off by discussing the disposition of their troops. Then, with Baron von Schweppenburg present, Rommel relates the details of their frustrating meeting yesterday, and an intense argument ensues. The old Prussian, bemused by "the young cub's" complaints, listens casually, nodding occasionally. Finally, the old man replies that while he understands Rommel's point of view, he nevertheless agrees with Geyr's theories of holding back the panzer reserves.

This does not make Rommel happy. He braces himself, and immediately goes over to the map table. Rommel now having been officially given command of the 2nd Panzer, he says that he has thought about it, and suggests that he put the 2nd Panzer both sides of the Somme River, near its mouth. That way, no matter which side of the river the invasion begins, half the division will be able to move immediately against it, while the other half struggles to find means to cross the river.

Von Rundstedt just frowns. It is bad enough that Rommel has wrangled another panzer division out from the shrinking mobile reserve, but now the fool proposes to position it straddling a river, like some fearful bull embarrassingly hung up on a fence.

"You know, my dear Rommel," he begins with a sneer, "I'm too old for these things," referring to their periodical conflicts. "But once upon a time, we old timers learned a little bit too."

"I take it you object," Rommel says coldly. He adds, "I have my orders from the Führer."

"Ah," the old man snarls and, losing his temper, he curses—something he rarely does in front of his surprised chief of staff.

He angrily walks over to the map table and points to Rommel's proposed position for the 2nd Panzer. "This set-up at Abbéville—half a division on the right, and half on the left bank... It's just no good. It ought to be *there*," he barks as he points to Amiens, "further inland."

Rommel silently looks at the map.

"But as far as I'm concerned, you do your own damned business in your own damned way." The old Prussian angrily turns away from Rommel.

Rommel glances at von Rundstedt, and then departs himself.

Returning to his headquarters irritated, Rommel finds out that the Allies naturally are doing their share to make his day miserable. In addition to air strikes against their communications infrastructure, they are now bombing critically important positions along the coastline day and night. A good-sized raid just today has knocked out the large Octeville naval battery, just north of Le Havre.

As a remedy against these attacks, Rommel borrows a common trick from his North African days. He has ordered his construction gangs to build a number of

Scheinbatterien—dummy batteries. Using cheap or natural materials, they begin to set up false positions, chosen by him, at various key locations around the coast.

While construction of these fake targets takes a degree of time and resources away from the real defensive work that is being done, the results prove worthwhile. A number of bombing raids are diverted to these worthless positions, and as a result, fewer real batteries are hit.

Before retiring that evening, Rommel shares his thoughts on today's meeting. First in a letter to Alfred Jodl, he writes:

> *In my view, any strategic airborne landing by the enemy is doomed to disaster sooner or later, PROVIDED we succeed in sealing the coast.*

Then he writes to Lucie:

> *Today I went to see Rundstedt. Things have not turned out the way I had believed they would on 21 March. One does not want a cabinet crisis[1] here, and I have to give in. Nevertheless, I'm going to have my own way in the essentials...*

*** *** ***

The subject of the invasion of Europe is again discussed at length during Hitler's daily main conference. In an April 9 report from *Fremde Heeres West,* Roenne reports:

> With the weather situation now favorable too, the general picture is rounded off in the previously reported sense of the launching of a major attack being possible at any moment. The timing of the attack is strongly influenced by political considerations, and despite countless rumors, pertinent concrete information has not become available.

A few more recent reports at different levels again suggest that the invasion might not even come this year. An aide to Propaganda Minister Goebbels today writes:

> The question whether the Allied invasion in the West is coming or not dominates all political and military discussion here.
>
> Goebbels is afraid that the Allies dare not make the attempt yet. If so, that would mean for us many months of endless, weary waiting which would test our strength beyond endurance. Our war potential cannot now be increased, it can only decline. Every new air raid makes the petrol position worse.

---

1   Rommel was informed of a communiqué that von Rundstedt had sent to OKW. He had told Hitler essentially that if the Führer and OKW did not allow him to command in the West his own way, then he would most likely "quit." Whether that meant tendering his resignation, asking to be relieved on conditions of bad health, or just plain retiring, was not made known. One thing was sure—Hitler was not prepared at this time to relieve the old man. So he rethought his decision to give Rommel the reserve panzers, the concession that he had magnanimously made back at the March conference.

Tuesday, April 11

Generalfeldmarschall Rommel goes on tour again, this time headed for Brittany. He travels over to St. Malo and discovers a number of problems needing correction. He continues on to several coastal towns and ports, noting details, amending directives, issuing counter-orders. He seems indefatigable, always on the move. His irritation grows as he continues to hear reports of so-called "experiments" being conducted over and over to see how effective offshore obstacles are. He is also fed up with the pessimistic attitude of some unit commanders. Mind and body need to focus for all of these men if they are to defeat this enemy. The orders, he grumbles, must be "executed precisely as given by the army group."

He moves on to the key U-boat ports of Brest and Lorient, covered by the 344th and 265th Infantry Divisions respectively. Overall, he is satisfied to see enthusiastic participation and adequate defensive construction results, despite supply hardships.

This brings up another problem today: sabotage. The Brest port area has been repeatedly harassed by local Resistance units.[1] There are many days when supply trains cannot get through because of damage to the rail line. And when that happens, the local SS lashes out, and the populace in turn reacts to their actions. One officer equates these actions to the savagery in Russia.

Rommel tackles this problem head-on. Reprisals against the people, he says, are not to be made. He orders heavier guards for supply depots and convoys, and more diligence on the part of the security forces. But he wants it clear that there are to be no atrocities.

The local SS authorities report these counter-instructions up the SS chain of command.

***

A major improvement occurs in the West. Because the crisis on the Russian Front has abated somewhat for now, OKW now starts transferring mobile reserves from the East back to France to refit and await the invasion. After all, spring is beginning. If the Allies invade now and there are no panzers to push them back...

As part of this good news, OB West is informed that the élite 1st SS Panzer Division is returning to France. The bad news though, is that not much is coming back. The division had taken severe losses in February, furiously assaulting the Russian Korsun pocket. Then in late March, as part of General Hans-Valentin Hube's First Panzer Army, the unit took a severe pounding in southern Russia. Encircled by a massive Soviet offensive, the soldiers had fought desperately to break out.[2] With the help of the newly arrived 2nd SS Panzer Corps, Hube's men had finally struggled out of the entrapment, fighting furiously as they retreated, losing or abandoning equipment right and left.

The trapped divisions had indeed finally escaped the pocket, but their desperate struggle breaking out, like their other recent engagements, had exacted a heavy toll. The 1st SS Panzer Division was shattered as a unit. It had started withdrawing to Belgium to refit, leaving just a *Kampfgruppe*.[3] It though, was in turn enveloped and forced to withdraw. Now its remnants will be joining the others in the West to recuperate and await the invasion.

This is the fourth time now that this division has come out of Russia in such a battered condition. Only last summer, after having been smashed in the battle of Kursk, it had been transferred to Italy to refit, leaving all its armor, transports, and equipment behind to be used by the 2nd SS Panzer Division *Das Reich*, which had to stay and operate against the Russians. LSSAH became part of Rommel's Northern Italy command, until the Italian political situation was resolved. Once the Germans had again taken firm control of the Italian countryside, the *Leibstandarte* had been transferred back to Russia again, right into the thick of battle. Now they were returning to France once more.

SS *Brigadeführer* Heinz Lammerding's *Das Reich* has fared even worse. It had been prepared to leave Russia for Italy as well after the Kursk campaign had failed. But an unexpected Russian drive towards Kharkov that autumn had kept it, the 5th SS Panzer *Wiking*, and the 3rd SS Panzer *Totemkopf* in Russia to deal with a powerful, determined, advancing enemy. Eventually surrounded along with the LSSAH's remaining *Kampfgruppe, Das Reich* too had fought its way out of the pocket.

Most units had left their equipment and vehicles behind and had been sent off (as a sort of Christmas present) to recover and refit, first to Germany, and then in early February to southern France. The remaining ad hoc battle group of some 5,000 men (less than one-quarter the size of the original division), had then continued on fighting a series of desperate, retreating actions. First the Soviet winter offensive, and then their spring offensive, had forced the weary battle group time and time again to meet the threat of an advancing enemy spearhead, moving frantically around like an overworked, battered fire brigade.

Now it is coming back to France, a shattered unit of only some 2,500 men. This is a far cry from the 19,000-plus that it had once mustered, not taking into account the thousands of casualties that had transferred into and out of the division during that time. The unit is not even rated as a panzer division anymore, merely as *Panzergruppe Das Reich*. So these remnants are being moved to southern France to rest and be refitted.

Von Rundstedt succeeds in getting LSSAH transferred to the Beauvais, about 70km north of Paris, and only 90km behind the coast. Unfortunately though, the new location is not near enough to the Channel to suit Rommel. He calls OKW and argues that this is still too far away from the coast. He wants the division moved next to the beaches.

This, Jodl replies tonelessly, is just not going to happen. He points out patiently, almost paternally, that these large mobile formations are their reserves, and therefore must be deployed strategically, not tactically. Besides, he argues, Rommel has to admit that this closer positioning is still an improvement.

Rommel agrees, but believes that it does not better assure them of success. It would still take a long time for them to reach any invasion site, and they would still get roughened up considerably before reaching there, even assuming that the invasion takes place nearby.

Along the same line of thought, he mentions that 12th SS Panzer is too widely dispersed inland. In the face of heavy enemy air attacks, it will take them at least 48 hours just to concentrate and move up to Caen. And 2nd Panzer is over 85km from the Somme sector where it is garrisoned on the coast. The units would take quite a pounding from the air as they slowly struggled to reach the English Channel.

---

1   French underground units in urban areas were usually referred to as the Resistance (*der Widerstand*). Those guerrilla groups in rural and mountain areas around the country were usually referred to as the *Maquis*.

2   The so-called Kamenets-Podolsky Pocket or Hube's Pocket. Two Russian fronts had cut off *Generaloberst* Hans-Valentin Hube's 1st Panzer Army just north of the Dniester river.

3   A loosely assigned improvised battlegroup varying in size from a battalion to a division, and created from other combat units. It was traditionally named after its commander.

Wednesday, April 12

Rommel continues his tour of the Brittany area. Just outside the strategic port of Brest, he watches a demonstration of a new type of offshore mine, manufactured locally. The trigger mechanism is a lever that extends from the concrete block enclosing the mine casing. When a vessel strikes the lever, the explosive is detonated.

The linkage design seems well engineered, and he approves. Now, if only the mine can remain operable for long periods of time underwater and withstand the currents.

In the area there are five centers that create and assemble the iron rail tetrahedrons that are going into the offshore barriers. They have averaged over 1,200 assemblies each. Again, Rommel looks for short cuts.

He later confides to his aide, "I have only one real enemy now, and that's time."

***

Von Rundstedt spends the day in his villa going over reports. For the last few nights, Allied bombers have conducted heavy air raids on French railyards, including those at Charleroi Montignes. Although damage is fair to moderate, this new strategy bears an ominous foreboding.

In talking to Blumentritt about the 2nd SS Panzer transferring from Russia, he is told the division is to be rebuilt with some 9,000 new recruits. The old Prussian snorts. Untrained boys, they are.

He turns his attention to other matters. Ah, the 65th Army Corps is conducting a V-1 war exercise at the corps' Paris headquarters...

***

Today, the Führer has no time to discuss the situation in the West. He is again in deep trouble in the East. The lull has unexpectedly ended. The threat is now down south. The 3rd Ukrainian Front is smashing deep into Romania, and the German southern flank is threatened. The Führer and his command staff search desperately for more units to plug the gap. Now that it is almost too late, he orders that the Crimea be evacuated. But at this point, the only escape route for his men is by sea from Sevastopol.

Undoubtedly, many will not make it.

During the day, some 450 enemy heavy bombers escorted by another couple hundred fighters bomb various targets in southern Germany and Austria, including Rommel's old residence, Wiener-Neustadt. Some 30 German aircraft are destroyed attacking the formations, against the loss of a dozen enemy aircraft.

Rommel, it turns out, was wise to move his home to Herrlingen.

Thursday, April 13

Today, Rommel is near the tip of Quiberon Bay at Plouharnel, inspecting 4/264, a naval battery made up of four old French 340mm guns. The Germans have mounted them on railway cars since the area has an excellent railway network. He is impressed with their 30km range.

Onward to the U-boat base at St. Nazaire. The units there have been working hard, and progress on the many barriers looks good. The landward defensive perimeter has been pulled in so that the 7,500-man contingent can better defend it. Over half of this force is made up of anti-aircraft personnel.

He moves on, traveling westward to the port town of La Baule, some 18km away. Good progress here, too. Rommel makes a few stops, then retires here for the evening, Word has been received that there will be a possible partisan raid this evening, so his quarters are heavily guarded throughout the night.

***

At La Roche-Guyon, *Generalleutnant* Gause is trying to stay busy and to justify his last few days at headquarters. He calls Günther Blumentritt at OB West and is told that OKW has given new orders: there will be no more motorized units transferred to the West. Blumentritt then tries to reassure him that von Rundstedt does understand the need to defeat the enemy at the shoreline if at all possible, and on this, the two commanders are in complete agreement.

Gause is glad to hear this. He is looking for some sort of good coup to go out with.

In the meantime, besides Gause leaving, the army group's headquarters staff is undergoing a few other personnel changes. The intelligence section has been permanently turned over to unpretentious *Oberst* Anton Staubwasser. Hans Lattman, Rommel's artillery specialist, has been promoted to *Generalmajor*. Other additions to the staff include Luftwaffe *Oberstleutnant* Wolfgang Queissner, who will be Rommel's liaison with air operations (few as they are). *Oberstleutnant* Olshausen has been assigned as their deputy transport officer. In addition, several staff officers, adjutants, clerks, communications specialists, and even a few historians are added to the growing staff. Things are getting busy these days.

***

Adolf Hitler has a conference with *Großadmiral* Karl Dönitz, head of the Kriegsmarine. The admiral complains that more resources must go into the U-boat program if they are to have any hope of countering the Allied invasion and making a dent in the Battle of the Atlantic. Hitler refuses, telling him that what he needs more than anything are tanks and fighters, the former to counter that "*verdammte russische Offensiven"* and still equip the panzers in the West, and the latter to combat the hordes of enemy bombers over Germany. "That's the alpha and omega of it," he says simply.

Priorities...

Today, American and British tactical assets begin to target coastal defenses along northern France. These are preliminary strikes for the upcoming invasion.

Friday, April 14

Today, Rommel starts out with a simple breakfast in his quarters at La Baule in Brittany. Then he is off eastward, past the port of St. Nazaire again to look at the positions in Nantes on the Loire River. Work there has progressed well, and after a few stops, he moves on further inland to the town of Angers. There he looks in on the Engineering School. After that, he has a brief talk with 10th Air Corps commander *Generalleutnant* Alexander Holle. The man reports proudly that his men are ready to fight.

A couple more inspections and Rommel begins his return. He stops once more at Le Mans to confer there with General Dollmann. Then it is back to La Roche-Guyon.

***

Generalleutnant Dr. Hans Speidel is at his home at Freudenstadt, Germany. After leaving Berchtesgaden early in April, he had gone home for a well-deserved leave. Tomorrow, he will report as chief of staff to his new command—Headquarters, Army Group B.

Speidel is a solid member of one of the conspiracy groups bent on overthrowing the Nazi regime. Most members simply want to kill Hitler. Others want him tried and convicted. A few desperately hope he just steps down.

By now, the conspirators are not just a few circles of dissatisfied Germans; they have grown into a full-scale underground movement. Because many of these collaborators are highly placed within the civilian or military organizations, their collective influence is somewhat powerful but unfortunately, also uncoordinated. Speidel had found out early on that, within the scope of secrecy and reason, they could manipulate or influence certain appointments to promote their own interests. So it was no coincidence that his name had been one of the two chosen by the General Staff to replace Alfred Gause. And for Rommel, who was a fellow Swabian and had known him as an infantry student a couple decades ago, he was a natural choice. Thus, he had been ordered to report to OKW immediately.

Speidel, a one-time assistant to dissident General Beck,[1] wants the Führer dead— period. Oh, to be sure, he had at one time tolerated Hitler and his schemes. But after Stalingrad, Speidel, working for General Hubert Lanz, became convinced that their leader had to go. And the more Speidel involved himself in the conspiracy, the more he had realized that Hitler had no other recourse but to die. So today, he receives a visit from a co-conspirator, none other than Karl Strölin, the *Oberbürgermeister* of Stuttgart. The mayor, who still calls on Frau Rommel from time to time, has also been in contact with members of the Goerdeler-Beck group,[2] and the the distant Kreisau Circle. All of them were part of what was being called by some in the SS investigating them as the *Schwartz Kapelle*.[3]

Strölin, on behalf of the rest of his group, has a specific task for Speidel: he is to win over Rommel to their cause. The field marshal must be ready to commit to whatever action the conspirators undertake, and be willing to represent Germany to the Western Allied commanders as needed. A true hero, the field marshal is one of the few men the West would listen to seriously.

Speidel agrees to sound out the field marshal in good time, although he admits it will not be easy. Strölin gives him some suggestions on how to approach this covert subject. The Stuttgart mayor of course knows the field marshal well, having, at Goerdeler's suggestion, already approached the field marshal to join them back in February. The French military governor General Stülpnagel, another plotter, is also a friend of Rommel's, having served with him at the Dresden Infantry School under Falkenhausen. Strölin suggests coordinating his efforts with him.

Caution must cover everything, though. Speidel must be very wary in his endeavors. The Gestapo is closing in on many of them. There already have been several arrests, and some of these have resulted in the imprisonment (and all that implies) of key members of the different groups. And those arrested might break down and implicate others at any time. Retired General Beck himself was rumored to be under a 24-hour watch by the Gestapo.

Speidel grimly listens to the mayor, determined, but apprehensive. The field marshal will not be easily won over.[4]

***

Today at the daily war conference at the Berghof, in contrast to the depressing news on the Eastern Front, positive reports on the defensive buildup in the West partially offset the Führer's depression. It seems that Rommel's optimistic spirit is back.

Propaganda Minister Goebbels observes:

> *The Führer is very enthusiastic about Rommel's work. Rommel has worked with exemplary effect in the West. He has an old score to settle with the British and Americans, is on fire with anger and hate, and has put all his cunning and intelligence into the perfection of the defensive works there. Rommel is the old fighter again.*

---

1   *Generaloberst* Ludwig Beck, retired now. General Beck had resigned his position as *Chef der Generalstab* in 1938, to protest Hitler's occupation of Czechoslovakia. Now he was one of the leaders of the conspiracy.

2   Dr. Karl Goerdeler avidly hated the Nazis. A professional civil servant, he had at first acquiesced to the new National Socialist principles back in 1933. He had even under their new regime become the Reich Commissioner of Prices in late 1934. However, Goerdeler had resigned in protest the next year, because the Nazis would not accept his advanced ideas of reforming local governments. Even more importantly, Goeredeler had strongly disagreed with their methods of asserting authority. And his refusal to fly the swastika from his office at the Leipzig city hall only furthered the friction.

In 1936, he was re-elected as mayor of Leipzig for another 12-year term. Despite his pointed criticism of them, the Nazis had still backed his appointment. Months later though, he found himself defying Berlin directly. He had been ordered by the party to remove the city's monument to the world-famous composer Felix Mendelssohn, a native of Leipzig, because Mendelssohn had also been Jewish. Goerdeler had bluntly refused the removal order. Mendelssohn he declared, had honored his home city greatly with his beautiful music.

Upset that this dictum had been challenged, Hitler personally ordered the statue removed. He realized, however, that an open confrontation with the mayor would look bad in the public eye. So working behind the mayor's back, Nazi officials had waited for him to leave town one day, before taking the sculpture down from its place in front of the concert hall. When Goerdeler had returned and found out that it had been removed against his express orders and in his absence, he had raged against the Führer. In protest, he had resigned as mayor. He had been fighting the Nazis secretly ever since then.

3   The "Black Band," or "Black Orchestra." See footnote for February 22.

4   Several authors have written that Rommel was already in on the plot in the spring of 1944. On the one hand, the weight of testimonial evidence from Rommel's memoirs and his family's postwar recollections points out that this simply is not true, no matter what Rommel felt about the war's outcome. Controversial historian David Irving strongly denies Rommel's involvement at that point in time. One cannot know for sure because all involved are now deceased, and before and after the attempt on July 20, Rommel almost certainly would have destroyed any incriminating evidence of his complicity in any possible coup.

Fred Majdalany for example, wrote that Speidel "represented Rommel" at that meeting of April 14, where he was given "(for onward transmission to Rommel) an up-to-the-minute breakdown of the plot." If this is the case, he represented an uncommitted field marshal. It has been confirmed by a number of sources that Dr. Strölin at that meeting did confer with Speidel on how to win Rommel over to their side, and it was for this reason that the updated status of the plot was discussed.

And yet, at least one other source (Brown) also describes a meeting between Rommel and Speidel at a lodge *a month before he reported aboard.* The meeting supposedly took place in the Marly Forest, surrounded by a cordon of *panzergrenadiers* from the famed (albeit resurrected) 21st Panzer Davison. At that meeting, supposedly attended also by General von Stülpnagel, General von Falkenhausen, General Lüttwitz, and General Schwerin, several ideas were supposedly discussed to make peace with the West and arrest the Nazi leaders, putting perhaps General Beck in charge. Again, this meeting was very unlikely, as Speidel was still in Russia, and the meticulous postwar entries of Admiral Ruge make no mention at all of the encounter at that time, though Rommel was indeed in the area.

Saturday, April 15

The Luftwaffe reports today at La Roche-Guyon are analyzed in detail. Enemy air activity has increased quite a bit in the last few weeks. An army coastal battery near Nieuwpoort[1] has been damaged, two of its four 155-mm guns knocked out. Other air raids further down the coast have targeted a number of radar installations, the port of Le Havre, and yet another coastal battery near Dieppe. Fortunately, damage was minor.

Other messages detail the progress of defense construction. Sizable numbers of enemy mines have been laid in various areas off Le Havre, north of Walcheren Island, and close to the Scheldt River, near Zeebrügge. Did this mean that the enemy was going to land near the Somme estuary? Possibly.

At the field marshal's bidding, his headquarters staff has requested that naval enlisted personnel be used to help move construction material along the coast of Brittany. And there is still no decision on where the concrete needed for several naval battery emplacements will come from, shortages being what they currently are.

***

Late that evening, a modest rain begins to fall over Rommel's château. Cold sentries shiver miserably as they stand glumly at their posts. Their soaked, camouflaged capes are wrapped tightly around them as they watch the rain come down. Bored machine gunners in their pillboxes occasionally sip a terrible concoction known as *ersatz* coffee and miserably watch the rain come down. Anti-aircraft crews have received permission to stand down.

A lone army car enters the wrought-iron gates and pulls up to the main entrance on the side of the villa. The right rear door opens, and a single, unknown figure emerges. As he stands up, light raindrops softly strike his immaculate raincoat and hat. The nearby sentries note the red stripe down the side of his trousers, signifying an army general.

Staff members come out to welcome him, grab his bags, and escort him inside. His luggage and raincoat are taken, and he is told that the field marshal is in, having just returned yesterday from a number of inspections along the coast. The newcomer's arrival is announced, and he is shown the way to Rommel's study. Calmly, the man walks in, comes to attention, and formally reports for duty.

The field marshal stands up and warmly greets the visitor with a tired smile, measuring him up. At 46 years old, he is of medium height with a squarish build, but not overweight. With his hat off, his tawny hair is still damp from the trip. He wears thin-framed spectacles on a lightly freckled, owlish face with a grave expression..

He is *Generalleutnant* Hans Speidel: Rommel's new chief of staff.

This man is an old acquaintance as well, a fellow Swabian. While not an aristocrat, he is certainly a stately, intelligent, well-educated man. Fluid in several languages, he holds a doctorate from Tübengen University. He is highly intelligent, decorous, cultured in the finer arts and advanced contemporary literary works, and an excellent equestrian. Another good reason why Rommel picked him as his next *Chef*.

Rommel asks him about his trip, and then as an opening gambit, chuckles that here they are again, back in France. Speidel is certainly no stranger to the country. He has fought here in both world wars, having once been the German military attaché in Paris. He was once chief of staff to the military governor of France, serving first under General Streccius, and then later Joachim von Stülpnagel, cousin to the more famous Karl-Heinrich. However, when the SS had taken over the judicial side of the military affairs in 1942, he had disgustedly transferred to the Eastern Front. Now he was back.

As they talk, the field marshal glances at the shiny Knight's Cross below Speidel's neck, just recently presented to him by the Führer himself for his part in the besieged Eighth Army's recent courageous retreat from Cherkassy.

As the two men relax in each other's presence, the dialogue eases up. At a certain point, the conversation shifts gears from high German to Swabian, that southern German dialect with which they had both been raised. Speidel tells him about his briefing at OKW, and that he has no specific instructions. "I am to assume the duties of chief of staff for you."

Rommel queries this: no instructions regarding policy? Speidel replies, "I was told that none were needed. Basically, if the enemy lands, we must just drive them back into the sea." Nothing more. Of course, they have yet to do that to the Western Allies. Still, they did give them a good deal of difficulty at Salerno, and the Anzio beachhead has been contained for nearly three months now.

"Those were the only instructions you were given?"

"Jawohl, Herr Feldmarschall."

They briefly talk over old times. They had met in the Argonne Forest during World War I, and later, between wars, their paths had crossed in the 13th Württemberg Infantry Regiment. Rommel remembers Speidel as a rather quiet but sophisticated fellow, very intelligent. And like Rommel, his father had also been a teacher. Now the field marshal finds himself warming up to the man. Yes, they will get along quite well.

Speidel, despite what he had promised Jodl at Berchtesgaden, and more along the lines of the conspirators' plans, does not go out of his way to give Rommel inspiration. On the contrary. He does not hold back the Eastern Front news, knowing that it will probably depress the field marshal. He wants to gain Rommel's trust by doing well in his new position, so always appearing to be honest and open with him is critical. He must at the same time weaken Rommel's hopes of winning the war if he is to have any hope at all of bringing him over to the side of the government conspirators.

Depressing him is easy to do. Rommel is starved for news, and Speidel willingly gives it to him. He fills him in on the latest situation on the Eastern Front, from which he has so recently come, including the latest updates from OKW. He tells him about the massive Soviet offensive last month; about the 1st Panzer Army entrapment; the setbacks in the center; the terrible winter conditions; the dismissal of von Kluge and the legendary von Manstein, a general Rommel holds in high esteem. In a depressed tone, Speidel goes into detail about his own harrowing experiences with the Eighth Army, how they had been encircled, and how they had to desperately fight their way out of the pocket.

Speidel speaks frankly, painting the already-bleak picture even darker. Presenting Germany's hopeless position in the war, he describes in detail how their eastern armies are losing hundreds of thousands of men and countless numbers of vehicles in the freezing cold, as so many veteran divisions are getting chewed up. He mentions the rumors of atrocities; the endless hordes of Russian units that arrive every week at the front from a seemingly endless source of manpower. He recalls the hours of pounding from the massive Russian artillery; the merciless savagery of the fighting; and the desolation everywhere from a scorched-earth policy carried out on both sides.

Speidel relates briefly how the Crimea is now totally lost. The new *Heeresgruppe Nordukraine* on the Southern Front[2] is in full retreat, while the weak Army Group Center (*Heeresgruppe Mitte*) is being forced back steadily. And of course, there is the next round coming up—the dreaded Russian summer offensive starts in a couple of months…

The effect of the news upon the field marshal is immediate and considerable. Rommel shakes his head increasingly as Speidel goes on. By the time his new chief of staff is finished, Rommel's good mood is gone.

Looking at Speidel, Rommel shrugs his shoulders and says, "Well, I don't think we have the slightest chance now of winning the war."

That evening, Rommel's daily diary entry reflects his change in disposition and how upset he is at von Manstein's dismissal. Will Rommel end up like him?

> *What will later historians have to say about these retreats? And what will history say in passing its verdict on me? If I am successful here, then everybody else will claim all the glory—just as they are already claiming the credit for the defenses and the beach obstacles that I have erected. But if I fail here, then everybody will be after my blood.*

Speidel's comments to the field marshal have obviously had considerable effect.

---

1   A small coastal town in the Western Flanders part of Belgium, about 10km down the coast (southwest) of Ostende.

2   *Heeresgruppe Süd* at the beginning of the month was renamed *Heeresgruppe Nordukraine*.

Sunday, April 16

After a welcoming breakfast with the staff at La Roche-Guyon, *Generalleutnant* Dr. Hans Speidel is given a full tour of the headquarters. His assigned quarters in the old Norman tower are excellent, and his office is to be just down the hall from the field marshal's study. He has time for an amiable chat with his predecessor, Alfred Gause, before he is taken in for a series of briefings to bring him up to speed on the army group's status.

Generalfeldmarschall Rommel though, is not at all in a good mood. The effect of Speidel's bad news about the East has carried over into today. He reads his morning reports with a feeling of depression.

Vizeadmiral Ruge, Rommel's naval advisor, is today returning from his two weeks' leave at the minesweepers' recreational home in Schwalbach, rested and fit. His assistant, Captain Peters, meets him at the Paris railway station that morning. Together they drive northwest down the Seine to the château. During the trip, after some pleasantries, Peters fills the admiral in on everything he has missed in the last two weeks, including General Speidel's arrival. In other developments, Admiral Würmbach has been reassigned, moving from commanding the naval forces in Denmark to those in the Skagerrak. Ruge shakes his head. Another step in the wrong direction. Admiral Krancke has sent them his latest naval assessment…

When they arrive at the château around noontime, Ruge immediately reports in to the field marshal and finds him in a somber state of mind—cordial, but humorless. Rommel solemnly relays the grave situation on the Eastern Front. He tells him about von Manstein being dismissed on short notice, and that things in the East are just getting worse.

Rommel pauses and then tells the admiral that, in his opinion, the military high command is now in a "confidence crisis." He thinks that this grave problem will only be solved by instituting mutual trust between the many different commands, across the varied services, and especially with the Führer himself. That trust, he admits, is not present right now. Even those few verbal commitments that he had so gracefully made to Rommel about the panzers at the March conference have not been confirmed in writing, much less acted upon. And if the past is any indication of how well he keeps his promises…

As the field marshal goes on about this, he again refers back to the critical problems in the East. The evacuation of the Crimea, he says quietly, has evidently turned into a rout.

Rommel shifts gears and tells Ruge he can get the full story about the situation in the East later from him. He fills Ruge in about the new chief of staff. Rommel then suggests that Ruge go out and greet Speidel. So the admiral emerges from the field marshal's study, finds Speidel, and gives him a hearty welcome-aboard. They talk for a bit.

As the afternoon goes on, Rommel struggles to regain his sense of purpose and to shake off this new depression. He decides to embark on one of his "armed promenades" with General Meise and Ruge. The few pheasants and rabbits that they encounter (but do not bag) help to improve the field marshal's spirits.

The mood upswing though, only lasts until he returns to the château. There a new problem confronts him. General Christiansen, commanding all Wehrmacht units in Belgium and the Netherlands, reports that he has just received orders from the Kriegsmarine that Naval Training Detachment 24, working on the Atlantic Wall in his area, will be transferred to Germany, possibly so that they cannot be committed to battle if the invasion begins up there.[1] More troops being taken away from the defensive effort; men that could have taken over duties in the secondary line of defenses, thereby freeing up more soldiers to man the coast. Rommel just shakes his head.

Late that afternoon, La Roche-Guyon receives a visitor from Rommel's past. Thirty-two-year-old *Oberst Freiherr* Hans von Luck arrives at the château in his Mercedes.[2] Rommel's old subordinate is on his way to his new assignment: the *Panzer Lehr* Division, commanded by another old acquaintance of theirs from North Africa, Fritz Bayerlein.[3] On the way to his new command, he has decided to pay his respects to the field marshal.

Von Luck is shown in to see *Generalleutnant* Gause. "Good to see you again, safe and sound," Gause says with a smile, as they shake hands. "I'm just initiating my successor, General Speidel."

They chat for a while in Gause's office. Von Luck fills him in on what he has been doing. After the collapse in North Africa in 1943, he was given a break from combat. Allowed a few weeks of leave in Berlin, he had been assigned in August as instructor at a panzer reconnaissance school in Paris. There he enjoyed the Parisian atmosphere, where his health (and his love life) had improved. In March 1944, at the end of a brief seminar in Berlin, he had been told that he was being appointed as commander of the panzer regiment in the newly forming *Panzer Lehr* Division in Western France.

Gause comments favorably on von Luck's new assignment, "And congratulations on your posting to France, where we must recon on a landing, sooner or later."

After a bit, von Luck asks him if he might say hello to the field marshal.

"By all means," Gause replies easily. "Rommel is rather depressed right now, because his arguments about how a landing should be met are getting nowhere with Hitler. He'll be pleased to see you. Take a little walk with him. It'll distract him." He prudently does not mention Russia.

Rommel is indeed enjoyably surprised by this visit from an old comrade. As Gause shows von Luck in, the field marshal rises and heartily shakes his hand.

"So good to see you again, Luck!" says Rommel, flashing his famous smile.

"*Danke, Feldmarschall.* You look well yourself."

Much better than he had last seen him, in fact. That had been in early March of 1943, when their now-legendary desert army had been surrounded by the British and the Americans. Rommel had been once more flying off to seek reinforcements from Hitler, although both of them had somehow known that he would not be coming back. Von Luck had gone into his tent to bid him farewell and to wish him, on behalf of Luck's battalion, good fortune. Rommel, a tear rolling down his cheek, had pulled down a photograph of himself and autographed it. Von Luck had been moved. Now, the old fox looks himself again.

"I'm glad that I can greet you here on the Western Front," says Rommel, as they stroll over to his French doors. "We've got something coming up in the weeks ahead. See that the regiment you're to take over is well motivated, and aware of the seriousness of the situation."

The colonel assures him that he will, and with that, they saunter outside into the château grounds. They talk at some length about the war. Rommel frowns. Knowing that he can trust the colonel implicitly, he confesses to von Luck that he does not think that they can win.

Von Luck asks what is to be done, then.

"I'm against any solution by force," Rommel replies, shaking his head. "I must somehow convince Hitler that we can no longer win the war; at the most we can only put off the end. As soon as the opportunity arises, I'll try to make it clear to him personally—in writing if necessary—that the war will be finally lost if the Allies succeed in setting up a second front here in the West."

Rommel smacks one hand into the other for emphasis as he speaks. "Every opponent who sets foot on French soil must be thrown back into the sea in the first hours. That can *only* be done if our panzer divisions are stationed right by the coast and if enough fighters are in the air, so they can be thrown against those powerful Allied air forces."

They continue walking. "But Göring has let us down once before in Africa," he says. "And at Stalingrad too, he failed to keep his promise to provide an adequate air bridge for the trapped Sixth Army. "And I don't believe in the 'thousand fighters' that he intends to send here."

They go on discussing the situation for a few more minutes, before turning to lighter, personal items. They eventually walk back to Rommel's study, and von Luck says his goodbyes.

"All the best to you, Luck," Rommel wishes him cheerfully, shaking his hand again. "I'll be visiting your division quite often in the coming weeks," he adds.

Von Luck replies that he will look forward to the visits.

"Remember," Rommel says as they part, "we must do our duty."

That night, buoyed by von Luck's visit, he writes Lucie about his new chief of staff and tries to be upbeat:

Speidel arrived yesterday. he makes a good and fresh impression. I believe it will work out well.

He still worries though, about Germany's shadowed future.

***

Von Luck unfortunately, is in for a surprise that evening: He has already been reassigned. When he reports to his commanding officer and friend, Fritz Baylerlein, he is told the bad news.

"My dear Luck," he tells him, "I had marked you down as commander of the panzer regiment; but I was told a few days ago to send you immediately to the reorganized 21st Panzer Division."

Seeing the surprise on von Luck's face, he adds, "Seems like your commander, *Generalmajor* Feuchtinger, has more pull at the Führer's headquarters. I really regret that I won't be able to have an old African campaigner in my division."

Upset, von Luck reports to Feuchtinger's 21st Panzer Division that night. He is to take over as commander of the division's newly formed 125th *Panzergrenadier* Regiment.

As things turn out, he will now play a key role when the invasion comes.

---

1 See entry for March 26.

2 The date of the visit is uncertain. Von Luck indicates only that it was some time after the first of the month. But Gause's remarks about initiating his successor put the arrival just after April 15, the date Speidel arrived at La Roche-Guyon. And Rommel was on the road for the following three days. Thus, the 16th is the most likely day for the visit.

   Von Luck had known Rommel for years. Rommel was one of his instructors at the Dresden Infantry School back in 1931 when von Luck attended as a cadet. In the spring of 1940, he had served faithfully under him in France as part of the recon battalion of Rommel's famed 7th Panzer Division. After participating in the invasion of Russia, he had been transferred in April 1942 to North Africa, commanding the 3rd Panzer Recon Battalion of the old 21st Panzer Division. Von Luck's battalion had been one of Rommel's favorite units.

3 Bayerlein, now 45 years old, had been a private in World War I, rising to the rank of *Feldwebel* before the war's end. He received a commission in the 21st Cavalry Regiment in 1922, and the start of world conflict had found him as General Guderian's *Ia*[3] during their headlong advances through Poland, France, and then on towards Moscow in 1941.

Monday, April 17

After a quick, early breakfast, *Generalfeldmarschall* Rommel briskly leaves his château, walking down the entrance steps, ready for another inspection tour. This trip is going to be up the northern French shoreline again, to the coastal positions along the Somme and Scheldt estuaries. This time, he is taking along with him Admiral Ruge and his new *Chef*, Hans Speidel. Gause will spend the next few days wrapping up loose ends and preparing to leave.

As Rommel walks out the side entrance into the courtyard, he sees a three-car convoy ready, along with escorting motorcycles and a small entourage. The third car is for the four reporters—well, war correspondents[1]—that are tagging along. In the trunk of the third vehicle are a number of special gifts for the men in the field. The field marshal is resuming his habit of handing out small, special tokens to any outstanding men who have made exceptionally good progress in their work. These tokens include harmonicas, concertinas,[2] or other nice trinkets.

Sometimes he gives away presents that have been sent to him by admirers back home. Occasionally, he will hand out packs of cigarettes or bags of cookies to those in the field as he asks them how they are doing or how their families are faring. For ranking officers, his gifts often include alcohol, of which he of course has little use for. If he finds out that a soldier comes from his native Württemberg, he will informally converse with them in their common Swabian dialect. They might share a laugh over a good joke, especially if only someone from that area would appreciate it. One of his favorites is, "What is the difference between a *'Schwab'* and a *'Schwob'*?" The answer is, "A *Schwob* is a *Schwab* who calls another *Schwab* a *Schwob*."[3]

Rommel briskly walks out through the main doors wearing his raincoat, baton in hand. Everyone is assembled around the shiny black vehicles, telling stories, talking about the war, or commenting on the weather. The war reporters have already taken the opportunity to engage the new chief of staff in conversation, feeling him out.

The field marshal comes down the steps and approaches the group chatting quietly next to the vehicles. He briefly greets each of them. Then they are off.

They leave La Roche-Guyon and head down river. Turning east at Rouen, they travel up to the coast and on to their first stop, the town of Ault. There they hold a conference with *General der Artillerie* Sinnhuber, commanding 67th Infantry Corps, one of his divisional commanders, *Generalleutnant* Paul Seyffardt, commanding the 348th Infantry, and their senior officers. Progress over the last three weeks has been significant, and the field marshal expresses satisfaction with the recent improvements, noting various types of obstacles set into the shoreline. He hands out three concertinas to the staff.

More inspections follow as they travel northeast up the coast. They stop around noon for lunch at St.-Valery-sur-Somme on the southern bank of the Somme estuary. Despite his rank, Rommel (and thus, his staff) settles for a simple meal from the local field kitchen. Wasting no time, they are off again, crossing the Somme, moving up the coast to the positions of the 344th Infantry, and then those of the 49th Infantry.[4]

Rommel's staff enjoy an amusing moment in the 49th Division area when the field marshal and his entourage come upon an unsuspecting guard. Startled, the man clearly is not expecting to be approached by so high-ranking and famous a general. Losing his composure and in a panic, he addresses the Desert Fox standing before him as *"Herr Major."* The field marshal wryly stares back at the guard and mercifully says nothing to him, although when he glances at Ruge a moment later, there is a twinkle in his eye.

At each stop, Rommel listens to more reports. The inspection party notes new obstacles, mines, and barriers up, but not nearly as many as they had seen earlier. More effort is obviously needed here. Rommel records in the army group's Daily Report:

> *The difference in the progress of the divisions in the completion of the offshore obstacles is astonishing and depends on the division commander's initiative.*

They finally stop at Le Touquet[5] for the night.

---

1 The reporters were famed Lutz Koch, 52-year-old *General der Infanterie* Hans Gert *Freiherr* von Esebeck, and two other reporters named Ertel and Podewils. The baron (as a newly-promoted *Generalmajor*) had in the spring of 1941 been given command of the 15th Panzer Division under Rommel in North Africa. Unfortunately, he was severely wounded in the face shortly thereafter and evacuated to Europe. Despite wanting to return to Africa, he was sent to Army Group Center on the Eastern Front, until he had in mid-February, 1944 been attached to *OB West* for "special duties." On April 1, he had been transferred to the Führer Reserve, and now served as a war reporter, sometimes accompanying Rommel on his tours.

2 See footnote for April 5.

3 *"Schwab"* was the regular, or high German term for a native of Swabia; *"Schwob"* [pronounced "Shwobe"] is the same term in the Swabian dialect.

4 *Generalleutnant* Felix Schwalbe commanding the 344th, and *Generalleutnant* Siegfried Macholz commanding the 49th.

5 Located next to the coast, about 20km south of Boulogne, on the southern bank of the Canche River.

Tuesday, April 18

Rommel, on an inspection tour along the northern French coast, is up early at his quarters in Le Touquet. Accompanying him, Ruge, and Speidel today, will be the local corps commander, General Sinnhuber.

The group gets an early start, beginning with *Generalmajor* Heinz Furbach's 331st Reserve Infantry Division, located in from the coast. After Furbach gives his status report, Rommel repeats his plans. Sure, he argues, it would be great if units did not have to move for a good 24 hours. But war is never fought under ideal conditions, and the men must be ready to react immediately.

They continue up the coast to the lovely, historic port of Boulogne, then around Cap Gris Nez, and onward to Otto Elfelt's 47th Infantry Division. Construction of offshore barriers here is coming along well, although for this area, stakes are more difficult to set than tetrahedrons because of offshore crosscurrents. Still, the 47th is luckier than most divisions along the coast, because it has its own 40-man concrete factory nearby. Even so, the firm is hard-pressed to keep up with demands for concrete supplies, and shortages often cause delays in shipments.

Rommel continues up the coast to Calais, where the High Command expects the Allies are most likely to land. Here, many formidable offshore barriers are well placed by now. The party stops for lunch, and then continues. As they move on, Rommel notes with satisfaction certain areas where man-made swamps have been created at spots along the shoreline, and in certain draws leading inland.

Still more inspections. The field marshal is relentless in his schedule. He is told that the 18th Luftwaffe Field Division[1] has had problems putting up anti-invasion barriers, mainly because there is just not enough help around. Most of the local residents have already moved away, "just in case." He suspects though, that part of the problem is their motivation. They are, after all, Luftwaffe personnel.

That day, Rommel notes in his diary:

> *Am carrying on with my inspection tour in the area of Calais, which I consider the most dangerous point. Here too, they could have achieved much more in strengthening our coastal defenses. I have indeed the feeling that the unit commanders have not yet recognized their responsibilities, which is the reason why I am so meticulous about details. I cannot stress enough to these commanders that it is in the West that the war will be decided.*

As the busy day stretches into the late afternoon, the inspection party finds itself approaching Dunkirk. They stop along the road that bypasses the town to admire the view. Dunkirk—where they had trapped the desperate British troops just four years ago, pushing them back into the sea. Now though, the small group stands and watches the port undergo an air raid.

They are mostly silent as they observe Allied bombers fly in, one wave after another, and make runs on the harbor facilities. The formations, coming in at 3,000 to 4,000 meters, meet a heavy curtain of accurate anti-aircraft fire as they approach their targets. Still, the awesome airpower of the enemy is certainly being brought home to all of them as the aircraft press on and the town gets pounded. Rommel marvels at how the explosions continue almost ceaselessly. If only the Reich still had that kind of power at its disposal…

Suddenly, one of the aides, acting as a lookout, shouts a warning, pointing excitedly out to sea. They all look out over the Channel where he is gesturing, Rommel with his binoculars. While they have been busy watching the bombers unloading over Dunkirk, a formation of some eighteen aircraft has peeled off from the next approaching main force and is now headed their way, seemingly focused directly on their own little group. Shouting directions to each other, the entourage scatters for cover.

A number of them run headlong into a ditch along the side of the road. General Sinnhuber groans loudly as he unfortunately lands on a pile of broken glass. Admiral Ruge and the new chief of staff get their uniforms scratched (to say nothing of their pride) as they scurry into some bushes and then struggle with the thorns. Naturally, sharp-eyed Rommel has found himself a nice thick patch of tall grass to disappear into.

Luckily for the group, no bombs come anywhere close to them, but they are rattled by the enemy aircraft passing low overhead. Embarrassed, they soon emerge from their hiding places, shaken up, rueful looks on their faces, cleaning or dusting themselves off. Rommel assures everyone that he is fine. Once again, they observe the continued bombing. The next wave approaches the town, and they note with smug satisfaction that a couple aircraft are shot down, landing in the sea. A few enemy air crewmen are lucky enough to bail out, and soon a harbor craft sails out to fetch them.

When the air raid finally ends, the disheveled spectators load up into their cars and continue on their way towards Neumann's 712th Grenadier Division.[2] They make their inspection and note with approval that a good deal of effort has been made here. They then continue on to *Generalleutnant* Casper's 48th Infantry[3] in the Ostende area. There the anti-invasion barriers are only being constructed in certain limited coastal areas. Rommel notes in his daily report:

> I was shaken to discover that entire strips of the coast… did not have any defense strongpoints whatsoever. If only commanders would travel more often, they would realize how much more there is to be done.

They stop for the night in the port of Breskens, splitting up to stay in different quarters. That evening, after rehashing the story of the enemy bombers outside Dunkirk, Rommel somberly reflects on the exercise of air power that he has today witnessed. It reconfirms for him what large numbers of aircraft can do to fortifications. And he knows what tactical bombers can do from personal experience, because he has personally been attacked by enemy aircraft several times. Most certainly he will be again.

How long will his famed luck hold out?

1 *Generalleutnant* Joachim von Tresckow, commanding. The 18th Luftwaffe Field Division was created in Soissons, France, under the command of *Oberst* Ferdinand-Wilhelm Freiherr von Stein-Liebenstein zu Barchfeld. It consisted of two Luftwaffe *jäger* regiments, an artillery regiment made up of captured Russian and French artillery, a small *panzerjäger* battalion, and some engineers. It was moved to its area between Dunkirk and Calais in April of the year before, assigned to the 82nd Corps. After the division was committed to battle in mid-August of 1944, it sustained substantial casualties, and OKW officially declared the 18th destroyed as a fighting unit on September 16.

2 Fifty-five-year-old *Generalleutnant* Friedrich Wilhelm Neumann, commanding. Neumann took over command in April 1942.

3 Fifty-one-year-old *Generalleutnant* Karl Casper, who took over at the beginning of February. The 48th was created on February 1 in Holland from the 171st Reserve Division.

Wednesday, April 19

It is a lovely but brisk spring day. Rommel, in the Belgian port of Breskens, is up early, as usual. A quick breakfast at his assigned quarters, and then he and his group are off. They assemble at 7 a.m. at the docks. They meet 89th Corps commander General von Gilsa and the local port commander, *Kapitän-zur-See* Frank Aschmann.[1]

The weather is cold, and an easterly wind has buffeted water out of the Scheldt. Because of this low water level, the "flagship" of the area, an armed yacht called the *Sarah* (supposedly once owned by ex-Prime Minister Neville Chamberlain), cannot carry them out to Vlissingen on Walcheren Island as planned, since its deep draft prevents it from crossing over to get them. The group must take the ferry. The waters are choppy, so the ride over is a bit rough.

They disembark and are taken to Vlissingen, where the conferences begin with Aschmann. While he has nothing prepared, he is acquainted enough with his island command to be able to answer questions. Rommel is satisfied with him.

Next comes *Generalmajor* Wilhelm Daser, commanding the 165th Reserve Infantry. He reports that over half of the 500 bunkers planned have been finished.

Rommel sees a number of problems. There are shortages that could have rectified by von Gilsa a while ago had he exercised better management. The new version "nutcracker" mine is just being started up here, and they are being laid too thinly and in some spots too close to the naval batteries. The concussion of the guns firing might accidently set them off.

Also, the unit commanders do not seem totally committed to his stop-them-on-the-beaches doctrine. Calmly and clearly, he spells out what he expects of them. One particularly slow army artillery commander is given a "heart-to-heart" talk by the field marshal.

They go back over to Breskens at 11 a.m. on the *Sarah*. Admiral Ruge is somewhat nervous during the crossing, because as they travel across the Scheldt, he notices that an enemy reconnaissance aircraft is spying on them. Yesterday's run-in with the enemy bombers outside Dunkirk is no doubt still fresh in his mind. Rommel is not worried, but they are all thankful when they make it back over without incident.

They depart southward for Brugge for another conference with 48th Division commander General Casper. Then they have lunch at the soldiers' mess.

As they eat, they listen to the radio. As is his custom, Rommel wants to hear the BBC newscast. A few of the men dining nearby are pleased that their field marshal will listen to an enemy radio broadcast with them.

National pride notwithstanding, they, like him, do realize that this can be a primary source of intelligence. General information about the war for line commanders is hard to come by, particularly now that the war is going against Germany.[2] Rommel has often in the past been attached to OKW and was thus privy to all the military activities of the Third Reich. Now though, he is cut off and badly informed about the general progress on the war. So he regularly listens to enemy radio broadcasts to glean some idea (even if it is colored by the Allies) of what is happening on the other fronts, and to get a sense of how his enemy is feeling.

That afternoon, they travel south some 66km to Tourcoing. There, Rommel visits *Generaloberst* von Salmuth in his quarters. The Fifteenth Army commander is laid up in bed with the flu, and Rommel wishes him well.

The inspection party goes on, traveling west another 60km towards an army base at Hazebrouck, where they are to watch some drills. There is some trouble getting into the area though, since the gate guard does not know who Rommel is and incredibly, seems never to have heard of him. He finally relents, after Rommel threatens to have him beaten.

The inspection tour continues southward, and finally returns to La Roche-Guyon, arriving there at 8 p.m. Rommel, tired from the trip, retires for the evening. Admiral Ruge soon joins the two chiefs of staff—soon-to-be relieved Gause and incoming Dr. Speidel—for some inspiring conversation. Gause recalls an action he took in late 1942, and Speidel recounts a harrowing incident in Russia. They talk about the war, and how badly it is going…

In his quarters, Rommel, before he goes to bed, records his latest frustrations with bureaucratic red tape:

> *I discovered shortages which could have been overcome had the local commander shown more initiative. This is additional proof that only there where I personally intervened and issued orders, has the steam been put on.*
>
> *Indeed, a point has been reached where written orders are no longer taken into consideration. Only there where I personally—often with an outburst of anger—have directed things, is something being done. This is sad and beyond the realm of military discipline, when one has to watch upon the execution of each order; but there is nothing else that I can do…*

Today, a special conference on aircraft production is held at the Berghof. Attending are Reichsmarshal, General Milch the Air Armament Secretary, and several senior Luftwaffe generals. Göring and Milch, by now bitter enemies, have had several sharp words the night before, so are today cold towards each other. They discuss the construction of underground bombproof aircraft factories, especially for the new Me-262 jet fighters. Göring to cover himself mournfully adds that he had wanted this some eight months before. "All this could have been ready long ago," he sighs.

---

1   Aschmann, the senior naval officer on Walcheren, carried the title of Sea Defense Commander for South Holland (See footnote for Tuesday, January 4.)

2   General war information had been scarce ever since early 1940 and the so-called Mechelen Incident. At the time, the Western Allies and Germany had been in the stagnant, so-called "phony war" since the end of the Polish campaign. Then on January 10, with planning for the invasion of France and the Low Countries in its final stage preparation, a Luftwaffe staff officer, one Major Hellmuth Reinberger, took off as the back passenger in a BF-108 *Taifun* ("Typhoon"—predecessor to the ME-109) for Köln. He carried with him several highly classified documents, including maps,

detailing the entire airborne component of the upcoming invasion of the Lowlands, scheduled to begin in one week. His pilot, Major Erich Hoenmann, became lost in thick winter fog and heavy clouds, so he descended to get a better view of the ground and possibly pick up a landmark. While standing up in his seat to get a better look at the river below (which he thought was the Rhine), he accidentally hit the plane's fuel switch, cutting off the engine's fuel supply. The engine sputtered and quit on them. Forced down, the pilot crash-landed at 11:30 a.m. on the east bank of the river below. After talking to a peasant passing by though, they found out to their horror that they had not come down next to the Rhine, but next to the Maas (Meuse) River instead, just inside the Belgian–Dutch border.

Reinberger then told his shocked pilot the nature of his top-secret documents, and that they had to destroy them at once. He ran into some nearby bushes to do so. He started a fire using a match (borrowed from the farmer when his own lighter did not work). Unfortunately though, a Belgian border patrol stumbled onto the scene. The pilot walked back to the plane to divert the patrol so that Reinberger could finish his task. The patrol, initially distracted by the pilot, right off spotted the smoke, and captured Reinberger in the act of burning his documents. The two were taken to the nearby military guard post for interrogation. Reinberger once more tried to destroy the remaining documents. He suddenly grabbed them and, lifting the very hot lid of a pot-bellied stove, he threw them in. The Belgian police captain though, Captain Arthur Rodrique, hearing him cry in pain, quickly seized them (burning his own hands in the process) and managed to recover ten burned pages of detailed plans, including a few sections of maps showing planned preemptive airborne drops.

Outraged, the Belgian government accused Germany to the world of deliberately planning aggression. They defiantly called up their reserves and quickly manned their border defenses. The French mobilized three armies. Hitler, seething with rage over this blunder, ordered the two men condemned to death (as prisoners though, they of course would not be executed) and fired General Hellmuth Felmy, the commander of 2. *Luftflotte*, and his chief of staff, Colonel Josef Kammhuber. Hitler eventually was forced to call off the invasion of the 19th and subsequently tried desperately to reassure the Belgians that he had no intention of invading their country. As a result of this leak, he also issued a directive on January 11, 1940 and ordered it posted in every headquarters. It stated in no uncertain terms that no German officer, agency, command—*no one*—was to have any knowledge of an operation in which he was not directly concerned or did not have absolute need to know. Security was to be the word from then on.

Both captured majors were evacuated first to Britain and then to Canada. Hoenmann's wife Annie, however, did not fare so well. The Gestapo, suspecting that the two men were traitors and were deliberately betraying their country, arrested her and subjected her to an intense, humiliating interrogation, one that she did not long survive. Their two sons were allowed to serve in the army, but were killed in action during the war.

One last interesting note. Many sources state that Hitler, his strategy now foiled, was forced to come up with an entirely new plan. A direct result of this incident was a revised plan, the final, brilliant *Fall Gelb* ("Case Yellow"), in which the Germans faked their original invasion plan and struck with their main force instead in the dense Ardennes, both bypassing the Maginot Line on the left and outflanking the BEF on the right. As it turned out, this change proved decisive in the fall of France.

Thursday, April 20

General der Panzertruppen Heinz Guderian leaves for France to attend a number of conferences there with the senior commanders. The main topic, of course, will be disposition of the panzers.

***

Generalfeldmarschall Rommel stays at La Roche-Guyon today, catching up on paperwork and chairing a number of sessions with his staff. They cover a wide variety of subjects, including the distribution of an incoming supply of "nutcracker" mines,[1] manufacturing more tetrahedrons, the areas along the coast where they are needed, and the repositioning of several coastal units.

When evening comes, the headquarters shifts into a festive mood. First of all, it is Alfred Gause's going-away party, and the staff has really put forth an effort to make this a festive occasion. Second, it is the Führer's birthday, now a national holiday, so the more celebrating that is done, the better it looks to outsiders.

The Duc du Rochefoucauld and his family, residing upstairs, above the noisy routine of this busy headquarters, have been invited to the evening's festivity, and they have graciously accepted the invitation. The duke's younger son, dressed in the uniform of the French Navy, calls on Admiral Ruge. As the admiral treats the young man to some tasty confections, he is told that the duchess would like a word with him. He goes to the main stairway to meet her, and soon she regally descends with some gifts for the party—a bouquet of lilac and four bottles of her best wine, a vintage 1900 claret.

The celebration begins. In attendance are Rommel, his senior staff officers, most of the army group administrative staff, and tonight's guests: the duke and his family, including their daughter Charlotte (who is proudly escorted by a number of Rommel's junior officers).

After a fine dinner, Rommel stands up and graciously addresses his audience. He prefaces his remarks with a set of well-intended congratulatory comments, recognizing the Führer's birthday, and noting the strength that their leader has given their country.

He then begins an oratory on the finer qualities of his outgoing chief of staff. He tells them of the struggles the two of them have endured together in the French campaign, and later in North Africa. Rommel of course outlines Gause's many and varied accomplishments during this time with great fervor, sometimes describing in detail a particular episode, or dramatically recounting some tale of woe that had befallen them.

At the end of his speech, after the applause finally dies down, Gause stands and addresses the field marshal. He tells Rommel what a privilege it has been serving a German legend (Rommel is embarrassed), and that he has enjoyed working with all of them. Formally recognizing members of the Kriegsmarine and the Luftwaffe, he beseeches them to strive to work together against the enemy, and to resist trifling power squabbles.

The final speaker is their Ia, *Oberstleutnant* von Tempelhoff, who puts in a few choice words welcoming the new chief of staff. He then expresses hope on behalf of the staff that Gause finds happiness in his future and satisfaction in his next assignment. Rumor has it that, based on Rommel's recommendation, Gause is going to get command of his own panzer division.

Then the "unofficial" part of the evening begins. In a now-relaxed mood, and amidst a roar of cheers and whistles, Gause is informed that, after careful consideration by the staff members, he has been elected the "Tetrach[2] of the Tetragoner," with a fancy (though unrefined) swamp ribbon, featuring a dark blue coat of arms with two Czech hedgehogs on it.

In the meantime, a choice set of musicians begin playing a number of popular songs, and melodious sound fills the halls of the château. The duke's daughter Charlotte becomes the life of the party and is waltzed around the dancing area many times by keen young officers. The senior officers spend their time happily conversing as they sip fine wine, laughing and enjoying sparkling conversation.

Even though there is work to be done the next day, the party does not wind down until about two in the morning—unusual for the staff, but appropriate for the occasion.

***

It is indeed the Führer's birthday. Today he turns 55, and the entire Reich is encouraged to commemorate this holiday. At the Berghof though, Hitler is depressed and does little to celebrate, what with the war going so badly and his health not so good. In a nice ceremony, with some pretty flower arrangements and decorations in the great hall, he stands next to an ever-watching Martin Bormann while over a hundred people wait in line to congratulate him on his birthday. Also attending are Göring and Admiral Dönitz. Still, he woodenly goes through the motions.

Staff photographer Walter Frentz takes a few photos of him with some close friends: Eva Braun and her sister Gretl, Herta Schneider, Martin Bormann, Otto Dietrich, Dr. von Hasselbach, one of his personal surgeons Dr. Karl Brandt and his wife Anni… The Führer's official photographer, Heinrich Hoffmann, a popular jokester, tries to keep the mood upbeat, but that does not work.

They move into the dining hall for the presents. Hoffmann shows everyone a new painting for the Führer's priceless collection, as many of the entourage look on.

As part of the ceremony, the Führer decorates one-armed General Hans Hube,[3] commander of the First Panzer Army, for extracting his encircled army from the clutches of the Soviets. Although the II SS Panzer Corps had helped rescue his army, his energies and valor were, the Führer happily says, what mainly counted.

Hube, nicknamed by his men "*der Mensch*" ("the Man"), managed to extricate nearly 300,000 men out of what became known as the "Hube Pocket" (the Russians call it the "Kaments-Podolsky pocket"). Hube is being awarded the Knight's Cross with Diamonds and is being promoted to *Generaloberst* for his valor, not just recently in the Hube Pocket, but also back in Sicily and Salerno. The Führer tells everyone that the man is in his mind, a true leader, and a prime candidate to become the next commander of the German *Heeres*.

Hitler perks up more when he and his entourage leave the villa and travel to Klessheim Castle in Salzburg to view a small parade of new weapons. Included in the display is the new Czech T-38 *Jagdpanzer*, and a modified version of the Vomag *Jagdpanzer IV*.[4]

Back in the castle, the socializing continues into the early morning hours. Finally after a good deal of leisure talk, decorated General Hube begs the Führer's leave, and requests permission to fly back to Berlin that evening on "personal" matters. Hitler affably agrees, adding that although the general's pilot is not very experienced at night flying, an experienced aircrew is at hand to back him up. All possible safety measures will be taken to ensure that the aircraft reaches Berlin safely.

***

In reality, very few others in the Reich really celebrate Hitler's birthday today, other than high government leaders. Most observe it, but few celebrate it—except of course, the fervent Nazi followers. Goebbels' radio address to the Reich of course is a fresh attempt at rousing the people to the national banner. His speech ends with a stirring tribute:

> We all wish him health and strength and a blessed hand. He must know that he can always rely on his people. When trial and danger is before him, we will stand more firmly behind him. We believe in him and in his historical mission, and believe that in the end he will be crowned with victory.
>
> He will be the man of the century, not his opponents. He gave this century its meaning, its content, its goal. Affirming the meaning and understanding the content, we will reach the goal.
>
> He points the way; He commands, we follow. We, his old and tested comrades, march in the first row behind him. We are tested by danger, steeled by misfortune, hardened by storm and trial, but also crowned with the first victories and successes of the coming new world.
>
> We are at the head of a countless multitude who carry and defend the future of the Reich. We defend the cause of the nation, which has found its visible form in the Führer.
>
> In this battle between life and death, he is and will remain for us what he always was: Our Hitler!

---

1 See entry for February 16.
2 The source here is Admiral Ruge. This term is probably either a misprint or a spelling variant. The admiral probably meant "tetrarch," a subordinate ruler. The term, originating in Ancient Greece

and later taken up by the Roman Empire, refers to a unit commander. A tetrarch commanded a quarter of a Greek phalanx.

3   *General der Panzertruppen* Hans-Valentin Hube. Born in Naumburg, Germany, on October 29, 1880. He entered the army and served throughout World War I. Just after the start of hostilities, he was seriously wounded in Northern France and lost his left arm. He recovered in a year and fought again, suffering again in 1918, this time from a poison gas attack. Hube, seriously wounded again during the invasion of Poland, still took part in every major campaign thereafter, becoming a prominent Panzer general. Hube was evacuated from Stalingrad on January 19 1943, only a few days before von Paulus surrendered the Sixth Army. He took a significant part in the defense of Sicily and later Salerno in 1943, before later taking command of 1st Panzer Army.

4   The *Jagdpanzer 38(t)* (Sd. Kfz. 138/2), was an excellent light tank destroyer, built on a modified chassis of the popular Czech Panzer 38(t) (which went out of production because its small turret could not accommodate a large gun needed to knock out later Allied tank models). Cheaper and easier to build than other tank destroyer models such as the *Jagdpanther* and *Jagdtiger,* its simple design made it mechanically popular, and its 75mm PaK 39 L/48 gun gave it the ability to destroy nearly all Allied tanks in service at long ranges (except heavy tanks). The model was later nicknamed by the troops the *hetzer* ("baiter").

The *Jagdpanzer IV* was one of the better light (26 tons) tank destroyers built during the war, entering production in January, 1944. Built on a *PzKw IV* chassis, it had a low, sloped silhouette and carried a high-velocity 75mm gun mounted directly in the fixed superstructure. Since it had no turret, a turret engine was not needed. The unit could thus carry up to 55 rounds, and was organized into anti-tank battalions for the panzer and SS panzer divisions.

Friday, April 21

It is early morning at La Roche-Guyon. The merriment of the previous evening is over. Gause attends a quiet, somber last breakfast with the staff that he will shortly be leaving. Rommel is already gone, having left earlier on an inspection tour. The festive air is long gone, replaced by an atmosphere heavy with unsaid comments, apprehension, and depression. Gause, nervous and upset, finally departs the château at 7:30 a.m. He is bound for the French capital to catch a train.[1]

After he leaves, his replacement, Hans Speidel, busies himself by taking care of a number of administrative details. OB West has approved the movement of the 77th Infantry Division to Brittany, specifically to the St. Malo area. It has also consented (only in theory) to allow the 21st Panzer Division to move from Rennes to an area between the towns of Flers and Argentan, south of Falaise, and some 65km southeast of the Bay of the Seine. OB West reports the approval as a *fait accompli* to OKW "in order to save time," although actual permission has not yet been officially given.

Power games…

As Gause discreetly leaves the château, Admiral Ruge departs in that direction as well to meet up with Rommel at a fortress engineering depot—the Hoyer factory. He finds the field marshal watching a demonstration of engineering contrivances. Modified mines and updated explosive devices are displayed. A number of new and makeshift devices are shown as well, a couple ingenious, a few crude, and some a product of sincere but uninformed minds. While a considerable amount of the time spent on fashioning these makeshift devices did not produce any substantial return, Rommel realizes that such is the nature of research. He later writes in his Daily Report:

> (W)e're badly equipped and should therefore take advantage of all help which technical knowledge can give us. For, against a strong weapon superiority, it is no longer enough to oppose [it with] the courage of our soldiers…

While he is in the factory, the air raid sirens go off. The deep blue sky is filled with condensation trails of the enemy bombers, but the bomb hits are distant and do not do much damage.

That afternoon, Rommel returns to the château and finds himself involved with, of all things, a women's issue. Supposedly, some time back, he had decided that all women up to the age of fifty were to be used on defensive barrier construction details, and he had given instructions to that effect. Now he finds out that a complaint has reached OB West from Daser's 165th Reserve Infantry Division area about women being forced to work on the barriers. A message received from Daser states that permission for such use of women can only come from OB West, since using women this way technically violates the 1940 armistice agreement.

Rommel, shaking his head, thinks about the situation a bit. He then calls OB West himself and talks to Blumentritt. He tells him that they have been using women quite successfully in the 348th Division sector to make "Rommel's asparagus." And these willing "volunteers" are getting paid quite well for their work. Rommel adds that anyway, he had not actually ordered this practice. He had only recommended it to his unit commanders, that's all. Evidently, the people at the 165th Reserve must have misunderstood him… No general, there is no such edict forcing women to work on the barriers.

Of course, if the SS had their way…

That night, he finishes a letter to Lucie that he had started the night before (the party had delayed him). In it, he writes about the two dachshunds, Ajax (now home with Lucie) and Elbo (at the château with him):

> *…Aldinger should bring Ajax along. I'll exchange him for a real hunting dog. The little one is too cute, but not quite housebroken. I'll send him to you later. Yesterday, he tore my pants for joy. Or do you want him right away?*

The field marshal is having Elbo problems.

***

In the late morning, just after he has awakened, Hitler is informed that on the way back to the front from his promotion ceremony, General Hube's Junkers flew into a mountain right after takeoff, just outside of Salzburg. He is dead.[2]

Shocked at the news, Hitler becomes quiet and somber, understandably depressed. He orders a state funeral for his remains[3] at the Reich Chancellery. The Führer will attend, as will the senior leaders of the Reich.

During the day, bombers from the Eighth Air Force bomb the vital railroad marshaling yard in Hamm, Germany. The largest such yard in Europe, it sits at the entry to the Ruhr valley industrial complex. The raids will leave the yards crippled for the rest of the war.

---

1   Gause about a week after D-Day was reassigned as chief of staff to one of Rommel's main critics, Geyr von Schweppenburg at *PanzerGruppe West*.

2   Most historians confirm that Hube was killed when the plane crashed into a mountain outside Salzburg. Some accounts state that he was headed back to his command at Army Group South. Yet still others state that Hube was badly injured in the crash while on his way back to Berlin and died soon after in a hospital.

3   The wrecked aircraft was so ravaged by fire that only Hube's charred, blackened artificial arm was recovered.

Saturday, April 22

This morning, Rommel awakens to the sound of raindrops gently pattering on his windowpanes and on the walkway outside his bedroom. These days, he loves the sound of rain. It is his ally. Silently he gives thanks for another day of bad weather. It is a sure sign that the enemy is not coming. At least, not today.

After breakfast, Rommel gets a visit from one General Kanzler, who reports on various problems with mine production. OB West has now focused attention on this as well (based on Rommel's investigation into this problem, he notes), and is working on starting up some new mine-producing facilities.

Despite Rommel's hopes for continued bad weather, a few hours later, the sun comes out, so his staff enjoy a quiet Saturday afternoon. There are very few phone calls, and it seems that not much seems to be going on. One morning report though, mentions a number of bridges in France and Belgium having been attacked by low-level fighter-bombers.

Today, *Heeresgruppe B* sends a detailed report to OKW on their progress so far along the coast. Rommel addresses the problem of units not cooperating. He writes:

> … (H)ere and there I noticed units that do not seem to have recognized the graveness of the hour, and some who do not even follow instructions. There are reports of cases in which my orders that all minefields on the beach should be alive at all times have not been obeyed. A commander of a lower unit gave an order to the contrary.
>
> In other cases, my orders have been postponed to later dates, or even changed. Reports from some sectors say that they intend to try to put one of my orders into effect, and that they would start doing so the following day. Some units knew my orders, but did not make any preparations to execute them.
>
> I give orders only when they are necessary. I expect them to be executed at once, and to the letter, and that no unit under my command shall make changes, still less give orders, to the contrary, or delay execution through unnecessary paperwork.

He also states that there is still a good deal to be done. He then issues a message to the men in his army group:

> We must succeed in the short time left until the offensive starts, in bringing all defenses to such a standard that they will hold up against the strongest attack. Never in history was there a defense of such an extent, with such an obstacle as the sea. The enemy must be annihilated before he reaches our main battlefield!

That evening, he receives an extremely interesting report. One of the few German recon planes that they have left flew a mission today (and actually survived). Around sunset, the aircraft discovered a convoy of over two dozen enemy vessels some five kilometers east of Dover. Half of the vessels were landing craft; the other half were mostly escorts.

So! The Allies are getting ready, are they? A surge of energy wells up within him. Well, he will be ready too.

It seems as though this force was carrying out some type of landing exercise. It must be a practice run, or else many more vessels would have been spotted. Rommel tells his staff to get further details. His officers are to press intelligence services for more information, but it will probably not do them much good. Now that Himmler's Gestapo has assimilated the army's Abwehr branch,[1] the quality of their intelligence reports, mediocre for the last year or so, has now taken a nose-dive. It is no great secret, either. Himmler's agents appear to be blundering clods, lacking the finesse, patience, aptitude, resources, or experience needed to gather quality information in the field. They jump on any rumor like eager bloodhounds, and Rommel has to smile when he imagines the Allied intelligence department heads laughing over some crazy red herring of theirs that the Gestapo might be investigating *en masse.*

No, as unsatisfactory as the old army counterintelligence agency had been, it had been a far sight more reliable than the inept SS staffs doing the work now. And the enemy is taking full advantage of the change, because more rumors than ever before have begun coming down the pipe.

Maybe the enemy will broadcast news about this exercise themselves, though it seems unlikely. Still, they seem shockingly good sometimes at tooting their own horns. So that evening, Rommel and his staff listen to the BBC for any hint of an exercise (or a landing), but the radio does not yield a thing.

If only they could get some real photo reconnaissance flights over there...

***

Today, Hitler meets Mussolini as his guest at Klessheim Castle in Salzburg. The *Duce* is in a foul mood, depressed, and demoralized. They talk about the situation in the West and of course, in Italy. Mussolini's ill humor becomes even darker when Hitler tells him that the Allies will probably start another offensive in Italy in the next six to eight weeks. Hitler tries to cheer him up by promising at that time to let loose new technical weapons that will rip into the English cities and turn London in to a pile of ruins. Still, when the meeting finally breaks up, the *Duce* does not at all seem convinced.

---

1   See entries for February 9 and February 11.

Sunday, April 23

Panzer Inspector-General Heinz Guderian is on tour in Northern Europe, visiting and inspecting the panzer units there. Today he is at Mailly-le-Camp, near the city of Rheims. There he talks to a number of panzer commanders about replacements, tactics, and general well-being. He will stay here a few days, before he goes on to Paris to call on Rommel and von Rundstedt.

***

It is another quiet day at La Roche-Guyon. There is no further word on the exercise convoy spotted the day before, as Rommel catches up on paperwork and makes a few phone calls.

Today, he tries once again to convert a "heathen" to his way of thinking. He writes a letter to Alfred Jodl about the necessity of having the mobile reserves close to the coast. Clearly, the decisions that had been made back at the Führer's conference in late March are not being implemented. His letter, he hopes, states what he has been preaching for months now (and the Führer had agreed with in March), concepts that he sincerely feels are correct. Once the invasion occurs, enemy airpower will paralyze their columns. Surely Jodl must see that. He writes:

> Provided we succeed in bringing our mechanized divisions into action in the very first few hours, then I'm convinced that the enemy assault on our coast will be completely defeated on the very first day...
> Contrary to what was agreed on March 20, however, they have still not been put under my control and they're lying too far back from the coast, widely dispersed.

Candidly, he refers to his clash on the 10th with von Schweppenburg:

> I've had some hard words with Geyr about all this, and I can only get my own way if he is put under my orders in good time.

He concludes:

> Failing the early engagement of all our mobile forces in the battle for the coast, victory will be in grave doubt. If I have to wait for the enemy invasion actually to _occur_ before I'm allowed to submit through routine channels an application for the panzer divisions to come under my orders and move forward, then they'll probably arrive too late.

Later in the day, he goes outside with his aide to unwind, take a walk, and enjoy the beautiful weather. He relishes this time before the storm, this period of quiet solitude before the war again savagely erupts in front of him.

He starts out tramping through the woods with a well-made shotgun under his arm and Lang at his side. It feels good to get out of the headquarters, and just go walking around the forest behind the château. It is a beautiful day, and the woods are alive with the rebirth of spring.

Clomping along in his boots, relaxed in spirit, his blue eyes darting everywhere as he takes in all the splendor of the afternoon, he is moved by the remarkable contrast of this enchanting scene with the horrors of war. Still, he feels an uneasiness in the pit of his stomach as the remembrance of the enormous responsibilities he carries comes back to him. If he loses this time, his country will be destroyed, because he knows that Hitler will never give up until every town in Germany is blasted to rubble. And if that happens, the name of Erwin Rommel will not after all go down as being a legendary leader. He will be lucky if he is not court martialed.

He mentions this to Lang, who promptly disagrees with him. He is a hero now, and always will be.

Rommel smiles at this blatantly loyal remark. Looking at Lang, he remarks, "How peaceful the world seems. And yet, what hatred there is against us. In an atmosphere like this, one cannot imagine that a war is on. And yet. It's upon me that the heavy responsibilities of the coming events will rest."

He pauses, and then continues. "To have responsibility is all right, but one can only withstand the judgment of history if one is successful. History takes account only of those who know victory. There is no art in being a warlord for a wealthy country that is richly endowed with all the materials for war."

"But I," he concludes, "I have to be satisfied with what little I've got, and try to defeat the enemy with only the most modest means."

He looks around at the woods, thinking about the ever-advancing Soviet armies. "And defeated they must be, if Bolshevism is not to triumph over us. Even then, supposing that we've defeated Great Britain and the United States; the war with Russia won't be over, because it has such enormous resources of men and raw materials. The war will go on."

He stops and gazes up at the treetops. "Perhaps though, perhaps then a United Europe will come forward to fight this enemy."

Rommel falls silent as Lang furiously scribbles the field marshal's words.

Neither of them knows that Rommel has just envisioned the Cold War.

Monday, April 24

At the Berghof in lower Bavaria, Albert Speer, Minister of Armaments, visits his depressed Führer. The war is still going badly in Italy and in the East. General Hube has just been killed in a plane crash, and the Führer's production heads, Speer included, are squabbling over who is responsible for what weapons, and why new Luftwaffe design production is stymied. Hitler has tried to clear the air of their differences, only to have Speer threaten to resign. Now the two make up. Hitler tells him to reorganize any way he thinks is best.

***

After a quick breakfast, Rommel leaves on another inspection tour. This time, he is on his way to check out units around the Seine estuary. For this occasion, since his driver Daniel is indisposed, Rommel drives his Horch himself. The second car carries Admiral Ruge, *Oberst* Freyberg,[1] and a war correspondent. Ruge's car struggles to keep up with the lead-footed field marshal, and the two cars finally part company at the outskirts of the ruins of Rouen, hit hard in recent weeks by Allied bombers.

Ruge and Freyberg stop in the city to call on *Vizeadmiral* Rieve, commanding the Kriegsmarine forces along the *Kanalküste*. There they spend a couple hours discussing the various target priorities for the naval batteries whenever the invasion comes. Rieve seems optimistic, especially in light of the defensive construction effort up until now.

In the meantime, Rommel, having driven on, visits various positions of Erwin Menny's 84th Reserve Division, located near Yvetot.[2] He instructs the units to move away from village positions, especially the unit's artillery. Otherwise, they would make easy targets for Allied *Jabos*.

By noon, Rommel is at Crasville-la-Rocquefort, some 28km north, where he is rejoined by Ruge and Freyberg. They dine there at a regimental headquarters before moving on southwest towards Le Havre. They stop and note an army battery of a half dozen 150mm guns that were hit in an air raid. To speed up work, a number of the tetrahedrons had been moved about during their handling and subsequently damaged. The inspection uncovers a few areas devoid of defensive barriers, especially across some coastal ravines. Again, Rommel shows the men there his unpleasant side as he harshly orders the local commanding officers to quickly rectify their problems. With the mood the field marshal is in, it is just as well that a cold fog rolling in from the Channel ends the local inspections.

The inspection party moves on to Le Havre, where they go over the defensive positions there, inspect the shore batteries, and tour the minesweeper flotillas with the sea commandant and the newly-appointed port commander.[3] Rommel likes what he sees, and his mood changes from irritated to pleasant.

That evening, they have dinner and some stimulating table talk at the port's enlisted mess hall. Rommel turns in early.

***

Von Rundstedt in his weekly estimate to OKW expresses concern that the "danger zone" for the invasion includes an area that stretches some 300 kilometers, from Caen northeast to the Scheldt estuary in Belgium.

***

Today, General Guderian spends another day at Mailly-le-Camp, near Rheims, visiting with more of his panzer commanders.

---

1   Freyberg was the IIa, the headquarters adjutant.
2   A small inland town about 52km by car southwest of Dieppe, or about 62km northeast of Le Havre.
3   Seeko Seine-Somme *Konteradmiral* von Treskow and the *Hako Le Havre*, 50-year-old *Generalmajor* Johannes "Hans" Sauerbray.

Tuesday, April 25

Today it is bright and sunny. In the port of Le Havre, Rommel is up as usual at the crack of dawn. Over breakfast, he talks with his accompanying staff members. Goodheartedly, they joke about yesterday's fog cutting short their inspections. Ravines, they decide, are to be cordoned off with barbed wire and anti-tank obstacles. Further inland, they can be defended just with infantry. Ruge points out that it would be a waste of labor fashioning steel barriers in areas of quicksand.

At 7 a.m., they are off. They first inspect the support positions of General Diestel's 346th Infantry Division.[1] Rommel is generally satisfied with the overall progress the division has made. He notes that a good deal more of his "asparagus" has been put up in open fields.

At divisional headquarters near Bolbec, he listens to Diestel's report, and then decides to address the men on defensive measures against airborne landings. His speech is unrehearsed, although the ideas are firm in his head.

"We will have to think in a very modern way," he explains to them. "You commanders will have to keep in step with all of the new technical developments. What can *we* do, you might ask."

He stands facing the men. "Well, we'll have to shape the ground around us in such a way as to inflict a defeat on the enemy during the landing phase. We cannot just rely on our artillery; artillery is only a coarse tool for striking at them."

He takes a couple steps, his hands behind him. "We must be ready at any time. Unfortunately, cooperation with the early warning service is still not perfect. We have to expect that the enemy will use the most advanced methods of battle against us.

"For example, they might try an airborne landing at night, just as they did in Burma—and yet, in the end, we will still win." He emphasizes those last words. "Like a cunning hunter, we will have to patiently lie in wait for the wild birds descending from the air."

He stops pacing and again faces the men. He makes a fist.

"Utilize the labor power of the local population. Pay them at once for work that they have rendered. Generally, use your personal charm and prestige on them. Sell them on the idea that there'll be less chance of an enemy landing where much work has been done."

"If you need wood, take trees from the villages. The troops will be moving out of them anyway. Remember, wire is scarce. If you must, use fence wire, and replace it later with supplies as they arrive. What is of greatest importance is that you pay for everything at once; not after weeks or months. The average farmer is glad if he has money to put in his purse."

He points his finger at the men. "*No forced recruitment.* I want only laborers who are indirectly recruited. And be considerate of your labor force. Try to keep their spirits up. Have the workers sing on their way to work. Do try to convince them that the work they do will assure them of their own security."

"Look," he continues as he begins to pace again. "The enemy will have a confoundedly difficult time getting out of the water. Then the moment will come when he tries to attack us from the rear. Remember: no counterattacks without artillery support!" His hand pounds his fist as he speaks. "Otherwise, our losses will be heavy. We must continue to fire! Fire! *Fire!*"

He pauses and looks at the men with burning eyes. "You commanders, make your officers versatile enough to be able to fight against airborne troops and panzer formations. An officer out there will have to know that. Experience has shown us that saturation bombing destroys our field positions. Dugouts are useless; so the best field solution is to place your men in widely spaced Hube holes.² Don't dig in along a line on the perimeter, but dig widely dispersed positions in the open fields. A good regimental commander will have to be with his troops in the field. They'll need you to steady them against an airborne attack."

He pauses and gazes at those officers in front. "Imagine," he says, "what it will look like to them. Imagine! Try to envision swarms of locusts falling out of a moonlit sky. They'll be all over you. So help your men—lead them. Show them by example. That's how we will win."

As he goes to sit down, they began applauding him. How could they not? His speeches in countless locations before now have boosted the morale of the men he addressed. This group is no different, and they cheer the Desert Fox for several minutes. Embarrassed, he finally excuses himself to go outside to watch an anti-tank exercise with self-propelled guns. The demonstration thankfully goes well. Yes, his men are learning. It has been, on the whole, a gratifying morning for him, and he is in good spirits.

He pauses to point out some new construction that needs camouflaging. Otherwise, he is content with their progress, enough so that he gives out as a reward a couple of concertinas.

At lunch, his good mood stays with him, and he reminisces with the attending men about his adventures as divisional commander in this area during the French campaign of 1940. He entertains them with a story about leading his panzer recon battalion as they smashed through a French division.

"I told them to hit the enemy hard, and to start shooting in all directions." And they did, firing their guns as they rumbled through the enemy lines. He tells them about how they rolled into the town of Petit Dalles, surprising the commander of an enemy artillery unit. They laugh good-naturedly as Rommel describes how they captured the French officer while he was taking a bath and getting ready to sit down to a plate of just-cooked fried chicken.

His audience eager for more, he continues. The next day, his *panzergrenadiers* assaulted the town of Fécamp on the coast, but were ultimately driven back by naval gunfire support from a couple enemy destroyers.[3] Rommel regrouped his men and took the town the next day, this time attacking it from the south, and away from the enemy vessels.

His next big engagement was at St.-Valéry-en-Caux, where the fighting was bitter. The enemy, entrenched on some steep cliffs, put up a formidable fight, protecting men being evacuated in the town. He finally overcame the enemy troops by concentrating his firepower on the strongest positions.[4] He goes on as the men listen to him intently, reveling with him in these old days of German glory.

He pauses and looks around him. He is out from the aura of past glory and returned to the harsh reality of now. Back then they had been bold and daring. Now they are desperate. Four years ago, his greatest warriors were at the front of his columns. Now, most of them are dead, captured, or starving on the Eastern Front. It seems that interspersed with some recuperated, disgruntled veterans are replacements, mostly old men, children, weaklings, some Soviet prisoners, and God knows what other foreigners fighting with them. And with these men he would either win or lose; upon their heads rested the outcome of the invasion…

That afternoon, they leave Bolbeck. Moving south, they arrange at Port Jérôme to take a ferry across the Seine, so that they can head for Quilleboeuf-sur-Seine. It is 12.30 p.m. as they board the ferry with their vehicles. Rommel notes that the river has swelled from the spring rain runoffs. He mentions the high waters to Ruge standing next to him. The admiral, in response, begins to tell him about the *Mascaret*—the traditional flood wave in this part of the world.

"In the spring and in the fall," he explains, "during the flood tide, the flood depth will reach a height of one to two meters."

"And it goes inland?" Rommel asks.

"*Jawohl*," Ruge replied. "It moves upriver, a seething wall of water, rushing forward at a speed of about 15 kilometers an hour."

Rommel looks out at the water, envisioning a large, advancing wave of seawater moving inland. He broaches an idea that they have discussed before, about using the tidal currents for transport in Brittany, and up north in the frozen Norwegian fjords. Ruge responds with his thoughts, and they talk about improving river traffic along the coast.

After some silence, Rommel suddenly turns to the admiral. "What do you think I would like to do more than anything after the war?" he asks.

Ruge has no idea.

"I would like to be manager of Europe's power systems," Rommel says with a smile.

"Electrical power systems, *Herr Feldmarschall*?"

"Yes! Imagine it, Ruge! I would reorganize them for the whole of Europe, according to modern centralized principles." He goes on, talking about how he would reorganize the electrical grids for Western Europe. The admiral half-listens, thinking that the field marshal would benefit Germany much more if he managed not just the power systems, but everything else as well; better that he run Germany, instead of having those idiots that were now in Berlin. But of course, he does not verbalize this.

Rommel has already changed subjects on him. "…and we simply must get on a better footing with the French," states the field marshal. "We need their cooperation badly. He looks at Ruge and anticipates the admiral's question. "Oh, not just for the moment, but for the long term as well. We need to sensibly rebuild Europe if we are to survive as a nation."

"Would that include rearming the French?" Ruge asks.

"Yes, it would," Rommel replies. "Right now they should be put in charge of the anti-aircraft defense of their own towns. Later on, they can begin to rebuild sections of their defense forces."

Rommel pauses and envisions a France united with and at the side of his Germany. An extension of the Vichy France experiment. After all, the French did make formidable opponents in 1940. They simply had been outmaneuvered, misallocated their panzers, and did not know how to use the *blitzkrieg*. But they were undaunted soldiers and plenty brave. They had proven that in World War I, withstanding Germany's relentless attacks for four years, eventually beating them to a standstill. And those fighters in the Resistance or the Maquis who were captured were like iron.

Yes, he concludes in his mind. A united Europe. Working and defending in unison, with Germany leading them. Together, they really could take on the rest of the world—something that Germany foolishly had tried to do on her own, or with those Italian dolts.

They talk some more about working with the French, ideas that he had discussed earlier in his speech to the troops. The conversation turns to addressing the French and people in general. The field marshal readily admits disliking the formal habit of addressing people in the third person. To him, it is far better not to, and to have a real conversation with that person. Ruge of course, agrees with him.

They turn to matters at hand as the ferry pulls up to the pier. The vehicles get unloaded, and the inspection goes on. Now on the southern bank of the Seine estuary, they take a shortcut along the river valley that gives them spectacular views of the fertile lands and chalky cliffs. After traveling about 40km, they reach the coast at Honfleur. There they meet *Generalleutnant* Reichert, commanding the 711th Grenadier Division. Together, they inspect the division's shore defenses, traveling southwest along the coast. Reichert tells him that his coastal batteries have taken a pounding from the air. Gravelines was hit on the 20th. However, a couple dummy battery positions have been hit as well. So the ruse seems to be working here and there.

Past Deauville near Bénerville-sur-Mer, they drive to the Mont Canisy naval battery, positioned on a 110-meter hill, overlooking both the Channel on the left, and the Seine estuary on the right. They note damage to the supports and mountings in the concrete pits. Rommel observes with some satisfaction that the actual French 155mm guns are themselves undamaged, though the ground around them has been so torn up by the bombs that moving ammunition to the guns is at present impossible. Rommel instructs Reichert to expedite repairs.[5]

The inspection party, studying the battery's design, concludes that naval casement styles are superior to their army counterparts. The gun emplacements are larger and thus need more concrete; but the shells are more easily available and the shield keeps the gun emplacement from tilting over as the result of a side hit. Rommel tells his officers to draft a memorandum to various commands instructing them to use the navy's design whenever possible—assuming of course, they can get their hands on the concrete.

They inspect a fake battery position recently pulverized by enemy bombs. Rommel listens with amusement to a corporal describing the air raid. The soldier had been bicycling past the dummy position when the intensive bombing started. Shocked by the sudden intensity of nearby explosions, he leaped off the bike, dived headlong into a nearby ditch, and burrowed into the ground. The *Gefreiter* recalled with fervor how, his hands over his ears and his eyes screwed shut, he had just lain there, terrorized, marveling at the force of what only could be described as some sort of saturated bombing of the position.

When the air raid finally ended and the enemy planes departed, the corporal slowly stood up, terrified and dazed, but unharmed. The dummy position was now nearly unrecognizable, testament to the power of the enemy bombers. Still stunned, he had shakily picked up his bicycle and had continued on.

Rommel's staff do some quick measuring. The nearest bomb had fallen only eight or nine meters from where the corporal had lain. He had indeed been lucky.

The group moves on southeast past Hougate to the Dives estuary, noting areas that have been flooded, and other measures taken. Rommel, delighted at the progress, hands out three concertinas to the men.

They move on to Cabourg where they conclude the inspection at the headquarters of the 711th Grenadier Division. After a brief stop, they turn homeward, heading back to Vernon to cross the Seine.

On the way back, Ruge gets to ride with the field marshal, and they discuss a number of subjects. As he drives, Rommel discusses his leadership methods. He admits that, though he tries to be civil most of the time, sometimes a gruff demeanor is the quickest and least painful way to get the desired effect.

He relates that, before the war, because of superior peacetime training, orders were carried out exactly as they were given. Today though, orders are often disregarded or even disobeyed, depending upon the circumstances. The Waffen-SS, for instance, never had a peacetime training schedule. So owing to their rigid determination to accomplish a mission, he believes that sometimes they do not carry out their orders, which often reults in harsh methods that reflect their own interests.

With surprising bitterness, Rommel frankly criticizes officer jealousy, no doubt reflecting on those who have turned against him because of his quick rise in rank and fame. He complains about their interfering with his mission and sometimes sidetracking critical issues. But he praises the troops for their efforts in camouflaging their positions, their surprising mobility despite their lack of transport, and their general ingenuity.

Reflecting on resourcefulness and leadership makes him think about the late General Hube. Rommel expresses his sadness and regret over the man's untimely death in that recent, fatal air crash. Hube, he states, was an inspiring leader, and had ways of getting out of a sticky situation. He had proved that repeatedly. And he had died senselessly, just on a routine trip after leaving the Führer. Men of his ilk should not have to endanger themselves by making needless trips like that, he concluded. A lesser officer should be sent in their stead.

After an awkward silence, he tries to lighten the subject. He tells Ruge about how his experiences as a hunter. Years ago, he had been put in command of the *Jägerbataillon* in Goslar, located in the beautiful Harz Mountains.[6] Soon after taking command, he was surprised to learn that, the unit's designator notwithstanding, none of his officers knew how to hunt game.

With typical Swabian resolve, he had set about remedying that deficiency. Countless times he had happily led his officers through the woods, usually on horseback, stalking deer. Unfortunately though, the first deer that he bagged was not the one he had been aiming at. So as a way of penalizing himself, he made sure that the next two deer he shot were imperfect in some way—the first had deformed antlers, and the second had antlers that were corkscrewed. Only then, he says, did he allow himself to take on a better-looking animal, this time a six-point buck.

He recalls that once, accompanied by the gamekeeper, he had the chance to get a good bead on a beautiful eight-pointer. But the rifle did not fire when he squeezed the trigger. Checking it, he found that the safety was still half-engaged. Carefully, he released the safety, holding the weapon tightly, in case it went off. It did not though. Rommel stood there wondering what to do, reluctant to cock the weapon again because the noise would startle his prey. Wordlessly, the gamekeeper handed him his own rifle, and again taking aim, Rommel took down the animal.

Rommel goes on a bit more with his hunting stories as their Horch now turns along the Seine River valley and travels southeast. He tells an amusing story about the time he tried to teach his son Manfred how to ride a horse. This was back when he was an instructor at the Potsdam Military Academy in the summer of 1935. Rommel had taken the boy, at the time six and a half years old, out one day to the stables. It was done in secret of course, because Lucie felt that Manfred was far too young yet to ride a horse. Since he was so short, his little legs did not reach the stirrups, so his father tucked them under the stirrup straps. As Manfred sat uncertainly on the animal, his father led it around in a circle with a rope tied to the bridle.

Unfortunately, the horse had suddenly bolted, and as Manfred fell off the animal, one foot slipped down and got caught in the stirrup. The horse dragged the boy along for a hundred yards or so, his horrified father running after them. At last, Rommel caught up to the animal, and managed to stop it and untangle the boy. Fortunately, Manfred came away from the frightening ordeal with only a gash on his head. Relieved and yet worried about the consequences he would face at home from his wife, Rommel took out a nice shiny five-mark coin, pressed it into the boy's hand, and told him, "If you tell your mother when you get home that you fell downstairs, you can keep this!"

The boy agreed. They returned home, but when Rommel quietly started dressing the wound with iodine, Manfred wailed from the pain. Fearful that they would attract Lucie's attention, his father angrily demanded the coin back. But his shrewd son had already hidden it. Fortunately, Lucie bought the falling-down-the-stairs story. But, Rommel concludes with a hearty laugh, he never took his son riding ever again.

As they travel along the Seine, the conversation turns serious. Rommel talks about how war will age a leader, especially military commanders. The early years (when they were winning) were much easier. Now though, they are in their fifth year of the war. Such prolonged heavy responsibility undoubtedly has exacted a heavy toll on their leaders (not to mention those that have died). Rommel of course does not include himself.

They finally roll into their headquarters just after 7 p.m., exhausted, but satisfied. The weary men sit down to dinner and start to relax. They are tiredly chatting about the trip when suddenly a loud explosion shocks them out of their seats. General Meise, smiling broadly, comes into the room. He has just introduced them to a newly designed glass fuse for their land mines.

After dinner, Rommel checks on the status of his panzers. Wanting to play the peacemaker, von Rundstedt has tactfully suggested that, in light of the difference between Rommel's and Geyr's suggestions, the panzers be positioned somewhere in-between.

Rommel set his jaw. No. The division is his to command. Enough nonsense. Turning to his staff, he directs that the 2nd Panzer is to move forward, until its lead elements actually touch the coastal positions at Abbéville.

While he is in the mood, he decides that it is time to move the 21st Panzer Division as well. Right now, they are situated over a large area in Brittany, centered on Rennes. He needs them to be closer to the coast. Since *OKW* has grudgingly given him administrative control of them, he can put them wherever he wants. And that is exactly what he intends to do.

He stares at the map of Northern France and focuses on the Calvados coast. Marcks' area. Currently, there is no armor nearby to back him up. Rommel makes up his mind. The 21st Panzer will move to the Normandy coast, just south of Caen.

***

In a conference at the Berghof in lower Bavaria, Luftwaffe Chief of Staff General Korten[7] makes the same argument to the Führer that Speer's assistant Karl Saur and Luftwaffe Air Inspector General Erhard Milch have been making for a while now: that they should shut down production of the new second vengeance weapon, the A-4 (*Aggregat-4*) or V2 rocket, and instead allocate precious production resources to fighter and tank production. "We won't see the A-4 this year," General Milch had predicted, and now General Korten is supporting this forecast.

Hitler refuses to do so (although he made the opposite argument yesterday to Dönitz when the admiral had wanted to increase priority to U-boat production), insisting that the V-2 development continue, because he sees a missile campaign against England as a critical way to smash the morale of the enemy troops getting ready to invade.

---

1   Fifty-one-year-old *Generalleutnant* Erich Diestel, commanding. Diestel, a decorated World War I veteran who had fought in Poland, France in 1940, and then on the Russian Front, took over this static infantry division in September, 1942.

2   The term was used to describe individual or paired dugout positions, from which non-armored infantry could fight against tanks. Named after General Hube, who had recently died in a plane accident leaving the Berghof (see entry for April 21).

3   This action happened on June 10, 1940, one of the destroyers being HMS *Ambuscade*, which sustained some hull and splinter damage from Rommel's panzers,. After evacuating troops, it returned to Portsmouth on the 12th and stayed there for three days of repairs.

4   In the process of the evacuation, French shore batteries sank a couple of their own ships in the harbor. Among them was the French cargo vessel *Granville*.

5   Just before the invasion, half the guns were moved into concrete positions on the side of the hill. When the invasion began, the three not moved were knocked out by naval fire from the British battleship *Ramillies*. The other half were camouflaged and moved around from time to time. Thus, they were able to fire against the British troops for a couple weeks after.

6   Rommel took command of the 3rd Battalion, 17th Infantry Regiment in October, 1933. At that time, a regiment's third battalion was typically a *Jäger* (hunter) battalion. These were specially trained infantry battalions, authorized to wear green instead of the traditional white. He was posted as an instructor to the Potsdam Military Academy in 1935. Interestingly, it was during this time that Rommel met Hitler for the first time.

7   *Generaloberst* Günther Korten, *Chef der Generalstabes der Luftwaffe*, the first general to campaign for a strategic bomber force in the Luftwaffe. He was appointed to chief of staff after his predecessor, Hans Jeschonnek, committed suicide in August 1943. Korten will die an agonizing death on July 20 when Stauffenberg's bomb explodes directly under the conference table and a wood fragment pierces him.

Wednesday, April 26

It is a beautiful morning in Northern France; sunny, with a northeasterly breeze. It is 6 a.m. as Rommel sits in his study at the huge inlaid Renaissance desk. As usual, he slept no more than five hours. Now he goes over the morning message traffic. The Luftwaffe 5 a.m. weather forecast: a fine high-pressure weather front; the Kriegsmarine report: clear weather in the Channel, and the normal picket boats are out in force.

Today's situation reports include an aerial recon message reporting several formations of enemy ships massing between Portsmouth and the Isle of Wight. Could this be it? The invasion at last? A bit early. He puts *Heeresgruppe B* on alert, just in case.

Hans Speidel leaves for Paris to attend a chief of staff conference at St.-Germain. They discuss various subjects. General Hoffmann[1] brings up von Salmuth's request to disperse into combat groups the 12th SS Panzer Division and put them between elements of General Reichert's 711th Infantry Division along the coast, between the Seine and the Dive Rivers. Speidel tells them that Rommel has denied the request. He knows well that von Rundstedt does not like the idea of the division close to the coast. Both agree on Rommel's policy of keeping the division together instead of it being parceled out. Although Rommel wants the panzer divisions close to the coast to be able to react swiftly, he wants each to be able to move and operate as a unit, hitting the beaches *en masse* in a coordinated attack, as they have been trained to do. Distributed between the infantry units, they would not be able to do this, and their effectiveness would be all but neutralized. That was the same blunder that the French had made against them in 1940. This is no time to repeat old mistakes.

At the conference, General Christiansen[2] asks Speidel for some reinforcements to help protect the west Frisian coastline.[3] He also wants to have the power to assume full command of all naval training units in the area if there ever is an invasion, as well as acquiring two reinforced grenadier regiments from Germany. Speidel tells him that the requests will be approved and forwarded on to OKW, although up until now, the Navy has refused to allow these units to suspend their training and join the conflict.

The conference breaks up in the afternoon. Speidel leaves to return to the château, but not before learning that General Heinz Guderian will soon call on von Rundstedt to discuss the displacement of the panzers.

***

Rommel remains at the château, tied up with a number of items besides the 12th SS issue. Disturbed by so many coastal batteries being bombed from the air, he orders the construction of more dummy batteries to throw the Allied bombers off. There is to be at least one fake battery for every real one along the coastline. And to further throw off the bombers, he orders dummy foxholes to be dug in a 100-meter circle around the real guns.

Then there are the Öst units. Made up of "liberated" Russian POWs, their fighting ability is marginal at best. Rommel wants the placement of these battalions re-analyzed, and to make damned sure that they put a good German unit on each side of them.

Lunchtime. Rommel eats lightly. The French good life is getting to him, despite his often-hectic schedules, and he seems to have put on some weight.

That afternoon, because he has started horse riding again to try to lose some of that weight, his staff present him with a nice gray-white mount. Beaming, he takes a ride on the sturdy, tame animal around the area, and notes afterwards with some disappointment, that the horse would have been a nicer gift for a 70-year-old country parson. As he dismounts, he comments, "The horse has so little temperament that I got quite impatient."

As his naval advisor looks at him in sympathy, he adds, "See, I also don't like boring people either." He pauses and adds with a slight smile, "But you most likely have already noted that." Ruge grins. Rommel promises though, to continue taking regular rides on the animal around the grounds.

***

That afternoon, the bridges at Mantes, down the road and upriver from La Roche-Guyon, are bombed, and the raid makes a raucous commotion as distant enemy contrails cross the skies over the bridges. Later, Rommel finds out that luckily the damage is minimal. Just as well. Otherwise, when they went out again, Rommel and his vehicle would have to use the local ferries to cross the Seine.

***

It is evening. Speidel, returning from Paris, relays to Rommel General Christiansen's request for emergency direct authority over the naval training units in his area. This has been an ongoing issue.[4] Rommel approves that request and the one to transfer two grenadier regiments to Christiansen's area. The approvals are forwarded on to OB West.

Early that evening, he writes letters to both Manfred and Lucie. To his son, he describes the thrill of having been on horseback again:

> *Just think, today I went riding for the first time since 1939...*

To Lucie, he writes of his animals:

> *The thoroughbred would have been quite suitable for a seventy-year-old clergyman, but there are others too...*
> *Last night the little one got away from Günther and came to sleep with me...*

He writes her about the recent bombings and discord among the Western Allies:

> *The invasion preparations have now just about begun with large scale air attacks. The damage here at the front is still negligible, but at the same time, this is a good thing, because the troops can slowly get used to these concentrated attacks.*
>
> *In England, morale is bad, one strike after another and the cries, "Down with Churchill and the Jews" and peace are getting louder. These are bad omens for such a risky offensive...*

After dining, Rommel and his staff discuss having a special dinner. The idea is to invite a number of VIPs to the château to wine and dine them—to socialize and (of course) try to incur favors from them. Rommel though, does not like the idea of having them all come in for one big dinner. He worries that this will dilute their efforts with each individual, because the discussions will be varied and not centralized. It will be hard to concentrate on any one guest. No, he wants to be able to go one-on-one with them.

Their planning session over, Rommel takes time out to see a movie, something he rarely does with his men. He and some staff members walk downstairs into one of two large reinforced makeshift caves that have been blasted out of the chalk cliffs by the engineers. One has been turned into a game room. The other, a large chamber that can hold nearly 400 men, has been turned into a makeshift movie theater. The same movie has been played for two or three days now, but it relaxes him somewhat, and he is grateful for the diversion.

His evening is ruined though after he returns upstairs. Stopping by the operations room on the way back to his quarters, he casually asks for a status report on the 2nd Panzer Division's progress as it repositions closer to the coast. Checking on his request, a staff officer finds out that the division has not yet started to redeploy.

His good mood quickly vanishes. Is von Lüttwitz[5] stalling on him? He would not dare. Is Rommel's order being countermanded? If so, by whom? Is Geyr von Schweppenburg trying to go around him? Maybe it was even Guderian. He is in-theater, and has seen von Rundstedt today. In any case, the delay is probably not the division commander's own initiative. Damn these people! Why can't they let him do his job?

Verbally he begins in front of his staff members to denounce all of those accursed "obstructionists." He is fed up with the lot of them. Stupid armchair generals! They are all just a bunch of administrators.

He angrily thumps his fist down on a table. "The panzer divisions are going to be moved forward," he growls, "whether they like it or not!"

The room goes silent. He glares straight ahead, waiting for someone to challenge him. Naturally, no one does.

With a final grunt, he leaves the room and stomps off to retire for the night.

1 Forty-nine-year-old *Generalleutnant* Rudolf Hofmann, Chief of Staff, Fifteenth Army. A World War I veteran, he later fought in Poland, France and Russia with the Ninth Army. After a period of illness, he was on May 1, 1942, promoted to chief of staff for the Fifteenth Army in France.

2 *General der Flieger* Friedrich Christiansen, Commander-in-Chief, Armed Forces, Netherlands.

3 Frisia is a stretch of coastland along the North Sea extending from northwestern Holland, through northwestern Germany, to Denmark. West Frisia corresponds to the northern part of Holland.

4 See entry for March 26.

5 Forty-seven-year-old *Generalleutnant* Heinrich *Freiherr* von Lüttwitz.

Thursday, April 27

By now, the Allies are deep into their preparations for the invasion. A steady stream of men and supplies has been unloading onto the British Isles for many months. Planning has advanced considerably, and intelligence reports are being harvested regularly so that landing site information is not only definitive, but also updated.

The army brass has argued for months that an early-morning landing at high tide would provide minimum exposure to fire for the men as they charge across the beaches. On the other hand, the navy strategists have countered that striking at low tide would be better for the landing craft. They would be better able to avoid the underwater mines and obstacles. A compromise is reached. The Allies will hit the beaches about an hour after dawn, and between one to three hours after low tide. Since the tide will be rising, it will give later incoming landing craft draft to maneuver (assuming many obstacles would be cleared by the assault engineers). And a mid-morning high tide would allow for a second one in the evening, thus giving better opportunity to unload supplies.

There are dozens of problems associated with the tide issues. High and low tide vary in time from one beach to the next, since the tide advances up the Channel. Total variance is 40 minutes from beaches Utah to Sword, so each beach will require its own H-Hour. This time factor discrepancy means that the beach furthest east, Sword, will be in broad daylight for the longest time between dawn and H-Hour, while the one furthest west, Utah, will only have about 40 minutes of daylight to pound the shore defenses before the troops land. The second high tide, needed to maximize off-loading, will not occur until well into the evening. Maximum favorable conditions for the air drop require light as well, but not so much early on in the evening, so that aircraft could still approach in darkness. Thus a full moon, rising around 1 or 2 a.m. would be best.[1] And low winds are vital, to minimize scattering; no greater than Force 3 (8–12 m.p.h.) on shore and Force 4 (13–18 mph) offshore. Although previous major landing operations (almost all of them in the Mediterranean) have begun in the dark early-morning hours, Eisenhower's top planners agree that this invasion must begin in daylight. There will be too many small craft operating over an expanse of five major landing locations. Daylight will be needed to simplify navigation and keep accidents to a minimum.

Another problem will be identifying targets from offshore. A huge armada of warships is being readied to provide an initial bombardment and subsequent naval fire support to the assaulting troops. The gun directors will have to be able to readily spot the targets if they are going to guide quick and accurate fire onto them.

The same is true in the air. For bombardiers to pinpoint enemy positions to knock them out, they will need daylight to see them. Naval and air planners calculate that least an hour of daylight is needed to neutralize enemy coastal positions enough for a successful landing. They want to have two hours, but army planners insist on a landing right at dawn.

The invasion, designated "Y-Day," has been targeted for June 1. The next two periods in June that fulfill all of these requirements are June 5–7 and June 18–20, although the latter period would have a new moon.

It is another warm, beautiful spring day at La Roche-Guyon. Mid-morning. Rommel is back in his study again, evaluating some reports that have come in. Boulogne was bombed again. One unusual (and disturbing) note was that the British for the first time bombed the offshore defensive obstacles as well. Was this the start of a new enemy tactic? He will have to watch this carefully.

A Naval Group West message reports the loss of the torpedo boat *T-29*.[2] The report of course states that the crew had fought valiantly against an overwhelming enemy force.

The latest orders from OKW have caused a stir. The Führer seems to be trying to kill two birds with one stone. He has decided to beef up the Brittany peninsula, and to reorganize the paratroop forces at the same time. He has ordered the II Parachute Corps, under the command of *General der Fallschirmtruppen* Eugen Mendl, to be relocated to France. This includes the 3rd and 5th Parachute Divisions, and the 6th Parachute Regiment from the 2nd. Rommel calls in Speidel and tells him to send a message off to OKW at once, requesting that the paratroopers be put near Rennes, so that they can move towards either St. Malo or Lorient if one or the other is ever threatened.

Admiral Ruge is gone today, off to Paris to see Admiral Krancke. Rommel hopes that meeting goes well. The two have had problems with each other.

***

After first meeting with navy fortress engineers to find out their plans to implement protective shields for their concrete emplacements, Ruge reluctantly goes to Krancke's headquarters.

Krancke's small minelaying fleet, between shortages and bombing attacks on them, has only been able to put down a couple of shallow water minefields off the coast of Dieppe. A couple of temporary minefields have also been laid in the Bay of the Seine, but these will only be effective for a little over a month.

The meeting with Krancke surprisingly goes rather well, all things considered. Krancke seems to have gotten over the fact that Ruge is not in his chain of command. They discuss an intelligence report that Eisenhower had taken command of the combined Western Allied strategic air forces on April 13. Well, that made sense.

Turning to naval matters, Krancke gives his reasons for not yet mining the Bay of the Seine and his plans for *Blitzsperren*[3] to be laid after the invasion had begun. They talk about other things too, including camouflage patterns, and the fates of the lost *T-29* and the damaged *T-27*. Once more, Ruge pleads with him to start laying the new Type-A coastal mine.[4]

Krancke pulls out several photographs of some ports of southeast England and the Thames estuary, taken at a distance by German air reconnaissance. He comments that they show little activity. He tells Ruge that as far as he is concerned, Cap Gris Nez and the northeast coast are not threatened by an invasion. He states that, in his opinion, the invasion when it comes will probably be somewhere between Boulogne and Cherbourg.

Krancke later reaffirms this theory in his estimate to OKW. To back up his claim, he explains that Allied air attacks against coastal batteries and radar installations are at present concentrated between Boulogne and Cherbourg, as are Allied minesweeping and minelaying operations. The enemy air formations have extensively bombed railroads and have interrupted traffic to the Channel coast, but not lines of communication to the Atlantic area. So, he concludes, the invasion when it comes will probably be further southwest, somewhere between Boulogne and Cherbourg, probably with the main effort against the Cotentin, the mouth of the Seine, or the mouth of the Somme.

***

Today, the last surviving remnants of the once-powerful 2nd SS Panzer Division *Das Reich* reach the southern French city of Toulouse by rail and begin disembarking. The division had been decimated in brutal fighting on the Eastern Front.[5] That battlegroup, now called *Kampfgruppe* Weidinger after its commander,[6] had somehow managed to continue on with its missions.

Finally, on April 8, as the fighting had tapered off, the survivors were deemed too unfit to continue. The battle group had gone into reserve, and a week later, had set off on foot for the nearest rail hub. They had departed the savagery of the East by train on the 20th, and were now getting off in Toulouse.

A total of just over 500 survivors derail—less than a battalion in strength, and less than a tenth the size of the original battle group.

***

Back at La Roche-Guyon, Rommel is troubled. Today he is to entertain an illustrious guest, General Heinz Guderian, to discuss yet again the recurring problem of placing the panzers. This discussion will be no small matter. The word of the *Generalinspektur der Panzertruppen* still carries much weight with the Führer. At 55 years old, Guderian is by now considered the creator of the German panzer corps, and the father of panzer warfare. Unfortunately, his concepts have not caught on with all of the German general officer corps, and his blunt manner of telling the truth as he sees it often borders on tactlessness. Still, his bullish determination to expand the role of the panzers is boundless, and in early 1938, he was chosen to lead Germany's first armored corps, the 16th Panzer Corps.

Like Rommel, his ascendancy to higher commands has been resisted by the general officer corps, and like Rommel, he is considered by most to be a foremost panzer expert in the field. To Rommel though, Guderian's credentials are far more impressive. With some time on his hands, the field marshal writes an early letter to his wife:

> *Dearest Lu:*
>
> *Tomorrow I am going to take a more extended trip to the southwest and south [of France].*
> *It looks now as though the British and Americans are going to do us the favor of keeping away for a bit. Still no sign of them. For our coastal defenses, this will be of immense value, for we are now growing stronger every day, every week—at least on the ground, though the same is not true for the air. But even that will change to our advantage again some time.*
> *My inventions are coming into action. Thus I am looking forward to the battle with the profoundest confidence—it might be in May, or perhaps not until the end of the month.*

A nice touch, he feels. Easing Lucie's mind from worry is the least that he can do. Besides, no doubt Himmler's men are checking out his mail regularly. This should keep them quiet. He continues:

> *What is Ajax doing? My little one[7] is touchingly affectionate and loves sweet things. He sleeps in my room now, underneath my luggage stand. He's going to be inoculated soon against distemper.*
> *Went riding again yesterday, but I'm feeling my joints pretty badly today.*
> *Guderian is due here this afternoon. The affair with Geyr von Schweppenburg—with whom I recently had to be very rough because he would not give way to my plans—has all been cleared up now by orders from above and decided as I wanted it.*

That afternoon they get word that Guderian will not show up today. One of his staff members phones around noontime to report that his visit will be a day late, because he is behind schedule. Also, the delay will allow Geyr von Schweppenburg to attend as well. More trouble. Now Rommel will be double-teamed.

That night, he has difficulty sleeping. Enemy bombers—the RAF, no doubt—pass over the château at times throughout the night, and although there are no air raids, the noise of their rumbling above unsettles him. Will they hit his headquarters tonight? He wonders as the night slips by.

***

A Luftwaffe reconnaissance aircraft late this afternoon has reported spotting a convoy of some seven merchant ships off Start Point, England.[8] Alerted by this report, German shore-based surveillance systems this evening have noticed heavier than normal radio traffic around Lyme Bay, somewhere around the eastward side of the point. At 23:17 p.m., two radar stations report possible contacts across the English Channel.

In response, Krancke orders two groups of S-boats to move into the area to investigate and do some reconnaissance.

---

1   For the invasion, the moon would actually rise at 6:30 p.m. on June 5.

2   *Flottentorpedoboot Klasse 1939*, Elbing class torpedo boat, the largest German T-boat built, equivalent in size to a US destroyer. Of the 30-some T-boats of various classes built during the war, there were only about half a dozen left in Admiral Krancke's possession at this time, testimony no doubt to the determination of the Allies to control the surrounding seas. Another T-boat, the *T-21 (Klasse 1937)*, had itself been damaged just a few weeks earlier and was at this time undergoing repairs in drydock.

   Three sister vessels—*T-24*, *T-27*, and *T-29*—had in recent weeks been minelaying in the Bay of Biscay. Early on the night of April 25, they ventured out again into the English Channel, along with a few *Schnellbootes*. Unfortunately, they were picked up on radar near St. Malo at 2 a.m. on the 26th by the cruiser HMS *Black Prince*, which was accompanied by four British destroyers out of Ushant: HMS *Ashanti*, HMCS *Athabaskan*, HMCS *Haida* and HMCS *Huron*. After a running gun battle along the Brittany peninsula, fought in the dark and at a distance, the T-boats attempted to turn back near the coast. *T-29* was detected and engaged west of the Seven Islands (*Sept-Îles*). She was sunk at 4:21 a.m. further west, near the Îles-de-Batz, by the *Haida* and the *Huron* (the *Haida* sustained damage from the battle as well). The *T-27* was also damaged, but managed to put in to St. Malo for repairs, along with the *T-24*.

3   "Lightning fields." These were last-minute, ad-hoc minefields to be immediately laid by all available vessels and naval bombers as soon as the invasion was impending or had begun.

4   The Type-A was an "oyster" mine, or pressure mine. They were also not permitted to be laid before the invasion began. This edict of the navy's was backed up by *OKW*'s agreement, so there was little that *Heeresgruppe B* could do to change Krancke's mind.

5   See April 11 entry.

6   *Sturmbannführer* Otto Weidinger, the division's commanding officer. *SS Oberführer* Heinz Lammerding, had turned the battle group over to him in early March and had left for France to reorganize the rest of his division.

7   Elbo, again, the younger of the two dogs that were given to him by *Organization Todt*. Strangely the smaller of the two dogs he usually refers to indirectly, as in "my little dog" or "the little one." Ajax, at home with Lucie, is usually cited by name.

8   Located on the western half of the southern coast of England, forming the left horn tip of Lyme Bay.

Friday, April 28

Just after midnight, nine 35-meter-long German *Schnellboote*[1] set out from Cherbourg on patrol to investigate earlier sightings. Avoiding a group of British MTBs watching their port area, they make their way northeast across the English Channel. They then begin a sweep, moving northwest towards Lyme Bay. They glide quietly through the water in two formations. The first group, of six boats, is *Korvettekapitän* Bernd Klug's *5. S-Flottille*, consisting of *S-100, S-136, S-138, S-140, S-142, S-143*, and the other group consists of *Korvettenkapitän* Götz *Freiherr* von Mirbach's *9. S-Flottille*: the *S-130, S-145*, and *S-150*.

Over an hour later, the half-dozen patrol boats of Klug's 5th Flotilla are cruising along the southern coast of England near a stretch of beach called Slapton Sands. The moon has just gone down, so the skies are not yet completely pitch black. The seas are calm.

Around 1:30 a.m., the German crews suddenly find themselves approaching several dark, medium-sized ships, the silhouettes materializing far ahead. The vessels are moving at about six or seven knots in a single-file column over 4 kilometers long, each with a clearly visible, splashy wake. The German skippers cannot know that they have stumbled onto the tail end of a major enemy naval exercise.[2]

In the black shadows, Klug's six patrol boats split up into three pairs: *Rotte 1* consisting of *S-100* and *S-143*; *Oberleutnant-zur-See* Goetschke's *Rotte 2*, the *S-140* and *S-142*; and *Rotte 3: S-136* and *S-138*. The three groups close in on the vessels from three different directions. As they slowly make their way forward, they focus hard, trying to identify what is ahead of them. There are a total of nine ships: a small leading escort, then a line of five vessels, followed by three more. All eight vessels, other than the escort, are similar-looking in configuration. Are they destroyers? Possibly. They do not appear to be merchant ships.

Initially puzzled why so many warships would travel that way, the Germans have recovered fast. Having crept up stealthily in the last few minutes upon the unsuspecting enemy—well, unresponsive at any rate—they now react quickly. It is now about 2 a.m. Taking turns, each *Rotte* swarms in at over 35 knots, swings around, and fires. *Rotte 3* goes in first, quickly unleashes all of its torpedoes, first from one side, then turning and firing from the other. *Rotte 2* moves in and shoots two fish, but they both seem to miss. The German skippers conclude that the vessels must have a shallow draft. *Rotte 1* is luckier, and several torpedoes run true and hit their mark. At least one vessel bursts into flames and starts to sink. One S-boat manages to get off a contact report at 2:03 a.m.

Now identifying these vessels as some type of American landing ship, the *Schnellboote* quickly close in again. Fires have broken out on two of the targets, providing better light for the patrol boats to see by. They charge ahead at full speed, firing their guns.[3] The enemy vessels fire back into the shadows, and at least two landing ships take the unprecedented decision of sporadically using searchlights to try to spot the German attackers. The small escort has turned around to starboard to meet the unexpected threat, but the *Schnellboote* are far too quick for it.

The red tracers in the night sky are immediately seen far away by the three boats of von Mirbach's 9th Flotilla. They quickly come about and cruise over to the area to investigate. Spotting the enemy landing ships at a bearing of 070 degrees, they too close in and attack. Once again, the vessels struggle to defend themselves from these unexpected, savage night raiders. A second escort speeds toward the area and the two begin to chase the patrol boats.

In the final ensuing attacks, *S-100* collides with *S-143*, damaging its superstructure. Clearly, it is time to leave. The Germans disengage and start to head south into the night.

By 3:30 a.m., the action is almost over. One of the strange-looking vessels[4] is seriously crippled, on fire, and barely moving in the water. It has already lowered a few landing craft, no doubt to pull it back to harbor. *S-145* attacks them with gunfire. Another ship has burst into flames, probably trapping scores of victims below deck. A third that was hit sinks immediately, probably sending hundreds of enemy soldiers and sailors to a watery grave.

The nine German patrol boats speed away, using smoke to mask their quick escape. Moving out of the area southward, they send out another contact report and head back to Cherbourg harbor, delighted at their handiwork, thankful to have escaped without harm, and also wondering what the hell they had stumbled into. They can only surmise the tremendous hornet's nest that they have stirred up in the enemy camp.

In the meantime, the entire Normandy coastline, forewarned by the report, goes on alert.

***

Rommel and his staff stay around the headquarters château, catching up on paperwork and other small odd jobs. Admiral Ruge takes time out in the morning to go through his mail, tend to some administrative details and, oddly enough, to finish doing his taxes. His assistant, *Kapitän* Peters, goes back to *Marinegruppenkommandos West* in Paris to again talk about the naval batteries using lateral observers.

Later that morning, Ruge sits down with Rommel and tells him about his meeting the day before with Admiral Krancke. Thankfully, Krancke did not pursue his earlier insistence that Ruge actually be subordinate to his own command, instead of reporting directly to Rommel. All was not forgiven though, and Ruge tells the field marshal about Krancke's determination not to mine the Seine until the invasion. Ruge describes Krancke's plans for *Blitzsperren* that could be laid after the landings have begun, and how they would be just as effective.

Rommel shakes his head as Ruge relays how he had objected to the idea, although he had not been vehement doing so. That could have triggered an angry response, and Krancke in retaliation could have gone back to his former peeve regarding Ruge's questionable chain of command. No, it was better for Ruge to let that sleeping dog lie for now.

Ruge tells Rommel how he had instead commented that he found it difficult to believe that the small Kriegsmarine forces would be able to lay a sizable quantity of mines in the presence of an overwhelming enemy fleet. Besides, it would take a good deal of time and effort to get the Type-A mine laid. Krancke had just refused point blank. Not until the invasion came. Anyway, the Kriegsmarine Naval Staff was afraid that, once the new type mines were laid, the Allies would recover one, figure out its secrets, begin to manufacture them as well, and then use them on German shipping in the Baltic area.

Today Rommel's staff prepares for the arrival of the Inspector-General of the *Panzertruppen*, who had been expected yesterday. He will be calling on them this evening.

That afternoon, while Speidel goes out for a walk, Ruge has some fun with Rommel's dog, Elbo, and provides comic relief for the staff. The admiral and Peters had found a huge land turtle yesterday afternoon, and they had brought it back to the château. Now, Ruge unleashes the lumbering reptile on Elbo. Naturally, the dog is at first terrified of the beast, but soon becomes bolder, finding the courage to stand his ground, barking louder and louder at the slowpoke intruder.

At 5 p.m. that afternoon, General Baron Leo Geyr von Schweppenburg arrives. After greetings are exchanged, he spends the next forty-five minutes talking to Speidel.

Around 6 p.m. that evening, General Guderian himself finally shows up with one of his staff officers. The Inspector-General apologizes for being late, but he has been in another part of France gathering information for OKW and was delayed.

As protocol demands, Guderian and Geyr meet with the field marshal and Speidel in the Grand Salon. Rommel hopes that the encounter will not turn out too explosively as he fears. He knows the meeting has been partially triggered by this recent trouble over moving the 2nd Panzer close to the coast, even though OKW had at last officially released the unit to his command. Guderian only administratively oversees the panzers. Geyr, still responsible for its training, is the one that has lost operational command of the unit. Clearly, these two have come to put up a fight about this move and the alarming trend Rommel has embarked upon.

Patience is needed here, Rommel reminds himself. After all, they mean well. They are all on the same side. Still, politics in the Wehrmacht is always a factor. At any rate, he is certainly not going to take any guff from Geyr. And Guderian, experienced as he is in panzer warfare, will not exactly be talking to any slouch. Rommel has a good deal of fighting experience himself, by now.

The meeting begins pleasantly in the presence of their senior staff officers. Guderian and Rommel warm up to each other. Although there has never been any love lost between them, they each respect the accomplishments of the other.

The three senior officers talk about the different theories that they believe will work best against the Allies. Rommel lays out his schedule and discloses that, like the 2nd Panzer, he is going to move the 21st Panzer closer to the coast, south of Caen. He has similar plans for the 116th Panzer. When he suggests that the remaining three panzer divisions in Geyr's command do likewise, the discussion heats up. Rommel of course staunchly defends his idea of digging in these units close to the coast. Guderian, as expected, supports Geyr's (and von Rundstedt's) theory of keeping them back inland, under Geyr's command (and not, it is implied, under Rommel's). Guderian's point is not unreasonable, at least on that point. If von Rundstedt is to command the overall theater, he reasons, and Rommel is defending the coast, someone else might have to command the panzers for the counterattack.

The baron attempts to mend the fences that he had torn down in their fiery meeting on March 29, now almost a month ago. To get on Rommel's good side, he softens his approach, apologizing for his sometimes blunt and rash behavior.

Guderian here points out that Geyr, with his valuable Eastern Front experience, is the obvious choice to command von Rundstedt's panzers. A decisive counterstroke from a large, inland reserve mobile force, coupled with a massive set of strikes from a held-back Luftwaffe contingent, would be crucial in defeating the invasion. The panzers, Guderian goes on to explain, are in his opinion effective because they are able to move and concentrate their firepower quickly over large distances. "How can they do that if they are stationary and exposed on the coast?"

Rommel is unconvinced. "I agree that they must maintain their mobility. But not inland."

Guderian pushes his point. "*Herr Feldmarschall,* the panzers *must* be positioned inland, away from the enemy navy. If they are not, their warships and air force will devastate the columns."

Rommel does not answer, staring down at the beautiful, luxurious carpet. "The landings in Italy proved that," Guderian adds gently, trying to sound logical.

"So shouldn't the panzers be put a set minimum distance away from the enemy naval artillery, and not move forward from that line?" Geyr adds.

The two fall silent as the field marshal gets up and begins pacing, trying to control his temper. He understands how they feel. He often used a mobile reserve successfully in North Africa. But the arrival of Allied airpower has changed all that. Unlike the Russians, the Americans and British use thousands of sophisticated aircraft to neutralize key targets, an upscale version of their own *blitzkrieg.* And he has seen many times what a massive air force can do to a moving column of vehicles, especially strung out in the open. With scores of enemy bombers ravaging mobile units, the enemy could very well stop their reserves cold and thus isolate the battle area.

So he tells them, "If you leave the panzer divisions in the rear, they will never get forward." Guderian and Geyr look at him, unconvinced. "Once the invasion begins, enemy air power will nearly stop everything from moving." Enemy *Jabos* would hit precious fuel sources. And what their aircraft missed, their navy would take shots at.

"*Herr Feldmarschall*," Geyr replies patiently, "if it is necessary, the panzers can roll by night. And sir, if it's critical enough, they can still move by daylight too, as long as we keep the spacing to at least 150 yards between vehicles."

Rommel stares at him. He must calm down.

"In the first place," he begins, controlling his voice, "once the landing takes place, 150 yards will not mean a thing. Allied fighter-bombers will dust off anything that dares to show itself on even a side road. In the second place, their navy has the capability to saturate an entire area with high-caliber shells. Intervals will not help, because the entire road area will be hit. We cannot use trains to move units, because the rail networks are all but destroyed. Also, American technology has made it possible for their ground units and aircraft to communicate with each other, and with their fleet. Anything trying to get to the coast will be picked up and their positions given to attacking aircraft or warships."

Rommel has seen this type of precision at work for the British in North Africa. And the well-armed, well-supplied technological Americans are even worse. He had grumbled more than once, "Those damned Americans fight their battles '*mitt dem Rechenstift*'"—with a calculator.

Movement in the dark would not be much better. Rommel has seen nights where the sky is lit up brilliantly with parachute flares, as ruthless enemy aircraft begin bombing their targets below, exposed to the harsh light of the aerial flares. Rommel pauses and remembers what those ruthless *Nachtjabos* had done to his beleaguered columns struggling to retreat from El Alamein.

Guderian, seeing that the discussion is deteriorating, speaks up. He repeats the importance of keeping the panzers inland, out of the way of the enemy navy and tactical support squadrons. "This is critical for several reasons, *Herr Feldmarschall*. For one thing, they will not easily be targeted. And besides, what if the invasion is at up Calais or along the coast up there?"

"Then they will withdraw and struggle northeast to get to the landing site," Rommel replies.

"But that's the point," replies Guderian gently. "If they are along the Normandy shoreline, it will take a great deal of time to pull them away from the coast and send them northwards to meet the enemy. That'll use up a lot of fuel too, you know. And by then it might just be too late."

"Well, my dear Guderian," Rommel says, "it won't make any difference anyway—not with the power the Allies have in the air. Whether it is 200 or 300 kilometers, it will take them days to get up to Calais, especially if many of the bridges are out.

And all that time, they will suffer greatly from massive air attacks. By then the invasion will be long decided, one way or the other."

Geyr, looking at Rommel, says sullenly, "Sir, in the desert you always fought off enemy attacks by outmaneuvering him. Now you want to put everything up front in a line, just like the French did to you in 1940. Remember what you and General Guderian did to them? Have you changed your way of fighting, *Herr Feldmarschall?*"

Rommel feels his face redden. Before he can speak though, Guderian is in the middle of it. "General," he admonishes quietly but reproachfully, "you are out of line."

Geyr looks over at him, then back at Rommel. "Excuse me, *Generalfeldmarschall,*" he answers apologetically. "I sometimes get frustrated. I am sorry."

Rommel nods. "I understand what you are saying. Look, don't you think I'd rather fight a mobile battle? Of course I would! I'd love to be able to maneuver freely around them, to concentrate my forces at one point and puncture their line. I'm just telling you that we will not be able to do that. At the landing point, they will have concentrated all of their naval strength, and most of their tactical airpower. Remember, General," he adds, staring at Geyr, "I've seen what just a part of their huge air force can do—you have not."

He pauses. Stay calm. "You mentioned North Africa. *Herr General,* those weeks we retreated from El Alamein, what was left of us could hardly move because of their constant bombing and strafing raids. Day and night. Up and down our lines." He thinks back to the terrific *Trommelfeuer*[5] he and his men received starting the night of October 23. It had continued on and off for long periods as they had time and time again been forced to abandon their positions.

"We couldn't advance without being stopped in our tracks. And we couldn't retreat without taking terrible losses. I can't remember how many times my own vehicle was strafed and run into a ditch, or how many times I had to duck for cover, with their bombs exploding a short distance from my head. Men only a dozen meters away were blown *himmelhoch.* There were times when staff officers right *next* to me were killed.[6] You just can't deploy well under those circumstances. They would cut your vehicles to pieces…"

Trying to get to the point, he tells them that he is well learned in fighting the British and Americans, and that as a matter of fact, he knows a hell of a lot more about commanding the panzer reserves in France now than they do. Rommel fiercely concludes that he is fully convinced that his method is right.

Guderian stares at the field marshal and realizes that he will not be able to change the Swabian's mind. It is like talking to a brick wall.[7]And Rommel does have a point about airpower. Guderian himself has observed how Allied aircraft often fly with almost arrogant impunity over various sections of France, including their training areas. And their bombers seem to be able to strike in significant numbers wherever they choose. So Guderian finally drops the subject and, following his lead, Geyr wisely does too. With the point of contention dropped, the conference is essentially over. Nothing worth mentioning has been achieved, but Guderian concludes that he will remember this conversation, and that this matter is not yet over.

Luckily, things perk back up again at dinner. Guderian talks about developing better self-propelled artillery and assault guns and, charming as ever, he is only too happy to quote portions of his *"Tigerfibel."*[8] Rommel and Guderian get along pleasantly enough through the evening, and Rommel hopes that Guderian will not fight him any more on the panzer issue.

---

1   Lit "fast boats": small German craft, equivalent to the British MTBs or American PT boats, many capable of cruising at speeds of 34–36 knots. The all-encompassing moniker "E-boat" was used for any German patrol craft, ranging from an armed motorboat to a large *Torpedoboot.*

2   Operation *Tiger.* One of the largest amphibious exercises secretly being conducted by the Allies in preparation for the Normandy Landings, involving a landing exercise for some 30,000 soldiers. These vessels are carrying American engineers of the 1st Engineer Special Brigade.

3   Each *Schnellboot* had a 37mm Flak gun at the stern and at least one 20mm Flak gun at the bow or amidships, along with a variety of machine guns. A number of the boats had 40mm cannon.

4   This was an American LST (*Landing Ship, Tank*). The idea was first suggested to President Roosevelt by Winston Churchill, telling him that they needed a ship that could carry and land tanks and heavy equipment directly onto a beachhead. At just over 100m in length, and with a draft of just 5m at full load, its maximum speed was 11 knots. The LST was armed with one 76mm gun, one 40mm gun and six 20mm antiaircraft guns. It carried seven officers and 204 enlisted men.

5   Lit. "drum fire," as a snare drum beat might give.

6   Rommel did not exaggerate. Many times he and his staff were bracketed by enemy air raids. On September 1, 1942, he personally suffered six such attacks. In one particularly close raid, a 20cm piece of red-hot shrapnel punched a hole clear through one of the shovels in his tent, and landed on his leg. Later raids produced more such incidents, with pieces of explosion fragments landing next to him.

7   Guderian later wrote about the field marshal, "He *always* wanted to have his own way."

8   Guderian's *Tiger Primer.* See footnote for February 12.

Saturday, April 29

Despite the fact that it is the weekend, Rommel plans on leaving for yet another tour of the coast. Intelligence reports from *Fremde Heeres West* have indicated that the enemy has substantial amphibious forces in the Mediterranean (as is evidenced by the Salerno and Anzio landings), and that a simultaneous landing in southern France is possible.[1] Since the barrier construction seems to be going well enough along the Channel, Rommel decides to go south one more time. His reasons for the trip are twofold: First, he is going to inspect the First Army along the Atlantic and the Nineteenth Army, now led by General Sodenstern.[2] However, he also wants to have a look at the Pyrenees.

It is early morning. *Hauptmann* Lang is sitting in the chief of staff's office, going through the morning communiqués for the field marshal. There is little new in the reports before him today, with one exception. In the early hours of the 28th, two formations of *Schnellboote* out of Cherbourg had stumbled onto a sizable convoy of nine enemy ships around Lyme Bay. Attacking with torpedoes, they had destroyed or damaged several enemy vessels. The S-boats certainly must have shaken up the Allies.

Of course, that swings both ways. When the landing craft had been reported at 3:25 a.m., the coastal defenses had gone on full alert. A follow-up message later indicated that a nearby enemy destroyer had evidently not been aware of the presence of the landing craft. So they were probably stragglers from a landing exercise. The coastal units eventually were told to stand down. Another false alarm.

Well, the field marshal will want to see that report. Then they will have breakfast with the staff and then leave for another inspection. They will embark on a long trip, heading down to the southern zones of France—the Bay of Biscay, the Pyrenees, and finally to the shores along the Mediterranean.

When the field marshal tours, his group normally travels in a convoy of just two cars. Today though, his entourage will include five automobiles. There will be several reporters on this trip. Along with Rommel will be Lang and his driver Daniel. General Meise and their operations officer, the cultured *Oberst* von Tempelhoff, will ride in the second vehicle and Admiral Ruge in a third. Five cars, and yet there will be no escort to attract attention. The commanders of the many sectors that they will travel through will not know that Rommel is coming, so that word of his trip does not reach the enemy. However, if they get in trouble, no one will know it.

Lang wonders again about what he will take for lunch along the way. The field marshal often maintains a spartan diet when on the move. Usually, they only take along a thermos of coffee or consommé, along with a few sandwiches. Often the field marshal will cross out a proposed menu that Lang has written and write out in big letters: SIMPLE KITCHEN MEAL.

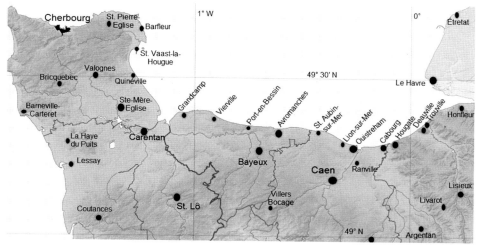

The Normandy coast. (Author)

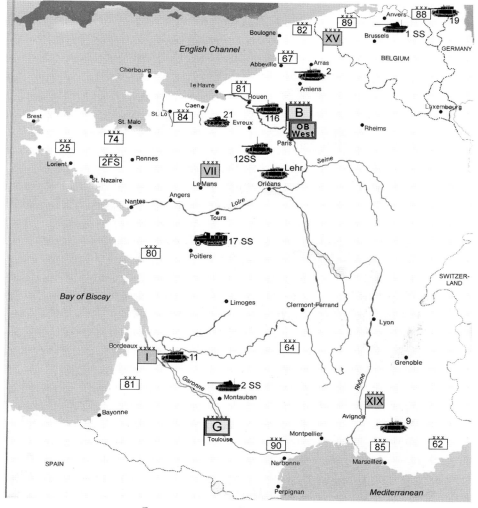

German major units, June 1944. (Author)

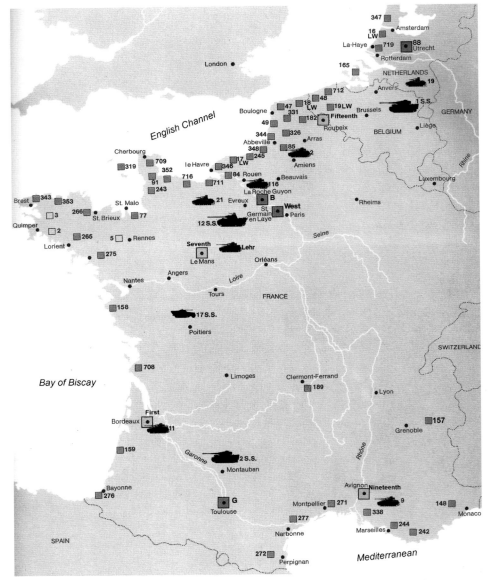

German division locations, June 1944. (Marshall Cavendish, Vol. 12, p.1565)

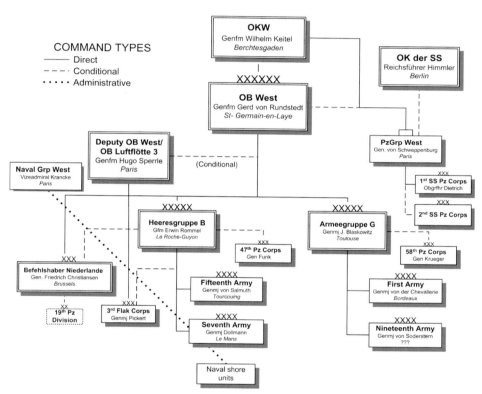

OB West Chain of Command, Spring 1944. (Author)

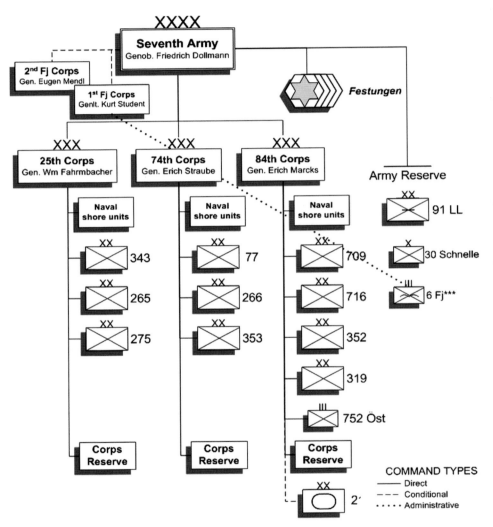

Seventh Army Order of Battle—June 1944. (Author)

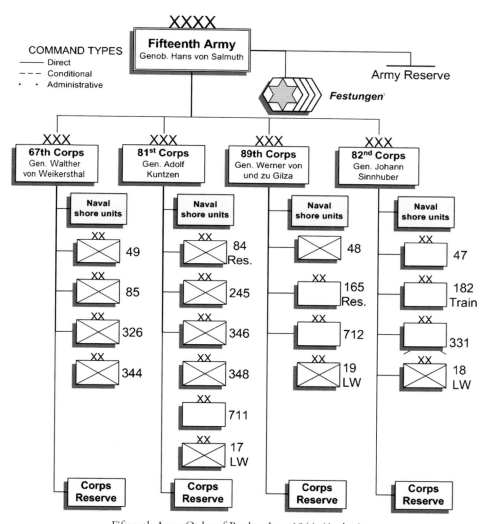

COMMAND TYPES
—— Direct
– – – Conditional
· · Administrative

XXXX
Fifteenth Army
Genob. Hans von Salmuth

Army Reserve

Festungen

XXX
67th Corps
Gen. Walther
von Weikersthal

Naval
shore units

XX 49

XX 85

XX 326

XX 344

Corps
Reserve

XXX
81st Corps
Gen. Adolf
Kuntzen

Naval
shore units

XX 84 Res.

XX 245

XX 346

XX 348

XX 711

XX 17 LW

Corps
Reserve

XXX
89th Corps
Gen. Werner von
und zu Gilza

Naval
shore units

XX 48

XX 165 Res.

XX 712

XX 19 LW

Corps
Reserve

XXX
82nd Corps
Gen. Johann
Sinnhuber

Naval
shore units

XX 47

XX 182 Train

XX 331

XX 18 LW

Corps
Reserve

Fifteenth Army Order of Battle—June 1944. (Author)

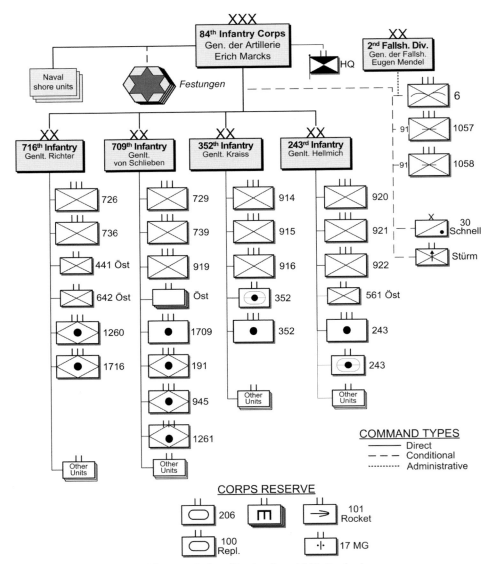

84th Corps Order of Battle—June 1944. (Author)

The main entrance to La Roche-Guyon, located on the right side of the château. It was from here that Rommel would leave for his inspection tours. (ABC Salles)

A recreation of Rommel's study at La Roche-Guyon. Note the historic tapestries on the walls. (*Rommel* teamWorx Television & Film GmbH, 2012)

Von Rundstedt visiting 1st SS Panzer Division in Beverloo, Belgium, March 1944. The division commander, *SS Oberführer* Fritz Witt, is to his right. (Bundesarchiv Bild 1011-297-1739-04A)

Hitler's birthday—April 20, 1944. (Frank, p.79)

The La Roche-Guyon ferry. With the bridge opposite the château gone and the Seine bridges bombed, this ferry was the only way Rommel could cross the river to inspect units in western France. (*Rommel*, teamWorx Television & Film GmbH, 2012)

The downed roadway bridge across the Seine River at Vernon, taken shortly after it was brought down. Rommel frequently crossed the river over this bridge on his inspections, until some six dozen B-26s bombed the town again on May 26, 1944 (the railroad bridge a bit further downstream had been destroyed on May 7). Along with this bridge, 50 houses were destroyed and another 150 heavily damaged. Some 45 people were killed and another 80 injured. (GiVerNet)

Rommel and Marcks somewhere along the Normandy coast — May 9, 1944.
(Bundesarchiv Bild 101I-300-1863-29)

Alfred Becker. His mobile artillery and rocket launcher creations were a big part in making the 21st Panzer Division a lethal unit. (National Archives)

General Johannes Blaskowitz, commander, *Armeegruppe G.* He was in Hitler's disfavor throughout the war. (National Archives)

Western Theater conference, May 8, 1944. Seated (l–r): Geyr von Schweppenburg, Johannes Blaskowitz, Hugo Sperrle, von Rundstedt, Rommel, and Theodor Krancke. Seated opposite them (out of picture) are their chiefs of staff. (*After the Battle*, Vol.141, p.13)

Rommel inspecting beach obstacles; April 1944. (Bundesarchiv Bild 1011-719-0243-33)

Field Marshal von Rundstedt greets General Guderian, May 1944. (Alamy (Sueddeutsche Zeitung))

Oberstleutnant Helmut Meyer, Chief Intelligence Officer, Fifteenth Army. (Cornelius Ryan Collection)

General Feuchtinger, commander, *21st Panzer Division.* (Bundesarchiv Bild 1011-300-1865-12)

Max Pemsel, Chief of Staff, Seventh Army. (Wikipedia)

Rommel inspecting the 21st Panzer Division, Spring 1944. At left is General Dollmann. In the center is division commander Feuchtinger. (Bundesarchiv Bild-1011-300-1865-10)

Rommel inspecting 82nd Corps, April 18, 1944. Next to him holding the map is Hans Speidel, and behind them is Helmut Lang. Corps commander Johan Sinnhuber is at far left. (National Archives)

Rommel inspecting at Riva Bella, May 30, 1944. Lang is behind him. Note Becker's improvised rocket launcher at the back. (Bundesarchiv Bild 1011-300-1863-35)

Rommel watching a Becker demonstration, May 30, 1944. Present (l-r) Hans von Salmuth (far left), Rommel, Friedrich Dollmann, Walther Buhle (OKW), Erich Marcks, and Alfred Jakob (OKW). Out of picture at left is Admiral Krancke. (Bundesarchiv Bild 1011-300-1863-09)

Rommel in his Horch, being driven by Corporal Daniel. (National Archives)

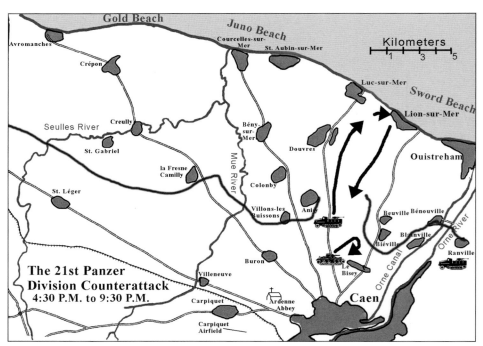

21st Panzer Division counterattack, D-Day. This was the most serious threat to the landing on June 6th. Although one regiment actually made it to the beach, it could not hold, and had to be withdrawn. (Author)

He then sometimes confuses poor Lang after handing back the now-corrected list by adding a contradicting comment, perhaps with a small shrug of his shoulders, "Of course, if you want to throw in a chop or two, that won't bother me."

Lang has settled this morning on a few sandwiches, some fruit, and some hot tea in a thermos. Not that it makes much difference what he takes along. Chances are, the field marshal will probably not even bother to eat it.

Lang finally takes the morning reports over to Rommel's study, and the field marshal goes through them. He notes the navy's *Schnellboote* report. He makes a note. His staff will have to look further into this incident.

In another navy report, two torpedo boats, the *T-27* and the *T-24,* had tried to break out from St. Malo, attempting to reach Brest. Unfortunately, they were once more intercepted off Île de Bas and attacked. Only one had made it back to St. Malo.[3]

Rommel finally gets up and walks down to the dining area with Lang. They are seated at the breakfast table with a number of staff officers, including Speidel. Rommel listens attentively to them as he eats breakfast.

The conversation is informal. His staff members are seldom constrained around their boss, and the talk this morning is casual and comfortable. The field marshal nearly always allows his staff to freely express their views. They are after all, *his* staff, handpicked by him, and he feels close to all of them. They in turn are completely dedicated to him.

Now as they sit at the table, each of them in turn brings up various subjects. Once in a while, they laugh comfortably.

With breakfast over, he becomes impatient to leave. Telling everyone "Well, I'm leaving," he pushes back his chair and stands. Most of them follow him down the hallway.

Just outside the main doors, Daniel waits, with both doors on the right side of the field marshal's beautiful, cleaned-up Horch open and waiting. Rommel turns to each of the staff members staying behind and bids them goodbye. He says a few parting words to Speidel, then walks down the concrete stairs and climbs into the front seat next to Daniel.

He looks at his watch. It is a little after 6 a.m. "Let's move, Daniel," Rommel says.

They drive down to the river and cross the Seine by ferry. On the west bank, they get in their customary three vehicles, accompanied this time by the other two cars for the reporters. The entourage departs southward.

They drive for some four and a half hours. At 11 a.m. they get to Nantes near the Loire estuary. They stop for lunch at the soldiers' mess hall there. Before sitting down, Rommel calls Speidel back at the château and gets updated on the latest reports. Nothing unusual. More bombings.

Despite the impatience of their customers, the two older French waitresses take their time. The men find it amusing that their dishes are served from the right, and even more so that Rommel himself is not the first one served. In fact, he must wait some time for his order. The attendants, unperturbed by their guest, seem to have their eyes on the younger men.

More driving that afternoon along the coast, passing the Loire estuary, continuing south. The towns go by—Pornic, St. Jean-de-Monts, Rochefort, Pointe de La Coubre…

They stop briefly here and there to visit elements of different units. This includes the headquarters of the First Army's 80th Corps,[4] Haeckel's 158th Reserve Division, Wilck's 708th Division,[5] and of course, units of the 17th SS *Panzergrenadier* Division *Gotz von Berlichingen*.[6]

At 8:45 p.m. that night, the small motorcade finally pulls into the town of Royan, about halfway down the Bay of Biscay on the Gironde estuary. They have traveled some 780 kilometers. Tired, they get settled in and dine a half-hour later. Most turn in afterwards, although Admiral Ruge, spending the night with the area Sea Commandant,[7] stays up to visit with his navy colleagues.

By the end of the day, most of the details about last night's German surface attack on the landing ships of convoy T-4 near Slapton Sands have been relayed up the Allied chain of command to SHAEF. The eight American LSTs carrying the 1st Engineer Special Brigade had been taking part in the Allies' only large pre-invasion landing exercise when they were struck by at least two groups of enemy E-boats.[8] Eisenhower himself is enraged over the matter. For one thing, the reports show that the Germans had been quite successful because the landing ship formations had not been zigzagging, but rather had been sailing in a straight line; perfect targets.

They had been led by just one escort, a small British corvette[9] that could only do about 15 knots, less than half the speed needed to chase after the E-boats. To make matters worse (and luckily for the Americans, unknown to the Germans), the small corvette could not communicate directly with the landing ships, because it was operating on a different radio frequency. It was also reported that once the German boats began attacking, many soldiers were ordered not to open fire and further give their vessel's position away. The American skippers, not knowing what to do, ended up circling their vessels, much like in the Old West.[10]

This attack is very bad news. The enemy probably now realizes that this exercise shows that the Allies are nearly ready to invade. The German radar and observation forces will no doubt be on special alert from now on for any other Allied movements, and surprise will now be much harder to achieve.

The preliminary casualty count from last night's E-boat attacks is reported as over 630 men lost, about three quarters of them US Army personnel. Two LSTs, 507 and 531, were sunk. A third, 289, was heavily damaged, barely making it back to port. A fourth, 511, was hit by friendly fire. The Allies only had a few landing ships to spare for the real invasion, and with the losses taken last night, the enemy attack has effectively taken out any reserve they might have had.[11]

Even more serious though is the report that nearly a dozen American officers[12] *presumed lost in the attack possessed considerable critical knowledge of the upcoming invasion. Some survivors reported that the E-boats had at one point puttered through the flotsam with small searchlights or flashlights on, apparently nosing through the wreckage for information.*

Enraged by this new security threat to their diligent precautions over the plans and objectives of their huge upcoming invasion, Eisenhower is livid. He harshly orders that the area be thoroughly, relentlessly scoured with frogmen, divers, capable swimmers— whatever it takes—until every single one of the bodies of those officers in question (and any incriminating papers they might have on them) is found.[13]

He wonders if the invasion might now have to be postponed...

---

1 Allied intelligence deception at work.

2 This used to be *Armee Felber,* named after its commander, *General der Infanterie* Hans-Gustav Felber. After Italy's collapse in August of 1943, Felber was relieved by *General der Infantrie* Georg Sodenstern, and the army renamed the Nineteenth Army.

3 Two Canadian destroyers attacked and the German vessels in response fired two spreads of torpedoes and turned to flee. The *T-27* mortally wounded the *Athabaskan,* but the *Haida* avenged her. Laying cover smoke and pursuing the German T-boats, she crippled the *T-27* with gunfire. Ablaze, the *T-27* grounded on a reef near Pontusval. She would finally be finished off by British aircraft and MTBs weeks later, on May 7. The T-24 though, made it back to St. Malo.

4 *General der Artillerie* Kurt Gallenkamp, commanding.

5 Admiral Ruge in his *Reminiscences* mistakenly refers to this unit as the 700th Infantry Division.

6 The division, created last October, was named after Götz von Berlichingen, a heroic 15th-century German knight. In one ferocious combat, he lost his right hand. Thereafter, he wore a prosthetic hand, which he defiantly kept clenched tight during battle. The division took his demeanor and adopted it as their own, their emblem being his clenched iron fist.

7 Forty-four-year-old *Kapitän-zur-See* Hans Michahelles. A torpedo boat officer in the 1930s, he became a naval liaison to OKH in the summer of 1941, before being put in charge of the port of Gascogne.

8 *E-boat* (enemy boat) was the all-inclusive generic term the Allies used for any German patrol craft.

9 HMS *Azalea,* a Flower-class ASW corvette, capable of no more than 16 knots.

10 Further inquiries uncovered other shortcomings. A second British escort, an old World War I destroyer, had been slated to escort the landing ships as well. However, it had returned early to Plymouth harbor for some repairs (left over from a recent minor collision), and the Americans were for some reason not informed. And at least one of the E-boat formations had been picked up by shore radar earlier that night, and both had been detected as unidentified contacts by other distant British escorts. The shore batteries around nearby Salcombe harbor had visually spotted the unidentified small craft as well, but they unfortunately were ordered not to fire on them, because that would have shown the Germans that the harbor was defended, and given away the battery positions. In all cases, the American vessels were never warned, partly because of the different chains of command, and partly because the Americans were operating on different frequencies.

11 This ended up being the costliest training exercise in all of World War II. When all the bodies had washed ashore, the official count rose to 749 lost, two thirds of them soldiers. Knowledge of both the exercise and the large casualty figures was covered up until the 1990s.

12 The final count was ten missing officers with top clearance and critical knowledge.

13 Luckily, they eventually were.

Sunday, April 30

After an early breakfast, *Generalfeldmarschall* Rommel and his group board a patrol boat in the port of Royan.[1] They steer south-southwest across the estuary. They pass the destroyer *Z-37* and circle her once in salutation.[2] The crew responds smartly, turning out in parade formation (they have been told that the Desert Fox is on that little patrol boat) and returning salutes. Rommel is moved.

Their cars are waiting for them on the other side, and they depart southward, towards Bordeaux. They pass a large section of coast recently ravaged by a forest fire. This fire had detonated or destroyed some five percent of the estimated 200,000 mines laid there. On top of that, this area is too lightly defended. Rommel makes a note. This area is commanded by First Army commander Johannes Blaskowitz and is technically directly subordinate to von Rundstedt. However, the First and the Nineteenth will soon combine to form a new army group[3]—so there is no need to stir up trouble. Therefore, Rommel does not comment on that area when he reaches Blaskowitz's headquarters at Bordeaux late in the morning. Ruge and the First Army staff go into conference, while Rommel and Blaskowitz talk privately for a short while.

Blaskowitz and Rommel continue their chat through a (thankfully) simple lunch, relating their past experiences. Rommel of course talks about North Africa, especially El Alamein, and Blaskowitz tells of his experiences in Poland in '39, and briefly goes over the atrocities that he protested against so vehemently.

By 1 p.m., they are on the road again on this beautiful Sunday afternoon. Next stop is the port town of Arcachon. Inspecting the positions, they find an oddity: a bunker near the water with its field of fire pointed inland, and not out over the approaching waves. Shaking his head, Rommel orders the corrective measures to be made.

Soon after leaving the town, the second car in the motorcade (Ruge's car) develops engine problems—no doubt partly due to the fast pace and the nearly ubiquitous flying sand particles near the coast. So Ruge heads directly for their night stopover, the picturesque town of Biarritz.[4] Rommel continues on, pausing here and there to note a position.

By 8 p.m., Rommel has joined Ruge in Biarritz, and they dine some 45 minutes later in the soldiers' mess. They are served on priceless Basque china. The field marshal finds himself as usual the center of attention, surrounded by smiling, adulating men. He beams and, rising to the occasion, he launches into one of his North Africa stories. This one is about his first retreat, and the resulting problems that he had experienced with that bombast, Italian General Bastico.

When he finally finishes his storytelling, the men make comments and ask questions, trying to get him to converse with them, interact with them. They seem to relish this special time with one of their most famous war heroes. Rommel in turn stays for a bit, trying to answer their questions, He listens patiently when a number of them tell some short stories of their own.

Attention briefly turns to a major in the Alpine Corps, who recalls occupying some Greek islands in 1943 against heavy resistance. While he is talking, Rommel takes a minute to relax and look around. He is a bit surprised to see that the mess hall is now packed. Men have come from near and far to see him and to hear him speak. The talk goes on for some time, with the men asking him about a variety of things like North Africa, the Italians, conditions in Germany, and the upcoming invasion.

He finally becomes aware that it is getting late and that he is keeping these men from their duties. Rising from the table, he thanks everyone sincerely for letting him dine with them. In turn, the officer in charge of the mess thanks him profusely for the privilege of eating in their mess hall. Rommel smiles.

He turns and starts to leave, when suddenly the men impulsively break out into rousing applause. They are clapping wildly, some of them in tears. They are cheering him, *der Wüstenfuchs*. Their hero. He is moved, and takes a deep breath to keep from breaking down in front of them.

As he stands there, too moved to speak, looking around at this emotional crowd, the applause quickly turns into an enthusiastic standing ovation. He gazes at them humbly as the spirited clapping and whistling continue unabated, with many cheering and yelling out his name. Despite his control, he finds himself trying hard to hold back the tears. A lot of these men, he realizes, had fought either directly or indirectly under him. All of them would clearly follow him anywhere. And many of them in doing so would probably die before the war was over.

He looks out at the faces of those men, many now crying openly. They are what is left of the best his country has given—proud, respectful, loyal warriors. They in turn are in awe of him, and he makes a unique emotional connection with them in a special moment of mutual respect.

They can see now that he wants to say something, so the cheering slowly dies down. Gazing at them, he finds it difficult to speak. With a slight tremor in his voice, he thanks the men sincerely for their warmth and fond sentiment. Then he turns and leaves.

It is a day he will remember for quite a while, this elegant dinner at Biarritz.

---

1 On the northern bank of the Gironde River.
2 The 2,637-ton *Z-37*, commissioned in July 1942, (KL Ullrich, commanding) was accidentally rammed and damaged by *Z-32* on January 30, 1944. She was later towed into Bordeaux, where her guns were eventually removed. They were to be used for shore defense. Repairs were discontinued on August 24, 1944 and she was decommissioned. That same day, the ship was gutted by fire and she was scuttled. Her hulk was finally scrapped in 1949.
3 Von Rundstedt had made this proposal to OKW back in March and had suggested that command go to the capable General Blaskowitz. OKW had agreed at the beginning of April.
4 Located on the Atlantic coast, a little over 200km south-southeast of Bordeaux, and some 30km from the Spanish border.

May 1944

Monday, May 1

It is 5:35 a.m. Rommel sits down for a quick early breakfast, once again at the soldiers' mess in Biarritz. Just before the officers are served, the staff, mostly *Luftwaffenhelferinnen*,[1] present the field marshal with a bouquet of flowers. It is a lovely arrangement, dainty lilies-of-the-valley from some secret (no doubt female) admirer. Rommel shakes his head with a smile, and those officers next to him beam and gently chide him as a couple photographers snap a few pictures. The smiles continue when several of the staff ask for Rommel's autograph and in general gush all over him.

After a very nice meal, the field marshal, his staff, and the reporters leave the mess, ready to depart, the *Luftwaffenhelferinnen* smiling from the windows. As Rommel walks towards his Horch at the curb, he turns to his chief engineer with a grin, points back towards the windows, and says, "You know, Meise, some of those girls are so darned attractive, I could almost be a rat!"[2]

Meise smiles back, knowing full well that the field marshal would never cheat on his Lucie.

They depart at 6 a.m. sharp for more inspections, driving across the southern base of France towards the Mediterranean. There is a heavy fog in the air, but as the morning wears on, the temperature begins to warm up, the sky starts to clear, and finally the sun comes out. Corporal Daniel's route becomes easier, allowing them to better enjoy the spectacular montages of the breathtaking Pyrenees off to their right.

The vehicles stop at a striking rocky formation near Perpignan, and Rommel lets the photographers take some photos of him there. "The British are bound to recognize that rock formation," he says with a grin. "Now they'll see that I've been down here, too."

The motorcade reaches the port town of Perpignan around 1:30 p.m. Rommel is puzzled to see policemen blocking off the side streets, and a large crowd gathered, evidently just to watch him arrive. There is a strong curiosity, no doubt, to see *"Le Renard."*

They drive to the headquarters of the IV Luftwaffe *Feldkorps* and have lunch with its commander, General Petersen.[3] Also present are *Konteradmiral* Schulte-Moenting and *Generalleutnant* Schack.[4] The conversation is interesting, as they discuss the concept of senior naval officers taking over defense of some major ports. The more senior officers should be capable enough.

After lunch and a quick report by General Schack, Rommel, accompanied by his recent lunch companions, heads southeast to the old town of Port-Vendres near the border. They make their way through the town, inspecting a number of positions, and notice a specially equipped anti-aircraft corvette in the harbor. Then it is back along the coast again, passing a number of defensive positions chiseled out of the cliff rocks, and a few areas strewn with deadly *Minengranaten*.[5]

More stops follow as they make their way northeast up the Mediterranean coast, enjoying along the way the breathtaking scenery and the beautiful mountains now behind them. They stop at Sète to inspect a fire control bunker located on a tall hill overlooking the town and its harbor. However, getting to it proves to be difficult, because the road up there is unpaved and stony. Hard on the tires, the path forces them to go slow. At the top, *Generalleutnant* Danhauser[6] meets them and gives his report.

They soon depart with Danhauser following. Their cars struggle down the steep hill over the rocky road before turning east. Admiral Schulte-Moenting, riding with Ruge, is somewhat upset by their seemingly quick pace, but stays calm and entertains him along the way with navy war stories.

The entourage finally arrives in Montpellier at 9:30 p.m., tired and hungry. They drive to the 271st headquarters, a small château just outside of town, where they are to be dinner guests of General Danhauser. Those who wish to change into something more comfortable before dinner are given only 12 minutes to do so—Rommel does not change for once, and stays in his high leather boots. Admiral Ruge decides to go to his room and change clothes and in doing so, is nearly late for dinner.

After dinner, *Generalmajor* Kaliebe[7] entertains them with various stories and anecdotes. There was the time he inspected a gun battery and after showing up and introducing himself, received the curt reply, "127mm," because the battery commander had obviously misheard what he had said.

***

This afternoon, while von Rundstedt is entertaining General Guderian at his villa in St.-Germain-en-Laye, his chief of staff is in his office, on the phone with his counterpart at La Roche-Guyon. Blumentritt has learned that Speidel is a cool customer, never ruffled. Blumentritt gets down to business.

He has a set of important instructions to pass on from Supreme Command, and he is rather sure that he knows how Rommel will take it. Generally, army group commanders do not like OKW telling them how to do their jobs, especially when the orders come straight down from the Führer, and Rommel is certainly no exception. He has a temper, and the wrong suggestion might upset him. Still, orders are orders.

The Führer at this point has become convinced that the enemy's main stratagem to deceive them about the invasion site[8] is just a ruse. So he has again somehow concluded that Normandy is a probable landing site for the upcoming invasion. Walther Warlimont had then called OB West for a status report on the Normandy defenses. Later that morning, Jodl had called Blumentritt too, telling him to remind von Rundstedt that the Führer felt the landings would probably occur along Dollmann's coastline. Now some time later, Blumentritt is pursuing this with *Heeresgruppe B*.

Blumentritt tells Speidel about the two phone calls and that the Führer now believes that the landing will probably be in Normandy. OKW wants an immediate estimate on General Marcks' chances of being able to defend the coast. Speidel is unsure of what Blumentritt wants to hear, and tells him that it is difficult to say precisely.

Blumentritt clarifies. "We need to know how strong the defensive wall is along the Normandy coast. Could General Marcks repel an invasion and airborne landing there if it came right now?"

Speidel pauses. "Yes," he replies carefully, "He probably could, eventually, given certain conditions. It depends on a lot."

Blumentritt presses him to be specific.

"Well," Speidel says thoughtfully. "For one thing, what kind of warning time he is given. The weather conditions. I suppose some luck would be involved as well. How quickly the reserve panzers could be released. What type of intervention the Luftwaffe would make…"

"Forget about the Luftwaffe," Blumentritt replies. "Could 84th Corps defeat the enemy?"

Speidel hesitates, and Blumentritt realizes that the other chief does not want to commit himself here. Well, Blumentritt has to press him for an answer. The question is coming from the Führer himself.

Speidel clears his throat and replies, "That's hard to say right away. I would have to have some time on this to give the Führer an accurate answer. Let me ask the field marshal when he gets back, and I'll give you a better answer as soon as I can."

This is an honest request. "*Gut.* Better make it today at the latest, though. General Warlimont stressed the fact that the Führer's pretty anxious about this. He wants this information as soon as possible."

"*Jawohl,*" Speidel replies. "I will get right on it."

General Blumentritt a little later calls Admiral Krancke at *Marinegruppenkommandos West* and relays to him the Führer's concerns about Normandy.

***

At La Roche-Guyon, important administrative matters have developed today. The 2nd Panzer Division is starting to redeploy, as per Rommel's insistent instructions. Word has come from OB West that the 155th Reserve Panzer Division is to disband. Most of its units are to go to the 9th Panzer Division.

In the meantime, 2nd *Fallschirmjäger* Corps and the 5th *Fallschirmjäger* Division have started moving towards Brittany. And the 91st *Luftlande* Division, commanded by General Falley,[9] will begin leaving for the Cotentin peninsula tomorrow.

Blumentritt calls Speidel again to set him in motion, and when the field marshal checks in that evening, Speidel tells him about the phone calls and the estimates that he has pulled together from their staff and from a quick estimate sent by General Pemsel at Seventh Army.

Speidel also tells him that Krancke at Naval Group West has informed the château that, because of the Führer's concerns, the Kriegsmarine is going to take additional measures. After some consideration, Krancke has decided to order some *Blitzensperren* be laid in the Somme River sector, between Le Havre and Boulogne. Because his forces are so meager though, the operation will have to be carried out by his fleet torpedo boats.

Speidel assures Rommel that he made sure that OB West received the requested situation report later that day, along with Pemsel's status report. Rommel approves.

---

1   Female staff in the *Luftwaffe*. Equivalent to American WAAFs.

2   Irving does not specify the exact day this occurred, only mentioning that it was "… during the last fatiguing weeks before the Normandy landings." However, May 1 is the likely day, because Irving stated that it occurred in one such mess hall or hostel, and this was one of the few times in May that Meise was with him.

3   See footnote for February 8.

4   Rear Admiral Schulte-Moenting commanded all naval units in the Provençe Sea Area. He had been *Großadmiral* Raeder's chief of staff, until Hitler dismissed Raeder in January 1943. *Generalleutnant* Friedrich August Schack was the commanding officer of the local ground unit, the 272nd Infantry Division.

5   "Mine shells." An anti-invasion device in which an artillery shell is imbedded along a cliff over a target area. If the shell is disturbed or the surrounding rock hit, the shell falls and explodes below.

6   *Generalleutnant* Paul Danhauser, commanding officer of the 271st Infantry Division.

7   *Generalmajor* Johanne Kaliebe, promoted to Chief Engineer of the Nineteenth Army on March 15, 1944.

8   Operation *Fortitude*.

9   Forty-seven-year-old *Generalmajor* Wilhelm Falley. A World War I veteran, he had fought with distinction on the Eastern Front in 1941, where he was wounded the next year. After that, he served on several training school staffs until early October 1943, when he returned to Russia and took over command of the 243rd Infantry Division. On April 25, *Oberst* Falley was transferred to France to take over the 91st Air Landing Division. His promotion to general came on May 1.

Tuesday, May 2

It is a lovely, warm spring day. *Generalfeldmarschall* Rommel, up early as usual, is on a tour of the Mediterranean positions—perhaps for the last time before the impending Allied invasion. He leaves with his entourage at 6:30 a.m., off to inspect the units along the coast.

They start with the nearest, the 338th Infantry Division,[1] and move eastward along the coast. Through La Marargue, then the ancient town of Aigues-Mortes and its historically preserved wall.[2] Onward to Le Grau-du-Roi, where they note the many barrier obstacles there. Further on is Port St-Louis, where they pass fields of plowed trenches. The staff officers note with amusement that these furrows will make excellent cover for airborne troops that might land nearby.

Onward to the area of the 244th and 242nd Infantry, then to Fos Plage, where the offshore barrier is a series of wooden stakes secured in concrete and topped by various types of mines. Farther inland, they pass a lagoon and many fields prepared against airborne landings with various cairns[3] strewn over the grassy knolls.

The tour continues to Port-de-Bouc, and finally to Couronne. There, Rommel finds himself facing an assembly of officers from the 242nd and 244th Infantry Divisions. Time for another one of his famous pep talks. Partially for effect (it never hurts to add spice to his talks) and partially because of the beautiful weather, he decides to give his speech outside. He stands atop of a small knoll facing inland, with the men gathering around him.

He starts off by telling them about the North African campaign.

"Look," he continues. "I understand that you men want to use your own experiences instead of the experiences of troops who have already faced the enemy. That's perfectly understandable."

He gazes at them steadily as he points his marshal's baton. "But men, time has just about run out for us. The clock stands at five minutes to twelve, and we can no longer take time to gather our own separate experiences on how to fight the enemy. That's why *I'm* here."

A few quiet cheers here. He goes on, trying to get them to see things his way.

"Don't get me wrong; what you've done so far is a good start." And it was, too. "But nobody should believe that our goal has been reached yet. This would only be the case if each company had its own concrete factory to make all kinds of offshore obstacles."

He goes on to explain his objectives in detail before winding up his talk.

"I have heard that the enemy is reputed to say, 'Kill the Germans wherever you find them.' Such behavior is alien to us. We fought as respectable soldiers; but we were just as tough as the others. The crushing defeat of this enemy attack on the coast of France will be our contribution to vengeance."

To his surprise, they applaud him and cheer. Somewhat embarrassed, he walks down the hill.

He dines that evening in Avignon with General von Sodernstern, commanding the Nineteenth Army.[4]

***

Adolf Hitler holds another conference for several of his top generals that afternoon. Rommel, on his Mediterranean tour, of course cannot attend.

Hitler, staring out the large window in the main salon, starts his situation monologue by once again reflecting his confidence in Normandy being the most likely invasion site. Especially, he adds, when recent intelligence reports have indicated that a large concentration of American ground formations has been identified in southwest England. A substantial number of British units have been pinpointed in southeast England as well. Two main troop movements have been detected, and Americans have been seen moving in and around Wales. British infantry units have been spotted moving in southeast England.

For the landing to be successful, the Allies have to secure a beachhead, stabilize it, and then build from it to go on the offensive. To do this, they need a large, ideally positioned, well-equipped harbor. There is, he concludes, "no better place on the whole coast than the Cotentin peninsula for this purpose."

Even though he has not as yet received a reply from Rommel's command on how Marcks would fare in repelling an attack (it has not yet arrived from OB West), Hitler has decided that whatever the troop strengths are in the Normandy area, they need to be increased. They are short of panzers, for one thing. At the end of April, there were only some 1,600 tanks in the West.

Hitler nods approvingly at hearing OB West's plan to have about 2,000 by the end of May. Still, it is not enough. He re-confirms his order for the II Paratroop Corps and the 5th Parachute Division to continue moving into the Normandy and Brittany peninsulas.[5]

In the meantime, to simplify command channels and at the same time elevate von Rundstedt's status, southern France needs an overall commander, an equivalent to Rommel in the northern half. General Blaskowitz is to be put in charge of the Nineteenth Army, as well as his own First Army. These two units are to become one command, known as *Armeegruppe G*.[6] Like Rommel's larger army group up north, it will fall under the theater command of OB West. Blaskowitz will get three panzer divisions for his area: the 9th, the 11th, and the eventually returning 2nd SS.

The conference goes on to cover the status of the coastal defenses. True, a lot has been done, but so much still remains. A recent report from Krancke's Naval Group West shows that of some 600 guns that needed casemates, only half have been completed, and a fourth are just being started. Even in the *Kanalküste* itself, only three quarters of 132 are finished. In Normandy, there are only 47 done, a little over half.

The Führer growls that he had ordered *all* casemates to be completed by the end of April. Jodl replies that, according to Rommel's reports, shortages in concrete, steel, and labor have slowed construction down considerably. The same is true for construction of the army battery sites.

The Führer just shakes his head.

The coastal areas also need additional air protection. Hitler commands that more flak units be sent to Normandy and Brittany. Additionally, more anti-tank weapons are to be moved there as well. Hitler tells them he wants the Seventh Army beefed up, and OKW begins to issue orders to that effect.

They'll have to do better than this if the coast is to be ready for the invasion.

***

Generalfeldmarschall von Rundstedt has had a busy week, including inspecting elements of the 17th SS *Panzergrenadier* Division. Today, as he usually does around 10 a.m., he goes over the morning reports. More attacks have been made on the rail complexes, including the marshaling yards at Cambrai and at Bethune.

A while later, he has a planning session with his staff members. They sit around a conference table in his command headquarters. He goes over to a map of northwestern Europe and stands there, a pointer in his hand.

"Here is where I think the attack will come," he says. He turns from his team, looks back at his situation map, and points to a spot along the *Kanalküste* near Boulogne. "If I were the Allies, I would hit us here, somewhere between the Somme estuary and Dunkirk." To the staff, it is a speech that by now they could almost recite themselves.

"It is the shortest distance across the Channel, and thus would provide for them the lowest amount of sea time, while giving them the maximum amount of air time," he says, glancing at back at them. "We learned that in 1940. Another reason is that striking here would give them the best chance to drive inland to the Ruhr area, which would cripple our industrial effort."

"Excuse me, *Herr Feldmarschall*," says Blumentritt, "But if you remember, intelligence has reported that the Allies have been well aware of our V-1 and V-2 rocket sites along this area. They would also be a primary consideration for choosing to invade through here."

"Exactly," von Rundstedt replies. "British bombers have been hitting these sites for weeks now. They have hit some three quarters of our 100 sites. Some we repair, some we let go, and some we make more defensible. London will be vulnerable when they become operational. The Allies cannot afford to let this happen."

A staff member asks if the rocket weapons are as powerful as they've heard.

The old man looks at him with a squint and croaks dryly, "It doesn't make much difference, if there are hundreds of them raining down upon you, does it?" That draws a short laugh from the staff.

The field marshal continues. "The coastal terrain is well-suited for a landing, and there are one or two ports in the area, such as Calais or Boulogne. *Ports*, gentlemen. The Allies need ports, or they will not be able to expand their beachhead. They just simply will *not* be able to supply their men."

"Anyway," he concludes, "I think that the invasion sooner or later will be here. It is just too lucrative a site to pass up. Oh, they may try to deceive us by making a diversionary landing at Brittany or Normandy, but the main effort, logically, has to be here. And gentlemen," he stresses, looking at his staff, "I want this area to be ready."

"*Feldmarschall* Rommel is, no doubt, working hard on that, sir," a staff member said.

The old Prussian grunts softly. "Yes, I know. Getting the beaches ready is driving him crazy. Well, no doubt, when the invasion comes, he will certainly be more at peace in his mind."

After the conference, the field marshal sits down at his desk and addresses an issue that has been weighing on his mind.[7] At the end of March, Witt's 12th SS Panzer Division was given orders to move closer to the English Channel, to better react to the invasion whenever it began. One component of the division, a panzer battalion under the command of SS *Obersturmführer* Walter Hauck, had loaded onto 24 railcars for the trip.

On the evening of April 1, coming in from Baisieux to the east, Hauck's train had been approaching the station in the town of Ascq[8] when suddenly a huge blast tore out a section of the track just ahead. The train stopped immediately and avoided the broken track, but a subsequent inspection revealed that the sudden stop had caused two of the flatcars to derail. Getting the flatcars back on the track again would cause a delay. In addition, several of the vehicles had broken their moorings. Luckily, no one was injured. However Hauck, already grouchy that day, while impatiently awaiting for the damage to be repaired, heard that this was the third time this area of track had been sabotaged. He ordered his SS stormtroopers to search the houses on each side of the track for the culprits and to round up all the men aged from 17 to 50.

Some 70 civilians had eventually been rounded up; they were walked back down the track almost a thousand meters and then shot in the back of the head. Another 16 or so were shot in the town itself through the night. A half-dozen more were arrested by the Gestapo, charged with planting the bomb, and shot by firing squad. Included in the dead were nearly two dozen French employees of the national railway system.

The incident had been published in the newspapers, and a protest had been made to OB West by the Vichy government. Furious, the French told the occupational forces in no uncertain terms that no German would be allowed at the funerals. Some 1,500 or so locals attended, and another 9,000 workers in the area had stopped work to observe a minute of silence for the victims. The SS reacted by giving Hauck a special commendation.

Although the shootings had been conducted by members of the SS, since operationally they fell under von Rundstedt's command, he had been delegated to respond.

A bit upset over the Resistance activities currently going on, von Rundstedt bears little sympathy for the victims, especially since they were all men. And so he responds:

> The population of Ascq bears the responsibility for the consequences of its treacherous conduct, which I can only severely condemn.

There is perhaps a slight tremble in his hand as he signs his name.[9]

---

1   Commanded by *Generalleutnant* René *Baron* de l'Homme de Courbière, having taken over from General Joseph Folttmann on January 5. Admiral Ruge in his book *Rommel in Normandy* mistakenly refers to this unit as the 388th Division. There is record of a 388th Training Division, but it was stationed in Norway, whereas the 338th is listed on almost all German Ground Order of Battle (GOB) lists.

2   In 1248, Louis IX began the Seventh Crusade from here, setting sail for Tunis.

3   A cairn is a mound of stones or small boulders erected usually as a marker or as a sort of memorial.

4   See footnote for February 7.

5   Admiral Ruge wrote that the initial order was made on April 27.

6   See *Armeegruppe* log entry for May 8, 1944.

7   Nuremberg document F-190, Exhibit RF-435, Page 141.

8   Just east of Lille.

9   After the war, some nine members of the SS, including Hauck, were tried in a French military court in Lille. They were all given death sentences, though the sentences were later commuted to various periods of imprisonment. Hauck was let out of prison in July 1957. The village never forgot the atrocity, and over the years, many dignitaries have visited to memorialize the shootings. Every Palm Sunday since 1945, the massacre has been commemorated in Ascq. Von Rundstedt was after the war tried for war crimes, but this incident was not one of them.

Wednesday May 3

Allied intelligence at this time is working hard to confuse the Germans and make sure that they do not know when the invasion takes place. At the same time, the Allies are doing everything possible to pinpoint and track all of the enemy ground units.

London becomes alarmed in this first week of May when a new FFI' report reveals that the massive, newly formed Panzer Lehr Division has returned from Hungary. What is worse, they learn that the division will not be stationed at Verdun in northeastern France as they had assumed. It has orders to move to an area between Chartres and Le Mans—much closer to the chosen invasion site than expected.

Generalfeldmarschall Rommel is still on tour in southern France. Today though, his inspection will end, and he is more than ready to return to his château. Perhaps that is why he and his group take their time at breakfast and start a bit later than usual. They leave Avignon at 7 a.m.

The entourage drives northward up the Rhône Valley. It is a nice day, and the trip home seems uneventful. They spot some German aircraft far off in the distance, but that is about it.

They stop for lunch at the soldiers' mess hall in Chalon-sur-Saône, south of Dijon. No one there has had any warning of who was coming, since the reservations had been made for an anonymous military group. So the shock and joy in the dining area are considerable when the men find out that their main guest is none other than the Desert Fox himself.

Although they are seated in a noisy open mess hall, the inspection group manages to talk over some new ideas for defensive barriers. They are constantly gazed and smiled at, sometimes covertly, sometimes openly, by the many nosy soldiers and auxiliaries around them, each eager to get a glimpse of Rommel. The field marshal finally turns to his audience and begins talking to them about a number of things, including better inter-service cooperation. There is no time, he explains, for bad feelings, jealousy, selfish goals, and blind ambition. They all have to work together now. Along those lines, he tells his staff and the reporters present that he is going to set up a special meeting for all non-commissioned officers in the near future.

The entourage finishes lunch and finally leaves the mess hall. They continue northward, up through Avalon, then Auxerre. The kilometers seem to stretch endlessly until they at last reach the outskirts of Fontainebleau, Rommel's old headquarters. The last car in the convoy becomes involved in a minor collision, but is able to keep up. Through Paris itself, then northwest, along the Seine. At 7:30, they finally reach La Roche-Guyon. Rommel is tired, but he feels good about the results of the trip. A lot has been done. Now he is eager to get in and call home.

As he clumps tiredly down the hall towards his study, Elbo sees him. The dachshund yelps gleefully and takes off from under the desk where he had been lying, headed straight for his master. Approaching Rommel enthusiastically and unfortunately a bit too fast, his young legs shoot out from under him, and he skids with a thud into one of the field marshal's boots. Rommel stops and laughs so hard that it shakes his whole frame. This was worth coming back to.

The group unpacks and later, everyone enjoys a pleasant late dinner. Afterwards, Rommel decides to phone Lucie to tell her he has returned from the south of France. It is late enough. Telephone traffic will be light by now.[2]

He sends her greetings and she sadly tells him that Ajax has been run over by an auto. He commiserates with her. Before they hang up, he asks her to send him a sketch of her shoe size. "I'm going to buy you a pair in Paris for June sixth."

It's her birthday. She will be fifty.

He tells his staff about the demise of his older dachshund, and they are sympathetic. Later, they all saunter down to the cave that is their theater, and watch a movie about farmers.

***

Generaloberst Johannes Blaskowitz leaves his First Army headquarters to take over his new command—*Armeegruppe G*. He is succeeded by General Joachim Lemelsen.[3]

***

Oberstleutnant Helmuth Meyer, the Fifteenth Army Intelligence Officer, is sitting in his office in Tourcoing, going over intelligence summaries of the latest enemy radio interceptions. Meyer, a short slim, thin-lipped 37-year-old officer, believes now more than ever that the efforts of counterintelligence units in the Wehrmacht are too often overlooked. He certainly believes that now as he reads the latest reports in front of him.

Meyer over many months had put together a tight little interception unit of some thirty men. His *NAST*[4] command had set up their headquarters close to von Salmuth's main command center in Tourcoing, near Lille. Meyer had trained these men in radio intercepts, and over the last few months, his men had made a concerted effort to gather every scrap of intelligence that they could so that they might deduce when and where the invasion would take place. All possible messages have been monitored, civilian and military. He even has had his men listen in on radio traffic between enemy jeeps and trucks across the Channel. And to be thorough, he has kept his men working in shifts to make sure all hours of the day are covered.

He fervently hopes that he has a better handle than most on when the invasion might occur. Von Salmuth himself has told him that the entire army group is counting on him, especially since (at least as far as he knows) his unit is the only special radio intercept signals center on the coast. Seventh Army does not have one, and he does not think *Heeresgruppe B* or even OB West has one either, testimony to the lack of importance the generals place on counterintelligence. And so, if for some reason his unit misses a vital message, it might prove disastrous for the whole army.

The problem of course, is to figure out which few intercepts are authentic and which are decoys, which is clearly most of them. Meyer though, is concentrating more than anything on one specific coded broadcast. A two-part coded message taken from the French poet Paul Verlaine is, according to the Abwehr, supposed to be the trigger signal. They had warned Meyer months ago that transmission of this poem would activate Resistance units for the invasion.

The first verse of the poem "*Chanson d'Automne*" was to be the key:

> *Les sanglots longs des violons de l'automne,*
> *Blessent mon coeur d'une langueur monotone.*[5]

The first line of the verse was supposedly to be transmitted on the 1st or 15th of the month in which the invasion was to take place. It would mean that the invasion would start within the next seven days. The second line when transmitted meant that the invasion would come within 48 hours. Meyer of course fervently hoped that the Abwehr intelligence was valid.

Unfortunately, the Abwehr was gone now, and High Command had little faith in Meyer's conclusions at this point, though they did appreciate his efforts. The problem, they explained, was mostly that there had been so many messages broadcast by the Allies over the last few months. They had all but given up any hope of their intelligence picking out any critical information. So many of the phrases made absolutely no sense; messages like "Jean sees no rain," or "Napoleon throws his hat," or "Tomorrow's molasses will bring cognac." What was authentic, and what was not?

But Meyer is pretty sure about the Verlaine coded phrase. He has always trusted Canaris, and now has come to believe that when those specific verses are transmitted, the balloon will soon go up.

God help him, though, if he ends up wrong.

Today, Prime Minister Churchill discusses several matters in a conference with the prime ministers of the Dominion. At one point, he reflects on the upcoming invasion and "the great operations which are pending." He tells them if Overlord fails:

> *We must either set our teeth and prepare for a longer war, or else reduce the severity of the terms which we are prepared to offer the enemy.*

He knows full well which of the two he would prefer. Hitler on the other hand, would welcome the other.

1 *Forces Françaises de l'Intérieur*—the organized, main component of the French Resistance.

2 Even though he was a field marshal, Rommel always adhered to the wartime measure of not making any personal phone calls to Germany before 8 p.m.

3 Fifty-five-year-old *General der Panzertruppen* Joachim Hermann August Lemelsen. An artilleryman in World War I, Lemelsen had after the war transferred to tanks and commanded the 5th Panzer Division in the French campaign. When Russia was invaded in 1941, Lemelsen commanded the XLIV Motorized Infantry Corps (redesignated a panzer corps June 1942). At best an average commander and reportedly easily depressed, he nevertheless led his corps at Kursk in 1943. His units suffered heavily in the battle, and as a result, he undertook questionable retreats back to the Dnieper River to recover. With this tarnish on his record, his corps had been transferred to *Heeresgruppe Süd* in September, and Lemelsen was transferred to the Italian Theater in November.

    Lemelsen's command of the First Army would be short-lived. One month later, just before D-Day, he would be replaced by *General der Infanterie* Kurt von der Chevallerie on June 4. Lemelsen was captured on May 2, 1945, and imprisoned as a POW until his release in October 1947, whereupon he turned state's witness and testified against Albert Kesselring at Nuremberg.

4 *Nachrichtenstelle:* Radio Intelligence Department.

5 "The long sobs of the violins of autumn; Wound my heart with monotonous languor." According to most authoritative sources, including Martin Gilbert (*D-Day*), the Verlaine code was in truth only targeted for one Resistance command network, code name "Ventriloquist," which operated just south of the city of Orléans. The Abwehr, not knowing specifically who the two-part message was for, misunderstood it to be a general call to all the Resistance and Maquis units in France. Still, they were correct in concluding that its transmission did tie in to the timing of the invasion itself, and so who the message was for was, in the end, irrelevant if the coded implication was correct.

Thursday, May 4

General Guderian is still touring panzer units in France. Today he is with the newly reformed 10th Panzer Division near Bordeaux. Unbeknown to him, his trip is being followed by the Allies via Ultra communications intercepts.

***

The weather is bad today. Rommel stays at his headquarters and starts catching up on paperwork. There is some action upriver: the bridges at Mantes are attacked again by *Jabos*. He takes some time off to wander up to the Grand Hall of the castle and join his staff outside as they watch the enemy make bomb runs on the spans over the river.

He finally drifts back inside and tackles some administrative details. OB West wants a couple of smoke-launching units placed further inland than Rommel wanted. More hassles...

Not much new in the local daily reports. Good news though, comes in from the High Command. One report states that the Führer, still believing Normandy to be a likely invasion target, has decided that the 91st *Luftlande*[1] Division, one of the few divisions left in the OKW strategic reserve, has been ordered to Normandy. Additionally, the *2. Fallschirmjäger Division*, now in Russia, has been ordered to the West as well. It is scheduled to begin moving into the Seventh Army area. One of its regiments, the *6. Fallschirmjäger*, is to deploy in Normandy, near St. Lô.

Today Rommel asks OKW to ask *Reichsmarschall* Göring for some anti-aircraft batteries. Specifically, he wants the III Flak Corps, which consists of four powerful regiments. Rommel wants to put them between the Vire and the Orne Rivers, to cover air assaults or bombing raids occurring there.

By now, Rommel's routine at the château is set. The meals taken with his staff are nearly always enjoyable, the dinners the best. Knowing his twelve staff officers' desire for his presence, the field marshal usually attends the evening meal. This is a change of habit for him; in Africa he had always dined in his van alone with his aide. The change he feels, is a positive one, because he meshes better with his staff. Table discussions are pretty much free and open, and anything broached can be debated without pressure.

Naturally, they often have guests, and usually the menu and wine lists are modified accordingly, although Rommel seldom consumes alcohol. He does have an occasional drink, but he never lets himself get sloshed. Usually, one or two glasses of wine is fine for him although, to the dismay of some of his more refined officers, he usually waters them down.

He usually shows little interest in food, but he does enjoy vegetables, usually spinach, beans, and endive salads. Company notwithstanding, Rommel insists that his diet generally be simple and plain. He does not want to be branded as a lavish, out-of-touch commander (like Jodl had accused von Rundstedt of being in January). This unfortunately gives his cuisine officer problems. The man had been a gourmet chef at a renowned hotel before the war, and Rommel's directives towards simplicity do not let him show off his talents as often as he would like. And yet, the boss at times does let him do his thing, especially when VIPs visit. The resulting, opulent courses often delight his staff, used to eating plain and simple.

When guests do visit, Rommel tries to keep the number down, usually to no more than two. Rommel finally revealed his reason to his staff in late April, when a staff member suggested inviting several guests over in a big group. Rommel had replied, "No, this will only lead to superficial discussions. I want to work on everybody individually; only this will bring results." Even then, very special fanfares were as a rule not made for callers; still, they usually enjoyed their stay.

Naturally, the field marshal always sits at the head of his dinner table, with Admiral Ruge to his right (unless they have a guest), and the chief of staff to his left. Manners at the table are usually relaxed. Rommel never smokes, but prides himself on allowing others to do so. Table talk is usually lively. He enjoys humorous stories, and has that rare ability (especially for a German general) of being able to laugh at jokes directed at him. But he does not tolerate dirty jokes. He is not a prig, but he deems such stories inappropriate, especially at mealtime. Thus, it has become an unspoken rule that off-color stories are not to be told at his dinner table.[2]

As a good host, Rommel does not as a habit try to dominate the conversation. He found out long ago that it pays to be a good listener, whether with his staff or with a guest visiting for the evening. He is open-minded, and any positive suggestions brought up at the table are discussed. If they are worth the effort, he makes sure that he or someone else follows up on them.

Rommel often follows dinner with a walk around the château, sometimes with Speidel, Ruge, or even Lang. They might chat about something that has come up that day. Sometimes, the field marshal reminisces about earlier (and happier) times. During his strolls, one of the field marshal's favorite places to stop is between two huge cedar trees. The trees give him a feeling of strength, serenity, and security, and the spot offers a magnificent view of the Seine valley and the sky to the west.

Although he usually retires around 11 p.m., he sometimes sits up with the Duc at night, making small talk over a rare drink.

This evening at dinner, Rommel, in good humor, tells more stories of his youth—this time, his hectic days as a lieutenant.

He writes to his wife around ten that night:

Dearest Lu:

Last night I came back from a long trip and called you right away. Too bad that Ajax is dead, but he was not so hot anyway.

"Ebbo" as Günther calls him, is too cute. You should have seen how happy he was when I came back. Of course he is still very playful and when he madly chases through the room trying to move forward but can't because he slips on the parquet floor, it just about kills me...

---

1   "Air Landing." An air-lifted division in which most of the men and equipment, unlike an airborne or parachute unit, come in by glider, including a few medium weapons such as light artillery, as well as some small vehicles.

2   Once Rommel, on an inspection tour along the coast, had sat down for a repast in the nearby officer mess. As they were being served, one unfortunate unit commander began to recount an immodest anecdote. He had just started his story, and had told just enough to let everyone know that it was off-color. Glancing at the field marshal, he felt a cold chill coming from Rommel's eyes. It stopped the man dead in his tale. He was very quiet the rest of the meal.

Friday, May 5

The weather is still rainy. *Generalfeldmarschall* Rommel and his staff spend the day tending to administrative details. Some of the officers have to go into the French capital and call on various commands there.[1]

Rommel himself has a briefing with several officers on losing offshore obstacles. Several are being destroyed or rendered ineffective. Many of the wooden ones and a few of the metal ones are washing up in the surf, or are drifting out with the tide, or are simply falling apart. Some are losing the mines attached to their tops, and many of these mines are becoming waterlogged and rendered useless. Other obstacles are just a lot of trouble and time to install.[2]

Rommel patiently tells them about the benefits of these barriers. That includes the psychological effect, both on the enemy, and on their own troops. Heaven knows, the defenders do not have much else to go on. Many are in isolated, exposed positions, facing a potentially overwhelming enemy. Their own navy consists of a few small patrol vessels, while the Allies are amassing a huge fleet. And in the air—well, the current joke is, if you see it flying in the daytime, it's American; if you hear it at night, it's British, and if you do not hear or see it at all, it is the Luftwaffe. What makes the joke worse is that the Luftwaffe would be the first to admit its truth, with an "oh-well" attitude. So the barriers are a way of giving the defenders some comfort and self-reliance.

After the meeting, General Speidel gets on the phone with the commander of the 309th Artillery Regiment about where to position a couple launcher brigades in the Loire River valley.

Word comes in that Naval Group West has granted permission to move two naval training units in Holland further forward. A small victory at last for the Army on this issue.[3] On another matter, Rommel turns down a suggestion from Fifteenth Army that Luftwaffe senior officers inspect and evaluate the anti-airborne landing obstacles, such as the "asparagus." He wants his staff to retain that right. He also rejects a proposal by Seventh Army General Dollmann that Straube's 74th Corps be moved from Brittany to Normandy.

Around noontime, Rommel receives a visit from a war correspondent, Lutz Koch.[4] He had been attached to the Africa Korps in 1942, rolling with them back and forth across the desert. He had periodically sent out news communiqués about their victories, receiving high praise from the Reich propaganda ministry, especially for his exciting eyewitness broadcast about the fall of Tobruk in late June of that year. Now he is ushered into the field marshal's study. As he looks around at the famous ornate tapestries and lavish furnishings of the historic room, he contrasts them with the simple, sandy, spartan tent that they had lived in when they had been in the harsh, North African desert.

Rommel, surmising what Koch is thinking, smiles smugly. "It's more *gemütlich* here, isn't it, than at Tobruk or El Alamein?"

Koch smiles back and replies, "*Jawohl, Feldmarschall,* but the worries are probably still the same, aren't they?"

"*Und ob!*" Rommel chuckles.

Koch looks up again at the tapestry over Rommel's desk, which had once hung behind Louis XIV when he had signed the famous Edict of Nantes in the seventeenth century. They walk over to the terrace doors and gaze out at the peaceful-looking river, while Elbo happily prances around at their feet. They observe the scenic springtime colors, the cherry blossoms decorating the trees in the distance. Below them, Rommel's rose buds are starting to bloom.

"*La douce France,*" Koch observes. Rommel agrees.

Koch notices that little Elbo has acquired a larger companion, a hound dog. "That's Treff," Rommel tells him. "The OT gave him to me."[5]

Koch smiles back and then returns his gaze to the lovely green countryside. Rommel sighs, and murmurs, "I love this country."

After a pause, Koch asks him, "And how do things look here on the Atlantic Wall?"

Rommel's face turns serious. "That only exists on the Channel coast. But it's a sure thing that they won't come there."

He starts to relate the enormity of the job that he has been given. He concludes, "I had to improvise everywhere, in order to somehow protect the coast and to add some depth to the defenses. I'm having everything mined and wired. Piles are being driven into the sea offshore, and other obstacles are being built in, loaded with some unpleasant surprises."

He shakes his head. "But a *wall* it isn't—not a visible wall. I know that full well…"

He turns to Koch. "Remember Tobruk? I knew I'd get away with that. But several months later, in the El Alamein position, I also realized that the battle for Africa had been lost. If you ask me now what my feelings about the situation are, I'm telling you: I'm having premonitions of bad things to come."

They talk some more about the war, and Rommel's pessimistic feelings come out, especially regarding the invasion of the Soviet Union, which deprived him of so many men and supplies that he had desperately needed to ultimately defeat the British in North Africa. Just a few divisions would have made the difference. And it now seems to be a fateful decision that will in the end cost them the war. Near the end of their talk, he says sadly, "If only Hitler had never started the war against Russia. That was his gravest political and military mistake. Today, this war has long passed its zenith."

He pauses and adds, "Let's hope that we shall get out of it decently and honorably." But in his heart, he doubts that they will.

***

Today the Führer at his noontime war conference again brings up the subject of an invasion in the West, and again mentions his concerns over Normandy, especially the threat that would bring to Cherbourg. Despite some misgivings by Jodl, Hitler tells him to again call Blumentritt at OB West and stress the strong possibility of Normandy being the location for the upcoming enemy invasion. Special efforts should be made to strengthen the area without committing OKW reserves.

The message goes out to OB West that day. They in turn relay the information to Rommel's headquarters, stressing that the Cotentin peninsula and Brittany, because of concerns expressed by the Führer, are to be immediately fortified.

Jodl, talking to Blumentritt at 7 p.m. confirms the information, adding that the Führer now believes that the Cotentin peninsula will probably be the enemy's first objective. He then again goes over with him the coming reinforcements to the Normandy and Brittany area. He stresses to him the Führer's belief that the Cherbourg peninsula will probably be the Allies' first objective when they land. Jodl points out though, that the Führer is not entirely sure that the main invasion would be near there.

"However," Jodl adds, "the Führer attaches particular importance to Normandy and the defense of Normandy."

Blumentritt promises to discuss the matter with von Rundstedt.

***

Later that day, after Koch leaves, General von Schwerin,[6] commanding the newly formed 116th Panzer Division, reports to Rommel at La Roche-Guyon. Von Schwerin had served with Rommel in North Africa in the spring of 1941, and the two had exchanged some heated words at that time. But that was long ago. Now, they have a pleasant chat. Rommel gives him a rundown on the disposition of their units in northern France. Despite Hitler's recent anxieties about the Normandy area, Rommel tells him that, "We expect the invasion on either side of the Somme estuary." Von Schwerin's soon-to-be well-equipped 116th Panzer is to be located inland, athwart the Seine River. [7]

That evening, Rommel is in good spirits. About the upcoming invasion, he dictates to Lang:

> *I'm more confident than ever before. If the British give us just two more weeks, then I won't have any more doubts about it.*

The British will in fact give him a month.

---

1   There were a number of major German commands in the capital area at that time. OB West was, of course, located outside the city itself, in nearby St.-Germain-en-Laye; but others were in the city itself. These included Krancke's Naval Group West, several naval ordnance centers, the Luftwaffe

main weather service, Gestapo headquarters, Sperrle's *Luftflötte III*, and of course, the headquarters of the Military Governor, General von Stülpnagel.

2   The Chief Engineer of Seventh Army, *Oberst* von Bodecker, recorded after the war that corroding mine detonators had rendered ineffective about half of the 13,400 mines that were laid in front of the 716 Infantry Division.

3   See entry for March 26.

4   Forty-one-year-old Lutz Koch had been a journalist since 1924. Now in uniform, once an army specialist, he had become an experienced radio news reporter and war correspondent. He had been attached to Rommel in North Africa. He had also often been with him in Italy as well. He would survive the war, despite being wounded four times at the front.

5   "Treff," according to Cornelius Ryan's notes, was a common German name for a hunting dog. It is an expression meaning "direct hit" or "bull's-eye," as in accurately striking the target.

6   Forty-four-year-old *Generalleutnant* Gerhard ("Gerd") Helmuth Detloff *Graf* von Schwerin. A World War I veteran, he started World War II as a staff member of OKH. In 1940, commanding a battalion in the *Grossdeutschland* Infantry Regiment, he fought in the French campaign, where he played a significant role in the battle of Sedan. He later fought in North Africa under Rommel, but there was friction between the two of them, and Rommel eventually relieved him. Von Schwerin later fought in Russia, taking part in the siege of Lenningrad, then distinguishing himself in the Stalingrad campaign, commanding the 16th Panzergrenadier Division. In March, he and the remnants of his unit were transferred to France, where they combined with the 179th Reserve Panzer Division to form the 116th Panzer Division.

7   It has never been determined if Rommel knew at this time that von Schwerin was in on the plot against the Führer. One thing was certain: Rommel could not know at this time that the 116th Panzer would not engage the enemy for over a month after the landings—not until mid-July.

Saturday, May 6

It is overcast today and cooler, with some light drizzle. Chief of Staff General Dr. Hans Speidel leaves the château for Paris, where he has a number of conference meetings with various unit chiefs of staff and unit commanders. The talks continue into the afternoon with Admiral Krancke,[1] the military governor of France, and Luftwaffe Field Marshal Sperrle's chief of staff.

Speidel and Krancke discuss a reorganization of the naval commands. Naval Group North is going to be disbanded, for one thing. On a more personal level, Krancke relays a request from *Großadmiral* Karl Dönitz himself that *Heeresgruppe B* detach Admiral Ruge for more important duties with the Kriegsmarine.

***

After several other meetings, Rommel checks the latest messages again in the afternoon. One bit of news interests him: the Supreme Headquarters report on the paratroop units that are being dispatched to Normandy and Brittany. He confers with Speidel on this and then, for clarification (and to satisfy his aroused curiosity), he puts in a phone call to OKW. After a while, Jodl comes on the line, stolid and brisk as always.

"Ah, *Herr Feldmarschall!*" the OKW chief of staff says cordially. "How good to hear from you. The Führer was just talking about you the other day…"

"*Herr General,* why did he order those airborne units to move to Normandy and Brittany? Not that I'm complaining, of course."

"Airborne units? Let me see… Ah yes, well, actually, I'm not really at liberty to tell the source, but suffice it to say that he has 'certain information' from one of our intelligence sources, telling us that Normandy is a likely place for the landing."

"Interesting," the field marshal replies. What does the Führer know that he doesn't? And why can't he be told?

He stays polite. "May I suggest that the airborne units be deployed around Rennes, so that they can move either towards St. Malo or Lorient?"

"An excellent suggestion, *Feldmarschall.* We shall take it under advisement." Rommel grimaces. Pretentious administrators.

"What about the status of the OKW reserves?" Another sore subject.

Jodl says soothingly, "Don't worry. The panzer reserves will *all* be released as soon as it becomes clear where the enemy landing point is. Another thing," Jodl says in a low voice, as though that would keep the enemy from hearing, "After the landing, Cherbourg is supposed to be their first strategic objective."

"Cherbourg?"

"*Ja.*"

Rommel wonders about the reliability of their source. "Then I request the *Panzer Lehr* Division be taken out of reserve near Chambois and moved to Bayeux."[2] He does not of course point out that Bayeux is right next to the coast.

"My dear Rommel," Jodl says politely. "You know how von Rundstedt will react to that."

"But if what you say is true, that part of the coast will need some sort of local backup if we are to stop the invasion. The defenses in that area are not finished yet." Rommel is using reverse logic on him.

"Yes, we know," replies Jodl. "That is a definite problem," he says in a concerned tone. Rommel's ploy has obviously worked.

Rommel comes to the area corps commander's defense. "General Marcks is doing his best."

"But there is a good chance that they will not be ready before the Allies come." It is not a question. "Furthermore," Jodl continues, "we have intelligence reports that British experiments at penetrating your present types of beach obstacles have been successful."

Rommel is surprised. "Are you sure?"

"Our source is pretty reliable. Maybe you should take the time to re-evaluate your plans."

"I'll look into it," Rommel answers thoughtfully. He hangs up and sits back in his chair. If the enemy has found ways to overcome his beach defenses, his defense plans will be in serious trouble indeed...

After some thought, he picks up the phone again and gets hold of General Marcks at St. Lô. He tells the corps commander that something has come up, and that he will be back out there again in a few days. Marcks (is that a touch of reluctance in his tone?) agrees to expect him.

Hanging up once more, Rommel sits in thought. If the enemy can get around his obstacles, he will have to come up with a new rabbit to pull out of his hat. He had better mention this news to Speidel tonight at dinner.

Looking back at the papers before him, he glances at the latest reports. More bad news. The German fuel industry has been especially hard hit by the Allied bombings. Always a critical weak point, this bottleneck is now a crisis.

In the latest report, national production is estimated to have fallen from 6,100 to 5,200 metric tons per day. And he has a feeling that these numbers are conservative.[3] Rommel knows what this statistic means. Low fuel supplies had haunted him nearly all the time in Africa. Fuel had been scarce, and when it had dwindled, his panzers began to starve.

As Jodl has requested, Rommel orders the drafting of a message outlining suggestions on strengthening the Cotentin peninsula and Brittany be for OKW. OB West will have to pass it on.

Speidel returns to La Roche-Guyon and immediately goes into Rommel's study to report on his meetings. He gives him Dönitz's request to transfer Ruge. Is this an end-around by Krancke to finally get Ruge under him? Probably. At any rate, Rommel knows how Ruge feels about the idea and perhaps remembers the lack of cooperation that he's been getting from the navy lately. So he denies the request.

Speidel again discusses with Rommel General Dollmann's idea of moving the entire 74th Corps staff to Normandy. Rommel once more turns it down.

Then the field marshal fills him in on his phone conversation with Jodl about the airborne units transferring, and about Normandy. So Speidel goes to his office and talks again to Blumentritt, this time by phone, regarding the Führer's recent speculation over the Normandy area. Blumentritt tells him that there is also some concern from OKW about the 243rd Infantry's main transport—in this case, horses. Also, they want the top portion of the Cotentin peninsula in general reinforced. This cannot be done though, by replacement with a larger unit. None are available, and OKW is not about to let them pull a division out of reserve. And of course, sending another infantry division to the West is out of the question. No, it will have to be done with a hodgepodge of smaller units.

To that effect, some rearranging is done with Seventh Army. The 243rd will be used to help put up obstacles in other areas of the Cotentin peninsula. In the meantime, several smaller Seventh Army units will move into the central peninsula area. These include the 700th Training Unit, the 206th Panzer Battalion near Cap de la Hague, and the Seventh Army *Stürm* Battalion.[4]

At around 4:30 that afternoon, there is a visit from State Secretary Ganzemueller, out of the Reich Ministry of Transport. He and Rommel sit over tea and discuss the critical shortage of transport. The secretary's news is not encouraging. When the invasion comes, he says sadly, most major transport movements will either be blocked or destroyed. Only limited transportation will be available, and this will mostly be at night.

A little later, a message arrives from OB West confirming that the *2. Fallschirmjäger Division* has indeed been officially transferred from the Eastern Front. It is to be positioned near the 21st Panzer Division.

In the evening, Rommel writes to Lucie:

> Now I'm here at my headquarters for a few days to run things for a change. There is so much work. Today I have a very big conference. There are still no signs of the British and Americans coming in the very near future. Every day, every week, is for us of invaluable importance. Every day we are getting stronger. My inventions are now being employed. I am looking forward to the battle with confidence. Perhaps on the 15th of May, perhaps at the end of the month.

That night, upriver from the château, the bridges at Mantes are bombed again. Many of the army group staff are unable to sleep because of the noise.

1 Krancke commands Naval Group West (*Marinegruppenkommandos West*).

2 *Panzer Lehr* was still in the process of returning to France from Hungary.

3 During that time, production actually fell from 5,850 metric tons per day to 4,820 metric tons per day.

4 The 206th Panzer Battalion was mostly made up of two dozen French Hotchkiss H-35s, a dozen Somoa S-35s, and a few old German *PzKw I* and *PzKw II* light panzers. Nearly a dozen of them were non-operational. The Seventh Army *Stürm* Battalion was an independent army reserve group, used as an assault unit. It had some 1,100 "shock troops" and four light howitzers.

Sunday, May 7

It is a nice cool day. Rommel and his staff prepare for tomorrow's OB West conference in Paris. Again, in light of the Führer's recent concerns over the possibility of Normandy being the target for the invasion, Rommel spends part of the day with his staff going over a number of improvement suggestions that have been made by Seventh Army staff. Rommel is gathering ideas to bring up at the conference. They discuss the following points:

1. OB West senior officers should agree for good that moving the entire 74th Corps to the Normandy area is unwise.
2. The 243rd Infantry Division must be repositioned from Brittany to the northwest corner of the Cotentin peninsula. Rommel says that he would normally not have a problem with that, except that at present, there is nothing that can take over the southwest coastline, short of a couple Öst battalions.
3. They might want to move just one regiment of the 243rd (possibly the 920th) to the Cap de la Hague–Cap de Carteret area. Rommel rejects this idea, as much of the 243rd is to be used to defend ports and man anti-aircraft batteries.
4. They should move the 2nd Luftwaffe Field Division into the 243rd's area. Speidel says that he will discuss this matter with Field Marshal Sperrle's staff tomorrow, but they will probably not like the idea. Instead, Rommel proposes to move the 6th Parachute Regiment further up the peninsula.
5. The 342nd Tank *Panzerzerstörer* Battalion should be kept where it is, deployed on the hills overlooking Cherbourg.
6. The Seventh Army *Stürm* Battalion could be moved around La Haye du Puits. Rommel agrees to this.
7. They should move the 100th Panzer Reserve Battalion inland.[1]

Lunch at La Roche-Guyon is spoiled by yet another aerial attack on the Mantes bridges upstream, as well as the bridges just downstream at Vernon. It seems as if the enemy bombers are trying to cut off the château from Western France. Still, the loss of these bridges to Rommel seems insignificant, since whenever he wants to tour westward, he just takes a ferry across the Seine. However, the idea that the enemy has recently been severing more and more supply links across major rivers like the Seine is disturbing.

That afternoon, they get a call from the Waffen-SS commander in Holland. His units have been asked to take over the left flank of the 16th Luftwaffe Field Division to bolster it. The SS commander gives the standard bureaucratic response: they cannot do that without specific, written permission from *Reichsführer* Himmler. The matter is put on hold.

A couple hours later, while Rommel is out exercising his two dogs, official word comes in from OB West on the reorganization and reformation of the reserve panzer divisions. The 155th Reserve Panzer will become the 9th Panzer. The 273rd Reserve Panzer will become the reconstituted 11th Panzer; and the 179th Reserve Panzer will be absorbed into the recently created 116th Panzer Division under General von Schwerin.

More word from OKW. Göring has (probably gleefully) turned down the request to relocate the III Flak Corps. The batteries are to remain scattered all over France to cover bridges. Rommel just shakes his head. It is a pity that Göring is such an ass. The III Flak Corps would have been a perfect anti-aircraft shield to put near the Calvados coast. Now that area will be weak in AA defense.[2]

***

While his staff prepares for tomorrow's conference, *Generalfeldmarschall* von Rundstedt reviews various status reports. He is irritated that the Allies are indeed taking advantage of Germany's weak air strength. They have begun hitting strategic supply line targets. Railroad centers and trains themselves are suffering badly at the hands of the enemy tactical air forces. Bridges over key rivers like the Somme and the Seine in the northeast are being struck regularly, as are those in the central region along the Loire.

This is quite possibly an attempt to isolate different sections of northwestern France from the northeastern section. What makes things worse is that OB West has lost another railroad repair battalion, transferred to the Italian Front. He had already lost one in January. Now he is down to three. To compensate, he must take construction workers off the West Wall[3] and press them into service onto the railroads. Over 25,000 workers are being diverted.[4]

He glances at a report covering railroad losses. Over 500 locomotives have been damaged by various low-level attacks. Their supply system in France is certainly taking a beating. By the beginning of May, in France alone, over 600 army supply trains had been backlogged. Many are being destroyed systematically. Allied air power has reduced an average running schedule of 100 trains a day in France to a mere 48; by the end of this month, his staff estimates that this number will be down to less than two dozen. Logic dictates that it will go down much further after the invasion comes.

His staff has responded by canceling all military leave and putting some 18,000 workers onto repairing the railways. Another 10,000 are slated to be committed to this endeavor in May, but von Rundstedt knows that will not make the difference. Their efforts will not keep them from singing the tune that Allied air command is calling.

Enemy bombing raids of March and April included airframe parts and assembly factories—eight in March, and almost two dozen in April. The enemy is also hitting various Luftwaffe airfields near the coast, either destroying the aircraft on a continuing basis, or forcing air units to relocate inland.

Enemy fighter escorts have started to get particularly brazen about this. Up until the end of March, they had merely flown along to accompany the bombers flying in for the raids. Starting in April, if a German airfield was along a bombing route and its fighters did not respond to the approaching raid, the escorts had in several instances actually come down to low levels and strafed the aircraft along the runways.

Air casualties are mounting steadily. The Luftwaffe, one report claims, lost over 2,000 aircraft in April, and von Rundstedt is sure that the actual number was substantially greater.

Later that day, von Rundstedt's staff finalizes preparations for the large commanders' conference scheduled for tomorrow afternoon, as well as sorting out preliminary administrative details for the creation of the new army group. The order will go out today. *Armeegruppe G* for southern part of France is now a reality. *Generaloberst* Johannes Blaskowitz has been appointed commander. He too will be at the meeting tomorrow to officially accept his new command. He had many bad run-ins with the Führer in the early years of the war. However, he is a solid officer, a veteran leader of the Polish campaign, an intelligent product of the *Generalstab*, and firmly supported by von Rundstedt for the position.

---

1   The *100. Panzer Ersatz und Ausbildungs Abteilung* (100th Panzer Replacement & Training Battalion, as it was officially referred to) consisted of about 28 light captured French and Soviet tanks, and one *PzKw III*.

2   In his defense, Göring wanted the batteries evenly spread across the main path that the enemy bombers used on their way into Germany. He also denied the request partly just to assert his waning authority. Technically though, although the Reichsmarshal naturally had overall say on the flak corps' deployment through *Luftflottenkommando III* (3rd Air Fleet Command Headquarters in Paris), tactically and operationally, the corps actually fell under the command of the *Luftgaukommando Westfrankreich* (Western France Air District Command).

3   The West Wall was Germany's defensive line, built opposite the Maginot Line and the border to the Low Countries. It was also called the Siegfried Line by the Allies.

4   Before D-Day, another 3,000 workers would be switched.

Monday, May 8

By this time, Allied intelligence is well aware of Rommel's change of strategic headquarters. While the objective of the air raids over the lower Seine is of course to knock out the bridges, they also provide cover for occasional reconnaissance missions sent to get a good understanding of the logistical network set up by the Germans to supply the Seventh Army. In that vein then, a special aerial reconnaissance mission is set for today. As medium bomber formations are sent to bomb the bridges upriver and downriver from La Roche-Guyon, a high-speed reconnaissance plane flies over the château. It desperately avoids deadly anti-aircraft bursts from flak positions located on both sides of river, especially near the ancient Norman tower. The aircraft manages to take a series of photos of both the château and the nearby town.

The Allies now have Rommel's number.

It is yet another pleasant day at La Roche-Guyon. After breakfast, Admiral Ruge sits down with *der Chef*, and they discuss in detail plans for the upcoming reorganization of the Kriegsmarine fleet command.[1]

That morning, the air raid sirens go off. Rommel and the staff members dutifully go down the villa's stairs and into the engineered air raid shelters of the adjoining chalk cliff. Luckily, no bombs are dropped in the area, although the railroad bridge just upriver at Vernon has been hit by *Jabos*.

When the air raid threat ends, it is back upstairs to continue business as usual. After a couple hours of talks and phone calls, Supreme Command has decided that, instead of deploying the remaining elements of the *2. Fallschirmjäger Division* to the center of the Cotentin peninsula, General Falley's *91. Luftlande Division*, also intended to be sent to France but originally to deploy near Nantes, will go to the Cotentin instead. To Rommel, this makes sense defensively. It seems better to put the 91st on the peninsula with its two fully equipped and fully manned regiments, then supplement it with Major von der Heydte's operational 6th *Fallschirmjäger* Regiment, which would then be ordered to the Lessay-Periers area, instead of sending the 2nd Division's two depleted regiments. The air landing troops would be better able to defend the roads in the region, while the exhausted paratroopers coming west from Russia would get to recuperate and rebuild.[2]

Around noon, Rommel and Speidel walk out the side entrance. Getting into Rommel's Horch, they depart for today's scheduled conference in Paris. They enjoy the spring day as they travel southwest down the northern bank of the Seine, watching the scenery as they discuss the upcoming meeting. They enter the beautiful capital city, and Daniel takes them to the luxuriant Hôtel Prince de Galles, where the conference is being held.[3]

They enter the hotel and are greeted by other officers already there. After a lavish late lunch, the senior officers move to a large, luxurious dark-wood paneled conference room in the hotel basement. Here the war conference is to be held. Present are the following senior officers:

- *Generalfeldmarschall* Gerd von Rundstedt, Commander, Western Theater; Chief of Staff, *General der Artillerie* Günther Blumentritt
- *Generalfeldmarschall* Erwin Rommel, commanding Army Group B, and Chief of Staff, *Generalleutnant* Dr. Hans Speidel
- *Generalfeldmarschall* Hugo Sperrle, commanding Luftwaffe Air Fleet III and also Deputy-Commander, Western Theater; Chief of Staff, *Generalmajor* Hermann Plocher.
- *Generaloberst* Johannes Blaskowitz, Outgoing Commander, First Army, incoming Commander, Army Group G; Chief of Staff, *Generalmajor* Heinz von Glydenfeld.
- *Admiral* Theodor Krancke, Commander, Naval Group West; *Vizeadmiral* Gustav Kleikamp, Commander, all naval forces in the Netherlands
- *Generalleutnant* Karl Stülpnagel, Military Governor of France
- *General der Flieger* Friedrich Christiansen, Commander, Netherlands; Chief of Staff, *Generalleutnant* Heinz-Hellmuth von Wühlisch
- *General der Panzertruppen Freiherr* Leo Geyr von Schweppenburg, Commander, Panzer Group West
- *SS Obergruppenführer und Panzergeneral der Waffen-SS* Sepp Dietrich, Commander, I SS Panzer Corps.

Goebbels' Propaganda Ministry takes occasion to make the conference a media affair. The reporters are allowed in to take pictures, and a couple short authorized newsreels are made. The media is told that this meeting is being held to concentrate on developing new ideas to directly repel the expected enemy landing. After the photos are taken and some film shot, the media leaves the room and the conference begins.

The main purpose of the conference is to brief everyone on the newly reorganized command structure in the West. General Blaskowitz seems somewhat nervous. At 63, he is slated to command *Armeegruppe G*,[4] officially created yesterday by OB West. It has been about four years since Blaskowitz has commanded a unit larger than an army, and this high appointment is courtesy of von Rundstedt's recommendation back in March when he had first proposed creating another army group. This new command means that Blaskowitz will again be in regular contact with OKW. Blaskowitz tries not to think about that. He already has enough enemies there, and of course, the Führer's disfavor.

Blumentritt details some significant changes. *Armeegruppe G* will now be responsible for defending southern France below a boundary line running from Tours to the Swiss border. It will be comprised of the First Army, under *General der Infanterie* Kurt von der Chevallerie, headquarters at Bordeaux, and the Nineteenth Army under *General der Infanterie* Georg von Sodenstern, headquarters at Avignon.

Blaskowitz adds that he will establish his own headquarters somewhere near Toulouse. Most of his command staff will be chosen by von Rundstedt.

Von Rundstedt is happy with the new command structure. It makes strategic sense to divide his forces into two army groups, addressing both operational and administrative issues. Just as importantly though, it dilutes Rommel's command authority in France, reducing him to a subordinate position, something the Prussian has been keen on establishing since the Swabian came to France last December.

Other matters are covered. A mobilization plan from Seventh Army commander General Dollmann is reviewed. The 243rd Infantry Division is to be redeployed up the western side of the Cotentin peninsula, and will be backed up by the 206th Panzer Battalion and 342nd *Panzerzerstörer* Battalion.[5] Also discussed are the airborne units that Rommel will be getting for western France.

Close cooperation in defense from the Kriegsmarine is discussed with Admiral Krancke. Then von Rundstedt and Rommel briefly listen to Luftwaffe plans for the invasion, presented by Field Marshal Sperrle. He tells them that when the invasion begins, the alarm will be sent to all Western air units.[6] Pre-made plans to attack the embarkation points and bomber bases will be immediately put into effect. Rommel insists that they instead hit the beaches, and Sperrle reassures him that there will be enough fighters and tactical bombers to do that as well.

Rommel, sitting between von Rundstedt and Admiral Krancke, puts on a good show of cooperative spirit. He is on the one hand happy that the new command structure clarifies the chain of command, and that hopefully duplication of orders will be minimized.

On the other hand though, there is still the question of the panzer reserves. Rommel retains tactical command of the 2nd Panzer and 21st Panzer Division, as well as getting the newly created 116th Panzer, which von Rundstedt suggests should be deployed near the Seine. An official directive from OKW dated the day before makes it official. However, Rommel still has no real power to use them. That means he cannot, without specific permission of von Rundstedt and OKW,

- relocate them closer to the coast or to another sector,
- combine them into a stronger mobile force,
- take immediate command of them when the enemy lands,
- or direct their training for immediate response and anti-invasion maneuvers.

Not that it is any consolation, but General Blaskowitz down south will have a similar limited tactical control (and thus, no operational control) over the reconstructed 9th and 11th Panzer Divisions, as well as the 2nd SS Panzer Division *"Das Reich,"* returning from Russia (OB West having issued the order the day before). But Dietrich's I SS Panzer Corps, the élite *Panzer Lehr,* and the 17th SS *Panzergrenadier* will remain under the strict control of OKW. OB West will retain full responsibility for the training and administration of these units through von Geyr's *PanzerGruppe West.*

After the conference ends and the generals chat for a while, Rommel returns to his château. Rommel later has Lang note in his diary:

Throughout the conference, Rundstedt was most kind and amiable.

On the other hand, Rommel has basically the same command control that he had that morning. And his main mobility problem has not been resolved. He must be able to move those panzers close to the coast, and to be able to take swift command of them when needed. Today's conference shows that he is still far from achieving that objective. Since von Rundstedt, Geyr, and Guderian are set against him on this (as he suspects, are Keitel, Jodl, and Warlimont in OKW as well), he must go along with this arrangement—at least for now.

Jodl has written to him their reasoning:

The enemy's intentions are at present so obscure, that some capability for strategic command must be maintained by means of keeping a separate, if modest, reserve. These High Command reserves will be released for operations—without further application by yourself—the moment we can be certain about the enemy's intentions and focus of attack.

That evening, Rommel relaxes and takes time to write to Lucie. Today, he writes to her about the dog the civilians gave him a few days ago to replace Ajax. He writes amusingly:

Dearest Lu:

The OT have now sent me a big, brown, smooth-haired hunting dog. It's young, good at following and affectionate, and has soon settled down to its new life. Elbo looked aggrieved at first, but he now has lots of fun with his playfellow. It was at feeding time that Elbo suffered badly at first.[7] Anyway, the two of them got me up the hill four times yesterday. I shall either send Elbo to you shortly or get you to look out for a dog for yourself. It's strange what a distraction these creatures can be, and how they can take your mind off your troubles.

Rommel finishes his letter, then begins to help his aide pack his belongings for another inspection tour. This one will start with the 84th Corps, as per his conversation with Jodl. He reflects back on all the media at today's conference. He does not mind the coverage, and is satisfied that newsreels recorded his optimism.

He goes over in his mind again the command problem regarding the panzers. It really bothers him to be nearly powerless on this issue, a feeling he is not used to. Of course, he might just go directly to the top. The Führer basically agreed with his concepts of defending the coast. So why not jump the chain of command and go right to him? Rommel has done it before. Besides, as a field marshal, he carries the privilege of having access to Hitler anytime he desires. Anyway, Rommel learned long ago that the last man to get to talk to the Führer will probably be the one to get his way.

Rommel feels that a trip to Berchtesgaden might be coming up.

By early May, 1944, the Allies have realized that the crucial matter of setting a day for the landing must be decided. The target date, originally called "Y-Day," had been set for June 1. Now the date has to be pinpointed.

Maximum favorable conditions for the air drop require light as well, but not so much early on in the evening, so that aircraft could still approach in darkness. Thus a full moon, rising around 1 or 2 a.m. would be best.[8] And low winds are vital, to minimize scattering; no greater than Force 3 (8–12 mph) on shore and Force 4 (13–18 mph) offshore.

Today, as the German Western leaders confer in Paris, Admiral Sir Bertram Ramsay, commanding the Allied Naval Expeditionary Force, sits down with General Eisenhower to determine an exact date. The admiral tells him that, according to moon and tide predictions, and judging from the estimated level of readiness by then, the earliest favorable time after Y-Day would be June 5 (Y+4) and 6 (Y+5)—weather permitting, of course. The moon would rise late the evening before, and low tide would occur just after dawn.

Ramsay tells Eisenhower that the weather will be their biggest worry. Based upon historical weather records of the Normandy coast, the planners have calculated that the odds that all the required weather conditions are met in the month of June are only one in thirteen. Still, even with the weather odds against him, Eisenhower tentatively decides on June 5. But he keeps open the 6th or 7th as well—just in case the weather on the 5th is unfavorable to launch the landings.

---

1   There has been some speculation as to whether or not Ruge and Speidel talked at all about matters pertaining to the conspiracy against the Nazi regime. Certainly Speidel was one of the plotters, and more than likely, Ruge was quite sympathetic to their cause. Since Speidel was going to accompany Rommel to the capital, he would be in close proximity to other co-conspirators in the Paris cell. Perhaps some secret documents would be passed, as well as some words.

2   The battle-weary elements of the 2nd Parachute Division (except von der Heydte's 6th Regiment, which was already in Normandy) had been taken out of Russia at the beginning of the month to briefly rest and refit in Germany, before they were ordered to Normandy. There they would refit, reorganize and train, but still be able to enjoy some relaxation and leisure in the peaceful French countryside.

3   "Hotel Prince of Wales" is a luxurious hotel, built in 1928 in honor of England's Prince of Wales, the future King Edward VII. It is located on the Avenue George V, named after his father. The hotel was so named so that the prince would stay there whenever he visited Paris.

     The conference was originally scheduled to be held at the OB West command bunker for security reasons, considering the ranking general officers that were attending. However, since most of them were bringing staff and support members, there simply was not enough room to accommodate them all. A hotel would be much more comfortable. It would be much easier for guest officers and staff staying overnight to simply go downstairs. And of course, von Rundstedt would use any excuse to enjoy dining out. In addition, the Propaganda Ministry was going to make this a media affair, complete with cameramen, photographers, and reporters. So the location was changed to this Parisian hotel commonly used by the Germans.

4   Partly because he has been in disfavor with the Führer and partly because it is smaller in size, Blaskowitz's newly created army group has not been given the regular classification of a *Heeresgruppe*. Rather, it is denoted as an *Armeegruppe*, an inferior designation often denoting a heterogeneous command or two combined armies of multinational groups—especially if only one was German and the other from a second-rate satellite nationality, such as Romania. Usually though, it was given to a smaller formation, often to ad hoc temporary commands (a point no doubt not overlooked by the commanders present). As such, his headquarters would not rate all the complete administrative and personnel allowances that were normally given to a full army group headquarters.

   While the new *Armeegruppe G* was much smaller than a true army group, there was a shortage of transport and of key organizational personnel. Still, the biggest reason for this lesser title was Blaskowitz's past relations with Hitler. Thus, the less-eminent term was in essence an affront.

5   The 206th, to be located between Cap de la Hague and Cap de Carteret, was an ad hoc unit created around Versailles in November 1943. It was composed of nearly four dozen miscellaneous light tanks, including captured French, Russian, and Czech models. German panzers were limited to outmoded *PzKw I* and *PzKw II* models. No information was found on the 342nd.

6   Luftwaffe High Command had decided that in case of an invasion in the West, the alarm code phrase "Dr. Gustav West," a euphemism for "*Dringende Gefahr West*" ("Extreme Danger West") would be sent.

7   The field marshal's dogs were limited to the ground floor. They were kept in his study, and were not allowed in the officers' dining room.

8   For the invasion, the moon actually rose at 6:30 p.m. on June 5.

Tuesday, May 9

Another sunny day at La Roche-Guyon. Having discussed with his staff the results of the senior officers' conference the night before, Rommel leaves with a few senior staff members on another inspection tour. Prodded by Jodl's report that the British had found ways of defeating his beach obstacles, and since the Normandy area seems to be the focal point of recent reinforcement activity and personal concern by the Führer himself, Rommel decides that another tour west is in order.

Having notified Marcks three days ago to expect him, his motorcade now leaves at 7 a.m. Rommel's big, rumbling Horch circles in the courtyard once and then rolls through the main gate. Trailing behind as usual is Ruge's old Mercury, with *Generalmajor* Lattman, their artillery advisor, sitting beside the admiral. The motorcade passes the beautiful linden trees on the left side of the drive, and turning left onto the main road, it enters the southwest half of the village.

They travel northwest with the Seine on their left, downstream to the town of Vernon, where they turn to cross over as usual. However, they find that the bridge there has been recently destroyed. So they are again forced to take a ferry across the big river.

Now finally on the western bank, they continue northwest to the small coastal town of Houlgate, just east of Cabourg. There they closely inspect some of the offshore obstacles recently erected. Rommel approves of the work being done. Out inspecting the obstacles, walking along the wet flats, the field marshal forgets how fast the tide comes in here (some three meters an hour), and suddenly they all find themselves scurrying off the beach to avoid the incoming waves.

They continue to the open battery near Hougate and inspect it. They find that it has been the target of a number of bombings, and some of the damage is plain to see. They continue on along the bay, southeast to Dives-sur-Mer, where 84th Corps commander General Marcks meets them. There they find that the recent dry spell has somewhat diminished the local attempts at deliberate flooding of the area. Hopefully, some spring rain will take care of that.

Onward, they turn and travel inland again, southwest towards the city of Caen. As they approach the outskirts, they discover an air raid in progress. They pull over until the bombing ends. While waiting, Rommel consults privately for a bit with Marcks in his Horch, while the staff members in the motorcade stand outside in the warm sunlight. After the two talk a while, they all proceed on into Caen.

Starting off the briefing, Marcks reviews the disposition of his units. The 716th and 352nd Divisions hold the Calvados coast, while the 709th and 243rd defend the northern part of the Cotentin peninsula. The 77th Infantry is moving from the Caen area southeast to the Sélune Estuary, just south of Avranches. The 21st Panzer Division will be just south of Caen. Good. Rommel nods in approval.

Major von der Heydte's newly arrived 6th Parachute Regiment of 3,450 men will move near Périers, and the 91st *Luftlande* division, initially slated for Brittany, will instead move to a position south of Valognes, high in the center of the Cotentin peninsula. The 206th Panzer Battalion, with its almost pathetic combination of French, Czech, and old German *PzKw I* and *II* tanks, is up in the northwest. The Seventh Army Shock Battalion and its 1,100 assault troops are on maneuvers out of La Haye-du-Puits.

One problem is the 352nd Infantry, which is defending the western part of the Calvados beaches. The division, still recovering from its losses in Russia, only has four good battalions and four coastal batteries, spread out along the coast around eight major bunkers. Rommel makes a note to have them reinforced by June with a few dozen pillboxes, some mortar pits, rocket-launching sites, and dozens of machine-gun nests.

There has been an increase in sabotage and small raids in the Brittany area in the spring, and a good deal of their supplies are coming from Allied air drops. Enemy activity has increased remarkably, with very heavy aerial reconnaissance of the coastal areas, especially over the Cotentin peninsula and the Orne estuary. Coastal batteries are getting bombed heavily. Fortunately this includes the dummy positions they have set up to fool the Allied bombers. Also targeted are supply bottlenecks, such as bridges, major intersections, and depots. Rommel seems a bit skeptical at Marcks' concern. The enemy air activity in this area is still less than it has recently been further north, in the Fifteenth Army area.

Marcks then covers his future plans. For one thing, he intends to further strengthen the Cotentin peninsula. He is heartened by the fact that since the peninsula is so narrow,[1] any unit stationed in the interior could move to just about any trouble spot along the coast of the peninsula, or to the beaches east of the Vire River. Still, he points out, the Channel Islands are vulnerable, although a landing on Guernsey is not likely, due to the heavy fortifications there. Jersey though, could be taken in a surprise air drop.

Rommel asks him where he would position another panzer division if they could get one released. Marcks points to the map, near the base of the Cotentin peninsula. "Near Carentan," he tells Rommel.

The field marshal nods in agreement.

Marcks goes over other problems. Obstacle construction will continue, despite material shortages. Cement is in critically low supply, and he has not received any for a week now. Scrap metal is hard to get too, so many of the obstacles are being made out of wood. Marcks' men have done some 80km of coastline, and some 170,000 stakes of "Rommel's asparagus."

Next up is *Oberst* Hans von Rohr, the Cherbourg fortress commander. His report on the readiness of the port details extensive progress, and Rommel is pleased. Next up is *Generalmajor* Edgar Feuchtinger, commanding the reconstituted 21st Panzer Division. Positioning his stout frame before a map, he rattles off a precise, updated order of battle—his *Schlachtordnung*. He reports on the increased deliveries of the new *PzKw IV* panzers. And his division is making its own efforts to create some ad hoc tank destroyers by continuing to install and secure German anti-tank guns on some old captured French armored chassis. Becker is hard at work.

Rommel tells Feuchtinger that he wants him to obtain an accurate layout of the road networks in the area to scope out the best routes for rapid mechanized movement. He also orders him to identify all possible open staging areas in the Cotentin peninsula that could be used to organize a mobile combat group for mounting a counterattack.

The field marshal, knowing Feuchtinger's lack of armored fighting experience (as well as that of a number of his division officers), goes into details. Every river crossing is to be utilized, he warns. They must move at night whenever possible, or else in bad weather. Long, strung-out columns, easy prey for enemy *Jabos*, are to be avoided at all costs. Feuchtinger estimates that his trucks and armored cars can reach Cherbourg in four uninterrupted hours, and the mechanized units in a day or so.

Rommel stresses upon him the critical importance of having contingency plans. They may have to move through areas blocked by paratroopers, debris and ruins; or fight in totally unsuitable terrain. "Cover *all* possibilities," he tells him.

They break for lunch and go over to a nearby restaurant in Caen. Afterwards, Rommel is off again with his staff, accompanied by Marcks and his own corps staff. They travel to the 1716th Artillery Regiment. Starting with the Riva Bella battery next to the Orne estuary and less than a kilometer north of Ouistreham, they inspect its gun positions. Then it's westward along the coast to look over the 150mm guns at the Longues-sur-Mer naval battery. At this time, Admiral Hennecke, the Cherbourg peninsula naval commander, joins them. Looking out over the bay, he tells the gathered officers, "If they come, they'll come here." It is not so important that he believes it—he just wants them to believe it.

From there, they continue westward along the coast, inspecting the beaches near Vierville.[2] After making some more comments and his staff taking notes, they move on to Grandcamp, next to the Vire estuary.

It is supposedly on this portion of the tour that Rommel stands overlooking a deserted beach, facing the Channel. There he once again tells those officers present one of his cardinal points—that the first twenty-four hours of the invasion will be decisive. And that, "*Für die Alliierten, und auch für die Deutschen, der längste Tag wird.*" ("For the Allies, as well as for the Germans, it will be the longest day.")[3]

They continue on across the Vire and pass the battery at Pointe du Hoc. Rommel is told that fierce bombing in mid-April destroyed one of the battery's six 155mm French guns. Because of this, the other five were covertly moved inland. They will be brought back to the bunkers when the invasion begins.

Rommel notes the lower air activity here than that over Dunkirk—further evidence to him that the blow will fall elsewhere. Still, his beach defenses in Normandy are progressing steadily, although they are much less advanced than those at Calais.

They move inland to Isigny-sur-Mer and inspect some flooded areas. They finally reach Marcks' headquarters at St. Lô around 8 p.m. that night, once again tired from the day's activities. Marcks puts on a decent meal for them. Afterwards, he and the field marshal have a long, interesting talk, while several officers take walks around the area before retiring to the guest quarters.

More reports come in of coastal batteries and bridges being bombed. Calais, Sangatte, Frethune, Marcouf... Morsaline...

That night, Rommel's official diary reflects his activity:

> *Have left on an inspection tour of the Cotentin Peninsula, since this seems to be the area where the Schwerpunkt of an enemy landing might take place. On the way I was impressed by the remarkable work and achievements of the 711th Division. It was certainly worth my spending so much time and energy on the construction of our defenses. Without these I would have looked with great anxiety upon the possibilities of enemy landings over here.*

Today, Hitler's doctor, 57-year-old Theo Morell, examines his only patient (who he identifies as mysterious "Patient A") and notes his high level of stress. He also observes advanced neurological problems. The nearly uncontrollable tremor in the Führer's hand is now present in one of his legs as well, a byproduct no doubt of the stress and a certain degree of psychological hysteria. A physical reason for this is, in the physician's mind, unlikely. The doctor notes in his diary:

> *Leg tremor, caused by agitation [invasion imminent, where?]*[4]

Today, British Admiral Ramsay orders the Allied naval forces in Great Britain to freeze all invasion plans by May 12, so that the deluge of changes, alterations, and augmentations do not overwhelm his planners.

Critical in their timetable will be a well-planned air offensive. Huge air fleets of fighters and bombers will have to hit preliminary targets all over Europe. Between April 1 and D-Day, the Allies will have flown over two hundred thousand bombing sorties over northern France, averaging one ton of bombs dropped for every sortie. They will lose nearly two thousand aircraft in doing so.

---

1 The average width is 35km, and the distance across the lower part between Lessay and Carentan is only 25km.
2 This will be Omaha beach.
3 Rommel had, according to one source, told this to his aide Lang earlier in the year, on April 22. However, Rommel was nowhere near this area on that day, and Ruge's detailed book gives no indication that Rommel was on the road that day. A quiet day, he wrote. Another source writes that the quote was made to Lang on April 2. Some sources even claim that the famous comment was actually never made, but rather conjured up as a dramatic vehicle when Cornelius Ryan was writing *The Longest Day* and later focused on during the filming of the movie. Still, Ryan himself, a reliable journalist, believed these words to have been spoken. Anyway, why else would he have so named the book?

According to Ryan (who gave no date to the quote, either in his book or in his notes): "They had stood on a deserted beach, and Rommel, a short, stocky figure in a heavy greatcoat with an old muffler around his throat, had stalked up and down waving his 'informal' marshal's baton, a two-foot-long silver-topped black stick with a red, black and white tassel. He had pointed to the sands with his baton and said, 'The war will be won or lost on the beaches. We'll have only one chance to stop the enemy and that's while he's in the water... struggling to get ashore. Reserves will never get up to the point of attack and it's foolish even to consider them. The *Hauptkampflinie* [main line of resistance] will be here... everything we have must be on the coast. Believe me, Lang, the first twenty-four hours of the invasion will be decisive... For the Allies, as well as the Germans, it will be the longest day.'"

4   Advanced modern theories suggest that Hitler's tremors were most likely due to some form of Parkinson's disease or as a result of the high levels of toxicity in his body from all the amphetamines he was being given.

Wednesday, May 10

After breakfast, Rommel's small convoy leaves St. Lô at 7 a.m. in a light fog to inspect the Cotentin peninsula. Admirals Ruge and Hennecke go with him. Featured in today's inspection tour will be several strongpoints along the coast.

Driving through Carentan, they stop at a coastal fortification identified as Strongpoint WN-5.[1] Rommel is not too happy with the design of this position, including the exposed open pits for the four 50mm guns, and the uncovered 37mm *Panzerstellung* R67 Renault tank turret. Plus, it is not fortified enough. Ramming blocks are too few. The anti-airborne "asparagus" behind is too scant. There are not enough Czech hedgehogs along the beach in front, and he sees no Belgian gates at all. Rommel vents his displeasure upon the 709th's divisional commander, von Schlieben, regimental commander Keil, and the company commander, *Hauptmann* Matz.

In response, one junior officer dares report to him about the difficulties getting his men to construct effective barbed-wire obstacles. Rommel is still upset at this point, and at the sudden interruption, he impulsively looks at the junior officer. Glaring at the young man, he snaps, "Let me see your hands for a minute, lieutenant." He obviously wants to show him that it is hard to assess the capabilities of your men if you are not there alongside them.

Leutnant Jahnke seems shaken by this command, but he dutifully complies. He removes his smooth, gray suede gloves and holds his hands out. The field marshal looks down and notes that they are scratched with small tears and have some calluses. This boy has obviously learned somewhere (probably in Russia) that good officers pitch in right next to their men to prepare defensive obstacles.

Rommel's anger subsides. He nods his head. "Well done, lieutenant. The blood on an officer's hands from fortification work is worth every bit as much as that shed in battle."

Jahnke, only 23, is a seasoned veteran of the Eastern Front and a Knight's Cross recipient. He wants to reply that he has had to work hard because his men are not trained in building modern fortifications, and are actually drawing on their experiences from the World War I. Instead though, the second lieutenant holds his frustration and merely replies *"Jawohl, Herr Feldmarschall."*

Rommel departs and continues up the coast, stopping to inspect the St. Marcouf battery. The position was hit hard in late April, and evidence of the damage is clear.

Further up the peninsula, the motorcade stops at the main battery near Morsalines. It sits on a hill overlooking a stretch of beach that runs northeast of the Vire Estuary.[2] The battery, located not far south of St. Vaast-la-Hougue and installed back in 1941, now has vegetation growing along the sides of the bunkers. The position consists of six 155mm captured French K416 guns, mounted in semi-open concrete positions.

Realistic camouflage nets hang in selected areas. Admiral Hennecke points out that the battery, having been there for a few years, has no doubt been located and pinpointed by the Allies, thanks mostly to the Resistance.

Rommel takes a tour of the area and sees bomb craters everywhere. Several of the six exposed main guns, as well as the secondary 75mm and 20mm flak positions, have suffered quite a bit from aerial attacks. A number of them have been partially buried by bomb debris, and several of the guns have been tipped over, the wheels on one side now sticking up into the air. The netting is therefore not fooling the bombers. No, concrete barbettes are needed to protect the guns from above.

The battery commander arrives and confirms what Rommel has seen. He reports that a low-level enemy air raid the night before destroyed two of the guns. The other four are damaged, having been hit hard by the RAF. The battery at Pointe du Hoc, as Rommel has already been told, had been hit too.

Rommel marvels that the enemy bombing patterns are so accurate. He is told, "They used special flares that turned the night sky into day, *Feldmarschall.*"

Rommel nods knowingly. He has seen nighttime flares used effectively in North Africa. He orders that the four damaged guns be moved back to an open but sheltered area some three kilometers inland, closer to Videcosville, and remain there, even after they are fixed. They can still be moved up in time.

When the battery commander expresses some indecision, Rommel shakes his head. "Don't worry," he replies consolingly. "The enemy cannot get a huge invasion fleet across the Channel without us having some sort of warning time from our recon sources. It won't take you long to move the guns back up into their bunker positions. In the meantime, I have a feeling that this not the last you've heard from the enemy bombers."[3] It makes sense, and the relieved battery commander replies that it will be done. It should not take long to move the guns back up into their bunker positions.[4]

Rommel's procession continues up the road towards Cherbourg. At 1 p.m., they stop at La Pernelle, a small town a few kilometers north of St. Vaast. Rommel gives a short speech there. A journalist records his words on tape.

They continue on to St.-Pierre-Église at the top of the peninsula, some 10km west of Barfleur. It is the strategic crossroads for the area, and through it runs a main rail line from Paris westward to the port of Cherbourg. There they are briefed.

Then lunch. As they often do, during the meal, the officers pull out a radio and tune in to the BBC, today broadcasting from a station just opposite Calais. Enemy broadcasts are usually a good source of some information, even if it is skewed to the enemy's viewpoint. And it is usually entertaining. They all relax, sit back, enjoy their meal, and listen to the news broadcast. There are the usual items about rationing, the British Parliament, and the royal family…

Then a news item comes on that surprises Rommel. The announcer reports the bombing of the Morsalines battery on the coast—the one that he has just been at. Is it a coincidence that the very battery he inspected that morning is in the news broadcast? Should security on his travels be re-evaluated?

But the announcer's next comments absolutely shock him. His eyes narrow as the radio voice quips sarcastically, "Well, *Herr* Rommel, you've finally managed to discover your battery at Morsalines—the one you didn't see on your last inspection trip because it was so well camouflaged!"

After a short stunned silence, his staff members react by blurting out a few dismayed exclamations as he sits back in surprise and tries to organize his confused train of thought.

How in the hell does the British news announcer know where he has just been? Perhaps the enemy knows their route. That could very well mean treason. This makes twice now in two days. They had originally planned to go on up to Cherbourg today, but he had decided to change their schedule last night when the evening's BBC announcement had mentioned that he would be touring the port facilities there on Wednesday. He had figured that by changing their schedule and not going where the British news had reported, he would throw off any possible attacks against his motorcade (either from the air or from partisans), as well as smugly show everyone that British radio was not always right. So he had altered their route. But it turns out after all that the laugh was on him. Now, only a couple hours after he has stopped at Morsalines, his visit is being broadcast by the BBC.

Perturbed and wary now, they cautiously continue the tour, ending up on the other side of the peninsula, before they start back for St. Lô. Luckily, they make it without incident.

That evening, he dines again with General Marcks. Reports coming in from his château include an OKW summary. It states that:

- The invasion will probably occur in mid-May, with the 18th the best pick.
- The most likely location will be Normandy, not Calais. The second is Brittany. (So much for the popular Straits of Dover presumption.)
- Heavy air attacks on very small areas are expected to accompany intense, severe naval gunfire support of the landing.
- The introduction of new weapons is quite possible.
- Possibly dense airborne landings could occur just before the landing.

Rommel spends the rest of the evening discussing with his staff and with Marcks today's events, the summary, and further ideas on new types of minefields and tactics they could employ.

That night he notes in his daily diary:

Am proceeding with my visit to the peninsula...

An Allied landing in this [Morsalines] area seems quite possible inasmuch as the enemy would not fear any menace to its flanks.... we cannot count upon the Luftwaffe. (In spite of that the gentlemen of the Luftwaffe sit on their high horses, supercilious as ever.)

It is indeed an impossible situation that I, as commander-in-chief of an army group, do not know what means the Luftwaffe will put into battle when the decisive moment strikes. After all, as Commander-in-Chief, I should know...

Today, the Allied air commands begin a concentrated campaign against German coastal radar installations and support sites, attacking between Ostende in the northeast and the Channel Islands off the Cotentin peninsula. Also targeted are radio and other communication centers. Fighter groups begin singling out these special detection networks all over northern Europe. Top priority goes to the large, long-range radar stations, because the Allies figure that they would be the hardest to repair and would take the longest time to put back in operation.

---

1   *Widerstandnest* Position #5. A *Widerstandnest* ("resistance nest") was an isolated strongpoint of resistance. The coastal division units were usually broken down into numbered pockets of troops (such as W-22, W-16, etc.) that were clumped into small fortified sections along the coast.

2   This includes what will be Utah beach.

3   Rommel of course was right. The battery was hit again the night of May 27, this time by Canadian bombers.

4   Unfortunately for the Germans, moving the guns back would turn out to be a critical mistake, because when the Allies landed at Utah beach, through faulty navigation, they accidentally came ashore at a section of beach some two kilometers southeast of their intended landing zone. Because of these two factors, the Morsalines battery could not effectively shell the beachhead, although they did respond and prompt several warships in the Allied fleet to fire upon the battery. The guns were eventually carted off to Cherbourg to be mounted within the fortress.

Thursday, May 11

Today, in a continuing pre-invasion campaign, the Eighth Air Force begins coordinated operations against Luftwaffe airfields, especially those less than 150 miles from the planned invasion beaches. This includes some 40 fighter airfields. Special emphasis will be placed on aircraft maintenance and repair installations. By D-Day, this effort will total some 90 such raids. The Luftwaffe though will suffer little, since most of their aircraft have already been moved inland. When this becomes evident to the Allies later in the month, they will discontinue their attacks.

In the meantime, the air effort continues against rail centers and marshaling yards. The ones at Chaumont, some 136 miles southeast of Paris, are hit.

It is a beautiful morning. Rommel is off again, his last day for this inspection tour before he leaves Marcks and heads back towards his château. Today, Rommel wants to wind it up inspecting the 21st Panzer Division. At present, it is the only panzer unit that would be able to immediately respond to any landing on the Normandy beaches. On instinct, Rommel stops at Falaise early in the morning, and drops in on the headquarters of the 100th Panzer Regiment, commanded by *Oberst* Hermann von Oppeln-Bronikowski.[1]

Rommel arrives around 8:15 a.m. They park, and the field marshal climbs out of his Horch and walks briskly over to the regimental headquarters. Von Oppeln is a decorated, well-seasoned panzer veteran of the Russian Front. Rommel expects no problems here. So it is unpleasantly surprising when he walks into the adjutant's office and is told that the regiment's gallant commanding officer is not around. Rommel, disappointed and impatient, asks that he be found immediately.

While the field marshal cools his heels, two of the regimental staff aides fly out the door and over to von Oppeln's quarters to get him. They find their colonel passed out on his bed, sleeping off a rousing night of heavy drinking. He is lying there still in yesterday's uniform, smelling strongly of stale alcohol and in need of a shave.

Excitedly they wake him, and the tired colonel opens one eye.

"*Herr Oberst,*" one of the aides says urgently. "*Herr Oberst!* Come! Please, *Herr Oberst! Feldmarschall* Rommel is here!"

Von Oppeln, groggy, partially sits up, his eyes still half-closed. "Who?" he barks. He is not in a good mood. He overdid it (again) the night before, and his head feels like it is going to split apart.

"*Feldmarschall* Rommel!"

Von Oppeln sighs, trying to wake up. "Rommel?" he grumps. "Did you say Rommel?!" He sits up and scratches his head. His tongue feels like sandpaper.

"*Jawohl, Herr Oberst!* He is here for an inspection!"

"*Ja, ja*," he grumbles in a tired voice as he staggers up out of bed up and tries to straighten his uniform. What on earth is the field marshal doing here at this hour? And him in bed. Well, no time for hygiene.

"Why the hell didn't anyone tell me that he was coming?" he yells.

"No one knew, *Herr Oberst!*" his aide replies excitedly. "He just came!"

Great. Just damned great.

Some ten minutes later, von Oppeln walks into the headquarters office. Rommel, who has been slowly losing his patience waiting all this time, notes with irritation that while the colonel has washed his stubbled face (for whatever that was worth), stale alcohol is still on his breath, and his uniform, smelling of tobacco, is wrinkled, smudged and disheveled. The man's face suggests the pain that is no doubt hammering in his head. Obviously, he had been actively carousing into the late hours and is hung over. Rommel, turns to him with a scowl.

"Good morning, *Herr Feldmarschall*," the colonel croaks politely, giving what he hopes is a disarming smile. Actually, he probably cannot even feel his face.

Rommel, his blue eyes blazing, explodes. "You're lazy *stinkers!*" he roars at the startled colonel, who winces in pain at the sudden noise. "What happens if the enemy invasion begins before eight-thirty?"

Von Oppeln, his head splitting and clearly suffering, is at a loss for words. Caught off guard, he resignedly shrugs his shoulders, wearily slumps down into a chair, and mutters with a sigh, "Catastrophe."

What the hell. They are going to shoot him anyway. Now would be a good time to do it.

The room goes deathly quiet as the other officers gape at the two of them with horrified expressions. How will the field marshal react? Amazingly though, von Oppeln's delivery is perfect comic relief, and it hits the field marshal just right. In the ensuing silence, Rommel, thrown off guard, cannot stop a slow smile from breaking across his face. He chuckles softly. The retort has amused him, and he obviously cannot chastise the poor guy any further. He plainly is hurting enough. Besides, von Oppeln knows his stuff. He is a Knight's Cross holder, he has cheated death by enemy fire several times in France and in Russia.

Still smiling, Rommel mercifully shakes his head in amusement and leaves the building with his staff. Chuckling softly, he heads for his car. He can almost hear the sighs of relief coming from inside.

He goes on to inspect the regiment. They have worked hard recently, preparing certain defensive positions. They have dug holes in the ground for their panzers to sit in, hull down, so that just the turrets are visible above ground. They have also buried munitions and supplies. Rommel is satisfied.

He makes sure that they run patrols and conduct exercises—not that they can set off much ordnance. It is too scarce. One or maybe two shots in a firing exercise is the most that can be allowed. Of course, once the invasion comes, they will be able to fire. He instructs that each panzer be allocated 100 shells for the real thing.

At the drill ground, he attends a presentation put on by some mortars, and by Major Becker's rocket-launching company. He has again done some improvising by taking stationary *Nebelwerfers* (fog or smoke launchers) and mounting them onto some of those French tracked vehicles.

Then comes a firing exercise to demonstrate laying down a smoke screen, Rommel watches awestruck, as several volleys of rockets are launched with one of the most awful noises that he has ever heard, and whomp into the ground in succession, the explosions starting a small forest fire. To him, the demonstration is an overwhelming success. He gives Becker his heartiest congratulations.

"Build me more," he says, beaming.

He goes on to view the rest of the division. He inspects von Luck's 125th *Panzergrenadiers*, noting that their 1st Battalion now has halftracks for transport. The 2nd Battalion now has a number of supply trucks, although some are odd models.

He converses with von Luck, who tells him more about Becker's strange self-propelled weapons. General Feuchtinger had a few weeks ago ordered him to drive to "*Sonderkommando Becker*" in Paris and familiarize himself with the new equipment. Von Luck had gone and had marveled at the ingenious mobile assault weapons Becker had managed to create out of old captured chassis, odd-caliber guns, and some scrap metal.

Still chatting, Rommel and von Luck wander off to talk to some more divisional officers. Food in this area, Rommel is told, is scarce. Potatoes are often rotten, and meat is very hard to come by. As for the French themselves—well, they tolerate the occupiers, but predictably do not like them at all. Rather, they treat them in a snobbish, haughty fashion. That is understandable, under the circumstances.

Finally it is time to leave. Rommel thanks the officers present for their efforts to remain civil with the local populace, and exhorts them to stay so. Angry Frenchmen is the last thing that he needs at this time, especially in light of the recent escalated activities of *La Résistance*.

He stops to have lunch with Feuchtinger at his division's staff quarters at St.-Pierre-sur-Dives.[2] There is one new detail for the division commander. Rommel has decided that, until he can get a sizeable panzer unit moved to the base of the Cotentin peninsula, the 21st Panzer Recon Battalion will have to deploy west some 100 kilometers to around Carentan. He instructs Feuchtinger to plan for moving them soon.[3]

He returns to his château that night. Tired, he goes straight to bed.

***

Today, von Rundstedt is on the phone with Keitel at OKW, complaining about his crippled rail supply network. The enemy air attacks in the last couple months have been devastating. Hundreds of locomotives have been hit. Von Rundstedt asks if he can be allowed to use prisoners of war to help repair his rail units. As a precedent, he points out that Kesselring had been allowed to do so a couple weeks earlier.

Keitel promises to ask the Führer.

***

At 84th Corps headquarters, General Marcks is thankful that Rommel has finally finished his inspection tour. He likes discussing defensive methods with the field marshal, but the man at times makes him feel decidedly uncomfortable. Now, sitting at his desk, he continues the letter he had started home:

> *These last few days, Rommel was again with me. We get along well, although we are very different. Everything here too seems to push the final decision. Perhaps it has come closer. It will come to us in May.*

He goes on:

> *Opinion at present is that the Tommies have decided to tackle me... I've been given a lot of fine new soldiers, and I've been busy unpacking them from their cardboard boxes and setting them up. This brings the number in my corps up to more than 100,000.*
>
> *It's highly gratifying to see the number and the quality of divisions that we can still turn out in this, the fifth war year! The latest to arrive here, the 91st Airborne Division, is a real élite one; we had nothing remotely like it left by 1918. So I'm looking into the future with a good heart, whatever they choose to throw at me. I've got this bad feeling that things won't start heating up until about my birthday.*

Marcks pauses and stares down at the paper. It is strange, but the night before when they dined, he and Rommel had actually enjoyed a pleasant evening, despite the fact that they occasionally disagreed on schedules. Marcks had once complained about all the work his men were doing on the beach defenses. He had grumbled that his men were getting "neither training nor rest."

Rommel had looked back at him and replied dryly, "My dear Marcks, which would they rather be—tired? Or dead?"[4]

They had later stumbled on the amusing fact that Marcks and the field marshal's wife had the same birthday—June 6. Marcks will be 53, while Lucie will turn 50.

Marcks now wonders what this birthday would bring him, besides another year to reflect back on.

He looks down and continues writing.

---

1   The 100th Panzer Regiment is the armored unit for the 21st Panzer Division. Later this month, it became the 22nd Panzer Regiment, to avoid confusion with the 100th Panzer Battalion.

   Forty-five-year-old Hermann Leopold August von Oppeln-Bronikowski had served in World War I as a lieutenant, winning the Iron Cross in 1918. Between wars, he became an award-winning champion horseman and actually won an Olympic gold medal in 1936. In 1939, he served as a panzer commander in Poland, after which he was transferred to OKH. In of 1941, he was sent to the Russian Front, where he served with distinction, having several panzers shot out from under him. A number of times he successfully led ad hoc forces himself against the enemy. Although considered an excellent panzer commander, he had problems with higher authority because he was an excessive drinker. He survived the war and died of a heart attack on September 9, 1966.

2 Located some 20km southeast of Caen.

3 For some reason, Rommel later changed his mind about this move, perhaps because of objections by von Rundstedt or Geyr von Schweppenberg. Interestingly, had the panzer battalion been stationed near Carentan on D-Day, they could very well have helped the Germans retake Ste.-Mère-Église from the American paratroopers that morning, or might have successfully counterattacked with von Heydte's parachutists against the Utah beachhead.

4 In the movie *The Longest Day* (for which Cornelius Ryan was a key consultant), Rommel makes the remark to Fifteenth Army commander Hans von Salmuth.

Friday, May 12

Rommel this morning finds himself in a sort of funk. The isolation of his position and the desperate urgency in his mission are starting to affect him. To get his mind off issues, he plays with Elbo and Treff.

Then he calls Jodl at Berchtesgaden and reports to him that the southern portion of the Cotentin peninsula is still devoid of any real strength. He suggests that they move the 12th SS Panzer Division there. Jodl replies that he will consider the request.

Air activities, he adds, are really starting to heat up. Enemy air raids, once just relatively minor occurrences, now disrupt a good part of northern France. Bridges get attacked repeatedly, usually in daylight. Trains are getting strafed almost with impunity. Coastal batteries are getting bombed up and down the Channel. Cities near the coast are being hit. Granted, a lot of the damage being reported is distorted. But there seems to be a fair lot going on right now. Some of the more poorly designed positions are suffering badly.

Jodl acknowledges that Luftwaffe reports show that coastal air bases are being hit hard too. Rommel asks him if this means some of the squadrons might move inland, and Jodl admits a few already have.

Great. If you look up and don't see it up there at all, it must be the Luftwaffe…

They discuss airborne operations. Rommel says that he has revised his estimate of the countryside. Having talked to a number of airborne troops, he realizes that the patchwork boçage country is well suited for airborne landings. It is relatively easy to land in open areas and then quickly hide in the trees.

Rommel also tells him that they need more cement. Supplies are very low, and Seventh Army is behind in its casemate constructions. Jodl patiently tells him that he is getting all the Reich can spare at this time.

Rommel closes by adding, "Just get me the 12th SS Panzer, that's all. The base of Cotentin is bare. And the paratroopers are right. Contrary to popular opinion, the terrain there is ideal for airborne landings. The hedgerows and ditches would allow the landing assault troops to find cover immediately, but would be difficult to reach if we had troops already there. And Marcks' men have not had time to put up enough obstacles for the area."

Jodl soothingly replies that he will look into the matter. Rommel finally hangs up, frustrated. He knows that the call has for the most part been in vain.

He spends the rest of the morning catching up on paperwork and issuing new orders for the redeployment of units in the Cotentin peninsula.

Reports of air attacks, bombings, strafings, and aerial reconnaissance, not to mention damage reports from aerial activity the days before, pour in to the château. Some of these attacks can be heard outside—distant rumblings; as of thunder.

Around noontime, Luftwaffe General von Barsewisch[1] is ushered into Rommel's office. Rommel does not mince words with him and lets him know how disappointed he is with them.

After the general leaves, Rommel has Lang enter into his Daily Report:

> I told him quite clearly what I expected from the Luftwaffe. It is incomprehensible how, within two years, we have let our air supremacy drop to its present level. The Luftwaffe, it seems, has been resting on its laurels and has not found ways to adapt itself to the present-day necessities of the war. I too, could have rested on my laurels but constantly renewed efforts were required of me, just as much as they were of the Luftwaffe.

The rest of the day at La Roche-Guyon passes fairly well. Late that afternoon, Rommel is visited by the Quartermaster of the Army, General Eduard Wagner. They discuss shortages and the war in general.

That evening, Rommel holds a lavish dinner for him, and the *Heeresgruppe B* staff is allowed to relax. The banquet is done in grand style. Wagner loves food, and Rommel is glad. He wants to score some brownie points with the OKH quartermaster. Perhaps he can secure some much-needed supplies, like *Panzerfaust* weapons.

Later on, Speidel has an opportunity to speak privately with Wagner, who is actually a fellow co-conspirator. They update each other, and discuss strategies on how to win the field marshal over. A little later, their business concluded, Speidel and Wagner return to the main study. No one is aware of what they have discussed. As they part for the evening, Speidel asks Wagner to tell his brother-in-law, Dr. Max Horst, on Stülpnagel's staff, that he promises to get in touch with him as soon as he can.

That night Rommel writes to Lucie. Part of the letter is about Treff and Elbo.

> *Thanks for all the things you sent me, especially the cheese sticks. I'm already busily eating them up. The two mutts have made friends. The little one is a scream. Treff got into a fight with a German shepherd yesterday. When I come, the two of them are so enthusiastic, and I can't get away, unless I take them for a walk in the park. The little one will probaby soon be with you in Herrlingen...*

He also mentions the dogs in his diary:

> *My two dogs are a great source of joy. Above all, they take away some of my preoccupation arising from the great responsibilities placed upon me. That is also the reason why I can hardly afford to deal with personal matters. Furthermore, I find it difficult to establish close contact with other people. A man in my position is doomed to loneliness.*

Administratively, there are at present more panzer divisions in France than there are operational headquarters to command them. The Waffen-SS has Sepp Dietrich's staff, and the OKW reserve panzers have Geyr's. An administrative "buffer" command is needed between Rommel and his own three reserve panzer units: the 2nd, the newly formed 116th, and the 21st.

To better help administer these reserve panzer divisions, OB West orders the 47th Panzer Corps headquarters to relocate from Russia to command these units.

General von Funck, a veteran of the Eastern Front, had been appointed the corps commander on March 5. He is a long-time friend of Heinz Guderian's, although Rommel knows him too. Rommel had turned over his legendary *Gespenster Division* to him in February 1941 so that he could go to North Africa.[2]

***

At the Berghof, the news from Italy today is not good. The American Fifth Army and the British Eighth Army are continuing their expected spring offensive, started the night before against the Gustav Line in Italy. The Allies are trying to move northward to join up with the troops at the Anzio beachhead.

Clearly, the Hermann Göring Panzer Division will not be going to France now, no matter what the Western commanders have been told.

---

1   *Generalmajor* Harl-Hennig von Barsewisch (mistakenly referred to as "General Bardewicz" in Ryan's notes source). Appointed *General der Aufklärungsflieger* (General of Reconnaissance Aircraft) in April 1942, he commanded the reconnaissance arm in northern France until late 1944, including the versatile seaplanes.

2   Fifty-two-year-old *General der Panzertruppe* Hans *Freiherr* von Funck. He had commanded a motor-machine-gun company in World War I. Between wars, he became a *blitzkrieg* pioneer, working with Heinz Guderian, expanding their theories on panzer warfare. He had been an important part of the 1940 campaign in France, and until recently had been commanding on the Eastern Front.

Interestingly, von Funck had initially been considered to take command of the German forces in North Africa because he had already been there in January, assessing the situation for the General Staff. However, Hitler considered him "too gloomy" about what could be done there after the British had thoroughly routed the Italians. So Hitler picked Rommel because (as he told an Italian diplomat) "he knows how to *inspire* his troops… This is absolutely essential for the commander of a force that has to fight under particularly arduous climatic conditions, as in North Africa or the Arctic."

Saturday, May 13

It is early morning. At 7 a.m., Rommel and his entourage depart headquarters again on another tour—this time to the Somme estuary. It is here that Rommel really thinks the invasion will come, and in light of the OKW assessment that the invasion might very well start any day now, he wants to make one more inspection of this area.

They travel northeast in a heavy fog, and call on the 2nd Panzer Division. They find various divisional units bivouacked in fields around the headquarters near Amiens. There are many others in the nearby woods as well, trying no doubt, to stay away from the eyes of the enemy *Jabos*. The fact that they lack any suitable anti-aircraft weapons is no doubt a big motivator for cover and camouflage. Still, they have obeyed his orders to stay out of the villages, and Rommel is satisfied to see that.

He talks to the new divisional commander, General von Lüttwitz,[1] who tells him that his division has indeed scouted and noted the best routes available for rapid deployment, whether they be straight ahead to the coast, up towards Calais, or southwest towards Le Havre. Like von Oppeln-Bronikowski, von Lüttwitz was once an excellent, decorated equestrian, although he is now overweight and haughtily sports a monocle. Working his way up the general ranks, distinguishing himself in Russia, he was finally given command of the recuperating 2nd Panzer in March.

Rommel notes that two bridges in the area have been destroyed by bombs, and getting supplies and reinforcements across the Somme River could pose a serious logistical problem when the invasion comes. Rommel suggests that the bridges be rebuilt just below the river surface, and that the center span be left off until it is needed. He stops and talks to some of the panzer commanders. At one point, he yells out, "When the enemy approaches, don't engage in operational maneuvers. Just keep shooting!"[2]

They move on towards Abbéville and inspect the 85th Infantry Division, located behind the coastal main line of defense. Arriving at divisional headquarters in the famous town of Crécy, they get briefed by the commanding officer, *Generalleutnant* Kurt Chill. The men complain to Rommel that they lack machine guns.

"That's no problem," Rommel tells them. "Then take the guns off the paratroopers when they drop in on you!" He instructs the senior officers to make sure the division is deployed against airborne assault, so that it can immediately defend itself. To make this strategy even more effective, he tells them to issue their men additional ammunition.

They move on to inspect the 348th Division and note the 230 stakes that have been installed along the beach. Continuing, they inspect a tetrahedron plant in Cayeux, and Rommel expresses dissatisfaction over the design they are manufacturing. "I want to have the most modern and the best model," he tells them.

They move on and stop to observe a demonstration of the new nutcracker mine.[3] A few are detonated effectively, and Rommel is satisfied. Then on to Le Touquet, noting several enemy bomber formations overhead as they drive.

That evening, the group stays at the soldiers' quarters in town where they enjoy a fine dinner. Rommel is in a good mood, having a sense of accomplishment from what he has observed today. Later, he writes in his diary about the fact that some had once dismissed him as being an inexperienced, unfit commander. However, as he did in France in 1940 and North Africa in 1941, he is again proving that he can do what others said was not possible—in this case, turning the Atlantic Coast, once considered indefensible, into a deadly weapon. Now he is going to disprove both of those viewpoints.

Unlike these naysayers though, Hitler had still been confident enough in him to give him a critical post, one that would ultimately determine the future of the Reich. So the hell with what the rest of his flunkies thought. He adds with a firm hand, *"Der Führer vertraut mir, und das gejuegt mir auch."*—"The Führer trusts me, and that's enough for me."

He will want to get an early start in the morning.

***

Today, *GroßAdmiral* Karl Dönitz is informed that his last surviving son, *Oberleutnant zur See* Klaus Dönitz, assigned to *Schnellboot S-141*, has just been reported missing in action, along with the rest of the boat's 18 crew members; it has apparently been sunk by a French warship.[4] It had been his son's 24th birthday, and he had been invited by his comrades to ride along and take part in a 10-boat night patrol northeast of the Isle of Wight. Klaus, because of who his father was, was normally not authorized to go on any such dangerous mission. When the admiral's younger son Peter had been lost nearly a year ago aboard *U-954*, Klaus had been removed from combat operations and had resorted to studying medicine. His ties to his old shipmates though, were strong. They were going out in a formidable force on a routine patrol, and he really longed for some action. So he had convinced them to secretly take him along.

Early on the night of the 12th, the S-boats of the 5th and 9th Flotillas slipped across the Channel in the early night and began stalking some shipping off Selsey Bill point. Suddenly, they discovered that two enemy destroyers were unexpectedly closing in on them. The boats stayed silent, trying to remain undetected. Using searchlights though, the enemy vessels spotted the *Schnellboote* and immediately engaged the group. In the ensuing action, one boat had been heavily damaged and *S-141* had unfortunately been destroyed. Klaus was missing in action.[5]

The despondent Kriegsmarine leader nevertheless goes ahead with the soirée planned that night for the Japanese ambassador. After it is over though, his wife collapses in grief over the loss.

Dönitz vows to take revenge on the British.

***

At Hitler's daily war conference, the subject of the upcoming invasion in the West is again covered thoroughly. Many seem anxious for the landing to begin, so that it can be thwarted and they can move on to concentrate on other battle areas. There is even a small concern growing that the landing may not come. Propaganda Minister Goebbels gets field reports from many civilian leaders who feel that way, although they are disheartened about the "air terror." Today he records in his diary:

> *The letters I am getting talk almost solely about the invasion. People are not only expecting, but looking forward to it. They're only afraid that the enemy may not try.*

It is late afternoon at La Roche-Guyon. The field marshal, having departed that morning to tour the coast, will be staying at Le Touquet this evening. Knowing this, his chief of staff is using the opportunity to invite a close friend to the château for dinner: Ernst Jünger. An established author, he is currently a *Hauptmann* assigned to the command of Military Governor General Stülpnagel in Paris. Like Speidel, both are in the secret *Schwartz Kapelle*. In fact, Jünger is one of Speidel's contacts with the group. He had managed to get himself appointed to Stülpnagel's staff to be close to Speidel and to Rommel. Now with Rommel gone, the chief of staff has bid the author over for dinner so that they can talk freely. Speidel will also get a chance to see an advanced copy of the peace manifesto that the plotters have created. They will put it into effect once Hitler has been assassinated.[6]

The two seclude themselves as soon as Jünger arrives, and Speidel eagerly goes over the draft. He makes some favorable comments, and offers a few suggestions. They then put the papers away and go to dinner. Afterwards, Speidel suggests that they go for a stroll around the grounds. Although it had been foggy earlier, the skies have cleared up. The two conspirators walk out into the garden and begin climbing up around the back of the château, enjoying the scenery as sunset begins. Naturally, they do not discuss politics as they pass a sentry here and there. Jünger himself is not the fidgety type, but he is amazed at the calm that Speidel radiates. The chief of staff seems to be in control of his world, as they trek, talking about the war. Speidel takes in the idyllic countryside and suggests in general how the future might be.

They hike up the hill above the château to the old Norman tower, noting the occasional anti-aircraft units interspersed around the countryside. They continue up the battlements. Here they decide to share a bottle of fine wine as they discourse.

With nobody in earshot now, they discuss various covert matters. Jünger asks if Speidel has made much headway converting the field marshal to the cause of peace. He adds that many of the other plotters are quite worried about it. Rommel is their best hope for a leader after Hitler is killed. He is the one man who everyone—the

Allies, the German people, and the Wehrmacht—will probably accept as a leader to end the war. If anybody can negotiate a peace with England and the United States, assuming such a thing is still possible, he can.

The two of them finally arise from sitting at the battlements and slowly meander back down around the Norman tower. Walking down the hillside, they leave the château area and begin strolling towards the little village of La Roche-Guyon.

They eventually stop and sit down overlooking the Seine. Speidel tells Jünger about his attempts to win over Rommel. He has indirectly approached the field marshal on the issue a couple of times. Despite the fact that Rommel was uncomfortable about the subject, they had discussed certain issues along a general vein. Rommel knows of course that they cannot possibly win the war—he has known that since North Africa. He still believes though that negotiations with the West are possible, not to mention highly desirable. Speidel points out that Rommel also feels that it is time to end the war, before Germany is totally destroyed. Negotiations might still be possible, if the right conditions are placed before the United States and Britain. With a slight smile, Speidel also tells Jünger that Rommel confided in him the belief that the Führer would have to step down for this to be possible.

They eventually get up and start walking slowly through a meadow. Speidel occasionally pauses to gaze at some flora or to admire a bush. He stops at one point, bends over, and picks a lovely flower, Standing up, he slowly twirls it in his hand, and then looks around him. How beautiful this Seine valley is. Flowers of all types are in bloom. Spring here is at its height.

After a short while, they start back, walking through one of the village's narrow streets. Jünger glances at Speidel, who just smiles back at him confidently. "Don't worry," he says, "The war in Europe will be all over by this autumn."

"What about the field marshal?" Jünger asks.

"I think he'll come around," is Speidel's assured reply.

Jünger is not so sure.

---

1   Forty-seven-year-old *Generalleutnant* Diepold Georg Heinrich *Freiherr* von Lüttwitz. A Prussian aristocrat and excellent horseman, he was a highly decorated veteran of World War I. An early believer in maximizing the use of motorized units, he commanded a motorcycle recon battalion at the start of World War II. Working his way up the general ranks, he served in most of the Eastern campaigns (as did his two famous cousins, Smilo *Freiherr* von Lüttwitz and Hyazinth *Graf* Strachwitz von Gross-Zauche und Camminetz). Although he was gravely wounded in the Polish invasion, he served dutifully in the East, and eventually was given the 20th Panzer Division. After the 2nd Panzer was all but destroyed in Russia, it was moved to the West to recuperate and reform, and von Lüttwitz was put in command.

2   Admiral Ruge records him as saying, "but open fire immediately."

3   See entry for February 16.

4   As it turns out, it was sunk by the Free French destroyer *La Combattante,* which had initially started construction as a British Type II Hunt Class destroyer escort in mid-January 1941. Damage from an air raid postponed its launch until late April 1942, at which time it was christened HMS *Haldon.*

On December 16, it was turned over to the Free French Navy, whereupon it was recommissioned as *La Combattante,* before being launched on December 30, 1942.

5 Of the S-141's crew of 24, the Allies fished six Germans from the Channel and took them prisoner. Klaus' body eventually washed up on the French coast. He was buried in Amiens. The admiral now only had one surviving child, his daughter Ursula.

6 Forty-nine-year-old Ernst Jünger had been for years a forthright opponent of the Hitler regime, one of the few authors left in the Reich that could speak out in this way. The Nazis had wanted for a long time to incarcerate or remove him, but they could not do so, because he was an accomplished author and had strong ties to the conservative industrialists and to the military. Jünger was also a popular, decorated veteran of World War I, having been wounded several times, and in 1918 was awarded Germany's highest honor, the *Pour le Mérite,* an award Rommel had also earned. Jünger was one of the youngest soldiers ever to receive the award.

As war loomed on the horizon, Jünger had continued to protest against the government in a low key. He had written in 1939 a controversial short novel called *Auf den Marmorklippen (On the Marble Cliffs),* an intense, although understandably veiled, critical allegory of a totalitarian government. The novel depicted folks living in a peaceful, coastal region that was threatened by a mindless group of hillfolk led by a jolly but ruthless leader (closely parallel to Herman Göring and Hitler), a leader who would establish a dictatorship based on brutality.

Sunday, May 14

After staying overnight at the soldiers' quarters in Le Touquet, Rommel this morning prepares to continue inspecting the Somme area, even though it is Sunday. They begin at 6:45 a.m. There is a light rain as they leave, but the field marshal enjoys the bad weather—it is now his ally. Every rainy day means another day without having to worry about the enemy invasion.

They start out by viewing the nearby positions of the 326th Infantry Division[1] near Montreuil. The 326th is another *bodenständige*[2] unit, part of the coastal secondary line of defense. Rommel is satisfied with the progress the officers have made. To help them better understand though, he takes time out once again to explain how he wants certain barrier details constructed. But he does approve of the dummy coastal batteries that have been erected, and praises them for the nearly 100,000 wooden stakes that even the local folks have helped to put up. On behalf of their efforts, he suggests that they hold a sort of builders' folk party, like a *Richtfest*. He smiles when a senior officer tells him that they are ready to "counterattack" any enemy landing. He goes on to explain about more barrier ideas that are being used in other areas, while stressing to them the need to keep in mind the agricultural concerns of the local farmers.

The inspection group moves on to Montreuil. There they inspect 82nd Corps' 191st Reserve Infantry Division. The commanding officer briefs Rommel and shows him on a map all the points where the Allied bombers have hit so far. They leave mid-morning and drive back towards Le Touquet, and then up the coast to Hardelot Plage, where they inspect some areas hit by air raids.

At noontime, they dine at a *Vergeltungswaffen* arsenal near Le Chatel, sharing some "one-pot stew" with the soldiers and local workers in a nearby underground warehouse bunker. There they confer with army commander von Salmuth himself. He warms up to Rommel, and the meeting starts off nicely. Von Salmuth congratulates the field marshal on his efforts, and in turn, Rommel hands out to the men a few concertinas. Various recipients gratefully accept them and then proceed to show their talent (or lack of it, as is more often the case) playing them. One bragging combat engineer boasts that there is *nothing* the combat engineers cannot do. But playing a concertina he has never tried, and he declines the generous offers to try one in front of the field marshal. After all, he isn't stupid.

Then they are off again, now to inspect Furbach's[3] 331st Infantry Division. A few hours later, they move on to *Generalleutnant* Baltzer's[4] 182nd Training Infantry Division—a light unit made up of seven badly equipped battalions lacking a great deal of ammunition and weapons. Rommel's staff notes that most of the battalions are to be transferred to other units.

A little after five that afternoon, they have another conference at the General Sinnhuber's 82nd Corps headquarters at Aire-sur-la-Lys.[5] There, Rommel commends everyone for the work that they have done in their area, including putting in scores of thousands of anti-airborne stakes. He also thanks them for the sacrifices that they have made so far for the Reich.

They finally head home, traveling south to Beauvais, and from there southwest back to La Roche-Guyon. When they arrive at the château at 8:30p.m., they are met in the courtyard by their headquarters band (such as it is), which has been augmented by more concertinas that he has supplied for them. The turnout puts Rommel in a good mood.

***

Today at noon, after a few morning hours of reading reports and some discussion with Blumentritt, *Generalfeldmarschall* von Rundstedt decides to go for a stroll. Blumentritt continues to worry about his safety whenever he goes out in public. Von Rundstedt reassures him, telling him that, although the residence is not closed off from the rest of the city, he has never been bothered.

To the chief of staff though, the problem is more serious than that. It is bad enough that the villa has little security, but the field marshal often likes to take one- to two-hour walks around the area, thus physically exposing himself to possible violence. Sometimes he just walks around town, the city park or up the hill to the girls' school. Or he might stop in a restaurant for a drink. He seldom lets anyone go with him, except sometimes his adjutant, and of course, he never carries any weapons. The only items he ever takes include an occasional walking stick and handfuls of chocolates and other sweets for children that he might encounter, Naturally, these chance meetings have increased in number over time, as word has spread from one child to another.

His officers worry about him as well; that every time he leaves for a promenade, he might get mugged or assassinated. They once tried to remedy the situation by assigning two guards to trail him at a distance[6] whenever he went on one of his walks. That idea though, did not work for long. His sharp eyes had soon noticed his followers, and after that, he began cracking jokes about his two "hangers-on." Still, they continued to show up whenever he went for a stroll, so he began to get devious. Sneaking out the back gate, he would begin his walk by going to a nearby park, or through the school grounds up on the hill. Then he would stroll along certain pathways and then suddenly duck into the woods or a building to elude his pursuers. And he was so smug whenever he successfully shook off his trackers.

Whenever he went on one of these excursions he enjoyed meeting the general public. Always civil, this field marshal, easily the most powerful man in Western Europe, often greeted them with a smile or a nod, and as he did, he would politely step aside, often into the street, to let oncoming pedestrians pass. Over time, there had been many such chance meetings with a number of important people, including

St. Germain's mayor, and once in a while, the *abbé* from the nearby monastery. Sometimes it was another German or French officer in "mufti." These encounters amused his adjutant, because if von Rundstedt chanced upon some important official, they would often react to him in the same way as he did to them. The two would each courteously greet one another, and then each would step aside into the road to allow the other clear passage. Then each would acknowledge the courtesy offered by the other, and step out of the road, thus meeting once again in a sort of comical dance. Flustered, each would smile, then perhaps they would inadvertently do the whole thing again.

No matter where he was, the old man really enjoyed a good meal. At the villa, he always ate alone, and one of his favorite entrées was a beef dish called *tournado avec moelle de boeuf*—with the bone on top, naturally. Of course, he ate much better whenever he went out, especially to an elegant restaurant. He would frequently sneak out a half-hour before noon with one or two staff members and walk up the Rue Alexandre Dumas to the restaurant in the Hôtel Pavillion Henri IV,[8] where he had initially set up his headquarters after the *blitzkrieg* campaign of 1940. There in that lovely 17th-century building, he would enjoy a couple of drinks and enjoy the ambiance, before dining or returning to his villa for lunch. Then later in the afternoon, he might come back to the hotel for a few more drinks before dinner…

---

1   Fifty-four-year-old *Generalleutnant* Viktor von Drabich-Waechter, commanding. A World War I veteran, he served the first part of World War II as a department head in the German Army Personnel Office (*Heerespersonalamt*) until 1942. After a time in the Führer Reserve, he was given command of the 326th Infantry Division at Narbonne, France on June 1, 1943. The division would be destroyed in Normandy in two months, and von Drabich-Waechter was killed at Le Mesnil on August 2.

2   Static division.

3   Forty-eight-year-old *Generalmajor* Heinz Furbach. His division, originally the 70th Shadow Division *Wahn*, was re-designated the 331st (static) Infantry in mid-March.

4   Fifty-seven-year-old *Generalleutnant* Richard Baltzer.

5   About 16km east of Boulogne.

6   His gardener recalled after the war that his two tails were usually "Gestapo men."

7   A special fillet of beef and oxtail, with its delicious bone marrow.

8   The Hôtel Pavillon Henri IV, located at 21 Rue Thiers, was about half a kilometer from the field marshal's villa.

Monday, May 15

This morning, *Generalfeldmarschall* Rommel sends for Admiral Ruge. Sitting in his study, the field marshal queries him about the damage the Allied bombings is inflicting upon their coastal batteries. It would be nice to move the guns around to frustrate Allied bombers. However, the large naval batteries are unfortunately set in permanent casements and thus, immobile. However, those batteries exposed near the shoreline will stand little chance of surviving a naval bombardment. Further inland, yet still well within range of the coast, they might survive long enough to inflict some heavy damage to any incoming amphibious landing. So Rommel discusses the idea of reducing the risk of damage from air attacks by moving some of the relatively more mobile army batteries back, especially those sitting out in the open. Relocate them a bit away from the shoreline. Ruge agrees.

They change subjects and Ruge talks about the weather. The meteorological conditions have been uncannily stable over the last six weeks (even though it is lightly drizzling right now), with no major storms to mention. So, despite a number of false alarms, where is the invasion? Every day of good weather now brings Rommel apprehension. If the main show is about to start, he should probably stay close to his headquarters.

They discuss other invasion points, including preventing the planned sabotage and demolition of the many small ports in the Seventh Army sector. Smashing the smaller harbors would not slow down the Allies much, and the mistrust, hate, and general annoyance that this would cause among the local population would not be worth it. On the other hand, it is vital that the larger seaports like Brest and Cherbourg be rendered useless...

Their conversation ends, and Ruge goes down the hall to talk over these points with Speidel. In the meantime, General Meise brings into Rommel's study a Dr. Brug. The inventor of an effective chemical fuse, he has been experimenting with artificial fog. Rommel is heartened to hear that he will be able to supply fog generators to hide positions on the Cotentin peninsula. Brug also reports that he now has an additional 1.2 million grenades available for the army. Rommel suggests that some be used as makeshift mines.

They are still talking around noontime when they are interrupted by Ruge. He tells Rommel that the Führer is on the phone, wanting to speak to him.[1] Speidel gets on the other line. Rommel usually gets Speidel to listen in on such calls. He does this for two reasons: first, to make sure that Rommel covers all points and does not miss anything; second, Speidel will witness what is said, and be able to corroborate anything that Rommel hears—just in case someone might want to dispute it.

Rommel picks up the phone and begins talking to the Führer. He makes sure that he reflects his positive attitude in his tone and in the upbeat report he gives. He describes the new multiple rocket launcher unit being developed by Major Becker in the 21st Panzer Division. Rommel claims, "I can well imagine that these could be fired from bunkers in broadsides of four dozen at a time. They travel 4,000 meters." He added that the division commander, the ever-resourceful and affable General Feuchtinger, has promised to make a number of them, with ammunition as well. Hitler sanctions the project and enthusiastically tells him to proceed.

Speidel, eavesdropping on the other line, after a while lets Ruge listen in too. For each of them, it is an eerie feeling to hear the Führer's hoarse voice in the receiver.

Speidel maintains a deadpan look as he listens to the leader he has secretly sworn to overthrow and, if possible, help assassinate. Ruge though is almost captivated, and his face carries a look of awe. He is fascinated just to hear the Führer's voice. Speidel continues to masks his scowl of disapproval at the optimistic tone. He is not happy at all, either to hear the voice of that asshole, or to see the field marshal so buoyant in talking to him. This will make it all the harder to win Rommel over and betray the man he is at present glowing to over the phone. Speidel did not like this task when it was conceived, and it seems that it will be even harder now. Keeping his composure, he listens to the conversation. Ruge does not realize the chill behind his expressionless look.

Rommel goes on telling the Führer about the positive mood in the area. "The morale here of commanders and troops alike is magnificent," he says confidently. "One corps has already planted nine hundred thousand stakes against airborne landings, and it's gotten hold of a million grenades to arm them with explosives over the next weeks."

Rommel's effect upon Hitler is noticeable in the Führer's encouraging vocal responses, and heartened by this, the field marshal makes a mental note to write to Lucie about the call.

One point the Führer makes is that the enemy might very well go for an invasion further west, because Cherbourg and Le Havre would serve as adequate ports for supply. Thus, "an attempt to form a bridgehead on the Cotentin peninsula in the first phase would seem quite natural."

The phone call finally ends, and the day continues. A report comes in from Dollmann at Seventh Army that its defense preparations along the coast are, for the most part, completed. Beach obstacles and paratroop obstacles have been set up, and dispositions of the troops have been made.

The army group naturally looks upon the report with skepticism.[2] Rommel will have to have a word with Dollmann about it.

That afternoon, work temporarily caught up, Ruge leaves for Paris to see Admiral Krancke to impress upon him the need to move any vulnerable mobile naval guns on the coast inland or into sheltered areas. Rommel and Speidel leave for the christening of a colonel's daughter just outside Paris. Rommel usually hates to attend these social affairs, but Speidel has coaxed him into making an exception this one time.

They arrive and the field marshal relents, softening up when he sees the baby. He lets himself be photographed with the child.

It turns out to be not too bad an affair. Rommel's old friend Fritz Bayerlein is present, having recently been promoted to *Generalleutnant* on May 1. Also attending is the military governor, General Karl von Stülpnagel. Speidel happily brings him over to meet the field marshal. These three "godfathers" converse for a while under a broad expanse of chestnut trees, again allowing themselves to be photographed.

The two leave the christening, Speidel headed for another meeting elsewhere, one much more clandestine. It is a perfect time. The weather is for once rainy, and the field marshal is on his way back to the château. Besides, he is already in the Paris area.

Speidel drives to the Hôtel Raphael where he meets his brother-in-law, Dr. Max Horst, the military governor, and another plotter. In private, they discuss further developments of the upcoming coup.[3] Max briefs his brother-in-law on the importance of keeping Rommel in on the plot. Perhaps it will be best if Speidel goes about it gently. Speidel agrees to do that.

***

Today, von Rundstedt in his weekly estimate to OKW continues to express his concern about the possible enemy landing area. He writes that the Allies "Need to win large and capacious harbors," and that the "danger zone" for the invasion includes an area that stretches almost 300 kilometers, from Caen northeast to the Scheldt estuary in Belgium. However, he stressed that "Le Havre and Cherbourg are primarily to be considered for this purpose; Boulogne and Brest secondarily. The attempt to form a bridgehead rapidly on the Cotentin peninsula in the first phase would therefore seem very natural."

Then he gets on the telephone and calls Keitel directly to formally lodge a protest. He has been told that, in light of the heavy enemy air attacks against their lines of communication, Rommel has renewed a request to have the OKW reserve panzers released to him, To put them in Rommel's control, so that he could place them near the coast, would be like throwing in their reserves before the battle has even begun. Keitel agrees, and promises that Rommel's request will go nowhere.

***

Today at the Obersalzberg, Hitler, Göring, and General Korten discuss a moral problem. The British and American air forces have near-total mastery of the skies now over Western Europe and going along with their strategic bombing campaign, their *Jabos*, involved in destroying the Reich's supply lines, are significantly increasing their attacks on trains, and sometimes even machine-gunning farmers and civilians. The public has responded angrily against downed enemy airmen, sometimes hanging them or just shooting them.

Unfortunately, hapless German pilots who are shot down in aerial combat are also meeting the same angry mobs convinced the fliers are the enemy, and are often having to fight off crowds brandishing shovels and pitchforks.

The leaders discuss what to do with these captured airmen and whether the Reich should allow this type of vigilante violence. Göring favors it, although he insists that those enemy airmen who actually fire on civilians be executed in the traditional way: by firing squad, and near the area where they came down. The problem, he tells the Führer, is that they have to actually identify the airmen who commit these intolerable acts as distinct from those flying over the Reich in other functions, such as escort duty or reconnaissance.

After some discussion, Hitler decides that enemy pilots can be executed immediately if they have committed special heinous acts, such as firing on German airmen in parachutes, or strafing civilians or public transport. Göring stresses though, that downed enemy airmen not committing these acts should not be subject to execution but treated in accordance with the Geneva Convention.

He still has some chivalrous respect for the enemy in the air, left over from when he served as a pilot in World War I.

Today, SHAEF holds a large day-long conference in the Victorian "model room" of St. Paul's School in London. The narrow, circular hard wooden risers are crammed with all levels of officer ranks from all varieties of service. In attendance on the lowest bench is King George VI himself, along with Prime Minister Churchill, Eisenhower, and all the top SHAEF commanders.

The purpose of the conference is to finalize all operational plans for the upcoming landing, scheduled to begin in three weeks. Many officers are for the first time meeting the other commanders that they will soon be coordinating their efforts with, in some cases sitting side by side with them. Everyone present knows what is at stake, and they all appreciate the critical importance of this epic operation. The tension in the room is understandably heavy.

Eisenhower, their military leader, is the first to speak. His warm tones and encouraging words inspire them all. He is followed one by one by his deputy commanders, and the morning goes on.

In the afternoon, the king himself addresses them with a short, unrehearsed address, followed by a stirring speech from Winston Churchill. Because many there know of his past reluctance to endorse the landing, he now tries to put on a show of support, growling with a slight hint of a smile, "Gentlemen, I am hardening towards this enterprise."

In the evening, an exhausted Rommel writes to Lucie about his phone call with the Führer:

> *He [Hitler] was in the best of humors and did not spare his praise of the work we've done in the West. I now hope to get on a little faster than we have been doing.*

Pausing, he finds himself thinking about the invasion date. He is puzzled, because it is now mid-May. He just cannot see what the Allies were waiting for; and such mysteries bother him greatly. He writes:

> *Mid-May already, and still nothing doing, although a pincer attack seems to have started in Italy, which may well be the prelude for the great events of the spring or summer.*

So why have the Allies not started in the West? The weather is perfect. Tides are right. What are they waiting for? They must be waiting for something else. To be better prepared? Or maybe for the start of the Russian offensive, which was probably going to begin in another six weeks or so. He continues:

> *I've been away for a couple of days, talking to the officers and men. It's quite amazing what has been achieved in the last few weeks. I'm convinced that the enemy will have a rough time of it when he attacks, and ultimately achieve no success.*

He thinks about his tours taking him away from his headquarters and adds:

> *I can't take many more big trips now because one never knows when the invasion will start. I believe only a few more weeks remain until things start here in the West.*

A few more weeks would make it early June.

---

1   While Ruge documents this call as having been made today, David Irving records it as being on the 16th and states that Rommel initiated the call. Rommel perhaps may have initiated the sequence by first calling the Berghof and asking to speak to the Führer at his earliest convenience.

2   About a week later, 84th Corps would report that its own defense construction program was only half complete.

3   Some sources, including Speidel himself a number of times, claim that Speidel and Rommel were also at an earlier meeting at a home near St. Germain—possibly the one where the christening took place. At that meeting, Rommel and von Rundstedt discussed with their chiefs of staff what might be done about Hitler and how. Rommel supposedly agreed to von Stülpnagel's plan for Hitler to be arrested, in exchange for the Allies stopping the bombing of Germany; but he also, according to accounts, insisted that no attempt to kill Hitler must be made. Supposedly, he also authorized a further meeting with Mayor Strölin and Baron von Neurath. Whether this meeting actually occurred is questionable.

Tuesday, May 16

Today, Allied Intelligence learns that the élite 6th Parachute Regiment under veteran Major Baron von der Heydte and the 91st Air Landing Division under General Falley are being moved to Normandy. The analysts begin to wonder if the landing site location has been compromised.

On the other hand though, an intercept of an enemy transmission to Tokyo from Japanese Ambassador Baron Ōshima[1] two days ago is a gold mine of information. He tells of an informal dinner that he attended, in which he had a chance to talk with Admiral Dönitz. Ōshima reports that the Kriegsmarine commander, bringing up the subject of the invasion, let out a planned strategy, confiding in him:

> My own belief is that the domestic and international position of both [*Great Britain and the US*] is such that they cannot avoid attempting an invasion. However, if a second front is not attempted, Germany plans to transfer powerful forces to the Eastern Front, relying on the strength of the West Wall and striking back at the enemy by other means.[2]

In other words, Germany would carry out in reverse the maneuver they had pulled off in 1917 when Russia had collapsed, shifting large numbers of units from one front to the other. The West, Dönitz inferred to Ōshima confidently, would be dealt with "by other means"; with the "vengeance weapons. The V-1 production is in full swing, and the V-2 not far behind."

The report states that as they chat, the German admiral opens up even more. He adds:

> Recently, I received a report from Marshal Rommel, regarding his inspection of various areas, including the fortifications along the Atlantic coast. Rommel is confident that Germany will be able to repulse the enemy no matter when or where they attempt to land. As a matter of fact, we Germans hope that the attempt will begin as soon as possible. Since England and the US possess very superior air forces, the German Army naturally expects them to carry out "carpet-bombing" attacks, but is confident that the German defense organization can easily weather such a bombardment.

Dönitz adds that, understandably, Hitler is reluctant to send any more reinforcements to the East until the invasion is thwarted.

Tomorrow, the information in this intercept will be given to the US Joint Chiefs of Staff.

Rommel stays at his château today to do more paperwork. He keeps a close eye on the latest situation reports, looking for any signs of an impending enemy operation. Bombing raids yesterday hit the V-weapons sites again, as well as a railroad yard at Somain.[3] Many aircraft were reported over the Loire River and over Liège in Belgium—possibly on reconnaissance missions.

Around noon, a special visitor shows up: General Bayerlein, Rommel's old friend from North Africa, now commanding the *Panzer Lehr* Division.[4] Having completed its part in the occupation of Hungary, the division had started back on May 1, with Bayerlein getting promoted from *Generalmajor* to *Generalleutnant*. The return trip was arduous. The railroads had taken a beating by Allied bombers, and their undersized, overworked locomotives strained to pull the heavy cars laden with the division's armor. There were many delays, once because a coupling broke and the rear section of the train was left rolling along. The division finally completed its return to France a fortnight later, setting up in several parks and forests some 45km from Chartres, hidden by day from Allied aircraft. Now Bayerlein is visiting his old boss.

They celebrate Bayerlein's promotion over refreshments and talk over old times. Then they venture outside for a walk in the park. They discuss the reserve panzers, and the Führer's continued vacillation between Rommel's theory of "hit them on the beaches" and Geyr's theory of "wait until they're ashore and hit them inland." Rommel reflects on those panzer generals who once commanded on the Eastern Front.

"Our friends from the East cannot imagine what they're in for here," Rommel says. The generals who had fought there had faced an enemy low on technology and aptitude, but having great numbers of uneducated men, that could therefore use mass frontal tactics and overwhelming numbers. This was not the case in the West though, and Rommel knew that, being one of the few field marshals who had experience fighting the Americans and British.

"It's not a matter of fanatical hordes to be driven forward in masses against our line, with no regard for casualties and little recourse to tactical craft," he says. "Here we are facing an enemy who applies all his native intelligence to the use of his many technical resources, who spares no expenditure of material, and whose every operation goes its course, as though it had been the subject of repeated rehearsal."

Rommel goes on. "Dash and doggedness alone no longer make a soldier, Bayerlein. He must have sufficient intelligence to enable him to get the most out of his fighting machines. And that's something these people can do. We found that out in Africa."

Bayerlein, fresh from operations in the East, agrees.

Rommel hesitates, frustrated. "You have no idea how difficult it is to convince these people," he says, referring to the General Staff again. "At one time, they looked on mobile warfare as something to keep clear of at all costs; but now that our freedom of maneuver in the West is gone, they're all crazy after it. Whereas, in fact, it's obvious that if the enemy once gets his foot in, he'll put every anti-tank gun and tank he can into the bridgehead and let us beat our heads against it, like he did at Medenine."[5]

Rommel continues, sensing that he is on to something. "To break through such a front, you have to attack slowly and methodically, under cover of massed artillery; but we, of course, thanks to the Allied air forces, will have nothing there in time. The day of the dashing cut-and-thrust tank attack of the early war years is past and gone. And that goes for the East too, a fact which may, perhaps by this time, have gradually sunk in."

He is reflecting his negative feelings—the hopelessness that he feels about winning the war, especially in the light of the overwhelming enemy in the East, and the awesome technology and material resources of the West...

That evening, Ambassador Abetz[6] comes for dinner. They have a nice discussion over a generous meal. Abetz was once a teacher, just like Rommel's father. They talk about life in the occupied Vichy zone, and about Marshal Pétain. Abetz confesses somewhat sheepishly that, although Vichy is some 400km south-southeast of the capital, he spends most of his time in Paris. Rommel nods thoughtfully.

A couple hours later, Abetz bids goodbye and leaves. Rommel retires, wondering about the upcoming invasion.

***

Today Adolf Hitler, mesmerized by what undoubtedly in his mind will be the devastating effects that his soon-to-be-operational V-1 program will have on England, decrees that the beginning of the air assault will be coordinated with a number of air raids and an artillery assault of British coastal towns by the long-range channel guns. The primary V-1 objective will be, of course, his top political target, London. This new unstoppable air offensive is set to start around June 2; the exact time this will all begin will be decided upon by von Rundstedt, who will send out the code word "*Rumpelkammer*"—"Junk Room."

***

This morning, General Blaskowitz arrives at his new army group headquarters. He has chosen a château in the tiny village of Rouffiac-Tolosan on the Garônne River, about six kilometers from the lovely city of Toulouse and roughly halfway between the headquarters of his two armies, the First and the Nineteenth.

He has a private discussion with his chief of staff, *Generalleutnant* Heinz von Glydenfeld, about how they will implement OKW's expectations for an improved defense. He then listens as the chief of staff gives him a brief rundown of his new staff.

That afternoon they are called together. Blaskowitz, about to address them for the first time at their new headquarters, faces them. He wants to tell them exactly how he feels and convey to them the importance of the situation. He begins by welcoming them to their new command, then gets right to the point. He tells them that he expects them to fully cooperate with each other, to mesh together as a good team. That will be critical when the time comes. He stresses that they do not have much time and their resources are quite limited. They will have to be effective and resolute, not worrying about the little stuff. Red tape is to be kept to a minimum.

"Remember," he says, "that bureaucratic work is non-productive and not conducive to success. Your emphasis should be on priorities and efficiency, and not on amenities."

Now warmed up, he proceeds confidently. Their first priority, of course, is their men. To do that, they have to work with them daily and communicate with them on their level. Commanders must have enough leeway to use initiative; the basics of good leadership.

In keeping with his command policies, all of his staff officers are to check out infantry weapons and attend training sessions in close combat. This, he says with a smile, will keep them bright-eyed and bushy-tailed. They chuckle good-naturedly, and he takes that for a good sign.

He finishes up by telling them that he hopes to see a "noble behavior among his officers, and in working with the subordinate ranks."

As they applaud him, he thinks to himself, God help us if we screw up now.

***

Today, the last night air raid against England for *Unternehmen Steinbock*,[7] Germany's baby blitz, takes place. This four-month air campaign against the British Isles has done little to affect them: 1,600 people have been killed, with another 2,000 seriously injured—small numbers compared to the hundreds of thousands of casualties that Allied bombers are inflicting upon the Reich.

In return, almost 500 German bombers and fighters have been lost.

---

1   Fifty-eight-year-old Baron Hiroshi Ōshima, the Japanese military attaché and ambassador to Germany for some ten years. See the footnote to January 23.

2   SRS 1302, dated May 14, 1944.

3   About 140km southeast of Calais.

4   Both Bayerlein and his biographer, P. A. Spayd, state that the visit took place on the 17th at La Roche-Guyon. But Rommel had left for a two-day inspection tour that morning. So the visit must have either taken place at the christening on the 15th, or on the 16th. Since Bayerlein talks about them walking through the park at La Roche-Guyon, the visit must have been on the 16th.

5   On March 6, 1943, almost three weeks after his victory at Kasserine Pass against the Americans, an uncertain and ailing Rommel, commanding *Armeegruppe Afrika*, had launched Operation *Capri* against the British position at Medenine. Montgomery's position stretched from the town northward some 20km to the sea. The bulk of his position, located northwest of the town, consisted of a dug-in semicircle of six fortified brigades, which included some 400 tanks and 600 anti-tank guns. Rommel, as expected (thanks to intercepted intelligence), feinted in the front and tried to maneuver around the left flank of the perimeter with a small force of tanks and *panzergrenadiers*. He was stopped cold, and had to give up the attack on the evening of the first day.

6   Forty-one-year-old Otto Abetz, ambassador to the French Vichy Government. Abetz's duties were many and varied. He was a special advisor to the Gestapo, German adviser to Pétain, oversaw people returning from intern camps, and controlled the media in the occupied zone.

     After the war, Abetz was arrested by the French and charged with a number of war crimes, including overseeing the deportation of thousands of French Jews to concentration camps. In July 1949, he was found guilty and sentenced to prison for 20 years. Like most convicted after the war, he was released early; in his case, April 1954. Four years later, he was killed in an automobile accident in Germany. Some speculate that the accident might have been caused by "persons unknown" in revenge for his activities during the war.

7   Operation *Capricorn*. See entry for January 21.

Wednesday, May 17

In their continuing campaign against German radar and communications sites, the Allied air commands today switch their main focus of attacks to night-fighter control centers and coastal battery fire control installations. By the end of May, some 42 major sites will have been hit.

This morning, Rommel and his staff prepare again for another inspection tour, this one to the Brittany area. He is a bit concerned about this trip, because he does not want to travel too far away from the Channel, as he had written to Lucie on the 15th. After all, the now-overdue invasion could come at any time.

They leave at 7 a.m. Under overcast skies, they first cross the Seine by ferry and then move westward, encountering an occasional light rain, welcomed by the farmers after the dry spell. After leaving Caen, they turn west and travel along the Normandy coast. On this trip, Rommel wants to check that Marcks is bringing all of his reserves up forward as he had been ordered. Inspecting the positions of the 352nd Infantry Division along the coast, Rommel notes that two regiments are preparing for a scheduled rotation. In three days, the 914th will come out of reserve and move onto the coastal positions, and the 915th will move off the coast and become the reserve regiment near Bayeux, along with the division's *Füsilier* battalion. The latter has been designated as a rapid deployment force, to reinforce any threatened sector Rommel approves.

Moving on to Carentan, they meet an officer of General Falley's newly arrived 91st Air Landing Division. This impromptu guide eventually leads them to Falley's new advanced headquarters in the Cotentin peninsula, although not without first getting them lost a few times. They roll in around 11 a.m. and Falley greets them warmly.

A conference immediately begins. Besides Rommel's entourage and Falley's staff, attendees included representatives of the OT. Its local leader and Falley's engineering officer give Rommel the now-common complaint that they are desperately short of cement; again, the same story. Transportation lines are being hit hard throughout northern France, not just by Allied bombers, but by the Maquis. Rommel's suggestions to remedy problems are numerous:

- Underwater bridges and supports through swamp areas
- Trails and clearings cut alongside roads through the boçage
- Smoke screens and anti-aircraft positions around critical supply points
- Get the Kriegsmarine involved in better navigation of the rivers.

Rommel stresses to them the need to overcome each of their concerns. They in turn protest, citing severe shortages, a lack of cooperation by the local residents, and little time, all of which are making their task difficult.

Rommel though, is in no mood to hear this. He repeats that they will just have to overcome every problem as it arises. When the OT leader replies simply, "*Herr Feldmarschall*, our men cannot do the impossible," Rommel glares at the man. He says sharply, "*Nothing* is impossible!"

And that of course, ends that.

At the end of the briefings, they enjoy lunch in Falley's spacious hall. The walls have been painted in a pattern that is supposed to simulate marble, but of course, does not. After lunch, Rommel's caravan continues on, driving across the Cotentin peninsula. They stop several times to inspect defensive positions and climb a number of hills that are covered with heather. The sun is peeking out from the heavy clouds by the time he stops south of Valognes in the center of the peninsula to pay a quick visit to the men of the 6th Parachute Regiment, commanded by Major von der Heydte.[1] All fifteen companies of this recently arrived 3,450-man regiment quickly assemble before the field marshal. He notes that many of the faces are not much older than his son's.[2]

Rommel is warmly greeted by von der Heydte, who served with him in Africa two years ago. Despite the fact that the paratroopers in the desert had never really been well-liked by the army units because of their snobbish, élitist attitude,[3] Rommel now takes the time to talk over some old times with him.

He then gets up before the regiment and gives the paratroopers a short speech. Two reporters cover his talk in a newsreel. After expressing confidence in their defensive preparations, he goes on to (unknown to him, prophetically) stress the need to be vigilant at all times.

"Don't think that they'll come on a clear day, and let you know ahead of time," he says to them warningly. He shakes his head. "Oh no. They'll come when you don't expect them. They'll suddenly drop out of the sky in gusts of wind and rain."

His audience appreciates his airborne analogy and seems impressed with his emphasis on staying alert at all times, even though Rommel himself does not give much credence to the idea of starting a large-scale operation in bad weather. The enemy might be able to drop a few paratroopers in bad weather (although certainly not in storms), but they would not be able to land assault troops onto a beach. *Seelöwe* had taught him that.

After a quick inspection, they turn south and head for Brittany. Just after 8 p.m., they roll into Val André.[4] They have a candlelight dinner with officers of the 77th Infantry Division and a unit of SS military geologists. Rommel singles out the geologists to praise them for their fine work on obstacle construction over the past few weeks, and then shares with them some popular stories of his past glories.

With a broad smile, he tells them about an old gray-haired French general that he had once encountered back in that hectic June of 1940.[5] The captured old Frenchman had patted him on the shoulder and had said to him in a critical but paternal voice, "You're far too fast, young man."

Then there was the time when his Africa Korps had, after a tenacious battle, finally taken the port of Tobruk. In one of the buildings they had discovered an opulent booty of English delicacies, including pineapples, some good beer, and canned crayfish. And later on, there was this one spunky New Zealand fellow who had been captured in the North African desert. A remarkable fellow, this "versatile General Clifton" as Rommel calls him.[6] He and the field marshal had a number of interesting discussions. In fact, in the middle of one talk, Clifton asked to be handed over to the Germans, instead of the Italians. Rommel told him that he could not, and that Clifton would have to go into an Italian POW camp. Clifton a couple minutes later asked to use the restroom. Going in, he promptly crawled out the window and escaped. Rommel chuckles at the memory, and adds that Clifton was recaptured a couple days later going down a desert path with a jerry can, tired and thirsty.

Rommel had taken a liking to him, and now expresses his admiration for the man's audacity, despite the fact that the prisoner ended up escaping some four times while in North Africa and subsequently in Italy, running his guards ragged as they looked all over for him.[7]

After dinner, Rommel takes on a sadder tone, telling his audience about how the Italians lost their will to fight as things became worse. He expresses regret over the many empty promises that General Cavallero had made to him.

Later that evening, before retiring, he takes a stroll along the wet beach with Ruge. They talk about things in general. It is low tide, and the two stop once in a while to admire both the evening and all around them the newly constructed defense obstacles. The last time he had stood here, the beaches had been empty. Now they are filled with all sorts of his anti-invasion devices—Czech hedgehogs, barbed wire, Belgian gates, mined posts… They have turned a beautiful coastline into a maze of death.

Rommel grunts with satisfaction, and then looks out over the dark waters, almost trying to pierce the night to see any approaching Allied ships.

---

1   Thirty-seven-year-old *Major* Friedrich-August *Freiherr* von der Heydte. A devout Catholic from an aristocratic Bavarian family, von der Heydte had joined a German cavalry regiment in 1925 and remained in the Army until the invasion of France in May 1940. At that time, he transferred from the 240th Infantry Division to the Luftwaffe airborne branch and was assigned to the 3rd *Fallschirmjäger* Regiment. After taking part in the airborne invasion of Crete (for which he was later awarded the Knight's Cross) and then the invasion of Russia in 1941, he served with distinction in North Africa under Rommel as part of General Ramcke's airborne brigade. In early September of 1943, when Italy surrendered to the Allies and broke ties with the Reich, the 2nd *Fallschirmjäger* Division, of which von der Heydte was now the Ia (Operations Officer), occupied and secured Rome as part of Fall Achse, the German takeover of Italy. In the middle of January 1944, after recovering from injuries sustained in a plane crash three months before, von der Heydte was given command of the 6th Fallschirmjäger Regiment, which was starting to form in Germany. He would later be promoted to *Oberstleutnant* on August 1, 1944.

2   Average age of the enlisted men in the 6th Parachute was 17½ years old.

3   Rommel himself had written, "The brigade had never been very popular with us, because following the normal Luftwaffe practice, they had always been demanding special treatment. They had sometimes wanted, for instance, units taken out of the line in order to husband their special troops."

4   A town along the Gulf of St. Malo, some 45km west of west of the U-boat port city of St. Malo.

5   It was June 12, at St. Valery, after Rommel had captured a dozen French and British generals, including the commander of the French IX Corps.

6   Brigadier General George H. Clifton, commanding the 6th New Zealand Infantry Brigade. Along with most of his headquarters staff, the New Zealander was captured by Ramcke's paratroopers on September 4, 1942. Rommel immediately sent for him and they had an interesting talk (described in Desmond Young's classic, *Rommel, The Desert Fox*). They chatted a couple more times after that (including after one escape in mid-September) about many different things, even Churchill's personality.

7   Regarding Clifton's escape, Rommel later wrote, "To put a stop to any such further nonsense of the kind, I had him shipped straight across to Italy." The next year, while in Italy, Rommel found out (erroneously) that Clifton had been transferred to and later escaped from an Italian POW camp by assuming the role of a *Hitlerjugend* leader (shorts, proper insignia, and all) and had made it into Switzerland. According to General Fritz Bayerlein, he was actually dressed on this attempt (his fifth) as a sailor of the merchant marine, and did not make Switzerland, but was captured near it, outside of Como. (Liddell-Hart, K.282)

On Clifton's eighth attempt, "the flying kiwi" (as he was now called by his fellow POWs) was wounded. While sitting between two guards in a moving railway car headed to Germany, he had suddenly made a break for it, diving out of one of the car's windows and onto the embankment. The guards shot at him, wounding him in the thigh. Finally, on his ninth try in March of 1945, he escaped from his POW camp in Silesia, and this time he was successful in getting out of Germany and making it to freedom. Interestingly, after the war, Young, gathering information for his biography, interviewed Rommel's widow, Lucie. One of the first things she asked him was whether General Clifton had ever made it out of the Reich. "My husband always hoped he would get out of Italy," she told him. "He had a great opinion of him."

Thursday, May 18

Rommel begins his day early. Starting out from Val André, he resumes his inspections. He stops at the headquarters of the 77th Infantry Division. The commander, General Stegmann,[1] gives his report. Rommel then stands and addresses the senior officers. He tells them that they are all to cooperate with the French, from the top on down. He tells Stegmann, "Let the enemy invade us now, but with trembling knees."

Continuing the tour, the motorcade moves westward, inspecting some glass minefields (actually, just the detonators are made of glass), and three manufacturing firms that are making his *Nussknackerminen*. On the road, they pass a lively, colorful battalion of Russian Tartars.

He makes several speeches that day, one at St. Malo, and another at General Eugen Mendl's *2. Fallschirmjäger Korps* headquarters in Quintin. Accompanying Mendl is Seventh Army's General Dollmann and most of the senior commanders of the units in northwest Brittany.

Before any briefings begin, Rommel has an open dialogue with these officers on a whole range of subjects. Among the subjects they discuss are: the varied effects of offshore and anti-airborne obstacles; different types of smoke screens and their limitations; the larger appetites of the younger troops and food supply problems; the idea of German officers teaching in local French schools; Russian soldiers pressed into their service, and their combat efficiency; fighting elements of the Resistance and the rules of war; effective techniques to move combat units quickly to the front; local jury-rigging and makeshift devices to make up for shortages...

Again, Rommel emphasizes the importance of not infuriating the locals. French cooperation at this time will be at its lowest, and it would be crazy for the occupiers to aggravate them now, especially when the invasion begins. Treat them well, he insists. Pay them or pay them off, quickly and reliably—especially the women, whose help is really gratis.

The officers for the most part seem to enjoy his positive tones, getting into the spirit of the briefing. They review the shortages in raw materials, especially concrete. When one general makes some snide remarks about the Kriegsmarine and their "mammoth constructions," the massive U-boat pens and the huge amounts of concrete and steel that have gone into their fabrication, Rommel smiles soothingly. He re-emphasizes the high degree of cooperation that he has experienced with their "naval brothers."

"We receive *many* advantages from the navy," he tells them, "such as the artillery fire control positions. The navy is the branch you are sitting on. Don't saw it off."

They review installation of the new Coastal Type-A mines. And of course, obstacle construction. Rommel hears that, around Farnbacher's 25th Corps, they have installed some 129,000 stakes and 35,000 tetrahedrons.

At another stop, he addresses an assembled group of unit commanders of the 5th *Fallschirmjäger* Division. Trying to ease their frustrations, he tells them, "We officers must be able to cope with all difficulties. There'll always be ways and means. We will have to be optimistic at all times."

He pauses for effect. "Even when things don't go right the first time, remember, there will always be a way out. The important thing is to perfect your training, and to use every possible means to strengthen your defenses."

He leaves with the paratroopers' good wishes. They head back, eventually returning through the Vire area. On the way, he stops at General Feuchtinger's 21st Panzer Division headquarters. This time, von Oppeln-Bronikowski is ready for him, and Rommel smiles as he remembers their last encounter. He sits down with von Oppeln, Feuchtinger, and the division's senior staff, and they discuss possible invasion scenarios. The field marshal makes sure that they understand his order that the 21st is *not* to move against any isolated airdrops without first getting permission from him.[2] In the meantime, he wants the unit commanders to get a good feel for the layout of the area. It will come in handy when the fighting begins.

After an inspection, Rommel decides to dine with the officers, and he speaks admiringly about the history of the division. After all, Feuchtinger, while not too popular a leader,[3] commands a new incarnation of what had been one of Rommel's favorite units in North Africa.

A major topic of discussion is the division's strange rocket launchers. Major Becker's group is manufacturing them in a sort of jury-rigged assembly line process, and Rommel now tells them that he expects them to fill a production order of a thousand units. Becker of course, balks at the amount. He admits feeling that this is beyond what his enterprising group can do in a short amount of time. But Rommel is insistent, and Feuchtinger reluctantly promises that they will do their best.

During the dinner, von Oppeln's previous encounter with the field marshal inevitably arises, and the story is good for a few laughs. Von Oppeln, embarrassed, takes on the good-natured ribbing of his fellow officers. Rommel glances at him with a look of smug revenge.

Driving home in the dark, they have some trouble around Falaise. The cars have to make a few detours and one or two stops to avoid low-flying *Jabos*. Rommel and his staff finally arrives back at the château around 11:30 p.m. Weary from the trip but content at what they have seen, they sit down in the officers' mess and have a quick debriefing as they munch on a late snack. It has been a long trip.

---

1 Fifty-year-old *Generalleutnant* Rudolf Stegmann. A World War I veteran of the Eastern Front, he later fought in Poland, France and then Russia. Seriously injured in mid-January 1944, he returned to active duty on May 1, taking over the 77th Infantry.

2 This directive would not be enforced in the early night hours of D-Day, mostly because Rommel was absent.

3 Although Feuchtinger commanded a panzer division, he had been trained as an artilleryman and had little combat experience. To make matters worse, it was rumored that he had a bad habit of frequently leaving his headquarters for some far-off tryst.

Friday, May 19

The weather is turning bad, so Rommel spends the day at his headquarters. He and his staff are due for their third and last (*Gott sei Dank!*) set of standard booster vaccinations. They have a number of briefings on their latest inspection tour, discussing various uses of the paratroopers. Also discussed is the idea of Type-A coastal mines being laid off Brittany. When will the navy start laying them in the Bay of the Seine?

Another subject is how to best make smoke-screen generators and use smoke screens. Also discussed are the many aircraft swarming daily over northern France; Major Becker's unique rocket launchers; and how to get more wood, steel, and concrete for the shore obstacles, and coal for the industries making them.

They go over some problems regarding the paratroop units. They are all short of men and need training. None of them has a full set of parachutes, except von der Heydte's 6th Parachute Regiment. Of course, that is not critical. They are not about to undertake any airborne landings, what with transport aircraft being so scarce and the enemy's control of the skies so effective.

Then there is the idea of an upcoming inspection with von Rundstedt and Marshal Pétain. OB West had broached the possibility of the Vichy France leader accompanying Rommel and von Rundstedt on a tour of the defenses, possibly this weekend. Rommel is agreeable to this, so they thrash out what protocols would be needed or "suggested" for the day.

That afternoon, Admiral Ruge drives off to Paris to talk to Krancke about a number of things, especially putting those damned mines in the Bay of the Seine.

After he has departed, Rommel is informed that two British commandos have been caught around the Somme estuary. Concerned, he tells Speidel to have them transferred to the château. Keitel's "Commando Order" of late 1942, demanded by an infuriated Hitler,[1] is after all, still in effect. Speidel will have to act quickly if they want to get their hands on these two before they are turned over to the Gestapo and shot. The orders are issued.

That night, Rommel writes another letter to Lucie:

> *Yesterday I returned from the west. Everything went well and according to plan...*
> *The weather is still cold and it's raining at last. The British will have to be patient for a bit. I am curious whether I can spare a few days in June to get away from here. Right now it's out of the question.*

Generalfeldmarschall von Rundstedt today sends a detailed report on his panzers to OKW. The 1st SS Panzer Division's roster is back up to some 20,000 men. He also lists the 2nd SS Panzer, headquarters in Toulouse, with some 55 *PzKw IV*s (46 still on order) and 37 *PzKw V*s (another 62 to be shipped). Other details are listed.[2]

That evening, he visits French Marshal Pétain at his headquarters, Château Voison, near Rambouillet.[3] Pétain, a hero of Verdun, had taken over the controversial position of Prime Minister after the fall of France and the 1940 Armistice. Since then, Pétain has headed the Vichy government.

Von Rundstedt knows that Pétain's relationship with Berlin has been shaky at best. After the fall of France, he had wanted to create an economic alliance with Germany. Most Nazi officials though, especially those at the top, did not favor one. To them, France was a vanquished enemy, just like the others. Hitler, who had fought there in World War I, saw it as just a satellite of the Reich, to be plundered for its raw materials and economy. After all, France had been the first country to declare war against them in 1939.

Deeper than that though, was a continuing feeling of smug revenge—fair vengeance for the defeat of 1918 and the cruel peace treaty that had been forced upon Germany. And so, despite Pétain's efforts, the Führer had kept France in her place. He does not care about making France an ally, or even converting it into an independent fascist partner. France is merely a defeated country, justly occupied and a part of the Reich.

Besides, to the top German officials, the French could not be trusted. They have had for years an active and rather effective resistance group. And in 1942, when the Americans had landed in North Africa, thousands of Frenchmen had hastily gone over to their side. Seeing a serious threat here, the Germans had felt compelled to occupy Vichy France. Hitler had at that time sent Pétain a long letter of explanation for the occupation, ending with:

> If *Marechal*, you have any wishes or anxieties, refer them to Field Marshal von Rundstedt.

As the months had gone by, the two field marshals, who in two wars now had been enemies, had conferred a number of times over various internal matters, including the shortage of vital goods, violence conducted by the Maquis, and the rebel gangs that prey upon road traffic, particularly to and from Southern France.[4]

Now von Rundstedt is visiting again, enjoying Pétain's company. He also wants to show him some of the defensive measures that have been constructed along the coast. So as they sit down together for some refreshments, the Prussian invites Pétain to accompany him and Rommel on a tour of the Atlantic Wall this coming Sunday. There is little danger of invasion at this time, and they will be able to find time to discuss various details that they observe along the coast. Naturally curious about how construction is going, Pétain accepts the invitation.

Von Rundstedt leaves the château satisfied, and instructs Blumentritt to notify Rommel's headquarters of the trip.

Later that day, Pétain, who himself has recently toured several towns in France, broaches the decision to Jean Tracou, the *Directeur du Cabinet*. Tracou pauses and then asks if he has considered the ramifications of such a trip. He points out *le grand jour* that Goebbels' propaganda ministry will make in the German media of this visit. They will gloat over images of the French prime minister and the German senior commanders touring defenses designed to thwart the invasion that in many eyes, would liberate France. Such images will no doubt infuriate the expatriates, as well as send a mixed signal to Pétain's own supporters.

Pétain, already in trouble with the Allies over his dealings with the Germans, begins to realize that the West and his countrymen will view this tour as a reaffirmation of his own support for the Nazis. Everyone knows that the invasion is coming, and to be in the spotlight now, seen at the side of the German commanders in France, seems foolhardy—especially if the Allies win, which currently seems very likely. Pétain is certainly no fool, and he now realizes the error of agreeing to the public inspection. He has to notify von Rundstedt that he will not be able to make the trip. His office will instead publicly emphasize the dangers of any bombardment of the coastal communities.

He asks Tracou to make the phone call.

Von Rundstedt, back in his villa, is notified about Pétain's change of heart a short time later and is of course saddened by the news. After all, he had only wanted to point out the defensive features of the Atlantic Wall and just "talk shop." Still, having no political agenda himself, he accepts the cancellation graciously and decides not to pursue the matter.[5]

---

1   The Commando Order was a highly confidential directive decreed by Hitler in 1942 after a series of escalating Allied raids, culminated by the Dieppe sortie and the Sark Island Raid in August. An operational order taken across the Channel by a British general and later captured stated among other things that German prisoners were to be bound. Angered by this, Hitler ordered Berlin to announce in early October that some 1,400 Allied prisoners (most of whom were Canadians that had been captured from the raids) would now be shackled. Hitler himself wrote in the Wehrmacht daily communiqué: "In the future, all terror and sabotage troops of the British and their accomplices, who do not act like soldiers but rather like bandits, will be treated as such by the German troops and will be ruthlessly eliminated in battle, wherever they appear."

England responded by shackling many German prisoners in Canada. Further enraged upon hearing this, Hitler discussed what to do about the matter with his senior staff advisers. On October 18, Keitel issued the Führer's top secret *Kommandobefehl*. It stated that "From now on all men operating against German troops in so-called commando raids, even if they are in uniform, whether armed or unarmed, in battle or in flight, are to be annihilated to the last man... Even if these individuals on discovery ... give themselves up as prisoners, no pardon is on any account to be given." The order also claimed that British commandos had been ordered to kill German prisoners (which was of course a lie). Only a dozen copies were distributed by Jodl the next day, with a special attached appendix dictating that the order was "intended for commanders only and must not under any circumstances fall into enemy hands."

2   The report, sent as an Ultra message, was intercepted by the Allies, and a translated copy would soon be in the hands of their intelligence analysts. They would note the updates, including a correction of an earlier mistaken identity: it was the 11th Panzer that was in southern France, not the 10th Panzer, as they had earlier thought.

3   A hunting château, located some 51km southwest of Paris.

4   After the war, von Rundstedt himself testified at Nuremberg, "I can only say that I did everything to help Marshal Pétain, with whom I was on terms of great confidence. I asked Hitler to define at last what position France was to have in the future Europe. I assisted Marshal Pétain to raise his Guards and tried to create a new French Army for him, though it did not grow into more than a regiment. I succeeded in obtaining more rations for the fine French railroad men who managed all our transports, and I tried to have their relatives who were prisoners of war returned to them, in the same way in which Hitler had approved after the Dieppe raid that the relatives of those in Dieppe, could return. We did what we could to supply the great city of Paris with coal and food, though the transport situation for the German Army was almost unbearably poor."

5   Pétain, who later fled before the Allied advance into Germany, eventually was returned to France after the war to stand trial for treason. He was found guilty and sentenced to death. In 1946, General de Gaulle commuted the sentence to life imprisonment. Pétain, lonely and now more or less a man without a country, eventually died on July 23, 1951 on the island of Ile d'Yeu off the coast of Brittany.

Saturday, May 20

Air activity over the English Channel has been heavy this week. The coastal batteries at Le Havre were hit yesterday. The 100mm battery at Merville was also bombed. The main gun emplacements survived the attack well enough, but the commanding officer, *Hauptmann* Wolter, was killed in his quarters.[1]

This morning at La Roche-Guyon, the staff is occupied with a "diversionary action" entitled *Landgraf,* with Military District 6.[2] During the exercise, the air raid sirens go off a number of times, but the château is not targeted. Just as well. Rommel is spending a good deal of his time there. After all, the invasion could come at any time, and he knows he cannot at present go home. But when Speidel requests a few days of leave over Pentecost, he readily consents. They can survive without their chief of staff for a while, and who knows when he will be able to see his family again. Speidel will leave in a few days, on the 23rd.

That morning, Rommel has a phone conversation with State Party Leader Karl Kaufmann, the *Gauleiter* for the Hamburg area.[3] Rommel wants to set up a conference to discuss improving shipping volume on the French inland canals to increase the volume of supplies. They set the conference for Tuesday, May 23.

At lunch, the field marshal and his staff are graced with the company of their superior officer. The grizzled old Prussian has brought along with him as a guest, his visiting son, Hans Gerd von Rundstedt, a medical lieutenant in the reserves, currently posted at The Hague. Also along are Blumentritt and *Korvettekapitän* Eduard Becker.

Together, they all enjoy a formal meal. Naturally, they discuss details of the invasion as they dine. Rommel expresses his puzzlement over the fact the Allies have not invaded as yet. Von Rundstedt growls in reply that he is in no hurry.

Von Rundstedt then tells them that Marshal Pétain has turned down his invitation to accompany them on the inspection tour for Sunday. His decision is understandable, although disappointing. They discuss the internal policies of the French and how they interact with German occupational rule.

Since Pétain is not going with them, the Prussian has now lost his interest in a full inspection of the coastal positions. He is though going to look at some of them with his son today. Rommel offers to go with him, but the old man tells him it is not necessary. Actually, von Rundstedt prefers that Rommel not go (though he does not say so). This way, the old Prussian can spend the time alone with his son.

Von Rundstedt states that this evening, Hans plans on going out to explore the Parisian nightlife with some fellow officers.[4] Von Rundstedt of course will not go, growling that he is far too old for that kind of thing. He will instead spend the evening sipping brandy, smoking cigarettes, and reading a good Karl May book or a detective story.

That afternoon, after OB West has departed, an army staff car drives up to the château courtyard. Two British prisoners, their khaki uniforms wrinkled and dirty, climb out, blindfolded and tired from a long, tense 240km drive. Their blindfolds are soon removed by their two escorts, and they are led away to a holding cell. They are given some sandwiches and tea, while a growling, vicious dog stands guard outside.

These prisoners are the two British commandos that Rommel was told about yesterday, caught snooping around the Somme estuary. Rommel's staff managed to keep them out of the hands of the *Sicherheitsdienst*[5] and take them into their custody, Rommel not only did not want them to get executed, but was curious about British commandos. Now they are here.

Staubwasser, Rommel's Ic, goes down to the cells and questions them. They are obviously commandos; the way they were caught and their physical build give them away. And even though the insignias have been torn off their blouses, the clean outlines of the Combined Operations emblem and the Special Services shoulder patch can be discerned. They are both lieutenants.

Although the two are relieved to be where they are, one prisoner, Lieutenant Roy Woodridge, refuses point blank to say anything else besides his name and rank. After that, he remains silent. In the other cell, the other prisoner, claiming to be a Lieutenant George Lane,[6] speaks a bit to his interrogator. He talks about mundane things and jokes with his captor; obviously a more promising subject.

Staubwasser finally tells Lane that he is being taken to another office for questioning. He and a guard take the prisoner to the army group operations officer. Von Tempelhoff, seeing Lane nervous, turns on the charm and tries to put him at ease. He begins conversing with him in English, which at first surprises the man, until von Tempelhoff tells him that his wife is English.

Von Tempelhoff tells Lane that, since the commando team was picked up at the Somme estuary, it is a good sign to him that the invasion will come there. (It is also one of the target areas popular with Rommel.) Lane just shrugs his shoulders and replies that he believes that area and the coastline north of it is too fortified for any kind of landing.

Staubwasser sighs. At any rate, could *Herr Leutnant* Lane tell him if "such commando spy missions are really necessary, if the invasion is imminent?"

Lane's eyes widen. He looks up at the two German officers and exclaims heartily, "The invasion is not imminent at all. You just overestimate our enterprising spirit!"

Von Tempelhoff smiles as Staubwasser grunts in reply. As the questioning continues, Speidel informs Rommel of the prisoners' arrival and that one seems pleasant enough to talk with. Rommel smiles and asks Speidel to bring the man to his study whenever Staubwasser and von Tempelhoff finish with him.

Speidel informs an aide to send word to the two staff officers. He then turns back to the field marshal and fills him in on their capture. Sometime around the evening of the 18th, the two had evidently been dropped off the coast by a British MTB, and had come ashore to investigate the construction of some of the obstacles that had been positioned along the shorelines of the Somme estuary. Perhaps they wanted to take apart a mine as well. When a patrol had discovered them, a second was dispatched as starshells began to illuminate the area.

The two commandos somehow slipped away from the searchers and circled back around to where they had hidden their dinghy on the beach. Paddling furiously, they hurriedly pulled it through the surf and put to sea. However, they found to their dismay that the launch that was their ride home had vanished. They were stranded in the dark off the enemy coast, and in pouring rain.

With the local Kriegsmarine contingent now alerted to their presence, their fate was sealed. Sure enough, a while later, as they struggled to row out into the main Channel, they were picked up by a patrol boat.[7] Speidel adds that, on the way over to the château, one of them had commented that the first thing their jailers had bluntly told them was that they were going to be shot as spies. "With that in his mind, *Herr Feldmarschall*," the chief of staff concludes, "this prisoner might try anything."

Rommel shakes his head. He replies reassuringly, "I doubt it, Speidel. Not to me. He doesn't have the authority, for one thing. Besides, I'm going to help them." He smiles. A little chat with an Englishman will be interesting. Yes, indeed.

So after questioning Lane, Staubwasser advises him with a serious face, "Please try to clean yourself up a little. In a bit, you are going to meet a very important person." When the prisoner looks up suspiciously and asks who, Staubwasser shakes his head and replies, "You will see." He starts out of the cell.

Lane stands up. "Please tell me," he presses. He is clearly worried. The Gestapo?

Staubwasser, near the door, turns around. Relenting, he replies, "Somebody very important. Very important indeed. Field Marshal Rommel." He then leaves the commando standing with a stunned look on his face. Let him think about *that*

In due course, the now clean but still suspicious British prisoner is brought blindfolded into Rommel's study. He is accompanied by an interpreter, Staubwasser, von Tempelhoff, and, just to keep things friendly, two armed guards. The field marshal, sitting at his desk in the corner of the room and gazing out the French windows at his terrace, rises to come around and greet the Englishman.

The blindfold is removed, and Lane blinks his eyes, adjusting to the light and to the incredible scene around him. Rommel examines the man. Lane is a solid rugged fellow, about 1.8 meters tall, with a broad forehead, a prominent nose, and large wide-open eyes, which are now staring at the field marshal. One of the benefits of fame.

Rommel notes that the prisoner, though standing at attention, begins taking in the lavish furnishings of the room—the historic tapestries on the wall, the exquisite wooden floor and plush carpets, the historic porcelain along the walls. Then his eyes return to the field marshal, looking again into his eyes, then to his *Pour le Mèrite*, then back to his eyes again. Rommel smiles, shakes his hand, and motions them all over to the squat round table near the windows. There a kitchen attendant has set up priceless bone china and two teapots.

They all sit down, and the field marshal begins the conversation, the interpreter following him closely. "So... You're one of those commando gangsters, *ja?*"

Lane, although nervous, shrugs his shoulders. "Well, I'm a commando, and proud of it. But I'm not a gangster. None of us are."

Rommel furls his brow. "Well, perhaps you aren't a gangster; but we've had some nasty experiences with you commandos. They haven't, shall we say, behaved as impeccably as they should."

Lane stays silent, on his guard now. Rommel turns his head and looks out one of his terrace windows, thinking about how to phrase the next sentence. He does not want to overtly threaten the man, but he wants him to realize that they have him over a barrel. He barely notices Staubwasser motioning for an aide to pour the tea.

"You know," Rommel observes, "you're in a bit of a spot. You *do* know what we do with saboteurs..."

Lane turns to the interpreter and replies, "If your field marshal thinks I'm a saboteur, he wouldn't have invited me here."

Hearing this from the interpreter, Rommel smiles. "So," he concludes with mock surprise, "you regard this as an invitation?"

Lane looks at him and replies solemnly, "I do, and I must say that I'm highly honored." With that, he bows majestically in his chair.

Everyone in the room laughs. Rommel smiles and changes the subject. "And how's my old friend General Montgomery?"

Lane smiles back and, now a little more at ease, answers casually, "Very well, thank you. I hear he's planning some sort of invasion."

Rommel plays along and arches his eyebrows. "Oh? You mean there really is going to be one?"

"Well, so *The Times* tells us, and it's usually reliable enough."

Still in a light tone, Rommel continues. "Do you realize that this is going to be the first time that the British have had to put up a proper fight?"

Lane scowls. "What about Africa, then?"

"Ah! That was child's play!" Rommel retorts affably with a wave of his hand. Looking back on it now, compared to the enormous forces that he commands in France, it actually seemed to have been.

He launches into a we-should-have-won speech. "The only reason I had to retreat there was that no more supplies were getting through to me," he replies truthfully. Which is why the British outgunned him at El Alamein. Now if the odds had been just even...

He states that Africa was just an unfortunate detour that had only delayed their inevitable victory. On the other hand, the British Empire, he explains, is meeting its doom. Its navy is slowly being pummeled at sea, with all its naval resources going to build merchant ships that keep going to the bottom. The RAF cannot expand in any real way, and is only holding its own because of the massive influx of American products. And England's real resource, its men, are steadily being killed off.

Rommel pauses. It is true, he continues, that Germany has sustained some costs; but mostly on the Eastern Front. Against the British, their manpower pool is tremendous. And that is why, in the end, the Reich will win out—superior manpower, highest quality equipment, and a determination to win, fired up by a pride born out of the depths of economic disaster and tempered by global shame…

Lane sits and listens to him, totally absorbed by the lecture, as the interpreter tries desperately to keep up with the field marshal.[8]

Rommel tells Lane that there is no need for the British to be consumed by this conflict. Germany is not their enemy. England and Germany have to unite and fight side by side.

Lane is obviously impressed by the monologue, but disturbed by the idea of such an alliance. "That, your Excellency, might be difficult at this time," he says slowly. "Many German policies repel the British."

Rommel's eyebrows go up. "Such as?" he asks.

The prisoner hesitates, clearly uncomfortable. Finally, looking Rommel in the eyes, he says softly, "The problem of the Jews."

Rommel stirs a bit, uncomfortable about the words. But he cannot let this man know it. They have to overcome their differences if their two countries are to unite. He forces himself to make light of the remark. "Ah, every country has its Jews. Ours are just different than yours. Or those here in France. Ah, the French! What a country!" Rommel continues on about the French. If Lane looked around, he would see a population at ease with life and its temporary occupiers.

The prisoner replies dryly that it has been kind of hard for him as of late to do that, since he has only been able to tour the country in blindfolds.

Rommel smiles. The man has a sense of humor. He replies, "Well, if you could, you would see how really happy they are…"

Rommel keeps talking, telling this fellow soldier from the other side what the new German movement has been all about. Its original purpose, he notes, was not to dominate, but just to make the country rise up to be the best there was. And others had found that unsuitable. Well, now they are paying.

Lane raises his hand a bit, almost as if in school, and requests permission to ask a question. Rommel pauses and then nods.

"Would your Excellency tell me whether you regard military occupation as an ideal situation for a vanquished country?"

Rommel thinks about the question and then answers tactfully, "The ideal situation is for a country to be run by someone who knows what they need. For that very reason, soldiers make the best rulers." He explains how soldiers are conditioned for the worst emergencies, and can handle crises better than civilians can. Soldiers are more ready for critical situations and have more contingencies to deal with them. That is why the Germans are able to run the French countryside so well.

"If you travel around occupied France today and keep your eyes open," Rommel repeats, "you'll see everywhere just how happy and contented the French people really are. For the first time they know just what they have to do—because we are telling them. And that's the way the man in the street likes it!"

They talk some more. To Rommel, Lane's points do not seem to carry much conviction. Talking of after the war, Rommel asks Lane if he thinks a military man could successfully handle Germany's reconstruction. Lane says he does. He also admits candidly that in his opinion, Rommel would be the right man for the job.

At some point in the conversation, von Tempelhoff interrupts. He has noticed that Lane speaks English with some sort of accent, possibly Eastern European. He observes that Lane has an accent. If Lane is indeed a British officer, why is this so?

Lane hesitates. Admitting to being a Hungarian Jew by birth would definitely be dangerous. On the defensive, he replies, "Because I am Welsh."[9]

"Ah, of course," von Tempelhoff replies as the German officers nod.

After what seems like a half-hour of visiting, the meeting is concluded, and the prisoner is ready to be escorted from the study.

"What will happen to me, your Excellency?" Lane asks a bit anxiously.

"We'll keep you out of the hands of our police, and my staff will take you and your friend to get safely to a prisoner of war camp," Rommel reassures him. "You have my personal guarantee on that, *ja*?"

Lane smiles back, obviously relieved and grateful, though embarrassed. "*Danke, Herr Feldmarschall*," he replies.

Rommel nods and smiles, and Staubwasser leads Lane off with Speidel, the interpreter, and the guards. The Ia lingers behind.

Rommel looks at him. "An interesting fellow," he ventures.

"Indeed he was, *Herr Feldmarschall*," von Tempelhoff replies.

"Make sure they get to a prisoner camp. I don't want the SS or the Gestapo to get their hands on them."

"*Jawohl*. Lane seems like a good fellow. I sort of took a liking to him."

Rommel looks at him with a smile. "I hope you're not going to marry *him* too?" Rommel chides, teasing Tempelhoff about his English wife.

Tempelhoff smiles. "*Pustekuchen!*" he replies. No chance.

They are still talking when, a few minutes later, Staubwasser comes back into the study, beaming. "Well, they're gone," he says.

Rommel glances over at him and replies, "Good. They should have a safe journey to their prisoner of war camp."[10]

Although obviously dismissed, Staubwasser remains standing, still smiling. Rommel picks up on it and raises an eyebrow. "What is it?"

"Well sir, when we left the room and were putting the blindfold back on him, he gripped my arm and begged me to tell him where we were."

"Oh?" Rommel's smile slips a bit. "You didn't, did you?"

"No sir," Staubwasser replies, frowning at the question, "although he persisted. He even swore that he wouldn't tell anyone."

Rommel shrugs. "I suppose it doesn't make too much difference. We're protected enough here, what with all the bomb shelters in the cliff and the flak positions. And anyway, I'm sure Montgomery knows by now where I am."

"*Herr Feldmarschall*," Staubwasser says, still smiling, "He wanted to remember the place, so that after the war, he can bring his wife and children back here and tell her that this was where he met the great Rommel!"

They all grin, and Rommel, chuckling softly, shakes his head, flattered.

Staubwasser adds that Lane was adamant about that, and vowed after the war that he would scour the French countryside until he found the castle.

It is only after the staff members have left his study that Rommel's smile fades. He had told Lane why France was so well off with the Germans here. And it made sense. Some day the French would be united with them. So why is he feeling so guilty? That question about the Jews. It has unsettled him.

That evening, several large formations of enemy bombers pass over La Roche-Guyon, no doubt on their way to the Fatherland.

---

1   *Hauptman* Karl-Heinrich Wolter was spending the night in his private quarters with his mistress when the bombing began. The building was demolished, and they both perished. *Oberleutnant* Raimund Steiner succeeded him.

2   *Landgraf* was a deception operation created by Army Group B to attempt to convince the Allies that the German defenses were stronger than they appeared. Dummy tanks and fictitious divisions were created for this. The operation was supported by specially prepared radio broadcasts.

3   Forty-three-year-old Karl Kaufmann was a founding member of the Nazi party, having joined in 1921. His close relationship with the Führer landed him the position of *Gauleiter* for the Ruhr valley and then for Hamburg in 1928. In 1933, the Nazi party made him *Reichsstatthalter* (Regional Governor) of the Hamburg district. In the fall of 1941, after the Hamburg population had suffered some from Allied bombings, Kaufmann petitioned and was granted permission to be allowed to seize homes owned by Jews, have them deported "east," and then turn over the seized property to Aryan Germans who had lost their own dwellings. Kaufman, arrested by the British in 1945, was as expected convicted of war crimes and sent to prison. He was released because of bad health and re-arrested a couple times before he was finally let out in 1953.

4   In the orderly's office of the command bunker at St. Germain, the younger staff officers had two large maps of Paris put up that showed nightlife entertainment. To update them, information was gathered from all visitors, who were asked to recount their Parisian experiences. On one map, numbered blue dots represented locations for a great meal; on the other, numbered red dots showed the locations of establishments where "something for the heart was to be found." Amusingly, von Rundstedt one day happened to come into the room. Seeing the maps, he went over to them as several young officers stood nearby. Studying the dots, he finally growled, "Here… Your red map isn't nearly full!"

5   The SS Security Service.

6   Sergeant George Jemru Lane, 29 years old, had actually been born in Hungary on January 18, 1915 as Dyuri Lanyi. A persecuted Jew, he had fled to England and after the war, became a member of the Hungarian Olympic water polo team. With the establishment of the Third Reich, Lane had seen how things were in Europe and moved to England. Given a commission in 1943, he eventually joined the infamous X Troop (made up of foreigners) of Commando Unit 10. It consisted of Europeans who had fled the continent, assumed new identities (especially since many of them were Jewish), and were now working for the British, raiding the French coast. This was Lane's fourth trip across the Channel, checking out mines off Ault. Woodridge was a sapper and mine expert who Lane had brought along to investigate German improvements in underwater mining.

7   The Germans never found out that Lane and Woodridge had brought some infrared photographic equipment to photograph the German Teller mines that they had found on their last couple missions. Fortunately, they managed to jettison the equipment into the Channel before they were captured.

8   Lane could speak a fair amount of German, but of course feigned ignorance at understanding it.

9   Pryce-Jones, David, "R.I.P. George Lane," David Calling, March 29, 2010.

10 Later that day, Lane and Woodridge were taken to Fresnes Prison near Paris. Again they were told that they would be hanged or shot, and Lane recalled later that he had even occasionally heard screams from other cells. Nevertheless, after a couple days, they were sent on to the officer POW camp in Spangenberg castle prison, 35km southeast of Kessel. Near the end of the war, while the prisoners were being relocated to avoid the approaching Allies, Lane was able to escape. After several dangerous days of hiding and running, he was finally liberated. After the war, he moved his family to the United States and became a stockbroker, but eventually returned to London. He died March 19, 2010.

Sunday, May 21

Today, the Western Allies launch Operation Chattanooga Choo-Choo, *a renewed, combined, concentrated effort to disrupt rail services in Western Europe. Dozens of fighter and tactical bomber groups, especially some 500 long-range fighters from Jimmy Doolittle's US Eighth Air Force, make low-level attacks on trains all over Germany. Air Chief Marshal Leigh-Mallory's Allied Expeditionary Air Forces send over 760 multi-national fighters on similar hunts over northern France. The initial results are impressive. The Eighth Air Force alone will eventually hit some 225 locomotives, destroying over 90 of them, along with several railroad stations, bridges, road crossings, barges, and of course, vehicles along the road.*

The attacks in France will force daytime railroad runs to be cut off in five days.

On this same day, another Japanese transmission to Tokyo from Ambassador Ōshima is intercepted by Allied Intelligence. It states that his main German contact, Under-Secretary Adolf von Steengracht, believes that the recent Allied attacks in Italy are meant to force the Germans to divert more divisions down there and away from the upcoming invasion. Von Steengracht also feels that some recent recon photos of southern England show that there are not yet enough troops there to mount a successful invasion. He also reports though, that a few partially covered photos of troop units in Scotland show (according to German senior officials) that a possible upcoming diversionary landing might very well be mounted against Norway.

Grinning among themselves, Allied Intelligence charitably give von Steengracht one out of three.

Recent reports have indicated that Allied tactical aircraft have been strafing civilians. A couple gun cameras taken from shot-down fighters have confirmed this, and when they were played at the Berghof, Hitler had watched civilians running out in the open and getting cut down. In response he had told Göring to select a couple captured pilots who had done this and shoot them. When the Reichsmarshal objects to executing pilots like that, someone on Jodl's staff suggests that the jail commandant just turn these perpetrators over to the SS. Again Göring and Keitel object to this "lynch mob" behavior. Göring suggests they be publicly tried in court for murder.

Based on the discussion, Luftwaffe chief of staff General Korten records the following:

Memorandum

The Führer has rendered the following decision regarding measures to be taken against Anglo-American air crews in special instances; downed enemy airmen are to be shot *Standgerich*[1] in the following instances:

1. In the event of the shooting of our own (German) downed air crews while they are parachuting to earth;

2. In the event of aerial attacks upon German planes that have made emergency landings, and whose crews are in the immediate vicinity;
3. In the event of attacks upon railway trains engaged in public (civilian) transportation;
4. In the event of low-level aerial attacks upon individual civilians (farmers, workers, single vehicles, etc.).

The memorandum will go to Warlimont, but is to be initialed by Jodl, Warlimont, and Keitel.[2]

***

Despite the fact that it is a heavily overcast day, there is heavy Allied air activity all over Europe, although there do not seem to be many enemy aircraft over La Roche-Guyon. Rommel spends the morning at the château, going over administrative details.

Around noontime, *Vizeadmiral* Rieve, commanding the naval forces for the *Kanalküste* out of his headquarters in Calais,[3] comes to the château to discuss Rommel's earlier ideas of pulling back the army coastal batteries from the shoreline. Rieve likes the idea, but points out a number of problems that this would entail, especially the lack of transport at this time for the heavier guns. They continue the discussion of this and of control of the coastal artillery with Admiral Ruge over lunch.

Afterwards, the two admirals go outside to walk off the meal. Rommel meets with Assistant Secretary Michel, from the military governor's office. Rommel complains to him about the shortages of coal and electricity for his units. Both commodities are needed to run lathes, generators, and plants that manufacture his war materials, especially the offshore obstacles and cement for the coastal gun emplacements.

Around 4 p.m., Rommel calls it a day. He, Ruge, Meise, Treff and Elbo go for a long promenade around the area, including through the town. It seems strange how the people, while they may notice the field marshal, do not bother him.

During the walk, the three officers chat about a number of things, including the country's leadership. The subject of removing certain "key leaders" from office is discussed—Keitel, for one. Also Göring, and Jodl. With Rommel leading the conversation, they explore the possibilities of how that could happen. Rommel eventually admits to his two staff members that he often feels troubled about such things happening. At any rate, they had all better be careful what they say to whom. It is one thing to grumble about the state of affairs, and quite another to be reported.

That night, he writes to Lucie of von Rundstedt's visit and about his talk with Lane. But then he also lets her know that things are getting close:

Dearest Lu:

Things were very lively in the air again yesterday. We ourselves were left alone. It's quieter today, so far. The enemy successes in Italy are very unfortunate. Strength on the ground was not unfavorable to us. It's simply that their superiority in the air and in ammunition is overwhelming, the same as it was in Africa. I hope things will go better here in the West. There's been no real air preparation so far. The damage caused some days ago has long since been put right.

We stand on the eve of heavy fighting, the most decisive battle of the war. Extraordinary things have been accomplished during the last months and weeks, and yet we are not as prepared as I would like to be. We still need more mines, more obstacles in the water and against airborne troops, still more artillery, anti-aircraft, and rocket projectors......

Yesterday, Rundstedt came here for a visit. In the afternoon I had a talk with a British officer who was quite sensible...

With *Panzer Lehr* now back from Hungary, they seem to sport a real chance of defeating the invasion. It is all a matter of knowing where it will start and reacting as soon as possible. Perhaps any day now...

---

1 A flying court-martial or "drumhead" court-martial, a term used for a quick proceeding done in the field, one in which the accused is given little or no chance to mount an effective defense.

2 731-PS, Memorandum from Chief of the Command Staff of the Armed Forces to the Deputy Chief of Command Staff of the Armed Forces, dated May 21. The memorandum was later used as evidence in the Nuremburg trials after the war.

3 Rieve, who replaced Admiral von Fischel on April 21, 1943, commanded four sectors: *Seeko Pas-de-Calais*, with headquarters at Wimille, *Seeko Seine-Somme,* headquartered at Le Havre, Hennecke's *Seeko Normandie*, its headquarters at Cherbourg, and *Seeko Kanalinseln,* its headquarters at Jersey. Rieve reported directly to Admiral Krancke.

Monday, May 22

In the morning, Rommel and Ruge travel southeast and upstream along the Seine to their alternate command center, a small, modest villa in the nearby town of Vernon. Accompanying them is war correspondent and good friend of the field marshal Lutz Koch.[1] Rommel wants him to write an article about this alternate site, hoping that the enemy will be confused and not know for sure whether he is spending his time here or at La Roche-Guyon.

At lunchtime, General von Salmuth arrives at this alternate site. He dines with them and then stays for a few meetings with Rommel early that afternoon.

Leaving Vernon a while later, Rommel returns to his château and goes over reports. Today, they seem favorable. The effort to strengthen Normandy continues. By now, additional units have fully arrived in the area: Falley's 91st Air Landing Division and von der Heydte's crack 6th Parachute Regiment. In addition, several army group reserve units have been moved there: the 206th Panzer Battalion, the 7th *AOK Stürm* Battalion, the 101st *Stellungswerfer*[2] Regiment, the 17th Machine Gun Battalion, and the 100th Panzer Replacement Battalion. Though these units are small in number, many of the men in these units are combat veterans or have been fully trained.

In the late afternoon, Rommel goes rabbit hunting with his aide Lang and chief engineer Meise. He feels that this is about all he can do at this point, as he awaits the invasion. His units by now know what to do and are working steadily on their defenses every day (and the Allied air forces on his nerves every night).

At one point, trudging through an open field, Meise and Rommel find themselves together and alone. For lack of anything better to talk about, Meise tries something he has never done before: he tries to engage the field marshal in politics. As he speaks though, Rommel interrupts him.

"Meise… Look, you and I can only talk politics if we're in an open field with nobody else in sight for two hundred yards all around." He goes on to say that in his mind, the Führer is and always has been a sort of brilliant visionary, who can quite be levelheaded and practical. "If you see him entirely alone, you can talk quite reasonably with him. But then 'Martin Bormann and Company' come in, and he reverts to his old form."

He pauses and adds, "Let's not talk about that."

***

Today's Situation Report from OB West reflects von Rundstedt's uncertainty about the landing area:

> OB West appreciates the situation as follows:
>
> The focal point of the enemy's concentration for invasion is in the South and Southeast of England. The Isle of Wight area is a focal point of preparations. The threatened main front is

still definitely the Channel front between the Scheldt and Normandy, as well as the northern part of Brittany, including Brest…"

In the meantime, new reports of Allied air activity come in. The rail lines all over France have yet again been targeted. A number of German airfields and railroad marshaling yards are hit in the Calais, Cherbourg, and Paris areas.

Paris, declared by the Germans to be an open city, like Rome, still comes under aerial attack, although it is a small, limited raid. The enemy aircraft fly in on careful, precise vectors and conduct strict bombing and strafing runs on parts of the Paris/ Orly airport.[3]

A half-century later, a bomb run like this will be termed a "surgical air strike."

***

Reich Minister Albert Speer begins a conference with the Führer that, on and off, will take place today and tomorrow. At the end of it, Speer will note the Führer's agreement with his view that:

> …in the West, even though building operations on the Atlantic Wall should be possible, the main duties of the OT should lie in the elimination of difficulties in transport, including those in the interior of France.

---

1   See entry for May 5.
2   Rocket launcher.
3   This is the first time that Brereton's tactical Ninth Air Force has hit the capital in force.

Tuesday, May 23

At La Roche-Guyon, Rommel has that noontime conference with State Party Leader Karl Kaufmann that he set up on the 20th. They discuss the problems of transportation along the inland rivers and canals. They also discuss (although in the abstract) possible consequences to Germany if the invasion fails and the Führer steps down from power. If he did, the other prominent Nazis such as Göring, Bormann, and Himmler would have to go with him. If that happened, government stability would depend upon the *Gauleiters* like Kaufmann to keep political constancy in the Reich until a peace could be secured with the Allies.[1]

That afternoon, the army group staff squeezes in a few games of tennis between air raid warnings. The Allies are at it again, bombing railroads and bridges.[2]

A series of phone calls is made to Germany. Rail transports are being held up at the border because the delousing operations there have fallen behind schedule.[3]

That evening, General Speidel in his bedroom up in the old Norman tower packs his bags, getting ready to go on leave. To him, this trip home will be an important one. He is going to confer with some of his co-conspirators in his province of Württemberg.[4]

***

Generalfeldmarschall Wolfram von Richthofen arrives at the Berghof in Bavaria. He has flown in from Italy to report directly to the Führer on the air situation there. First though, he attends a preliminary morning air production meeting in the SS barracks. Göring of course chairs the meeting. Von Richthofen is struck by the difference in attitudes between the old-school veterans like Milch and those wanting change, like Armaments Director Karl Saur.

Just after noontime, the Luftwaffe field marshal meets the Führer, who to him appears older. He still though, carries himself regally, and despite rumors, he does not seem at all nervous. On the contrary, he acts like a man charged with a historic mission, calmly letting his destiny unfold before him.

Von Richthofen gives his briefing on both the military and the political status in Italy. Each facet is getting bad. The setbacks at Cassino and Anzio though do not seem to perturb the Führer. Time, he says, is their ally. He even boasts to Richthofen that, as a matter of fact, from a political standpoint, Germany has already won the war.

Later on, around 3 p.m., *Reichsmarschall* Göring and his air production people join them in the villa's Great Hall. With them is famous fighter ace Adolf Galland. Although the view of the Alps is spectacular, the unheated room is somewhat chilly. They are all here for the *Jägerstab* report, the update on the production of fighters. Today's reports will include the status of the long-awaited new jet airplane, the Me-262. Hitler listens to standard fighter details as he absent-mindedly gazes out his grand window at the breathtaking mountain view below. Field Marshal Erhard

Milch, in charge of aircraft production, then begins his report on the projected figures for production of the new jet-fighter—

Hitler whirls around. "Jet-*fighter*?" he asks sharply. "I thought the 262 was coming in as a high-speed bomber."

Surprised at this, Milch replies hesitatingly, "*Mein Führer,* for the time being, it is being manufactured as a fighter."

Hitler looks intently around at the group and asks, "How many of the 262s already manufactured *can* carry bombs?"

Milch is now thoroughly rattled by the Führer's abrupt, somewhat harsh tone. He meekly tells him, "None, *mein Führer.* The Me-262 is being designed exclusively as a fighter aircraft."

After an awkward moment of silence, Milch goes on defense. Hitler is ominously quiet. Milch explains that the 262 has been designed as a swift fighter aircraft. To be redesigned now as a *Jabo* and hold bombs, its frame would have to be strengthened considerably. That would take a lot more precious design time. Even then, its payload would be limited; it would not be able to carry more than one 500kg bomb.

The Führer erupts into a furious tirade. Another screw-up! He had wanted a jet built that could carry bombs to the upcoming Western invasion site and smash through the enemy air armadas. Instead, they are getting ready to make another fighter. He fumes, "Who pays the slightest attention to the orders I give? I gave an *unqualified* order and left nobody in any doubt that the aircraft was to be built as a fighter-*bomber*."

As Milch tries to goes on, Hitler snaps, "Never mind! I only want one 250-kilo bomb! … How much do they weigh?"

Armaments Director Saur replies with statistics on the weight of the aircraft's cannon, protective armor, and ammunition. Hitler adds the numbers up as they are given. Together, the total weight is over 500 kilos.

"You don't need any guns," he replies with an evil grin. "The plane is so fast, it doesn't need any armor plating, either. You can take it all out."

He turns to *Oberst* Edgar Petersen, head of the Luftwaffe experimental research station at Rechlin, and asks if this is not so. The colonel of course nods in agreement. "That can be done without any difficulty," he replies.

Trying to salvage the situation, Milch pleads for the Führer to listen to other air experts who have come with him, but none want to speak up. In a brave attempt, General Galland begins hesitantly. An abrupt retort from the Führer, though, silences him after a dozen words or so.

After a short tense moment of silence, Milch tries again to appeal to the Führer. Raging, Hitler cuts him off and begins to berate the man.

Desperate and agitated, Milch hesitates, then again speaks up. "*Mein Führer,*" he cries pleadingly, "the smallest infant can see that this is a fighter, not a bomber aircraft!"

Infant?! Hitler deliberately, dramatically turns his back on the field marshal, a clear sign that this part of the meeting is over and a curt dismissal to the group. Milch is clearly on the way out. One of Petersen's assistants to his left in a very low voice whispers, "*Aufschlagbrand.*"—Shot down in flames.[5]

After leaving the main hall, Göring follows the Führer's lead and turns on his own production leaders, berating them. Milch, for whom Göring already has a long-standing personal resentment, naturally gets the brunt of the heat.

A short time later, Göring meets outside the great hall with Keitel, Milch, Armaments Minister Albert Speer, and several key industrial leaders who had come to brief Hitler on war production and the effects of the enemy bombing raids.[6] With the previous Me-262 fiasco fresh in his mind, Göring pleads with the industrialists not to be too pessimistic in the meeting. The Führer is already upset enough. And of course, with more bad news about the air war, Hitler might very well unload upon him again.

They all join Hitler in the cold (physically and socially) Great Hall. They discuss the impact of the Allied air campaigns upon German industrial output. The industrial leaders are under no illusions and stick to the facts. At first Hitler tries to put a good spin on the discussion and gives them his commonly used phrase, "We've been through worse crises." The industrial leaders, though, tell it like it is, and he is forced to ask them for their objective opinion. They give it to him. If the air war does not get any better, German production (and thus, the war) will be lost.

After leaving the Great Hall and entering the anteroom, Göring again starts up with a post-conference berating, this time rebuking the industrialists. They should not have burdened the Führer with such bad news. They could have dispensed with the needless anxieties and kept their pessimistic nonsense to themselves.

The guests are all eventually ferried down the mountain to the *Berchtesgadener Hof*, a luxurious hotel in town. With the fiery conferences now over, the members of Hitler's private inner circle hesitantly come down from their upstairs rooms for the social part of the day. With coats on, they patiently wait in the vestibule for their daily excursion across the valley to his *Mooslahnerkopf Teehaus.*[7]

Depressed, Hitler finally joins them wearing a hat and a black cape, holding his walking cane. They leave for their daily afternoon trek to the tea house less than a kilometer away.

***

In Berlin, General Hans Cramer arrives. He had been the last *Befehlshaber* of the Africa Corps before being captured in 1943. For medical reasons (acute asthma), the Allies, through skillful negotiations with the Red Cross, allowed him to be repatriated. Having been imprisoned in England, he was taken from the London Cage[8] near Kensington Palace to a formal dinner with General George Patton, commanding First US Army Group. He had then been given a thorough tour of the Operation *Neptune* assembly area. They had driven by various military staging areas in what seemed to be southeast Britain, although he could not tell for sure. Signposts, street signs, and names had all been removed or changed. The units are all supposedly ready to hit the Calais area.[9]

The next day, Cramer had been taken to the docks and allowed to board the Swedish ship *Gripsholm* for home. He had arrived in Berlin on May 23.

Now he reports to OKH Chief of Staff Kurt Zeitzler. Tomorrow he will go to Berchtesgaden, and eventually wind up in France on Geyr von Schweppenburg's staff. He is full of details of what he has seen—an enemy invasion force that, evidently, is getting ready to hit the Pas-de-Calais.

***

In the late evening, several German minelayers venture into the English Channel to lay segments of several new ad hoc minefields—*Blitzsperren*. Unfortunately for them, they are pounced upon by both the Royal Navy and the RAF, and take heavy losses before retreating to port.

The intercepts by Allied intelligence of the Kriegsmarine Enigma signals have proven to be invaluable again.

---

1   Kaufmann after the war claimed that the conversation was much more specific, and that they openly discussed the idea of forcing Hitler from power.

2   Over 800 bombers hit central and secondary rail marshaling yards all over France and Belgium. Nearly 60 bombers hit three coastal batteries, and over 120 fighter-bombers hit trains in France.

3   Delousing is a process in which individuals are treated with insecticides or insect repellents to get rid of lice on the head, body parts, and clothes. Typically during the war, an insecticide powder was used, usually sprayed onto the individuals. It was not a pleasant procedure.

4   Sources are conflicting or vague on whether or not Rommel knew this.

5   Erhard Milch, not a brilliant man, had made a number of strategic blunders, some of them political, some of them related to air production. After the dismal failure of the Luftwaffe in the Battle of Britain and its lackluster performance in the opening phases of *Barbarossa* in 1941, Milch, disillusioned with Göring, had gone to Hitler with Goebbels and Himmler and stated that Göring had to be replaced. Hitler turned them down, and the Reichsmarshal never forgot the betrayal. Even worse, Milch made a number of strategic air planning blunders that put the Luftwaffe in a critically weak condition by 1944. His heavy emphasis on design research came at a crippling sacrifice to production. This incident on the Me-262 became the final straw. Six days after this meeting, Petersen informed Milch that Göring had replaced him as head of air armaments. Hereafter, the Air Ministry would be run by Karl Saur. It was suggested to Milch that he take a vacation. He did, a broken man.

6   They included: Professor Carl Krauch, minister of the Reich's chemical industry; Paul Pleiger, Reich Commissioner for Coal and director of several key fuel plants; *SS Obersturmbannführer* Heinrich Bütefisch, director of the I.G. Farben synthetic fuel Leuna Works; E.R. Fischer, Chairman of the Board for I.G. Farben; and Kehrl, head of the Planning and Raw Materials Branch.

7 The *Mooslahnerkopf Teehaus* was less than a kilometer from the Berghof, and Hitler frequented it. It should not be confused with the *Kehlsteinhaus* ("Kehlstein House"), otherwise known as the Eagle's Nest. Built atop the nearby Kehlstein mountain in the Bavarian Alps, it was a birthday gift given to the Führer on his 50th birthday, April 20, 1939. Access was via a 124-meter high elevator. Hitler though, had a bit of acrophobia (a strange condition for one who loved living on a mountain!) and so he rarely went up there. The *Kehlsteinhaus* survived the war and today is a popular tourist attraction.

8 The London Cage was the headquarters of the War Crimes Investigation Unit and Combined Services Detailed Interrogation Center. It was located in a large mansion on the corner of Kensington Palace Gardens and Bayswater Road. Here, all captured prisoners of high rank were interrogated by special intelligence teams. Naturally, all cell conversations between prisoners were bugged.

9 It was, in fact, a grand ruse. It was quite a tour that the Allies put on for him. Cramer was led to believe that they were motoring through southeastern England, when in fact he had been driven through a good part of central and southwestern England. Guy Liddell, director of British counterintelligence 1931–1952, kept a detailed diary of British intelligence activities, and it paints a different picture of the repatriated general. According to Liddell's March 4 entry, General Cramer, soon to leave his POW camp, made a pleasant speech to the British commandant. Cramer with a smile confessed that, now that he was being sent back to Germany, he could admit that he himself was by blood one-quarter English. Cramer confessed that, "Every time he looked out of the window and saw his very smart guards, he was proud of his English blood. He then donated to the BAO in the name of all the officers of the Africa Korps as a token of their gratitude for the British gentlemanly (sic). He then gave the BAO his Africa Korps armband from his uniform with the remark that not even [General] Arnim was entitled to wear that."

Liddell also records that Cramer admitted that he "was not at all looking forward to his interview with Hitler. He would however have to give a full report on the last days in Tunis and on his stay at No. 11 Camp. About the latter he could say nothing but good. He would however, tell Hitler the truth about von Arnim, whose behavior in the camp was the worst possible propaganda for the German army, and Cramer apologized for it to the BAO."

Wednesday, May 24

This morning, the army group staff at La Roche-Guyon is busy with a number of details. Rommel though, travels to a nearby army ordnance center and watches several demonstrations. He later records his experiences in his Daily Report:

> Left to inspect a new "artificial fog" apparatus. The smoke, produced through the mixing of Nebelsäure[1] with burned chalk, is thick and suitable for the troops. Unfortunately our supplies of Nebelsäure are limited. On the other hand, I learned that back home several million smoke grenades are stocked up. It is irresponsible on the part of the authorities not to have issued these so far. However, this is another proof that one must always be on the lookout to find things out. If it hadn't been for this visit, I still wouldn't have known about the smoke grenades.
>
> Another pleasant experience was the display of a new submersible machine gun used in conjunction with an aiming mirror. I ordered its immediate production. At the Buck factory, I was shown another smoke-producing agent created by the mixing of ammonium and oil with burned chalk. Though not too thick, I ordered its immediate adoption by the troops. There I also saw beach-lighting installations which, built in with the wooden poles along beaches, will certainly have an irritating effect upon the enemy.

He orders a number of them put into service as soon as possible.

Admiral Ruge goes to Paris that afternoon, to visit various headquarters, trying to scare up some cement supplies. Enemy air activity is not too bad for road travel, although reports have shown that the rail centers, bridges, and airfields are getting hit heavily. Ruge's car has to make a wide detour around one downed bridge because of enemy fighters patrolling nearby.

General Speidel, having been granted leave over Pentecost, departs today for home around 9 a.m. Others of Rommel's staff spend part of the day talking to various officers at Luftwaffe command specifically, Sperrle's *3. Luftflotte*. They are trying to secure some flak batteries for coast defenses.

The outgoing mail includes a letter written yesterday by the field marshal, addressed to Alfred Jodl. In it, Rommel asks him to coerce Hitler into starting up the V-1 missile program as soon as possible. This would give the Allies one more reason to attack von Salmuth's sector, the more heavily defended area of the coast. And, if Rocket Command could somehow direct the missiles at the Allied embarkation points, that would help them a great deal.

That evening, after they have all returned to the château, they hear on the radio that Stuttgart has once more been bombed, and it sounds like the city had taken a pounding. Not surprising perhaps, since the Reich propaganda ministry has maintained the impression to the world that construction of aircraft and panzers, "is going on full blast." It would be better, if the Reich did not brag so much in the media about production. Perhaps air raids might diminish.

That night, for the first time, large formations of enemy bombers fly right over the château. The staff is forced to go downstairs into the air raid shelters.

***

Today at the Berghof, Göring has another conference with his senior staff about aircraft production.[2] They had taken a pounding yesterday from the Führer over the Me-262 issue, and now, clearly, Göring is on a mission: to reaffirm the Führer's orders (and of course, clear himself of blame).

His staff estimates that the Me-262's airframe will have to undergo a major modification to be able to carry a bomb. That might take another five months.

Hearing this, Göring explodes. "You gentlemen appear to be stone deaf, the lot of you! I have referred again and again to the Führer's order: he doesn't care two hoots about getting the Me-262 as a fighter but wants it only as a fighter-bomber."

He pauses and glares at them. "The Führer must have the strangest impression of you. From every side, including Messerschmitt, he was left in doubt about this, right from the start. And then, in my presence,[3] Messerschmitt told the Führer that his company had provided right from the start for it to be manufactured as a *Jagdbomber*. And now suddenly it is impossible!"

Oberst Edgar Petersen again repeats the structural problems that the change would entail, and how the engines would have to be redesigned.

Göring asks how soon the Me-262 can start production as a fighter-bomber. Petersen takes a deep breath and in a wild guess to save the situation, replies about three months.

Göring scowls at him. "I would have been grateful had you uttered ten percent of these remarks yesterday!" He pauses. "The Führer says, 'As far as I am concerned, you can cremate the fighters!' He needs an aircraft which can force its way through by virtue of its sheer speed, despite the enormous mass of fighters guarding the invasion forces."

He shakes his head in wonder. "What no civilian dares to do, simply ignoring superior orders, you gentlemen venture to do time after time after time! The most undisciplined bunch in Germany, our own Wehrmacht—and our officer corps!"

In the afternoon, *Generaloberst* Korten tells Göring that he thinks the invasion will not come for a while. He says, "The invasion appears to have been postponed. Otherwise, we wouldn't be having these big air raids on the Reich again," referring to the recent American bombings.

Again Göring shakes his head. They still do not get the point…

Today, the Allies, continuing their pre-invasion air strikes, launch a combined Western Allied effort to destroy all the bridges in northern Europe. Those flown in France are designed to further isolate the Normandy area. By D-Day, all 24 major bridges over the Seine between Paris and Rouen will go down, as well as a dozen other river bridges.

1   Smoke-acid. A combination of chlorine sulfonic acid and sulfur trioxide. The dense fog that resulted from the mixture could even be used in the winter, since the freezing point of this mixture was well below the coldest European winter temperatures.

2   Field Marshal von Richtofen is absent, having returned to Italy.

3   At a conference in Insterburg in November.

Thursday, May 25

Rommel stays at his château, tackling some paperwork. The weather today is beautiful, but no particular enemy activity is noted outside of the intense but getting-to-be-common Allied bombing raids. Air targets today are varied: the Longues-sur-Mer naval battery; the rail yards at Blainville, Charleroi and Belfort; a couple of airfields, including the Paris/Orly airport yesterday. Some coastal targets are hit, as well as a few V-1 rocket sites. But the enemy seems to be giving the Seine bridges a break today. That's good.

So where are the Allies? Where is the invasion?

Around noon, Rommel gets a visit from *Oberst* Walter Reinhard, the chief of staff for the 47th Panzer Corps. Reinhard is the advance party for the corps' headquarters unit. The 47th had once been a powerful panzer corps, and the command staff officers were all veterans of countless battles on the Eastern Front.[1] Now this cadre has left Russia, coming westward to France. Their new assignment is to coordinate Rommel's panzers and to reinforce his command of the army group. The corps is going to organize and take charge of the three panzer divisions of which OKW had finally released tactical command to Rommel—the 2nd, the newly formed 116th, and the "phoenix" 21st, still busily re-equipping itself just south of Caen.

No less experienced than the unit's chief of staff is its commanding officer, General von Funck.[2] He had fought well in Russia, commanding for two years Rommel's 7th Panzer Division. On December 7 of last year, von Funck had been promoted to acting commander of the 23rd Corps, and on March 5 of this year, he and his staff had been promoted to command the 47th Panzer Corps. Yes, von Funck is one of the oldest and most experienced panzer commanders in the German Army.

Rommel and Reinhard have a nice visit, and Rommel tells him that he looks forward to seeing his commanding officer tomorrow at a formal luncheon the army group is throwing.

A few hours later, Rommel is told a wild French rumor that he and his staff have packed up and left La Roche-Guyon. He chuckles at that. No, he is not quite ready to leave the lovely château just yet.

On a more serious (and upbeat) note, he is informed that the deadly coastal KMA minefields are to be started shortly. About damned time. Ruge had been pleading with Admiral Krancke for over two months now to accelerate production and distribution of the KMAs. Krancke had resisted, though. He was having sections of the Bay of Biscay mined, and that had to be finished first.

Krancke works well enough with Rommel under normal circumstances. Yet everyone knows that he and Friedrich Ruge do not get along, and because of this, Krancke will drag his feet when it comes to matters of working with or for the army. And as far as he is concerned, Ruge is no longer in the Kriegsmarine; he is just another one of Rommel's army flunkies.

Rommel makes a note to speak privately with Krancke on that matter. After all, they are all going to have to work together, especially if they are to get out of this mess with their heads still on their bodies.

That afternoon, Rommel tries to take his mind off things by going on an exhaustive but fruitless rabbit hunt. After he returns, he has a brief conference with von Rundstedt's propaganda chief.

***

At the Berghof, General Hans Cramer has made a report to the Führer. Cramer has been repatriated because of a serious lung problem (contrived, boasts Cramer). He tells Hitler about the vast weapons depots that the British and Americans have shown him.

Hitler is taken in by his report. Dr. Sonnleitner though, Foreign Minister von Ribbentrop's liaison officer, sees through the sham. The British doctors have allowed him to fool them on his medical condition, he explains to the Führer. There is no way a German general could have faked a serious lung condition, especially to a prison doctor. And why were the Allies so eager to show him all of those weapons centers in southeast England? Sonnleitner, having spent a few years himself as a political prisoner in Austria, knows that no matter how smart a prisoner is, the captors are always smarter. No, he concludes, Cramer has not hoodwinked the Allies. They have hoodwinked *him*. This has all been staged to lead Cramer into spreading strategically false conclusions to the German High Command.

But Hitler is not so sure. "Whatever," he replies to Sonnleitner. Still, true or not, no matter what, Rommel needs to hear this story. Cramer is to be sent to see *Generalfeldmarschall* Rommel and tell him what he has seen. "Especially," Hitler adds, "the special tanks, and where he had seen the most landing craft."

Cramer is to leave immediately.

---

1   The 47th Panzer Corps had recently suffered badly in the Soviet Union. Part of the Eighth Army, it was surrounded in Kirovograd by the sudden Russian offensive of January 5. The 47th, tired from recent battles and standing in the center of the Russian advance, bore the full onslaught of the enemy attack, and their command staff was overrun by medium tanks in the early morning hours of January 9.

2   See also entry for May 12.

Friday, May 26

At La Roche-Guyon, some reconnaissance photos arrive. Taken on the 24th, they include some good quality shots of the southwestern English ports of Bournemouth, Poole, Portland, and Weymouth, crowded with all sorts of invasion vessels and landing craft. Perhaps Calais will not be the target area, although Rommel still thinks that the Somme estuary will be the invasion area.

Now committed to staying at his headquarters as much as possible, Rommel today holds a special luncheon for General Wolfgang Pickert, the new commanding officer of the III Flak Korps.[1]

Pickert took command two days ago and established his headquarters just south of Amiens. The flak corps was formed in late February. It consists of about 12,000 men in 24 batteries and features four anti-aircraft (*FlakSturm*) regiments of 40 88mm dual-purpose guns each.[2] This is clearly a sizable unit to deploy against the hordes of enemy aircraft that will dominate the skies over an invasion site. Although Göring had back on May 7 refused to allow Rommel to relocate the units to Normandy, Pickert might be persuadable.

Rommel receives Pickert warmly, and they talk over lunch. A little later, they are joined by *General der Fallschirmjäger* Kurt Student, commanding all the airborne troops. Having dissolved the XI *Fliegerkorps*, he had in its place formed the *Fallschirmjägerkorps* and had last March established his new headquarters near Nancy. His parachute school at Dreux[3] was now busy with new recruits, eager to learn how to jump out of an airplane (even though there were few to jump out of). Also joining them is General von Funck. A nice social gathering; the men discuss various aspects of the air war and the situation in the West.

They discuss Göring's refusal to relocate the flak batteries to Normandy, and Pickert tells Rommel that he agrees with the decision. The flak regiments, widely scattered eastward, are protecting the bridges over the Seine, even though, dispersed as they were, they offer little effective power against any Allied air force flying over. Moreover, they also provide some defense against bombers trying to fly into Germany. In addition, a few batteries protect V-2 production centers, a high priority for the Führer.

Pickert tells Rommel he has other concerns. His men have been softened by *la belle vie* of France (something Rommel sympathizes with). Many of his officers are young, impetuous, usually with no experience in actual combat; certainly not like Pickert has seen on the Eastern Front. While he defends his batteries' locations operationally, he objects to the fact that most of them are semi-permanently fixed and kept immobile, stagnantly located around other established anti-aircraft sites. Pickert realizes that together, his batteries can potentially pose a much more formidable weapon than at present. They are entirely motorized, one of the few such anti-aircraft units in the Wehrmacht. Still, a good deal of training for combat operations and how to work with ground forces when the invasion comes will be needed.

After the guests leave, Rommel receives a scolding phone call from State Secretary Theodor Ganzenmueller, in the Ministry of Transportation. Rommel tries to tell him that he needs additional transport space for supplies, but is cut off by the state secretary, who proceeds to complain to Rommel about the meddling into the affairs of transportation by *Gauleiter* Kaufmann on Rommel's behalf. While Ganzenmueller keeps a civil tone (after all, you do not berate a field marshal and a national hero in the Third Reich—unless of course, you have a death wish), he does tells Rommel to kindly keep Kaufmann (and anyone else Rommel is contemplating) the hell out of transportation matters.

Yes, he admits dully, the Ministry is aware of the acute transportation problem in France right now because of the bombings, but trying to get things done using Kaufmann is *not* the proper way to do things. From now on, the field marshal is to go through proper channels.

Rommel hangs up disgruntled and grits his teeth. Politicians…

***

Admiral Ruge drives to Paris to the headquarters of Security Area West, and then off to Naval Group West. Luckily, he is already on the northern bank of the Seine and thus does not have to cross over. It is just as well. By now, all the bridges over the river have been hit by Allied air attacks, and all rail traffic across the river is blocked. The Germans of course are trying hard to repair the bridges, but their efforts are infuriatingly being stifled daily by the enemy. The Allies observe repair efforts on these bridges, and whenever a repair nears completion, the enemy bombs it again.[4]

Ruge finds out from a radar expert at Krancke's headquarters that the radar installations along the Channel have in the last couple weeks also been hit pretty hard by the enemy, but that of the eleven major radar installations that had been damaged by the bombs, all but one are back in service again.

***

This morning, several key officers of the 12th SS Panzer Division have been mysteriously summoned to their divisional headquarters at Tillières-sur-Avre.[5] Worried, they report to the main building and are amazed to find their wives sitting there. At the orders of the division commander, *Brigadeführer der Waffen-SS* Fritz Witt, the ladies have been brought from all over Germany to their headquarters for a last liberty with their husbands.

Witt senses that the invasion will come soon and when it does, many in the division will be killed. He magnanimously tells his officers, "Since there is going to be no leave for anybody from now on, you can all go to Paris for two days and then say goodbye at the *Gare de l'Est.*"[6]

The men understand only too well. One officer confides to his wife, "We are for it," and gives her his personal effects—just in case.

***

That afternoon, a number of senior generals are taken to the Berghof for an audience with the Führer. His speech focuses on reinforcing what Himmler had told them before lunch. He starts out comparing the Jews to simple bacteria invading the Reich host, and talks of the problems Germany had been plagued with because of these bacterial Jews. Removing them from their positions of power in the Reich, he points out, has allowed the offspring of thousands of middle-class Germans to move up, while simultaneously cleansing the German revolutionary movement of their taint.

Addressing a common theme, he rhetorically asks if perhaps the manner of their removal could be done more humanely. He shakes his head dramatically. "My dear generals, we are fighting a battle of life and death. If our enemies are victorious in the struggle, the German people will be extirpated.[7] The Bolsheviks will butcher millions upon millions of our intellectuals. Those who escape the bullet in the nape of the neck will be deported..."

He goes on for a while, interweaving the "bestial" reasons for the war's necessity, graphical descriptions of the air war's effect upon the country, and the removal of the accursed Jews. He occasionally pauses for applause or verbal approvals.

The subject of the impending invasion in the West is not even addressed.

---

1   Forty-seven-year-old *Luftwaffe General der Flakartillerie* Wolfgang Pickert had once commanded the 9th Flak division in the East, attached to von Paulus' ill-fated Sixth Army to dealt with Russian bombers. He had been at Stalingrad with his unit when it had nearly been annihilated at the end of 1942. Pickert had been one of the lucky ones flown out of the surrounded Sixth Army that winter.

2   These batteries, created around the cadre of what used to be the 11th Motorized Flak division, were now grouped into four antiaircraft regiments. The 1st *Stürm* Flak Regiment had been created out of the 431 Flak Regiment (of the 16th Flak Division) and the headquarters of the 32nd Flak Regiment. Likewise, the 2nd was created from the 653rd, the 3rd from the 37th, and the 4th out of the old 79th. The batteries had been given special training in both anti-air coverage and mobile ground warfare (hence, the designator "*Stürm*" had been added to give the units a ground assault rating). The 103rd *Luftnachtrichten* (Signals) Battalion rounded out the corps.

3   A small town some 65km west of Paris.

4   Bridges along the Loire River were for the most part left alone, so that the enemy did not discern the general location of the invasion area.

5   About 110km west of Paris.

6   Paris' East train station terminal, one of the oldest railway stations in the capital, a historic favorite.

7   The word he used was *ausgerottet*, which means to be totally destroyed or more graphically, to be yanked out by the roots.

Saturday, May 27

Whitsun Saturday[1] is a lovely day at La Roche-Guyon. The temperature is up, although there is a breeze coming off the river to bring relief from the warm morning. After Ruge fills him in on his meetings yesterday, Rommel leaves to see the smoke generator plant that he visited on the 24th. Progress has been made. He orders the manager to accelerate their program for production.

He returns to the château for lunch. These days, he dares not go anywhere very far. The invasion could come any day now. All this enemy air activity in the last few weeks must have some significance. Something will probably be happening soon. He can almost feel it. Besides, his troops know enough by now about how to construct their barriers, and work is steadily going on all along the coast. Every day makes them more prepared, better able to meet the enemy. So where are they?

That afternoon, he and some staff members go on yet another "armed promenade" to work off lunch and to relieve some of the strain of waiting. The few rabbits they come across are too small to shoot. However, since previous hunts have usually proven fruitless, they try something different. They bring along a few ferrets to go down the rabbit holes and chase their prey out. Unfortunately, this tactic backfires on them, because the ferrets decide that the nice rabbit tunnels are cool places to rest. The frustrated hunters end up having to dig their ferrets out.

When they eventually return to the villa, they find out that official word has come down from *Luftflotte III* headquarters in Paris. General Pickert, after having dined with Rommel (yesterday's sumptuous feast thrown for him must have helped after all), has relented some. He is going to allow one of his four regiments, the *1. Flak Regiment*,[2] to relocate to Normandy. Their role however, will be strictly as an air defense weapon, and they will not be used at all in ground operations.

Two more of the flak regiments will stay with the Fifteenth Army, with one regiment on each side of the Somme estuary between Montreuil-sur-Mer and just north of Abbéville. The fourth regiment will be held in Army Reserve. It will stay on the right bank of the Seine, upstream from Tréport, to continue covering the river bridges, now repeatedly getting hit hard by enemy air attacks.

Rommel, expecting to get more batteries into Normandy from the other three regiments, is upset.

***

General Hans Speidel is at home in Freudenstadt, Germany. He is entertaining two prominent guests: pre-war Minister of Foreign Affairs, Baron Konstantin von Neurath, and the *Oberburgermeister* of Stuttgart, Karl Strölin. They are part of another contingent of the *Schwartz Kapelle*.[3]

In Speidel's study, they exchange their ideas on removing the Führer from office, and how the Western commands could coordinate their operations with them, once the plotters had made their move. Some contacts have been made with the Western Allies, and these will be used when needed. Speidel briefs them on his dealings with the field marshal and how far he has progressed. Von Neurath reviews the reasons why Hitler is the crux of the problem, having followed his present policy. He states what they all know well: none of the Allies will deal with him, and so he has to go, for the good of the country.

Von Neurath needs to know how willing Rommel would be to help lead the government if the conspiracy succeeds. The plotters agree that they would like to make their move before the Allied invasion takes place. Speidel knows from reports coming into his office that time is getting short. Strölin and von Neurath tell him to plead with Rommel to be ready to take over when the coup is initiated, either as head of the military, or as the leader of the country.

It will be a hard sell.

***

Brigadeführer Fritz Witt, commanding the *12. SS Panzer Division Hitlerjugend*, enjoys his 36th birthday with his senior officers and their wives at Tillières-sur-Avre. The champagne flows freely at the celebration as the SS officers relax and have a good time. Witt does not know that this will be his last birthday.[4]

***

In the large picture room of the Berghof, the Führer is today entertaining the Japanese ambassador, Baron Hiroshi Ōshima. He has been lecturing him on general strategy. Also present are Walther Warlimont, General Jodl (who seems bored), chief of staff Wilhelm Keitel, his eyes gleaming at the Führer's words, and Luftwaffe adjutant Nicolas von Below. Except for Keitel, the senior army officers are uncomfortable about the Führer telling a foreigner about strategy points that perhaps should not be mentioned. After all, telling senior Nazi politicians what they might do is one thing; or even late at night, when the Führer, reclined in an easy chair, reflects some thoughts about military plans to the attending ladies. They are, after all, simple souls. And besides, who could they relay the information to? However, telling foreigners is something else entirely, even if they are supposed to be their allies.

Now the Führer turns to Germany's military situation. He starts with the Italian front. "It is," he says with authority, "on the Italian front that the fighting is now most acute." Looking at the Japanese ambassador, he continues. "England and America have thrown against us an infinitude of weapons and materials. In my opinion, the main object of this new drive is to lure German military strength to that theater, and we are therefore not making too great an effort to prevent the loss of territory. Instead we are gradually retiring, and in doing so, we are inflicting huge losses on the enemy."

"And, by the way," Hitler declares, turning towards Keitel and von Below. "I am not sending any more planes to help defend Italy." He looks at Jodl. "And we have also decided to establish a new defensive line running from the Alban Hills on the west coast to a point south of the Grand Sasso Mountains, and finally to a point north of Pescara on the east coast…" Hitler has decided to call this new line "Position C." Of course, moving back to this fortified position means having to give up any serious idea of defending Rome.

The subject turns to the Eastern Front. Hitler says, "We Germans have known all along that the Axis should have defended along the Don. But Hungary and Romania never could grasp that fact. Now however, the flames are close to their own borders, and the Hungarian and Romanian forces are more aware of the peril. So far, they have stood up rather well." He does not mention that this is especially true since Germany marched into Hungary in mid-March, occupied the capital, and "re-educated" the Hungarians.

The Japanese ambassador speaks up. "Do you know from which direction the Russians will strike?"

Hitler turns to him and thinks about the question. "I think," he replies, "that the Russian assault will be two-pronged. In my opinion, they'll head northwest from the Lvov area and penetrate into central Poland." After a moment, he adds, "And they will also invade Romania. I think though, that the drive from Lvov will come first, and an attempted invasion of Romania will come afterwards.[5]"

Ōshima changes the subject and asks Hitler about the upcoming Western Europe invasion. The Führer starts to pace. "I believe," he begins, "that, sooner or later, an invasion of Europe will be attempted. I understand from recent reports that the enemy has already assembled about 80 divisions in the British Isles.[6] Of that force, only eight divisions are composed of first-class fighting men with experience in actual warfare."

Ōshima asks "Does your Excellency believe that these Anglo-American forces are fully prepared to invade?"

"Yes" Hitler continued, "I believe that they are fully ready to invade us."

The Japanese ambassador considers this and then asks him, "Then sir, I wonder, what ideas you may have on how the invasion will be carried out?"

The Führer stops pacing and pauses. "Well, as for me, judging from relatively clear portents, I think that diversionary actions will take place in a number of places—against Norway, Denmark, the southern part of western France, and the French Mediterranean coast. After that, when they have established bridgeheads in the Normandy and Brittany peninsulas, and have sized up their prospects, they will then come forward with an all-out second front across the Straits of Dover."

Hitler pauses. "We ourselves would like nothing better than to strike one great blow as soon as possible." He looks down and begins pacing again before he goes on. "But that will not be feasible, if the enemy does what I anticipate... No, their men will be dispersed. If that's the case, we intend to finish off the enemy's troops at the several bridgeheads. The number of German troops in the West still amounts to about 60 divisions."[7]

Ōshima, sitting calmly at the large round table, replies, "Remember, sir, our last meeting? You told us that if it turned out that there was no invasion, you thought that you might blast southern England with rocket guns, and then maybe find an opportunity to take the initiative again on the Eastern Front. Well, since then," continues the ambassador, "the Anglo-Americans have been bombing the Channel area more heavily than ever... I wonder, sir, if those weapons you were going to use against England have not been destroyed?"

The senior Wehrmacht officers hold their breaths. What Ōshima is suggesting may be construed as indirectly accusing the Führer of either holding out on their Japanese ally or not holding up their end of the war. To anyone else in Europe, that would be a capital offense.

"No," replies the Führer irritably. "Those guns are in an arsenal made of impenetrable concrete. They are in no danger."

The other men in the room relax. That could have been explosive.

"If the Anglo-Americans do not stage an invasion," Ōshima continues, unaware of his close call, "would it not be a little dangerous to return your troops to the Eastern Front?"

Hitler scowls at Ōshima. "Well," he replies after a moment, "I have no intention of waiting forever for them to come. I will give them two or three more months. If they don't come then, Germany will take the offensive."

He pauses. "By that time, we will have finished organizing and equipping additional forces. We will have between 60 to 70 fresh divisions, including over 40 panzer and *panzergrenadier* divisions.[8] Then, we will be in a position to attack. I have already exceeded my goal for SS divisions; twenty-five of them are now practically organized and equipped."

Warlimont feels a tug at his sleeve. Looking over, he sees one of the Führer's aides. There is a telephone call for him in the antechamber. Warlimont excuses himself from the room as the Führer and the ambassador begin talking about aircraft production. A thought suddenly occurs to him. What if the Japanese somehow tell the enemy of German intentions? He shakes his head. The Japanese would have nothing to gain from that. No, they would not knowingly tell the enemy.

He is right. They will not—knowingly. But he cannot know that Ōshima will radio a full transcript of this conversation to Tokyo in a few days. Very soon after that, less than a week before the invasion, the Ultra intercept will be in the hands of the top Allied commanders in Europe.

1 The day before Pentecost.

2 The *1. Regiment* consisting of two anti-aircraft battalions, would later be nearly destroyed in the Falaise Gap.

3 Some sources (especially Hans Speidel himself) state that he was at the meeting on behalf of and personally representing Rommel. Others maintain that Speidel was just trying to uphold the reputation and historic image of the field marshal, and that he had not as yet actually approached him on the plot—at least not fully. Even if Speidel had sounded out the field marshal on the idea, chances are that Rommel's part in the conspiracy at this time was probably minimal.

4 On June 14, a naval barrage targeted his divisional headquarters at Venoix (then a western suburb of Caen). Shrapnel from a shell explosion hit him in the face, killing him. He was buried there at Venoix, but later his remains were moved to the German military cemetery at Champigny-St. André-de-l'Eure.

5 Hitler had guessed wrong. The Soviet Union's offensive on June 23 would come not from Lvov southeast of Warsaw, but instead from the Belorussian Front at the center of the line; and the Soviets would not strike westward towards Poland, but northwest, towards Lithuania and Estonia.

6 *Heeresgruppe B* had estimated some 85 divisions, about eight of which were airborne. *Fremde Heeres West* overestimated as well, concluding that there were about 79. Actually, at the end of May, there were the equivalent of only 52 Allied divisions in England: 20 British, 21 American, 5 Canadian, 1 Polish, 1 Free French, and a number of brigades and special battalions.

Interestingly, since the SS now had overall control of German Intelligence (see entries for February 9 and February 11), all Army intelligence reports were funneled to headquarter units from SS headquarters. There, Security Branch commander *Generalleutnant der Polizei* Ernst Kaltenbrunner would regularly modify Roenne's estimates of enemy strength in Britain downward for the Führer. As a result, Roenne began to inflate his numbers to offset this practice. At some point in time, Kaltenbrunner suddenly stopped amending Roenne's numbers, which resulted in the overinflated estimates.

7 This does not include another six divisions in Denmark and about 12 operational divisions across the North Sea in Norway.

8 The boast, of course, was a wild exaggeration. At that time, Germany could not hope to create that number of new divisions without taking some from the hard-pressed Eastern Front.

Sunday, May 28

Today is Whitsunday.[1] It is another beautiful day at La Roche-Guyon. Rommel and his staff are perplexed. Where the hell are the Allies?

To pass the time away, there are a number of tennis matches today. For those wishing to stay indoors, several ping-pong battles are fought.

Enemy air activity seems low today. However, the Allies are not as idle as the army group staff thinks. The Romanian oilfields at Ploesti are hit by a few hundred enemy bombers.[2] The Allies had struck Germany's oil production facilities hard on May 12. This is the second phase, and its effect will cripple German oil (and thus, manufacturing) production.

In Western Europe, railroad marshaling yards in northern France, Belgium, and central France are hit again, while rail lines are attacked by tactical fighter-bombers. The V-1 sites are hit again, as are a few coastal positions. And of course, rail bridges along the Seine and Somme rivers are hit once more. By D-Day, all the Seine bridges will be down.

That afternoon, Rommel decides to takes time to ride with his aide to the beautiful Choisy Forest. On the way, Rommel talks about Herman Göring and his lack of character. Rommel speaks ill of the Luftwaffe, too, and discusses how things have become as bad as they now are.

Rommel sums it up for Lang, telling him, "While the others were building up their air power, we were fast asleep. Now we're paying the penalty. My impression is that the people around the Führer often didn't tell him their real opinions about the situation."

They enjoy a stop or two, admiring the scenery before they drive over to the expansive villa of the Marquis de Choisy. The count is related to the Duc du Rochefoucauld, whose château Rommel is currently using. Back in 1940, after his wild ride across France, Rommel had met the count and had found him to be a perfectly charming man. The family was sympathetic to the Germans, and the count's son had even gone as far as to join the army and had fought a few years on the Eastern Front. The count's young daughter has often visited her relatives at La Roche-Guyon; the countess herself is a spry and energetic woman.

Today, the frail old man greets him warmly, and Rommel visits with the couple. The countess' bitterness towards the British comes out in her remarks. Rommel in turn tells the count about how the Germans and French—all of Europe, for that matter—must stand up together if their crusade against Bolshevism is to be won.

They have a nice get-together and discuss the war and the future.[3]

Around sunset, Rommel and his aide return to their château. That evening, they once again mingle with French royalty. The two of them join the Duc du Rochefoucauld in the family's upstairs quarters. They pass on the felicitations of the count's family, and stay up with the duke, enjoying a laid-back, informal talk with this languid old man. Rommel feels at ease talking to him.

When Lang and Rommel finally arise to leave, the Duke, overcome with emotion, urges his family to stand for a toast. Raising his glass, he declares, "To Germany's victory." Rommel thanks him and retires.

---

1   A feast of the Catholic Church commemorating the descent of the Holy Ghost upon the Apostles, forty days after the Resurrection of Christ. A popular holiday in France and Belgium, it is also known by many as "Pentecost." The day is called "Whitsunday" (White Sunday) because of the white garments which were worn by those who are baptized at this time. Whitsunday first became a Christian feast in the 1st century, though there is little evidence to show that it was observed, like Easter.

2   Over four hundred bombers of the American Eighth Air Force.

3   After the war, the restored French government understandably charged the Marquis with collaboration with the enemy in wartime. He was found guilty and condemned to death. By order of Charles De Gaulle himself, he was hanged.

Monday, May 29

With the invasion looming near, Allied Intelligence is trying to keep an updated appraisal of the German ground forces, especially in and around Normandy. Through key radio intercepts, the Allies have now confirmed that the 6th Parachute Regiment and the 91st Air Landing Division have been relocated to the Cotentin peninsula.[1] This has raised considerable concern about the American airborne landings planned for that area. German paratroops and glider infantry on the edges of the assigned drop zones will seriously jeopardize achieving initial objectives and add greatly to the airborne fatality list.

In the Colleville area, the Resistance agent there has finally determined that major elements of the veteran 352nd Infantry Division have been relocated north to the Calvados coast, beefing up the left flank of the bodenständige 716th Division. Two regiments of the 352nd now occupy positions across the western half of the beach, across what is scheduled to be (unknown of course, to the agent) a major Allied landing area, designated "Omaha beach."

Based on that agent's report, the local Resistance leader near Grandcamp sends his routine report using his normal communications route. In this case, that happens to be with carrier pigeons. The French have been using them as message couriers to England since 1940, but only in areas where radio reception is poor or where wireless use would be too risky. One pigeon was also carried by agents parachuting into enemy territory and released upon a safe landing, to let headquarters know that the agent had made it down safely.

The French have found pigeons to be an ideal method of communication, because they cannot be weakened, jammed or detected, like radio signals. They are silent in their travel, and if spotted, are relatively hard to hit. On the other hand, they are on the whole quite unreliable for getting to their destination, and can only carry small messages or diagrams. Moreover, setting up and maintaining such a system is also often difficult, especially since each bird can only be used a couple times. So their successful return rate since 1940 has only been about one flight in nine.

There are several reasons for the low reliability rate. For one thing, the birds are parachuted into France and sometimes die in the drop, are intercepted by the Germans, or are turned over by the local citizenry. It is, after all, a serious offense to be caught with them. And especially in the last year, the Germans have become quite aware of spy carrier pigeon mail systems and their value. These birds are now considered dangerous contraband material.[2] Of those that have been successfully released, several were given only mediocre training, and of course, sometimes bad weather played a decisive role. So as a precaution to increase their reliability, the Resistance has started to send two birds at a time.

Over time, these feathered couriers have naturally become fair game for sport by troops stationed on the coast. A good pastime for the Feldgrau along the beaches has become practice target shooting at birds when they spot them, especially pigeons. The amateur hunters usually conduct their sport with shotguns, although any small caliber firearm is considered acceptable. On the whole, the participants are lousy shots, especially at such a small target often unexpectedly flying out towards the Channel at over 80 km/hour.

Usually the shootings result in a clean miss on both of them. Occasionally, the hunters might wing one bird, but that is rare. As a result, the message (if there is one; sometimes there is nothing to report) usually has a good chance of at least getting over the English Channel.

Even if the hunters on the beaches are lucky enough to hit one bird, very rarely do these potshots ever get both of them. On this particular day though, the 716th's shooters are quite lucky. They get both birds. In fact, one of the dead pigeons will land close by and fall into German hands.

The report of the veteran 352nd being moved up to the coast never makes it to Allied headquarters.[3]

Generalfeldmarschall von Rundstedt's summary report for the day notes intensive bombings on the Seine River bridges.

> OB West appraises the situation as follows:
> Systematic bombing, especially of all traffic installations within the zone of OB West, by the enemy Air Force… demonstrates the enemy's intention of destroying and disrupting the traffic network, and thereby, troop movements and supply services [from the coast] to the far rear areas. Successful attacks carried out recently on the Seine bridges have considerably interfered with the cross-river traffic, and thereby cut off the Channel front north of the Seine from direct contact with the Seine estuary and Normandy.
> This may indicate enemy designs on Normandy.

Despite his report though, von Rundstedt still maintains that the main assault will come at the Pas-de-Calais. In any case:

> It is true that the hour of invasion draws nearer, but the scale of the enemy air attacks does not indicate that it is immediately imminent.

He rereads that last part again. Has he overplayed that point? Enemy air activity has stepped up and is playing havoc with their transportation system. He has already read Rommel's report that the coastal construction is coming along, although the attacks on the transportation systems are "having a bad effect on the situation." Maybe he should revise that last part.

He thinks about it and decides not to. The conclusion might have a calming effect on Hitler.

Of course, if his report turns out to be wrong…

***

Today Rommel stays at his headquarters and fills out several reports. In the evening, General Walter Buhle and his associate General Jakob[4] arrive at the château. Tomorrow they will go together to watch a number of demonstrations, including Major Becker's new "toys."

The two generals stay for dinner and since they will attend Rommel's conference tomorrow, agree to stay the night. At dinner, they discuss tomorrow's agenda. After an evening walk, they turn in.

Late on in his quarters, Rommel hears the explosions of yet more bombs as enemy air raids strike again. He writes to Lucie:

> *The Anglo-Americans have in no way let up from their incessant bombardment. The French in particular suffer from it terribly—in 48 hours, there have been three thousand dead among the people. Our own losses are in general only moderate. Many dummy installations have been ripped apart.*

He considers that what he has written might sadden her, so he switches to a lighter subject, the dogs:

> *I am so glad that the little one pleases you so much.[5] Treff is very quiet and obedient on a hunt.*

He pauses. That was true. The dog did well on their "armed promenades." He continues:

> *I am very satisfied with the big brown hunting dog. Most of the time, he lies next to me at the desk. When I get up he hopes to come along. On the hunt he heels and immediately reacts to a whistle. The other day he attacked a German shepherd so that it was difficult to separate the two mutts.*

He is tired. Time to end the letter.

> *That's all for today.*

---

1   See entry for May 16.

2   To counter this threat, the Germans sometimes made extensive searches of houses along the coast, and occasionally dropped their own containers of "spy pigeons."

3   One source claims that no pigeon ever carried information about the redeployment of the 352nd, but that seems unlikely. Steward Bryant though, analyzing material written by the 352nd Division's chief of staff as an American POW after the war, confirms the fact that the Resistance did use carrier pigeons, provided by British SOE (Special Operations Executive). In this case, they were being sent by a French resistance cell operating out of Cricqueville, a couple kilometers inland behind Pointe du Hoc.

4   Buhle replaced Himmler in January 1944 as the army Chief of Armaments at the suggestion of Armaments Technical Department Director Karl Saur. General Jakob was in charge of Engineering and Fortifications for the German Army.

5   Rommel had evidently sent Elbo to Lucie, as he indicated on May 8 and May 12.

Tuesday, May 30

It is morning. Rommel leaves La Roche-Guyon in a motorcade for a conference and weapons display on the coast. With him and his staff[1] are General Buhle and General Jakob. Despite recent Allied air attacks on the northern European rivers, the bridges at Mantes are still thankfully intact, though several bombs have landed several times around the island sitting between them. However, when the convoy arrives in the town, they are told that there are already a number of enemy air formations flying high above. The cars are quickly driven over the bridges and continue on to Riva Bella, just west of Ouistreham, where the conference and demonstrations are to take place.

Already assembled there are Admiral Krancke, Rommel's corps commanders (including 47th Panzer Corps commander von Funck), the two army commanders, von Salmuth and Dollmann, and their two chiefs of staff, Heinz Meyer-Bürdorf and Max Pemsel. There are also a number of senior officers from the nearby 21st Panzer Division, since they are conducting the special weapons demonstrations. After arriving, Rommel has a chance to greet Major Hans von Luck, an old comrade from North Africa. Photographers in attendance take a number of pictures of the attending officers.

Featured in the demonstrations will be some innovative multiple rocket launchers that have been fashioned by the 21st's manufacturing wizard, Major Alfred Becker. He has been busy coordinating component shipments from his factory, Alkett in Berlin, to his multi-talented workshops in Paris, which have jokingly become known as his "Special Headquarters," *Besondererkommando* Becker.

The demonstrations, especially the effect of those whooshing missiles, are hugely successful and impress everyone there. Becker also demonstrates some of his ad hoc hybrid armored assault guns. He has added armor plating shipped from the Alkett factory onto the old French Lorraine armored carrier chassis, and using his industrial connections, obtained for them the latest radios. In doing so, he has so far created some two dozen Marder SP tank destroyers by mounting onto them 75mm PAK40 tank guns. Similarly, he has created some deadly self-propelled artillery by mounting FH18 105mm howitzers onto some four dozen old French Hotchkiss H-35 tank frames. Other French light tank chassis were given reinforced armor, and an anti-tank gun.

All of these homemade armor assemblies, put together by his Paris detachment, are deployed, mostly to the 21st Panzer. Some officers in the *panzergrenadier* regiments had at first laughed hysterically at the odd-looking, horrific, homemade contraptions. However, after having trained to work with them, and seeing their potential, the *panzergrenadiers* have been forced to admit that these mobile tank destroyers are good substitutions for the *Jagdpanzers* they were supposed to get.

There are also a number of smoke generators shown. Hopefully, they will effectively screen the beaches from the landing craft; that is, if there are enough of them, and they are in the right place at the right time. General Buhle promises to send all there are from Germany

After the presentation, General Marcks gets a chance to talk to General von Salmuth. He tells him of the problems that he is having along his Calvados coastline. The 352nd and the 716th Divisions have an 80km stretch of beach to defend. "It's the weakest sector of my whole corps," Marcks admits worriedly.

He continues voicing his concerns about a landing in this area. He had told Geyr von Schweppenburg the same thing a few weeks before when the panzer general had visited his corps headquarters. Marcks had told Geyr that he was not worried about a landing on the western side of the Cotentin peninsula, but that he was concerned about the beach area east of Carentan. Now he is telling von Salmuth the same thing. But his concern does not seem to be registering too heavily upon the senior generals. Then there is the short supply of concrete…

The conference begins and the senior army commanders give their situation reports. Then they all break for lunch, provided by a small but adequate field mess. The officers sit at tables under a lovely thick canopy of trees. Just as well, perhaps. Enemy air activity is bustling, as usual these days. Rommel remarks that he is surprised the Mantes bridge over which they traveled to cross the Seine this morning is still functional.

After lunch, Rommel closes the conference by addressing all of his commanders. He pleads with them to stay alert, and to be ready at all times. "You shouldn't count on the enemy coming in fine weather," he tells them, "and by day."

Sadly for him, he will end up ignoring his own advice.

Rommel, Buhle and Jakob then ride off to tour the defensive barriers along the coast. Rommel takes the opportunity to show the OKH generals the progress the men have made, and the new types of obstacles they have erected. He does not know it, but this will be his last tour of the invasion area before D-Day.

Eventually, the officers start back towards La Roche-Guyon. They make a few stops at some deployment areas of the 21st Panzer Division. Again Rommel gives the "stay alert" speech. His friend von Luck is present here again, as he was at the conference. Rommel expresses his anxiety over the fact that the enemy has not yet come. Will they ever? This long period of no activity is beginning to have an effect on his men, even the new recruits, fresh from Germany. And the nice weather, the peaceful French countryside, and the good wine are not helping matters.

In the late afternoon, members of Rommel's staff, returning ahead of him, experience a harrowing crossing at Gaillon, about 20km downriver from the town of Vernon. All seems well as they arrive in the town and see that the bridge is intact. However, when they get close, they find themselves in the start of an air raid. As they approach to cross, the first bombs start falling around the bridge spans. They stop and wait for the initial wave to finish. Then the vehicles, with the staff members craning their anxious heads up to spot approaching enemy bombers, make a mad dash across the river. Less than an hour later, the bridge is down.

When Rommel later approaches that bridge, the damage has been done. With the Vernon and Louviers bridges out as well, Corporal Daniel has to drive them further upstream to Mantes. When they arrive though, Rommel sees that the bridges there are also gone.[2] Probably all of the bridges along the Seine between Rouen and Paris are now destroyed or in the river. Daniel is forced to backtrack downstream along the southern bank to just opposite the château, where they have to cross the Seine in a boat.

In a similar fashion, various ferry services are operating. But many supplies will now have to travel long out-of-the-way routes to get to units along the western coast.

---

1 Including Admiral Ruge, General Meise, General Diem, and Colonel Lattman.
2 The last one standing, the highway bridge, was successfully taken out by bombs dropped by 36 B-26s of the 386th Bomb Group.

Wednesday, May 31

This morning, *Generalfeldmarschall* Rommel takes a quick trip upriver to check out those destroyed bridges at Mantes that he saw yesterday. While several enemy formations fly overhead, he then backtracks downriver past his château to see the ones first at Vernon, then further on at Gaillon. Obviously the Allies wanted the bridges down to isolate the northeast coast from northwest France. But which side is the target area? Or will it be somewhere in Brittany? And this isolation effect—is it for an actual upcoming operation, or is just a prelude for something that will go down in a few months? What is the overall strategic general plan? Is this perhaps some kind of a feint for another operation somewhere else, like a strike at Norway? Intelligence had picked up some clues about something like that...

After returning to the château, Rommel checks the tide tables and decides that they will be unfavorable for invasion in early June; no high tide at or near dawn. The nearest such period would be June 20. And that would also coincide with the end of the Russian spring thaw, which is when their dreaded summer offensive is expected to begin. But the date ranges would be different if the Allies decide on a mid-tide or a low-tide landing.

He thinks about this. A landing at high tide seems the most rational. They would still be somewhat vulnerable to his high-tide barriers, but they would avoid many of the medium-tide obstacles and the few low-tide ones his men had managed to set. Most of his beach defenses constructed to date have been based upon that assumption. He feels that the Allies will not land at low tide, because the assaulting troops would struggle ashore along a much greater distance. Exposed in the open kill zones, they would make easy targets, and it would be far more likely for his defenders to inflict heavy casualties. Follow-up waves would be vulnerable as well, similarly struggling across open ground.

Then there is the weather. Weather predictions for early June are not favorable for an invasion either, despite a full moon scheduled for less than a week into the month. If a storm hits, he might be able to make a last quick trip to Germany. He had been planning on going home for a few days in June for weeks now, and it seemed as though conditions might accommodate him.

He has three reasons for the trip. First, he wants to arrange a private audience with the Führer. He does not have an appointment, but he can easily get one. Field marshals after all, have full access to the Führer. Among other things, Rommel is going to try to convince him to let him take control of Sepp Dietrich's I SS Panzer Corps. Still a part of OKW reserves, it is garrisoned far inland, and cannot move without orders from the Führer. Rommel wants to place the divisions at various locations much nearer to the coast. And if they are his to command, they can be released much faster, and thus more quickly react to an invasion. One of the divisions, the 12th SS, he would put at the base of the Cotentin peninsula.

And while his shopping list is out, he will also renew his request that the Führer order the other three regiments of Pickert's *III Flak Korps*, as well as a *Nebelwerfer* brigade, be moved west of the Seine into the Normandy area. If the enemy lands there, these few units will be critical. If the enemy lands near the Somme estuary, he can reinforce the area from all sides. And of course if the enemy lands at the well-defended Calais area like the High Command expects, they will not stand much of a chance.

On a private note, he wants to try to reason with his old mentor; to let him see how badly the war was getting. Normally, Keitel would sense this and try to block or delay his immediate access. But this time he is going around the back door, through his friend, General Schmundt, the Führer's army adjutant.

His second reason for going on leave is personal and quite simple. Lucie is having her 50th birthday (he himself is 52). She'll be one year older on Tuesday, June 6. His present to her will be that new pair of fancy shoes from Paris that he had promised her back on May 3, when he had asked for her shoe size.

His last reason for leaving is to just rest and mentally recuperate; to relax before having to deal with the intense commitment to the upcoming epic Allied invasion.

Today, there are two prominent visitors at the château. General Guderian's elder son, Major Heinz Günther Guderian, comes for lunch. Close to his father and following in his footsteps, he has risen through the officer ranks of the German Army, including becoming part of the General Staff. Indoctrinated into the *Panzerwaffen*, often near or with his father, he has witnessed and taken part in the blitz campaigns that had made Heinz senior a legend in the German Army. The major, now nearly thirty, is now the Operations officer of the newly created 116th Panzer Division.[1]

In the afternoon, Sepp Dietrich stops in to discuss the status of the panzer divisions. Dietrich is happy that the 1st SS joined him last month. He now has three divisions under his command: The 1st SS, 12th SS, and 17th SS *Panzergrenadier*. Dietrich reports in about how the panzer units are building up in strength, detailing the accomplishments they have made so far. To help him, Rommel instructs his staff to transfer another hundred men from the 100th Panzer Reserve.

Rommel confers with Dietrich about deployment, stressing that he wants to not only get firmer operational control of the panzers, but also to move them. He tells Dietrich that he will try to persuade the Führer to let him move 12th SS from the Evreux area to the base of the Carentan peninsula. Dietrich admits that he does not mind, although he laments that his corps command would then be really spread out—from Belgium to Carentan to the Loire River Basin. Rommel sympathizes, but insists that it is necessary. There is no armor backup for the western part of Normandy.

Later that day, Rommel and Intelligence Chief Staubwasser have a short meeting on a number of intelligence reports that have come in from *Fremde Heeres West*. They agree that their estimates of Allied strength are far too high. Because of this and other factors, Rommel feels that there will be only one major landing, and not a diversion followed by the main one, as OB West and OKW have believed up until now.

They discuss the probability of a preliminary airborne assault. Jodl and OKW are convinced that the Allies will preface their landing with a large one. High Command feels they can only effectively land in the late afternoon or around sundown. The amphibious landing would then come right afterwards, at night. It makes sense. If they land at night, the German gunners will have difficulty picking out their targets, thus reinforcing the low-tide landing theory.

On the other hand, having thought about it, Rommel comments that he feels OKW has underestimated the effectiveness of his new beach obstacles—his "devil's garden." When they had started on them back in December, the Atlantic Wall construction had not been too far along. But his people have made considerable strides in the last few months. He reasons that for the many Allied landing craft to first get around the many new and different types of barriers, high tide or low tide, they would have to see what they were doing. Clearing the way would be a considerable undertaking. The critical point though, is that the enemy will have to get a large number of men and supplies ashore very quickly before the Germans can react effectively. Naturally, the best time do that is during the day. Hence, a daylight landing.

"No matter what Berlin says," he comments thoughtfully, "the engineering part of the amphibious landing would probably start at or just before low tide, and in daylight, to clear the beaches for the landing craft." He pauses and thinks about that. "That means though, that the airborne assault would have to come the night before. And since they would need some light to see where they are dropping, there would have to be moonlight..." Otherwise, they would not be able to hit their objectives properly. The men would be scattered all over the countryside.

He lets that sink in. A morning landing so that preliminary engineer pathfinders could clear some corridors through the obstacle belts would imply an airborne assault the night before. And it would have to be a moonlit one, because landing at night would be hazardous enough for the paratroopers. Dropping a large force down in pitch blackness would severely cripple their ability to organize and to be effective—two critical elements the airborne troops would need in their plan if they had any hope of achieving their objectives before the Germans had time to react and neutralize them.

Staubwasser agrees that this sounds logical.

Rommel stares at a map of his belts of beach obstacles. Suddenly, possibly coming from his *Fingerspitzengefuehl*,[2] Rommel wonders if the enemy might actually plan a low-tide landing to better circumnavigate them.

It makes some sense. Still, all those months of working on high-tide obstacles... Well, no matter. They were not wasted. The higher belts would still hamper landing activities and supplies coming in at high tide and some of those coming in at low tide. Right now though, he has to concentrate on a possible low-tide landing.

"When are the next periods of good moonlight and low tides at dawn?" he asks.

Staubwasser consults the charts. The next combination is coming up soon, between June 5 and 7. The one low-tide period at dawn would be between the 12th and the 14th, but without a good moon.

"Then we should stay on alert up to and during those periods."

Staubwasser mentions Rommel's trip.

"Well, it'll just have to wait—unless of course, the weather is bad."

"I would think that they would need at least a week of good weather," says Staubwasser.

Rommel figures on them requiring at least four or five days straight. So now all he needs to go home is bad weather on the 5th.

As if in answer to Rommel's wish, that evening, a fierce thunderstorm covers the area.

***

Generalmajor Max Pemsel spends a good part of his day updating and then analyzing the latest maps of the Seventh Army beach areas. Defense construction is improving, but not fast enough. Shortages are plaguing them, and the quality of many formations is questionable at best.

There are so many foreigners now in their units, many of whom were once enemies. Over a quarter of their troops are Russians, with some 23 *Östentruppen* battalions stretched out along the Channel coast. In Marcks' 84th Corps alone, eight of them are Russian. This has caused a number of problems, some political, some logistical. Even communicating with them is difficult. And truth be known, against an Allied landing, they probably will not put up much of a struggle, if any. Rommel has grumbled to Pemsel more than once that one of his biggest problems is where to put the damned Russians. Von Rundstedt on the other hand, was glad that he had started using them back in 1942.[3]

Regarding armor, Seventh Army only has two panzer battalions. The 213th is made up of old, obsolete French equipment, totally useless against an aggressive, modern force. No worries though, Pemsel thinks sarcastically. It has been sent out to the Channel Islands, where it will be useless once the landings began. The other, the 206th, is located on the western side of the Cotentin peninsula. It has about four dozen panzers, all of them obsolete.[4]

Unit transport is lacking, and so many units have had to resort to horses, bicycles, and motorbikes to move supplies. Those regimental commanders lucky enough to have command cars (usually old, beat-up French vehicles) are restricted because of fuel shortages to using them only once or twice a week. To partially remedy this, Rommel and Dollmann have thought out three contingency plans for the invasion.

1. If Normandy is attacked, the following will be routed to the landing area: all available Seventh Army mobile forces, to be moved by rail and when close enough, by road; one division from each of the coastal areas of St. Malo and St. Nazaire; and one reinforced regiment from each of the *bodenständige* divisions in Morlaix and Lorient. Eventual reinforcement of the beachhead area will come from the army group panzer reserve and some additional seventeen divisions, some from interior sectors.

2. If Brittany is invaded, singular plans to move reinforcements by rail will be implemented. They specify specific routes, rest areas, supply points, contingency paths for detours, and special instructions for bottlenecks and gorges. Special traffic control units and *Aufgang Kommandos* will expedite movement to the western coast. These plans have been reinforced through training, drills, and practice exercises these last few months. Of course, with the Allied bombers hitting the railyards and trains, execution of these plans seems questionable.

3. If another area outside Seventh Army's area of responsibility is invaded, a third set of similar movement plans will be initiated to get as many units to the fighting area as possible.

Pemsel will later go over these invasion contingency reaction plans again with his staff.

***

An enemy air raid today destroys a section of the Luftwaffe communication trunk between Paris and Rouen. Teleprinter and phone lines between Paris and Rouen, Rennes, and Caen will be out for at least three days.

---

1 Ironically, when the war ended, Guderian and his son found themselves prisoners of war in the same camp (Allendorf, and then Neustadt). The son noted with surprise how his father, now freed of the tense, critical responsibilities that he had carried daily in the war, took up gardening with relish. He also began playing bridge for the first time in his life, and, as his son later recalled, "did so light-heartedly." In a fitting tribute to his father, Heinz Günther in 1967 also became *Inspekteur der Panzertruppen* in the West German Bundeswehr.

2 A sixth sense or instinct, something that had served Rommel well in North Africa.

3 Von Rundstedt had proposed using Russian POWs back in October 1942 to flesh out his units, "if no political or other reasons are opposed to this move, which I cannot judge." He reasoned that the Russians were "satisfied with very little," and so would be easy to feed and find quarters for. They were on the whole simple individuals, and as such were not swayed by effective propaganda. In addition, no Russian POW spoke French, so he would be a good deal easier to control. In conclusion, von Rundstedt said simply, "If he does not behave, he can simply be shot."

Technically, *Östentruppen* units were usually classified as either infantry or cavalry types and deployed as such. Thus, an *Öst Bataillon* was an infantry battalion that was usually composed of an odd mixture of Russians, Hungarians, Latvian, and Polish prisoners of war or deserters.

4 See footnote for May 6.

June 1944

Thursday, June 1

It is just after 8 a.m. at OB West in St.-Germain-en-Laye. The staff is busy taking care of a number of details. The most important is *Generalfeldmarschall* von Rundstedt's upcoming inspection tour. Near the end of last month, the old man had informed them that he was going to review part of the Seventh Army coastline in early June. So they started to plan his itinerary, with several stops that would include various towns in Western France. Today, they are finalizing the journey.

Itinerary for June 6, 1944

1030	OB West motorcade will leave St.-Germain-en-Laye heading for Dreux.
1115	*Brigadeführer* Fritz Witt, commanding the 12th SS Panzer Division *Hitlerjugend*, will meet the motorcade at the outskirts of Dreux and guide them through his division's assembly area, Laigle, and on towards Argentan.
1130–1200	The field marshal will inspect several units along his route.
1230	*Generalmajor* Edgar Feuchtinger, commanding the 21st Panzer Division, will meet the motorcade at the Argentan exit and guide them through the Fleurs area.
1300	Stop for a brief lunch with a unit of the 21st Panzer.
1330	Back on the road again. The motorcade will drive to Vire, and then continue on towards 84th Corps headquarters at St. Lô.
1600	Arrival at 84th Corps headquarters. The headquarters will arrange for the motorcade's meals and quarters.
Evening	Brief staff discussion with corps and divisional commanders.

Itinerary for June 7, 1944

0800	OB West motorcade will leave St. Lô and drive to Coutances. A stop for an inspection of *Östentruppen* in the 752nd Regiment.
0900	Inspection of the 635th *Öst* Battalion and then the 521st Security Battalion.
0930	Continue on from Granville through Avranches, Pontorson, Mont-St.-Michel, and Dol. After crossing the 84th/74th Corps boundary, the 77th Division commander will guide the motorcade on to St. Malo.
1200 (about)	Inspection of the SS Geologist battalion.
1330	Short lunch.
1400	Inspection of St. Malo defense installations.
1430	Leave St. Malo and drive on to Dinard. 77th Division will provide auto and ferry transportation.
1500 (about)	Inspection of defense positions up to and including St. Brieuc.

| 1630 | Continue on to 2nd *Fallschirmjäger* Corps headquarters at Quintin. *General der Fallschirmjäger* Meindl's staff to provide meals and quarters. |
| Evening | Brief staff discussion with unit commanders. |

Itinerary for June 8, 1944

0930	OB West motorcade will leave Quintin to inspect 2nd *Fallschirmjäger* Corps units on its way to Loudeac. From there, on to Merdrignac.
1030	The 5th *Fallschirmjäger* division commander, *Generalleutnant* Gustav Wilke, will meet the motorcade at the west exit of Merdrignac and lead them through the division's assembly area. Inspection of various units and preparations against paratroop landings will be made.
1300	Brief lunch at the airborne divisional headquarters in Bourges.
1400	Short rest.
1500	Motorcade to continue on to Fougères, Mayenne, and then Alençon.
1700	Arrival at the military government headquarters #916 in Alençon for the night. The headquarters will provide security, meals and quarters.

Itinerary for June 9, 1944

| 1030 | OB West motorcade will leave Alençon and drive to Dreux. |
| 1300 | Arrival back at St.-Germain-en-Laye. |

Additional details

- The motorcade will consist of two automobiles and eight men—two drivers, three guards, the Commander-in-Chief, *Oberst* Cullmann, and the field marshal's son, *Leutnant* von Rundstedt.
- Assignment of vehicles, drivers and guards, as well as their weapons and ammunition, will be made by OB West commandant. The paymaster will provide for ration cards and travel allowance.
- Only those representatives and officers mentioned in the orders will take part in the various parts of the inspection trip.
- The quarters of the Commander-in-Chief on the Rue Alexandre Dumas will be guarded inconspicuously while he is away.
- Responsibility for security, meals, and quarters on the trip will be that of the unit where the Commander-in-Chief is staying.

Von Rundstedt himself is in his quarters at his nearby villa, looking over the latest roster of his armies. At present, including the eight divisions in Holland and Belgium, he commands some six dozen divisions,[1] plus dozens of odd battalions. Of his total force, over half of them, 34 to be exact, are considered *bodenständige*, or static reserve. They can at best only be used in limited, fixed defensive operations. Two of his divisions are airborne, without any airdrop capability, of course. Though the remaining 23 are considered fit for combat, only about 13 are actually mobile infantry.

He grunts softly. The term "mobile" here is being used in the loosest sense of the term. It usually covers a wild mixture of any sort of transportation, from horse-drawn wagons, to bicycles, to motorbikes, and a wide ad hoc variety of old pre-war cars and trucks, along with a light smattering of actual supply trucks and a few prime movers.

He turns his attention to his armor. In addition to the infantry units, he has nine panzer divisions and one *panzergrenadier* division. Both he and Rommel can be thankful (not to mention relieved) that their mobile forces have been built back up again. Most of their missing panzer divisions, sent off to save the East, have finally been returned to France to nurse their wounds and to prepare for the invasion. A few smaller components are either still in transit or getting ready to move west, but the bulk of the panzers are back. Actually, von Rundstedt had never really objected too much to sending units eastward, and even had volunteered to send divisions to Russia a number of times when things there looked especially critical. After all, he had been a principal commander on the Eastern Front for nearly a year. In fact, he would just as soon look at a map of the Eastern Front as one of Western Europe.

Many of these panzer divisions are of course, still somewhat understrength from action on the Eastern Front, testimony to the ferocity of the Soviet army. Three of them are élite SS units—the 1st SS, 2nd SS, and the 12th SS. His one *panzergrenadier* division is also SS, the 17th SS *Panzergrenadier "Gotz von Berlichingen."*

The 1st SS Panzer, one of his strongest divisions, can now boast a complement of over 21,000 men. Others, including the two that have not yet arrived in the West, cannot. The 9th SS Panzer, for example, still in transit from the East, could not come up with 13,000. Although still short of men, SS *Brigadeführer* Fritz Witt's latest report for the 12th SS Panzer is that training is all but complete, and the unit is ready for offensive action.

A serious problem is a shortage of tanks. The 1st SS Panzer was allocated 200, but currently has a total of 88, and only 38 of these are Panthers. Rommel's 2nd Panzer, actually one of the better equipped divisions, has a total of just 69 out of 162 tanks authorized, and only 25 are Panthers. Bayerlein's *Panzer Lehr* is the only division that boasts a full panzer complement, with a total of 183 tanks. No, the new panzers are not coming fast enough.[2]

The lone *panzergrenadier* division, because it is an SS division, enjoys a larger authorized complement than its army equivalent. Yet in reality it is still much weaker than its organizational table would indicate, even though it now musters 17,321 men, a thousand short of its full authorized strength.[3]

Of these ten panzer units, four are designated as OKW reserves, technically under his control, but in reality, subject to release only by the Führer himself. Their locations are scattered all over his command. The 12th SS Panzer and *Panzer Lehr* are centrally located inland, between Normandy and the Somme. The 1st SS Panzer is rebuilding far up in Belgium, between Brussels and Antwerp. The 17th SS *Panzergrenadier*, under the command of SS *Brigadeführer* Werner Ostendorff, is located south of the Loire River, around Thouars.[4]

He looks at the map in his study. Three more panzer divisions are under Rommel's direct operational control. The rebuilt 21st, with its many substandard vehicles (so many in fact, that it really should be rated as a *panzergrenadier* division), is located near

Caen. Its two regiments of *panzergrenadiers* are on either side of the Orne River, and the division's panzer regiment is south of the city. Von Rundstedt had suggested that it be put further west, perhaps south of St Lô. Rommel had countered by suggesting instead that the 12th SS be moved close to the Vire estuary. Von Rundstedt had said no. The 12th SS was part of the panzer reserve and would remain so.

Rommel's other two panzer divisions, the 2nd and 116th, are located northeast of the Seine, in the Fifteenth Army's sector. With the bridges all knocked out at this point, movement in response to any threat in the western provinces could be a problem.

Three additional panzer units are allocated in southern France, in Blaskowitz's *Armeegruppe G*: The 11th Panzer is inland from Bordeaux, the 2nd SS Panzer is about 70km north of Toulouse, and the 9th Panzer is near Avignon.

Beside these ten divisions, one more has just now started to arrive in France. It is the 19th, which had struggled its way out of the Hube Pocket in the East. Now exhausted and depleted by vicious fighting in the East, it is down to less than a quarter of its former size. Like many other armored units before, it is coming west, specifically to Holland, to recuperate, refit, and reform. And like most of the others before it, the 19th Panzer is leaving most of its equipment and supplies behind, components that will be used by other units on the Eastern Front. So the 19th in its present condition will not by any means be a viable unit to use, and von Rundstedt does not intend to commit it to any combat.[5] The men need a well-earned rest.

On top of these 11 divisions, OKW has promised that the II SS Panzer Corps, consisting of the 9th and 10th SS Panzer divisions, will be shipped to the West whenever the invasion starts. Of course, von Rundstedt has been promised these units before.

Against his fortified command, Army Intelligence has estimated that the Allies could probably land nearly seven full, top-grade divisions at any viable landing area on just the first day, supported by some five or six regiments of artillery, maybe a half-dozen battalions of engineers, and a couple tank regiments. In strategic support, it is estimated that they could initially drop up to four paratroop divisions, followed by another two or three over a few days.

Von Rundstedt pauses and considers his upcoming inspection trip. Although its purpose is to inspect the various units in western France, he is not going to push himself too much. And his son coming along will make the time go better…

Von Rundstedt sighs and looks at his watch. Around 11 a.m. Time to take a break and go for a walk. He grabs his walking stick and leaves out the back door of the villa. He will stop for a drink somewhere as soon as he ditches his shadow that is tasked with following him…

***

Today, the Führer allows the head of the Kriegsmarine, *Großadmiral* Karl Dönitz, to go on leave. It is his first since the start of the war.

***

Generalfeldmarschall Rommel goes to his study after breakfast and looks over the morning reports. A few hundred bombers hit some radio and radar stations on the coast the night before. However, the navy reports that there are many still operating. That's good.

He wonders yet again about when the invasion will come. Why didn't they attack last month? There had been something like 18 days of near-perfect weather. May had even ended on a bright, sunny day. And the tides had been favorable. Everyone knows by now that the Allies are in a high state of readiness. The landing, he reasons—*if* there is to be one—should have come by now. More and more, it seems like the invasion will probably tie in with the expected Soviet offensive. That would put it somewhere around late June, after the late Polish thaw ends.

He still feels that the main landing site will be some distance up the coast—away from Normandy, somewhere in the Fifteenth Army sector. For one thing, Allied reconnaissance flights spotted up there have outnumbered those over the Seventh Army by a 2-to-1 ratio. Still, he cannot take any chances. All of *Heeresgruppe B* is in an alert status, although it is a low-grade one.

His fundamental problem remains of course, still not being able to get all the panzers positioned near the coast. Unfortunately, even if he does get his way and all the panzer divisions are allowed to relocate to his direct control, he will still have a big problem moving nearly all of them once the invasion comes. Spread out all over France right now, one or maybe two might be close to the landing site whenever the time comes; but that means that most will be some distance from the target area. He needs somehow to get the panzers redeployed as soon as possible.

Transportation is a big issue. Most of the mobile units in the responding divisions will just have to make their way by road, vulnerable to strafing. With the situation as critical as it is, he will also have to rely on the badly beat-up French rail system to move as many panzers as he can as close to the invasion site as possible. The measure of his counterattacks will rely upon the efficiency of the OKH Quartermaster and upon the French rail system—the same system that has been getting such a heavy pounding lately by the Allied air forces.

The biggest bottlenecks are the various river networks running inland from the English Channel, especially the Seine itself. Von Rundstedt has established special bridge restoration units to repair them as soon as possible. Protecting them while they work are flak units, including major components of Pickert's *III. Flak Korps*.

Construction of barriers continues. Complicating things is the shortage of cement, partly due to the increased enemy bombings of the railways. There is a coal shortage too. The cement installation in Cherbourg has had to close down last month because of a lack of coal. His men are trying to get some shipped by canal up to Rouen, but that will be slow.

Rommel takes a break to confer with Assistant Secretary Berndt,[6] a member of Goebbels' Propaganda Ministry. They discuss how to psychologically influence the enemy at the actual moment of invasion. Rommel is not leaving any stone unturned.

Things at the château seem quiet today, so just after lunch, Rommel takes advantage of the good weather. He and *Hauptmann* Lang take a ride up to the coast for yet another look at the coastal defenses. They travel northeast to inspect the fortress at Dieppe and the shoreline up there, covered by Sanders' 245th Division and *Generalmajor* Seyffardt's 348th Division.

While examining the beach installations, he is told that the incomplete 170mm battery near Ault has in the last few days been bombed twice.[7] He directs that the guns be withdrawn to shelter until the concrete emplacements are finished.

Back from his inspection early that evening, physically tired from stomping along the coast today, and generally fatigued overall from the intense activities of the last few weeks, he gets a visit from the military governor of Belgium, General von Falkenhausen. They relax in Rommel's study and talk about the war. To the visiting friend, Rommel's demeanor seems changed, reflected in a strange pessimism, uncharacteristic for him. Perhaps the field marshal feels differently now about the future, has been disturbed by recent events in the progress of the war, or is just mentally and physically fatigued from the rigorous schedule he has kept for the past few months. At any rate, he seems to the military governor a different man than when they last saw each other in Brussels at the end of February.

The more they chat, the more von Falkenhausen is convinced of this. With a possible massive invasion looming near, Rommel, feeling the stress of the heavy responsibility that is upon him, is no longer enthusiastic and optimistic. Rather, he seems sadly resigned and somber about Germany's chances of coming out of this war in a relatively good condition, something the visiting general himself has been convinced of for a while now.

Von Falkenhausen later writes:

> [W]hen I repaid the visit on June 1, 1944, at La Roche-Guyon, he had changed and wholeheartedly adopted my view.

That evening, Rommel sits back and relaxes at a small celebration party given by his staff. His Operations chief, von Tempelhoff, has been promoted to *Oberst*—a full colonel. They also use the opportunity to bid a heartfelt farewell to *Oberst* Heckel and a few other officers who have been in their quartermaster staff for a while.

***

It is dark now. Fifteenth Army Signals Center is busy with routine interceptions of BBC transmissions. As usual, they are all analyzed for content.

The enlisted watch operator, *Unteroffizier* Walter Reichling, is sitting at his desk with his headphones on, listening to the end of the BBC 9 o'clock news. It is almost time for the "French speaking to French" special messages that are regularly sent to the Resistance in occupied Europe.[8] The phrases are simple yet cryptic, and no meaning can be discerned from them, unless that code has somehow been divulged to their center beforehand by Intelligence.

Reichling is always especially alert for any of those coded phrases. Those they know about, though, are rare. Usually the messages they receive are nonsense, red herrings made up of innocuous phrases sent to confuse them. Still, Reichling's boss, *Oberstleutnant* Meyer,[9] is a thorough man and has always insisted that his men record and examine everything intercepted for later analysis on any possible meaning or patterns. Once in a while, they are rewarded for their diligence when an authentic code for a particular underground group is picked up. Strangely, there seem to have been quite a few of those lately, over a hundred in the last couple days. Intelligence has determined that many of the recent authentic messages are the first half of two-part personal message triggers.

Reichling is bored as he goes on listening to the BBC's news broadcast. A couple of somewhat interesting tidbits, and some reports about the progress of the war. Still, certainly nothing of significance. Finally, the news comes to an end, and Reichling is glad. Here comes the interesting stuff: the messages to the Underground.

ICI LONDRES—LES FRANÇAIS PARLENT AUX FRANÇAIS. VOICI NOTRE HUITIEME BULLETIN D'INFORMATION. MAIS ÉCOUTEZ TOUT D'ABORD, QUELQUES MESSAGES PERSONNELS...

The messages begin. He makes sure the recorder is working, taking down these simple sentences. Some moments later, he frowns as he listens to the next message. His eyes suddenly fly open in astonishment as he begins to write it down. Quickly he checks to make sure the wire recorder is still recording what he is hearing. Moments after this message ends, he rips off his headphones, grabs the paper, tells his assistant to keep listening, and goes running down the corridor, racing out of the intercept bunker.

He dashes over to Meyer's special command bunker and heads directly for Meyer's office. He flings open his office door and goes in.

The office is actually a spacious room divided by a partition. Meyer works on one side, and his superior, Fifteenth Army Chief of Staff, *Generalleutnant* Rudolf Hoffmann, works in the other. A large square opening in the center of the wall allows them to converse and exchange messages.

"*Herr Oberstleutnant*," Reichling says breathlessly, "Pardon me sir, but the first part of the message. It's here." He hands Meyer the paper with the message notation and the time on it.

Meyer looks up sharply. "The Verlaine poem?" he replies, standing up.

"*Jawohl, Herr Oberstleutnant.* I just heard it."

Meyer grabs his hat and quickly follows Reichling over to the watch office. He listens to the recording of the wire intercept, nodding. It is indeed the first verse of the code. Admiral Canaris' information has evidently been right. It looks like the invasion will now come in a couple of weeks. They have to notify all major commands right away.

Meyer takes off for General Hoffmann's villa. As he quickly walks into the living room, Hoffmann looks up and growls, "*Ja?*"

Meyer hands him the paper with Reichling's scribbles on it. "Well, there's the message. It's here," he tells the Chief.

Hofmann is quiet, studying the paper. "The Verlaine poem, *Herr General*," Meyer adds. Has he forgotten?

After another second or two, Hoffmann asks, "Are you sure?"

Meyer replies confidently. "We just recorded it."

Hoffmann pauses. "Very well," he says. "I'll put Fifteenth on alert immediately. Make sure the other commands get the word."

"*Jawohl, Herr General.*" Meyer leaves as Hoffmann picks up the phone and orders Alert One, the second highest alarm.

Meyer runs back to his office and immediately gets on the phone to the Intelligence Officer at *Heeresgruppe B,* Anton Staubwasser. Meyer tells him that the first part of the Verlaine poem has just been intercepted. Staubwasser acknowledges and tells him that he will pass the message on to the field marshal and to his chief of staff. Meyer hangs up and then calls OB West to tell them as well.

After making the two calls, still excited, he begins preparing a formal, follow-up teletype message that will immediately to go out to OKW, OB West, Seventh Army, and *Heeresgruppe B,* while that simple French verse continues to echo in his ears:

"*Les sanglots longs des violons de l'automne...*" The long sobs of the violins of autumn...

***

This evening, *Oberst* Oskar Reile, head of *Abteilung III der Abwehrleitstelle Frankreich* (German counterintelligence in France), is in his headquarters in the Hôtel Lutetia in Paris, analyzing dozens of intercepted coded messages for the French resistance cells in the Underground. He has been doing this now for many months, monitoring and investigating radio traffic. From going over these intercepts, he strongly suspects that the invasion target is going to be the Normandy area. He also has determined that many of these messages are the first half of two-part personal message triggers. So far, he has intercepted a few hundred of them. Most, he knows, are decoys. But since February of this year, the Abwehr had cracked enough of the French Underground to know that, when they were broadcast, many would signal an upcoming major operation, probably the invasion. Even more importantly, they knew in several instances which code phrases to listen for.

Tonight, Reile's men have intercepted over a hundred of these first-part messages, most to the Brittany and Normandy area. However, they get excited just after 9 p.m. when they intercept the first line of the Verlaine poem. Two hurry over to his office and inform him of the intercept. The invasion will now supposedly come within two weeks.

Reile considers that. Such a flurry of messages had been sent at the beginning of May, and German Intelligence had accordingly gone on the alert. However, nothing had ever come of them, and finally the Germans had concluded that this had been a ruse.

So was this the real thing? It seemed to be. To support this, his office has noted that those resistance cells that the Allies know or suspect the Germans have infiltrated have so far not received any such key messages.

Reile, not taking any chances, informs OB West (through Gestapo headquarters, which is now handling Abwehr activities) of the intelligence alert, and then Berlin.[10] Reile's message strangely is not sent to *Heeresgruppe B*. He assumes that OB West will forward it.

***

At OB West, von Rundstedt's Ic, Wilhelm Meyer-Detring, is on leave, so his deputy takes the call. Reile tells him about the two-part alert messages being sent, and about the Verlaine trigger line. He recommends that the Seventh and Fifteenth Armies be put on alert. The deputy thanks Reile for the call. He makes a note of it and does no more. Meyer-Detring, like von Rundstedt, puts little credence in espionage-related matters, so late last year, he told his staff to ignore such BBC "alerts." And since Rommel now commands the Seventh and the Fifteenth, let him alert them.

***

The evening of June 1 at Berchtesgaden has been relatively calm. Operations Chief General Alfred Jodl has settled down into his evening routine at his temporary residence named after him, the *Jodlhaus*. About 2,200 square meters, it is a quaint three-storey square house built into the side of a grassy slope, with a concrete wall in front of the steps leading up to the second level. His superior, Field Marshal Keitel, has his own separate residences in the complex as well, about a hundred meters away. The *Keitelhaus* is a larger, charming three-storey manor, with an impressive arched entryway, a large overhanging roof, and full balconies around the upper stories. Most of the OKW staff stays at the Strub Barracks on the other side of town.[11]

Their headquarters are located a few kilometers down the mountain in the *Klein Reichskanzlei*—the "Little Reich Chancellery." Since the actual *Reichskanzlei* was far away in Berlin, the Führer in 1935 decided to create a secondary semi-permanent chancellery just outside Berchtesgaden. So in 1935, he ordered this alternate *Reichskanzlei* built in Stanggaß, a valley suburb on the northwest edge of Berchtesgaden,. It is only a few miles from the Berghof (although still a good half-hour drive through the town and up the main winding road to get there). Jodl though is seldom there. He spends most of his time either at the Berghof with Hitler, or in his quarters here.

Despite the fact that the Führer's mountain compound has grown tremendously in size over the last five years, none of the senior military personnel actually stay with him at the Berghof. Top leaders like Göring, Speer, Jodl, Keitel, and Himmler get to have their own residences in the compound. Most of the OKW staff though, work and sleep outside the immediate area, far below the mountain, close to the *Klein Reichskanzlei.*

Jodl is now sitting at his desk, tired from the day's activities. It is not that he minds staying at the *Jodlhaus.* He must admit that the accommodations are fine. Rather, he is just tired of going back and forth all the time. Not just locally up and down the Obersalzberg mountain between his headquarters, the Berghof nearby, and his own quarters, but also periodically between Berlin, Rastenburg, and Berchtesgaden. Staying in the enclosed compound at Rastenburg in East Prussia was like living in a labor camp in the middle of the woods. And working at the Berghof is like operating in a monastery, subject to the whims of a brilliant but somewhat insane abbot. In general, Jodl's own staff worked out of a train half the time. This included Walther Warlimont, who had his own Section L (Operations) located in its own special railcar car at the Berchtesgaden railway station.

Jodl's thoughts are interrupted when his aide comes in and hands him a teletype message. Meyer in Fifteenth Army Intelligence has intercepted the first part of the Verlaine code. If one is to believe the report, the invasion now is supposedly not far off. Jodl reads the message with a scowl. To him, it is just more spy cloak-and-dagger crap. And stuff like this by now is not that interesting to him. Anyway, he is pretty sure that after von Rundstedt reads it, he will put all of France on alert, so Jodl decides he does not need to.

He sets the dispatch down on his desk, along with the rest of the day's message traffic, and forgets about it.

---

1   While actual numbers vary, most sources agree that von Rundstedt commanded anywhere from 58 to 60 actual divisions at this time, not including various detached or independent units.

2   The husky Tiger I and Tiger II tanks (*PzKw VIa* and *PzKw VIb*) were rare. The deadly *PzKw V* "Panther" was starting to come off the production lines in increasing numbers. Unfortunately, huge numbers of tanks were needed immediately, and the good ones were going to the Eastern Front. Because of that, older model *PzKw IVs* and *PzKw IIIs* were still being produced and put into combat units, such as the 21st Panzer, supplemented by whatever else they could scrounge up,

including a few French tanks, which were nearly useless against even a Sherman tank. To increase their survivability, the German engineers had beefed them up with extra armor plating and better radios.

3   There were only six rifle battalions, organized into two regiments. Their transport, like that of most of the divisions in the West, was haphazard, utilizing a variety of vehicles, including some vintage Italian trucks. Two battalions moved around on bicycles. The panzer battalion had no tanks at all, but rather 37 assault guns. The anti-tank battalion was two-thirds understrength, only having one company of 12 self-propelled guns, instead of the intended three. The *Flak* battalion, while it featured a dozen towed 88mm guns, only had four-fifths of its required personnel. An armored recon battalion and a small headquarters unit rounded out the division.

4   About 110km southwest of Tours.

5   The 19th Panzer would eventually be sent back to Poland in July 1944, and a month later, it would take part in subduing the Warsaw Uprising. In September, still on the Eastern Front, it would try to stabilize the German defensive line near the Vistula. Continually forced to retreat, it finally surrendered to Russian forces at the end of the war in Czechoslovakia.

6   Thirty-nine-year-old SS *Brigadeführer* Alfred-Ingemar Berndt, Assistant Secretary of Propaganda. A strong Nazi supporter and once a famed journalist, Berndt had taken over the central Propaganda Department in 1941 for Goebbels. Berndt knew Rommel quite well. Back as a lieutenant, he had first joined Rommel's command staff in North Africa and had served as Rommel's aide-de-camp, a sort of Nazi party representative, keeping Rommel's diary. Berndt proved himself to be tough, boldly courageous, and when necessary, direct, even with his superiors (which Rommel used to his advantage whenever anything unpleasant needed to be reported to the Führer, especially since Berndt was now also a Party official and a close assistant to Goebbels).

   Although he now ran a large part of the Propaganda Department, he had taken back his rank as an SS officer (he had joined in 1934). Thus, if he came to Rommel's headquarters in his SS uniform, that would have been an unusual sight. A good friend of Rommel who had helped create the field marshal's image in the media, he was a stout fellow, with wavy hair, and an incurable streak of curiosity that caused him to want to poke into everything he came across. Still, Berndt remained a fiercely loyal Nazi.

   In a letter to Lucie on the morning of May 27, Rommel had noted Berndt's upcoming visit. Evidently, it had been postponed.

7   The battery was hit again on June 4 by the 386th Bomb Group.

8   This special BBC segment of the news, "*Les Français parlent aux Français,*" ("The French speak to the French") first began in July 1940, right after the fall of France. It was transmitted for a variety of communication purposes, many of which were innocuous, such as for congratulations or to celebrate certain personal occasions. Some messages were made up and just sent to confuse the Germans. Many of course, were used to relay coded instructions to the French Underground, either collectively, or most often, to individual local cells. This radio segment continued on the BBC until the end of August 1944.

9   *Oberstleutnant* Helmuth Meyer, Intelligence Chief (Ic), Fifteenth Army. See May 3 entry.

10 OKW passed the information on to the unemotional Colonel Roenne, head of the expert staff at *Fremde Heeres West,* which evaluated enemy intelligence reports and passed on that information when it was appropriate to lower army echelons. Roenne did nothing.

11 A two-year project began in 1936 to build a large military barracks complex in nearby Strub for the *2. Abteilung, 100. Gebirgsjägerregiment.* After the war, it was used by the American Army until 1995.

Friday, June 2

It is another lovely day in France, with a slight, cool breeze in the air. Again, no real signs of Allied activity regarding any landing operations. A radio broadcast gives them the gloomy news (although the announcer put a very positive spin on it) that Rome is now nearly in the hands of the Allies. The military situation in Italy is getting even worse, now that the Allies have broken out of their Anzio landing area. It seems likely that Rome will soon fall.

Generalfeldmarschall Rommel, at the request of the Führer, puts out a directive granting fortress commanders greater powers of authority regarding the defense of their assigned areas.

That afternoon, Rommel, some of his staff members, and a few local hunters go on a *battue*[1] with the Marquis de Choisy. Treff accompanies them. They all trample around in the woods for a few hours but only manage to scare up a few squirrels. The hunt though, does allow them some splendid views of the placid Seine River valley on this nice day, so the afternoon activity is not completely wasted. They have plenty of opportunities to take in the beautiful scenery, only spoiled by a view far off in the distance of enemy aircraft bombing a bridge crossing.

***

Early this afternoon at the Berghof, Alfred Jodl talks to Hitler about the upcoming invasion in the West. There are some reports of Allied troop movements down into southern England that occurred at the end of May, but analysis is inconclusive. Jodl's staff has been checking moon phases and tides, with an eye towards Cherbourg. Hitler is told that a favorable time period for invasion exists between the 5th and the 13th of June.

He is also informed from the Gestapo in Berlin of an intelligence alert coming from *Oberst* Oskar Reile, in charge of counter-intelligence in France. The first half of over a hundred key trigger phrases had been transmitted by the BBC to the French Resistance According to his intelligence, D-Day will occur in less than two weeks. When the second halves of the phrases are sent, the invasion should be launched within 48 hours.

The Führer's concerns today, though, are elsewhere. Listening to the lunchtime briefings and studying the latest combat reports, he concludes that the situation in Italy is getting much worse. Rome is about to fall, and German units are starting to retreat. So he orders the 19th Luftwaffe Field Division, now renamed the 19th *Luftwaffe Sturm* Division, to relocate from Holland to Italy.[2] OKW General Warlimont is furious about this decision and knows that the commanders in the West will be as well.

***

Today, OB West receives two communiqués from OKW. The first, a teletype message, informs them that, since the 21st Panzer Division has recently successfully demonstrated the importance of multi-barrel rocket launchers (the weapons demonstrations on May 30), a thousand captured BM-8 82mm Russian rocket launchers will be shipped from the Replacement Army in Germany to them for that purpose.

The second, a radio message from Keitel under instructions, reminds von Rundstedt that the Führer in January and again in February had issued directives declaring certain islands and fortified port areas to be considered *Festungen*. As such, their commanding officers are directly answerable to the Führer and receive their orders only from him.

In the early afternoon, OB West issues its noon status report. It states that, despite the temporary period of bad weather approaching from England, there is continued heavy Allied air activity, with several raids around Boulogne.

Later on, von Rundstedt gets a phone call from the Army's chief operations officer at OKW, *Generalmajor Freiherr* Treusch Baron von Buttlar-Brandenfels. Although the call is for the field marshal, Blumentritt takes it because the old man hates to get on the phone and avoids it whenever possible.[3] They discuss emergency alerts, and in what conditions they are to be sent. The agreed-upon codewords "Imminent danger" (*drohend Gefahr*) would put all forces upon maximum alert.

Von Buttlar, speaking for Jodl, wants to know why the old man has not already put his forces on a higher state of alert. It seems to OKW that the Anglo-Americans could come at any time, and there are some indications that the invasion will begin soon.

Blumentritt first assures von Buttlar that they are indeed ready for the invasion. He adds that after careful consideration, OB West feels that such an emergency alert would mostly just affect rail transportation, because their military units (he says modestly) are already in a high state of readiness, and do not need much more warning. An emergency alert would immediately force them to mass all of their rolling stock, so that large units, reinforcements, and supplies could be quickly transported into the danger area using pre-arranged plans that had been formulated after exhaustive statistical analysis.

Unfortunately, this in itself would be difficult using their hard-pressed weak rail assets, hit so hard by Allied bombings. Blumentritt (with the old man next to him, prompting at times) cites some statistics to prove his point. They have assembled a few groups of extra railcars, but that would not be enough when the time came.

Von Buttlar feels the situation is not that grim. Blumentritt assures him that it is. If an emergency alarm is declared, the last small reserve that they desperately need to supply the population, the economy, and war production will be gone. That in turn will create new problems. Unemployment and strikes will rise, especially at the defensive supply plants. War production, already crippled by Allied air raids, will grind to a halt. Supplying larger cities with basic necessities will be difficult, angering the population, and at a time when it is most critical to keep them content. So, Blumentritt concludes, the commander-in-chief feels that these threatening conditions should be avoided for as long as possible.

Von Buttler reluctantly agrees, but adds that he will have to talk to Jodl about this.

Blumentritt whispers this to von Rundstedt, who nods. Blumentritt in a deferential tone adds that, on the other hand, they might declare some local alerts, especially in economically inessential areas such as central France, where the Maquis is occasionally active. A local emergency alert could improve their counter-operations against insurgents and restore civil order.

***

Late in the afternoon 84th Corps commander Erich Marcks is standing on a long, sandy bluff near Arromanches-les-Bains, a small coastal hamlet about midway between the Vire and the Orne estuaries. Tomorrow, he will inspect parts of the 914th around Brévands. Now though, he is overlooking the English Channel with a few of his staff officers, including his aide, *Hauptmann* Jobel. As he feels a breeze coming in off the Channel, he leans on his good leg and gazes intently out over the water, lost in thought. He is probably visualizing enemy ships, laden with troops and tanks, anchored offshore, while swarms of enemy bombers at varying altitudes, protected by groups of enemy fighters circling overhead, buzz towards where he is standing at the moment.

He continues his gaze out over the choppy waters. His gut feeling, that has served him so well in the past, now tells him that von Rundstedt is wrong about Calais being the invasion target. Nor is it the Somme estuary as Rommel has proposed. And though the skies are starting to get cloudy, they would nevertheless make a good screen for a surprise landing—that is of course, if the weather does not get too bad, and if the Allies have enough men and the right equipment. Of those latter points, Marcks has little doubt.

His idea of a landing along a western shoreline is further evidenced by the recent enemy air raids that have targeted all those east–west bridges along the main rivers and railroads of Northern France and Belgium. The Allies are trying to isolate western France from the rest of Europe. And though there was intensive enemy air reconnaissance throughout the Calais and Normandy area all last month, the air activity along his coastal sector is now ominously quiet; too quiet.

Still staring intently out over the water, he slowly comments, more to himself than to anyone present, "If I know the British…" He glances over at his aide as his cane points out to sea. "If I know the British, they'll go to church next Sunday for one last time, and come Monday…" He pauses and adds, "After Tuesday, they won't have another chance for the tides until June 28–29."

Marcks stares out over the water again. Yes, something is up. He can sense it.

He turns again to look at his aide. "Army Group B says they're not going to come yet, and that when they do come, it'll be up at Calais. So I think we'll be welcoming them on Monday, right here," he concludes, poking his cane in the sand.

He turns back to look out at the Channel. He fervently hopes that he is wrong, but that hunch in his mind and that accursed ache in his stump somehow tell him that he is not.[4]

---

1   From the French word meaning "beaten." A type of hunt where herders beat the brush in front of the hunters (bird hunting) or towards them (ground hunting).

2   In Italy, the 19th would become a part of the 14th Panzer Corps and constantly fight rear-guard battles on the Frieda Line against several larger American units, before finally falling back on Livorno. At the end of July, depleted, it would be disbanded and sent back to Europe. In Denmark, it would became the cadre from which the 19th *Volksgrenadier* Division would be formed.

3   Von Rundstedt avoided phone calls, especially making them, mainly because he was hard of hearing, but also because he was impatient. The right party had to be found and put on the line, and even then connections were often weak and full of static. Anyway, by now, von Rundstedt had become quite vexed with the High Command, and his attitudes towards their dictums had become decidedly lackadaisical.

4   Marcks of course was right on the money. Monday would be June 5, the original planned day for the invasion. Of course, the general had no knowledge at that time that a storm would hit the coast that day, delaying the invasion by 24 hours.

Saturday, June 3

Morning at La Roche-Guyon. The weather in France is still fairly nice, although the skies are much cloudier, it is cooler, and the wind has picked up a bit. At the château, the normal, day-to-day administration of the army group continues. Rommel is in his study as usual, going over the new reports. The latest Luftwaffe meteorological forecast predicts a storm coming in. That is good news for him. It looks like his trip home is on.

He scans the incoming message traffic. A group of enemy bombers the night before hit one of their radio jamming stations near Dieppe. Another group bombed four of his coastal batteries in the Pas-de-Calais.

Included in the dispatches are three significant reports, all of them disconcerting. The first is a communications intelligence summary. Army operational centers all over England have gone on radio silence. Rommel briefly feels a slight chill go through him. In the desert, radio silence usually meant that the enemy was getting ready to attack. Here in Western Europe though, after all the waiting he has done, this development could mean anything. Besides, in the last few months, a few of these periods of radio silence have come and gone. This one, like the others, probably, hopefully, is not significant. Still, he had better not take any chances—not this late in the game.

As if to reinforce his concern, a second disquieting message from the Luftwaffe reports that Allied aerial reconnaissance in France has increased significantly the last few days. The enemy is getting quite nosy now for some reason. He writes out a memo to Speidel, requesting that the Luftwaffe immediately try again to conduct some aerial reconnaissance flights of its own over all the British southern ports.

The third noteworthy message is from General Marcks at 84th Corps. He reports that his sector is seriously behind schedule in building defensive barriers. This, Marcks explains, is due to a lack of supplies, inferior materials, and a shortage of power. Marcks estimates that the defensive construction program in his zone is only about half done. Rommel also notes his copy of a message Marcks has sent to OB West, requesting eight to ten small trains be put at his disposal to speed up the placement of casements in his coastal defenses. Rommel smirks. Not much chance of getting those trains from the old man.

Rommel thinks about Marcks' report for a bit, and then writes out another memo for his staff. *Heeresgruppe B* is to request of OB West that, regarding all special construction undertakings and supply shipments, those that are slated for coastal defense be hereafter given the highest priority.

Fortified by a forecasted storm coming their way, Rommel is thankful that a possible Allied landing in the low tide/good moon period between June 4 and June 7 is now probably just an academic question. He is considerably relieved.

He finally stands up, stretches, and leaves the study to go have his usual early breakfast. Lang as always waits in the hallway to accompany him. After eating, he chairs a conference concerning that battalion of SS military geological engineers in the Seventh Army sector. They are excellent at helping with the defensive barriers, but Himmler wants to withdraw them to Germany. The army can complain all it wants, but in the end, they are Himmler's unit.

Orders from OKW via OB West arrive. The 19th *Luftwaffe Sturm* Division is going to be transferred out of Belgium. It is slated to travel south through Blaskowitz's *Armeegruppe G*, and then on to Italy to fortify the crumbling line there. Other matters come up, but they only carry a part of the field marshal's interest. Though tired, he is restless, because he is looking forward to his trip today to Paris.

A number of staff members pursue by phone some mundane subjects such as smoke candles and smoke-creating acids. Later that morning, two army generals from the *HWaA*[1] promise Rommel that the manufacture of those multiple rocket launchers that he recently saw demonstrated will continue by Major Becker's men.

A new message comes in from the central SS intelligence branch in Berlin, now the army's main intelligence source since the SS took over the duties of the Abwehr. The message reports the interception of the Verlaine poem's first verse, and concludes that the invasion can be expected within the next two weeks. Maybe the low tide/full moon period of the 5th/6th/7th. On the other hand, Dönitz's naval headquarters has dismissed the interception as bogus, possibly part of an enemy exercise. So many variables…

Thinking about it, Rommel requests that just in case, the Luftwaffe lay some *Blitzsperren* in both approach channels around the Isle of Wight. Between the lethargy and the inadequacy of the Luftwaffe at this time though (in contrast to the full preparedness of the Allies), this request is probably not going to be carried out.[2]

Early that afternoon, under cloudy skies, Rommel wearily climbs once again into the front passenger seat of his Horch, with Lang in the back. Daniel starts the car, and they drive off towards the metropolitan capital.

First, they call on von Rundstedt in St.-Germain-en-Laye. The old Prussian and his chief of staff greet them at his villa. Blumentritt immediately notes Rommel's fatigue. The two field marshals and Blumentritt sit and have tea.

While they are chatting, they are presented with *Generalmajor* Hans Cramer. Now refreshed from having taken leave and mindful of the Führer's specific instructions, Cramer fills them in completely on everything the Allies showed him. He recounts the tour he was given on the way to the harbor where he was to board a ship to be repatriated. He describes in detail the many weapons and vehicle depots that he saw—supposedly, the FUSAG[3] units that were ready to go, located in what was probably southeast England…

Cramer concludes that, from what he had seen of the Allied units, it seemed to him that the enemy would hit somewhere either below Calais, or near the Somme estuary, the second of which just happened to be Rommel's pet theory.[4]

They all discuss the information. To the old man, this is more confirmation that the invasion will come at Calais. Rommel is not so sure. The Allies must have had some good motive for showing Cramer all of that stuff. To perhaps discourage the Germans into giving up? Hardly. Much more likely, it was to throw them off the track...

Cramer eventually leaves them.[5] The two field marshals then discuss the status of the defenses along the coast and the upcoming bad weather. They talk about Rommel's trip home. Both of them agree that it is a good time for it, what with the upcoming storm. Anyway, Rommel needs the break. Blumentritt will later note that Rommel seemed "tired and tense...a man who needed to be home for a few days with his family."

Rommel now formally requests to go on leave in Germany from June 5–8. Von Rundstedt immediately grants it.[6] They chat for a while longer on minor details. A panzer battalion from *Panzer Lehr* will be fitted with *PzKw V* tanks and then probably sent to the Eastern Front. Enemy bombing of their transportation lines continues. Tactical enemy units across the Channel have gone on radio silence...

Von Rundstedt tells Rommel that he too is going to take advantage of the bad weather. He has scheduled an inspection trip of Western France and is going to take along his son. The itinerary has been radioed to OKW He mentions that he will inspect a couple of their Russian *Östentruppen*, and they smile at the thought. That will be interesting.

Rommel finally takes his leave. Von Rundstedt and Blumentritt sincerely wish him a safe trip and a pleasant leave. As Rommel starts to walk out, he looks over at von Rundstedt and Blumentritt. "There's not even going to *be* an invasion," he says with a slight huff. "And if there is, then they won't even get off the beaches!"

He and Lang pile back into black Horch and set off for downtown Paris, Rommel intent on getting those birthday shoes for Lucie. He ends up purchasing a beautiful pair of handmade gray suede shoes—size 5½, just as she had told him.

On the trip back to the château, it starts raining. Rommel gazes out at the passing French landscape. The timing for his leave seems good. The weather is confirming the latest meteorological reports. The task of landing now would be at quite hard. Nor are the tides right. They are scheduled around the 5th and 6th to be low in the morning. OKW has agreed with him that this would not be suitable for a landing, since, as Rommel has often reviewed, the assault troops would have to travel hundreds of yards further across an exposed beach to reach the cliffs. This longer distance would naturally result in many more casualties. It was upon this premise that most of the Atlantic Wall obstacles have been laid out and positioned.

He sits back in the Horch, wrapped in thought. Granted, the extra time would let his men fire more shells at the enemy; but there is, he acknowledges uneasily, a positive aspect to partially offset this drawback. Landing at low tide would allow the assault force to more easily avoid and better dispose of the impeding but exposed high-tide beach obstacles. It might also allow the enemy to bring in heavier equipment a little faster, and with less difficulty.[7] Would it be worth getting shot at for a longer period of time? He does not think so. No, Rommel is pretty sure that they would come in at high or at least medium tide. They had before.

Even so, this continues to bother him. When he arrives at La Roche-Guyon, he gives Speidel a summation of his trip. He then goes to his study and drafts out a formal instruction to partially ease his concerns. Fearful now of a possible low-tide invasion, Rommel orders his units to continue with their huge offshore barrier construction program, but to now concentrate on low-tide obstacles. Most areas have finished, or are over three-quarters finished, with the high-tide barriers. The two mid-tide barriers are coming along; but many of the low-tide barriers have not even been started yet, especially in the Seventh Army sector.

Now that the even lower spring tides are here, Rommel wants the men to take advantage of this temporary condition and set up as many as possible of the low-tide belts that have taken so long to get started. Especially since intelligence reports have stated that the Allies had practiced a few low-tide landings recently. The rush program is to have a completion date of June 20. While his units might not be able to reach that target, at least they will understand that there was a matter of urgency here. He writes down a message to be sent to his unit commanders:

> The enemy has conducted repeated invasion maneuvers at low tide, which means we may have to take such an invasion seriously into account.

A really rushed program could get a good many completed in a few weeks.

> You are to complete this by June 20.

Oberst Staubwasser, Rommel's Ic, receives a report from Reile's counterintelligence group on the two-part message system for the Underground and the significance of the Verlaine first line. Never having been prewarned about these two-part trigger messages, his written response in his daily assessment reflects his skepticism, and the incoming bad weather shows that the radio silence across the Channel is just a ruse. He writes:

> The increased transmission of alarm phrases by enemy radio since June 1 for the French underground cells is not, on previous experience, to be interpreted as an indication that the beginning of the invasion is imminent.

Chief of Staff Speidel countersigns the report.

That evening, Rommel pursues some final details for his trip. He notes in his diary:

> *The most pressing problem was to speak to the Führer personally on the Obersalzberg, convey to him the extent of the manpower and material inferiority we would suffer in the event of a landing, and request dispatch of two further panzer divisions, an AA Corps, and a Nebelwerfer brigade to Normandy.*

Now, if only the Allies give him a few more weeks. It looks like they just might...

Allied Intelligence, after examining some recent aerial recon photos of the Normandy coastline, finally begins to suspect that some elements of another infantry unit have relocated along the Calvados coast, east of the Vire estuary. It is probably the veteran 352nd Infantry Division, which had been further south, although intelligence analysts have heard nothing of this move up until now from any Resistance groups.[8] They therefore theorize that these few units, even if they are indeed part of the 352nd, have only recently relocated to the coast for a "defensive beach exercise" and probably will withdraw as soon as it is concluded. Still, major commands should probably be notified.

General Bradley, commanding the American units scheduled to land in that area, will not find out about the "temporarily" reinforced coastline for another 48 hours—after his flagship puts out to sea on June 5, and a little over four hours before the naval assault begins. And the American troops hitting this strip of beach will not know until it is too late that this entire area has been permanently reinforced and fortified by a veteran infantry division, and that these seasoned troops have been alerted and are patiently awaiting their arrival.

This coastal strip has been designated by the Allied planners as Omaha beach.[9]

It is late evening. Although the weather is bad, the Fifteenth Army's Signal Center in Tourcoing is busy as ever, intercepting different BBC transmissions. A weary *Oberstleutnant* Meyer is listening to some of the broadcasts himself tonight, even though he desperately needs some sleep. This is the third night in a row that the first line of that *verdammte* Verlaine poem has been picked up. Meyer had been led to believe that the first line would only be transmitted once. Could these repetitions indicate some kind of operational cancellation? Or are the Allies just playing a ruse? Perhaps they are just making sure that the Resistance receives the word? That makes sense. Maybe it is a sort of "standby" indicator... Why couldn't intelligence work be easy once in a while?

Some time before 11 p.m., he is called to the phone by *Unteroffizier* Reichling. Listening to this excited voice, Meyer is told news that makes his heart begin thumping wildly. His signals unit has just intercepted a high-speed radio teletype dispatch from an American news agency, the Associated Press. The chilling message reads:

URGENT PRESS ASSOCIATED NYK FLASH—
EISENHOWER'S HQ ANNOUNCES ALLIED
LANDINGS IN FRANCE.[10]

As Meyer grabs his hat and hurries out of his office, he fights down the panic rising in his chest. The Allies have already landed? How? And where? Certainly not around his area. So where? And if the enemy has landed, why have they not sent that second Verlaine verse that Berlin had warned would come first? Had his team missed it? If so, he would be in deep trouble.

At any rate, he has to alert all the major headquarters immediately. But they will certainly want to know the location of the landing. What on earth should he tell them? A response of "I do not know" would not go over well at all. That would look really stupid on his part.

His staff alerted, he quickly scans the incoming message traffic for any other clues, but there are none. No radar reports, no sightings, no phone calls, nothing. Everything seems boringly normal.

The intercept simply has to be a ruse. The second part of the Verlaine message has not come yet. Besides, there is absolutely no indication of any trouble anywhere; just the normal enemy air activity. If there has been a landing, sure as hell *somebody* would have said something. In the absence of any corroborating reports to the intercept, he is forced to bet on Canaris's information being right. Of course, Berlin has been wrong so many times before. He has no idea how many intelligence reports he has received in the last few months, giving them information that had later proven to be either partially or (more often) completely wrong.

And yet…

He looks down at the message again. He makes his decision. He is going to go out on a very dangerous limb and hold off hitting the panic button for now. Still, he calls his superior, General Hoffmann,[11] and tells him of the news flash. Hoffmann reacts by telling Meyer to stay on it, and to damn well find out for sure. And that is just what he will have to do.

It is getting on to midnight. So much for his social life—or for sleep…

***

Today at the Berghof there is a wedding. Gretl Braun is to wed *SS-Obergruppenführer* Hermann Fegelein, a member of Heinrich Himmler's staff. The reception goes off elegantly, and afterward, photos are taken, followed by a party at the *Kehlsteinhaus*.[12] The stylishly dressed Eva Braun, *"Die Chefin"*[13] as the other ladies refer to her (with mixed emotions), is the darling of the evening, along with her sister Gretl, of course.

By 9:30 p.m., a good part of the Allied invasion fleet is either making its way through the heavy seas or is in the process of leaving the many English harbors. The weather has been rough and even seems to be getting worse. Some of the vessels have already been at sea for days now. Hundreds of other vessels are still in port awaiting either their turn to depart, or a temporary stand-down order from Eisenhower's headquarters.

The Supreme Commander has started a meeting with his command staff just north of Portsmouth at Southwick Manor, which is now Admiral Ramsay's headquarters. With them is SHAEF's head meteorologist, 43-year-old RAF Group Captain James M. Stagg, who has the misfortune of telling Eisenhower that weather conditions in the Channel will be too stormy to permit even minimal conditions for a landing on the 5th. The invasion must be called off and the fleet recalled. Eisenhower, a stern look of concentration on his face, sits immobile, weighing his options.

He decides to postpone his decision for just a few hours, in hopes that the weather might show signs of letting up.

---

1 *Heereswaffenamt*, the Armaments Office of the German Army. The two generals were its director, *General der Artillerie* Emil Leeb, and Operations Coordinator, *Generalleutnant* Erich Schneider.

2 At the end of May, *Luftflotte 3* only had on the books some 900 aircraft, of which only about 650 were actually deemed operational. General Kammhuber's *Luftflotte 5* in Norway had fewer than 200 serviceable aircraft.

3 First US Army Group—Patton's fictitious command, as part of Operation *Fortitude.*

4 Cramer of course had indeed been set up by the Allies. The tour had been a carefully staged drama, enacted for his benefit. See entry for May 23.

5 After more medical attention (he really did have an asthmatic condition, but it was not serious), Cramer was eventually assigned to Geyr von Schweppenburg's PanzerArmee West.

6 Rommel had already spoken to Jodl about taking a few days off twice by phone. Initially, he had suggested that he leave whenever circumstances permitted to call on the Führer at Obersalzberg and update him on the situation in the West. In a second conversation, he had reiterated the suggestion, and then had asked Jodl if he could coordinate this with a stopover at his home in Herrlingen, to celebrate his wife's birthday. Jodl had agreed, and had told him to just drive straight from there the next day to Berchtesgaden. Jodl tentatively set their conference up for June 7. Rommel had then spoken by phone about the idea to von Rundstedt, who was agreeable. So Rommel's request was no surprise to von Rundstedt, merely official formality.

7 This was exactly what Eisenhower, Bradley, and Montgomery had concluded.

8 See entry for May 29.

9 When the Americans landed at Omaha on D-Day, instead of coming up against one battalion of the inferior and undersized 716th Infantry, they instead came up against three entrenched full battalions of the veteran 352nd. To make things worse, the addition of the 352nd to the coastline allowed the 716th to shorten its own line, which in turn resulted in most of its troops being able to man the positions facing the British and Canadians at Gold, Juno, and Sword.

10 The broadcast was logged in the US at 4:39 a.m. EST. That would make it 11:39 p.m. British Double Summer Time or 10:39 p.m. German Central Time (see note 1, page 12).

11 *Generalleutnant* Rudolf Hoffmann, Fifteenth Army Chief of Staff.

12 This is the Kehlstein tea house, which came to be known as the *Adlerhaus*—Hitler's Eagle's Nest.

13 The female equivalent of "The Chief," the common informal title for the Führer.

Sunday, June 4

In the dark early morning hours of Sunday, the fierce storm that had come up the day before continues to rage across the Channel. The Allied invasion fleet, slogging through the howling winds and stormy seas, struggles to make headway. If the landing is to begin on schedule when the weather (hopefully) gets better, they will have to continue on through crashing waves for another whole day before H-Hour comes on the morning of June 5.

At Southwick Manor, Eisenhower meets around 4:30 a.m. (BDST[1]) with his staff. The Supreme Allied Commander is briefed on the bad weather by Group Captain Stagg and his meteorological staff. Eisenhower is reluctantly but defiantly told by one of Stagg's three separate team leaders, Sverere Petterssen,[2] that the weather is still too rough for a landing; the invasion must be postponed until conditions improve. Another briefing is given by the head of the American weather team, 38-year-old Colonel Irving Krick, who claims that in his opinion, conditions are good enough to go. In the end, Krick's position is dismissed as too optimistic.[3]

Eisenhower ponders the three choices open to him. He can postpone the assault for one day and pray real hard for a better break in the weather (and that his five-thousand-ship fleet is by some miracle not detected at sea). Or, he can move back the invasion two weeks to the next period of low tides at dawn, again hope for good weather, and if so fly his airborne troops in on a moonless, perhaps cloudy night. His third choice is to call the whole thing off and reschedule the invasion for July—to hope for better weather at that time, while risking both detection of his plans and a blow to Allied morale.

Montgomery tells him that he's for going ahead anyway, no matter what the weather report says. Several other senior members agree.

Eisenhower ponders the many complicated factors facing him, and at 5:15, he makes his decision. He elects to postpone the landings for 24 hours, hoping that the weather might break enough so that they can go on the 6th. All Allied radar jamming operations are called off, so that those stations in the German naval radar network that are still up do not set off any alarms.

The codeword "Ripcord 24" is sent to the Allied fleet approaching the French coast in the heavy seas. The word goes out: D-Day has been postponed for at least a day.

Most of the few thousand ships already at sea immediately begin to turn around and head back to port. Inevitably, as things often happen in war despite the best of plans, some units do not receive the recall, even though it is repeated to make sure that everyone gets notified. Everyone does not. One force of minesweepers is only 35 miles from the beaches when they finally get the word.

Another slow convoy of some 135 vessels,[4] Task Group U2a out of Salcombe and Dartmouth,[5] sails as a part of Force U (slated for Utah beach). It carries elements of the 4th Infantry Division in dozens of landing vessels and their escorts. Not receiving the recall, it sails onward towards France at six knots, totally unaware that the invasion has been delayed. Further radio signals to the convoy commander prove to be fruitless.

At last, in desperation, two destroyers turn around to bring back the runaway convoy before it reaches the French coast and tips the enemy off about the whole operation. Unfortunately, because of the stormy seas, the escorts are unable to find the missing convoy.

At the same time, aircraft are also dispatched to the search, braving the early morning tempestuous elements in a gallant attempt to locate these ships. But time is starting to run out. With the weather bad, it will take the planes some time to reach and then find the convoy, even though the search is much more effective from the air. And after the ships are found, the plane may have a problem convincing the convoy commander that the delay has indeed been made, and to turn the convoy around—all before the vessels are detected from the French coast.

After a couple hours of desperate searches by air and by sea, the wayward convoy is finally spotted by a British Walrus reconnaissance biplane.[6] It is now dawn, and the convoy has traveled almost 100 miles and is some 30 miles south of the Isle of Wight.

The pilot immediately sees that the ships are still dutifully headed for their assigned positions off the Normandy coast, struggling forward across the high waves. Frenzied signaling from the aircraft does not sway the convoy commodore. He knows that the Germans (as he had been briefed), using captured American planes, could quite possibly pull a stunt just like that. His orders are to ignore any such local signals, and that is exactly what he does. After all, his contingent of men and cargo will be desperately needed at Utah beach tomorrow morning.

The frantic pilot braves the storm's winds and dives the little pusher-engine aircraft down to a scant hundred feet above the water. Through a cracked open window in the plane, he drops a signed, coded message in a canister down at the commodore's ship. The canister just misses the vessel and plummets into the heavy seas.

The convoy sails on.

There are a number of German radio stations working in the early hours. Many have been recently hit by enemy raids, including the key listening station at Ferme d'Urville.[7] This is the headquarters for the German "Y" Service, their main radio intercepting organization in Western Europe. This station, like several others along the English Channel, is still operational, although barely. Luckily, tonight there is not much enemy traffic on the air.

Several undamaged radar stations are also routinely sweeping the Channel that evening. Their signals clear significantly after a few hours and are now relatively unmolested by enemy jamming stations across the Channel. It is just as well. The German radar units are having enough problems as it is. All night, the winds and heavy waves have been creating many false echoes on their scopes, coming and going as the sea and wind patterns constantly change. So tonight, true radar returns off vessels at sea are particularly hard to detect.

At least one radar station though, picks up a few formations of aircraft headed for the Straits of Dover. No doubt, an enemy bombing raid. The station reports them and their position, and then tracks them as they fly southeast across the Channel. The targets turn out to be coastal batteries at Calais and Wimereux.

Another operating station begins to detect an oddly large amount of surface activity in the western part of the Channel. Careful analysis shows that this does not look like any natural formation of false echoes brought on by the weather. No, something seems to be out there.

The radar report is immediately routed to Admiral Hennecke's naval headquarters in Cherbourg. The other operational radar stations are all alerted, and the one tracking the echoes is told to stay with the signal and to advise headquarters immediately if the contact pattern heads for the French coast.

The dauntless British pilot circling over the wayward contingent of Force U2a does not give up—way too much is at stake. He somehow has to convince this rogue convoy to turn back. Hurriedly, he writes out his own note to the convoy. The co-pilot sticks it into their last canister, and they dive down, hoping this time to somehow drop the container onto the commodore's ship. The aircraft makes a very low pass and miraculously, in this second try, the canister lands on the deck of the flagship.

The wrapped package is taken to the convoy commander, who opens it and reads the scribbled message inside. While the convoy sails on, he studies its meaning, trying hard to determine if it is genuine, the nagging worry of what-ifs now foremost on his mind. He realizes that if the message is authentic, he could quite possibly ruin the entire operation—the invasion itself.

The pilot, now low on fuel, is forced to return home, cursing the storm and that stupid convoy commander down there. Frustrated, the radio operator transmits the convoy's position back to base.

After fifteen minutes of deliberation, the still-skeptical commodore, having discussed the issue at length with his officers, at last grudgingly admits that the message just might be on the level. Reluctantly, he breaks radio silence and calls his debarkation port for a confirmation of the delay. They are now just 36 miles from the coast of Normandy. The commodore is directed by a distraught, nearly frantic harbormaster to turn about immediately and head back for England. The order goes out to the vessels, and slowly, cumbrously, the multi-columned formations at last begin to come about. Bucking the rolling swells, the convoy finally completes its turn and makes its sluggish journey in the heavy seas northwestward. It is almost 9 a.m.[8]

As dawn nears, a few German coastal radar operators are tracking the set of contacts they had picked up a few hours before. The plotting crews are starting to get tense as the formation appears to be making its way southeast across the Channel. The contacts seem to be on a course for somewhere in the Seine Bay. One watch commander, edgy because he knows what this many contacts implies, has kept his eye on the blips over the shoulder of his seated operator. Unfortunately, there is no way that the contacts can be checked out. The bad weather has kept the German outpost ships and minelayers in harbor, and the few Luftwaffe recon aircraft still in Western France are grounded.

About 40 minutes later, the tracked positions of these unknown contacts (and there have to be many, because of the size of the return) slow and then become stationary. Gradually they begin moving back northwest again towards Weymouth Bay. After another hour, the fuzzy echoes become lost in the radar returns from England's ground interference, the rain, and the choppy waves.

Since the blips have disappeared, the radar crews are eventually told to stand down. Perhaps this was a crazy Allied exercise in the tempest. Maybe the enemy navy was testing its radar capabilities. Or possibly just a case of false echoes from the storm seas. Nevertheless, a report will have to be written and sent through proper channels, although in light of the results, it will probably now be filed and forgotten. Admiral Hennecke's Headquarters at Cherbourg is not contacted again.

The Allies are very lucky. The rogue convoy remains undetected.

***

At the Army Signals Interception Center near Fifteenth Army headquarters, a bleary-eyed, tired but happy *Oberstleutnant* Helmuth Meyer emerges from the communications bunker that he has stayed awake in most of the night. Turning to his on-duty sergeant, he gives some last-minute instructions, and then wearily trudges off to get some sleep.

Admiral Canaris' predictions still appear to be right. The second Verlaine verse has not been transmitted, and despite that tremendous scare that the American news flash had given him last night, nothing unusual has happened.[9] The break of day has thankfully revealed no enemy fleet off the French coast. Just a lot of bad weather. Still, God only knows what tonight will bring.

If he only knew…

***

At La Roche-Guyon, dawn is gray and misty. The town is still wet in the aftermath of the brutal storm that had first hit the Channel. Torrents of rain and heavy winds have ravaged the dry land. The worst of the storm for now has abated inland, and in the fog, the château stands like something out of a gothic horror story. The road in front of it is as usual devoid of traffic, more so because it is Sunday. The countryside is deserted, except for the sentries in their camouflaged capes dotted throughout the area. In a short while the hour will change, and the bell in the Church of St. Samson in the town will sound the Angelus, to let the villagers know that it is time to stop a moment for silent prayer.

Rommel is in his study, reading the latest messages. He has been up since 3 a.m., listening to the early morning sounds outside. It had still been raining while he was in the bathroom. Now the rain has subsided somewhat.

The weather forecasters predict that bad weather will continue for at least another three or four days, with heavy swells and rain over the English Channel. The winds are between Force 5 and 6 and forecast to go up to Force 6 at the Pas-de-Calais, and up to Force 7 at Cherbourg. Gales in the Channel average 48 km/hr. The heavy cloud base is low—275 to 550 meters—and the storm in the Channel is producing waves over two meters high. The Kriegsmarine report also details the stormy seas in the Channel, and that it will be at least two weeks before meteorological conditions and the tides are again right for an invasion. Altogether a lousy time for an invasion.

He picks up the latest situation report:

> The continuation and systematic increase of enemy air attacks and more intensive minelaying in our harbors with improved mining equipment indicate an advance in the enemy's readiness for invasion. Constructional work on the defense front is being impeded by further deterioration in the transport situation and in fuel supplies (shortages of coal).
>
> Constant enemy air attacks obviously concentrated on bridges over the Seine, Oise, and to a certain extent, over the Aisne, also coastal defenses in the Dunkirk-Dieppe sector and on the northern and eastern sides of the Cotentin.
>
> Attempts to cripple rail transport continue, with raids on marshaling yards and on locomotives. Whereas attacks on bridges have led to destruction or serious damage to all the crossings over the Seine between Paris and Rouen, damage inflicted on coastal defenses is still comparatively small.

He puts down the report and stands, rubbing his eyes. He yawns, stretches his arms, and winces as a dull pain runs through his lower back. His lumbago is acting up again. He glances at his watch. It is almost 6 a.m.

He wanders over to the French window on his left and glances out through the rain rivulets trickling down the glass pane. Peering into the gloom of the early morning, he makes out what is left of his rose garden on the terrace. His poor roses suffered badly in last night's storm, and now pedals, twigs, and broken plants lie haphazardly all over the veranda.

Bolstered by the bad weather and reassured by the Luftwaffe official weather reports predicting continued rain and winds, he makes what history will record as one of the unluckiest decisions in his career. He decides to take the trip home.[10] It will give him a quick rest before the main event begins, which could be coming up. Besides, he wants to try once more to persuade Hitler to give him control of the panzers.

He leaves his study and sees Lang waiting for him in the hallway.

"Ah, good morning, Lang," he greets his aide warmly. "Are we ready to go?"

Lang smiles and replied, "*Jawohl, Herr Feldmarschall.*" They wander off together for breakfast. Walking into the dining room, they are warmly greeted by the senior staff members. As they sit down (Rommel taking his customary seat at the head of the dining table) and are immediately served, the seven staff officers continue talking. Rommel occasionally joins in with a remark or two. They discuss his upcoming meeting with the Führer. General Meise reminds him, "And make sure, *Feldmarschall,* that you get me more mines."

They discuss the main goals of the meeting. First, they must convince the Führer of the seriousness of the situation in the West. Second, to get the supplies that they desperately need to prepare to meet the landings. Third, they must convince the High Command to release the reserve panzers to them, so that they can be repositioned much closer to the coast.

Rommel listens patiently to his staff as he sips his tea and spreads some honey on his buttered slice of white bread. Once in a while, he checks the time. The conversation eventually becomes informal. He feels a bit tense about the trip, but stays in good humor. At one point during the meal, noting the quality of the food on their plates, he looks down the table at his aide and asks mischievously, "Lang, do *all* the men at my headquarters get the same sort of breakfast?"

Lang smiles back at him. "*Jawohl, Feldmarschall,*" he replies, "But it isn't served quite as pleasantly as this." They all laugh affably.

With breakfast over, he checks his watch at 6:47 a.m., and suddenly announces, "Gentlemen, here I go."

Rommel leaves the dining room heads for the main entrance, his officers filing out behind him. Other staff members have gathered along the corridor and stairs to wish him well. Walking slowly, he takes the opportunity to shake their hands and murmur an occasional comment to one or another.

Accompanying Rommel for the trip is his Operations chief, von Tempelhoff. They will travel in a two-car convoy. No flying home this time. The Führer has insisted that if general officers want to fly anywhere, they have to ride in an aircraft with at least three engines, and be accompanied by an adequate fighter escort. Rommel does not want to tie up so many critical aircraft, especially with the heightened enemy air activity. Anyway, he prefers to travel by car.

Lang will ride with Rommel and Corporal Daniel. The newly promoted von Tempelhoff, on his way home to see his wife in Bavaria, will ride in the second vehicle. driven by a sergeant. As the field marshal has ordered, their leaving is a secret outside the headquarters. No one has been informed of their trip, much less their itinerary. Rommel's Horch will not fly his customary field marshal's banner on the front bumper. And he has insisted that the two cars will have no escort to attract attention. With any luck, he will get home by mid-afternoon.

Outside, Rommel turns to von Tempelhoff and invites him to ride in the front car with him and Lang until their turnoff. Von Tempelhoff's driver can follow in the second car behind them. The colonel accepts the invitation, and climbs into the back of the Horch. Lang, carrying a thermos of consommé and some small sandwiches for them to eat along the way, gets in after him and closes the door.

Rommel then turns to Speidel and says a few parting words.[11] They shake hands gravely, and pause briefly. Speidel looks at his superior solemnly and says quietly, "Good luck."

Rommel smiles slightly, and then climbs into the front next to Daniel. He momentarily turns around to look at Lang and von Tempelhoff in the back. He beams as he raises the shoebox, to show them that he has not forgotten Lucie's birthday present.

They are finally ready to leave. "We can go now, Daniel," Rommel tells his driver. It is about 7 a.m. as they leave the château for Germany.[12]

***

With Rommel having departed, the empty morning seems to drag on at La Roche-Guyon. The weather continues to be bad for the rest of the day. And with the field marshal gone, this Sunday is like a holiday routine. A couple of incoming calls deal with whether or not inland shipping should operate in the bad weather.

Speidel dispatches a message to OKW, reporting that *Heeresgruppe B* might stand down its two armies during the bad weather, so that they might get some rest after the low-grade alert they had been on for a while now. He also adds that enemy air activities still indicate the Straits of Dover as the likeliest landing area.

***

Generalfeldmarschall von Rundstedt begins writing his weekly estimate to OKW in the afternoon. After going over the strengths of the panzer units, he turns to the infantry. Those that had been drafted in the 22nd recruit wave have fleshed out several of his corps. The training of those in the 25th wave is progressing acceptably.[13]

He quickly tires of the details. Jotting most of the major points down, he sets the report aside. He and Blumentritt will finish it on Monday, the 5th.

***

Along the eastern shore of the Cotentin peninsula, more pigeon target practice. Today, Sergeant Günther Witte, a crew member of the nearby 1262nd Army Coastal Regiment, takes aim at a pigeon headed out towards the Channel, flying close to the ground. Witte, a crack shot, fires his rifle and incredibly hits the bird, which falls to the ground. Investigating his catch, he finds a small metal capsule attached to one of the bird's legs. Inside the capsule is a coded message written on a small scrap of rice paper, along with what appears to be the dispositions of the German units on the peninsula.

Witte turns the capsule in, and a report is filed to go up the 709th Infantry Division chain of command.

***

Admiral Krancke at *Marinegruppenkommandos West* is finishing up his latest situation report. His available forces look pathetic. Less than half a dozen fleet torpedo boats, some minesweeper flotillas, several score auxiliary craft, and his biggest punch, five squadrons of S-boats.

There are also the U-boats. Some three dozen are operational in the Bay of Biscay. Eight of them have the new schnorkel. Another 15 coastal units are in immediate range of the English Channel and can strike at the invasion fleet once the landings begin. He cannot though, direct and coordinate their attacks; the U-boats are under Dönitz's command.

Mining operations have been pathetic. His minelayers have only been able to put down three minefields this month, all near the Pas-de-Calais. Mining around the Cotentin peninsula has hardly begun. Their plan to replace the mid-Channel minefields laid last year had been postponed a few times and was finally called off in March, partly because there just were not enough mines available, and partly because intensive Allied radar operations would have spotted the operations and easily noted the areas for avoidance or for sweeping.

Krancke feels that that their minefields in deep water will probably be virtually obsolete by the middle of this month. It is true that a few simple minefields were laid in the Bay of the Seine a couple months ago, but they were only designed to be effective for a little over a month. With supplies short, Krancke determines that if the invasion were to come now, patrol boat mining operations would only provide "nonessential" help against the enemy.

On the positive side, the recent enemy bombings have not damaged his land units as badly as he had feared. His radar stations for instance, have not all been knocked out, not by a long shot. And only eight naval guns have been put out of action, five in the *Kanalküste*, and three in the Normandy area. He is sure that an invasion will not come until a widespread, aggressive bombing campaign is carried out against the coastal batteries. And that is just not happening, although recent raids indicated that this strategy might have already started.

Krancke states in his report:

> The anticipated mining operations to renew the flanking minefields in the Channel have not been carried out. On the way to the rendezvous at Le Havre, T-24 fell behind because of damage from [a] mine, "*Greif*" was sunk by bombs, "*Kondor*" and "*Falke*" were damaged by mines, the former seriously. The 6th Minesweeping Flotilla likewise on its way to Le Havre to carry out KMA operations reached port with only one of its six boats, one having been sunk by torpedoes and the other four having fallen out through mine damage, air attack or sea damage. The laying of KMA mines out of Le Havre therefore could not be carried out."

Krancke's report's summary accurately reflects his views. If the invasion comes, he believes it will probably be at the Pas-de-Calais—that is, *if* it comes. Like Rommel, he is seriously beginning to doubt that the invasion will take place at all… The furor across the English Channel is starting to look like a gigantic, elaborate deception, just to keep them armed along the French coast, and their divisions away from the other fronts, where they would do some good. And the enemy might very well keep up this façade for many months yet, continuing to prepare. Germany would have to maintain some sixty divisions just sitting along the coast, while meanwhile it would continue losing in all the other theaters. Krancke sees this as a solid strategy, because eventually, the German army groups in the West would get so weakened from transfers to the other, threatened fronts that an invasion here would be sure to succeed.

Yes, the admiral can feel himself starting to relax. The enemy does not look like he is going to come soon. He glances again at that meteorological report. And especially not in bad weather.

When he receives a message from *Fremde Heeres West* that the first part of the Verlaine poem and a number of other important personnel messages have gone out to the Resistance. Krancke writes in his war diary:

> *Although it is hardly to be assumed that the invasion will be announced in advance, it must be admitted that these "messages personnels" would certainly cause acts of sabotage in connection with the traffic and communications network, and also insurrections, all of which would pave the way for the invasion proper.*

Krancke issues one last set of orders before he departs for Bordeaux to wind up some mining operations in the Bay of Biscay. Because the weather is scheduled to be bad for the next few days, he suspends minelaying operations. Thinking about it, he decides to add naval patrols to the order. After all, there will be nothing out there to see in those heavy seas and high winds except rain, so why risk losing an S-boat? He has damned few left as it is.

The Allies have had a distinct advantage over the Germans for weather predictions, and this will prove to be crucial now. The Germans no longer have meteorological facilities and vessels as far west as the Allies do. Their Greenland, Spitzbergen, and Jan Mayen Island weather stations have been captured, evacuated, or destroyed. Their weather ships in the Atlantic have all been captured or sunk. They therefore cannot know that an abrupt weather change has taken place in the Atlantic, and that a significant break between storm fronts rapidly approaches the Channel, It is a break that will bring minimal weather conditions needed for an invasion.

Today, Seventh Army commander General Dollmann is having lunch with five of his officers. Edgar Feuchtinger has dropped in as well. The prevailing feeling at the lunch table is one of optimism. Most believe that the long-awaited invasion will not even come this year. The Allies would have launched it in May, when the weather was great. June is a tricky month, as evidenced by the current storm.

One or two officers sitting at the table do not share this optimistic belief and express concerns about the invasion date. But all of them are pretty sure that nothing is going to happen for a few weeks. And certainly not with this storm brewing in the Channel.

Just to be sure though, Max Pemsel has started making a complete survey of the Normandy defenses.

The officers finish eating and sit around afterwards chatting some more. Feuchtinger will finally return to his headquarters at St. Pierre around 6 p.m. Dollmann plans on retiring early, because he is going on an inspection tour in the morning.

***

Adolf Hitler is still enjoying the beautiful, idyllic scenery of Obersalzberg. In one of today's meetings, he and Albert Speer discuss turning over aircraft armament production to Speer's own War Ministry. Göring will be furious. Too bad. He is not the Führer's favorite son these days. Production of the V-1 is going well, so today, Hitler orders the unit preparing the weapons to stand by for operations in the next week or so.

Later that afternoon, Josef Tito, the Slovakian prime minister, visits the Berghof, and Hitler brags to him about the new weapon. "If the British came to us now with any kind of peace-feelers," he boasts, "I would prefer to tell them to keep their feelers…" He pauses. "At least until the invasion."

***

Rommel's two cars have traveled along the Seine River to Paris, and from there, take the main highway towards Châlons-sur-Marne. They continue across France, through lovely Saverne, and eventually come into beautiful Stuttgart. There, Lang parts from them and, in a change of plans, takes the second car, originally assigned to von Tempelhoff, so that he can have some type of immediate transportation. Lang heads for his 400-year-old townhouse in Gemünd. Daniel drives on, passing the Herrlingen turnoff, and goes into Ulm. There they drop off von Tempelhoff and his driver at the railroad station, where they will catch the next train for von Tempelhoff's hometown of Munich. Daniel then turns the Horch around, and drives the field marshal back to his townhouse in Herrlingen.

They pull into his driveway around 7 p.m. that evening. The stiff-jointed field marshal gets out of the car and stretches. Elbo is excited when he spots him, and begins barking excitedly and jumping up and down, his tail wagging eagerly. Lucie warmly meets him at the door. Aldinger, his aide in residence, helps Daniel bring the bags in, while Rommel goes upstairs and changes.

Lucie of course is glad to see him. She often worries about him, especially when he runs around from one hotspot to the next. She knows that he thinks of himself as being charmed, but she often frets that one day his luck might turn on him. And now he looks very tired and spent from the tension of his responsibilities. Well, she is making his favorite dish for him—Swabian-style *Spaetzle mit Kalbsbraten.*[14] That would help.

Their son Manfred joins them. Now over six feet tall, the fifteen-year-old towers over his father. His thick glasses go well with his quiet demeanor and his dark hair. He speaks comfortably with his father in his own strong Swabian accent.

They sit in the living room for a bit as the field marshal unwinds from the trip. He tells them about the upcoming visit with the Führer, and that troubles Lucie. They discuss the issue at length.

Later, they sit down to dinner. Rommel comments favorably on the casserole. Since neither he nor Lucie has a much of a taste for wine, they instead sip on some blackberry and cherry fruit juices with the meal.

After they have eaten and their aides have cleaned up the dining room, the field marshal and his wife sit down again and relax. Manfred goes to his room to read, while the two of them talk about his upcoming meeting with the Führer. He confides in her about his hopes and expectations of the visit. She has always understood and made an excellent sounding board for him. He admits to her that he has worried for months now about his degenerating command capabilities as the war has turned steadily against Germany. He worries that, if the invasion fails, Hitler will never surrender and will drag the country down in ruins.

Lucie sympathizes, telling him that the Führer will surely listen to his concerns. He looks at her pointedly, and she shrugs. The Führer, brilliant as he is, has a screw loose somewhere in his head.

She asks if he should even be away at this time. He reassures her. The weather is bad, even if there is a full moon. The latest reports seemed to confirm this. Enemy activities levels are relatively low. So he does not expect any attacks at this time. Not until at least mid-June, or more likely, early July, the next full moon.[15]

At 9 p.m., Rommel phones Speidel at La Roche-Guyon to tell him that he has arrived safely and shared a nice evening with his family. Speidel has little to report, and so the call is not long. Rommel tells him that he will phone in an update on his itinerary as soon as he finds out from Schmundt when his appointment with the Führer will take place.

After the call, Rommel talks some more with Lucie. They turn in around 10 p.m. He has no doubt that he will sleep well tonight.

9:30 p.m., BDST. Eisenhower, dressed as always in his olive-green battle-dress uniform, walks into the library of Southwick Manor. He and his staff must decide whether to give the word to start Operation Neptune, or to delay the invasion again, this time to at least mid-late June, or maybe even mid-July.

Chief Meteorologist Staggs starts off by reporting that if the invasion had taken place on the 5th, it would have been a total catastrophe.[16] *He then delivers the good news that electrifies the tension in the room; an upcoming 3-day period of barely tolerable conditions is still scheduled to arrive early in the morning, and at the moment appears to be on track. The rain will subside, and the 25–30 knot winds will abate some. Clouds will be heavy, but not continuous. And by Tuesday morning, visibility should be good enough to allow naval fire support to spot their targets. All three of Staggs's weather teams agree on this.*

Eisenhower is now faced with a tremendous decision. Another postponement now could easily spell disaster. The next tolerable tidal period would start on June 19; but it would be relatively moonless.

A postponement would also create a logistical nightmare. Those men already loaded onto the hundreds of transports would have to disembark again. In most cases, they would be unloading onto piers and assembly zones already crowded with other units that were slated to follow them ashore in France. Complex schedules would have to be refigured. And of course, morale would take a big dip.

On the other hand, there is no promise that this short break in the weather will be as good as predicted by the American weather team, nor that it will last. To make matters worse, postponing the invasion by 24 hours has meant that, should he give the word to now go on the 6th, low tide will now occur about an hour later, coming now at 5:15a.m.. The American landings will therefore be at least an hour later, coming between 6:15 and 6:45 BDST.[17]

Then there is security. Waiting until July would add more enormous risks to keep the time and place of the invasion secret, not to mention giving the enemy more precious time to prepare. In the next two weeks, the Germans could learn of the invasion site, and the critical element of surprise would be lost. An intercepted "Ultra" message gives the Allies the latest Luftwaffe weather report, which calls for more bad weather. The Germans will not be looking for an invasion at this time. So the critical element of surprise (assuming the enemy does not know about the invasion date and location) would for now be solidly on their side.

As the debate goes on, Admiral Ramsay[18] *breaks in with a time concern. If they are indeed going to go on the 6th, some units in various distant harbors will have to be notified within the next half hour. It is because of refueling considerations, Ramsay explains. If these forces sail any later and are recalled, they would not be able to return and be refueled for a possible landing on Wednesday, the 7th.*

Eisenhower turns to each of his senior commanders to get their opinion. His chief of staff, Bedell Smith, thinks they should proceed with the landings. The air commanders, Air Chief Marshals Tedder and Leigh-Mallory, are not so sure. Montgomery, like yesterday, wants to go. They discuss it some more.

The room finally falls still as Eisenhower, sitting with his hands clasped, stares down at the green baize table. The silence stretches on as the men look at him, waiting for his historic decision.

At 9:45 p.m., Eisenhower finally makes up his mind. Still staring at the table, he slowly says, "I am quite positive we must give the order... I don't like it—but there it is." Looking up to the men, he concludes solemnly, "I don't see how we can possibly do anything else."

They will have a final commanders' meeting at 4 a.m. That will be the last opportunity they will have to break off the operation. But there is little chance of that now.

---

1   That was 3:30 a.m., German Central Time.

2   Stagg oversaw the efforts of three separate forecasting teams. This key briefing for the British was given by 46-year-old Norwegian meteorologist Sverere Petterssen. Living in the United States when the war had broken out, he had gone to Britain and had helped in weather planning for Allied bombing raids. Now he predicted continued bad weather for the next day.

3   Interestingly, Eisenhower also received a cable from the Russians advising him to postpone as well. An invasion later in the month of course, would have been timed with their own mighty summer offensive, which began on June 22.

4   Sources vary on the count. One makes it 150 vessels. Another source says 77 British LCT, 61 American LCT, 4 escorts and a rescue tug.

5   Located near the southwest tip of England in Devon, about 20 miles southeast of Plymouth.

6   The British Supermarine Walrus was a small, antiquated single-engine amphibious biplane designed strictly for air reconnaissance. Used mostly by the Fleet Air Arm, it was the first British aircraft to feature a fully retractable main undercarriage, with either an all-metal fuselage (Walrus I) or all wood (Walrus II). First flown in 1933 and outdated by the middle of the war, they still were valuable for patrolling the western approaches to Great Britain. Each carried a pilot, copilot, and a crew of one or two airmen. The Walrus was only 10 meters long and had a wingspan of 14 meters, with a single pusher engine mounted in the rear of the top wing. It had a top speed of just 215km/hour and a range of about 960km. Production was halted in 1944, by which time a total of about 740 had been built.

7   On the night of June 1, a group of 200 Halifaxes and Pathfinder Mosquitoes had attacked this station near Cherbourg, but had been unable to score any hits because of the haze and cloud cover. The target was again hit on the night of June 3.

8   Operational Report, USS PC.484.

9   See entry for June 3. The shocked Germans finally concluded that the transmission was either an error or a hoax. It was in fact an accident. A 22-year-old teletype dispatcher in the Associated Press had been making practice perforated tapes on a disconnected teletype to improve her typing speed in preparation for the actual landings. An editor had interrupted her with a report to transmit immediately, a summary of a recently monitored Soviet war report on the radio. Not realizing that a fake message was started on the tape, she dutifully typed out the report, and then ran the tape on a live teletype, thus immediately transmitting both messages to the world. Of course, the announcement was quickly noticed and cut off midway through the Russian report. However, the damage had been done. The dispatcher, when told what had happened and its enormity, collapsed and had to be sedated. Despite the mishap, she was not fired. Eisenhower's aide, reacting to the incident, was not bothered. Eisenhower, he commented, had bigger worries.

The details of this unusual story are covered in my book, *Bust Eisenhower: The Message that Almost Ruined D-Day.*

10 The perhaps surprising controversy as to when Rommel left for home has pretty much been settled. The most authoritative writers of the invasion—Ruge, Irving, Ryan, Fraser, Reuth, Toland (*Adolf Hitler,* pp.890)—put his departure date at June 4. Others have stated that it was June 5, including, surprisingly, Rommel's own chief of staff, Hans Speidel (*Invasion 1944*). Other authors simply leave the date out (such as pioneer biographer Desmond Young in *The Desert Fox,* and Harrison in his exhaustive *Cross Channel Attack*). Most eyewitnesses though (Lang, Tempelhoff, Ruge, and Rommel's own wife and son), as well as the Army Group B War Diary, confirm that his departure date was indeed the 4th.

11 Admiral Ruge wrote that Rommel had at some time recently thoroughly discussed with Speidel the measures to be taken in case of an attack. That statement could be given a critical eye, considering Speidel's actions two days later in the early morning hours of the 6th.

12 The details of Rommel's trip to Germany at this momentous time are covered in my book entitled *Rommel's Fateful Trip Home: June 4th to June 6th, 1944,* 2014.

13 When the Reich began calling up men in 1939, it was carried out in waves. From each wave called up, the men were either assigned to existing infantry units or used to create new ones. There were some 35 waves called up during the war. From the 22nd wave, called up in November 1943, five new infantry divisions were formed. The 25th wave, called up in the first two months of 1944, created six.

14 Roast veal stew with German noodles.

15 Rommel once told Lang, "If [*the invasion*] is going to come at all, it will be around the middle of June, sometime around the 20th, when the moon is full." Attacking during a full moon was a pattern that he had noticed in North Africa. The British seemed to prefer it, and he often did too. He had expressed this idea to his wife and son as well.

16 Amazingly, decades later, the American weather team leader, Irving Krick, was still claiming that if his optimistic predictions had been followed and the invasion launched on June 5, it would have been just as successful.

17 Many sources have indicated that the Allies (specifically, the Americans) hit the beaches exactly at low tide. This is very close. The first waves of Americans came ashore at or near 6:30 a.m., BDST. According to data taken from the English Channel Handbook prepared by the British Admiralty and included with all US Navy operational orders, low tide for June 6 at St.-Vaast-la-Hougue (north of Utah beach) was to be at 6:04 a.m. and again at 6:28 p.m. High tide was to occur at 11:04 a.m. and 11:40 p.m.. At Port-en-Bessin (east of Omaha beach), these figures respectively were 6:21 a.m. hours and 6:45 p.m. for low tide, and 11:36 a.m. and 11:57 p.m. for high tide. Thus, extrapolating, low tide on Utah beach would be about 6:12 a.m., and about 6:18 a.m. for Omaha beach. Low tide at the British beaches would occur around 6:26 a.m.

18 Admiral Sir Bertram Ramsay, the Commander-in-Chief of the Allied Naval Expeditionary Force.

Monday, June 5

Shortly before 1 a.m., two Royal Navy midget submarines, X20 and X23, surface off the Normandy coast. With heavy seas in the Channel, no German patrol boats are in the area.

These two small five-man subs are the first Allied vessels to reach the invasion site. Their mission will be to guide the many incoming vessels and landing craft to the British and Canadian landing areas.[1] Having arrived at their target destination at daybreak on the 4th after a long, 36-hour trip across the Channel (in bad weather), they have quietly sat submerged on the bottom all day, waiting to go into action.

Now as they make final preparations for their critical mission, they receive a coded message: "Ripcord 24." The invasion has been postponed for at least a day. So they will have to submerge again, and sit on the bottom of the English Channel for another 24 hours before they can surface and find out if the invasion is on.

Eisenhower has decided to launch the invasion. The orders go out at once to the Allied fleets. Nearly six thousand ships of all types set sail once again from various points all over England in the early morning hours. Spearheading the task forces are waves of various-sized minesweepers. There are over 290, including the ones already working at sea. They must all clear wide channels through the German minefields, so that the task forces can safely pass through.

The 1,200-plus warships in these fleets include seven battleships[2]. Four are British: HMS Nelson, Rodney, Ramilles, and Warspite. Three are American: the USS Arkansas, the old Texas, and the illustrious Pearl Harbor veteran, Nevada.

Steaming besides them are numerous smaller escorts, including 23 cruisers, over a hundred destroyers and destroyer escorts, some 360 corvettes and motor torpedo boats, and several hundred frigates, sloops, cutters, buoy layers, gunboats, and many others.

Sailing with these warships are the vital key to the entire campaign: the invasion fleet. This assault flotilla consists of some 4,000 amphibious assault and special purpose vessels, and includes some 1,500 landing craft.[3]

At 4:15 a.m. BDST,[4] Eisenhower meets one more time with his meteorologist, Captain Staggs, and his team leaders. Stag reconfirms his assessment of the two-day break in the bad weather. Though conditions will then get worse, he explains, they will not get bad enough to stop invasion supplies from landing.

This is the final moment. If he is going to postpone the invasion again, it must be done now. After some deliberation, the room gets quiet. Finally, Eisenhower decides. He stands up, looks at his senior officers and says, "Okay… We'll go."

The others immediately stand up and start to leave. He orders the "It's on" messages be sent to confirm the invasion date for the 6th by quipping, "Let 'er rip."

The others scurry out of the room, a thousand tasks to perform.

For the Allies, there is now no turning back.[5]

Oberst Professor Dr. Walther Stöbe is in his central office, studying the latest weather conditions. He is the chief meteorological officer for not just for the *Luftflotte 3* headquarters in Paris, but for all air units in Western Europe.

His command center is located on the second floor of the Luxembourg Palace in Paris. It is an ornate building, and even though the Nazi flag flies out front, the Germans, in deference to French sensitivity, have been ordered never to take a picture of the building with the flag flying. Stöbe does not see how that makes much difference, what with the many German military personnel that come and go through its doors.

Today, the weather, as anticipated, is bad. The Wehrmacht generally assumes that no invasion will come if visibility is only a couple of miles and the wind strength is at least 4 on the Beaufort scale, with the sea at Force 4 or 5, making waves between 1.5 to 2.5 meters high. Occasional weather recon flights over the North Sea are made, but as a rule, they are next to useless to predict what might be coming out of the west. And there are currently no U-boats in the area to take meteorological measurements. Lacking any evidence to the contrary, it looks like the winds will continue to be high, and that the sky will get increasingly cloudy. And it is going to continue to rain.

Reports record the winds around Cherbourg near Force 7 and at Calais near Force 6. There are no indications at this time that these conditions will change anytime soon. The cloud base is less than a thousand feet, lousy conditions for any tactical aerial operations, and certainly prohibitive for any sort of airborne landing.

It is a pity that they are no longer getting reliable weather reports from their hidden weather stations in Greenland. Over the last couple years, the Allies had played a cat-and-mouse game with them, conducting search parties over vast areas, weeding their meteorological units out. In response, the Germans had been forced to slowly evacuate those that were left. They have lost their key weather stations on Jan Mayen Island, Greenland, Iceland, and Norway.

Nevertheless, anyone can see that the weather is far from ideal right now, and this will probably continue for a few days. So the chance of an invasion coming is nil. Dr. Ströbe confers with his top aide, Major Ludwig Lettau. They agree that no large enemy operations will be forthcoming, at least for the next 48 hours. So Stöbe tells Lettau to give their staff members the day off. Most of them immediately begin planning on touring or carousing through the Parisian hotspots. In the meantime, Stöbe decides that he had better phone in his weather report to von Rundstedt's headquarters.

He calls his liaison officer at OB West, "Heeres" Mueller,[6] and gives him his assessment of the storm. Mueller promises to write it up and forward it on to the field marshal.

***

Early morning. Seventh Army is still on a low-level alert. That there is any alert at all is testimony to all of the air attacks that have recently been made upon the Seine, Loire, and Somme river bridges.

Marcks and the staff of the 84th Corps are indoors today, catching up on paperwork, especially with the weather so bad. The chief of staff, *Oberstleutnant* Friedrich von Criegern, is going through some reports. Marcks' intelligence officer, Major Hayn, is logging in a strange report that has been sent from the 709th Division. A report concerning a dead carrier pigeon.

According to the report, the bird had been shot by an *Oberfeuerwerker* in the 709th Infantry Division early yesterday morning along the Normandy beach. On the leg of the dead bird had been found attached a small aluminum tube containing a modest scrap of paper with a coded message of numbers, letters, and a drawing of a small image, possibly a fox. Both the tube and the paper rolled up within have been taken to the 709th's headquarters for analysis.

Well, this message confirms at least one thing. The Resistance in the area is still using carrier pigeons to send messages across the Channel. Marcks will be interested in this.

Hayn turns to look out his big window across to the beautiful cathedral, and to the skies beyond. He does not think anyone will be landing soon. The weather continued to be bas, with winds in the English Channel at Beaufort Force 5 the sea at Force 4 or 5. In some places, it is raining. Hopefully, the Allies will give them a break.

More than likely, the paper clipped to the bird contains troop dispositions. Anyway, tomorrow the tube and its message will be sent to Army Intelligence in Paris. They will have the time and resources to analyze the code.

***

Late this morning, Adolf Hitler chairs a meeting on Portuguese tungsten imports. He then attends his noontime OKW conference. Most of the time is spent discussing the loss of Rome and the withdrawal of the Tenth Army as the Americans advance up the Italian boot.

That afternoon, the Führer has a lengthy talk with Speer and Jodl about bridges. Speer, having recently noted damage by an Allied air raid and read reports of the Seine bridges going down, has suddenly realized that the enemy could knock out all the Rhine bridges in one day. A landing in the North Sea would then become feasible, and a blitz down through Germany could effectively neutralize all the units in France.

When he mentions this at the conference, Jodl dryly comments to the architect, "I suppose you are now, on top of everything else, becoming an armchair strategist as well." Hitler though, finds merit in the argument, and they spend some time making plans to set up smoke screens around the Rhine bridges. There are no further discussions on conditions in France.

The Führer later attends a meeting about the production of diesel trucks.

***

Throughout the 5th, nothing unusual is reported to *Heeresgruppe B*. General Speidel, in charge while Rommel is away, considers it to be a quiet day. There have been no recon flights this month, so no photo-intelligence reports have to be analyzed. There is, in short, nothing that plausibly indicates that an invasion might be on its way. On the contrary, it is dreary outside, raining at times.

***

Rommel is up early and spends the day at home in Herrlingen, lounging around in relaxed attire with Lucie and Manfred. With them is a guest, Hildegarde Kircheim. Her husband had been with Rommel in North Africa.

Although he enjoys his relaxation, he spends some time going over what he will discuss with the Führer. Interestingly, his notes are peppered with small drawings, because he thinks that they will make his point much better to the Führer and the High Command.

He chats with his wife and son at different times during the day. He tells them about how the French rail lines are getting pounded by Allied aircraft. An idea comes to him. "You know," he says, "we should use the French canals and rivers to move up our supplies and reinforcements..." He pauses and thinks about it. "We could use specially built concrete boats which could be easily camouflaged, and they would move at night. This'd give us an extra arm in our supply problem."

Later, he calls General Schmundt, Hitler's army adjutant, to arrange for a meeting with the Führer. Schmundt tells him that they could probably have some time in the next day or two—probably on Thursday, the 8th. Schmundt will call him back later to confirm this.

Rommel spends part of the evening talking to Manfred and Lucie about glass mines, before retiring early.

Around 9:15 p.m., *Oberst* Oskar Reile telephones OB West from Gestapo headquarters. He reports rather excitedly that many second-part triggers of two-part messages are being broadcast to the Resistance on the BBC, including the Verlaine poem. The first parts had been sent on June 1. Now these messages are being sent to the various groups, probably instructing them to start committing acts of sabotage.[7]

To make sure that OB West truly understands what this implies, he personally goes over to St.-Germain and gives a summary to von Rundstedt's counterespionage officer, Major Brink. Brink knows that their Ia, Bodo Zimmermann, must be informed immediately, So he decides to give the report to him. Before he leaves though, he calls Major Doertenback and tells him to find the Operations chief immediately and verbally inform him of the information.

Reile then informs Berlin. He also passes the information on to the unemotional Colonel Roenne, head of the expert staff at *Fremde Heeres West,* so that they can pass it on to lower army echelons. Reile does not send the information to *Heeresgruppe B,* because he assumes that since the coastal armies are now under Rommel's direct command, he will alert them.[8]

***

9:18 p.m. General von Salmuth is in his quarters, playing a boring game of bridge with his chief of staff and two other officers. They are suddenly interrupted by *Oberstleutnant* Meyer, who comes in out of breath from running.

"*Herr General!*" he exclaims. "The message! The second part—it's here!"

"What?" replies von Salmuth tiredly as he looks up.

Meyer explains in an agitated state that the second part of the Verlaine poem has just been picked up. If their intelligence information from the Abwehr is right, the invasion will now come within the next 48 hours.

Von Salmuth thinks a moment, then calmly orders the Fifteenth Army once again to full alert—to *Alarmstufe II.* Meyer remains standing, waiting for more. The general looks up, sees that he has not moved, and says politely, "*Danke,*" to dismiss him.

Meyer hesitates, then quickly leaves. The other three officers remain silent as the general calmly looks back at his cards, returning to the game. After a pause, he looks up at the other players and, as if to explain his reaction, he quips, "I'm too old a bunny to get too excited about this."

Meyer runs down the hallway to initiate the alert. Quickly he begins drafting a priority message to go out to various commands. He will send a similar message out to all general headquarters. To expedite things, he will also telephone OB West to forewarn them.

As the message is being prepared, he wonders if the second Verlaine verse will be repeated. Probably.[9] His message soon goes out:

Teletype No 2117/26
Urgent

To: 67th Corps 81st Corps 82nd Corps 89th Corps
Military Governor Belgium and Northern France

Army group B
16th Flak Division[10]
Admiral Channel Coast
Luftwaffe Belgium and Northern France

Message of BBC 2115, June 5 has been processed. According to our available records, it means "Expect invasion within 48 hours, starting 0000 June 6."

***

This evening, a strange event takes place at Rommel's headquarters. His chief of staff, the overthrow plot foremost on his mind, has taken the liberty of inviting by phone a number of guests over for dinner. The list includes many co-conspirators from the Paris section of the secret anti-Hitler resistance. With unusual Teutonic humor, he prefaces his unexpected invitations with the wry phrase "The Old Man's gone away."

Included are several interesting guests. Among them are General Wagner, Colonel List who had served in OKW, Consul Pfeiffer, and Speidel's brother-in-law Dr. Max Horst, who works in military administration. There is "war reporter" and good friend Major Wilhelm von Schramm. Speidel told him when he phoned, "We can really have a night discussing things."

There is also outspoken author/philosopher Ernst Jünger, now a captain serving with the military governor of France. Jünger brings with him the finished secret 30-page peace manifesto that he has written, entitled *Der Friede*.[11] It details a plan on how the conspirators intend to make peace with the Allies after Hitler is either overthrown and imprisoned—or just killed. It also envisions a plan to create a new united Europe, something Rommel himself has spoken favorably about at times.

The dinner must be delayed because Jünger, the key guest, is late arriving. Having discovered the main bridge at Mantes is down, he has had to take another route to the château. He does not arrive until 9 p.m.

The get-together makes for an interesting evening. Both before and during dinner. a number of discussions and conversations are held on a variety of subjects, Closer to the main theme of the evening, they also talk about "the insufficient development of Hitler's future plans." After the sumptuous repast, about half of the guests take a stroll through the château and around the grounds, while a colonel relates a number of amusing stories in one parlor.

At about 9:30, the others go up to Speidel's quarters in the Norman tower and begin going over Jünger's written 30-page peace proposal, to be given to the Allies after Hitler's demise. Plans involving the field marshal are also discussed privately between Speidel and Jünger. The plotters need his name to give credence to their coup if and when it occurs.

Just after 10 p.m., Speidel is told that he has a call from the Operations desk. It is Staubwasser, the Ic. He tells Speidel that the second verse of the Verlaine poem has been intercepted, and that von Salmuth has put Fifteenth Army on alert.

Speidel excuses himself from his guests, walks down to Operations, and discusses the message with the intelligence chief. Should Seventh Army be put on alert too? Speidel suggests that he call OB West and adds, "Go with what they say." He then casually returns to his guests.

Staubwasser calls and reaches Operations Officer Bodo Zimmermann, who tells him that, because of the weather, Seventh Army need not be alerted. So Staubwasser hangs up and forgets the matter.

The army defending Normandy is not being put on the alert.

***

At Seventh Army headquarters, Max Pemsel is getting concerned. There is a *Kriegspiel*[12] planned for the next day at Rennes, which was scheduled back on May 26. Despite Pemsel's recommendations, too many key officers have departed this evening, citing the weather and Allied bombing as excuses for leaving early. Even General Dollmann had departed, but he soon returned to headquarters. He planned on leaving a couple hours before dawn for Rennes, so that he could help Mendl set up the scheduled wargames.[13] Even Rommel, perhaps the key figure in the command chain, is at home with his family. So is his operations officer. Most of Seventh Army division commanders are gone. Von Schlieben, commanding the 709th, Hellmich, commanding the 243rd, Falley, with the 91st Air Landing Division… The list goes on.

After some deliberation, he drafts a message:

COMMANDING GENERALS AND OTHERS SCHEDULED TO
ATTEND THE *KRIEGSPIEL* ARE REMINDED NOT TO
LEAVE FOR RENNES BEFORE DAWN ON JUNE 6TH.

It was strong enough, but not too harsh. And any evidence of a possible landing would surely be detected before daylight, although dawn would be the critical time. Not that anyone expected anything, especially with the storm that had hit the Channel.

The chief of staff shakes his head. It is going to be a long night.[14]

Around 10:30 p.m. (BDST) in England, hundreds of C-47s start their motors. The sky is dark, and heavy clouds are hiding the moon. Destination: Normandy.

German radar operators at the still-functional installations in Normandy soon begin to notice that their units are being heavily jammed. Operators in the Calais area note a number of strange radar returns. They are probably ghost echoes from the heavy seas. Surely they cannot be large numbers of many ships and aircraft approaching the straits. Still, the information is passed on up the chain of command and to the Luftwaffe.

***

Generalfeldmarschall von Rundstedt is enjoying an evening with his son at his villa on Rue Alexandre Dumas. He has had a nice Monday. Getting up around 11 a.m., he found the weather rainy and overcast. He washed and dressed, and finally entered his villa's first floor study around noontime. There, he quickly went through the day's business, finding nothing unusual. Dr. Strobe had phoned in a weather report calling for rain and gusting winds. Good. The old man's schedule would be light, and he would soon be free to spend the rest of the day with his boy.

He held a short meeting with Blumentritt to finalize their "Estimate of Allied Intentions," the weekly report that they had to sent to OKW that day. Earlier, they had received from Foreign Armies West the latest situation report of the enemy status:

> The enemy command is continuing its endeavors to conceal its invasion plans by all means of the war of nerves. Dissemination of items pointing to a postponement of the invasion due to political differences alternates with announcements of imminent attack. The presumable objective of these machinations is a gradual blunting of German vigilance in order to create the conditions required for a surprise success.
>
> Against this must be stressed as the only concrete, but decisive fact, the state of preparedness for the take-off of about 60 enemy major formations in the South of England, of about ten in the central zone of England, and from five to six in Scotland. There is as yet no evidence that embarkation has begun, though considerable concentrations of shipping have been noted.
>
> Movements along the lower Thames indicate that formations (among them the Ninth Armored Division) are being moved towards the large harbors in that area, which will be used, perhaps, to relieve the harbors on either side of Dover which lie within the range of German gunfire.

Von Rundstedt looked over the report that he and Blumentritt had written, based on everything that had come in. He read:

> The systematic and distinct increase of air attacks indicates that the enemy has reached a high degree of readiness. The probable invasion front still remains the sector from the Scheldt to Normandy... and it is not impossible that the north front of Brittany might be included... [but] it is still not clear where the enemy will invade within this total area. Concentrated air attacks on the coast defenses between Dunkirk and Dieppe may mean that the main Allied invasion effort will be made there...[but] imminence of invasion is not recognizable.

Although his estimate mentions the enemy's high level of readiness, it does not bother him. He is echoing what OKH is implying, while still keeping his own conclusions vague. The Allies are ready to move, and can land just about anywhere; but as yet, there is no immediate prospect for the *Grossinvasion*.

The weekly estimate over with, the old man went over his travel plan with Blumentritt for tomorrow. Finished with the itinerary, he was done for the day. He told Blumentritt with a smile that he and Hans-Gerd were going to dine at one of his favorite restaurants—the Coq Hardi, near Bougival.[15]

Father and son departed by auto for the restaurant at around 1 p.m. They spend the next couple hours dining in luxury. With the meal over, they did a bit of shopping in the small local stores before returning to St.-Germain under drizzling skies. They retired for a relaxing late afternoon and evening in the field marshal's sumptuous château. Tomorrow, they will begin his tour of the Atlantic. He plans to leave his villa in the morning. The first day, they will tour the Normandy section.

***

Around 10 p.m., after Hans-Gerd has gone to bed, Blumentritt walks in on the old man with a special message. Meyer-Detring has received a communication from Fifteenth Army Intelligence. The second line of the Verlaine poem has just come in. If Army Intelligence (now under the SS) is correct, the invasion is only one or two days away. Blumentritt needs to know if von Rundstedt wants to alert the two armies along the coast.

Von Rundstedt looks skeptically at his chief of staff without even looking at the message. He doubts that there is any truth to it. He does not believe in any of this spy nonsense anyway, and he sure as hell does not believe that the enemy would risk tipping the Germans off that they are coming, just to get some *Widerstand* fighters active.

"Blumentritt," he growls, "do you think that a commander like Eisenhower would announce the invasion over the BBC?"

Of course, when the Old Man put it that way… "Well, sir," the chief replies, "Even so, von Salmuth is alerting the Fifteenth Army."

The field marshal snorts derisively. He pauses and looks up. "Well, pass the information on to OKW and to Blaskowitz."

"Shall we order a general alert?"

"No," the field marshal barks. "Especially not in this weather."

Thousands of Resistance fighters, alerted by hundreds of special coded messages that have been broadcast by the BBC (including the Verlaine verse), prepare to execute dozens of different missions against their four-year oppressors. They uncover hidden explosives, guns, knives, and other weapons or equipment that they will need in the next 48 hours.

Each of their missions has some significance to the upcoming invasion. Many of them will have to do with cutting communication links, while others will attack transportation routes. They will damage bridges, block roads, or cause breaks in rail lines, including the Avranches, Cherbourg, and Caen rail lines into St. Lô.

All of these missions are designed to further isolate western France.

This afternoon, the Führer is getting a fecal examination by his doctor for his meteorism.[16] That evening, they will hear Roosevelt on the radio, broadcasting the liberation of Rome.

***

While von Rundstedt enjoys his evening in his villa, *Oberst* Bodo Zimmermann is in the OB West senior officers' mess, located in a spacious French residence some 300 meters away. This home had also been appropriated when the field marshal had first relocated his headquarters to St.-Germain-en-Laye. The ground floor had been turned into a mess hall and recreational area, while the bedrooms upstairs had been converted into quarters for some of the senior officers, including Zimmermann.

Bodo Zimmermann is in his mid-fifties, about 5'8" tall and of medium-slim build. He considers himself good-looking and fit for his age. A concise and precise officer, he is usually relaxed and confident, although some consider him to be arrogant at times. Well, perhaps he is.

Tonight, after changing clothes in his quarters, he had come downstairs, and he and some 30 other officers had sat down at the long dinner table to a common meal.[17] There had been the simple salad and the beef course (extra vegetables, of course, cost an individual extra), along with some French cheese and an adequate red wine. The conversation had been heated and centered, as usually was the case, around the upcoming invasion. But the officers, he has noticed, seem decidedly pessimistic in their views, and he finds that disturbing. The Allies have gone to great lengths to display their total command in the last month. Supply lines, one logistics officer pointed out, were being regularly strafed and bombed. Around this time last year, a daily average of 200 supply trains would enter the Parisian rail network. Now that daily average is down to less than ten.

Most of the officers (just like the old man) express little confidence in their famed *Atlantikwall*. It is a paper tiger, a bluff that the Allies will soon deliberately and determinedly call. The predominant opinion at the table was that the *Schwerpunkt* would be somewhere along the beaches between the Vire and the Orne estuaries, weakly defended by a hodgepodge of second-rate units, undermanned, underqualified, and unreliable.

"And," one officer had added, "it's a good bet that the Allies know it, too." Zimmermann, smoking a cigar as he often did, had to agree.

That point had been driven home in early April. Zimmermann had been studying some recent aerial recon photos that the Luftwaffe had been lucky to have taken along England's southern coast. Studying the photos, he had noted on a couple of them some unidentified flat-surface vessels that were being towed. They seemed to resemble some type of floating platforms, an analyst had noted. Well, it was obvious that they were somehow tied in to the invasion. But how? Weapons platforms? Perhaps to ferry tanks across the Channel? No one in the headquarters knew.

Sometime later, a connection had unexpectedly come to mind. He remembered back to a trip that he had taken before the war to Algiers. There he had noted with interest similar type concrete platforms, being used offshore to unload cargo. These makeshift wharves were being used as a sort of offshore "artificial harbor." The concept had been a novel one, and because of that it had stuck in his mind. After viewing the photos, Zimmermann had later sent a detailed report of his analysis to Admiral Krancke at Naval Group West, but Krancke had dismissed the idea of portable harbors as "unrealistic and highly improbable."

Zimmermann is still in the dining room, talking with some fellow officers around 9:30 p.m., when an orderly comes in and informs him that Major Doertenback has arrived and urgently needs to see him. Zimmermann follows the orderly into the adjoining anteroom. There Doertenback is standing, agitated and out of breath. The major reports in an excited tone that their counterintelligence men have deciphered a message from the BBC to the French Underground, a sort of call to mobilization.

Zimmermann is skeptical. Normally a traditionalist, he distrusts most spy reports, just like his boss. He is tempted to dismiss the Verlaine poem warning.

A short time later, Major Brink arrives and tells Zimmermann that Colonel Reile has intercepted other recent trigger messages. He sees the threat of a landing soon. Now Zimmermann decides it is time to act.

Picking up the phone there in the anteroom, he puts in a call to General Blumentritt at the field marshal's villa. He tells him about the deciphered message. They already know, having been warned by Meyer. Wearily, while not initiating an alert, von Rundstedt authorizes the transmission of a warning message to all commands. Drafted, it reads:

> Several phrases known to us since the autumn of 1943 to give brief notice of the start of the invasion, were broadcast for the first time today by the British radio.
>
> While we cannot expect that the invasion itself will be announced in advance by radio, it is to be anticipated that the sabotage acts prepared against our transport and communications networks in connection with the invasion, and perhaps armed uprisings as well, are to be set off by these messages.

The message goes out to all commands.[18] The copy for *Heeresgruppe B* is addressed to the attention of Hans Speidel.

Phone calls from OB West go out to all major Western European commands stating that code words broadcast by the BBC will summon French Resistance units to rise up in the next night or two, and that this should be considered a general warning. *Heeresgruppe B* is to go to *Alarmstufe II*. All other commands are to increase their vigilance. The phone calls are followed up by confirming messages.

***

Admiral Hennecke in Cherbourg has spent a relaxing day, bolstered by the forecast his staff has given him that the weather will continue to be foul for several days. That means that the next date on which similar conditions of tide, moon and overall weather situation necessary for a landing would coincide would not be until the second half of June.

He has therefore enjoyed a relaxing, informal day. After all, he deserved it. Last night had given him some jitters. That radar report from that coastal station had shaken him up. And the tides and the moon phase for the next three days would be ideal for an amphibious landing. What if the Allies decided to go anyway, despite the bad weather? He had been relieved that everything had turned out for the best. The radar contact had faded away into the night.

So today the headquarters enjoys a nice day of bad weather. That evening, since no alerts have been received, he attends a small social function. Having gone to a concert given by a German "USO" troop, he has asked a number of performers back to his villa. He is now listening with his wife to one of his senior lieutenants playing Schumann's "Papillons."

As the music wafts on, the admiral hardly notices that one of his lieutenants is called to the phone. The call is from the battle headquarters in the tunnel below the villa. They relay a report for the admiral. The staff member returns to the room and comes over to him with the message.

"Some very heavy air raids on towns and roads in the coastal area, *Herr Admiral*. Other strong bomber formations are reported from the Calvados coast."

The admiral, his eyes never leaving the musicians, gently nods his head in acknowledgment and calmly glances at his watch. It is 11:30 p.m.

About ten minutes later, another message is relayed to him. Luftwaffe headquarters in Paris has reported that 50–60 twin-engine aircraft are approaching the Cherbourg peninsula from the west. Could this be the long-awaited invasion? The musical performance is immediately broken up.

***

It is ten minutes before midnight. Just north of the town of Picauville near the Douve River is Château Haut, the headquarters of the 91st Air Landing Division, recently arrived in Normandy. The commanding officer, *Generalleutnant* Wilhelm Falley, is getting ready to leave for the wargames in Rennes.[19] He has stated that he is not worried about any possible Allied activity tonight. "There's nothing to fear in this filthy weather," he had snorted to his Operations officer earlier.

Despite his sarcastic crack though, he does have some concerns. The presence of several enemy aircraft flying overhead worries him. So as an afterthought, he leaves orders for his men to be especially alert tonight. Then he and his logistics officer, Major Joachim Bartuzat, climb into his staff car with its pennant of black, white and red flying off to the side, his driver, *Gefreiter* Baumann, also a paratrooper, at the wheel. The car moves off with a rattle of stones under its tires, bound for Rennes.

***

General Marcks at his headquarters in St. Lô is resigned to spending the rest of the night there. He too would probably have left for Rennes that evening, had he not become so immersed in planning for the next day's exercise to be held there. And besides, he has a suspicion that his staff wants to give him a small party. After all, he will be 53 on Tuesday. So he decides to delay his departure until the next morning.

As midnight approaches, he is still studying map after map, analyzing them for the upcoming exercise. He almost always wins these exercise, mostly because of his orthodox attack and defense doctrines, and this time, he is to be the enemy yet again. This exercise will simulate a large-scale airborne landing, followed by a full naval assault.

The theoretical target will be Normandy. And Marcks is going to play Eisenhower.

He is correct about one thing: his staff is indeed planning for him a small birthday celebration. Major Hayn, his intelligence officer, and their chief of staff, *Generaloberst* von Criegern, have organized the event, having secured a number of bottles of a fine Chablis.

This evening has shaped up to be an interesting one. Starting at 10 p.m., reports had starting coming in of huge aircraft formations flying in over the area, even though, despite a full moon, the weather was still overcast, and far from ideal. Did the presence of these aircraft mean anything? Was this the beginning of more raids? Or possibly an airborne assault? Marcks had wondered.

Major von der Heydte, commanding the 6th Parachute Regiment, had shown up earlier that evening to accompany Marcks to Rennes and get a chance to talk to him. When Marcks had told him that he was going to delay his departure because he was busy planning for the exercise, von der Heydte, expressing some disappointment at not having the opportunity to talk, and not wanting to make the trip alone, had returned to his headquarters just north of Périers to spend the night there.[20]

As midnight approaches, Marcks studies map after map for the upcoming exercise. Hayn, von Criegern, and the few other senior staff members check on their modest preparations, while a few more enemy bomber formations fly overhead. They wonder how their stern, no-nonsense commanding officer will react to their seemingly adolescent gesture of celebrating his birthday.

Finishing up, they are getting ready to surprise him when suddenly a nearby flak battery opens up, rattling the window panes, momentarily distracting them. Briefly startled by the unexpected burst of fire, wine bottles and glasses in hand, they grin sheepishly at each other as the battery outside pounds away up into the night's sky.

Running out of their bunker, they catch a glimpse of an enemy airplane going down, smoke and flames billowing behind. The two-engine aircraft had evidently flown over at a low altitude, and the nearby flak battery that they had heard, some 50 meters away from them on the roof of the high school next to the nearby St. Lô cathedral, had opened up on it, apparently successfully. The gun crew yells gleefully, "We got it! We got it!"

Shaking their heads, the corps staff officers walk back into the bunker to grab their refreshments, the sound of more enemy aircraft continuing some distance away.

***

It is almost midnight. The Guernsey Island Luftwaffe radar crew has been plotting since 11 p.m. on their *Freya* and *Wurzburg* radars many incoming slow-moving air contacts approaching the French coast. They are told that a counterpart army signals unit has been picking up several formations as well. What is significant is that several of these formations appear to consist of heavy two- or four-engine aircraft, many of which appear to be closely followed by a small, fuzzy ghost echo, probably just that in this weather. However, the phantom echoes could also possibly be gliders.

After studying the tracking some more, the Luftwaffe commanding officer decides that it is time to raise some alarm. He gets a hold of the regimental commander at headquarters, *Oberst* Oelze, and gives him a full report on the contacts.

The regimental commander thanks him for the information and in turn immediately calls General Marcks' headquarters. The duty officer there tells him that none of the senior officers are available at the moment, including Chief of Staff von Criegern, and Operations Officer Hasso Viebig. One is attending an army group conference in Paris, another is at the moment attending a birthday celebration for the corps commander, and another one is on leave…

The frustrated regimental commander explains to him that some alert must be sounded. Several enemy aircraft are coming in from the north. He adds, "I think a major operation against the mainland is coming."

The duty officer sighs and promises to see what he can do.

The regimental commander hangs up, unconvinced that the man will do much.

1 Each sub carried an 18-foot navigational beacon that would shine a green beam out to sea (but not visible from the shore). In addition, they would use a short-distance radio beacon and an underwater echo sounder for the minesweepers.

2 Surprisingly, there has been some confusion as to which capital ships participated in the Normandy invasion, despite readily available information. The seven battleships listed here took part in *Overlord* and *Neptune*. The battleships HMS *Rodney* and HMS *Nelson* would not take part in the initial bombardments of the beaches that early June 6, but would instead be held in reserve roles. One account describes HMS *Rodney* shelling the 15-inch guns of the Le Havre battery later that fateful morning. After D-Day, the 16-inch firepower of both these battleships would be added to the fleet, and they would take part in many naval gunfire support activities for the beachhead; but not directly at the beginning of the invasion.

3 Exact figures again vary, and greatly. Theodore A. Wilson in breaks the 1,500 landing craft figure down into the following: 229 LSTs, 241 LCIs, over 900 LCT, and about 60 US Coast Guard 83-foot cutters, used to rescue troops and crewmen in the water. These figures did not include all of the extra landing craft—real, damaged, or dummy—that were put into the Dover area to simulate preparations for the "other" invasion at Calais with Patton's fictitious First Army. John Mann puts the figure at 4,126 landing ships and craft.

4 That was 2:15 a.m., German Central Time.

5 Again, the Allies were lucky. If Eisenhower had decided to postpone to the next low-tide period, June 19, he would have found himself delayed yet again, because on the 19th, one of the most violent three-day storms in years smashed into the English Channel. Eisenhower would have had to postpone until July. He later wrote Captain Staggs, "I thank the gods of war we went when we did!"

6 Major Dr. Hermann Mueller. The nickname "Heeres" (army) is a play on words "Hier ist" (Here is) and comes from the fact that he was not a civilian. Earlier in the war, all of the meteorologists assigned to the various high-level commands in Western Europe had been civilians, working directly for and on permanent loan to the Air Ministry. They were eventually pressed into service as Luftwaffe officers, including Stöbe, who was given the highest rank of *Oberst*. When Mueller, an army major, was posted to OB West as Stöbe's liaison, he of course was the odd man out, and nicknamed "Heeres."

7 Hundreds of such acts would be committed over the next few days. Unfortunately, the Resistance and Maquis would pay dearly for them. In Northern France alone, nearly a thousand suspected members would be shot or rounded up and executed. Another four thousand would be exported to labor or concentration camps.

8 Reile could not know that, for some reason, Rommel's intelligence officer, *Oberst* Staubwasser, was never initially told about these two-part trigger messages and what they meant.

9 The second verse would be broadcast a total of fifteen times that day.

10 The 16th Flak Division, a part of *Luftflotte 3*, was located in Belgium. It consisted of three Flak Regiments (the 37th, the 129th, the 132nd, and the 531st) and a *Luftnachtrichen* (Signals) battalion. It would later see heavy action in Operation *Market Garden.*

11 "The Peace." Jünger had started the document last year. It would not be published in its entirety until 1947.

12 Wargame. This particular wargame conference was to be held in Rennes, starting mid-morning on June 6, chaired by *General der Fallschirmjäger* Eugen Meindl, commanding the 2nd Parachute Corps. Ironically, the wargame was to be an exercise centered around an enemy airborne assault, followed by a few amphibious landings.

13 Most sources agree that Dollmann had not left for the wargames, but had turned in for the night.

14 Other senior officers missing include: 21st Panzer commander Edgar Feuchtinger, somewhere in Paris; SS General Sepp Dietrich in Brussels; Admiral Krancke, down in Bordeaux, and von Rundstedt's intelligence officer, Col Meyer-Detring who was on leave in Paris. Even *Groß Admiral* Karl Dönitz was with his family in their home in the Black Forest.

15 The Coq Hardi ("Dauntless Rooster") had been for many years a world-famous five-star restaurant. It was about 5.5km away on the Quai Rennequin Sualem, along the southern bank of the Seine River. Decades later, it was sold, renovated, and reopened as "Chez Clément."

16 Equated to tympanites, which is a flatulent distention of the stomach; the presence of gas in the stomach intestines.

17 The recollections made here were made by Zimmermann in June of 1958. How much of it is true and how much of it the memories of a "Monday morning quarterback" can only be speculated.

18 Fifteenth Army log records the warning being received at 10:33 p.m.

19 The exact time General Falley left is questionable.

20 One biographer wrote that von der Heydte had an ulterior motive, wanting to discuss with Marcks a possible anti-government resistance movement. For instance, was the general aware of an existing plot to assassinate the Führer? Or did he know that his cousin von Stauffenberg was involved? This suggests that the major was somehow involved in the plot. Indeed, his name was later found written on a document seized by the SS. Fortunately it was misspelled, and, in a wryly amusing twist, according to the laconic story, some unsuspecting officer named Von der Heide, an officer who was then serving on the Eastern Front, was subsequently arrested and had to spent the rest of the war in prison.

Tuesday, June 6—Part One

According to German clocks, it is midnight. Thousands of Allied aircraft swarm over the northwestern coast of France, following the routes the pathfinders took an hour ago.

From the northwest come planes carrying the advance elements of the American 101st and 82nd Airborne Divisions. As they pass between the islands of Guernsey and Jersey, searchlights stab at the murky night, occasionally accompanied by blasts of multi-colored anti-aircraft fire—vain attempts by the enemy units on those islands to find the source of the many engine noises in the dark skies near them. As the aircraft pass over the mainland, other German anti-aircraft units begin firing.

From the northeast, flying slowly over the coastline, come more aircraft carrying paratroops of the British 6th Airborne.

At 12:15 a.m. over an hour after the pathfinders and the dummies have arrived, the airborne troops begin jumping into France. The gray-black skies fill with thousands of silk chutes as paratroopers leave their aircraft into the dark of night.

On the ground, thousands of French Resistance fighters start leaving their homes and shops to begin to make their contribution to the operation. Cities all over northern France begin experiencing communications problems and other small acts of sabotage. Major cities like Paris, Le Mans, Lille, Orléans, Cherbourg, and Bordeaux, as well as many smaller cities in the Normandy area such as St Lô, Caen, and Avranches, begin to suffer radio problems. Wireless sets start to experience high electronic shrieking, as Allied jammers dropped to Resistance groups begin operation.

Ground communications lines between many German headquarters go dead, and many conventional telephone lines suffer similar fates. Several units, physically cut off somewhat by the recently bombed river bridges, are now having problems reaching each other as well.

General Erich Marcks is in the map room at his headquarters in St. Lô. As the cathedral's bells start to chime midnight, his staff officers enter the room apprehensively to accost the corps general with their birthday surprise. After a moment, Marcks becomes aware of their presence and gazes up at them in calm surprise through his wire frame spectacles. He slowly rises to greet them, his wooden leg creaking as he does. They nervously wish him happy birthday, and he smiles and waves his hand. They crowd in, now at ease and grinning.

They open another bottle and fill their glasses before coming to attention and raising them to formally toast their commanding officer. They drink to his health and wish him good fortune for the forthcoming year. He thanks all of them sincerely. They get him to slice the ornate, richly flavored birthday cake they have procured. Decorated on the top is his name, the town, and the date: June 6, 1944.

The quick, modest birthday celebration soon ends, and Marcks goes back to his long table, a glass of chablis still in his hand, to study the maps again and wrap up his plans for tomorrow's *Kriegspiel*. He will leave at dawn. However, he is a bit concerned that the air activity overhead is continuing this late in the night. Heavy engines, probably bombers. But they seem slow moving…

At 1 a.m., General Marcks is still at that table, finishing up his plans on the maps of the exercise area. He will probably be one of the last to arrive at the *Kriegspiel* exercise tomorrow, even though Dollmann had scheduled it some nine days ago. No matter. Marcks' theatrically late arrival notwithstanding, he is particularly looking forward to the exercise. Most of the divisional commanders have agreed that it will be a fascinating one. And of course, Marcks has prepared for this role as if it is the real thing.

Sitting beside his map table with various charts spread out before him, tired, he wipes his brow. It is a warm, humid late spring night. He glances at his intelligence officer, the only one with him in the room.

"Hand me the map of the Pointe du Hoc area please, Hayn." The major dutifully hands it to him. Marcks' theoretical target is Normandy.

Marcks had been the enemy before. Last February, his Allied forces had landed along the Calvados coastline. He established a firm beachhead and moved his landed units west and southwest, to occupy all of Normandy and Brittany. Now he will play Eisenhower again, only this time, he will have three airborne divisions to initially drop into the Normandy countryside. Marcks has no doubt that he will win the exercise, and in doing so, show the generals how easily they could lose if it were the real thing.

Von Criegern comes back into the room, and Marcks talks to him informally, their conversation casual and relaxed. Marcks is only half-listening to what his chief of staff is saying. He is ready. All he will have to do tomorrow morning is to grab his charts and papers and leave. It will not take him long to get to Rennes. Besides, he is too tired to travel now. It is late, and the wine has not helped. As if all that is not enough, his leg is bothering him again. Still, he hesitates to retire for the evening. Judging from the air activity, something seems to be happening.

At 1:11 a.m., the ringing of the field telephone on his desk interrupts their discussion. Calmly, Marcks picks it up and answers. The call is from Karl Bachus, the 716th Division Ia[1] from their headquarters in Caen. As Marcks listens, his eyes widen. The fatigue seems to magically vanish from his face. His whole body begins to stiffen as he stands up, almost as though he is bracing himself, his other hand clenching the edge of the table tightly.

He looks at von Criegern and nods to him, motioning him to come listen in. The general is told that enemy airborne landings have taken place northeast of Caen, east of the Orne estuary, somewhere around Ranville.

The receiver crackles with static as they hear the report. "The area seems to be along a line between Bréville-sur-Mer and Ranville… more reports of paratroopers along the northern fringe of the Bavent forest."[2] Marcks looks at von Criegern who is scribbling notes, trying to get everything down. The objectives for the second set of reports appear to be the Dives River bridges and the crossings over the Orne.

Countermeasures, Marcks is told, are in progress. Marcks tersely tells Bachus to keep them advised and then quietly hangs up the field phone.

The call has hit them like a ton of bricks. No one says a word as the senior staff members are quickly called in. Marcks analyzes the report with interest. Surely, this is not a massive raid. No, it has to be tied to some amphibious landing. Yes, this is probably the prelude to the invasion, but where will the enemy land?

One staff member suggests in an unsure voice, "Perhaps these paratroopers are only exceptionally strong groups who have come to establish contact with the Resistance." After all, it had been only yesterday that several leaflets had been dropped on the Brittany port of St. Malo, carrying the cryptic proclamation that *La carotte rouge est quittée*.[3] And 84th Corps had noted a recent dramatic increase in coded radio traffic.

After a moment of silence, Hayn slowly shakes his head. "No," he responds thoughtfully. "The drop is too near to the main line of resistance. The Resistance wouldn't dare do that." He continues. "These jumps have been made much too near our main combat line to be of any use for stirring the FFI[4] in our sector into action." He pauses. "If your opinion were right, it would mean that a fundamental change in the attitude of the civilians in our corps area had taken place. Up until now, the peasants of Normandy—slow, but jovial, pleasure-loving fellows—have refused to take part in any act of sabotage." Unlike the more active groups operating to the West in Brittany.[5]

Marcks orders 84th Corps on alert. His staff meanwhile has put away most of their work. One thing is for sure—the wargames will now be canceled.

Marcks suddenly realizes that his staff is looking at him intently. He says gently, "We've called out the alert. Now, let's wait and see."

In the meantime, time to notify higher authorities. He tells von Criegern to contact Max Pemsel at Seventh Army headquarters immediately. It is 1:15 a.m.

God help them now.

***

Speidel's party at La Roche-Guyon finally breaks up after midnight. Most of the guests are returning to Paris, and the trip will take longer than usual since the Seine River bridges are out. At 1 a.m., Speidel turns in to go to bed. A few, like Admiral Ruge, decide to stay up a while, drinking fine brandies, telling stories.

***

It is just past 1:15 a.m. at Seventh Army Headquarters. Max Pemsel, ready to turn in for the night, is told he has a phone call in Operations. Whoever it is had better have a good reason for keeping him up. It is von Criegern, Marcks' chief of staff. Pemsel listens to him report on the paratroop landings. Pemsel turns to a staff member and orders him to wake the entire army staff up immediately.

He and von Criegern then briefly discuss the reports and agree that this is probably the beginning of the invasion. Pemsel ends the call by instructing von Criegern to keep him informed of all developments.

Pemsel immediately noted in the phone log at 1:35:

> Chief of Staff LXXXIV [84th] Corps reports: Since 0030 parachute jumps in area east and northwest of Caen, St. Marcouf, Montebourg, astride Vire and on east coast Cotentin. LXXXIV [84th] Corps has ordered Alert II.

Pemsel orders the entire Seventh Army be put on alert. Then he calls General Dollmann's quarters. and tells him that there have been several reports of airborne landings in the Calvados area and in the Cotentin peninsula. "General," he concludes, "I believe that this is the invasion. Will you please come over immediately?" Dollmann tells him he will, as soon as he gets dressed.

Taking a deep breath, Pemsel picks up the phone again and nervously calls Speidel at La Roche-Guyon. The chief of staff has to be woken up to come to the phone. Pemsel passes on the reports of the paratroop landings. Speidel takes the news in a calm sleepy voice and in turn promises to immediately call von Rundstedt's headquarters.

Right after the call, Pemsel notes in his diary:

> The long-awaited invasion has begun.

They will all be busy tonight.

***

Speidel, now awake, notifies all major commands of the airborne sightings. Reports now coming are perplexing and often contradictory. Some of them are illogical, placing reports of enemy sightings in wildly irrational locations.

Not having a clear picture yet, he decides to wait and see what develops. This will pretty much be his drill for the whole night.

***

At 1:23 a.m., the staff at the OB West headquarters bunker first gets the word of the paratroop landings from Naval Group West. They are also informed that Marcks' 84th Corps is on full alert. Blumentritt and von Rundstedt are woken up at their villa.

Around the base of the Carentan peninsula, scattered American paratroopers start to get organized. Groups of one or two find others, and they in turn merge with other clusters to form squads and then platoons. Some find their locations. Those not too far from their objectives set out for them. Many scamper up telephone and telegraph poles to cut the lines, to further isolate the Germans in the area.

By 1:30, reports are reaching General von Salmuth in Tourcoing. Then comes a phone call from *Oberst* Wise, chief of staff for Kuntzen's 81st Corps headquarters near Rouen. He reports enemy paratroopers landing in Deauville, 15km up the coast, and around the 711th's headquarters at Cabourg. Fighting is supposedly going on all around the buildings. Wise tells von Salmuth that the noise of battle can be heard over the receiver. No other details are available at this time.

To von Salmuth, this sounds crazy. His army is already on full alert, and though enemy air raids have hit Calais, nothing much else seems to be going on. To find out, he calls the divisional commander, General Reichert. Finally getting through, he growls, "Reichert, what the devil is going on down there?"

Reichart had been sitting in the officers' mess with other officers, exhausted after a hard day of training, sipping calvados,[6] wondering about the heavy enemy air traffic, when a flight of slow-moving aircraft had flown over. He had dashed into his command bunker to get his pistol, and returning in the dark, he spotted paratroopers floating down over his quarters. Two had landed on his lawn and had been immediately captured. He and his men were desperately trying to defend the divisional headquarters when von Salmuth called.

Reichert now replies, "My General, if you'll permit me, I'll let you hear for yourself." He holds up his receiver to the doorway. Von Salmuth waits a moment, listening sullenly. Suddenly, his eyes widen as he distinctly hears machine-gun fire in the background. "Thank you," he promptly responds, and hangs up. He then calls Speidel and tells him that, at the headquarters of the 711th, "the din of battle can be heard."

Von Salmuth immediately raises the Fifteenth Amy alert to Level II. Then he picks up the phone again to call *Heeresgruppe B.*

***

1:45 a.m. General Marcks at his headquarters continues analyzing the reported locations of the paratroop drops. A few more sightings have come in. One group of British paratroopers has had the nerve to come down right on the lawn of Reichert's 711th headquarters. Marcks could just imagine the look on the division commander's face.

The phone rings. *Oberst* Hamann[7] at the 709th headquarters in Valogne. The colonel relays that enemy paratroopers have been reported just south of St.-Germain de-Varreville, near the base of the Cotentin peninsula. Another group has been sighted west of the main road to Carentan, near Ste.-Marie-du-Mont. More groups of enemy paratroopers have been spotted along both sides of the Merderet River, and on the road between Ste.-Mère-Église and Pont-l'Abbé.

Marcks asks him about any firefights. He replies that there are some going on at the river crossings. "Have they identified any of the units yet?" Marcks asks.

Yes. 3rd Battalion of the 919th Grenadier Regiment has identified a few prisoners as belonging to the American 101st Airborne Division.

As staff members try to contact the 84th's division commanders, Hayn orders the French postal service in the corps' area shut down, Marcks continues plotting the new drops. Scattered all over the map, he cannot make out the enemy's main objectives.[8] He does though, quickly decide that this is the main event—the invasion. He orders the message "ALARM COAST" be sent, the coded phrase that put the coastal units on maximum alert for an invasion.

The alarm goes out over the service telephones (the civilian phones are not operating, courtesy of the Maquis). It is coming up on 2 a.m. when he calls Speidel at *Heeresgruppe B* again and tells him that this is the invasion.

***

It is 2 a.m. Günther Blumentritt, still tired from having been awoken a half-hour ago, is called to the phone. It is Eduard Wegener at Naval Group West.[9] He reports airborne landings around Caen, and radar contacts near the entrance to the English Channel. Wegener says that Admiral Hoffman, Blumentritt's naval counterpart, is convinced that this is the invasion.

Blumentritt though is not quite convinced. There had been no evidence of any enemy shenanigans the evening before. And besides, the storm…

"In *this* weather?" he challenges. Blumentritt hopes this is a false alarm, because he's tired. "Maybe you've picked up sea gulls," he ventures hopefully.

Wegener's reply is icy. "Surface contacts, *Herr General*. Confirmed by several stations."

"Well, I still don't believe it, but I'll pass on your report."

"Yessir. And Naval Group West is alerting all the ships and ports along the coast."

Hanging up, Blumentritt is depressed. Doesn't anyone look outside anymore? Who invades in storms?

***

Just after 2:09 a.m., a couple still operable German radar stations start seeing large areas of "snow" all across their screens for a good part of the night. There appear to be two very large bomber groups headed for Germany. And a number of vessels have been picked up by surface radar, apparently headed for Le Havre. At the same time, German radar and communications networks are being jammed.

In the next hour, these contacts turn out to be a hoax as they disappeared back into the English coastline. But now, one of the repaired radar sets has picked up a large number of ships in position off the Normandy shoreline. Naval Group West in Paris is contacted.

***

It is 2:10 at *Heeresgruppe B.* The headquarters has received incoming messages of airborne landings further up the coast, in the Fifteenth Army sector. Also, Admiral Ruge has received reports of straw dummies that explode upon landing. They are being dropped all over the 84th and 47th Corps area. Speidel, weary from the party earlier in the evening, now concludes that any naval assault will probably be elsewhere, possibly near Calais. Perhaps the field marshal is right. The invasion may come near the Somme estuary.

Shortly after talking to von Salmuth, Speidel receives another phone call from Max Pemsel. More paratroopers in the lower Cotentin peninsula, including near Carentan. Pemsel tries to convince Speidel of the seriousness of the situation, contending that this is a major operation. To back that up, he tells Speidel of a report from *Admiral Kanalküste*[10] that ship engine noises in the Channel have been heard east of the coast of the Cotentin peninsula.

When asked, Pemsel replies that there are no immediate radar reports of any vessels in the Channel. Most of the radar networks along the Bay of Seine have been taken out by bombs. A couple naval observers though, have reported possible ship movement around Cherbourg.

Speidel calmly reassures him, replying that, "The affair is still locally confined. All of the paratroop drops are either diversions, bomber crews that are bailing out, or dummies."

Pemsel is understandably in disbelief. These are all dummies?

Speidel patiently explains. In one or two reports, the "paratroopers" were just rubber dummies fitted with roman candles. The explosions when they went off convinced the German troops that there were real airborne troops in the area.

After the phone call, Speidel enters into the war diary:

> Chief of Staff Army Group B believes that for the time being this is not to be considered as a large operation.

If some of these sporadic landings are by real paratroopers, it is probably a large reinforcement to the French Resistance. Someone needs to do something.

Speidel sighs, picks up a phone, and tries to get a hold of Feuchtinger at the 21st Panzer headquarters. Feuchtinger is not in. No matter. They have given the 21st

Panzer standing orders: in the event of an enemy paratroop landings, move out and attack them immediately.

***

At about 2:15, Fifteenth Army gets a phone call from *Heeresgruppe B.* They have reports of strong airborne landings in several locations in Normandy, as well as continued flights of gliders. There are reports of firefights on the Cotentin peninsula. There has also been a report in one area of booby-trapped wooden dummies being dropped.

***

Around 2:45 a.m., Admiral Theodor Krancke is sleeping in a hotel room down in Bordeaux. He had gone down there to inspect the naval forces along the southwestern coast of France. Most of the vessels currently operating in that area were conducting mining operations in the Bay of Biscay.

He is awakened by his aide. *Konteradmiral* Hennecke in Cherbourg is calling. When Krancke gets on the line, Hennecke reports that paratroopers have landed somewhere below the St. Marcouf naval battery along the eastern coast of the Cotentin peninsula. The battery commander insists that this is the invasion. Krancke tells Hennecke to alert his forces.

Krancke immediately calls his Naval Group West headquarters in Paris. Wegener, his Operations officer, tells him that airborne landings have been reported near Caen, a considerable distance from the St. Marcouf battery. OB West is sure that this is only a diversion, but Wegener adds that his staff feels that this is the real thing. Several ship contacts have been detected.

At 3 a.m., Krancke calls Wegener back and instructs him to alert everyone. The destroyers in Royan are to sail up the coast towards Brest. He tells Wegener to send a few torpedo boats into the Seine Bay to find out what is happening. Although the U-boats are under Dönitz's direct authority, Krancke orders that the coastal boats be made ready to put to sea to repel an invasion fleet.

Wegener tells him that their staff is getting organized. Their chief of staff, Admiral Hoffmann, has also received reports of surface targets from a couple of radar stations near the Atlantic side of the Channel. He and Hoffmann are convinced that this is the invasion. Krancke tells him to notify OB West and OKW immediately of the recent radar reports. Wegener replies that they are in the process of doing that. Krancke thanks him.

After hanging up, Krancke hurriedly gets dressed. Leaving his quarters, he quickly walks across the darkened courtyard of the Bordeaux naval headquarters and up to the commandant's quarters. He is worried. He knows that the second Verlaine verse has been broadcast, and that the Fifteenth Army was on alert.

He wakes up the Bordeaux naval commandant and tells him what has been reported. They sit in the commandant's drawing room and discuss the situation. Krancke admits that he cannot understand how any type of enemy operation could possibly be afoot, not with Force 6 seas in the Channel.

They discuss the radar contacts. Wegener had told Krancke that the radar returns could not be completely confirmed. There was such a large area of them. The radar operators are convinced that either this is some new type of enemy jamming device, or every ship in the Allied fleets is headed for France.

***

3 a.m. General Wilhelm Falley, sitting in the back of his Dusenburg, orders his driver to stop the car as they approach a clear intersection, some twenty miles south of Coutances. As the car stops, two guards walk over. Falley and Major Bartuzat get out and identify themselves, bringing the guards to rigid attention.

He tells them to relax, and then asks how long they have heard planes flying by. One of the men has just got on so he does not know. The other one though has been on for two hours and replies that he has been hearing aircraft engines all through that time.

"So have I…" replies Falley thoughtfully. They all fall silent as they hear aircraft fly above them, headed north in the night sky. Too much is going on. And a little earlier, the guards had seen flare markers being dropped. Markers meant pathfinders, and that strongly indicated enemy paratroop landings.

"This is no routine attack, Bartuzat," Falley says. "I don't like it," he adds.

He thinks about it. They hear enemy bombers flying overhead, headed for targets inland, the sound of their engines loud and harsh.

Falley finally decides. He tells Baumann, "Turn around. Back to the command post." War games or not, they are returning to headquarters to see what is going on.

They climb back into the car, the sound of its running motor almost impossible to hear over the overhead din. Falley tells the driver as he gets in, "Let's get back to headquarters right away."

Baumann turns the staff car around in the intersection and they speed northward, towards Picauville again.

They do not know that, by the time they get close to their headquarters, it will have been overrun by American paratroopers.

***

At 3:15, General Kraiss, commanding the 352 Infantry Division, summons his regimental commanders. He tells them about the airborne drops, then turns to *Oberstleutnant* Karl Meyer, commanding his reserve regiment, the 915th, with

1,750 men. He orders him to lead his men away from the Bayeux area to look for paratroopers. He is to probe inland west-southwest behind the division's left flank. The companies will have to load up, some in tired old French Otrag trucks, some on confiscated bicycles, and many simply on foot. They are to head towards the Cerisy Forest.

One thing is critical, Kraiss adds. If Meyer does not meet any real resistance and the invasion comes, they are to return as fast as possible to augment those on the coast. So Meyer will have to stay in contact with division headquarters by radio. Meyer acknowledges.

Kraiss wished him good luck, and Meyer leaves. It will take him almost an hour to move all of his men out and get his *Kampfgruppe* on the road.

By 3:35 a.m., assault craft are being lowered from Allied transports in preparation for the landings that will soon follow. Hundreds of Allied soldiers begin warily descending swaying nets into scores of landing craft. Many men are tired from lack of sleep. They have been aboard transports for days, and are finally getting ready to assault their targets.

Shortly after 4 a.m., as Allied aircraft roar overhead, the first wave of the American assault craft begin their 1½-hour trip in towards the beaches. They have an 11½-mile run. Each of the five sea lanes is marked with buoys for traffic control.

The landing has begun.

3:40 a.m. Max Pemsel is busily filtering messages coming into Seventh Army headquarters. A major airborne drop has come down along the east bank of the Orne River, and another has landed over on the left, around the Vire and Merderet Rivers. Marcks is probably right. Chances are, the landing will be on the coast, somewhere in the middle.

A dispatch is passed to Pemsel. Communications have been lost with Ste.-Mère-Église.

***

It is now after 4 a.m. At OB West, von Rundstedt and Blumentritt have been monitoring the incoming messages for the last three hours. *Fallschirmtruppen* have landed sporadically over an extensive area, and an amphibious assault now seems likely. In reaction to the paratroop reports, he had ordered the 12th SS Panzer and *Panzer Lehr* divisions alerted around 2:45. The 12th SS Panzer was to form up its units and get ready to roll towards Caen. Bayerlein's *Lehr* was told to prepare to do the same.

Finally, von Rundstedt decides that it is time to bring up the panzers. Rommel is in Germany, so at 4:25 a.m., von Rundstedt orders *Panzergruppe West* to "reconnoiter in force into 711th Division sector." To keep OKW informed, Blumentritt calls

Warlimont and informs him what they are doing. They follow up with a message at 0445, formally requesting that the panzer reserves be released:

> OB WEST IS FULLY AWARE THAT IF THIS IS ACTUALLY A LARGE-SCALE ENEMY OPERATION IT CAN ONLY BE MET SUCCESSFULLY IF IMMEDIATE ACTION IS TAKEN. THIS INVOLVES THE COMMITMENT ON THIS DAY OF THE AVAILABLE STRATEGIC RESERVES… IF THE 12TH SS AND PANZER LEHR DIVISIONS ASSEMBLE QUICKLY AND GET AN EARLY START THEY CAN ENTER THE BATTLE ON THE COAST DURING THE DAY.

On the Cotentin peninsula, firefights have turned into skirmishes as both sides collect their forces and begin probing the enemy for weak points. Bands of American paratroopers roam the countryside, struggling to join up with their regiments and move to their objectives.

One such group of four soldiers from the 508th Regiment of the 82nd Airborne, led by Lieutenant Malcolm Brannen, is walking down the small road towards nearby Picauville. Suddenly, a black car comes speeding down the road at them. Brannen yells, "Here comes a car! Stop it!"

The Americans fling their weapons up and yell at the approaching vehicle to halt. The occupants either do not hear or chose to ignore them, so the GIs open fire.

General Wilhelm Falley, having turned around, is impatient to get back to the 91st headquarters. As his Dusenberg barrels along a minor road, he says to Baumann, "Drive faster. It's light already."

They are almost there, only a few kilometers away. He is tired from the wasted trip, and worried about all the air activity overhead. Something is up. Hopefully, army headquarters will figure it out before it is too late. Some sort of big enemy air operation has started. A paratroop drop perhaps? They have not seen any chutes, although it has been cloudy.

The car turns into a side road. Far in the distance, Falley can barely make out the upper floor of the château he is using for his headquarters… If the enemy is already on the ground, his regiments will have to find and attack them immediately, before they can group themselves into a solid defense. As soon as he gets back, he will order a full issue of ammunition. And then they—

The still night is suddenly shattered by the sound of automatic fire. The car's windshield spatters with little starbursts as bullets slam through it. Bartuzat, sitting in the front passenger's seat, immediately sags and falls to the side, struck in the face and the chest.

Baumann swerves the car violently and loses control. The vehicle careens back and forth across the road, tires screeching loudly as he desperately tries to compensate with the wheel. With a final rattle of stones, they leave the right side of the road and lurch into a short stone wall. Both Bartuzat and the driver are ejected from the car by the impact. Bartuzat is thrown violently onto the ground. His Luger slithers away from him, bounces once in front of him, and lands next to the road.

Dazed, Bartuzat begins crawling towards the pistol a few yards away. He becomes aware of the enemy soldiers racing towards him. Are they American? He yells in English. "Don't kill! Don't kill!" as he edges away from the car and closer to his weapon.

Lieutenant Brannen sees at a glance that the officer still in the car is out of commission. He looks back to the man on the ground. He sees his arm stretch out, apparently for his pistol. "Stop!" Brannen yells. The German continues reaching for the Luger. Coldly, the GI levels his Thompson and fires at the figure below him. One bullet hits the man in the head, blood briefly spurting up in a high geyser before subsiding.

The lieutenant walks over to the car and examines the passenger. He notices that the officer in front, slumped down, has red stripes on the sides of his trousers, gold epaulets, and an Iron Cross hanging around his neck. This might be someone important. He sees the man's hat lying on the seat, picks it up, and reads "Falley" on the inside sweatband. He rips the name out to send back to headquarters. Maybe they will know who this joker is.[11]

5:00 a.m. in Cherbourg. Dawn is about an hour away. Admiral Hennecke is in teletype contact with *Oberleutnant zur See* Walter Ohmsen, commanding the large naval gun battery at St. Marcouf. The battery is about 8km northwest of the large beach area next to the Vire estuary. The battery commander had earlier sent a message detailing a status report, and that an air raid around 11 p.m. had knocked out all six 75mm anti-aircraft guns. The gun crews had tried to repair two after the raid, and were still working on them.

Now the commander is on the teletype again. Hennecke's eyes widen as he reads the message. The battery has sighted many vessels. Presumably they are the enemy's, but Ohmsen wants to make sure.

Hennecke replies immediately:

> ANY VESSELS SIGHTED BOUND TO BE ENEMY SHIPS. PERMISSION TO OPEN
> FIRE. AMMUNITION TO BE USED SPARINGLY.
> MESSAGE ENDS. OUT.

***

5:15 a.m. Alfred Jodl is spending a quiet morning in his quarters. Up at 5 a.m., he is having his usual light breakfast of a soft-boiled egg, a thin slice of toast, and a cup of coffee, before leaving his quarters.

The news from Italy is bad. With Rome fallen, Kesselring's men are pulling back, desperately trying to stave off an Allied breakthrough. Walter Warlimont has been ordered to go see Kesselring and scope the latest situation.

As if on cue, Warlimont calls. Up since 4 a.m. following the airborne reports in Normandy, he now reports the situation to Jodl. He tells him about OB West's teletype message requesting release of the reserve panzers, and his own subsequent phone conversation with Blumentritt. "OB West wants to move them into the invasion area immediately," he concludes.

Jodl hesitates before responding with a simple question: "Are you so sure that this is the invasion? According to the reports I've received, it could very well be a diversionary attack… you know, part of a deception plan."

Jodl decides. "OB West has sufficient reserves right now," he states. "They should try to clean up the attack at present with the forces at their disposal."

Warlimont acknowledges, stunned. No reinforcements? He is not going to argue with Jodl, though.

Jodl, perhaps perceiving the surprise in his deputy's voice, finishes by calmly observing, "I do not think that this is the time to release the OKW reserves." Jodl also says that he is not going to awaken the Führer about this. He had only gone to bed a couple of hours ago taking some sleeping drugs. Typical.

Warlimont questions this, and Jodl responds, "We must wait for further clarification of the situation."

Warlimont understands and says, "Sir, in view of the Normandy situation, shall I proceed to Italy as planned?"

Jodl thinks about this, and replies, "Yes… Yes, I don't see why not."

***

Warlimont hangs up, shaking his head. He looks at Baron von Buttlar-Brandenfels who is standing next to him, and who had heard most of the conversation.

"I sympathize with Blumentritt," he says. "This decision is absolutely contrary to my understanding of what the plan was to be in the event of an invasion."

Warlimont stares down at the phone. This information will not be well received. Still, he is not in a position to argue with his boss. Sighing, he picks up the receiver again and telephones Blumentritt in France.

Blumentritt comes on the line at the command bunker and tells Warlimont that, based upon the information coming in, this enemy operation is more than likely the actual invasion, and that the apparent target is Normandy.

Walther replies that he will pass that along. In the meantime, he adds reluctantly, the release order for the reserve panzers will have to be postponed until the situation becomes clearer. The Führer himself will release them at that point. But the panzers cannot move without his approval, and he has only been in bed a couple of hours.

Blumentritt in an angry tone demands to know who countermanded the order.

"General Jodl," Warlimont replies. "He feels that would be the decision the Führer would make if he were awake."

Blumentritt voices his objections loudly, his tone cold and biting. Walther sympathizes, but he is just doing his job.

***

When Blumentritt tells von Rundstedt that OKW will not release the reserve panzers, the crusty old field marshal becomes furious. His face turns bright red, and his speech becomes almost incoherent. He yells that he wants confirmation of this insult. So their Ia, Bobo Zimmermann, calls OKW back to confirm the surprising decision, and to try to get it changed.

Zimmermann's call goes through to the Strub Barracks. But this time, instead of Warlimont taking the call, von Buttlar-Brandenfels does. He has just gotten off the phone with Jodl.

Zimmermann asks for confirmation of the release delay, and von Buttlar coldly gives it to him. Zimmermann starts protesting, telling him that the order is crazy. Von Buttlar's reaction is swift.

"These divisions are under the direct control of OKW!" he barks. "You had no right to alert them without our prior approval. You are to halt the panzers immediately."

Zimmermann, distressed, tries to argue the point. "Sir," he says, "if we cannot use the panzers now, the Normandy landings will succeed, and then all types of unforeseeable consequences will follow."

Von Buttlar though is adamant. "You are in no position to judge," he replies curtly.

Zimmermann is shocked. If OB West was in no position to judge, who the hell was?

Von Buttlar cuts the argument short by snapping, "Nothing is to be done before the Führer makes his decision. Do as you are told!" He slams the receiver down.

Blumentritt and Zimmermann walk in to von Rundstedt's office and find the field marshal half-sitting on the front edge of his desk, glaring at the floor. The Old Man is really pissed off. This is not going to be easy.

The old Prussian looks up at them. "*Ja?*" he grouches.

Zimmermann tells him about the phone call as von Rundstedt begins to seethe. Blumentritt tactfully suggests that he call the Führer himself. After all, he has the privilege as a field marshal to be able to go over OKW's head.

The field marshal glares at his chief of staff. Does he know what that would mean? Being hard of hearing, it is embarrassing to not hear a sentence, or misunderstand it. And to do that to someone important on the line... Besides, he does not want his voice secretly recorded, so that his comments might be used against him later. Worst of all though, it would look like he was begging. He would have to swallow his noble pride and grovel to that house painter. He imagines the Führer grinning as he humbles himself into the phone.

He grits his teeth. He will never call that Bohemian corporal. He is an aristocratic Prussian, a true blue-blood. He despises that Nazi bastard and his commoner background. For months now he has been treated like a figurehead in the West. There was that humiliating war conference in May. And now that he is just trying to do his job, those martinets around Hitler are playing power games, trying to cover their fat butts. Yes, well, the hell with all of them. He will never crawl on his knees to them, no matter what the situation—war or no war.

***

At Berchtesgaden it is about 5:30, and the birds are just starting to sing. Dawn will shortly break against the beautiful backdrop of the Obersalzberg mountain, and a lovely Austrian sky.

At the Berghof, Admiral von Puttkamer, Hitler's naval aide, has been told about the airborne drops. Does he wake up Hitler after only a few hours' rest?

Hitler at this point in his life is an insomniac. He stays up into the early morning hours, and only turns in when he can no longer stay awake, to sleep fitfully for a few hours. On the evening of June 5, as was his custom of late, he had stayed up well into the early morning hours, entertaining Eva Braun and some of her young female friends with his stories and trite chit-chat.

The Führer had finally gone to bed at 3 a.m. To make sure that he slept well, Dr. Morell had given him a sleeping drug. Obviously, the Führer would be in no mood to receive any news, good or bad, after less than three hours' sleep. And the admiral felt that Hitler should be in good spirits before hearing about some paratroop landing in France.

So the admiral decides not to wake him. "Besides," he comments to an assistant, "there isn't much to tell him anyway."

***

Along the Calvados beach near Ste.-Honorine-des Pertes,[12] the night is nearly over. It has, all things considered, been somewhat eventful for Major Werner Pluskat, commanding the three batteries of the *1. Abteilung, 352. Artillerie Regiment*. Awoken just before midnight in his gloomy château in Etreham[13] by the sound of anti-aircraft fire, he had immediately phoned his regimental headquarters to find out what was going on. He had spoken to Karl Ocker.[14]

"What's going on?" he had asked.

Ocker had replied "I don't know yet," adding that when he found out anything, he would call back. But the continued bombing up the coast had worried the major. Instinctively, he called Major Paul Block, the 352nd's Ic, at division headquarters. Block had replied, "It's not clear yet. We think American paratroopers are landing to the left of us, but I'm not sure." The reports were very sketchy.

After hanging up, Pluskat had considered a possible airborne attack to his west and wondered what to do. Should he get up and go to regimental headquarters? Or to his command bunker on the shore? Or was this just another one of the many false alarms they had been given over and over in the last few months? In the end, he just tried to go back to bed. But Block's report, the bombings, the sporadic anti-aircraft fire... It was difficult to go to sleep.

Twenty minutes later, regimental headquarters had called back. Ocker told him that the invasion was probably beginning, and that he had better alert his unit. So Pluskat got dressed and woke up his two ordnance officers, *Leutnant* Fritz Theen and *Hauptmann* Ludz Wilkening. They grabbed a driver, and together with Pluskat's dog Harras, they all climbed into his small command Volkswagen and drove north about four kilometers to his fortified, advanced command bunker, located on a cliff overlooking the bay.[15] They had arrived there after one o'clock in the morning.

Pluskat had found that all was quiet at the bunker. As the hours crept by though, they noted a tremendous amount of air activity going on, although actual glimpses of aircraft were sporadic. Bombing raids continued far up the coast around Boulogne, and many aircraft formations had flown by in the clouds, both to the east of them and to the west. Some groups seemed to be going inland, and some seemed to be headed back out to sea, towards England. Later, a small bombing raid actually flew over their bunker, the bombs falling somewhere inland. Occasionally the quiet sound of the waves was broken by sporadic gunfire far off to the west; evidence perhaps of the few sketchy reports that he had received from regimental headquarters about possible enemy airborne landings.

However, that had been the extent of the excitement for the night.

Now Pluskat, tired and somewhat calmer, stands in his command bunker, gazing with his powerful binoculars through the narrow aperture out into the dark Channel and at the shore to each side of him. For several hours now, he has periodically swept the area thoroughly and painstakingly for any signs of enemy activity. He is emotionally drained from the night's apparent activity. Out here alone with his men, he feels isolated, vulnerable. The sea though, seems tranquil despite the recent storm, and the dark skies, though cloudy, occasionally glow from the backdrop of a full moon. It is now exceptionally quiet, the misty stillness in the air heavy.

The sky to the east is just starting to lighten up. Dawn cannot be far away. Pluskat will soon get to return to his quarters and finally go back to bed, another long night over. No invasion, it seems. But those reports of *Fallschirmjägern* landing to the west bother him.

The men in the bunker rarely speak, and when they do, it is in low tones. They are busy listening for something, anything. But there is nothing. Dead silence, except for the rolling sound of the waves.

Pluskat turns to Theen and Wilkening, now talking quietly. "Still nothing out there," he tells them. "I'm about to give it up." He sighs, walks over to the aperture, and once more scans the horizon for any signs of activity... No, nothing... Empty sea... Not one—

He stops his sweep and gazes hard through the glasses at the center of the bay, tensing up. Something there! A vessel? He peers hard through the glasses. No, not just one; several…

He lowers the binoculars and steps back in amazement. Pausing, he raises them again, his heart pounding. The dim dark-gray horizon is starting to fill with all sorts of vaporous vessels, a ghostly armada materializing out the mist, moving in slow, steady, precise formations towards the coast—towards *him*.

He hands the glasses to Theen and says in wonder, "It's the invasion. Take a look."

Theen raises the glasses, observes the massive ethereal fleet of ships coming closer, and says in shock, "*Mein Gott*. It's the invasion." He gives them in turn to Wilkening, and the captain confirms it.

Pluskat quickly grabs the phone and calls Block at division headquarters and tells him. "There must be 10,000 ships out there!" he adds.[16] "It's unbelievable… It's fantastic. This must be the invasion."

Block is calm on the other end. "No… Look Pluskat, are you really sure there are that many ships? The Americans and the British together don't have that many ships."

Angrily, Pluskat snaps, "For crissakes, come and see for yourself!"

Block, still skeptical, and asks calmly, "Which way are these ships heading?"

Pluskat, staring at the enemy vessels slowly closing in, yells, "*Auf mich zu direkt!*"[17]

But Block still remains dubious. Pluskat, disgusted with him, growls, "Aw, the hell with you," and throws down the receiver.

Some ten minutes later, hundreds of Allied warships begin their bombardment of the Normandy coast. Scores of projectiles of all calibers start slamming into the beaches and the bluffs, raining down from different distances and angles, shelling the five major beach areas—Sword, Gold, Juno, Omaha, and Utah. Swarms of Allied aircraft fly over the shore, headed for coastal targets, unworried about any interdiction from the Luftwaffe.

The firing of the mighty battleships is distinct, and the massive thuds from their large guns can be felt a few miles away and heard for many more. The recoils from the gun turrets slam the warships sideways, setting up small tidal waves that drench the troops standing in the nearby small craft as they head in towards the beaches. A silent enemy battery on Pointe du Hoc takes a terrific beating, and portions of the point collapse and fall into the sea.

Inland and far away from the shelling, the three panzer divisions closest to the Normandy area have been on alert status for hours, biding their time, and still in or near the same areas they have occupied since midnight. They have performed a number of innocuous and relatively unimportant duties as they await orders from above to march, supposedly towards the Calvados coast.

Fritz Witt's 12th SS Panzer Division is scouting out the local areas. One regiment is reconnoitering up the road towards Caen. Another is moving into and around Lisieux to the southeast, looking for reported paratroopers near there.

The massive *Panzer Lehr* is spread out all around near the town of Chartres, ready to move. Bayerlein and his men have been standing around for hours now, impatient.

The story is not much different for the 21st Panzer, closest to the beaches. Many of its units had finally been given marching orders by their now-returned, frustrated commanding officer and are technically on the move, although slowly. Most of the division is experiencing traffic problems as it approaches the outskirts of Caen from the south. Those elements along the eastern bank of the Orne River have sent forward a few patrols and are poised to attack, expecting the go-ahead to start a major assault to recapture the two bridges over the river and the parallel canal. Couriers are sent to divisional headquarters with requests to advance. The answers are the same—get in position on the road, be ready to move out, and hold until further orders.

***

Over the next five hours, Marcks' headquarters in St. Lô receives many airborne landing reports. As a few groups of prisoners taken east of Caen identify the 3rd Parachute Brigade of the 6th British Airborne Division. Reports from the 709th Infantry sector in the Cotentin peninsula have identified prisoners taken from the 501st and 505th Parachute Regiments, part of the American 101st Airborne Division.

The 84th Corps staff continues feverishly—Hayn later writes, "humming like a beehive"—to plot the report positions and issue orders. But in their minds, they have no doubts about what is happening, and that a landing is coming. The wait is finally over. The months of agonizing suspense, ended. The many false alerts, and the seemingly endless, mentally (and often physically) numbing hours of tensely manning their posts, the training, the many analytical hours of theorizing and discussions, the hours of preparing defenses, and the agonizing wait for an enemy who never showed up—over.

One thing is sure. General Marcks' men have no illusions at all about where the landing is going to be.

By now the Allied fleet and air forces have pummeled the target beaches, and thousands of Allied troops are hitting the shores of Normandy.

D-Day has come.

1   Cornelius Ryan wrote that the caller was the division commanding officer, General Richter. Paul Carell agreed with Jon Lewis' account (*Eyewitness D Day*) that it was the operations officer on the line. Studying Ryan's interview with Hayn, it seems Lewis was probably right. Ryan's information was based upon a postwar interview with General Richter, who told him that he himself had made the call. Perhaps then, the chief of staff actually initiated the call and Richter had then come on the line. Jacobsen's biography of Marcks does not specify.

2   The Bavent Forest is about 13km east-northeast of Caen, between Escoville and Troarn. Here elements of the British 3rd Brigade/6th Airborne Div. had landed. Their objective, among other things, was to destroy the five bridges across the Dives River to prevent any enemy counterattacks on their left flank from Fifteenth Army's 711th Division.

3   "The red carrot has left."

4   *Forces Français de l'Intérieur*—the main French Resistance group.

5   According to Paul Carrell, Hayn adds, "This is the invasion." This claim though, is unsubstantiated in any other account.

6   A delightful Norman apple brandy, popular with the occupational troops in the area.

7   With the commanding officer (*Generalleutnant* Karl-Wilhelm von Schlieben) departed for the wargames in Rennes, Hamann was the acting commander of the 709th Division.

8   It should be noted here that although hundreds of aircraft ended up dropping their airborne troops in the wrong areas—sometimes way off course—this did have one significant good effect. Airborne troops being dropped all over bewildered the Germans even more than the paratroopers. Also, at least the paratroopers, as lost as they were, knew what was going on. The Germans though, with spotty reports, commanding officers departed for the wargames, and communication problems, could only guess what was going on.

9   *Kapitän zur See* Edward Wegener, *Generalstabsoffizier Ia* (Operations Chief), *Marinegruppenkommandos West.*

10   *Vizeadmiral* Friedrich Rieve took command April 22, 1943. Originally called, *Marinebefehlshaber Kanalküste,* it was renamed on February 1, 1943.

11   There are different versions of this incident. Brannen himself gave conflicting accounts after the war. In almost half the descriptions, it was Falley who was thrown from the vehicle and Major Bartuzat in front was killed immediately. Others state the opposite, and a couple accounts state that there were actually four in the car, not three. The driver, Corporal Baumann, survived the ambush and was taken prisoner. He attests that it was Falley who had been riding in the front seat and was killed immediately when the Americans opened fire.

12   About 4.5km west of Port-en-Bessin.

13   Pluskat's 1st Battalion headquarters. The villa was devoid of any furniture, and Pluskat himself slept on a folding cot.

14   *Oberstleutnant* Karl-Wilhelm Ocker, commanding the 352nd Division's artillery regiment.

15   Pluskat's command bunker was located in WN-59 (see footnote for May 10), just to the east of Omaha beach.

16   In the movie version of *The Longest Day*, the figure used was 5,000.

17   In the movie (for which Ryan co-wrote the screenplay), the discussion is with Ocker, not Block. Ocker asks him *"Mein lieber Pluskat, welchen Kurs haben diese Schiffe?"* ("My dear Pluskat, on what course are these ships heading?"), and Pluskat yells back excitedly *"Auf mich zu direkt!"* ("Right for *me!*")

Tuesday, June 6—Part Two

It is quiet at the Rommel home in Herrlingen. Dawn has broken. A few birds chirp in the distance. Otherwise, it is the peaceful silence of another day.

There are a number of people staying in or near the villa, besides Rommel and his wife Lucie. There are the servants, Karolina and Private Loitsl. There is also Mrs. Hildegarde Kircheim, and Daniel, his driver. And Manfred is home, on leave from his Luftwaffe anti-aircraft defense unit in nearby Ulm.

Lucie is still asleep, as is Manfred, in his room. But the field marshal is up early, still in his dressing gown. This is a special day: Lucie's 50th birthday. Rommel has made arrangements with the servants to have bouquets of sweet-smelling flowers from the fields in each of the rooms. The field marshal is in the drawing room, enjoying a small breakfast. His wife's presents are gathered on the table. Later that morning, he will carefully lay them out, putting last-minute touches here and there. Naturally, the handmade Parisian shoes that he had bought her will be the centerpiece of the gift array. They are a special edition of platform-style, gray suede pumps with black heels, and as a layer in the sole, there is a suede strip that runs around the shoe. And of course, they are her size: 5½.

He smiles in anticipation of how she will react when she sees them. This should be a good day.

Sometime around 6 a.m., the phone rings. Surprised, Rommel walks over to answer it. Maybe it is General Schmundt calling about his appointment with the Führer.[1]

"Yes," he says, "Rommel here." Instead of Schmundt though, he is mildly surprised to find his chief of staff on the line. Rommel greets Speidel amiably, "Well, Speidel. What's up?"

He feels himself go numb as Speidel reports that "some sort of an attack" has been made. There have been a number of airborne drops in the Normandy area., and some as far northeast as across the Somme River. The reports are confusing. Rommel listens in stunned silence. An invasion? In lousy weather? Did the enemy know he was home?

Speidel tells him that there is as yet no sense of scale about the airborne assaults, and concludes that he is not sure whether or not this is just a "Dieppe-type" of attack—possibly to divert their attention—or the prelude to the actual invasion.

Rommel replies tersely, "Well, find out—and *fast*."

Speidel acknowledges the order and reports to him what steps he has taken so far. Rommel indicates his approval, and adds, "I'm returning as fast as I can make it."

Speidel has thought about this. He believes that Rommel should hold off leaving, in light of the importance of his trip home, both personally and officially (the upcoming meeting with Hitler). Speidel decides that Rommel should wait a bit until they better assess the situation.

He conveys this to Rommel. "I do not think you should leave right away, *Herr Feldmarschall*," he suggests, "but I think that you should wait before making any decision until I ring you back." Speidel could get some more information and better determine what was going on, and if this was an actual invasion or just a diversion. After all, there had been no reports as yet of naval task forces.

Rommel is persuaded by Speidel's logic, and grudgingly agrees to consider it. His mind racing, he slowly climbs the stairs to his bedroom. Just in case, he is going to pack. Lucie, now awake, can tell that he is quite upset about the phone call, but she wisely decides not to ask him about it. He does not tell her what has happened, but merely starts packing.

***

Staff members at Rommel's headquarters are at this time optimistic about this whole landing thing. Many of the staff, up most of the night, have gone to bed. After all, things seem to be going well. OB West has ordered the reserve panzer divisions towards the coast. No one at La Roche-Guyon knows that OKW has countermanded the order.

The 21st Panzer Division, alerted since midnight, is now moving towards their jump-off points against the enemy. One target: the British paratroopers on the east bank of the Orne, holding the two bridges near Bernville. Von Oppeln's panzers are awaiting Feuchtinger's word to advance north. And in addition to the infantry units mobilized and ready on the coast, three full panzer divisions are thought to be on their way into the troubled area.

Unfortunately, no one remembers General Pickert and his III Flak Corps, located on the other side of the Seine. He is not informed about the invasion that morning, so he goes on an inspection tour. He gets the news when he returns. He immediately drives to Paris. The flak units will not get the word until mid-afternoon.[2]

Speidel's own complacency is shaken a short time later, when at 6:15 a.m., almost an hour after daybreak and a quarter of an hour past sunrise, he gets a call from Max Pemsel. Pemsel tersely lets him have it. Word has come from the 21st Panzer headquarters. An Allied naval bombardment off Normandy started at about 05:30. There. That ought to jolt him.

Speidel is indeed surprised by the information; but he still stubbornly persists that this is a ruse, and that the main effort will be somewhere else.

Pemsel tells him he has received sporadic reports from units telling him that they have heard sounds of combat, and can see ships out on the bay. But they have no clear description of what is going on. Pemsel comments, "I'm fighting the sort of battle that William the Conqueror must have fought—by ear and sight only."

Speidel argues his case to Pemsel. He is nothing if not intelligent, and his points this morning, despite his fatigue, are no doubt effective to Pemsel, who is surprised that Speidel still refuses to believe that the invasion has come. By the time Speidel finishes though, he has Pemsel again convinced that he is probably right—so much so in fact, that Pemsel later writes in his own war diary, against his better instincts, that the purpose of the bombardment is as yet unknown at this time, and quite possibly a diversionary tactic.

It is 6:28 a.m., about an hour and a quarter after low tide.[3] A light mist, combined with dust and the acrid smells of cordite smoke created by the naval bombardment, fills the air. American troops begin to land among the obstacles at the water's edge and assault two stretches of shore that they have designated Utah and Omaha beaches. The landing craft at Utah carry the advance elements of the US 4th Infantry Division, while to Omaha go the US 1st and the 29th Infantry. It is H-Hour for the Americans.

Tensely awaiting the 4th Infantry along Utah's nine-mile beach are several scattered strongpoints, covered by several machine-gun positions along the shore. In addition, there are a dozen batteries in the area in various conditions capable of ranging in on the beach.

One of the strongest positions remains the St. Marcouf battery, manned by 300 men. Three of the 210mm guns have been installed, although only two are casemated. Allied air raids had slowed down the process considerably since April, and the bombings of the night before took a heavy toll on the battery. Some 600 tons of bombs knocked out all of the anti-aircraft guns, including the six 75mm guns. And a couple of uncoordinated ground attacks in the early morning by scattered elements of the 101st Airborne have kept the battery crews off-balance as they try to repair the guns.

Some two kilometers southwest of the Marcouf Battery is the Azeville Battery. Its field of fire is not as good as the one at Marcouf.

The Americans are not opposed as they near the shore. Fortunately for them, there are few enemy batteries still operational, and any firing quickly becomes the target of Allied counterbattery fire, plentiful and accurate. Also, many bombs and shells miss the coast and explode in the sand, at the water's edge and out to the incoming breakers. These misses have detonated many planted German mines—obstacles that the Germans had counted on to take out a number of the landing craft.

The American landing craft hit the beach, and the troops of the 8th Infantry Regiment scramble ashore with little opposition. They discover that they have landed over a mile south of their intended spot, a navigational error caused partly by the hazy air, and partly by the lateral cross-current moving southeast. Unknown to them, it is a lucky error, since the area that they drift into is considerably less fortified than the beaches a mile up the coast; and they are that much further from the Marcouf Battery. They decide to let the error go and bring in the successive waves to the same area.

At Omaha beach to the east, it is quite a different story. The worst fears of the assaulting troops are about to be realized. The battle-hardened 916th and 726th Grenadier Regiments are waiting for the enemy landing craft to come into range. Their main batteries are better concealed and mostly still intact, because the 1,285 tons of bombs that were supposed to hit them have fallen mostly inland. This is due to the heavy clouds and the inaccuracy of the over-compensating Allied bombers.

The beach defenders hold their fire until the assault craft are close. They then open up with a terrific tumult, pouring a devastating fusillade into the boats struggling to make it to the beach. The surviving craft, sometimes coming in abreast with only a foot between them, finally reach the water's edge, and their bow ramps flop down into the surf. The men inside, poised to jump out, are now exposed to murderous machine-gun fire. As they surge forward into the chest-high swirling waters, many are mowed down like wheat. The bullets cut into their numbers as they desperately try to make it out of the water and onto the sand. They have to get out of the open immediately, mostly because it is lethal out there, but also to make room, because the next wave will be landing in twenty minutes. But soldiers are falling everywhere, hit by incoming fire. Death awaits the Americans.

One primary target is a German heavy-caliber battery atop Pointe du Hoc, a spit of cliff jutting out into the bay a couple miles from the western end of Omaha beach. Some 225 men of the American 2nd Ranger Battalion approach the point in ten British landing craft, plowing through the rough waves and strong crosswind. They will have a good deal of trouble taking the position, only to realize that the guns are not in the bunkers and have somehow been moved to another location.

Although the British and Canadians are scheduled to hit Gold, Juno, and Sword beaches between 6 a.m. and 6:30, they have decided to go in later than the Americans, and thereby catch the tide going back in. This will help them avoid many of the relatively few low-tide obstacles, while giving the ships more time to bombard the shore. Unfortunately, the seas are too rough for any more delays, so they begin heading towards the beaches. They immediately run into problems making headway in the choppy waters. The British finally hit Gold beach at 6:25 a.m., and Sword beach five minutes later. The first wave of Canadians land at Juno beach from 6:45 to 6:55 a.m.

One of the greatest threats to the Germans is on Gold beach, where elements of the 50th (Northumbrian) Infantry Division are splashing ashore. Among them are a significant number of tanks and motorized vehicles, elements of the British 8th Armored Brigade. General Montgomery wants to be sure that he weights the punch of his first waves with armor. He wants them to be ready for the panzers that he fears will soon come tearing over the bluffs and crashing down upon his men.

At 6:45 a.m., Fifteenth Army Headquarters receives a call from Max Pemsel, updating them on the situation. He acknowledges that there has been a naval bombardment, but no actual invasion has yet been reported. He also states that Seventh Army will be able to cope with the situation themselves. General von Salmuth, hearing the news, comments with glee that the invasion must have already failed. He then promptly goes back to bed.[4]

***

Around 7 a.m., *Obergruppenführer* Sepp Dietrich at his I SS Panzer Corps head-quarters calls the command center of the 12th SS Panzer Division. Based on the reports he has been given, he places them under the command of General Kuntzen's 81st Corps. They are to contact corps headquarters in Rouen. In the meantime, the entire division will soon be ordered to move up, assemble around Lisieux, and stay there to await further orders. The puzzled regimental commanders just shake their heads.

***

7:30 a.m., Jodl telephones OB West to get a situation update for the Führer when he wakes up. This time von Rundstedt himself picks up the receiver. Taking up the cause his staff members have fruitlessly pursued for the last few hours, the old man bluntly gets to the point. The panzers must be released immediately to deal with the landing. As von Rundstedt strains with his bad hearing to catch every word coming from the receiver, and with Blumentritt listening in on an extension, Jodl again turns him down. He insists again that, even if there is a landing (and that has not been confirmed), the panzers must not be released without orders from the Führer. The 12th SS, already in the process of moving some elements northwest of its bivouac, must be halted at Lisieux. *Panzer Lehr,* still on standby and ready to move out, is to remain where it is.

***

Von Rundstedt slams the phone down and clenches his teeth in rage. Stupid, self-righteous clerk! Jodl can be such an ass. Von Rundstedt stares at his two senior officers. Like him, they realize the consequences of this delay.

The old man sighs, shrugs his shoulders, and grumbles that he is going to get some breakfast. He stops at his office door and adds bitterly without turning around, "If anybody needs me, I'll be out pruning my roses." He leaves to walk back up the hill to his villa.

***

8 a.m. General Feuchtinger is getting upset. He is again on the phone with General Marcks, who has just told him that he has spoken to Berlin, and that the 21st Panzer is now a part of Marcks' Corps, and his to command. That being the case, Feuchtinger is now to turn his entire division around and to go back south to Caen

which is probably a traffic madhouse by now, because the city is being threatened by the British landing at the beaches. From there he is to cross the Orne, advance north towards the British landing area and crush them. The beachhead, Marcks tells him, is the highest priority. Engaging the paratroopers will just have to wait.

When Feuchtinger, trying to hold his temper, snidely points out that somebody has to keep the airborne troops at bay, Marcks agrees. Reconsidering, he allows him to leave behind one panzer recon company from the 22nd Panzer Regiment.

Feuchtinger hangs up the phone, mad as hell. After hours of maneuvering into position, he and his men have just begun to engage the British paratroopers on the east bank of the Orne. Now it is all for nothing!

Feuchtinger orders the panzer recon company to stay behind to deal with the British paratroopers, but he also decides to leave von Luck's 125th *Panzergrenadier* Regiment behind as well. No matter what, a lot of time will be wasted as the rest of the division moves back southwest to Caen, where it will cross the river and the canal and then move up along the west bank towards the beachhead.

***

8:30 a.m. General Marcks is talking to General Kraiss, commanding the beleaguered 352nd Division. Kraiss is nearly frantic. His units are taking heavy casualties and are starting to run low on ammunition. Yes, the enemy is still well pinned down on the beaches, but he does not think that he can keep them there for long. The Americans have taken severe casualties, but they just keep landing, jamming themselves at the base of the cliffs. Sooner or later, they will wear Kraiss' troops down and break out.

He tells Marcks with disgust that Meyer's reserve task force is lost, and Meyer's radio must not be working. Kraiss has scouts out looking for them. Marcks shakes his head, and orders Kraiss to keep him posted.

The enemy has apparently landed in five main areas. The two beachheads on the left are American. Two on the right are British, and the third between them is probably Canadian. The assault troops are supported by an enormous fleet, whose size has dumfounded his observers. The hundreds of aircraft flying overhead gave testimony to the air support that the enemy has committed. And there are the enemy *Fallschirmjägern*. On the left, the American 82nd and 101st Airborne have been identified. On the right flank is the British 6th Airborne, stubbornly holding onto the Orne River crossings.

At 9 a.m., Baron von der Heydte, commanding the 6th Parachute Regiment, calls Marcks. His men are moving towards Ste.-Mère-Église. He has seen the invasion fleet, and he too is stunned by its panorama.

"This is the invasion," he tells Marcks.

***

Activity on the Obersalzberg is increasing. Goebbels at 4 a.m. had brought reports of parachute and glider landings in Northern France, and one report of ship engines heard offshore. Reports from OB West, and another from *II. Fliegerkorps* coming in at 8 a.m., state strong enemy landings between Dieppe and Cherbourg.

Konteradmiral von Puttkamer is definitely worried. His staff have picked up on the radio Allied broadcasts of an invasion in northern France. Something is definitely afoot. What to do? Should he wake the Führer? Reports are sketchy. After some deliberation, he goes to the phone and calls General Jodl at the Little Chancellery. The admiral tells him that there are "definite indications" that an invasion is underway, and he tells Jodl about the Allied broadcast.

It looks like it is time to wake up the Führer. Jodl agrees, and tells him that he will be in his office if needed.

Puttkamer hangs up and take a deep breath. Nervous, he finds Schmundt, Hitler's army adjutant. The news will be better coming from him. The adjutant agrees, and a few minutes later, walks into the Führer's bedroom and wakes him up.

They walk out, the Führer having donned a robe. Armed only with a marked-up map of the area, Schmundt gives him a short synopsis of what has been reported. Hitler calmly listens, and then serenely sends for Keitel and Jodl.

By the time they arrive an hour later he is dressed, but not so pleasant. They talk about the little information that has come in. Between Le Havre and Cherbourg, some large enemy landings have occurred in the early morning. Jodl adds that more are expected, but OB West does not know where.

Jodl also tells him of von Rundstedt's order to move the reserve panzers forward, and that he personally has countermanded the order until they have a better overall picture of what is happening, and the Führer can decide himself where to move them.

Hitler approves of that, and Jodl is relieved to hear it.

The Führer at this point is not sure if this is the primary landing. Twice he has said, "This is *not* the main invasion," Now though, he starts to wonder. "This might indeed be the beginning of the invasion," he says, "but the enemy's intentions in Normandy are only diversionary. I'm sure that the main landing will come somewhere else." He repeats that point again.

The briefing quickly over, he suddenly looks up at them. "Well?" he barks, "Is it or isn't it the invasion?" Before they reply, he turns and walks out.

***

At 9:10, Pemsel at Seventh Army calls Speidel. He has been calling all night with reports, trying to get Speidel to understand what is happening. Finally, he stirs the man out of his complacency by tensely reporting that a massive landing had taken place on the Normandy beaches, and that the beach defense zone has been breached in several areas. They discuss what to do for a good half-hour.

A few minutes later, Blumentritt calls to tell them that Jodl has again forbidden movement of the reserve panzers until Hitler releases them. Still, Rommel's headquarters stays optimistic.

About 10:12 a.m., Speidel decides that it is time to call Rommel back and tell him the news.

***

At Herrlingen, the hours go by slowly. Rommel is packed now and ready to leave if need be. Trying to kill some time between pacing, Rommel fusses with the gift arrangements on the table. The more he tries to act normally though, the more concerned he gets. He talks a bit with Manfred, trying to explain to the boy what might be going on.

A knock on the door of the drawing room startles him out of his reverie. It is the housemaid, Karolina. Coming into the room, she exclaims, "*Herr Feldmarschall* Rommel is wanted on the telephone!" It is 10:15 a.m.[5]

Rommel walks out to the phone. It is Speidel. He confirms Rommel's worst fears as the blood drains from his face. The invasion has begun. It is in Normandy. As the chief of staff adds some early details, Rommel listens in silence. He must return at once and tells Speidel that he will do so. Tersely, he gives orders to hold the beaches.

Lucie, having come into the room while he was on the phone, can tell immediately that the call has changed him. Her husband is now once again terribly upset, and there seems to be a thick layer of tension in the room.

He stands there for a moment after having talked to Speidel, staring at the wall in front of him, lost in a jumble of thoughts. He tells Lucie the shocking news. "The invasion has begun. I must return immediately." Standing there, still stunned, he finally adds softly, "*Wie dumm von mir… Wie dumm von mir…*" How stupid of me…

Quickly regaining his composure, he yanks the receiver up again. When an operator comes on the line, he thunders, "A *führungsblitz*[6] call to the Führer's headquarters, at once!"

The operator hesitates. Such an order has tremendous ramifications for her. It carries absolute top priority in the telephone system. Not just anybody could order such a thing, and its misuse would carry the harshest of reprisals. The poor girl hesitates, not knowing whether to really clear the line for him or not.

"Dammit, girl," he snaps impatiently, "this is Rommel speaking! Give me a line at once!"

That does it. His call finally goes through, and he reports to OKW what he knows of the situation, and that he is returning to his headquarters immediately.

When the call is finished, he stomps upstairs to change into his uniform. Confronting his male servant, Private Rudolf Loistl, he orders, "Get my Daniel up here with the car at once... And get Lang to meet me at Freudenstadt."

As Rommel hurriedly packs to leave, Loistl gets on the phone and calls Lang's home. Fortunately, Lang answers the phone. Loistl fills him in and tells him that the field marshal wants to meet up with him in Freudenstadt. Loistl then informs the field marshal that he has Lang on the phone. Rommel comes downstairs and gets on. He speaks briefly to Lang, telling him of his intentions to return, and the need for haste. He tells Lang to meet him in Freudenstadt at noon.

After he has hung up, Rommel realizes that Lang cannot possibly get there by noon. Grumbling irritably, he calls Lang back and changes the rendezvous time to 1 p.m. Von Tempelhoff will just have to manage to somehow return on his own.

Rommel is ready to leave in fifteen minutes. With the others outside, he and Lucie as usual say their goodbyes privately behind the closed front door.[7] Daniel drives his car around front. Manfred comes in and tells them. Hearing this, Rommel kisses Lucie and puts his hand on his son's head. "Well Manfred," he says, "you and I will try to win the war."

Manfred replies, "*Auf Wiedersehen, Papa.*" They all walk out to the Horch, Rommel gets in the front, and the car takes off down the driveway.

Obviously, Lucie's birthday party is ruined. Lucie walks back into the living room. Seeing *Frau* Kircheim, she tells her in an excited voice that Rommel has already left for France. Mrs. Kircheim can see that Lucie is worried, both for her husband, and for Germany itself. The two ladies talk for a while about the phone call.

Finally, resigned to another birthday without Erwin and disheartened by her husband's abrupt departure, she reluctantly tries on her husband's gift. Perhaps the saddest irony to befall the German hero that day is the fact that the fancy, stylish, gray Parisian suede shoes that he had prided himself on getting his wife for her birthday do not fit her.

***

Lang slowly hangs up the phone, shocked by the two phone calls. Clearly, the field marshal is deeply upset. Lang heard it in his voice. And on top of that, the field marshal is *never* indecisive about anything.

Lang snaps out of the daze. He tells his mother what he is doing, then goes to his room and begins packing feverishly for the return trip. Why did Rommel change the meeting time? Probably so that Lang could get there in time. Then what? Return to France? Or, maybe to still see the Führer.

Lang leaves his mother about ten minutes later.

***

In a late-morning conference at the Berghof, Hitler unrolls a large map across a marble table. He points to the Seine Bay and updates Göring on the situation. He says jubilantly, "They're landing here and here," pointing to the Calvados coast; "just where we expected!" Göring grins back and agrees. Now his squadrons should be able to fly west, storm in over the landing areas, and wreak havoc in the enemy rear areas. The reputation of the Luftwaffe, which has suffered so badly this last year, will finally be restored.

By late afternoon, the mood at German Supreme Command has reached a strange pinnacle as optimism reigns. The enemy is now going to pay dearly for daring to step ashore on occupied Europe! In Göring's jubilation over now being able to act, he sends his staff a congratulatory message, thanking them for the great prepatory work they did in the months before the invasion.

At Hitler's formal noontime conference, his military staff, anxious, agitated, and worried over the news, is surprised when he walks in with a confident smile and pleasant demeanor. He tells them that this invasion is just a ruse and the real one will come sometime later at another location. This opinion has been reinforced by von Rundstedt's report to them late that morning: "Still no clear picture whether we are seeing a diversion or the real attack." He adds that what he has wanted for a while now has finally come to pass. Referring to the Western Allies, he says with a grin, "I am face to face with my real enemies!"

Today's schedule calls for a reception at nearby Klessheim Castle which is too important to cancel. He is to meet with Hungarian Prime Minister Horthy, Czechoslovakian leader Josef Tito and Romania's Marshal Antonescu about improving their war industrial effort. So after the conference, he is driven to the castle in Salzburg at noontime. When he enters the reception room, he beams at his guests. "It's begun at last!" he says. "Now, we can give them a nice little packet!"

Two hours after greeting the Eastern European dignitaries, he has another meeting. In it he goes into a short rant about Göring's Luftwaffe being absent over the invasion area, and how they only have a meager 327 aircraft to oppose the entire invasion. Still happy though, that the enemy have committed themselves, he mulls over OB West's plea to release the reserve panzers, and finally agrees at 3:30 p.m. Then he returns to the Berghof and has a late meal with a few Nazi party senior officials, their wives, and his mistress, Eva Braun. Now though, he starts to worry, sipping tea, quietly sitting with his guests.

He takes a nap for an hour in the evening, and finally has another conference at 11 p.m. to get updates on the situation. Even though the reports of the enemy landings show a strong effort, he remains convinced that this invasion is only a diversion.

By late afternoon, the crisis on Omaha beach is over. The sun has come out. The light winds blowing in from the Channel have thinned the haze and smoky fog created by the explosions, carrying the murky smog inland. Allied bombers and fighters have renewed their attacks on the fixed German positions atop the bluffs and on key artillery positions inland. Several aircraft are coordinating their attacks with the infantrymen.

Ammunition for the surviving German coastal batteries has now nearly run out. With no supplies forthcoming, they are forced to slacken or cease their fire. Allied sappers have finally blasted holes in the anti-tank dike just below the bluffs and facing the beach. The surviving Germans are now retreating.

The Americans at Utah beach, not having had nearly as much trouble as their buddies on Omaha, are exiting the coast area in substantial numbers as they move inland to join the fighting there. Most of the batteries on Utah have either been overrun or are out of shells and must be destroyed.

British and Canadian troops have been moving forward since noon. A couple small inland towns have already been captured. The British 3rd Infantry Division is moving on to Bénouville, while the Canadians push past Ver-sur-Mer, some 2½ miles inland.

The British 6th Airborne troops defending the Caen canal bridge have been relieved by Lord Lovat's commandos. This links the assault troops from the beach with the paratroopers.

Meanwhile, von Luck's panzergrenadiers on the east bank of the Orne have fallen back…

Rommel, having met up with Lang, is racing hell-for-leather across the countryside, Freudenstadt now a couple of hours behind them. As the minutes tick by, Rommel stars glumly at the road ahead, crazy with impatience and concern. The critical battle upon which so much depends, the struggle that his people know he has to win, has started over thirteen hours ago in his absence. Every minute another drop of blood in the life of Germany falling to the ground. He has to get back soon.

At the Calvados beaches, his men are fighting the most important battle of their lives while their leader, the great Desert Fox, is taking a joy ride across France. In the past they had followed him, and had fought and died for him, because he was always right next to them, usually in the worst sector, sharing their dangers, joking with them, encouraging them, coordinating them, as he commanded often desperate situations right from their midst. He had learned that when they talked about following him anywhere, their favorite expression was *Er hat die Strapazen mitgemacht.*[8] Well, he has certainly missed the boat this time. They had been hit, and he was at home, lounging around. His *Fingerspitzengefuehl* that had worked so well in North Africa has failed him.

It isn't fair. He had sacrificed so much for so long, and now at the most critical time, he has erred in going home. The Führer will be furious, and probably not care for his motives or listen to his reasons. He will just scream at him. The field marshal will permanently lose his mentor. Worse, Hitler will take it out on the German people and they will end up fighting to the end, as their country is reduced to ruins.

Glancing at Daniel, he impatiently urges his driver on, saying, "*Tempo! Tempo! Tempo!*" The Horch surges ahead as Daniel gives it more gas. Rommel stares ahead at the road rushing at them. Lang has never seen Rommel so despondent.

Around 4:30 p.m., Rommel tells Daniel that he wants to stop in the next city and phone in for an update on what is going on. Ahead of them is Rheims. Daniel replies that they will get there in about a half-hour. This is of course not good enough for Rommel, but he cannot lash out at Daniel. He is doing his best.

About 25 minutes later, the Horch rolls into town, still 140km east-northeast of Paris and 220km from headquarters. They pull up to the commandant's headquarters. Lang immediately gets out and goes inside to secure a phone to call La Roche-Guyon, Rommel close behind. The field marshal is given a phone in an office and after a small delay, finally gets hold of Speidel. Rommel spends the next fifteen minutes getting updated. Lang walks back outside to the car again to make sure it is getting refueled and serviced.

Speidel fills Rommel in on the situation. Summarizing, he admits that Normandy is indeed a large Allied operation. However, he also adds that this does not discount the possibility of future major operations somewhere else. The chief of staff still feels that this is not the main invasion effort.

Rommel does not pursue that at the moment. He does not want to waste time arguing with Speidel about that. Impatiently, he drops the subject and asks about the German panzer counterattack.

"There has been none as yet, *Herr Feldmarschall,*" Speidel replies. "The closest division to the assault area is the 21st Panzer. The division itself is ready, but it is awaiting further reinforcements before it advances."[9]

Rommel is aghast. What had happened to his counterattack-at-once instructions? "Get the division moving into the attack right now!" he rasps. "Don't await further reinforcements. Attack at once!" The conversation ends, and Rommel dashes back outside. The call has lasted less than fifteen minutes.

Lang can see immediately by the look on Rommel's face that the news is bad. They pile back into the car, and Daniel starts off again, no one saying a word.

The three of them travel on in silence. Daniel is busy driving, and Lang does not dare intrude on the field marshal's thoughts. Rommel suddenly slams one gloved fist into the other and bitterly quips, "My friendly enemy, Montgomery."

A while later, Rommel tries to recover his hope. Perhaps it is not too late to change the outcome. If they can muster their forces quickly enough and reinforce the 21st's panzers when they eventually go in with some assaulting infantry battalions, they still might stop the enemy long enough to let the big panzer divisions arrive and finish the job. "My God!" he says aloud. "If the 21st Panzer can make it, we might just be able to drive them back in three days." Rommel is clearly trying to think positive.

He is also clearly having a hard time about it.

***

It is at 4 p.m. at the front. Without realizing it, the Germans are playing their last card to destroy the beachhead. The 21st Panzer Division, finally in place to attack the British late in the afternoon, prepares to begin its long-awaited counterattack.

Marcks' orders to the commanders are clear. Fight through to the coast. Stop for nothing or no one. Forget retreat. Gottberg and his force of 35 tanks will take Périers Ridge, about 5km from the coast. Oppeln himself will lead the other group of 25 tanks to take the Biéville ridge on the right. The 192nd *Panzergrenadier* Regiment will then push through the middle, and go on to reach the coast.

General Marcks himself arrives at the scene. Walking up to Oppeln, he says simply, "Oppeln, the future of Germany may very well rest on your shoulders." Marcks' tired eyes stare at him through his wire-rimmed glasses. "If you don't push the British back into the sea, we shall have lost the war."

Oppeln hesitates to say anything in return. Taking a deep breath, he salutes and replies, "General, I intend to do my best." What the hell. If he dies, he dies.

Marcks returns his salute, then turns and hobbles over to General Feuchtinger and exchanges a few words with him. Oppeln takes a last look at them, and then walks over to where his unit commanders are.

Marcks and Feuchtinger turn around and climb into Marcks' command car. They drive over to the lead armored scout car of Rauch's 192nd *Panzergrenadiers*. Marcks slowly gets out and looks at the anxious faces of the men around him, loaded up and ready to move out against the enemy. Solemnly pointing forward with his cane, he says loudly, "Press on to the coast."

Oppeln meanwhile, apprehensive and worried, climbs into his command tank. As he checks the skies for aircraft once more, he spots a small command vehicle approaching from the coast. The driver must have seen Oppeln's command pennant, because he drives over to his tank. Sitting in the back of the vehicle is a dusty, smudged General Richter, commander of the 716th Division. Oppeln climbs out of his *PzKw IV* and greets him. Richter is full of anguish, tears making trails in the dirt on his face.

"General, are you all right?" asks Oppeln.

Richter takes a deep breath and wipes his eyes. His voice trembling, he dismally replies, "My troops are lost. My—my whole division is finished."

Oppeln is surprised. Surely some elements are left. Someone has to still be fighting, or else the enemy would have advanced much further by now. Finally, he said, "Well, what can I do, sir?"

Richter says nothing. After a short pause, he just dejectedly shrugs his shoulders.

Oppeln feels compelled to say something more, something encouraging. He replies softly, "We'll help as best we can."

He pulls out his map and shows it to the grief-stricken general. "Where are their positions, sir?" he asked.

Richter glanced over at Oppeln's map and stays silent, his hands at his sides.

Oppeln presses him. "Sir, will you point them out?"

Richter seems not just distressed; but also disoriented. He finally looks up and gazes past Oppeln. Slowly, he shakes his head. "I don't know," he murmurs. "I don't know…"

Oppeln glances at his watching subordinates. They are clearly worried.

At 4:30 a.m., the advance begins. From Lebussey, Oppeln's panzers attack on the right, and Rauch's 192nd *Panzergrenadiers* fan out to his left.[10] But the advance of *Panzergruppe Oppeln* is stopped cold by deadly fire from what seems to be a few enemy tanks and anti-tank guns along the well-protected, well-camouflaged Biéville ridge ahead of them.[11] Four panzers are picked off in succession by the dug-in, hidden, longer-range guns of the British. The enemy continues firing, and as has occasionally happened in the past, von Oppeln's own tank is again shot out from under him, along with almost a dozen other new but antiquated short-barreled *PzKw IVs*. Von Gottberg's panzer battalion on his left spreads out to the west and manages to make it to the hills around Périers before dug-in British anti-tank guns and nearby tanks destroy six units. However, von Gottberg is determined to break through, and continues on resolutely, changing his attack direction again and going further to his left. Near Mathieu, he gets ambushed again by a few British tanks, and another three *PzKw IVs* are knocked out.

The 192nd Regiment though, moving forward on his left, gets lucky. Smashing through between the Canadians to their left and the British on their right, they break through the still-forming enemy lines and press forward, onward, all the way down to the sea. Reaching the shore, they relieve a few beleaguered units. But as they try to consolidate their position, they realize that no help is going to come to support their advance. Sitting out there on the beaches, with the psychological impact of the huge naval armada in front of them and enemy units closing in from both sides, they quickly realize how exposed and cut off they are.

As they contemplate withdrawing, von Oppeln, although he has been stopped on their right, has not given up. He learns about the 192nd's breakthrough to the coast. With part of his regiment now dug in and ordered to hold, the rest get ready to follow the 192nd up the middle and exploit the breach. Oppeln begins to brief the other group of four dozen panzers on where to follow the *panzergrenadiers* to the shore. General Feuchtinger drives up and agrees with his plan, and the men begin to move out.

But Feuchtinger's confidence drains away at about 8 p.m. when, looking up, he sees the unmistakable sight of hundreds of parachutes descending in front of and possibly even behind the dug-in forward positions of his other panzers. He panics, thinking that this is a British airborne reaction to his counterattack, and that the landing paratroopers intend to cut his men off. Concerned about his rear, Feuchtinger calls off the entire attack on the beachhead and orders von Oppeln to withdraw all elements of these two advanced regiments to a new position behind the present line.

Von Oppeln reluctantly gives the orders.[12]

***

Marcks' men in the end cannot stop the advancing enemy coming ashore. Even at Omaha, the crisis begins to end in the early afternoon as the Americans start getting off the beach. The clearing weather makes it worse, as the Allied air force and now closer navy both pitch in to support the men beneath the cliffs. The Germans, low on ammo, shocked by the day's fighting, taking heavy casualties, and seeing little relief, slowly begin to fall back.

***

Von Rundstedt, infuriated over the panzer episode, is in bad temper all day as he struggles to get a hold of the situation.

***

Rommel's Horch continues on its speedy trek to La Roche-Guyon. Daniel, as ever, is silent as he drives them at breakneck speeds down the various roads. Lang, alone in the back, suffers the bumps silently. He is glad that the field marshal has now apparently partly recovered from his self-recrimination. Rommel at one point turns halfway around, and says fervently, "I hope there isn't a second landing right now from the Mediterranean."

He pauses briefly. How spectacular it would be to lead the mighty forces that the Allies possess… Deep into this image, he says slowly, "Do you know, Lang… If I was commander of the Allied forces right now, I could finish off the war in fourteen days." Having said that, and deep in thought, he turns back around and once again stares at the road ahead. Lang feels terribly upset and helpless. He remains silent as the car speeds on. Evening is approaching.

Allied tactical aircraft continue to swarm over the invasion area. Caen is bombed again, and Vire will be hit at 8 p.m. German vehicles moving up towards the front along inland roads are repeatedly strafed. American and British medium and heavy bombers continue to pound the defensive positions as darkness approaches.

The Allies have now landed the staggering figure of over 155,000 troops onto French soil. They control an area about 15 miles long and almost six miles deep—over 80 square miles. On the negative side, casualties just on Omaha beach are terrible. Bodies are strewn everywhere, and those units surviving have lost about 50 percent of their men and vehicles, as well as about three-fourths of their heavy weapons and supplies, including tanks. The disorganized beachhead will not be able to withstand a determined panzer counterattack. The British are doing better, and before dawn comes, they will have landed a total of four divisions.

The Allied fleet is relatively safe from naval attack, although 36 U-boats will put to sea from the Bay of Biscay in the next 24 hours. None will reach the Allied shipping lanes for at least a week.

Pitifully few German aircraft—maybe fifty or so of various types—have been available to scramble against the enemy landing. They have been thwarted by its formidable air cover. Several aircraft attempting to pierce the umbrella are shot down.

The evening report at 84th Corps is not good, and Marcks' staff is in a dejected mood. Between the American airborne assaults and the landings at Utah beach, the left flank of the developing front has all but collapsed. The Germans hold the center, but have made some major concessions to the British and Canadians on their right flank. Bayeux, held by the 915th Grenadier Regiment and supported indirectly by elements of the 21st Panzer, is about to fall. The mighty guns at the Pointe du Hoc had been moved back beneath camouflage, under Rommel's orders, so that they would not be bombed. A daring American commando raid in mid-morning had captured the guns where they sat, ready and waiting to deliver devastating fire onto Utah beach, stacks of shells next to them. The Americans had simply spiked the guns.

The one small glimmer of sunshine is the 21st Panzer's continued assault west of the Orne River. Elements of the 192nd *Panzergrenadiers* have broken through the enemy lines and have reached the coast at Luc-sur-Mer. But the panzers on their right, trying to widen the attack corridor, have been stopped, picked off by enemy anti-tank guns. And on the other side of the Orne, more bad news. Von Luck's 125th *Panzergrenadiers* have run up against a heavy barrage, and have been forced to fall back through Escoville. He will have to be reinforced by the 4th Panzer Company before he tries again.

No attacks by the Kriegsmarine have been reported, and only a few dozen German aircraft have been sighted in the invasion area all day. So much for Göring's promise of a thousand aircraft.

The status portion of the briefing concluded, Major Hayn stands. It is his turn now. The Ic starts out by flatly stating that this is the main invasion.

Marcks, normally easy-going (but thorough), is in a foul mood. Rommel is on his way back from Germany, and so is incommunicado. One hell of a time to leave France. The Führer had slept undisturbed until the late morning, and then had still held off making a decision. Those damned panzers had been frozen in reserve for hours, with everyone in the Supreme Command sitting on their thumbs. Von Rundstedt's had tried to get them to act, but had failed. Many at OKW probably are still wondering if the real invasion has actually come. Hell, the Allies had even announced the landing on the BBC! What do they need, a written invitation? Where are the replacements? Where are the supplies? The reinforcements? Who the hell is running logistics? Marcks' men are fighting desperately against an overwhelming enemy, using up their ammo and dying as they give ground.

"Damn!" Marcks finally snarls aloud, startling his staff. He forces his attention back to Hayn.

Three parachute divisions, Hayn is stating, have been identified so far in the assault: the American 82nd and 101st Airborne Divisions on the left flank, and major elements of the British 6th Airborne on their right. That is over half of the Anglo-American airborne force that is known to be based in England.[13]

Hayn checks his notes and continues. The American 1st and 4th Infantry Divisions have been identified ashore. So why, Hayn argues, would the Allies commit these first-line units—not to mention most of their airborne force—to a diversionary attack? Would they use their second-line divisions for the main assault? Hardly.

Hayn looks at his audience and holds up a paper. "Just take a look at Major Wiegmann's report from the Caen area. This is what it says." He glances at the paper. "The 3rd British and 3rd Canadian Divisions were identified before noon. Now we also know that the 50th Northumbrian and the 7th Armored Divisions are present. That leaves only the 51st Highlanders and the 1st Armored Division to make up Montgomery's entire old Eighth Army from North Africa!"[14]

Hayn knows that he is right, and makes his conclusion. "If this isn't the invasion, then what units are they going to use for it?" Hayn's argument makes sense. Marcks agrees with Hayn, and orders that the report be sent up the chain of command.

The intelligence officer at Seventh Army (Vorwerk) and the one at OB West (Meyer-Detring) later will agree with Hayn and endorse his report. But they will still have trouble convincing von Rundstedt that this is the real invasion.

***

At about 10 p.m., Rommel finally reaches the village of La Roche-Guyon. Daniel slows down as they roll through the outskirts. As they move quietly through the main street, the town seems deserted. The black Horch finally pulls off the main road, turning down the entrance driveway, and enters the well-guarded courtyard. As the car screeches to a stop next to the main steps, Lang jumps out and runs ahead to inform General Speidel that they have returned.

Hustling into the main hall, Lang slows down, puzzled. Incredibly, he is hearing—yes, that is music! Baffled, he listens intently, and recognizes a Wagnerian opera. It is definitely coming from the chief of staff's office. Stunned for a moment, he starts to get angry. The future of Germany is being desperately fought for out there, perhaps has even been lost by now, on the very beaches that this headquarters was assigned to protect. The field marshal is feeling miserable, but the chief of staff is playing records. Suddenly, the music grows louder as the door opens. Speidel comes strolling out, a serene look on his face.

Lang looks him straight in the eyes, laying aside for a moment that he is only a captain speaking to a general as he snarls, "How can you possibly play *opera* at a time like this?!"

Speidel, ever cool, smiles graciously in return, and replies, "My dear Lang, you don't think that my playing a little music is going to stop the invasion, now do you?" Lang is too shocked to reply.

Speidel sees the field marshal striding down the hallway in his long gray field coat, grim-faced, his baton gripped tightly in his right hand. Glancing briefly at Speidel, Rommel walks directly into his office and, clasping his hands behind him, begins studying the map. Speidel closes the door to begin their private conference. It is going to be a long one. Naturally, the aide is not invited.

Lang stands there a moment, fatigued and dejected. It has been a terribly long drive, and the day seems to be going horribly. Still, there is nothing that he can do right now—at least nothing that would help the field marshal.

Lang finds his way into the dining room and collapses at one of the tables. Tired, he gets up, pours himself a cup of coffee, and then sits down again. Gazing over, he spies another officer reading a newspaper. The other officer looks up affably and asks with a smile, "How was the trip?"

Lang cannot say anything. He can only stare at the man.

***

Rommel, now in the chief's office, begins studying the situation map. He shakes his head and grumbles, "That's one hell of a mess!" Speidel begins telling him the measures that he has taken.

As the field marshal listens to Speidel's briefing, he finds himself even more concerned. On the right flank, the British have secured a beachhead 20 miles wide and 3 to 6 miles deep. They threaten Bayeux in the center, which is barely holding on, defended by remnants of the shattered 915th Grenadiers.

On the left flank, the Americans have broken through on the southeastern part of the Cotentin peninsula and are driving hard inland. To the right of the Vire River, the enemy has taken horrific losses in trying to get ashore. However, the onslaught of enemy assault troops on the beach has ended. The Americans have somehow broken through the defense of the cliffs and are now slowly moving inland.

All in all, the Allies have landed at least six divisions, with elements of others arriving even now. Three airborne divisions have been so far identified, two American and one British. They have secured the exits to the beaches in many places along both flanks.

The enemy beach areas have been more or less sealed off by the Germans, but all the local reserves have been committed. Ammo is at a low level, and the men are doing without a lot of support all along the front. Very few supplies are getting to the front. Morale is down (Rommel personally blames himself for that), and everyone is probably wondering where the hell the panzers are.

The 21st Panzer have made a desperate limited thrust between the Canadians and the British, and some *panzergrenadiers* had actually reached the coast in one or two points; but the lack of reinforcements and an unexpected Allied air drop in their rear forced them to pull back. Rommel questions that decision, but since it is already a *fait accompli*, there is no use in creating a stink over it.

On the positive side (Rommel is thankful that there is one), *Panzer Lehr* and 12th SS Panzer are slowly moving up for a counterattack, although reports indicate that they are struggling under repeated air attacks. Rommel grimaces at that. How many times had he told them?

2nd Panzer Division can be moved from the Somme, and 2nd SS Panzer down in southern France getting ready to trek northward. In addition, the 17th SS *Panzergrenadier* Division in midwest France is also getting ready to move towards the invasion area. Thus, Rommel will gain at least four panzer divisions and one *panzergrenadier* over the next few days to move against the invasion site. But will it be enough? Or is it already too late?

Rommel had preached all of these months that unless the Allies could be pushed back into the sea in the first few hours (now highly unlikely), Germany would lose the war. He hopes that he is wrong in this case. But he usually is not. Still, he *had* miscalculated the invasion date…

With a successful enemy invasion launched and possibly another to come soon, as well as a number of key officers absent at this time, Rommel is sure that there will be repercussions from the Führer. Looking at his anxious chief of staff, Rommel finds the need to reassure him. He says, "Good work, Speidel. If I had been here, I could not have done anything else than what you have done and the actions you have initiated."

The field marshal spends the next two hours getting updated on what has happened, working past midnight. One of the first items is to contact OKW and request that all the first-rate combat regiments from the Fifteenth Army be sent to Normandy, to be followed by the second-rate units at the Pas-de-Calais. OKW, still figuring that the main thrust is yet to come, turns him down. They do though, allow him the use of the 346th Infantry northeast of Le Havre.

Calling them back later, he asks that the 35,000-man garrison stuck on the Channel Islands be moved to the front. Again he is turned down. If the Channel Islands were evacuated, the Allies could march right in and use them as a staging point for further smaller amphibious landings, not to mention create airstrips there.

He also asks for the two panzer divisions stationed in southern France, the 9th and the 10th, to be released. Again, patiently, OKW refuses his request. The 17th SS and 2nd SS though, are already getting ready to move.

Rommel then tries contacting a few Seventh Army units, but most radio communications are being jammed, and many of the land lines are still out because of bombings and Maquis activities. He does though, at one point, get through to Max Pemsel at Seventh Army headquarters. "You've *got* to stop the enemy from getting a foothold, whatever happens!" he yells into the phone.

Rommel also gets through to 21st Panzer, and orders them to attack at 8 a.m., along with the 12th SS Panzer, which is suppose to have arrived by then. Bayerlein's *Panzer Lehr*, hounded by the enemy *Jabos*, will take some time to get to the front.

Rommel looks again at the map. The 21st Panzer is dug in on the eastern flank and south of Caen. The 716th Division, reduced to the size of a few battalions and 12 pieces of artillery, is grimly hanging on. The 352nd is holding its own, but its supplies are running critically low, and no relief is getting through. The division's engineer battalion, the last of the reserves, has moved from St. Martin-de-Blagny and joined the 916th Regiment, waiting for another attack in the Colleville area.

The 30th *Schnell-Brigade*,[15] commanded by *Oberstleutnant Freiherr* von und zu Aufsess, has left Coutances and is on its way to the front. But given the fact that they can only travel by bicycle, and considering the heavy enemy airpower, they will probably not reach the invasion area until mid-morning.

A couple hours later, those still awake at the château are exhausted, ready to call it a night. As the minutes wear on, everything along the front has wound down—except of course, the Allied buildup along the beaches, but even that is reported as slacking off some. A lot has happened, and tomorrow is going to be a very busy day indeed.

Some time past midnight, Rommel finds himself with his aide again. By now Lang too has heard of the failure of the 21st Panzer's attack the day before. Naturally, he is crushed. The invasion seems to have succeeded. According to Rommel's own theories, the first day would be the most crucial. Have they already lost? Looking at the field marshal sadly, he asks, "Sir, do you think we can drive them back?"

Rommel glances over at him wearily and shrugs. He slowly spreads his hands. "Lang, I hope we can. I've nearly always succeeded up to now."

It is quiet in the villa. The field marshal suddenly realizes that it is late. They have both had a long trip. Now he reaches over and pats his aide on the shoulder. "You look tired," he says, almost paternally. "Why don't you go to bed? It's been a long day." It had been a long day—the longest day, he had once called it. Well, that was certainly true for Lang and him.

The exhausted field marshal turns away and, already lost in thought, slowly walks down the oak-paneled hall to his office. He gently closes the door behind.

On the coast, the Allies, far from being in a celebratory mood, move at breakneck speed to consolidate their bloody beachheads. They are pretty sure that they are there to stay, but you just never know. The wise ones keep looking over their shoulders for swarms of German tanks to descend upon them.

Besides, there is not much to celebrate at this point. There is a long road ahead of them, the fight has just begun in France, and thousands of their comrades already lie dead or dying at their feet.

---

1   The exact time at which Rommel was first informed of the invasion remains to this day a mystery. Many sources state that Speidel made the first or the only phone call (depending on the source) between 6 and 6:30 a.m. Others claim only one, including the headquarters war diary, which logged only one call to Rommel at 10:15 German Central Time (GCT). Also, Ryan in his book (*The Longest Day*) and Mitcham (*The Desert Fox In Normandy*) state this.

Regarding the time and number of calls, two of Ryan's sources seem the most reliable. One was an interview with Manfred Rommel on July 9, 1958, some 14 years later, and another was with Lang at his home in Gemünd the same day. Each stated that the first phone call came around 5 a.m. (certainly early enough in the morning), and that the second call came later at the verified time of 10:15. Also, Speidel told Ryan in an interview that he called Rommel initially "around 6 a.m." Ryan though, only included this call in a footnote and questioned Speidel's accuracy, despite the corroborative testimony given by Captain Lang, Manfred Rommel, and von Tempelhoff. Koch states in his book (*Erwin Rommel, die Wandlung eines grossen Soldaten*) that Lucie told him the first call came around 6:30 a.m.

Ryan doubted that there was ever a first call. He stated in his notes, "There seems to be grave doubts in my mind that Rommel received a phone call at 5 a.m. on the morning of June 6, because it is not recorded anywhere in the official o.d. west [sic] diary. There's even a doubt in my mind that Rommel was naturally at his home. There is a possibility that Speidel was unable to get the field marshal and did not contact him until the time that is specified in the war diary which was 10:15 on the morning of June 5 German time."

This second 10:15 a.m. call has some credence through the fact that Speidel was not notified of any actual landings until General Pemsel at Le Mans called him around 9:05 a.m. However, Pemsel did call at 6:15 a.m. to report a naval bombardment, but Speidel concluded that its purpose was not clear, and that it might be a diversion for an attack elsewhere. Testimony from Mrs. Kirchheim at the Rommel home that day also supports the 10:15 call time (See Irving, p. 442), as does of course, the army group war diary, and the Army Group B Telephone Log.

Testimonies given by Lang and Tempelhoff are enough evidence to support Speidel's claim that there were indeed at least two phone calls. Perhaps General Speidel's time of 6 a.m. was just an estimate,. This discrepancy would then confirm both Lang's and Manfred Rommel's claims of the first call at 5 a.m. The first call could very well have occurred to give the field marshal a "heads up," and as such would not be considered official.

David Fraser (*Knight's Cross,* p. 485) wrote that Speidel first called Rommel at 6:30 a.m. to tell him about the airdrops, but that Rommel later called him back at 10 a.m. It was at that time, Fraser wrote, that the field marshal was first told by Speidel about the amphibious landings that had occurred in Normandy.

A few other sources claim that Rommel received the only word of the invasion between 6 and 7 a.m. (e.g., Patrick, p.82). One even wrote that Rommel was in contact with elements of the 1st SS Panzer Corps at 6:30 a.m. This is highly unlikely. If Rommel had been fully alerted before 7 a.m., he certainly would have been dragging his heels in leaving for the front at 11:40 a.m. The testimonies of those present at his villa in indicate that he was indeed called early, but not actually informed of the invasion until later in the morning.

Unfortunately for the modern historian, a number of omissions and corrections were later made to the *Heeresgruppe B* War Diary. General Speidel admitted this after the war. Instructions for these

JUNE 1944 • 585

changes came from or were made by Rommel, Speidel himself, or by the Operations officer, von Tempelhoff. Ostensibly, the "adjustments" were made to prevent any retribution upon anyone when Adolf Hitler himself ordered a subsequent investigation. Suspicious and smelling treason in the air, he demanded a full inquiry to find out why so many key commanders had been away from their headquarters on the day of the invasion. The log changes in the army group diary were later made to protect those individuals who had indeed been away at that time, including von Tempelhoff, Lang, and of course, Rommel himself.

2 Pickert would survive the war. He would be promoted to General, Flak Artillery in March of 1945, and would end the war commanding the entire flak contingent of the Luftwaffe.

3 See footnote for June 4.

4 Von Salmuth wrote, "At 6 a.m., since it had been daylight for an hour and a half, I had my chief of staff telephone Seventh Army again to ask if the enemy had landed anywhere yet. The reply was, 'Fleets of troop transports and warships big and small are lying at various points offshore, with masses of landing craft. But so far no landing has yet taken place.' Thereupon I went back to sleep with a calm mind, after telling my chief of staff 'So their invasion has miscarried already!'"

5 See earlier footnote on time of calls.

6 An emergency command call. It was to be given the most direct phone line available, taking priority over any other telephone call then being placed.

7 According to *Frau* Rommel, the field marshal made it a habit of never showing affection and overt emotion for his wife or son when any members of his staff were present.

8 "He shared the gaff."

9 Speidel was not updated yet on the attack developing against the British at Sword beach.

10 Von Luck's 125th were left on the east bank to deal with the British paratroopers.

11 Anti-tank guns of British 27th Armored Brigade's Staffordshire Yeomanry Regiment, along with several British Shermans (American-made). Von Oppeln's *PzKw IV Ausf.* C and D models with their low-velocity KwK-37 75mm gun did not have the range or the penetration capabilities of the British anti-tank guns or the British Shermans (385 m/s muzzle velocity, compared to the Sherman's 619 m/s).

12 While Ryan and Mann state this time, Irving puts the time at 7:20 p.m., and Mitcham as late as 11 p.m. Irving and John Mann describe the drop as gliders, while the others refer to them as parachute drops. Actually, they are both right. Feuchtinger and von Oppeln saw parachutes. This was a pre-scheduled airborne supply drop containing canisters of supplies. The drop was merely misplaced, and landed in the wrong area. Added to this though, was another air landing spotted on Feuchtinger's right an hour later. This second airdrop was the mislocated 230-glider contingent of the British 6th Airlanding Brigade that was reinforcing, also according to schedule, the two parachute brigades that had been dropped in the predawn hours. This force would only lose one aircraft.

Paul Carell (*Sie Kommen!*) later wrote the highly questionable statement that the glider drop was a deliberate move on Montgomery's part to foil the German counterattack, and that Montgomery "...employed his glider fleet and dropped regiment after regiment of British airborne troops into the German corridor." This was not the case. Most of the drop was made up of supplies.

13 The other unit was the British 1st Airborne; Montgomery had originally wanted to drop it around Caen on June 8, but the idea was vetoed by Air Marshal Leigh-Mallory.

14 Hayn was more accurate in his assessment than he knew; the 51st Highlanders were also being landed at that very moment.

15 Mobile infantry brigade.

Epilogue

Field Marshal Rommel stayed up that whole night, getting updated on the military situation. He spent the next couple days trying to organize some type of counterattack against the beaches. He did not succeed. Aerial supremacy, as he had feared, became a crucial factor in the first 48 hours after the landing. Around the infuriating time of 4 p.m. on the afternoon of the 6th, Fritz Bayerlein's *Panzer Lehr* Division was finally released through General Dollmann to move out. His men, having waited next to their vehicles now for over fourteen hours, were finally directed to move towards the invasion area. Unfortunately for them, the cloudy skies had cleared, and that afternoon, Allied fighters and fighter-bombers swarmed down upon Bayerlein's columns. They became disrupted, and he lost 20 to 30 vehicles before dusk, with more damaged. Nor did it end there. Moving through the darkness, he was continually harassed by night attacks. The enemy aircraft dropped flares to see the moving columns below before they pounced. Rommel's grim predictions were coming to pass.

And this was just the beginning. On the morning of the 7th, as their relentless march continued towards the beaches, the panzer troops suffered even more. They struggled through cratered road junctions patrolled by fighters. Delays in front of damaged bridges made them sitting ducks for the *Jabos*. Moving along narrow roads with trees or hedgerows on each side hindered quick dispersal, and the columns struggled moving along routes that would have been free of enemy air interdiction those first dark early morning hours of the 6th. By the end of the 7th, Bayerlein's division had lost 40 refueling tank trucks, 70 trucks carrying men or supplies, five tanks, and over seven dozen half-tracks, prime movers, and self-propelled guns.

The 12th SS fared no better. Although a few components did arrive at the front, they did so piecemeal, and the line units for the most part had either been disrupted or disorganized from incessant aerial poundings. They would not be nearly enough to make any kind of a dent against the rapidly solidifying beachheads.

Neither panzer division was ready for any kind of a counterattack until the 8th—and even then, they still had units on the road as they tried to regroup for a counterattack.

The after-story revolved around four critical factors: total Allied aerial supremacy overhead and naval supremacy from the sea supporting the beachhead; a vicious, meat-grinding *Materialschlacht*;[1] brilliant enemy deception as to if and when another—presumably the main—invasion would come; and last, the ultimate failure of the German supreme military command structure to successfully deal with the situation.

Allied airpower though, was perhaps the deciding factor. All over France, supplies and men trying to get to the front were stymied and waylaid by Allied aircraft. The air war against supply depots, bridges, road centers, and railroad marshaling yards continued. The Loire River bridges, which unlike the Seine River bridges had been relatively untouched up until now (for fear that it would tip the Allies' hand on the landing location), were now hit full force. The air war expanded to other parts of France, Holland, and Belgium. Priority targets were any and all German units moving in columns, especially if headed towards Normandy.

The Luftwaffe, trying to keep its word, sent squadrons of aircraft west towards the front. But many of the pilots were new, and they were thrown against the masses of enemy formations piecemeal. They achieved little.

Out in the English Channel, the Kriegsmarine fared no better. All attempts to attack the amphibious force met with grave results. Torpedo boats approaching the fleet were sunk. S-boats were either turned back by aircraft, damaged, or sunk by surface craft. U-boats were hunted mercilessly as they struggled to reach the landing area, and most that survived were depth-charged several times before they could get close enough to attack.

German movement to the front continued. Some mobile units like the 2nd Panzer and the 1st SS in Belgium took far too long to reach the fighting area. The 17th SS *Panzergrenadier* had to move up from the Loire valley. The 2nd SS Panzer had to take a long trek from southern France to reach the landing area, while the relatively close 116th Panzer was not even committed before the first week in July. Eventually, most of the panzer divisions in France ended up at the front where they were slowly ground up on a static defense line.

The ground war would drag on for weeks, turning into the "material slugfest" that Rommel feared might happen. On the other hand, four factors worked against the Allies: the fierce determination of the panzers, the natural defense of those maddening cross-sections of hedgerows, Field Marshal Montgomery's failure to take Caen on D-Day, and Rommel's personal direction. The Allies had established a bridgehead, but could not go further.

The events at Normandy quickly became enmeshed with the other distant warfront issues. Rome had been liberated, and the Allies were moving up the Italian boot. And the Russian summer offensive, which started as expected in late June, rolled forward and in the end, all but destroyed an entire army group. And Rommel's relationship with the Führer was about to become toxic.

The Allies, led by General Patton's fiery August offensive, finally did break out of the beachhead. Defeat in the West was now a foregone conclusion.

---

1   A war of attrition, where fresh men and material come in on one side and leave the battlefield either dead or wounded on the other.

Glossary

Ia. Generalstabsoffizier—The First General Staff Officer in a unit headquarters. The chief Operations officer, he is in charge of the Operations Division, overseeing command and control of the command's sub-units. He also is responsible for leadership, training, transportation, housing, anti-aircraft defenses, writing the war diary, situation analysis, and maps. Equivalent to the US Army's G-3.

Ib. Generalstabsoffizier—The Second General Staff Officer in a unit headquarters, the Chief Supply and Transportation Officer. He is in charge of the Supply and Quartermaster Division. He oversees all matters relating to supply, replenishment, movement of supplies, rations, ammo, and the movement of wounded and prisoners.

Ic. Generalstabsoffizier—Third General Staff Officer in a unit headquarters, the chief Intelligence officer. He oversees all matters relating to intelligence, including gathering it and presenting it. Also in charge of discipline. Equivalent to the US Army's G-2.

IIa. Generalstabsoffizier—Chief Personnel Officer (Adjutant), responsible for all personnel.

IIb. Generalstabsoffizier—Responsible for all enlisted personnel, and the bureaus of the unit staff.

Abteilung—A widely used generic term for a battery, battalion, department, branch, or special unit. Often referred to a detachment or improvised battlegroup put together for a special set of operations. In the German Army, it was usually a battalion, especially in the armored, cavalry, and artillery branches.

Abwehr—The *Wehrmacht's* Intelligence security service that specialized in various aspects of counterintelligence.

Admiral Kanalküste—Naval Command Headquarters for the Pas-de-Calais area, located in Calais. Originally *Marinebefehlshaber Kanalküste*, it was renamed in 1943. It consisted of four naval commands: Pas-de-Calais (at Wimille), Seine-Somme (Le Havre), Normandy (Cherbourg), and *Kanalinseln* (island of Jersey).

Alarmstufe I & II—Alert Levels I & II. Full alert for an army unit.

Armeegruppe—A small, sometimes ad hoc army group, usually a command of one large army and some odd units or two small adjacent armies. It often fell under the auspices of the area *Heeresgruppe*. Because it was smaller or temporary, an *Armeegruppe* did not rate the full administrative support a *Heeresgruppe* was given.

Armeekorps (AK)—An army (usually infantry) corps that had two or more divisions and attached units.

Atlantikwall—Hitler's famed Atlantic Wall, built to thwart any Western Allied invasion.

Aufgang Kommandos—Straggler and roundup collection units.

Ausführung (Ausf.)—Modification series, version, or variant. Each major German weapon (aircraft, tank, etc.) model underwent various modifications and updates as the war progressed; these changes were grouped into different series editions; thus, a *PzKw III, Ausf C*, was a Mark III tank, Modification Series C.

Befehlshaber—A unit commanding officer. Often the title for a large command, unit, or area. For instance, the *Befehlshaber der Unterseeboote* (*BdU*) was the Commander-in-Chief of the Submarine Force (*Grossßadmiral* Dönitz).

Belgisches Gatter—"Belgian gate." 1½- to 3-ton two-meter-high barricade gates used as underwater obstacles. They were constructed of heavy steel angles and plates, mostly built before the war to be used as tank obstacles. They were set up in the breakers along a beach to tear out the bottoms of landing craft.

Blitzsperren—Lit. "Lightning fields." Special minefields to be quickly laid by all available vessels and bombers as soon as the invasion was impending.

Berghof—Lit. "Mountain House/Villa." Hitler's mountain retreat on the Obersalzberg mountain in Bavaria, a few thousand feet above the town of Berchtesgaden.

bodenständige—Static. An informal term used to denote German infantry divisions serving in France that had very limited field mobility. Created under Field Marshal von Rundstedt's reorganization of 1942, this type of division was used for coastal defense, garrison, or occupational duties. A static division was similar in makeup to the German standard triangular infantry division, in that it consisted of nine infantry battalions. However, they were smaller in size and made up of second-rate or third-rate troops, such as POWs, overage conscripts, "liberated" foreigners (who often could not even speak German), or recovered casualties. A *bodenständige* division did not have a recon battalion, only three (not the customary four to six) artillery battalions (non-motorized), and very little (if any) transport.

Brigadeführer—SS rank of brigadier general (equivalent to German Army *Generalmajor*).

Chef der Generalstab—A unit's chief of staff.

Ersatz—Reinforcement, replacement, or substitute.

Fallschirmjäger—A paratrooper. Parachute units were equipped with the latest weapons and played a critical role against the Allies in 1944, functioning as ad hoc battle groups. By then, their role was limited to being élite assault units, due to the crippled nature of the *Luftwaffe*. However, they still kept the honorary designation of being airborne.

Feldgrau—Lit. "Field gray." Nickname for the average German soldier; derived from the color of their uniforms.

Feldwebel—German Army rank of sergeant.

Feste Plätze—Fortified area. Commanded by a Fortified Area Commandant. Essentially equivalent to a fortress, as specified in *Führer* Order No. 11, March 8, 1944.

Festung—Fortress.

Fingerspitzengefuehl—A strange, sixth sense that gave one the ability to discern upcoming danger, a hidden problem, or even an enigmatic change to take advantage of a situation. Supposedly, Rommel had it on the battlefield.

Flak—Short for *Flugzeugabwehrkanone*. An anti-aircraft gun or unit. Flak units were created at the beginning of the war to deliver concentrated zones of anti-aircraft fire, either at key positions or in urban areas. A *Flak Regiment* (*FlakR*) usually became mobile (*Sturm*), comprised of three or more Flak battalions.

Flugzeug—Aircraft.

Freiherr—German aristocratic title of Baron.

Fremde Heeres West—Foreign Armies West. The intelligence branch of the Army High Command, responsible for determining enemy ground order of battle, and the main intelligence source for lower commands.

Führer—Lit. "Leader." As an adjoining word, it referred to a unit leader or commander. Used alone, in the Third Reich, it was reserved exclusively for the German commander-in-chief, Adolf Hitler. This title referred to him as the supreme head of the Nazi Party, the German state, and of course, the armed forces. His complete formal title was *Der Führer und Oberste Befehlshaber der Wehrmacht des Grossdeutschen Reichs.*

Führerbefehl—A direct order from Adolf Hitler. It carried the highest priority and importance, to be executed immediately.

Führerhauptquartier (FHq)—Hitler's main field headquarters, which included his entourage, his command staff, and all the extra personnel that travelled with him. Quasi-mobile by necessity, they traveled back and forth with him from Berlin to the Berghof, to Rastenburg.

Führersonderzug—Hitler's special train, mordantly code named *Amerika*. Sometimes serving as an advance command post when Hitler was traveling, it was pulled by two locomotives and included an armored Flak car at each end.

Führungsblitz—An emergency command phone call, taking priority over any other telephone line/call then being placed.

Gauleiter—The leader or highest-ranking Nazi official in a region (*Gau*), responsible for all matters of politics and economics, labor mobilization, and civil defense.

Geheime Staatspolizei (*Gestapo*)—The Reich's infamous secret police, responsible for investigating and pursuing attempts against the state and safeguarding it against traitors. Established by Hermann Göring in 1933, it was taken over a year later by Himmler, who was given the title of *Reichführer*. Over the course of the next eleven years, it became the most feared and hated state organization in the world.

General der …—The rank of general; equivalent to the US Army rank of lieutenant general. This rank required specifying the individual's specialty. Types included: *Infanterie* (Infantry), *Artillerie* (Artillery), *Kavallerie* (Cavalry), *Panzertruppen* (Armored), *Pioniere* (Engineers), *Flakartillerie* (Anti-Aircraft), *Luftwaffe* (Air Force), and *Fallschirmtruppen* (Paratrooper).

Generalfeldmarschall (shortened form *Feldmarschall*)—Field marshal. This historic title was the highest rank possible in the *Wehrmacht*; equivalent to the US Army rank of General of the Army. A field marshal supposedly had the rare privilege of being able to request a private, personal audience with Hitler whenever he desired.

Generalleutnant—German rank of lieutenant general; equivalent to US major general.

Generalmajor—German rank of major general; equivalent to US Army rank of brigadier general.

Generaloberst—German rank of colonel general; equivalent to US Army rank of four-star general.

Grenadier—An historic German term often used for heavy infantry units, originally referring to the task and type of weapon carried, in this case hand-thrown explosives (early grenades). Later in the war, most German regular infantry regiments were reclassified as grenadier in the hopes of increasing morale by alluding to their élite counterparts of the past.

Gruppe—A force of units. An army *Gruppe* could be an ad hoc formation of variable size. A large army group was called a *Heeresgruppe*, a smaller or ad hoc one (smaller staffs, usually temporary in nature) was called an *Armeegruppe*.

Gruppenführer—SS rank of major general (equivalent to an Army *Generalleutnant*).

Hauptmann—German Army captain.

Heer—The German Army organization.

Heeresgruppe—Army group. An army command consisting of two or more armies.

Heeresküstenartillerie—Army coastal artillery. A term created in 1940, used to supplement their naval counterparts along the coastline of the Atlantic Wall.

Heereswaffenamt (HWaA)—The Armaments Office of the German Army. Located in Berlin, it was created in 1919 to develop and oversee production of German weaponry.

Hilfswillige—Auxiliary volunteers (non-German), mostly foreign prisoners of war (usually from Russia) forced into uniform and service for the Reich, unlike foreigners who "volunteered" (*Freiwilligen*). The "Hiwis" were used only reluctantly, often limited to auxiliary duties, such as supply or defense preparation.

Hitlerjugend (HJ)—The "Hitler Youth." A paramilitary youth association created and strictly controlled by the Nazi Party in 1933 to indoctrinate and motivate male teenagers into Nazi culture and ideals, preparing them for military service, especially into the SS (*Schutzstaffel*). They were unfortunately also used to provoke, torment, and otherwise discriminate against various groups targeted by Nazi doctrine.

Kampfgruppe—Battlegroup. A loosely assigned unit created from improvised combat units of various sizes. They were usually named after their commanders.

Kanalküste—The coastal area of the English Channel nearest England at the Dover Straits.

KMA—Küstenminen A (Coastal Mine, Model A). Of simple design, it was used in shallow areas. It consisted of a concrete base in which a 75kg charge was placed. Above it was set a metal tripod and a triggering device.

Konteradmiral—A rank in the German Navy, equivalent to a US Navy rear admiral.

Kriegsgefangener—A prisoner of war.

Kriegsmarine—The German Navy.

Küstenartillerie—Coastal artillery unit.

Landser—The common German soldier; equivalent to the American GI.

Leibstandarte SS Adolf Hitler (LSAH or LSSAH)—"Life Guard" or "Body Guard." Title of the 1st SS Panzer Division. Organized and commanded by Sepp Dietrich in 1940, it adopted as its divisional symbol a skeleton key over a shield in his honor ("Dietrich" in German means "skeleton key," or "lock pick"), and also perhaps symbolizing with it their ability to overcome or "unlock" any position they attack.

Luftflötte—Air Fleet. Corresponding to a numbered American air force, it was a major, self-sustaining military unit in the *Luftwaffe*. It consisted of up to a thousand aircraft, with its own supply, maintenance, transport, and administrative units. The *Luftwaffe* consisted of several *Luftflötten*, each comprised of two to four *Fliegerkorps*.

Luftlande—Air landing unit. Similar to a paratroop or airborne unit, but usually delivered mostly by glider, and in doing so, capable of taking aboard small air transportable mobile units (such as personnel cars and small artillery pieces).

Luftwaffe—The German Air Force.

Major—German Army major, equivalent to its US counterpart.

Marinegruppenkommandos West—Naval Supreme Command Headquarters, Western Theater (Naval Group West). A naval command over all surface naval units in Western Europe; the U-boats were controlled directly by *Großadmiral* Karl Dönitz through the *Befehlshaber der Unterseeboote* (*BdU*).

Materialschlacht—A war of attrition and supplies. In 1944, Rommel was worried that if the Allies made it ashore, the struggle for France would turn into this, a production war that Germany could not hope to win.

Militärbefehlshaber—The Army military governor of an occupied territory. In Western Europe, there were two: *Militärbefehlshaber in Belgien und Nordfrankreich* (Belgium and Northern France, General von Falkenhausen), and *Militärbefehlshaber (in) Frankreich* (France, General von Stülpnagel).

Minengranaten—"Mine shells." A simple type of anti-invasion device in which an artillery shell is imbedded along a cliff over a target area. If the shell is disturbed or the surrounding rock hit, the shell falls and explodes below.

Mufti—A military expression referring to civilian attire worn by someone who normally wore or was entitled to wear a military uniform. Examples include civilian hat or a scarf.

Nachrichten-Führer—An army signal corps officer, usually on an army headquarters staff.

Nationalsozialistische Deutsche Arbeiter Partei (NSDAP)—National-Socialist German Workers' Party. The infamous Nazi Party.

Nebelwerfer—Lit. "Fog or smoke launcher." Originally referred to a 100mm mortar that fired a chemical weapon, such as gas or smoke. Unlike in World War I though, gas or chemical attacks were outlawed and never to be used. Thus before the war, these units were modified to operate small mobile rocket launchers for use against concentrations of light infantry. For intelligence purposes, the term remained for these rocket units that replaced the smoke weapons as a ruse to fool the Allies.

Nussknackermine—"Nutcracker" mine. A type of German ad hoc land explosive, derived from the *KMA* mine, created by Rommel in February 1944 and later adopted by Naval Group West in the spring.

Oberbefehlshaber (OB)—Commander-in-Chief, usually referring to a theater or branch of service and not a combat formation. Oversaw far-ranging strategic regions by controlling all troops or forces in a major geographic area.

Oberfeldwebel—German army rank of master sergeant.

Oberführer—SS rank, between the ranks of brigadier general and colonel.

Obergruppenführer—SS rank of lieutenant general (equivalent to German Army rank of *General der Infanterie* or *General der Panzertruppen*).

Oberkommando (O)—A strategic, high command, such as *Oberkommando des Heeres (OKH)* for the army, *Oberkommando der Kriegsmarine (OKM)* for the navy, and *Oberkommando der Luftwaffe (OKL)* for the air force.

Oberkommando der Wehrmacht (OKW)—The German Combined Armed Forces Supreme Headquarters. Its location moved to wherever Hitler was currently staying, be it Berchtesgaden, his advance headquarters *Wolfsschanze I* in Eastern Prussia, or Berlin. Whenever he stayed at the Berghof in Lower Bavaria, *OKW* would be located in and around the nearby town of Berchtesgaden.

Obermarineberater (OMB)—Chief Naval Advisor.

Oberst—German rank of colonel.

Oberstleutnant—German rank of lieutenant colonel. Equivalent of lieutenant colonel in the US Army.

Obersturmbannführer—SS rank of lieutenant colonel, equivalent to army *Oberstleutnant*.

OB West—*Oberbefehlshaber West*. Supreme Command, Western Theater. As such, Field Marshal von Rundstedt operationally controlled all *Wehrmacht* forces in Western Europe.

Organisation Todt (OT)—The Todt labor organization, a paramilitary government construction force that consisted of construction engineers, workers, and foreign civilian workers, often forced into labor (especially towards the end of the war). It was established 1933 under Dr. Fritz Todt, and taken over by Todt's successor, Albert Speer, in February 1942, after Todt died in a plane crash.

Östentruppen—Eastern troops. Russian or East European prisoners of war or in some cases, "liberated" soldiers who had been coerced into switching sides to fight for Germany.

Panzer (Pz.)—Armor or armored vehicle. When used in combination with other unit types (such as *Panzerabwehrkanone (PAK)*—Term for an anti-tank gun, mostly used at the tactical level to describe various calibers of defensive and offensive anti-tank weapons.

Panzerartillerie or *Panzerpionier)*, signifies the unit is motorized and equipped to operate with the armored units. A *panzerdivision* was an armored division, typically composed of a panzer regiment, two *panzergrenadier* regiments, self-propelled artillery, tank destroyer battalion, mobile artillery, support battalions, and a headquarters unit.

Panzerfaust—Lit. "armored fist." A German hand-held anti-tank rocket weapon; equivalent to an American bazooka.

Panzergrenadier—A term referring to armored infantry and nearly always a component of either a panzer division or a *panzergrenadier* division. The men moved and fought with armored transport vehicles such as halftracks, prime movers, and armored cars.

PanzerGruppe West—Armored Forces Command, Western Theater. Commanded by General Geyr von Schweppenburg.

Panzerjäger or *Jagdpanzer*—A tank destroyer; a motorized, armored, anti-tank vehicle.

PanzerKampfwagen (PzKw—Lit. "armored battle vehicle." The German formal term for a tank. Corresponding to the American term "Mark," it denoted a model number when followed by a

Roman numeral. Thus, the Allies' term "Mark IV" was based upon the German counterpart, *PanzerKampfwagen IV (PzKw IV)*.

Panzer Lehr—Lit. "Armored Training/Demonstration." A panzer division, one of the few designated just by name, considered one of the best in the German Army. It was formed to act as a bulwark against the upcoming Allied invasion of France, but its creation in the view of many historians was considered a critical mistake, because manning it pulled experienced training instructors and troops out of the schools and put them into combat.

Pour le Mérite—The classic German medal, created in 1740 by Frederick the Great, for the highest bravery, equivalent to the US Medal of Honor. During World War I, it was popularized by Germany's fighter aces, who earned it by shooting down single-handedly twenty enemy aircraft. It was actually the British who gave the award the sobriquet "Blue Max," referring of course to the color of the medal, and to Max Immelmann, the first German fighter ace to earn it.

Reichskanzlei—The Reich Chancellery in Berlin.

Ringständ—A small, hardened fortified position in a fortified line mounted in the ground flush to the surface, consisting of a hollow, round or octagonal fighting hole or expanded foxhole encased in concrete. It featured a major weapon such as a heavy machinegun or assault gun. Either open or encased, it usually held one or two men, and sometimes had a metal ring on to mount the traversable machinegun.

Ritterkreuz—The Knight's Cross. A distinct military decoration awarded for outstanding service instead of bravery. Higher levels included with diamonds and with oak leaves.

"Rommelspargel"—Lit. "Rommel's asparagus." A nickname given by Germans along the French coast to the formations of stakes (often topped with an explosive device) installed in the open fields behind the beaches to thwart inland glider landings.

Schnell—Lit. "fast" or "mobile." *Schnelltruppen* usually were intended to be motorized troops although a *Schnellebrigade* was actually bicycle troops and not motorized.

Schnellboot (S-boot)—Small German motor torpedo attack boat, equivalent to a British MTB or an American PT Boat. Called "E-boats" ("enemy" boat) by the Allies, they operated along the English Channel, attacking shipping and controlling areas. Displacing from 60 to 125 tons, they were armed with two or four torpedo tubes and a couple light guns. Crew averaged from 12 to 20 men.

Schützenpanzerwagen (SPW)—An armored personnel carriers; usually referred to as halftracks. Infantry either rode in the open on top or within an enclosure.

Schutzstaffel (SS)—Lit. "protection detachment" or "protective squad." Refers to the Third Reich's infamous praetorian guard. It was established in 1925 as Hitler's bodyguard, a small paramilitary organization amidst the German political and social revolution of the 1920s. Himmler was appointed its leader in 1929, and under him, it became the enforcer for the Nazi party. As such, it eventually controlled all other branches of government, ruthlessly carrying out all racial policies of the Reich, including mass extermination. The SS over the years grew into a complex organization, a fourth branch of the *Wehrmacht*, and eventually became totally independent of it (as indicated by the fact that members wore the national emblem on their left sleeve, instead of over their right breast pocket as the *Heer* did).

Schwerpunkt—The main point of force; the place where the main assault would come.

Standartenführer—SS rank of colonel.

Tigerfibel—"Tiger Primer." A publication written during the war by panzer expert Heinz Guderian. Designed in a sort of black-and-white comic-book format, it was an excellent primer on tank warfare and maintenance of the Tiger tank, written in verse, with some pages in a humorous vein.

Torpedoboot (T-boot)—German fleet torpedo boat. A patrol vessel, much larger than a British MTB or American PT-Boat and comparable to a destroyer escort. The older ones were originally designed in the 1920s as destroyers (*Zerstörer*), but were reclassified as large torpedo boats in the 1930s.

This was because the *Kriegsmarine*, bridled by the Treaty of Versailles, was only allowed to have a small, limited amount of destroyers. The later vessels carried a complement of about 110 and were over 90 meters long.

Untersëeboot (U-boot)—Lit. "Underwater boat"; the infamous German U-boat submarine.

Vergeltung (V-1, V-2…)—Lit. "Vengeance/Revenge." Hitler's unmanned air force that was launched against the English civilian population in retribution for the Allied bombings of Germany. The first such weapon was the V-1 ("Buzz bomb," as the British dubbed it, because of the droning sound it made in flight), a small pilotless flying bomb that served as a surface-to-surface land-attack missile. The second was the V-2 rocket, the first medium-range surface-to-surface ballistic missile ever constructed. The term was suggested by Goebbels as a propaganda response to the "V for Victory" code that was springing up in enemy camps.

Vizeadmiral—German Navy rank of vice-admiral, equivalent to the German Army rank of *Generalleutnant*.

Waffen-SS—Fully militarized combat formations of the SS, the Nazi party military arm. The term originated around 1940 for that portion of the SS whose personnel were organized into military fighting units. Though part of the larger SS structure, the Waffen-SS was a front-line fighting organization that encompassed over half a million men by the end of the war. Often committing atrocities, most Waffen-SS developed a reputation for fighting fanatically and bitterly against their enemies.

Wehrmacht—A term used to describe the combined German military armed forces from 1935 on. Although the term was often erroneously used to refer to just the German Army, it included all the armed forces, consisting of the German Army (*Heer*), Navy (*Kriegsmarine*), and Air Force (*Luftwaffe*). For ground operations, the *Waffen-SS* were tactically a part of the *Wehrmacht* as well.

Wehrmachtführungsamt (WFSt)—The OKW Operations office, the most important division of *OKW*. It controlled planning, combined operations, transportation, communications, and even elements of propaganda for the Armed Forces. Heading the division was Operations Chief Alfred Jodl. The main component of this office was the *Wehrmachtfuhrungsstab* (WFStb), the Armed Forces Operations/Command Staff.

Widerstand—The French Resistance.

Widerstandsnest (WN-)—"Resistance Nest." One of many common small, isolated, single, self-contained defensive strongpoints located along a defensive front, smaller than a strongpoint (*stützpunkt*). They were manned usually by no more than a platoon of men; each was given a number for identification purposes. The category was created by Field Marshal von Rundstedt in May 1942 and incorporated into the Atlantic Wall.

Wüstenfuchs—"Desert Fox." The term coined in 1941 for Erwin Rommel because of his early successes in North Africa against the British.

zur besonderer Verwendung (zbV)—For special purposes or special use. Often used for ad hoc units, it was used more frequently as the war progressed.

Appendix A
Rommel's headquarters at La Roche-Guyon

The château of La Roche-Guyon, which became Rommel's headquarters on March 9, 1944, is located about 64km northwest of Paris, roughly halfway between the capital and Rouen, and just 165km from Le Havre on the coast. The large estate had been the home of the Ducs du Rochefoucald since the 17th century. The château is located above the sloping northern bank of the Seine at a large U-shaped river bend; behind it is a steep chalk cliff. The first castle here was dug entirely into the cliff, hard to spot with a casual glance. In the 12th century, a new main building, protected by a wall, was built at the foot of the cliff, while above it rose a solid circular tower of stone, built by the Normans around the 10th century. A protective double stone enclosure shaped like a spur was also built around the rising keep, which was connected to the manor by a secret passageway dug into the rock. Next to the château and to its left is the small village of La Roche-Guyon, with about 540 inhabitants in 1944.

The complex was administratively taken over on March 17, 1943 by the German forces, who installed a flak battery on the hill above the château. Just down the main street was the town's Kommandant's office. Near the town center is the 15th-century church of St. Samson, on the Rue des Frères Rousse.

Because the bridge next to the château was destroyed in June 1940 (see below), anyone wishing to cross the Seine had to take the local ferry. There were also road bridges at the nearby towns of Mantes and Vernon. All in all, the château's location was off the main routes, but within easy access of them, and importantly for Rommel, close to the coast.

The château is elegant and spacious, although there was much work to be done to prepare it for Rommel and his staff. Because of the building's age and solid construction, utilities were somewhat challenging, and creating enough living and working space for an entire army group headquarters was a problem. Engineers dug out more tunnels in the cliffs, for such things as extra offices, storage, a makeshift movie theater, and of course, safe air raid shelters.

The chateau itself had lavish rooms, not overly spacious or luxurious but comfortable and well furnished. The solid walls were a few meters thick and stayed cool, even in the summer. In the late winter of 1944 though, the building was downright cold.

Rommel chose as his quarters an unpretentious ground-floor stateroom, as simple as his uniforms. His study, also on the ground floor, was a tall room, entered through a large door from a corridor richly paneled in oak. The room, decorated by the Duchesse d'Enville in the early 18th century, was a long, high-ceilinged, wooden-floored chamber. The south wall opened through two high beautifully designed French windows onto a lovely rose garden and terrace.

Next to the French windows was a priceless, inlaid, Renaissance desk catty-corner in one corner of the room. Rommel had been told that Louvois himself had signed the revocation order for the Edict of Nantes on that desk in 1685, so he made sure that the top was kept clean and simple. He only allowed himself one telephone on it. His neat piles of papers were limited to the latest messages and any report he might be writing, along with one simple black pencil. There were no photos of Manfred or Lucie, and he kept his letters from home discreetly put away in the drawers. (On one occasion, Gause inadvertently came into the room as Rommel was admiring a picture of Lucie that had been enclosed in her latest letter. Embarrassed, he hurriedly put the photo down and spread some maps over it. Rommel was pretty sure his chief of staff had seen the photo, but never said anything about it. Gause, embarrassed over the incident, discreetly decided not to either.)

The wooden floor was well-polished, with one or two valuable carpets on it. The oak-paneled walls had priceless 18th-century Gobelin tapestries hang on them, with ancient porcelain vases and lamps arranged below. On one wall hung a portrait of a hooded Duke François de la Rochefoucald, 17th-century ancestor of the present holder of the title, and writer of French maxims. Adjoining the study was a lavish library with priceless volumes, many of which date back over 200 years.

The army engineers did a remarkable job adding rooms to the cliffside. They installed a communications room, a theater, administrative offices, storage rooms, and a couple adequate shelters deep in the chalk cliff, so that the staff of some 20 officers and 80 enlisted need not worry about air raids.

The stables on the left, which had once housed some of the most magnificent horses in France, were renovated into offices for Rommel's intelligence officers. The wine cellars were consolidated considerably, and a large part of the freed space reinforced with concrete and turned into air raid shelters for the staff.

Rommel and his senior staff of course got to stay at the château. Junior staff officers and senior enlisted men stayed in a large adjacent building, where the naval advisory staff also worked. The remainder of the headquarters personnel had to find quarters in town. More anti-aircraft protection in the form of several batteries rose up from the valley floor—"like tall organ pipes," as one observer solemnly put it.

The bridge over the Seine—*le pont de La Roche-Guyon*—had once been a splendid structure. Heralded at its dedication on July 7, 1935 as the longest bridge in France, the structure had an unfortunately short life span. Less than five years later, on June 9, 1940, to slow down the blitz advance of the oncoming Germans, the French blew it up with 400kg of explosives placed at the base of the bridge's abutments. And according to a few local inhabitants, the demolition was badly executed, a testimony to the confusion war often creates.

The local populace, according to the story, had been forewarned on Friday, June 7 of the demolition plan, but no definite time was specified by the authorities. Nevertheless, the army engineers (*Génie*) had reassured the civilians, promising to stop refugee traffic across the bridge an hour or two before the charges were set off (an assertion supported after the war by statements made by members of the city council). By Sunday, civil authorities had moved their offices across river to the southern bank, as had the military units in the area. That afternoon, just before 2 p.m., the local military commander received a report of German mobile advance units approaching the area. The military unit at the bridge, perhaps with an element of panic, suddenly began blocking off traffic to the bridge. A scant five minutes after that, the demolition charges were detonated.

Only the people near the bridge had been given any final warning (brief as it was), and many were unaware that the bridge was even going to be destroyed, especially the unsuspecting refugees that were moving through the area. Many fleeing over the bridge had barely made it across when the barricades had gone up. So understandably, when the charges were set off and the bridge collapsed, chaos also erupted. The tremendous detonations destroyed the bridge, but explosive concussions, as well as flying splinters and fragments, did considerable nearby damage as well.

The demolition prompted an immediate panic, among both the local villagers and the throngs of refugees moving into the area—many homeless—that had planned on crossing the river here to flee from the advancing enemy. Making matters worse, all the governmental officials and workers had already evacuated across the river, so no authority was left to take charge of the refugee traffic. Many soldiers, cut off from their units and now a part of the fleeing civilian crowds, angrily threw down their weapons and ripped off their shirts and tunics, shouting, "Treason!"

The truly sad note to this was that the Germans did not approach the area for another 24 hours, finally rolling into the town around 4 p.m. on Monday afternoon. That had been nearly four years ago, and ever since then, to cross the river at this point, one had to take a small ferry; or go out of one's way, upstream to Mantes, or downstream to Vernon. This would be a minor but decidedly irritating drawback to requisitioning the château for Rommel's headquarters.

Appendix B
Von Rundstedt's headquarters at
St.-Germain-en-Laye

On the night of March 4, 1942, just von Rundstedt was reappointed *OB West*, an RAF air raid attacked the Renault factory at Boulogne-Billancourt, a nearby western Parisian suburb. A few stray bombs hit the area of St.-Germain. One stray all but destroyed the house across the street from the Pavillon Henri IV, von Rundstedt's base, as well as damaging the hotel itself. His staff at that point decided that a protected building was needed for the command staff. When Hitler was told of the air raid early the next year, concerned for the Prussian's safety, he immediately ordered a location be chosen for a bunker complex to be built for his strategic headquarters command. So the field marshal and his staff had chosen a beautiful, discreet, secluded location nearby. The picturesque area included a rolling hill, a nice terrace, a breathtaking little forest, a nearby castle, and several large villas, all which could be requisitioned if necessary for the headquarters staff.

On an old limestone quarry below a hillcrest, at 20–24 Boulevard Victor Hugo, OT laborers divided into three 400-man teams started working in shifts around the clock for seven months to build a three-floor concrete command bunker. The solid, thick concrete structure was finished in late 1943.

The 2,000-square-meter blockhouse headquarters at first only included several offices, a large map room, eating and restroom facilities, and an infirmary. It was about 100 meters long and 50 meters tall, with some five meters or so underground. The bunker complex had vine-covered concrete walls up to 60cm thick, and a good part of it was constructed deep into the hill, almost under the boulevard and part of the nearby school grounds. There were no windows; just two deeply set portholes in front, from which guards could peer out at visitors. Slides covered the ports in case of an attack. Several apertures were built into the walls, mainly for air venting and circulation.

There were only two entrances: a set of reinforced double doors at each end. Those around the corner from the field marshal's path down the hill were the main entrance. They were accessed from an iron staircase of 13 steps and then through a small iron gate. Inside the front door wes a marble-floored foyer. Just off this vestibule, a circular staircase with brass banisters wound its way upward to bedrooms above.

The second entrance at the other end of the front was designated for workers and supplies. Adjoining the back end of the blockhouse deep under the hill were several natural cave areas. The engineers made use of them to build enlisted quarters. The men were packed into small rooms, with hooks affixed to the walls to hold the bunks. Fortunately, toilets and other restroom facilities were numerous. Additional was been made of these small underground caverns to construct several air raid shelters. The entire building was completely air conditioned and centrally heated. The floors were red and white ceramic tile, and the beige ceiling was acoustic.

The ground floor housed the generator room and the other utility rooms, including the kitchen. Inside the generator room was a special escape passage that the staff officers could use in case of an emergency. It ran underground for about a kilometer and a half before coming out into a private home overlooking the Rue Felicien David.

The walls between offices were over a meter wide, and a thick steel door to each office slid to open or close. Each door (except those to the offices of von Rundstedt and Blumentritt) had a small glass inspection port in the center, so that visitors could be visually identified before being allowed entry. Each door also had affixed instructions for occupants. Each office had a metal barrel inside carrying a charcoal gas-filtering agent, through which the air was cleansed before entering the room. However, the door must be shut completely and levers engaged for the room to be able to withstand a gas attack.

Of course, being the strategic headquarters for the Western Theater, the offices were well furnished. The interiors were generally decorated with beautiful draperies, plush furniture, and elegant walnut paneling. Just off the front entrance on the main floor was the hallway. Von Rundstedt's office (although he seldom went there) was off that hallway and in front of the dining room. It was not very large: 4½ meters wide by 7⅓ meters long, and about 2⅓ meters high. It had two radiators for warmth in the winter, and an adjoining small restroom. The main feature in the office was an heirloom Louis XV desk. Von Rundstedt often enjoyed sitting behind it and reading a novel. Near his office was a map room, and he often updated the maps himself.

Next to his office was that of his adjutant, the room about half as large as his. Blumentritt's office was across the hall: about the same size as the field marshal's, but divided up into two areas: one for the chief of staff, and one for a secretary or aide.

The bunker normally held over a hundred people, although it could accommodate up to three times that number. Staff included various administrative and communications personnel, including a number of *Kriegshelferinnen* (Army volunteers). All in all, it was an excellent and safe location for the strategic staff charged with overseeing the defense of Western Europe.

Overlooking the bunker at the top of the hill was a French girls' school (today the Lycée d'Albret). Its four three-storey buildings, built in 1911, have dormer windows below peaked gray-slate roofs, a common design in Europe. The buildings are laid out in a U-shape, with a playground at the mouth of the partially enclosed area. Next to the playground was a small house, once occupied by the school headmistress. This structure was turned into a complex telephone exchange, linking *OB West* with the major commands in Europe, Germany, and of course, the Supreme Headquarters, wherever it happened to be at that moment.

Near the bunker was built a communications center. For air protection, the surrounding area included a number of anti-aircraft positions, as well as several fire stations. The school had to be partially requisitioned by headquarters for additional personnel to work in the command blockhouse down the hill. Half of the school became a garrison for German troops, and the mixing of German uniforms and girls in pink overalls around the buildings evoked concern from the locals. Other staff members had quarters in homes on the Rue Thiers and the Rue de Lorraine.

For von Rundstedt's personal quarters, the Villa David, located behind the girls' école at No. 28 Rue Alexandre Dumas, was chosen. It was a petite three-storey, twelve-room villa on a well-landscaped half-acre lot. It sat atop the gentle hill in which the block headquarters building, some 300 yards away, was partially buried. Few people knew that he lived there. A high wall and permanently secured, stout iron gates kept things that way. There were only two ways in: through a special walkway cutting through the school, or by an inconspicuous door in the wall next to the Rue Alexandre Dumas.

In the villa, there was a mirror in every room. The old man's bedroom was on the first floor, with a large window that overlooked the girls' school at the top of the hill. His room was adorned with two paintings built into the wall. They were not particularly good works of art and depicted French provincial scenery. The dining room had a large cozy fireplace, with yet another mirror above it. Blumentritt lived with him in the villa: his bedroom was upstairs.

The villa of course was guarded by sentries. One stood at a sentry box in the front garden area next to the main gate, which of course was always closed. Another endlessly walked a careful perimeter around the well-tended grounds, although von Rundstedt strictly forbade any guard from stepping on the grass. His staff had worried that despite the two guards, the villa could be easily accessed. Anyone could just walk in and start trouble. Von Rundstedt had argued that, although the residence was not closed off from the city, he had never been bothered. His officers had not been happy with that. Well, too damned bad. The old man liked the way he lived, because he could enjoy a private life there that was quite comfortable, very simple yet ostentatious.

The field marshal usually worked at the villa. He avoided going down to the blockhouse unless there is a pressing situation, conference, or whenever he has to use the communications complex to make a long distance phone call.

He also entertained VIPs at the villa, although the hapless Blumentritt disliked breaking the news to him about any guests coming. Von Rundstedt always made sure any formal repast was set for 1 p.m. That way, he could always make an excuse to his guests that he had work to do or another engagement to attend. And though he never ate much, he ate even less at these engagements to encourage his visitors to finish faster. Even so, they easily bored him, and he often looked for some pretext to excuse himself from the monotonous monologue—all to the amusement of his staff. Usually, he stopped working around 4:30, at which time he entertained a few of his officers over tea.

Whenever he went to the command bunker, he left his villa through the back door. He walked across the roomy courtyard, heading for the gate in the railed fence. Next to that back gate was his modest rose garden, tended for him by his gardener, M. Ernest Gavoury. The old servant faithfully tended to all flowers there, and von Rundstedt, who loved gardening, spent many hours of his spare time talking to the old Frenchman and fussing with his roses.

The field marshal strolled through the back gate, and then through a specially built passageway in one of the buildings to enter the school recreational area. He then walked down a gentle winding path that not only provided a beautiful view of Paris in the distance (he could see the Eiffel Tower on a clear day), but was elegantly landscaped as well. The manicured lawn on each side was interspersed with all kinds of bushes, small flower beds, sycamores, poplars, and birch trees scattered around the grounds. Going down the path, he passed a small knoll on his right, similarly landscaped with trees and bushes. At the bottom of the hill, he turned right and approached the nearby bluish-green blockhouse built into the base of the knoll. The front of the blockhouse, covered with ivy, was also camouflaged, so that it was difficult to spot from either the Boulevard Victor Hugo or the Rue Alexandre Dumas.

The complex was later expanded, with several more rooms and offices being added to the basement of the command bunker, expanding it to 40 rooms. At the same time, the nearby communications network was improved and an air raid shelter added—in the beautiful garden, to von Rundstedt's disgust.

Reference Notes

A good part of the information that was used in this book came from almost a dozen distinct sources. As with other works I have published, one of my foremost sources was the amassed material of interviews, logs, official documents, and superbly detailed data collected by Cornelius Ryan for his classic, *The Longest Day*. A surprisingly vast amount of information, I discovered to my astonishment (and delight) had never made it into his classic account. Among this material were three detailed personal interviews of Rommel's trip home, given by Helmuth Lang, Hans-Georg von Tempelhoff, and Rommel's two immediate family members: his wife Lucie and son Manfred. My heartfelt thanks to Douglas McCabe, curator of the Cornelius Ryan Collection at the Alden Library of Ohio University, Athens, Ohio for his cooperation, his insight into the material and into Ryan's methods, and for his unswerving assistance in helping me gather the information that I needed.

My second major source was Friedrich Ruge's daily reminiscences. The admiral kept a remarkably detailed account of the daily activities of Field Marshal Rommel.

Two other major sources that I found very useful were *Hitler's War* and *Trail of the Fox*, both written by the now-controversial David Irving. Despite the furor that was raised over his later claims about the Nazis, Irving was and remains one of the most fastidious, detailed researchers ever, a trait I confirmed in several talks with him. This biography of Rommel is perhaps one of his greatest works, a book that stands as an impressive piece for this or any period. Despite the controversy he has stirred, his material has proven to be highly useful.

I found a surprising amount of detailed correspondence information from Reports 40 and 50, prepared by the Canadian National Defence Headquarters. Additional reminiscences and reflections of the period by German senior officers were found in the US Army Military History Institute's Archives Branck in Carlisle Barracks, Pennsylvania.

Other major sources used included Fraser's biography of Rommel and Rommel's own papers edited by B.H. Liddell-Hart. Of course, no account of Rommel's activities would be completed without Desmond Young's classic biography. Additional details came from works by Hans Speidel, Paul Carell, and Gordon Harrison's excellent accounts of the invasion. I also drew heavily from the works of Max Hastings, Samuel Mitcham Jr., and John Keegan.

My primary sources on Field Marshal von Rundstedt's activities include the two biographies written by my chief of staff Günther Blumentritt, David Isby, and Charles Messenger. Detailed information on the units in France came from George Nafziger's excellent works on the German Order of Battle and from George Forty.

Bibliography

Books

Ambrose, Stephen E., *D-Day June 6, 1944, The Climactic Battle of World War II*, Simon & Schuster, NY, NY, 1994.

——————, *Pegasus Bridge—June 6, 1944*, Simon and Schuster, Inc., NY, NY, 1985.

Astor, Gerald, *June 6, 1944, The Voices of D-Day*, St. Martin's Press, New York, NY, 1994.

Balkoski, Joseph, *Utah Beach, The Amphibious Landings and Airborne Operations on D-Day*, Stackpole Books, Mechanicsburg, PA, 2005.

Barnett, Correlli (ed.), *Hitler's Generals*, Grove Weidenfeld, NY, NY, 1989.

Below, Nicolaus von, *At Hitler's Side: The Memoirs of Hitler's Luftwaffe Adjutant 1937–1945*, Stackpole Books, Mechanicsburg, PA, 1980. (Geoffry Brooks, Trans.)

Bennett, Ralph, *Ultra In the West—The Normandy Campaign 1944–45*, Charles Scribner Sons, NY, NY, 1979.

Berger, Sid, *Breaching Fortress Europe—The Story of U.S. Engineers in Normandy on D-Day*, Society of American Military Engineers, 1994.

Blumentritt, Günther, *Von Rundstedt: The Soldier and the Man*, Odhams, London, 1952.

Boyd, Carl, *Hitler's Japanese Confidant: General Oshima Hiroshi and MAGIC Intelligence, 1941–1945*, University Press of Kansas, Lawrence, KS, 1993.

Breuer, William B., *Hitler's Fortress Cherbourg*, Stein and Day, NY, NY, 1984.

——————, *Hoodwinking Hitler: The Normandy Deception*, Praeger Pub., Westport, CT, 1993.

Brickhill, Paul, *The Great Escape*, Fawcett World Library, NY, NY, c. 1950.

Brown, Anthony Cave, *Bodyguard of Lies*, Harper & Row, NY, NY, 1975.

Buffetaut, Yves, *D-Day Ships—The Allied Invasion Fleet, June 1944*, Naval Institute Press, Annapolis, MD, c. by Brassy Ltd, 1994.

Carell, Paul, *Invasion—They're Coming!* (Revised) Schiffer Publishing Ltd., Atglen, PA, 1994, trans. by David Johnston; Originally published as *Sie Kommen!* by Verlag Ullstein Gmbh, Berlin.

Center of Military History, US Army, *Omaha Beachhead*, US Govt. Printing Office, Washington, DC, 1989.

Chicken, Stephen, *Overlord Coastline: The Major D-Day Locations*, Biddles Ltd., Wood-bridge Park, Guildford, Sussex, England, 1993.

Colvin, Ian, *Admiral Canaris—Chief of Intelligence*, Colvin Press, 2008.

Cooper, Matthew, and Lucas, James, *Panzer—The Armoured Force of the Third Reich*, St. Martin's Press, NY, NY, 1976.

Cooper, Matthew, *The German Army 1933–1945: Vol. I: Rebirth*, Kensington Publishing, NY, NY, 1978.

Darlow, Stephen, *D-Day Bombers: The Veterans' Story*, Grub Street, London, England, c. 2004.

Davis, Richard G., *Carl A. Spaatz and the Air War in Europe*, Center for Air Force History, Bolling AFB, DC, 1993.

Delve, Ken, *D-Day: The Air Battle*, Arms and Armor Press, Ramsbury, England, 1994 & 2004.

Dept. of Military Art and Engineering, *The War in Western Europe, Part I,* US Military Academy, West Point, NY, c. 1952.

Doherty, Richard, *Normandy 1944 The Road To Victory,* Spellmount Limited, Kent, England, 2004.

Drez, Ronald J. ed, *Voices of D-Day,* Louisiana State University Press, Baton Rouge, LA, 1994.

Farago, Ladislas, *The Game of the Foxes: The Untold Story of German Espionage in the United States and Great Britain During World War II,* David McKay Company, Inc., NY, NY, 1971.

Farrar-Hockley, Anthony H., *Student,* Ballantine Books, Inc., NY, NY, 1973.

Fest, Joachim C., *Hitler,* Harcourt Brace Jovanovich, Inc., NY, NY, 1974.

Ford, Ken, *Battle Zone Normandy: Sword Beach,* Sutton Publishing Ltd., Gloucestershire, England, 2004.

Forty, George, *The Armies of Rommel,* Arms and Armor Press, London, 1997. US distribution by Sterling Pub. Co. Inc., 387 Park Avenue South, NY, NY, 10016–8810.

Frank, Dr. Bernhard, *Hitler, Göring and the Obersalzberg,* Anton Plenk KG, Berchtesgaden, Germany, 1989.

Fraser, David, *Knight's Cross: A Life of Field Marshal Erwin Rommel,* Harper Collins Publishers, NY, NY, 1993.

Friedrich, Otto, *Blood and Iron,* Harper Collins, NY, NY, 1995.

Fuchs, Thomas, *The Hitler Fact Book,* Fountain Books, Los Angeles, CA, 1990.

Galante, Pierre, and Silianoff, Eugène, *Operation Valkyrie: The German Generals' Plot Against Hitler,* Harper & Row, New York, NY, 1981.

Giziowski, Richard, *The Enigma of General Blaskowitz,* Hippocrene Books, NY, NY, 1997.

Guderian, General Heinz, *Panzer Leader,* Da Capo Press, NY, NY, 1996, first c. 1952.

Guderian, Heinz Günther, *From Normandy to the Ruhr: With the 116th Panzer Division in World War II,* The Aberjona Press, Bedford, PA, c. 2001.

Harrison, Gordon A., *Cross-Channel Attack,* US Army in World War II, The European Theater of Operations, Office of the Chief of Military History, US Department of the Army, Washington DC, US Government Printing Office, 1951.

Hastings, Max, *Overlord: D-Day and the Battle for Normandy,* Simon and Schuster, NY, NY, 1984.

Heston, Leonard L., M.D. and Heston, Renate, R.N., *The Medical Casebook of Adolf Hitler,* University Press of America, 1980.

Hoffmann, Peter, *Hitler's Personal Security,* MIT, Boston, MA, 1979.

Hogg, Ian, *Fighting Tanks,* Grosset & Dunlap, London, England, 1977.

Hooton, E.R., *Eagle in Flames: The Fall of the Luftwaffe,* Brockhampton Press, London, England, 1997.

Horthy, Adm. Miklos, (Andrew L. Simon, ed.), *The Annotated Memoirs of Admiral Miklos Horthy, Regent of Hungary,* Robert Speller & Sons, NY, NY, 1957.

Hoyt, Edwin P., *Hitler's War,* McGraw-Hill Book Co., NY, NY, 1988.

Irving, David, *Goebbels: Mastermind of the Third Reich,* Focal Point Publications, London, England, 1996.

_____, *Göring: A Biography,* Avon Books, NY, NY, 1989.

_____, *Hitler's War,* Focal Point Publications, London, England, 2002.

_____, *The Rise and Fall of the Luftwaffe: The Life of Field Marshal Erhard Milch,* Focal Point Publications, London, England, 1973, Parforce UK Ltd., 2002.

_____, *The Trail of the Fox,* Thomas Congdon Books, A/elec., Parforce UK Ltd., 2001, 2005.

Isby, David C. (ed.), *Fighting the Invasion: The German Army at D-Day,* The Military Book Club/ Greenhill Books, London, England, 2000.

Jacobsen, Otto, *Erick Marcks, Soldat und Gelehrter,* Gottingen, 1971.

Jodl, Luise, *Jenseits des Endes*: Leben und Sterben des Generaloberst Alfred Jodl, Verlag Fritz Molden, Wien, München, Zürich, 1976.

Junge, Traudl, (Melissa Müller, ed.), *Until the Final Hour: Hitler's Last Secretary,* Arcade Publishing, NY, NY, 2002.

Kaufmann, J.E., and Kaufmann, H.W., *Fortress Third Reich: German Fortifications and Defensive Systems in World War II*, c. 2003, Da Capo Press, Cambridge, MA.

Keegan, John, *Guderian*, Ballantine Books, Inc., NY, NY, 1973.

_____, *Rundstedt*, Ballantine, NY, NY, 1974.

_____, *Six Armies in Normandy*, Viking Press, NY, NY, 1982.

Kershaw, Robert J., *D-Day—Piercing the Atlantic Wall*, US Naval Institute Press, Annapolis, MD, 1994.

Kirk, Tim, *The Longman Companion to Nazi Germany*, Longman Group Ltd, Essex, England, 1995.

Koch, Lutz, *Erwin Rommel : Die Wandlung eines grossen Soldaten*, Verlag Walter Gebaur, Stuttgart, Germany, 1950.

Lee, Bruce, *Marching Orders—The Untold Story of World War II*, Crown Publishers, New York, NY, 1995.

Lenton, H.T., *Navies of the Second World War—German Surface Vessels I and II*, Doubleday & Co. Inc., Garden City, NY, 1966.

Lewin, Ronald; *Rommel: As Military Commander*, Van Nostrand Reinhold Co., NY, NY, 1968.

Lewis, Jon E. (ed.), *Eyewitness D-Day: The Story of the Battle by Those Who Were There*, Carroll & Graf Publishers, Inc., NY, NY, 1994.

Liddell-Hart, B.H., *The German Generals Talk*, William Morrow, NY, NY, 1948, 1975.

_____, *The Other Side of the Hill*, Pan Paperback, 1978.

Lucas, James, *Das Reich: The Military Role of the 2nd SS Division*, Arms and Armor Press, London, England and NY, NY, 1991.

Luck, Hans von, *Panzer Commander: The Memoirs of Colonel Hans von Luck*, Dell, NY, NY, 1989.

Macksey, Kenneth, *Guderian: Creator of the Blitzkrieg*, Stein and Day, NY, NY, 1975.

Majdalany, Fred, *The Fall of Fortress Europe*, Doubleday and Co., NY, NY, 1968.

Man, John, *The D-Day Atlas—The Definitive Account of the Allied Invasion of Normandy*, Facts on File, Inc., 1994.

Manvell, Roger, *The Conspirators—20th July 1944*, Ballantine Books Inc., NY, NY, 1971.

Margaritis, Peter, *Rommel's Fateful Trip Home: June 4th to June 6th, 1944*, CreateSpace Independent Publishing Platform, 2015.

Mark, Eduard, *Aerial Interdiction—Air Power and the Land Battle in Three American Wars*, USAF Special Studies, Center for Air Force Studies, 1992.

Marshall, Charles F., *Discovering the Rommel Murder: The Life and Death of the Desert Fox*, Stackpole Books, Mechanicsburg, PA, 1994.

Megargee, Geoffrey P., *Inside Hitler's High Command*, University Press of Kansas, 2000.

Messenger, Charles, *Hitler's Gladiator: Sepp Dietrich*, Brassey's Defence Pub., NY, NY, 1988.

_____, *Rommel: Leadership Lessons from the Desert Fox*, The World Generals Series, Palgrave Macmillan, a division of, St. Martin's Press LLC, NY, NY, 2009.

_____, *The Last Prussian: A Biography of Field Marshal Gerd von Rundstedt 1875–1953*, Brassey's, Oxford, England, 1991.

Mitcham Jr., Samuel W., *Rommel's Last Battle: The Desert Fox and the Normandy Campaign*, Stein and Day, NY, NY, 1983.

_____, *The Desert Fox in Normandy: Rommel's Defense of Fortress Europe*, Praeger, Westport, CN, 1997.

_____, *Triumphant Fox: Erwin Rommel and the Rise of the Afrika Korps*, Stackpole Books, Mechanicsburg, PA, 2009.

_____, *Defenders of Fortress Europe: The Untold Story of the German Officers During the Allied Invasion*, Potomic Books, Inc., Dulles, VA, 2009.

_____, *Panzers in Normandy: General Hans Eberback and the German Defense of France, 1944* (1st ed.), Stackpole Books, Mechanicsburg, PA, 2009.

_____, *Retreat to the Reich: The German Defeat in France, 1944*, Praeger Publishers, Westport, CT, 2000.

Mitcham Jr., Samuel W., and Mueller, Gene, *Hitler's Commanders*, Cooper Square Press, NY, NY, 1992.

Mitchie, Allan A., *The Invasion of Europe—The Story Behind D-Day*, Dodd Meade & Co., NY, NY, 1964.

Morison, Samuel Eliot, *History of the United States Naval Operations in World War II, Volume XI, The Invasion of France and Germany, 1944–1945*, Castle Books, Edison, NJ, 1957.

Nafziger, George F., *The German Order of Battle: Infantry in World War II*, Stackpole Books, Mechanicsburg, PA, 2000.

_____, *The German Order of Battle: Panzers and Artillery in World War II*, Stackpole Books, Mechanicsburg, PA, 1995, 1999.

_____, *The German Order of Battle: Waffen SS and Other Units in World War II*, Combined Publishing, Conshohocken, PA, 2001.

Chandler, David G., & Collins Jr., James Lawton, USA-Ret., *The D-Day Encyclopedia*, Simon & Schuster, NY, NY, 1994.

Oldfield, Barney, *Never a Shot In Anger: The Informal, Inside Account Of The Strange War Bedfellowship Of The Military And The War Correspondent*, Duell, Sloan, & Pearce, Inc, Chicago, IL, c. 1956.

Patrick, Stephen A., *The Normandy Campaign, June and July 1944*, Gallery Books, NY, NY, 1986.

Penrose, Jan, ed., *The D-Day Companion*, Osprey Publishing, NY, NY, 2004.

Perrault, Gilles, *The Secret of D-Day*, trans. from French by Len Ortzen, Little, Brown and Company, Boston, Mass., 1964.

Persico, Joseph E., *Nuremberg—Infamy on Trial*, Viking/Penguin Group, NY, NY, 1994.

Read, Anthony, *The Devil's Disciples: Hitler's Inner Circle*, W. W Norton & Co., NY, NY, 2003.

Read, Anthony, and Fischer, David, *The Deadly Embrace*, W.W. Norton & Co, NY, NY, 1988.

Reuth, Ralf Georg (Marmore, Debra S. and Danner, Herbert A, translators), *Rommel: The End of a Legend (Rommel, Das Ende einer Legende)*, Haus Books, London, England, 2005.

Reynolds, Michael, *Steel Inferno—1 SS Panzer Corps In Normandy*, Sarpedon, NY, 1997.

Richards, Denis, *The Hardest Victory—RAF Bomber Command in the Second World War*, W.W. Norton & Company, NY, NY, 1994.

Rommel, Erwin, *The Rommel Papers*, B.H. Liddell Hart, ed., Hartcourt Brace, NY, NY, 1953.

Rose, Norman, *Churchill—The Unruly Giant*, The Free Press, New York, NY, 1994.

Ruge, Friedrich, *Rommel in Normandy*, Presidio Press, San Rafael, CA, 1979.

Ryan, Cornelius, *The Longest Day*, Simon and Schuster, NY, NY, 1959.

Shirer, William L, *The Rise and Fall of the Third Reich*, Simon and Schuster, NY, NY, 1959.

Spayd, P.A., *Bayerlein: From Afrikakorps to Panzer Lehr*, Schiffer Publishing Ltd., Atglen, PA, 2003.

Speer, Albert, *Inside the Third Reich*, The Macmillan Co., NY, NY, 1970.

Speidel, Hans, *Invasion 1944*, Paperback Library, NY, NY 1950.

_____, *To Remain Ready for Action: On the Occasion of the 70th Birthday of General (ret.) Dr. Hans Speidel*, Greven and Bechtold, Köln, Germany, 1967.

Speidel, Hans, *We Defended Normandy*, Herbert Jenkins, London, England, 1951.

Spielberger, Walter J., and Feist, Uwe, *Sturmartillerie: from Assault Guns to Hunting Panther*, Aero Publishers, Fallbrook, CA, 1967.

Stillwell, Paul (ed.), *Assault on Normandy*, US Naval Institute Press, Annapolis, MD, 1994.

Sweeting, C.G., *Hitler's Personal Pilot—The Life and Times of Hans Baur*, Brassey's Inc, Dulles, VA, 2000.

Tillman, Barrett, *D-Day Encyclopedia: Everything You Want To Know About The Normandy Invasion*, Regnery Publishing, Washington, DC, 2014.

Toland, John, *Adolf Hitler*, Vol. 1 & 2, Doubleday & Co. Inc, NY, NY, 1976.

Van Der Vat, Dan, *The Atlantic Campaign, World War II's Great Struggle at Sea*, Edward Burlingame Books, Harper & Row, Publishers, NY, NY, 1988.

Van Der Vat, Dan, *The Good Nazi: The Life and Lies of Albert Speer*, Houghton Mifflin Co., NY, NY, 1997.

Waller, John H., *The Unseen War In Europe: Espionage and Conspiracy in the Second World War*, I.B. Tauris, London, England, 1996.

Warlimont, Gen. Walter, *Inside Hitler's Headquarters 1939–45*, Presidio Press, Novato, CA, English version c. 1964; Weidenfeld & Nicolson, London, England, 1964.

Westphal, Sigfried, *The German Army In The West*, Cassell, London, 1951.

Wilmot, Chester, *The Struggle for Europe*, Collins, London, 1952.

Wilson, Theodore A., *D-Day 1944*, The Eisenhower Foundation, Lawrence, KS, 1971 & 1994.

Wilt, Alan F., *The Atlantic Wall, 1944, Hitler's Defenses for D-Day*, Enigma Books, NY, NY, 2004.

Wistrich, Robert S., *Who's Who in Nazi Germany*, Routledge, NY, NY, 1995.

Young, Desmond, *Rommel: The Desert Fox*, Berkley Books, London, England, 1950.

Zaloga, Steven J., *D-Day Fortifications in Normandy*, Osprey Publishing, NY, NY, 2005.

_____, *The Devil's Garden: Rommel's Desperate Defense of Omaha Beach on D-Day*, Stackpole Books, Mechanicsburg, PA, 2013.

Zetterling, Niklas, *Normandy, 1944*, J.J. Fedorwicz Publiching, Inc, Winnepeg, Manitoba, Canada, 2000.

Institutes

U.S National Archives, Washington, DC

Walker, Kenneth. *The Enemy Side of the Hill, World War II German Military Studies*, Vol. 1, July 30, 1949, US Army Historical Division.

US National Historical Society

Parton, James (ed.), *Impact: The Army Air Forces' Confidential Picture of World War II, Vol: Onward Toward Tokyo*, National Historical Society, Harrisburg, PA, 1989.

US Army Military History Institute, Archives Branch, Carlisle Barracks, PA

MS B-339—A Study in Command, Volumes I, II III.

MS B-308—Generalleutnant Bodo Zimmermann, OB West, Atlantic wall to Siegfried Line, A Study in Command, October, 1946.

MS B-597—Pickert, Pickert, *General der Flakartillerie Wolfgang, Das III. Flakkorps in der Normandie-Schlacht*

MS C-099–General Walther Warlimont.

US Army Adjutant General's Office, Washington, DC

German War Diary, *Wehrmachtführungsamt*, German Military Documents Section.

Canadian National Defence Headquarters, Ottawa, Canada

Report No. 40—*The Campaign in North-West Europe, Information from German Sources—Part I: German Defense Preparations in the West*, Directorate of History, Historical Section (GS), Canadian Army Headquarters, April, 1951, edited July, 1986.

Report No. 50—*The Campaign in North-West Europe, Information from German Sources—Part II: Invasion and Battle of Normandy (6 Jun to 22 Aug 44)*, Directorate of History, Historical Section (GS), Canadian Army Headquarters, October, 1952, edited July, 1986.

Magazines and Periodicals

Bryant, Stewart, "D-Day: German Infantry at Omaha Beach," Jewish Virtual Library, 2002.

Pallud, Jean Paul, *After the Battle, Vol. 141: "The OB. West HQ At Saint-Germain-en-Laye,"* Battle of Britain International Ltd, London, England, 2008.

Ramsey, Winston G. (ed.), *After the Battle, Vol. 19: "Guide to Hitler's Headquarters,"* Battle of Britain International Ltd, London, England, 1977.

The Cornelius Ryan collection

The Cornelius Ryan Collection contains all the articles, notes, and materials that Ryan used to write his three famous books: *The Longest Day*, *A Bridge Too Far*, and *The Last Battle*. The detailed, complete collection is located in the Archives and Special Collections division of The Alden Library at Ohio University, Athens, Ohio.

The Longest Day

Box 26—Military Documents and Analyses
Box 27—Various Interviews
Box 28—Chronologies
Box 29—Research Synopsis

Special sources

AHB/BAM, "Telephone Log of the German Seventh Army from June 6 to June 30, 1944," Translation VII/70, 512.621.

Grint, Keith, *Leadership, Management, and Command: Rethinking D-Day*, Palgrave MacMillan, NY, NY, 2008.

MIRS/MR-)T/5/45, Handbook of the Organisation Todt (OT), MIRS, London, March 1945, declassified May 3, 1972.

Mission du Patrimoine, Direction des Affaires Culturelles, Château de La Roche-Guyon booklet, *"La Roche-Guyon sous L'Occupation,"* 1996.

Showalter, Dennis E., "The Convenient Opponent: The Wehrmacht and D-Day," Kansas State University, Manhattan, KS, 1995.

Internet sources and notebooks (int)

German GOB—6 June, 1944, David Caldwell, 1998 (website unavailable)
Third Reich in Ruins, http://thirdreichruins.com/miscbldgs2.htm
Wikipedia, https://www.wikipedia.org